The Handbook of Communication Rights, Law, and Ethics

## Handbooks in Communication and Media

This series provides theoretically ambitious but accessible volumes devoted to the major fields and subfields within communication and media studies. Each volume provides experienced scholars and teachers with a convenient and comprehensive overview of the latest trends and critical directions, while grounding and orientating students with a broad range of specially commissioned chapters.

**Published**

The Handbook of Applied Communication Research, *edited by H. Dan O'Hair and Mary John O'Hair*
The Handbook of Public Sector Communication, *edited by Vilma Luoma-aho and Maria-Jose Canel*
The Handbook of European Communication History, *edited by Klaus Arnold, Paschal Preston, and Susanne Kinnebrock*
The Handbook of Magazine Studies, *edited by Miglena Sternadori and Tim Holmes*
The Handbook of Rhetoric and Organizations, *edited by Øyvind Ihlen and Robert L. Heath*
The Handbook of Communication Engagement, *edited by Kim A. Johnston and Maureen Taylor*
The Handbook of Financial Communication and Investor Relations, *edited by Alexander V. Laskin*
The Handbook of Global Media Research, *edited by Ingrid Volkmer*
The Handbook of Global Online Journalism, *edited by Eugenia Siapera and Andreas Veglis*
The Handbook of Media and Mass Communication Theory, *edited by Robert S. Fortner and P. Mark Fackler*
The Handbook of Psychology of Communication Technology, *edited by S. Shyam Sundar*
The Handbook of International Crisis Communication Research, *edited by Andreas Schwarz, Matthew W. Seeger, and Claudia Auer*

**Forthcoming**

The Handbook of Peer Production, *edited by Mathieu O'Neil, Christian Pentzold, and Sophie Toupin*
The Handbook of Listening, *edited by Deborah Worthington and Graham Bodie*

# The Handbook of Communication Rights, Law, and Ethics

## Seeking Universality, Equality, Freedom and Dignity

Edited by

Loreto Corredoira
Complutense University of Madrid Madrid, Spain

Ignacio Bel Mallén
Complutense University of Madrid Madrid, Spain

Rodrigo Cetina Presuel
Harvard University Cambridge, USA

WILEY Blackwell

This edition first published 2021


*Registered Office*
John Wiley & Sons, Inc., 111 River Street, Hoboken, NJ 07030, USA

*Editorial Office*
111 River Street, Hoboken, NJ 07030, USA

For details of our global editorial offices, customer services, and more information about Wiley products visit us at www.wiley.com.

Wiley also publishes its books in a variety of electronic formats and by print-on-demand. Some content that appears in standard print versions of this book may not be available in other formats.



*Library of Congress Cataloging-in-Publication Data*

Names: Corredoira y Alfonso, Loreto, editor, author. | Bel Mallen, Ignacio, editor, author. | Cetina Presuel, Rodrigo , editor, author.
Title: The Handbook of communication rights, law, and ethics : seeking universality, equality, freedom and dignity / edited by Loreto Corredoira, Complutense University of Madrid, Madrid, Spain; Ignacio Bel Mallén, Complutense University of Madrid, Madrid, Spain; Rodrigo Cetina Presuel, Harvard University, Cambridge, USA.
Description: Hoboken, NJ : John Wiley & Sons, 2021. | Series: Handbooks in communication and media | Includes bibliographical references and index. | Contents: Freedom as the essential basis of communication rights / Ignacio Bel Mallén -- Human dignity : a revolutionary principle in a cosmopolitan society / Javier Gomá -- Communication rights in an internet-based society : why is the principle of universality so important? / Loreto Corredoira -- Communication rights in the United Nations system : from declarations to soft law / Leopoldo Abad -- Universality vs. standardization : the privatization of communication rights on social media / Rodrigo Cetina-Presuel -- U.S. and international communication rights frameworks and the pursuit of global consensus / Erik Ugland -- Communication rights and their messages : news, opinions, ideas and advertising / Ignacio Bel Mallén -- Subjects of communication rights : a special study of minors / María Isabel Serrano Maíllo -- News : objectivity and truth / Justino Sinova -- Journalists, confidentiality and sources / Lorenzo Cotino Hueso -- Addressing the risks of harms caused by disinformation : European vs American approaches to testing the limits of dignity and freedom of expression online / Divina Frau-Meigs -- The law and ethics of journalism in a changing world : new professional realities and challenges for communication professionals / Fernando Gutiérrez Atala -- Data protection as a limit to communication rights. A general vision of European data protection / José Martínez Soria -- Regulation of internet intermediaries and communication rights / Joan Barata -- Imperiling community memory : the European right to be Forgotten's tampering of search engine results / Krystie Byrum -- The crime of historical denialism as a limit to freedom of expression : a European glance German / Manuel Teruel -- Hate speech in the United States and abroad : finding common ground / Chris Demaske -- Political communication and electoral campaigns in Europe : the search for international standards / Rafael Rubio -- One servant cannot serve two masters : a struggle for divided loyalties of media regulation in East Asia / Grace Leung & Richard Wu -- Latin American thinking in communication and advances in communication rights / Rolando Guevara Martínez -- Media disorder and the future of journalism : international developments and the challenge of WikiLeaks / Jane Johnston & Anne Wallace -- Public communication and sustainability in a post-truth era / María José Canel Crespo -- Freedom of expression on social networks and doxing / Pedro Anguita -- The emerging threat of Artificial Intelligence algorithms and synthetic media : a consideration of journalists' responsibilities / Muira Nicolette McCammon -- Journalism routines depend on clicks : best practices for using metrics in journalism / Martza Zapata Vazquez -- Epilogue : why communication law and ethics need each other / Ignacio Bel Mallén & Marisa Aguirre Nieto.
Identifiers: LCCN 2020047064 (print) | LCCN 2020047065 (ebook) | ISBN 9781119719403 (hardback) | ISBN 9781119720737 (paperback) | ISBN 9781119719519 (pdf) | ISBN 9781119719496 (epub) | ISBN 9781119719564 (ebook)
Subjects: LCSH: Mass media--Law and legislation. | Freedom of expression. | Freedom of information. | Freedom of speech. | Telecommunication--Law and legislation. | Right to be forgotten. | Data protection--Law and legislation.
Classification: LCC K4240 .H355 2021 (print) | LCC K4240 (ebook) | DDC 342.08/53--dc23
LC record available at https://lccn.loc.gov/2020047064
LC ebook record available at https://lccn.loc.gov/2020047065

Cover image: © metamorworks/Getty Images
Cover design by Wiley

Set in 10/12pt ITC GalliardStd by Integra Software Services, Pondicherry, India
Printed and bound by CPI Group (UK) Ltd, Croydon, CR0 4YY

C109962_050421

# Contents

Preface viii
*Monroe E. Price*

**Introduction** **1**
*Rodrigo Cetina Presuel and Loreto Corredoira*

**Part I Communication Rights: Principles** **7**

1. **Freedom as the Essential Basis for Communication Rights** **9**
   *Ignacio Bel Mallén*

2. **Dignity, a Revolutionary Principle in a Cosmopolitan Society** **20**
   *Javier Gomá Lanzón*

3. **Communication Rights in an Internet-Based Society: Why Is the Principle of Universality So Important?** **30**
   *Loreto Corredoira*

4. **Communication Rights in the United Nations System: From Declarations to "Soft Law"** **47**
   *Leopoldo Abad Alcalá*

5. **Universality vs. Standardization: The Privatization of Communication Rights on Social Media** **57**
   *Rodrigo Cetina Presuel*

6. **United States and International Communication Rights Frameworks and the Pursuit of Global Consensus** **75**
   *Erik Ugland*

**Part II Communication Rights: A Study of Subjects and Messages** 87

7. Communication Rights and Their Messages: News, Opinions, Ideas, and Advertising 89
*Ignacio Bel Mallén*

8. Subjects of Communication Rights: A Special Study of Minors 100
*Isabel Serrano Maíllo*

9. News: Objectivity and Truth 111
*Justino Sinova*

10. Journalists, Confidentiality, and Sources 121
*Lorenzo Cotino Hueso*

11. Addressing the Risks of Harms Caused by Disinformation: European vs. US Approaches to Testing the Limits of Dignity and Freedom of Expression Online 135
*Divina Frau-Meigs*

12. The Law and Ethics of Journalism in a Changing World: New Professional Realities and Challenges for Communication Professionals 147
*Fernando Gutiérrez Atala*

**Part III Studies in Comparative Communication Law** 157

13. Data Protection as a Limit to Communication Rights: A General Vision of Data Protection in Europe 159
*José Martínez Soria*

14. Regulation of Internet Intermediaries and Communication Rights 172
*Joan Barata*

15. Imperiling Community Memory: The European Right to be Forgotten's Tampering of Search Engine Results 185
*Kristie Byrum*

16. The Crime of Historical Denialism as a Limit to the Freedom of Expression 195
*Germán M. Teruel Lozano*

17. Hate Speech in the United States and Abroad: Finding Common Ground 205
*Chris Demaske*

18. Political Communication and Electoral Campaigns in Europe: The Search for International Standards 217
*Rafael Rubio*

19. One Servant Cannot Serve Two Masters: A Struggle for Divided Loyalties of Media Regulation in Hong Kong 228
*Grace Leung and Richard Wu*

**20. Latin American Thinking in Communication and Advances in Communication Rights** **241**
*Rolando Guevara-Martínez*

**21. Media Disorder and the Future of Journalism: International Developments and the Challenge of WikiLeaks** **253**
*Jane Johnston and Anne Wallace*

**Part IV At the Intersection of Law and Ethics: Challenges in the Age of Algorithms, Disinformation, and Post-Truth** **265**

**22. Public Communication and Sustainability in a Post-Truth Era** **267**
*María José Canel*

**23. Freedom of Expression in Social Networks and Doxing** **279**
*Pedro Anguita R*

**24. The Emerging Threat of Synthetic Media: A Consideration of Journalists' Responsibilities** **292**
*Muira Nicollet McCammon*

**25. Journalism Routines Depend on Clicks: Best Practices for Using Metrics in Journalism** **303**
*Mariza Zapata Vásquez*

**26. Epilogue** **315**
*Ignacio Bel Mallén and Marisa Aguirre Nieto*

Index 319

# Preface

## Monroe E. Price

I happily accepted the invitation of the editors – Profs. Loreto Corredoira, Ignacio Bel, and Rodrigo Cetina – to introduce this important work. The very occasion of our meeting resonates with the ambition of this book. I met the editors in 2019 at the annual conference of the International Association for Media and Communication Research (IAMCR), an organization long committed to exploring ways to enrich the flow of ideas of communication and society across cultures, across systems, across theoretical approaches. This book is emblematic of what might be called the exploratory spirit of the IAMCR. The collection is designed to underscore *communication rights* as that idea has flourished within the traditions of the editors and in conversation with competing and complementary ideas developed in other traditions.

The book is timely for many reasons. There is an imperative resulting from the massive transformations in media technology and in the tsunami of change that goes under the name of social media. The world is, and has been for recent decades, a jurisdictional and cultural experimental zone for testing or imposing policy, with the force of circumstances driving governments, civil society, political parties, nongovernmental organizations, and others in conflicting directions, confronting issues of power, impact, and conformity to norms.

Dramatic shifts – in geopolitics, in technology, and in institutions, create a demand for rethinking the relationship between media technologies and freedom. Recourse to first principles and review of historic traditions can, in such a context, lead to new insights. That is the significant effort of this book.

In my own work,[1] I have tried to think about alternate ways of characterizing large-scale efforts to shape systems of information flow. "Communication rights" in this approach are nestled in and products of other expansive themes or tendencies. These overall themes are sometimes posed as foundational rights (prescribed, one could find, in the International Covenant of Civil and Political Rights) or constructed through observation of what societies actually do. Examples, from my work, include these actions of major forces in the information space: the shaping of strategic infrastructures for channeling, encouraging, or restricting media flows or the invention and uses of forceful narratives (call them strategic narratives) to affect public behaviors and institutional choices. All this occurs under an umbrella of complex

[1] Monroev Price is Professor Emeritus at the Annenberg School of Communications, University of Pennsylvania and at the Cardozo School of Law, Yeshiva University in New York.

*The Handbook of Communication Rights, Law, and Ethics: Seeking Universality, Equality, Freedom and Dignity*, First Edition. Edited by Loreto Corredoira, Ignacio Bel Mallén, and Rodrigo Cetina Presuel.

operations that I have described under the term "Markets for Loyalties." How these ideas relate to communications rights or how communications rights flourish under technological and political pressures – this becomes the ongoing challenge.

## Strategic Infrastructures

Everywhere about us, we see the material remnants of historic approaches to governing speech and society, and this volume – in its array of authorial backgrounds – manifests a variety of experiences with regulating freedom of expression and communication from different countries around the world. These distributed studies yield a catalogue of techniques used to mobilize, affect, or otherwise regulate and control societies. Technologies change: fax machines in dissident Eastern Europe, audiotapes in revolutionary Iran, flash drives in Cuba, smartphones in Egypt, sophisticated apps in Hong Kong. We aspire to explain how these technical interventions become effective tools for furthering freedoms but sometime become hijacked, melded with surveillance in ways subversive of an original goal. We recognize that it is not the technology alone, but the system design advanced by major communicators that is telling in these instances. Powerful communicators, and those who seek power, advance an infrastructure of information flow that will further their strategic objectives. We have paid too little attention to these broad efforts at global, regional, national, and community structures for information flow and too easily resort to familiar formulae of words to describe them.

Who, one might ask, are the architects of strategic infrastructures? Who sees themselves as empowered to articulate, demand, implement, or force the adoption of particular information infrastructures (or resist them)? These include **those who seek a flow of images that reinforces sovereignty**; those who wish to ration the import of potentially destabilizing advocacy; those who consider their state to be vulnerable to communal violence. But infrastructure design is also significant for those who advocate a full and free independent marketplace of ideas. Each of the authors in this volume brings to the table, at least, an implicit architecture, an implicit conception of infrastructure.

Those who design satellite systems or cable television systems, who recommend the loci of undersea cable, or transponder regulation are all engaged with strategic infrastructure. Just to reinforce the point, it is not the hardware alone that defines a strategic infrastructure and its freedom-related or control-related potential. Cell-phone towers, surveillance cameras, satellite dishes, and flickering television sets, do not fully tell the story. One needs to know the legal and policy setting. "Freedom" is the combination of the technologies, themselves and the institutions that surround them. And that is true of communications rights generally.

A few examples of information infrastructure that help explain the complex relation to freedom are: the satellite and cable system of Singapore, which permits large-scale access to information necessary for a modern business society, combined with an explicit set of norms and the machinery to enforce them; the now-obsolete Dutch system of allocation of broadcast time to ensure that pluralist values in the society are recognized and performed; and in more modern times, concerns with Internet shut-down capabilities (as in Ethiopia, Cameroon, and Kenya). **Ithiel de Sola Pool wrote brilliantly about technologies of freedom,**[2] but the burden of this approach is that no technology is intrinsically an instrument of freedom. Indeed, some technologies of freedom have had Trojan-horse effects; by design, they have been engines of surveillance and betrayal.

[2] See Pool, Ithiel de Sola. (1984). *Technologies of Freedom*. London: Harvard University Press.

## Strategic Narratives

I turn now to what I call strategic narratives, which are increasingly in the tool kit of states and movements as strategic communicators. Strategic narratives include stories a society tells about itself or stories that those outside seek to impose. Strategic narratives are of the same family as propaganda and include how a society is made to think about itself, fully understanding that how a society perceives itself influences what policies it adopts. And "narratives" are a theater in which these positions are honed. Narratives of fear and destabilization, for example, lay the groundwork for more cautious and restrictive regulatory outcomes. Narratives of freedom generally embolden participation and encourage entry.

Who are the manufactures of strategic narratives? On what might be called the positive side, the Freedom Online Coalition is a consortium of states that recognizes the need for a narrative to foster adherence to a relatively strict regime of non intervention in the regulation of social media. They further a narrative of freedom that supports, as it were, a strategic infrastructure. Some powerful states insist on an open social media structure (the strategic infrastructure) and they advance a global narrative that reinforces it. The EU invests in a bedrock narrative that supports its internal strengthening and its capacity to advocate for freedom throughout the member-states and beyond. As is true both for the EU and the Freedom Online Coalition, the capacity to maintain a strategic narrative is itself a matter contested. A final example: Ukraine, in the information conflict with Russia, developed a strategic narrative for domestic and global, as did Russia. These strategic narratives were used to justify uses of law and uses of force to further some voices and restrict others.

The contributions in this volume imply an important point about the political economy of strategic narratives and their relationship to freedom that is worth examining. We must study not only the operation of a single strategic narrative (such as the narrative of the need for free and independent media) but the *mix of narratives*, their interaction and changing patterns in their production, what might be called, as these techniques become more potent, the *cauldron of narratives.*

For example, it has been a difficult time for *narratives of freedom*. In Europe, the idea of "illiberal democracy" has grown, often at the cost of institutions that were constructed precisely to advance pluralism, the rule of law, and independence – basic aspects of freedom. This is mirrored elsewhere, including for example Myanmar, where promising narratives have dimmed. We can see how, the impact of narratives turns, partly on geopolitical trends. China and its Belt and Road Initiative gains a significant narrative focal point, much like the Marshall Plan of the late 1940s and 1950s as it sought to further ideas of democracy and freedom in post war Europe

There has also been a concerted attack on the very engines of narrative that are most supportive of freedom. In the United States, the press – or major elements of it – are characterized as "enemies of the people." In Russia and elsewhere, non local NGOs, often the backbone of civil society and the instruments of freedom, are outlawed and harassed. Similarly, we are witnessing how delegitimization has become a hallmark of narrative production and how computational propaganda has industrialized this delegitimization.

A volume such as this, is written within the context of a globalized world and virtually borderless communication enabled by the Internet. This cumulative approach emerged after a twentieth-century push for the recognition of universal human rights.

A cauldron of narratives approach requires that we think more about the loci of a narrative's invention, more about the institutions and organizations behind the narrative, and more about the interplay and interactions among often competing narratives. It is in a cauldron of narratives that state intervention in social media can be more effective. Russia invested heavily in its RT channel as part of a cauldron of narratives, and it has been an effective investment. China has organized its Global Television Network to render more available its perspective on global news. And the US has rebranded many of its efforts as the US Agency for Global Media. These are all part of a changing context for the production of narratives.

The meaning of communication rights is affected by shifts and changes in strategic narratives, by the locus and intensity of strategic production of socially significant narratives. Communication rights incorporate who participates in narrative production, including the decentralization of narrative production – through social media and the Internet. In terms of the cauldron of narratives, the affordances of the Internet and social media – are more about enlarging the *freedom to produce narratives* than it is about *the production of narratives of freedom.*

## Markets for Loyalties and this Volume

All of this ties to **Markets for Loyalties**, a concept that helps bring together notions of strategic infrastructures and strategic narratives and the valuable insights from the contributors to this volume. Those who yearn for communications rights do so in countless contested markets for loyalties where struggles to define who can affect the information field and how are battled out. Markets for loyalties exist where large-scale entities compete for power. These include states, religions, movements, ideologies, political parties, "all those for whom myths and dreams and history can be converted into power and wealth." In their ongoing shuffle for allegiances, these "sellers" use technologies – in conjunction with other tools I have mentioned – strategic narratives and infrastructures to expand their sway. They use force, law, subsidy, and negotiation to intensify their reach or to facilitate or limit entry for others. The operation of such markets can help us understand the relationship between technology and freedom.

The 2019 IAMCR meeting where I was introduced to this volume occurred in Spain, and I will conclude with two examples of the working of markets for loyalties from there. The long struggle between "the center" and Catalonia is a case study in how a market for loyalties works, and how vying "sellers" use a repertoire of tools to alter the passions of audiences in the market. The "center," we can call it "Madrid," at many points used law, force, subsidy, and technology to drive home the idea of a more unified Spain, seeking to limit the capacity of the Catalan movement to expand and entrench. And when and where a pro independence or Catalan party was in control, it used its authority and leverage similarly, deploying technology, such as control of public television and other mechanisms to reshape political allegiances. Control of narratives and influence on infrastructure were dramatic factors.

The Catalan example underscores this question: in the next decades, if information warfare and propaganda expand, what control will the home state demand in terms of management of the information space? We may, in fact, be in for a period of **information mercantilism**. In a period of populism, some political leaders emphasize control of immigration as a necessary element of statehood. And, similarly there is a populist turn in control of the export and import of goods. States, asserting sovereignty, will use borders to restrict, even more than now, the flow of ideas. States, particularly authoritarian states, act to immunize their populations from what they consider destabilizing ideas and advocacy.

The confluence of these issues is explored in the contributions gathered by the editors to this volume. That is as it should be: we seek general and universal meanings for "freedom," but realize it also has a specific meaning in each specific market. Yoani Sánchez turned simple flash drives into technologies of freedom to enable thousands of Cubans to read or watch what would otherwise be unavailable. In this volume, Ignacio Bel Mallén examines the different meanings of such freedom, and in its different aspects, also contributing a chapter on the relationship with communication rights and messages. Joan Barata and Lorenzo Cotino Hueso examine expression not only as a freedom, but as a right that includes duties and obligations. One more example of the relation of law and technology to freedom that is extensively discussed. Many "sellers" or advocates in these markets rely on the important principles in Article 19 of the International Covenant on Civil and Political Rights. Rodrigo Cetina Presuel, Erik

Ugland, and Leopoldo Abad Alcalá, examine what the universality of such a right means today, particularly in the context of current technological developments, while others like Chris Demaske, analyze what common ground exists for the justifications for its limitations, particularly in relation to hate speech, while others like German Teruel Lozano analyze limits related to historical denialism. José Martínez Soria, in turn, explores limitations related to data protection while Krystie Byrum explores the tensions between the right to be forgotten and collective memory online.

The right to receive and impart information is applicable explicitly, regardless of frontiers, i.e., state boundaries. This aspect of communication rights, along with the importance of its universality, is examined by Loreto Corredoira in the opening chapters of this work, and that serves as the framework from which academics from various continents examine more specific topics around flows on information and the rights that enable them. Javier Gomá Lanzón, in turn, analyzes their relationship to human dignity and Rolando Guevara-Martínez approaches communication rights, and these concepts, through the lens of the most important Latin American authors.

I cannot finish this preface without also mentioning the contributions made by other authors in this volume to explore all of these questions, and others related to communication rights: emerging online threats and emerging international standards to face them and the evolving landscape of communication law in relation to journalism, media regulation, or elections. Justino Sinova explores objectivity and truth, while Isabel Serrano Maíllo concerns herself with the rights of minors and Divina Frau-Meigs analyzes the implications of disinformation for ethics and Fernando Gutiérrez Atala explores the professional realities of journalism in our rapidly changing, ever-evolving world. Other authors like Muira Nicolette McCammon and Pedro Anguita R. explore emerging online threats and explore them from points of view at the intersection of law and ethics while Maria José Canel uses the same framework to explore public communication and sustainability within the context of post-truth. Jane Johnston and Anne Wallace contribute a study on WikiLeaks and what these and other media disorders, mean for the future of journalism while Mariza Zapata Vásquez analyzes journalism driven by online metrics. Grace Leung and Richard Wu describe current challenges in media regulation and media freedom in Hong Kong and Rafael Rubio explores the emerging international standards for regulating political communication and electoral campaigns. Finally, Marisa Aguirre Nieto and Ignacio Bel Mallén provide an epilogue in which they highlight the important and complementary connection between Communication Law and Ethics and why they should be studied together.

I conclude here, as I did in a keynote in Madrid, by drawing on Picasso's monumental *Guernica*, perhaps the most famous and powerful paintings of the twentieth century: It was painted by the artist in response to the bombing and near annihilation in 1937 of a small Spanish town in the Basque country. The bombing, by the Nazis, was authorized by Franco for a testing of German technology for aerial warfare. This painting as a meditation on anxiety in the face of the brutal technologies being unleashed. But it is also about strategic narratives and creative modes of affecting the range of influences in a market for loyalties. For me, the painting captures the desperate unease with onrushing technology and its potential to crush the human spirit. It is about the power of creativity in resistance. The durability of the image is a reflection on the artist's contribution to strategic narrative.

We are at a different moment of a different onrushing technology in a differently uncertain world. *Guernica* could be a metaphor for our efforts as scholars and citizens, or citizen scholars: sounding an alarm, reaching beyond the ordinary, absorbing and reflecting the perils of dangerously collapsing norms. In the search for technologies of freedom, there is a need to help a wounded society cope with dramatic and bewildering change.

# Introduction

Rodrigo Cetina Presuel and Loreto Corredoira

The year 2018 marked the 70th anniversary of the proclamation of the Universal Declaration of Human Rights (UDHR). Article 19 of this document could not be more relevant today: "Everyone has the right to freedom of opinion and expression; this right includes freedom to hold opinions without interference and to seek, receive and impart information and ideas through any media and regardless of frontiers."

Using the declaration as a framework, this volume explores the relationship between the legal and ethical dimensions of communication from a variety of perspectives. In particular, this work concerns itself with exploring contemporary interpretations of communication rights through a complex understanding of freedom of expression and its different aspects, taking into account the freedom to seek, impart, and receive information and ideas as well as the inherent responsibilities tied to the exercise of these rights in democratic societies. This is explored through examinations of the universality of communication rights, their relationship with human dignity, their importance for free societies but tied to understandings that conceptualize them beyond this freedom aspect and dig into both their legal and ethical obligations as well as their role in promoting equality among peoples.

In this handbook, academics and researchers, seasoned and young, examine questions related to communication rights in general as well as to communication law and ethics in particular. The volume contains works that analyze what the essential and universal elements of communication rights are and where their limits lie, what freedoms and duties they entail and how they shape the role of both citizens – as individuals and as a collective – and the press – as individuals, collectives and a democratic institution – in contemporary societies.

This volume pools efforts to present all kinds of perspectives in the field and representing voices from different parts of the world through the authors that have contributed. While most works analyze our current reality, often shaped by modern communication technologies in general and Internet in particular, others take a more foundational approach and ask more perennial questions related to the very nature of communication rights and their ethical and legal justification.

Some contributors, mainly from Spain, but also from Latin America, build upon the work of José María Desantes (+2004), a Spanish academic who held the first chair devoted to the study of Communication law at a European University in 1976. The purpose of exploring the works of an author who fully believed in the universality of communication rights is two-fold: first, to

*The Handbook of Communication Rights, Law, and Ethics: Seeking Universality, Equality, Freedom and Dignity*, First Edition. Edited by Loreto Corredoira, Ignacio Bel Mallén, and Rodrigo Cetina Presuel.

produce the first ever English-language work that collects the most relevant of Desantes' ideas – he only published in Spanish during his lifetime – in order to start a conversation with researchers from civil law and common law countries who base their work in other theoretical frameworks that study communication law; and second, to identify the ideas and concepts present in Desantes' work that are universal and that intersect with concepts from other approaches to communication law. The ultimate purpose is to create bridges that allow one to overcome the language barrier and start dialogues that show the path forward toward identifying a universal set of communication law concepts that help build a global theory of communication rights based around their universal characteristics but that, nonetheless, acknowledge and respect existing differences.

While this volume does admit for variations in terms and for classical, and still widely used acceptations such as "*freedom of expression*" or "*free speech*," the term "*communication rights*" is preferred by many of our contributors, who embrace doctrine published from 1948 onwards, also taking into account influential work and jurisprudence produced in the United States; works, regulation, and jurisprudence from the European Union and its member states; from other countries around the world and from international legal systems. Influential Latin American authors are also given their due and concepts and frameworks such as those introduced by Antonio Pasquali (+2019) or Jose Marques de Melo (+2018) are very present in this work.

Terms like "*communication law*" are preferred in order to allow concepts like the French "*droit de l'information et de la communication*," the Spanish "*derecho de la información*" (the term preferred by Desantes) or "*First Amendment Law*" as used by some in the United States to engage in dialogue that avoids confusion with related concepts such as, for example, "*access to information*" or "*information law*."

The task of tackling phenomena related to communication rights demands linguistic and conceptual analyses of terminology (for example, *communication*, *information*, *facts*, *opinions*, and *ideas*) that have different meanings and connotations across languages. For this purpose, a compromise was necessary.

This compromise is justified by the fact that this work is published in the English language and, as it concerns itself precisely with universality, "*communication rights*," "*communication law*," and "*communication ethics*" are terms that allow for a global dialogue to emerge from the various chapters in this work, despite any terminological differences between academic disciplines, legal systems, and languages. Using these concepts as a bridge, allows us to successfully compare the implications of the phenomena we alluded to earlier, while avoiding possible confusions in terms of terminology.

Such a compromise also enables the possibility of translating into English, sometimes for the first time, contributions from many notable authors from non-English speaking countries around the world. For example, in the very first chapter of this book, Prof. Ignacio Bel (a coeditor of this volume) reviews the basic ideas contained in Desantes' *La información como derecho* (*Communication as a Right*), an essential reference on the areas of communication law and the ethical duties and rights of journalists, a work that is essential reading in Spanish Communication Law doctrine that has also influenced the rest of the Spanish-speaking world.

Seeking universal definitions goes beyond enabling academic exchange that uses accurate terms. Because terms are defined in different ways in different languages, they also enjoy different degrees of constitutional protection in different countries. Divergences in this respect also reflect the very different legal traditions that exist around the world. This book intends to be a contribution toward more universal definitions of communication rights that can lead to more universal conceptions that nonetheless respect existing differences by fostering dialogue among nations and their different legal traditions, and their historical, social, and economic realities.

Beyond terminological explorations, by comparing the substance of communication rights in online and offline environments, this volume examines how these concepts and their ideological foundations can be adapted and updated to serve present and future societies, whatever the communication platform or medium. Comparison also allows authors to shed light on how certain aspects of communication rights endure without the need of updating and are still valid for helping societies face new communication-related challenges.

Much has changed, but so much remains the same. All this means that while Article 19 of the UDHR is the starting point for thinking about communication law and communication rights, there is a constant need to revisit communication rights, and to rethink certain aspects, particularly in the context of current technological developments.

Many of the core concepts of communication rights ought to be reinterpreted in light of the challenges that arise from a constantly connected society. And yet, many other concepts still apply, whether we are talking about information dissemination in traditional media such as newspapers, or on social media platforms such as Twitter or Facebook, even as new types of media made possible by recent technologies pose new challenges that ought to be evaluated from the points of view of communication law and ethics.

In recent years, social networks have been viewed in many quarters as platforms that threaten democracy itself and that present substantial challenges to communication rights.

For example, they are held responsible for enabling a system for the uncontrolled dissemination of unfounded rumors, disinformation, and misinformation (so-called fake news). For some governments, the press itself is also seen as the enemy and the main cause for the spread of alleged disinformation. Governments also see a great threat in online whistleblowing and have sought to criminalize the journalists that also use these as their sources.

Though these are in many respects, new challenges, journalists and editors have in fact always had to face the challenges posed by biased sources, disinformation, misinformation, a lack of factual rigor, and the need to rely on confidential informants and, of course, the hostility of those in power that the press seeks to hold to account. It is here where more universal reflections related to communication law and ethics gain relevance for the purposes of identifying the constants that allow communication professionals to respond to these challenges as well as those aspects that must change and that allows us to identify the legal and ethical norms that are still effective in solving those challenges.

Though recent technological innovations, for example, those related to artificial intelligence, mean that even some regulation in these areas is already outdated, the principles of communication law still apply to media forms that are in constant change. Radio and television are no longer limited by the need for a license from a regulatory authority, as content can be broadcast via the Internet. Audiovisual content, including the news, can be spread easily over the Internet at near instant speeds and without regard to national borders. Governments usually struggle to keep the pace with their regulatory efforts and face difficult jurisdictional challenges as a result of these technologies.

Social media networks, as they exist today, are also seen as a threat to the communication rights of individuals. This may be because the platforms wield great power over individual expression online and exercise it opaquely and inconsistently, sometimes with the complicity of states that fail to hold these companies responsible for undue interferences with the communication rights of individuals. This may also be because platforms fail to protect other individuals from harmful expression such as hate speech, discrimination, and other forms of technology-enabled vitriol, abuse, and trauma and, because states face difficult jurisdictional questions when trying to protect rights that are often infringed upon, beyond their national borders.

A good number of the works contained in this volume deal with analyzing what must change in communication law as we know it today and how our understanding of communication rights needs to evolve to better face the aforementioned challenges. Throughout the works contained in the four sections of this volume, solutions are sought in the universal aspects of communication rights through exercises in comparative law and the examination of doctrine from different parts of the world that responds to different legal traditions. Often, our contributors examine these questions from the perspective of communication ethics or by combining communication law and communication ethics in their analyses, highlighting the links between both.

**Part I** of this handbook, **Communication Rights: Principles**, includes six chapters that present the essential principles and ideas that give shape to a communication law framework that pays special attention to the intersection, or sometimes clash, between different legal conceptions and models across the United States, Europe, Latin America, and other parts of the world. Chapters explore the different aspects of communication rights, freedom as its essential component, dignity as a central principle, with special attention to universality, its importance, the prospects for a global consensus and technological developments that may threaten such universality.

This first part analyzes communication-related freedoms and rights as they are formulated and applied in jurisdictions across the world. The subjects covered include their origin and their recognition in constitutions around the world and international instruments – from the concepts of "freedom of expression" and "freedom of the press" in common law and the first bills of rights to the constitutions of modern European and Latin American states that speak of communication rights in terms closely related to the Universal Declaration of Human Rights, the International Covenant on Civil and Political Rights, and other international treaties.

**Part II** of the volume, **Communication Rights: A Study of Subjects and Messages**, concerns itself with concepts and issues around communication law as the linchpin of the rights and duties of journalists, which encompass, among other things, source confidentiality, fact checking, corrections, and attributions. Together, the rights and duties of the profession give media outlets and their owners special privileges – in areas such as professional secrecy and independence – but also entail special duties rooted in the protection of the communication rights of every member of society.

Thus, the second part of the book specifically tackles questions that are particularly relevant for the study of journalism in communication law and ethics including communication rights in relation to news and ideas, or in advertising, the protection of journalistic sources, the rights of minors, objectivity and truth, disinformation and the challenges that the Internet poses for the practice of journalism and the essential duties of professionals in responding to those challenges.

**Part III** of our volume, **Studies in Comparative Communication Law**, is dedicated to comparative communication law studies on some of the major challenges our discipline faces today, such as data protection, the role of Internet intermediaries and the challenges they pose for communication rights, the tensions between the right to be forgotten and collective memory, international standards for political communication in the context of electoral campaigns, and studies on limits to free expression such as hate speech in the United States – and the search for a common ground in other legal orders – or the crime of historical denialism from an European perspective.

Other chapters in Part III analyze communication rights through the eyes of the most important Latin American thinkers to highlight the challenges specific to this region; the future of journalism from the perspective of the learnings derived from legal responses to WikiLeaks from an international perspective but, in particular, from the point of view of Australia; and current challenges related to media regulation in East Asia, particularly in the case of Hong Kong.

**Part IV** of the book, **At the Intersection of Law and Ethics: Challenges in the Age of Algorithms, Disinformation, and Post-Truth**, analyzes key issues in contemporary law and ethics such as post-truth within the context of public communication related to sustainability; online phenomena that can harm communication rights and other human rights, for example, doxing or synthetic media and how journalists can respond to these phenomena as well as the current realities in journalistic practice, such as the use of online metrics in the profession.

In general, and throughout its four parts, the volume also analyzes emerging questions that are shaping current debates in the world of communication rights including state and private surveillance; data protection and the right to be forgotten; the role of large private corporations on the Internet in protecting – or harming – communication rights; the effects of hyper-concentration of media and social media and the free flow of information online; the use of algorithms and other automatic systems for distributing and even generating news, journalistic and information sources, and ensuring access to public information, as well as the harms that technology enables. These and other topics help shape the ways in which not only communication, but communication and journalism are taught today.

As a whole, this volume seeks to identify and define concepts, questions, and universal themes that have had a consistent presence in communication law and ethics from the very beginning and will continue to be present in the future making the case for the need to study communication law and ethics together, as one discipline.

The aforementioned serve as the essential and timeless subject matter that has helped define, and will continue to define, the work of those of us interested in the study of communication law and ethics.

Overall, this volume offers guidance on how to understand the rights and duties of citizens as it relates to the free communication of their opinions and ideas and their liberty to seek, receive, and impart information, their communication rights. It also offers guidance and insights for professionals, corporations, and lawmakers based on the analysis of the mistakes of the past so that we can avoid repeating them in the future. Our aim is to offer a global picture of communication rights, through the lens of communication law and ethics, making the case, as it can be read in our overall conclusions in the **Epilogue** of this volume, that indeed, **Communication Law and Ethics need each other.**

We have been lucky that prominent scholars from all parts of the world have contributed the many different perspectives collected in this volume. Our most heartfelt thanks to all of them.

Rodrigo Cetina Presuel and Loreto Corredoira
Boston and Madrid, August 2020

# PART I

# Communication Rights: Principles

# 1

# Freedom as the Essential Basis for Communication Rights

Ignacio Bel Mallén

This chapter argues that no right can be exercised without freedom. Within this framework, I analyze the classic concept of freedom, which has served as the basis for the fight to secure rights for the press, book publishers, and individuals for the past 17 centuries. Freedom is what all human actions have had in common when people have claimed rights from the powerful, from the right to print without fear of censorship to communication rights as they appear in the Universal Declaration of Human Rights (UDHR) and as they have been studied by scholars.

There have been many authors based in the fields of law and politics, and even sociologists, who have analyzed and addressed the UDHR, from the points of view not only of human rights and the foundation of human beings' liberties and rights but also of their relationship with politics, culture, and ethics. These authors include, among others, Desantes, Glendon, Romain Parmenteir, Oraa, Gomez Isa, and Gimbernat. Not surprisingly, the recent commemoration of the 70th anniversary of the declaration has made this important universal manifestation of human rights topical once more.

Since the beginning of their existence, humans have felt the need to express themselves and to communicate with other humans. For Aristotle, as Azurmendi (2015) highlighted in examining the remote antecedents of communication rights, politics is "society's founding activity," an idea that connects with the clear relationship between communication and community (in Spanish at least). People have always sought ways, whether physical, visual, or oral, to fulfill this innate need to form relationships. Through most of the long history of humanity, these relationships were created spontaneously, without restrictions or conditions, with the only difficulties being those imposed by the current state of media and technology at any given point in history. Primitive societies were not conscious of the concept of freedom to communicate, because they exercised that freedom naturally. This is what Desantes calls "the spontaneous freedom of the classical world" (Desantes Guanter 1977, p. 46).

These beginnings make sense because the need for freedom, as a basis for communication, is not perceived until freedom of expression or communication is restricted by an act of force for whatever physical, legal, or political reason. The right to communication has been termed *ius communicationis* by F. de Vitoria to frame it as a social right, as Corredoira and Sánchez Férriz have pointed out.

*The Handbook of Communication Rights, Law, and Ethics: Seeking Universality, Equality, Freedom and Dignity*, First Edition. Edited by Loreto Corredoira, Ignacio Bel Mallén, and Rodrigo Cetina Presuel.

Various studies on Francisco de Vitoria focus on his contributions to the promotion of human rights in the early sixteenth century. José María Desantes (Desantes Guanter 1999) considers him the first precursor of communication rights in his work *Francisco de Vitoria, precursor del derecho de la información* as does Ramón Fernández (2003) in *Los derechos Humanos. Antología*. De Vitoria did not write directly; his legal work *Lectiones* has been handed down to us from his students.

## The Existence of Freedom Prior to Rights and States

From the moment in history when communication rights began to be restricted – I refer here to the first formulations of these rights, such as "the freedom to print" or "freedom of press" (Virginia Declaration of Rights of 1776) – a fight for unconditional freedom of expression began. In many cases, it would prove a difficult battle. During this long period, all political structures tended to limit the freedoms of their citizens, particularly in the area of information, in terms of both what could be said (speech) and what could be published (the press). This was done in the service of the ruling classes and was a product of their lack of understanding. They believed themselves to be the exclusive holders of these freedoms and to be the ones vested with the power to concede these freedoms – with limitations – on citizens. A clear example of this is seen in absolute monarchies in Europe. If we understand freedom to be, in the words of Castro Fariña, "the absence of barriers" (Castro Fariñas 1970, pp. 31–44) then absolute monarchs established a broad range of barriers to freedom of expression.

As the years passed and Western states began to form in the eighteenth and nineteenth centuries, it appeared that the situation would improve because positive declarations of rights appeared, and these promoted the freedom of citizens as a basic principle. During this period, constitutions made the effort to include freedom, albeit in general terms, as one of their basic principles. While the emergence of states promoted citizens' freedoms in one sense, it also severely delayed the arrival of the era of human rights.

This reflects a crude reality. States, which conceded certain freedoms to citizens, limited those freedoms in pursuit of their own interests, and these limitations were not always legal or consistent with citizens' rights. Up until the twentieth century, states ignored the idea that the concept of freedom, as a fundamental human attribute, clearly precedes the creation of political structures. Indeed, states thought that they were the first to grant freedom to people and, therefore, had the right to define and limit that freedom in a way that suited their political and social goals. And so, they codified and enshrined the concept of freedom into their laws and into the first constitutions.

This perception posed a challenge to individual rights because states understood freedom not as a reality existing prior to the creation of states – or, indeed, as something intrinsic to all human beings – but instead as an attribute created and established by the state. Not even Thomas Paine's ideas in his work *The Rights of Man* (1791) had much impact at first, despite his great influence on the United States' declaration of independence. Paine argued that the rights of man are innate and precede all else: "The Revolutions of America and France are a renovation of the natural order of things, a system of principles as universal as truth and the existence of man, and combining moral with political happiness and national prosperity."

In the Spanish and Latin American contexts, Francisco de Vitoria is also considered a pioneer, as previously mentioned, when it comes to the communication rights that we enjoy now.[1] He asked the Spanish Crown for "just titles" (a version of innate rights) for the peoples of

[1] See the various studies on Francisco de Vitoria, who promoted human rights in the early sixteenth century. José María Desantes considers him the first precursor of communication rights in his work *Francisco de Vitoria, precursor del derecho de la información*, 1999, especially pp. 35–68. See also de Vitoria's work published by Ramón Fernández in 2003, *Los derechos Humanos. Antología*, particularly pp. 242–243. De Vitoria did not write directly; his legal work *Lectiones* has been handed down to us from his students.

Spanish America at the beginning of the sixteenth century. When the New Laws of the Indies were promulgated in 1542, they drew on de Vitoria's views on human rights and policy.

This allowed the state to limit freedom when it felt that such freedom was not being exercised along lines that served the state's interests. The problem during this historical period is that the state, which conceived and defined freedom under specific circumstances, could limit that freedom until it no longer existed. What was the root cause of this? Put quite simply: the act of basing freedom on the state rather than on human beings.

This gave rise in subsequent centuries, principally the nineteenth and twentieth, to laws and even constitutions that, on paper, were clearly liberal but that in their daily implementation supported dictatorships in which the exercise of freedom was non existent – for example, Sweden's 1991 law on freedom of expression, which is one of the four fundamental laws that comprise the country's constitution, or the Dutch reformed constitution of 2018. This illustrates the conservative concept of freedom subjugated to the political idea of order.

Clearly, this situation had negative consequences on the consolidation of all rights, including communication rights. The idea that human rights are a positive and complementary consequence of the exercise of human freedom is incorrect. Freedom *per se* is a way to exercise rights, and it neither precedes nor follows from rights. Rather, freedom is an attribute of rights. No right can be exercised without freedom. And there is an even more important idea at work: human rights, which allow humankind to fulfill its existential needs, precede the existence of states and are rooted in the human condition itself. Rights are innate to humans: they are born with a person and belong entirely to that person until the moment of their death.

## From Freedom of Expression to Communication Rights

The true sense of freedom can be understood when we consider it as a form in which a right is exercised – in this case, communication rights and their three facets (seek, receive, and impart) as these are analyzed in this work. In this way, the exercise of liberty can be understood perfectly as a way to facilitate the development of human rights, since rights cannot be exercised without freedom. The two concepts represent two sides of the same coin, though there is a substantial difference between them. Freedoms, particularly public ones such as freedom of expression or freedom to join a union or political party, are innate to man, yet they are regulated by the state by virtue of its authority to establish the extent of the freedom defined in its laws and regulations. From this perspective, freedom is a concession from the state, which becomes more democratic when it concedes more freedom, but which always retains the possibility of limiting freedom in the name of the so-called public good in order to protect other assets. This is the case, for example, with official and judicial secrets as well as with regulation of telecommunications.

In contrast to freedom, human rights are not conceded by the state nor do they have their origins in the state. They fall under the authority of humankind and are innate to it; they are born together with the individual and accompany that individual throughout their life. The role of the state is to recognize human rights in this way and protect the ability of individuals to exercise those rights. The exercise of human rights requires freedom, which must be conceded by the state in sufficient measure to allow a meaningful exercise of those rights. This is the double task of the state: to recognize rights and to guarantee their free exercise.

If society struggled initially to achieve desired levels of freedom, the struggle today is to make states recognize the rights of their people and protect the exercise of those rights. It is, and will remain, a difficult struggle, just as it was difficult to win freedom. Without a doubt, the day will come when eventually all rights will be recognized everywhere in the world. Communication, particularly information and communication technologies, has a role to play in achieving this objective; it serves as a reference point for people lacking, completely or partially, the human rights that are innate to them.

### Freedom of Expression Lies at the Foundation of Communication Rights

Understanding this idea requires an understanding of the true concept of freedom; otherwise we will find ourselves with so-called frustrated freedom. Freedom, historically the fruit of constitutional revolutionary conflict, was granted by the state, which as lord and master of that concession also established the mechanisms of its development. In the event that the state does not follow those mechanisms, it assumes the authority to limit or even suspend that freedom. Freedom in this case is "given" or "granted" and does not have the status of a citizen's right. Rather, it is a prerogative of the state.

Under these circumstances, which are extreme but unfortunately common, freedom can become illusory or at least uncertain, regardless of how explicitly it is enshrined in a constitution. The cause of this situation – and, paradoxically, the solution – is that humans cannot be the victim of a continuous fraud. As a result, people tend to rebel against a lack of freedom. People's yearning for freedom, which is real, makes them fight constantly, since, in the words of Desantes (Desntes Guanter 1974, p. 28):

> The rights of people to achieve their existential aims are equivalent to the aims themselves, which precede the state and are rooted more deeply than the state.... [Similar to] the condition of being attributable to human personality ... freedom can be saved only when it considers itself to be what it really is: the emanation of a right, or one of the forms of exercising a right.

This is the true meaning of freedom, which is constituted as the essential foundation for exercising any right. But freedom is an attribute, not a foundation. The foundation is the right, and direct exercise of a right requires freedom. This clearly explains why the fight for freedom has been at the core of history and how it has been possible to obtain the communication rights. Thus, since 1948 we have not spoken of a freedom of expression arising out of the will of the state, but rather of a fundamental human right that exists in people purely because of their existence. This human right is enshrined in Article 19 of the UDHR.

## The Long and Difficult Road to Communication Rights

On December 10, 1948, over 70 years ago, the UDHR was approved in Paris under the auspices of the United Nations (UN). It is no exaggeration to consider this date epic in the history of human beings because it ended an extremely long stage of widespread fighting and conflict that initially had simple freedom as its goal but later sought the state's recognition of individual rights. This date marked a "before" and "after" in the history of humankind and its consolidation as a holder of natural rights (see Suksi et al. 2015).

The UDHR ended a process that, if we restrict ourselves only to the most recent centuries, began in 1628 when the *Magna Carta Libertatum* was written in English, or even in 1215, when the Magna Carta was approved by King John of England (Sánchez Ferriz and Corredoira 2017). The Magna Carta was followed by the Petition of Right (1628). This petition is considered by many historians[2] as the first great political declaration of rights. Its 11 articles aimed to guarantee not only principles of political freedom but also those of individual freedoms. For example, it forbids arbitrary detention and extraordinary courts, and it guarantees the right of the accused to due process and to respect their rights as these are recognized in the kingdom's laws and statutes.

Here, it is also appropriate to mention, for its indirect influence, the implementation of the Habeas Corpus Act (1679) for accused and imprisoned individuals, which aimed to protect the individual, prevent their arbitrary transfer, and guarantee compensation for damages

[2] See, for example, Suski et al. (2015).

arising from illegal transgressions of their rights. This document made transgressors legally responsible for their actions and established fines and penalties.

The Petition of Right lasted barely two years. Then in 1689, the Bill of Rights was signed which, for the first time in history, expressed the principle that the king's authority does not have the force of law and that the law is above the king. It also recognized the public's right to petition and the right to vote freely, and it established judicial guarantees and the protection of public freedoms.

This declaration was followed by others in Europe and North America. In North America came the Virginia Declaration (1776), the US Declaration of Independence (1776), and the US Constitution (1787). The Virginia Declaration comprises 16 articles that establish a series of rights that, because of their content and language, seem to be precursors of what we understand today as human rights. The declaration considers individual rights to be natural and inalienable – a historical first.

The Virginia Declaration establishes, for example, separation of powers (principally executive and legislative powers); it affirms the equality of men; it proclaims, for the first time, the primacy of civilian power over military power; and it establishes the right to justice and freedom of religion. Its Article 12 affirms that "freedom of the press is one of the great bulwarks of freedom and cannot be restrained by a despotic government."

This is the first great declaration related to freedom of communication, in this case, freedom of the press.

Jefferson drew heavily from the Virginia Declaration to draft the US Declaration of Independence, and the content of the Virginia Declaration was reaffirmed by the US Constitution, together with its amendments. From the perspective of freedom of expression, the most important amendment is the first one. It was proposed on September 25, 1789, and enacted on December 13, 1791. The First Amendment establishes that:

> Congress shall make no law respecting an establishment of religion, or prohibiting the free exercise thereof; or abridging the freedom of speech, or of the press; or the right of the people peaceably to assemble, and to petition the Government for a redress of grievances.

In the European context, it is necessary to mention the Declaration of the Rights of Man and of the Citizen (1789), published in France, where Jefferson was serving as US ambassador at the time. This declaration clearly paved the way for the concept of fundamental rights of the citizen, and it enumerates which rights should be considered essential. A good example is the first article, which affirms that "men are born and remain free and with equal rights" – a wording quite similar to the first article of the UDHR – and that men are "endowed with reason and conscience, [and] should behave fraternally towards one another."

The French declaration continues by speaking of political rights (national sovereignty, representative government, primacy of the law, and separation of powers) as well as of individual rights (resistance to oppression, presumption of innocence, and the right to property). Two articles on individual rights stand out from the perspective of information law and ethics. Article 10 states that "no one may be disturbed for his opinions, even religious ones, provided that their manifestation does not trouble the public order established by the law." The phrase "no one may be disturbed" is echoed by the UDHR's wording of "no one shall be subjected to arbitrary interference." Article 11 states that:

> The free communication of thoughts and of opinions is one of the most precious rights of man: any citizen thus may speak, write, print freely, except to respond to the abuse of this liberty, in the cases determined by the law.

In the twentieth century, in the wake of the trauma of World War II, the UN Declaration (1942) was a notable achievement. In this document, 26 states declared themselves unified in conflict against the Axis powers and committed to remaining united after the conflict in order to found an international organization whose mission would be to promote peace in the world. This agreement led to the UN Charter (1945), which created the conditions for the UDHR (1948), the final step in the long journey to establishing the primacy of human rights in the face of tyranny and abuse of the law. This was the culmination of a long process of searching for and formulating fundamental rights that would allow society to improve human dignity following all the violence of the twentieth century, primarily because of the two world wars that occurred between 1914 and 1945. The fundamental idea behind the UDHR was to establish major human rights that would impede the violations of human dignity witnessed in the twentieth century.

This is the meaning of the UDHR, which brings together the principal fundamental rights that, at the time, constituted the essence of human dignity. The declaration had a clear ethical force, even if it was not legally binding. The importance of its contents and the moral force of the rights declared therein led it to influence legislation adopted by the UN's member states. This legislation may have differed somewhat from state to state, but its purpose in all cases was to promote human rights within each country.

One of those rights, which was doubtless quite important given the rapid development of media at the time, was the right to freedom of expression, which, until that point, had been the focus of the fight for the right to freely express opinions and ideas. It was time – and this is also the perception from the declaration – to move from fighting for freedom of expression, as people had in centuries past, toward turning that freedom into a fundamental right. The moment was propitious to grant expression free of government interference as an essential part of society, the status of fundamental right. In this way, the universal right to freedom of expression emerged.

Article 19 of the declaration states, "Everyone has the right to freedom of opinion and expression; this right includes freedom to hold opinions without interference and to seek, receive and impart information and ideas through any media and regardless of frontiers." This article establishes the basis for communication rights, the right to communication for all citizens of the world through universality of subject, medium, content, and geographic location. The development of this right was a significant achievement. It amounted to a qualitative leap that allowed the creation of communication rights as a human right that should be respected and protected by the state.

This leap would gradually become more effective as national legislatures incorporated the UDHR's principles into their own laws and constitutions. Indeed, the goal of the declaration was to serve as the ethical and legal source for the development of national and supranational legal instruments that would make communication rights fundamental.

## International Agreements on Human Rights: The International Covenant on Civil and Political Rights

The UDHR is one of several universal declarations and international agreements that aim to strengthen the existence of human rights in various fields of endeavor. Just within the realm of communication, which is the focus of this volume, two agreements followed the UDHR: the International Covenant on Civil and Political Rights and the International Covenant on Economic, Social and Cultural Rights. These declarations were adopted by the UN General Assembly in its Resolution 2200 on December 16, 1966, when the agreements were opened for ratification by member states. The agreements ultimately entered into force on March 23, 1976.

One of the disadvantages of the UDHR is its nonbinding nature in relation to the national legislation of member states. From the start, it was more an ethical declaration; it was important, but did not have legal weight because it could not be enforced. The Human Rights

Committee, as Subedi (2017) points out, has a certain moral authority, but it is not a guarantor. Following the first announcement of the UDHR, many set about translating its contents into a unified international treaty in order to give it full legal backing. This would not be achieved until 18 years later, with the approval of the International Covenant on Civil and Political Rights in 1966.

Initially, the idea was to create a single treaty that reflected the unitary, indivisible character of the human rights enumerated in the UDHR. However, confrontations among the UN member states, which were divided into classical capitalist and Marxist camps, necessitated the splitting of the rights into two covenants in 1948. The first agreement, which was ratified by a larger number of UN member states, deals with civil and political rights and establishes oversight and monitoring mechanisms for ensuring its implementation. The second agreement, covering economic and social rights, is more general and does not stipulate adequate monitoring mechanisms.

Perhaps the most important aspect of these two covenants is that they are legally binding on the states that have ratified them. Therefore, they represent a transition from ethical declarations of human rights to legal definitions of them. For this reason, these covenants have an importance that is similar to or even greater than that of the UDHR in many parts of the world, particularly in English-speaking countries. These two covenants, together with their supporting protocols and the UDHR, make up what is termed the International Charter of Human Rights.

It is instructive to examine the first of the agreements, the Covenant on Civil and Political Rights, whose importance is expressed in its Preamble. (The two covenants' preambles are the same, reflecting the desire for unity between the two agreements.) The third paragraph recognizes that:

> in accordance with the Universal Declaration of Human Rights, the ideal of free human beings enjoying civil and political freedom and freedom from fear and want can only be achieved if conditions are created whereby everyone may enjoy his civil and political rights, as well as his economic, social and cultural rights.

Article 2 clearly establishes the legally binding nature of the covenant's contents:

> Each State Party to the present Covenant undertakes to respect and to ensure to all individuals within its territory and subject to its jurisdiction the rights recognized in the present Covenant, without distinction of any kind, such as race, colour, sex, language, religion, political or other opinion, national or social origin, property, birth or other status.

Two articles of this covenant are fundamental from the perspective of information and provide a detailed, extensive endorsement of Article 19 of the UDHR. Article 18 of the covenant establishes:

1. Everyone shall have the right to freedom of thought, conscience and religion. This right shall include freedom to have or to adopt a religion or belief of his choice, and freedom, either individually or in community with others and in public or private, to manifest his religion or belief in worship, observance, practice and teaching.
2. No one shall be subject to coercion which would impair his freedom to have or to adopt a religion or belief of his choice.
3. Freedom to manifest one's religion or beliefs may be subject only to such limitations as are prescribed by law and are necessary to protect public safety, order, health, or morals or the fundamental rights and freedoms of others.
4. The States Parties to the present Covenant undertake to have respect for the liberty of parents and, when applicable, legal guardians to ensure the religious and moral education of their children in conformity with their own convictions.

Though this article refers fundamentally to religion, I quote it because it describes freedom of thought as a right of all people and as an essential part of the freedom of opinion and of the freedom to manifest the beliefs mentioned in the third point. It is therefore clearly related to freedom of expression.

Article 19 declares:

1. Everyone shall have the right to hold opinions without interference.
2. Everyone shall have the right to freedom of expression; this right shall include freedom to seek, receive and impart information and ideas of all kinds, regardless of frontiers, either orally, in writing or in print, in the form of art, or through any other media of his choice.
3. The exercise of the rights provided for in para. 2 of this article carries with it special duties and responsibilities. It may therefore be subject to certain restrictions, but these shall only be such as are provided by law and are necessary:
   a) For respect of the rights or reputations of others;
   b) For the protection of national security or of public order (*ordre public*), or of public health or morals.

Even without detailed interpretation of the article's contents, the similarity of these provisions, especially the first two points, to Article 19 of the UDHR is striking. Perhaps the great innovation in both the UHDR's Article 19, and that of the covenant, is that their third paragraphs clearly establish the responsibility related to the exercise of communication rights. Such responsibility already appeared in the Declaration of the Rights of Man and of the Citizen (1789), though, there, it was not identified as a communication right. The third paragraph of Article 19 creates a responsibility for communication rights, but on many occasions, it has not been truly understood, since it has been used as a basis for limiting that right.

With the enactment of these two covenants, particularly the one on civil and political rights, the contents of the UDHR were reaffirmed. To be sure, other covenants, declarations, and resolutions have contributed to human rights, yet the passage of these two covenants in particular marks the final and definitive step in the establishment and defense of human rights related to information.

## Other Declarations to Consider

In the previous sections, I have discussed the principal declarations of human rights at a global level. We must remember that one of the objectives of the UDHR was to serve as a basis for different supranational organizations and, later, individual countries to reaffirm its contents within national borders. Indeed, a series of declarations followed that reaffirmed the defense of human rights in different geographic areas of the world, with consequences for communication.

The relevant declaration in Europe, for example, is the Convention for the Protection of Human Rights and Fundamental Freedoms, approved in November 1950. Based on the principles of the UDHR, Article 10 of this convention reaffirms the principal ideas of Article 19 of the UDHR, in nearly identical words:

1. Everyone has the right to freedom of expression. This right shall include freedom to hold opinions and to receive and impart information and ideas without interference by public authority and regardless of frontiers. This Article shall not prevent States from requiring the licensing of broadcasting, television or cinema enterprises.
2. The exercise of these freedoms, since it carries with it duties and responsibilities, may be subject to such formalities, conditions, restrictions or penalties as are prescribed by law and are necessary in a democratic society, in the interests of national security, territorial

> integrity or public safety, for the prevention of disorder or crime, for the protection of health or morals, for the protection of the reputation or rights of others, for preventing the disclosure of information received in confidence, or for maintaining the authority and impartiality of the judiciary.

In my opinion, two years after the UDHR was approved, in which no restriction was contemplated, this European convention, together with the reproduction of the content of Article 19 of the 1948 declaration, initiated the promulgation of a series of restrictions on communication rights under legal cover.

Another important statement was the International Covenant on Civil and Political Rights of 1966, which, in Abad's opinion (2015, pp. 58–59), made it possible to correct the "shortcomings over the regulation of communication rights in the UHDR." For this author, this document's major contribution is its establishment in its Article 19 of limits on the exercise of UHDR Article 19 through its "emphasizing that the exercise of the right provided for in Article 2 (practically identical to UHDR Art. 19) entails special duties and responsibilities … and may be subject to certain restrictions that must be expressly set by law."

In Latin America, the most important declaration is the American Convention on Human Rights, which is also called the Pact of San José, since it was signed in San José, Costa Rica, in 1969. It entered into force on July 18, 1978. Article 13 refers to freedom of thought and expression in these terms:

1. Everyone has the right to freedom of thought and expression. This right includes freedom to seek, receive, and impart information and ideas of all kinds, regardless of frontiers, either orally, in writing, in print, in the form of art, or through any other medium of one's choice.
2. The exercise of the right provided for in the foregoing paragraph shall not be subject to prior censorship but shall be subject to subsequent imposition of liability, which shall be expressly established by law to the extent necessary to ensure:
    a) respect for the rights or reputations of others; or
    b) the protection of national security, public order, or public health or morals.
3. The right of expression may not be restricted by indirect methods or means, such as the abuse of government or private controls over newsprint, radio broadcasting frequencies, or equipment used in the dissemination of information, or by any other means tending to impede the communication and circulation of ideas and opinions.
4. Notwithstanding the provisions of para. 2 above, public entertainments may be subject by law to prior censorship for the sole purpose of regulating access to them for the moral protection of childhood and adolescence.
5. Any propaganda for war and any advocacy of national, racial, or religious hatred that constitute incitements to lawless violence or to any other similar action against any person or group of persons on any grounds including those of race, color, religion, language, or national origin shall be considered as offenses punishable by law.

For African nations, the document of reference is the African Charter on Human and People's Rights. It was written by a group of experts appointed by the Organization of African Unity (OAU). In 1981, the draft was approved unanimously at the 18th Assembly of the OAS, and it entered into force in 1986. Articles 8 to 11 contain provisions related to freedom of expression (freedom of religion, assembly, and association), with Article 9 recognizing an individual right to share information and to express and disseminate opinions "within the law."

Among Arab-speaking countries, an Arab Charter on Human Rights was agreed at the League of Arab States on September 15, 1994, but no member state ratified it. The charter was updated in 2004 and entered into force in 2008, when seven members of the League of Arab States ratified it. Article 26 affirms: "Everyone has a guaranteed right to freedom of belief, thought and opinion."

Finally, one must say that human rights law and human rights theory are very much alive and continue to develop around the world. Authors like Nussbaum, centering their theories around human dignity and the universality of what makes us "truly human" (2003, p. 41), propose that governments should ensure that people develop essential human capabilities that allow us to use our minds, imaginations, and thoughts "in ways protected by guarantees of freedom of expression" (Nussbaum 2003, p. 41) and that allow us to "participate effectively in political choices that govern one's life" (Nussbaum 2003, p. 42). For this, communication rights must not only be guaranteed but actively fostered by states.

## Conclusion: The UDHR as the Basis for Modern Communication Rights

This chapter began by analyzing the concept of freedom as a basis and foundation for human activity, particularly in the field of communication and, more precisely, information. With the struggle to ensure that states recognized rights and guaranteed the freedom to exercise them rather than simply granting limited rights to citizens, communication ceased to be regarded simply as an attribute of freedom and instead became the object of bona fide communication rights. Humankind's tenacity gave rise to successive and ever more complete declarations of the essential rights that make one human.

The UDHR invoked freedom as a natural support for the right to information. This chapter concludes with a focus on that document as a foundation for communication rights, as well as the foundation for a set of legal and ethical norms that led to the development of what is conceptualized here as subject, object, and contents. This was an essential step forward in the characterization of communication as a right.

As pointed out, the UDHR is a text that has ethical authority but no legal support or guarantees of legal implementation. Some might have thought this would pose a challenge to the formulation of communication rights. Nothing could be further from the truth, since the declaration has contributed to the progressive constitutionalization of this right in countries with a Napoleonic legal tradition, and it has served as a legal precedent to guide legal decisions about communication issues in countries with a common law tradition.

Analysis of the legal-informational communication reality in a broad range of countries, based on their constitutions and legislation, indicates that the internationality of communication rights is alive and well. Little by little, without hurry though also without pause, the image of a universal right to information is arising through the unified force of diverse national laws. This is a profound development of the guidelines laid down in the UDHR in 1948. It is natural to find opposition – even unconscious resistance – to the gradual global acceptance of the principles laid down in Article 19 of the UDHR. Such resistance can take on forms that even violate the contents of the article, but modern reality, technological advances, and the development of new communication systems are creating an unstoppable march toward universal laws that ensure the right to information.

This trajectory also reflects the importance of universal public opinion regarding the achievement of international communication rights in the sense that community ideas are internationally valid and can be shared among all peoples. Globalization strengthens the possibilities for universality and will undoubtedly contribute to universal communication rights. So do different approaches to human rights that link them to human capabilities that are, in turn, made universal by identifying the essentials of human dignity, of what makes us "truly human."

This is reflected in the successive international declarations, such as the European Convention on Human Rights of 1950, the International Covenant on Civil and Political Rights of 1966, the Pact of Costa Rica of 1969, the African Charter on Human and Peoples' Rights of 1986, and the Arab Charter of Human Rights of 2004. These documents refer to communication in practically the same terms as Article 19 of the UDHR. This highlights the importance of the UDHR in ensuring that countries around the world acknowledge the existence and importance of communication rights and other human rights and the aspiration that societies and political systems continue strengthening their commitment to the protection of these rights by respecting and implementing international and regional human rights treaties.

## References


Abad, L. (2015). El derecho a la información en los textos universales (estudio del artículo 19 de la DUDH). In: *Derecho de la Información. El ejercicio del derecho a la información y su jurisprudencia* (ed. I. Bel and L. Corredoira), 49–68. Madrid: Centro de Estudios Políticos y Constitucionales.

Azurmendi, A. (2015). El proceso de la configuración del derecho y la Información. In: *Derecho de la Información. El ejercicio del derecho a la información y su jurisprudencia* (ed. I. Bel and L. Corredoira), 31–47. Madrid: Centro de Estudios Políticos y Constitucionales.

Castro Fariñas, J.A. (1970). *De la libertad de prensa*. Madrid: Fragua.

Desantes Guanter, J.M. (1974). *La información como derecho*. Madrid: Editora Nacional.

Desantes Guanter, J.M. (1977). *Fundamentos del derecho de la información*. Madrid: Fondo editorial Cajas de Ahorros.

Desantes Guanter, J.M. (1999). *Francisco de Vitoria, precursor del derecho de la información*. Madrid: Imatique.

Fernández, R. (ed.) (2003). *Los derechos Humanos. Antología de Francisco de Vitoria*. Salamanca: Editorial San Esteban.

Nussbaum, M. (2003). Capabilities as fundamental entitlements: Sen and social justice. *Feminist Economics* 9 (2–3): 33–59.

Paine, T. (1791). *The Rights of Man*. London: J. Johnson.

Sánchez Ferriz, R. and Corredoira, L. (2017). La compleja configuración de un derecho-libertad poliédrico, el Derecho a la información.: Referencias históricas. *Revista de derecho político* 99: 11–48.

Subedi, S. (2017). *The Effectiveness of the UN Human Rights System: Reform and the Judicialisation of Human Rights*. London: Routledge.

Suksi, M., Agapiou-Josephides, K., Lehners, J.-P. et al. (eds.) (2015). *First Fundamental Rights Documents in Europe*. Cambridge, UK: Intersentia.

# 2

# Dignity, a Revolutionary Principle in a Cosmopolitan Society

Javier Gomá Lanzón

Dignity is the most revolutionary concept to come out of the twentieth century. It is endowed with such transforming power that the mere mention of it, as if it were a magic word, has been enough to overcome enormous obstacles that have held back the moral progress of humanity. In the past few years, it has advanced dramatically. And yet, in spite of the extraordinary influence of this concept, philosophy, strangely enough, has simply ignored it for the last two centuries. It has never been a subject of philosophical reflection.

It might be said that this omission is strange because this concept escapes the boundaries of philosophy and is present in innumerable aspects of life, including many different legal contexts. Indeed, an in-depth discussion of it as a philosophical concept is particularly pertinent for a volume that focuses on the universalization of rights. For dignity, in addition to being the foundation of equality, is a *sine qua non* for the enjoyment of freedom. And the concept was incorporated in twentieth-century international law's most important texts. It can be found, for example, in the Preamble of the Charter of the United Nations (1946), the Preamble and Article 1 of the Universal Declaration of Human Rights (1948), the Preamble and Article 1 of the International Convention of Civil and Political Rights (1966), and the Preamble and Article 1 of the Charter of Fundamental Rights of the European Union (2002).

In this book, authors such as Corredoira, Bel, and Abad analyze the main international documents that, in the context of communication and the exercise of freedoms, have inspired its subtitle: *Seeking Universality, Equality, Freedom and Dignity.*

Dignity is the inspiration of countless ethical debates, such as those that arise in the field of bioethics (abortion, euthanasia, genetic manipulation, and cloning). Among many others, it is at the origin of social causes like trade unionism, feminism, or animalism. And, as recently as the present century, it triggered the social movement of the *indignados* (the indignant), though those involved felt no need to define, even in simple terms, what it was that provoked their wrath and brought them onto the streets in protest.

Schopenhauer summarily dismissed the Kantian concept of dignity and, in doing so, set in motion a tendency that has dominated the world of philosophy from his day to ours and either ignores or disdains the notion. A good example of the former (ignoring the subject) is the *Diccionario de filosofía* by Ferrater Mora (2009), which makes no mention of the term throughout its four volumes. Neither does the more recent and much more extensive (2800 articles) *Routledge Encyclopedia of Philosophy* (Craig 2000), which is even more surprising. As

*The Handbook of Communication Rights, Law, and Ethics: Seeking Universality, Equality, Freedom and Dignity,* First Edition. Edited by Loreto Corredoira, Ignacio Bel Mallén, and Rodrigo Cetina Presuel.

far as disdain is concerned, examples abound in both the juridical and the bioethical fields, the most eloquent of which could be the strident title of an article which Steven Pinker published in 2008: "The Stupidity of Dignity."

Years, decades, even centuries go by and dignity continues to be ignored or seen as hollow and lacking any theoretical prestige. Though there has been a certain revival of interest in the concept of dignity over the past decade, particularly in a historical or applied context, it still remains to be defined and is still untouched by philosophical thought.

Perhaps this persistent omission is due to some characteristic that is inherent in the concept and which, if it is not allowed for, makes it unpalatable for philosophers. Petrarch, a fourteenth-century Latinist and humanist, refers to this elusive nature of dignity when he reports that, even in his times, writings on the misery of the world proliferated but on the subject of dignity there was only one. To explain this imbalance, he argued that knowledge of the misery in the world did not require special study; it was so widespread and abundant that it was simply enough to open your eyes. Dignity, on the other hand, was much less obvious and required arduous speculative study, carried out in the face of resistance to the natural tendency and lacking a tradition on which it could be founded:

> I do not deny that the misery of the human condition is great and of many classes and has been wept over in many a book; but if you look in the other direction, you will see many things that make it joyful and blissful; yet, if I am not mistaken, no one has written about this and there are some who began but desisted because it seemed to them that they had chosen a difficult subject, which was dry and contrary to what others had written, and in any event more arduous than they had expected; because human misery is so great that it is clearly manifest to all, but human happiness is so small and concealed that it is necessary to dig deep in order to show it to those who do not believe. (Petrarch 1978, pp. 460–461)

## The History of Dignity

The history of dignity is usually recounted by using, one after the other, select texts taken from the Western literary canon, which employ the word with special intention and frequency. Such a history cannot preclude a certain number of essential names – Cicero, Mirandola, Kant – but the arid juxtaposition of quotations, in itself lacking eloquence, becomes more intelligible when inserted into a wider context, namely the debate between misery and dignity that permeated European cultural tradition up to the Renaissance.

In this debate, there are three principal viewpoints. First, there are those who believe that, in this world, the reign of misery is absolute and that there is no kind of dignity. Second, there are those who admit that there is misery but also acknowledge that there is dignity. Finally, there are those who only see the excellence and gravitas of humankind and take no interest in the rest.

The first group created a new literary genre to express their pessimism: the *consolations*. A consolation is a treatise, cultivated first by philosophers and later by rhetoricians, which is directed at someone who has suffered a calamity, a typical case being a man or woman who has lost a child. Authors in this genre strive to accumulate arguments that bring solace and relief to the sufferer. The consolations by Seneca and Plutarch that have survived coincide in the strategy of their argument – which is anything but comforting – by attempting to convince the sufferer that no death is an evil because the only evil worthy of pity is to be alive. The best thing, they say, is not to be born, and, if we have been born, the next best thing is to die soon.

Cicero is the initiator of the second group. The *Consolatio*, which he wrote after the death of his daughter, has not survived, but we do have his thoughts on the misery of death in a number of his writings, notably the *Tusculanae*. The subject of Book I of this treatise is his own death, a source of unhappiness for those who, he says, are not wise; and the subject of Book III is sadness (in Latin, *aegritudo*) upon the death of a loved one. In this sense, the work can be classed in the genre of the consolation, though the vitality of his own personality shines through its pages.

According to Cicero, philosophical meditation teaches us that death is only an apparent evil, whether we believe that the soul is immortal, as Plato did, or that it disappears along with the body. And this supposition does not lead, as it does with Seneca and Plutarch, to a disdain toward life but, on the contrary, makes room for dignity. The source of dignity is two-fold. If we strive to live *well* instead of simply to live *for a long time*, life will never have been brief. Our conscience is consoled, before death, by the memory of a worthy life: "But death truly is then met with the greatest tranquillity when the dying man can comfort himself with his own praise. No one dies too soon who has finished the course of perfect virtue" (*Tusculanae Disputationes*, 1.45). The second source, which is added to this satisfaction, is the solicitude that the virtuous have for posterity and that encourages them to carry out exemplary acts that will bring them posthumous glory and lasting memory, and thus endow human dignity with an influence that outlives the short-lived period of an individual life.

In Cicero, the recognition of a person's dignity in this world is supplemented by a daring extension of its subjective basis. We must remember that *dignitas* in ancient Rome implied status, rank, and a higher position in comparison with others in the same hierarchy. It is not an inborn quality but inherent in an office, which can be won or lost, and there is not one single dignity but a multiplicity of them. At the end of the Roman Empire, the lists of official positions continued to receive the name *Notitia dignitatum*.

Cicero introduces an important novelty into this state of affairs. In Book I of *On Duties*, he states that the general virtue of a person (honorability) is made up of four special virtues – prudence, justice, magnanimity, and *decorum* – which entail different types of duties. He defines *decorum* as "that which corresponds to the excellence of the person, where his nature differs from other living beings," and the duty that is peculiar to this virtue consists of disciplining the impulse to pleasure and subjugating it to reason (Kapust 2011). The ability of reason to impose obedience on impulse gives humans – all humans without exception – a distinctive dignity. For the first time, Cicero universalizes dignity in all men and women, placing them at the same level because they are endowed with reason, in contrast to the lower animals, which, being devoid of reason, are, as a result, devoid of dignity.

The dignity that, in Cicero, redeems the misery of this world is also worldly, since it is rooted in human nature, whereas in Innocence III, who in about 1195 issued his treatise *De miseria humanae conditio*, that dignity, which he does not reject, is supernatural: it is the hope of being saved by Christ and, after death, of attaining citizenship of Heaven. Centuries later, the humanist Bartolomeo Fazio, with the express intention of completing the diptych that Innocence III had left unfinished, wrote *De excellentia et praestantia hominis* in 1447. In this work, he signaled, as Petrarch did also, the puzzling lack of books on the subject. For Fazio, a human being's excellence stems exclusively from his immortal soul, which cannot be enhanced by anything originating in this corrupt world.

Petrarch also belongs to this second group, and in the work I referred to before, "On Sadness and Misery," he shares the conviction expressed by Innocence III that the greatest excellence of a human person resides in his supernatural destiny. At the same time, he adds a new tone: as a Christian humanist, he is able to perceive and enjoy the beauty of nature, the perfection of the human body, and the wonders of the arts and sciences that dignify our human condition and the contemplation of which banishes the general sadness (*aegritudo*) that oppresses us and which is all the more dangerous, he maintains, if it has no specific cause.

Finally, the third group includes those writers who praise the dignity of humankind and pay no attention whatsoever to his misery, as if it did not exist. An important author in this group is Giannozzo Manetti, who in 1452 wrote *De dignitate et excellentia hominis*. The first three volumes are a hymn of praise of the perfection of the human body and soul and postulate an ideal of happiness and plenitude immanent in this world, not as a substitute of the next, and incompatible with the defense of that misery, which had been tirelessly repeated in innumerable previous writings. For this reason, Book IV does not complete the unfinished treatise of Innocence III but, on the contrary, explicitly refutes it.

Giovanni Pico della Mirandola opens his well-known *Oratio*, written in 1485 (with a second version in 1488), and later called "On the Dignity of Mankind," by stating that he is dissatisfied with the reasons usually proposed to justify the great dignity of humankind and that he believes he has finally understood why, among all living beings, the human being is most worthy of admiration. God created the world by conforming to eternal archetypes and then realized that none of them could be used to form humankind; so He created humankind "without a precise image." Then He spoke to Adam and explained to him the eccentric nature of his dignity, saying that it derived not from possessing a specific place or gift within Creation but from having the freedom, similar to divine freedom, to create himself as he wished and to choose, according to his own will, the determination of his nature. So, if in Cicero, it was reason that distinguished humankind from beasts, here it was an absolute and limitless freedom.

This history would be incomplete if we were not to mention the *Diálogo de la dignidad del hombre* (*Dialogue on the Dignity of Man*), which was published posthumously by the Spanish writer Fernán Pérez de Oliva (1494–1531), and which is a dialogue between Aurelio, who takes the side of human misery, and Antonio, who defends human dignity. The most interesting feature of this Renaissance essay, in comparison with previous writings, is that it sets out the two opposing versions, one after the other, without deciding between them, and leaving that decision to the good sense of the reader. Furthermore, this dialogue acts as a gateway to later Spanish literature, since, for the first time, it is not written in Latin, which, until then, had enjoyed a monopoly on writings on such an elevated subject. Written in the vernacular, it is also innovative in that it is not written in the discursive style of the treatise or sermon, which had been prevalent in classical tradition.

## Dignity in Kant

Kant dignifies the concept of dignity by integrating it into his sublime moral philosophy. But he does not define it either and, if we discount the *Metaphysical Foundations* (1785), where he uses the term 16 times, it only occurs very occasionally in his work. Rather than being an essential component of his system, it tends to be a synonym for words that *are* essential: autonomous subject, self-legislating I, end in itself, compendium of the humanity of humans. The second formulation of the categorical imperative states: "So act as to treat humanity, whether in thine own person or in that of any other, in every case as an end withal, never as means only" (Kant 2008, p. 46). Kant could have reformulated that imperative, with identical meaning, by simply saying: "Act in accordance with the dignity of which you are the bearer."

Two distinctions in the works of Kant serve to introduce his idea of dignity. In the *Critique of Practical Reason*, he differentiates between happiness and dignity: "Morality is not properly the doctrine of how we should *make* ourselves happy, but how we should become *worthy* of happiness" (Kant 1898, p. 227). In our pursuit of happiness, which Kant identifies with pleasure or desire, we resemble brute animals, who instinctively seek the same satisfaction. Therefore happiness, pleasure, sentimental wellbeing – aims of the morality of English empiricism (Hume, Smith) – do not do justice to the loftiness of the human condition. In contrast to that sentiment-based ethic, Kant posits the ideal of an autonomous subject, who only obeys the universal-impersonal laws that his reason acknowledges, not only independently of experience and feeling, but even perhaps in spite of them, so that the struggle with his own instinctive inclinations will shed an even more favorable light on the grandeur of human morality. We might add that persistent adverse fortune may well stifle our desire for happiness because, however much we practice all the virtues, we will only be increasing the probabilities of achieving happiness, without, however, any guarantee of success. But nothing in this world – no circumstance whatsoever – can deprive us of the privilege of living our lives with dignity and of always acting in accordance with that dignity that belongs exclusively to us. Therefore, what is uniquely universal and distinctively human is not to be happy but to be worthy of being happy, and that dignity, which is worthy of happiness, but which this world does not provide, justifies Kant's postulation of a God and a future life where dignity and happiness finally coincide.

A foretaste on Earth of this future heaven would be the "kingdom of ends" that Kant imagines in the *Metaphysical Foundations*. In respect of this kingdom, the philosopher articulates the second of his interesting distinctions. "In the kingdom of ends," he writes, "everything has either value or dignity. Whatever has a value can be replaced by something else which is equivalent; whatever, on the other hand, is above all value, and therefore admits of no equivalent, has a dignity" (Kant 2008, p. 52). There are, therefore, replaceable things that are not valued by their intrinsic worth but by their instrumental utility in obtaining other goods, whereas there are beings, like those belonging to the human race, that are not replaceable because, of themselves, they are endowed with intrinsic value. The immoral act par excellence would therefore be objectification, by virtue of which, man is treated as an object and is dehumanized because he is given the treatment reserved for things that only have a price.

In conclusion, up to the time of Kant, dignity is understood to be a distinctive feature of man and is associated with some positive quality, which is exclusive to him – in Cicero, reason, in Mirandola, freedom, in Kant, morality – and which imposes on the bearer certain duties of validation. It is not by chance that the history of dignity begins with Cicero's *On Duties* and culminates with Kant's famous exclamation: "Duty! Thou sublime and mighty name" (Kant 1898, p. 180). The being, which distinguishes itself from brute animals because it possesses reason, freedom, or morality – qualities that give that being a particular dignity – is expected to act in accordance with that dignity. The duty to confirm or perfect the original, intrinsic dignity ends up by producing a selective effect because, in fact, only a person who fulfills those duties can rightly call themself worthy. This idea is also confirmed in Kant's work, where the concept continues to preserve hints of aristocratic overtones: following the lines of his argumentation, full dignity belongs not to *all* men and women but only to those who are morally *the best*.

## Dignity is What Gets in the Way

The historical itinerary we have just examined invites us to draw some provisional conclusions about the essence of dignity.

Only the human being fully and unconditionally possesses the quality of being irreplaceable, unexchangeable, an end in itself, and never a means. The following example is a rough illustration of the fundamental idea. Let us imagine a public highway that is under construction and has to pass through some private property: the state is empowered to expropriate the land by paying a fair market price, since a private interest should yield to the higher public interest. The land can be expropriated, but naturally the owner can never be, not even in the name of the common good or collective progress. From this, we can deduce a rule: private interest yields to a general interest but, in turn, general interest yields to private dignity, for which there is no possible fair market price.

So, dignity could be defined precisely as that which cannot be expropriated and makes the individual *resistant to everything*, general interest or common good included. Ever since Aristotle claimed in *Politics* that "the city-state is prior in nature to the household and to each of us individually" (1253a), civic virtue has required the citizen to give way to the priority of the common good. But even virtue understood in these terms has its limits, the principal of which is dignity, that intimate quality of the individual, resembling a diamond in its beauty, brilliance, and strength, which resists any good cause that involves the collectivization of the individual.

In the name of dignity, the citizen opposes the Machiavellianism of reasons of state, both old and new, and when it demands his collaboration saying that many others already collaborate, his reply will be what could be the motto of dignity; "Although others do, I won't."

In the name of dignity, the citizen opposes the possible tyrannies of majorities, which are not all-powerful – not even if they are democratic – and he rejects the utilitarian law of the happiness of the greatest number.

We should not expect the concept to provide a definitive solution, like the answer in a crossword, to the myriad of situations that raise so many subtle questions on applied ethics (bioethics, technology, business). Those who criticize the emptiness of the concept probably suffer from excessive expectations and feel disappointed because they find that there isn't a recipe book to resolve dilemmas that are best resolved by applying prudence in each particular case. There is always a hiatus between the theory of the concept and the reality of experience, which nobody can expect to bridge once and for all with norms that are so universal that we will be relieved in the future, as if we were robots, of the bother of thinking and deciding. Dignity presents itself only as a humanist principle of antiutilitarian orientation, which frequently falls foul of the desire to legitimize moral actions by their advantageous consequences for many or for the majority (consequentialist ethics).

So dignity might also be described as something that is a *hindrance*. It makes committing iniquities more difficult, of course; but, more interestingly, it also sometimes hinders just causes, such as material and technical progress, economic and social efficiency, or public utility. And this hindering, obstructive, and paralyzing effect, which often accompanies dignity and which makes us stop and consider, opens our eyes to the *dignitas* of precisely those who are a hindrance, because they are no longer useful, they are left over, always threatened by a history that would advance more quickly without them. So, if to begin with, dignity resembled a luminous aura surrounding only perfection, its meaning is now widened to include the dignity of imperfection in all its forms, which are often even more powerfully and visually noticeable.

The transition from a state of nature to one of civilization is manifest in a social organization that gives preference to the residual, the surplus, dignity's favorites; that preference might be exemplified, in our daily urban experience, by an expensive car that has been driving at speed but has to pull up and stop because of a distracted child or an awkward old person slowly walking over a crosswalk. In the world of nature, the struggle to survive is won by the strongest or the best adapted. Humankind enters that combat in better conditions because it has substituted ferocious teeth and sharpened claws for symbolic language and technology, which have worked the miracle of adapting nature to its needs and of dominating the other species. Having reached a certain level of social evolution, without any apparent evolutionary advantage, the human species, allowing themselves a luxury, which apparently only they can enjoy, raises up a humanitarian ideal that overturns the law of the *survival of the fittest* prevailing in the natural world and puts in its place a new and revolutionary law of the *survival of the weakest*.

Perhaps the first vestige in history of recognizably human behavior was found only a couple of decades ago in the excavations at Dmanisi (Georgia): the fossilized remains of hominids who lived in the area 1.8 million years ago. Among them was a jawbone, which exhibited the peculiarity of not having any teeth. It must have belonged to an old person who was unable to feed themself and needed the cooperation of the group to ingest a mash of prechewed meat. There is no other record of a prior fossilized hominid with such a great loss of teeth and remodeling of the jaw. There is no information either regarding primates with a similar degree of tooth loss. Before the Dmanisi discovery, there were no known cases of longevity either in hominids or chimpanzees, which in any event never outlived the postreproductive period. Once the basic biological function to ensure the perpetuation of the species had been accomplished – reproduction with transmission of the genetic heritage – the individual was headed towards a quick death. Why prolong life? Evolution is blind in respect of old age, a sheer biological absurdity.

Dmanisi certifies the birth of group cooperation, which was antievolutionary, antinatural, and antiutilitarian – in other words, genuinely human. The old fellow served no useful purpose, and in spite of that, the group considered him worthy of care and protection. The first flashing glory of dignity occurred at Dmanisi.

## Egalitarian Dignity

In premodern tradition, full dignity was still reserved for those who deserved it. In fact, the concept survived without any significant conflict in a highly hierarchal society in which there were different dignities and abundant discrimination. But, as I have already suggested, the concept bore within itself the seeds of its own improvement. Sure enough, the twentieth century brought about a mutation of its essence, which did not occur, as usually happens, through the influence of the teachings of a renowned philosopher or of a prestigious school of thought inspiring a program of political action; it occurred, in the absence of the learned, through ordinary people and the force of events.

This mutation of essence implied, in the first place, the substitution of the old distinction of aristocracy and an extension to include all the members of the human race – something in the nature of an *aristocracy of the masses.* All people, for the sole reason that they belong to the human race, possess it equally and forever. Furthermore, this egalitarian dignity is now perceived as *self-grounded,* not depending on another authority that acts as its foundation (reason, freedom, morality); *full* from the outset and not needing any later improvement, nor subject to loss, wastage, or depletion through possible misuse by the bearer; *absolute* and not relative to others, men or animals; and finally centered, not on the duties that it imposes on the bearer, but on his *right to demand* it be universally respected by others – all of which prepare the ground for the doctrine of universal rights.

Democratic dignity is received at birth and entitles the bearer to rights without any moral virtue on his part, rights that are valid even if the original dignity is belied by the odious indignity of a subject's life.

Dignity is inalienable, indefeasible, and inviolable; though it is undeserved, it is nonetheless worthy of respect and, in a certain way, places the rest of humanity in a position of owing.

It is unique, universal, anonymous, and abstract. And, consequently, it is also cosmopolitan; in other words, it is the same for all human beings on the planet.

An idea such as this, in spite of appearing to be a truism, is neither "natural" nor "normal," which is demonstrated by the fact that no one seems to have missed it in the course of previous millennia. It has to be understood rather as if it were an exceedingly difficult lesson to be learned collectively, a lesson that is not written in a revealed book or in the book of nature.

It is, as it were, a moral truth that has recently established itself with the majority as a result of recent historic events of unspeakable inhumanity, which have created a consensus, in negative terms, that such events should never, under any circumstances, be repeated.

Something that is evident is perceived, as such, by those whose senses are trained to perceive it – which is what happens in the perception of artistic perfection or philosophical or scientific truth. Therefore, the reason for people's dignity depends on their education. Kant's distinction between dignity and price is again useful to encapsulate the multiple objectives of education into two: training professionals and training citizens.

A professional is a person who has learned the rules of a trade and applies them with competence in order to make a living by supplying a product or a service for which the market is prepared to pay a price. A country with competent professionals has the stamp of a truly modern country. Together, with the training of professionals, the second objective is to educate that same individual to become a *citizen*, which means someone who is aware of their dignity. A rounded education not only becomes the source of practical and profitable skills but also prompts the citizen to be aware of their own dignity and instills self-respect into themselves, to avoid what Kant describes as "to find himself, on self-examination, worthless and contemptible in his own eyes" (Kant 1898, p. 259).

The ancients, at the times when they were not engaged in *negotium*, recommended the cultivation of *otium cum dignitate*, a complacency in that intimate feeling about the value of each individual, subject neither to price nor the rationality of the marketplace. Price and dignity are not locked in irreconcilable antagonism, but there is certainly a tension between them, which has no definitive solution. And, if there is a conflict, dignity prevails, because, both in chronologic and anthropologic terms, we are citizens first and professionals second.

## Inviolable but Violated a Thousand Times

A common criticism leveled at dignity and repeated by its adversaries is that it cannot be objectively and rationally explained and that it is, therefore, indemonstrable.

There is no doubt that dignity is the postulate of a value, not an empirical fact observable by the senses. It does not resemble, for example, an identifiable object, or a logical deduction, or a juridical law. Its essence is of the moral realities, like bravery, decency, compassion, which are not *apprehended* by scientific reasoning but which are *recognized* by feelings, even before they can be defined. Whatever dignity may be is learnt, not in the logical definition of scholarly treatises, but in the direct intuition of its essence, which is revealed by a specific example.

The law requires that something should be done and, if it is not obeyed, the law imposes it coactively. But in the realm of morality, unlike that of legality, it would be futile to order someone to be virtuous: *you cannot tell people to be good; you invite them to be good.* Every example of virtue includes an invitation to do the same and to make it generalized. And naturally this is also true of the practical acts of dignity. But it is not true of that innate and original dignity that every human being possesses by the mere fact of being. One thing is what a person does, which can be worthy or unworthy (pragmatism) and another is what he or she is (ontology). And, as I have said before, the democratic concept of original, *ontological* dignity remains intact in spite of reiterated unworthy *praxis.* This dignity is not a fact, not even a moral fact, but a postulate, an attribution that, with the passage of time, has widened its subjective basis. This growth does not come about through an invitation, as in the case of virtue, but through *scandal.*

The witness of an action, which had been morally invisible in the past, surprises himself on contemplating with sorrow what he suddenly perceives to be an act of violation. At that moment, the witness has implicitly applied to the victim, and the group to whom the victim belongs, a dignity that tradition had obstinately refused to afford him. Novels in the nineteenth century, for example, familiarized readers of the time with the injustices suffered by abused women, abandoned children, impoverished masses, debtor prisoners, and exploited workers. These novels showed readers, for the first time, that sectors of the population who historically suffered discrimination possessed the same dignity as the privileged by highlighting the scandal produced by such wretched situations. In the majority of cases, dignity is recognized by its absence, when the respect due is missing, because it is then that unquestionable truths are clearly evident. And the feeling of scandal is not usually limited to benevolent compassion but sooner or later unleashes an active movement of social reform aimed at bringing to an end those situations of indignity that are now judged to be intolerable.

Egalitarian dignity has been ranked as sacrosanct, and yet it is no secret that, in fact, it continues to be violated a thousand times a day. However, there is an important difference between the violations of the past and those of today: the dignity of women, children, workers, or the poor may continue to be violated, but today no one can do so without *degrading themselves*. For centuries, a woman's body, for example, could be constantly violated without punishment and even without reproach, because that action, given one name or another, or none, had become invisible in the normalcy of total masculine domination. Today, many women continue, unfortunately, to suffer violations, but now the violator can only carry out his repugnant act by degrading himself morally while creating revulsion around him and in himself too, if he is not totally corrupted.

The revulsion produced by indignity shows humanity the path towards moral progress.

## A Conclusion and a Proposal: Cosmopolitan Dignity

Of all the human groups who have persistently suffered discrimination since the earliest times, one of the most affected has been foreigners. Over the centuries, law and civilization have made great strides of progress for those living within their own frontiers; but very often, those who were born outside those frontiers were, all too often, considered barbarians or savages and received the treatment accorded to slaves, an intermediate status between that of a human being and an animal. In this respect too, perspectives have evolved drastically in our time. Over the past few years, many voices have been raised to condemn the restrictive policies that Western governments have applied to migrants from other parts of the planet, who flee from war or poverty. They are indignant at the closure of frontiers or the expulsion of migrants, which they consider to be contrary to elementary humanitarian principles. The fact that their condemnation and anger are, in many cases, fully justified should not prevent us from seeing the unusual novelty that one and the other imply in strictly comparative terms: they both presuppose the tacit recognition, unprecedented in history, of the full dignity of all men and women without distinction as human beings, irrespective of whether they were born on one side of the border or the other.

The Spanish poet Antonio Machado formulates the original intuition with admirable precision when his character Juan de Mairena says: "No one is more than anyone else" (Machado 1986), which is same as saying that "however much a man is worth, there is nothing greater than his worth as a man." The statement that "however much a man or a woman is worth, he or she has no greater worth than that of being a man or a woman" is the basis for the categorical statement I made earlier, that dignity is "unique, universal, anonymous, and abstract." In effect, if there is no greater dignity than that of being a man or a woman, then all the other attributes (birth, sex, fatherland, religion, culture, race) on which a wide variety of ancient dignities were based in the past become mere accidents with no moral relevance and simply fade away. The difference between the president of the most powerful nation in the world and a homeless person, a migrant who swims across the sea to reach the promised land, or a person in prison for serious crimes is accidental, irrelevant, because there is nothing greater than common dignity. Though the variety of possible circumstances is humanly enriching, all individuals belong equally to the common lot of mortals.

It is often repeated that death is the great equalizer; but before death arrives, in our lifetime, we have all been made equal by our common dignity of origin.

## Egalitarianism Leads Straight to Cosmopolitanism

The cosmopolitan ideal would like to see the establishment of a single citizenry for all the inhabitants of this global polis that is our planet. Before being a member of a state, a nation, or a country, each individual is firstly a citizen of the world. Because they belong to the same species, individuals have a generic citizenry from which are derived the rights that every state should always respect, even though the individual is not granted the citizenship that every state can give. Perhaps we will never attain and perhaps it may not even be desirable to attain the world state that Kant longed for (the world ruled by one universal government), but powerful tendencies can be seen on all sides that converge on the future construction of a cosmopolitan civil society.

In the final analysis, cosmopolitanism means simply that: there is only once race, the human race, and only one principle, individual dignity.

## References

Craig, E. (ed.) (2000). *Routledge Encyclopedia of Philosophy*. New York: Routledge.

Ferrater Mora, J. (2009). *Diccionario de filosofía*. Barcelona: Ariel.

Kant, I. (1898). *Kant's Critique of Practical Reason and Other Works on the Theory of Ethics*. London: Longmans, Green, and Co.

Kant, I. (2008). *Fundamental Principles of the Metaphysics of Morals*. New York: Cosimo.

Kapust, D. (2011). Cicero on decorum and the morality of rhetoric. *European Journal of Political Theory* 10 (1): 92–112.

Machado, A. (1986). *Juan de Mairena 1 & 2*. Madrid: Cátedra.

Petrarch. (1978). *Obras I. Prosa, De los remedios contra la próspera y adversa fortuna*. Madrid: Alfaguara.

Pinker, S. (2008). The stupidity of dignity. *The New Republic* (28 May).

# 3

# Communication Rights in an Internet-Based Society

## Why Is the Principle of Universality *So Important*?[1]

Loreto Corredoira

The foundations of the universality of communication rights were laid down in Article 19 of the Universal Declaration of Human Rights (UDHR) and confirmed in Article 19 of the International Covenant on Civil and Political Rights of 1966. Both texts define three communication rights: *seek*, *receive*, and *impart*. These three activities are at the heart of how the Internet is used across the world today. These three facets of the right also shaped the discussion that took place at the World Summit on the Information Society (as stated in ITU 2003). This chapter discusses the threats to communication rights that originate from the Internet and its universal or mass nature. Though there are many such threats, they should not hinder efforts to ensure the universal application of these rights. The "universal subject" in the information society and the rights that this subject possesses are described in this chapter.

A decade ago, I reflected on UDHR Article 19 (Corredoira 2007) in the context of Web 2.0. My primary focus was how this Article relates to the integration of new forms of public participation in media as well as to the new messages and methods that the Internet makes possible for industries and individual professionals. Since the use of the Internet became widespread in the mid-1990s, the universalization of communication rights has become even clearer. A range of stakeholders has emerged: a public that participates in and contributes to discussions in the media; media channels run by "digital natives" who require no license to broadcast or "print"; and social networks that democratize the communication of information and facilitate many channels for seeking it – sometimes from disruptive sources (Wasserman 2017, p. 72) – and for contributing to collaborative journalism.

Without any doubt, the guarantees contained in the generic right I have just analyzed or in the different "Bills of Rights" that contain them are, as Stephens (2005) says, insufficient. This is why it is useful to deconstruct this generic right into three rights: to seek information and ideas, to receive information and ideas, and to impart information and ideas. As a matter of fact, almost all international texts that recognize and interpret this "standard" do so while highlighting the "multifaceted" nature of freedom of expression, what we call, communication rights in order to reflect better this poliedric nature.

[1] This research was started during the Del Amo Scholarship stay at Berkeley, California (Summer 2017). This work was also produced as part of the Ministry of Science Projects DER2015-65810-P as well as the PID2019–105334RB-I00. Loreto Corredoira is Principal Researcher with Rafael Rubio of the last one.

*The Handbook of Communication Rights, Law, and Ethics: Seeking Universality, Equality, Freedom and Dignity*, First Edition. Edited by Loreto Corredoira, Ignacio Bel Mallén, and Rodrigo Cetina Presuel.

According to both Padovani (Padovani and Pavan 2006) and Raboy (Raboy 2004, pp. 345–359), communication rights originated in the United Nations Charter as described by D'Arcy when he proposed the "right to communicate," a different concept than "communication rights" but that shares with the latter the idea that we are in need of a more extensive, fleshed-out right or set of three rights:

> International recognition of the centrality of information to human rights dates back to the UN Charter, where article 19 states that "Everyone has the right to freedom of opinion and expression; these rights includes the right to hold opinions without interference and to seek, receive and impart information and ideas through any media and regardless of frontiers."
>
> (Padovani and Pavan 2006)


> International recognition of the centrality of information to human rights dates back to the UN Charter, where article 19 states that "Everyone has the right to freedom of opinion and expression; these rights includes the right to hold opinions without interference and to seek, receive and impart information and ideas through any media and regardless of frontiers."
>
> (Padovani and Pavan 2006)


Yet it was not until 1969 that another concept, that of a universal "right to communicate" emerged in the words of Jean D'Arcy, former director of the Radio and Visual Service at the Office of Public Information for the UN:

> The time will come when the Universal Declaration of Human Rights will have to encompass a more extensive right than man's right to information, first laid down-twenty one years ago in Article in 19. This is the right to communicate.
>
> (D'Arcy 1969)
>
> "The time will come when the Universal Declaration of Human Rights will have to encompass a more extensive right than man's right to information, first laid down-twenty one years ago in Article in 19. This is the right of man to communicate.
>
> d'Arcy (1969)

Twenty-five years from the rise of the Web, the appearance of artificial intelligence (AI) in journalism and marketing, the digitalization of the commercial world, and the sharing economy are all trends that make it necessary to reassess the foundations of communication rights.

In the spirit of "updating" communication rights enshrined in the UDHR – rights that, as we will see in other chapters of this book, are the natural evolution of the "freedom of expression" of the eighteenth and nineteenth centuries – the Declaration of Principles, also known as the Geneva Declaration (International Telecommunications Union 2003), of the World Summit on the Information Society (WSIS) was approved in 2003. This declaration, which was supported by the UN as well as by the International Telecommunications Union (2003, 2014), established the universal nature of the information society and that no one can be excluded from those benefits. Therefore, the text was revised and included an update of the concept of communication rights by introducing the concept of the *right to communicate* we have referred to earlier. Among the things that the right to communicate sought to ensure was the "universality" of Internet access, something that the legislation of many countries does not guarantee. In light of the risks of a digital divide between countries and individuals, the declaration recognizes that "everyone, everywhere should have the opportunity to participate and no one should be excluded from the benefits the Information Society offers" (ITU 2003). Thus, a new dimension to communication rights, universality of access was highlighted and entered our contemporary conversation around communication rights and what they seek to guarantee.

Other distinguished academics such as Danieli, Stamatopoulou, and Dias (1999) as well as Birdsall (2007), have reflected on the ins and outs of that declaration, which will be the subject of several pages in the current volume. In particular, O'Flaherty (2012, pp. 627–654) has focused on freedoms related to communication, and more precisely on the "right to communicate." Works such as those edited by Corredoira and Cotino (2013) or Bel Mallén and Corredoira (2015) or the study by Arellano (2012) serve as references for the most relevant freedoms and rights in the Latin American context and that also make it necessary to speak of communication rights, not just of a unidimensional right to freedom of expression.

## Threats to Communication Rights Arising from the Internet and Its Universal or Mass Nature

At the time this chapter was being written, the media was broadcasting Prime Minister Theresa May's announcement (Bienkof 2018) about the need for the United Kingdom to bring in laws to prohibit harassment of public personalities on social networks. This is not an isolated case. Throughout 2017, many political leaders and national and supranational democratic institutions – for instance, Macron in France,[2] the Spanish government, and the European Union (Alandete 2018) – considered placing limitations on communication in places that we could term "3.0" in order to refer to the services of the information society, especially after the explosive expansion of the social Web.

It is also worth mentioning the revolution represented by virtual currencies such as BitCoin, which is now traded on Wall Street.[3] These pose a challenge to sovereign states, some of which are now demanding special security measures be put in place. This was the European Union's response (European Commission 2017) following the exposure of computer system vulnerabilities during the massive Wannacry ransomware attack. But let us not confuse monetary or fiscal policy, which have no basis in human rights, with communication rights, which enjoy the status of basic human rights. Constant technological change creates growing uncertainty as computers' processing speeds accelerate and algorithms that publish content on leading websites and social networks (Facebook, YouTube, and Twitter) become more sophisticated. These changes are altering society in a way that has legal consequences and certainly poses ethical challenges.

Recently, websites such as Facebook[4] have made major changes to their policies, and sometimes these have gone in the opposite direction to those made in the radio and television industries. Google is also repositioning itself having created and disseminated content through Google News since 2002. These changes are coming about in response to regulation of the information ecosystem. In Spain, Google News ceased operating in 2016 after a so-called Google tax or fee for press clipping or links to newspapers was approved. Even more recently, these platforms have shifted their business strategies and sought partnerships with major news outlets – for example, through the Google AMP initiative or Facebook News. These partnerships raise questions not only about the role of social media platforms as news organizations themselves, but also about the impact that a greater level of media concentration may have on communication rights (Cetina Presuel and Martínez Sierra 2019).

Death threats have a greater impact when they are published on Twitter or Facebook than when they are printed. There is undoubtedly greater sensitivity among the public – and politicians – to websites where free expression can circulate without being detected by potential critics. "Bullying," sometimes by "trolls" or bots, has become a dreaded threat. Such Internet activity seems more threatening than if it happened on TV or in a printed newspaper. Are

[2] Press conference by Emmanuel Macron. https://www.pscp.tv/w/1mrGmZQokVdJy. (no longer available)

[3] Trading of BitCoin on Wall Street since December 2017 can be followed at http://quotes.wsj.com/fx/BTCUSD (accessed January 13, 2021).

[4] Facebook announced a major change in January 2018. See online press release at https://about.fb.com/news/2018/04/inside-feed-meaningful-interactions/ (accessed January 13, 2021).

threats harmful only when they travel, hidden away, through the dark corners of the Internet? No, as telephone harassment can also be a nightmare. The multiplying effect of social networks is to increase the dissemination, but not the nature, of criminal acts. Harassment, fraud, and threats are illegal acts in and of themselves, regardless of the medium or form of the message. Spanish courts have already established the concept of legal responsibility for Tweeting and reTweeting (Corredoira 2017).[5]

It seems that the universalization of communication mediated through the Internet is creating risks and potential "plagues" arising from the basic human behavior of communicating and sharing. The Internet is generalizing the right to receive and disseminate information to the many rather than the few, which is a strongly positive phenomenon, and yet sovereign states tend to be on guard because they see this as a development that leads to the emergence of potential enemies.

Along these lines, the European Union is even considering reducing anonymity on social networks and platforms such as YouTube and Vimeo. The governments of France, Spain, and Portugal[6] made this request as part of the debate that took place as the EU's Copyright Directive (Directive 2019/790) was being debated. This request was met with considerable resistance within the sector owing to its potential to restrict communication rights on the Internet[7] as well as offline.

As mentioned, it is important to return to the foundations of the universality of these rights and understand their basic features. These rights apply equally to private and professional individuals using digital media. This is also the case in the United States under First Amendment doctrine, as Ugland analyzes in Chapter 6 of this volume.

## Who is the "Universal Subject" in the Information Society, and what Rights does this Subject Possess?

If "everyone" has communication rights, such that "everyone" is the "universal subject" of them, that "universal subject" can be differentiated from the "professional subject" (that is, a journalist working with any medium or format of dissemination) as well as from the organized or corporate subject. By this, I mean that this subject also includes media, as Desantes (Desantes Guanter et al.1994) commented: "Universality also applies to the communication medium for an obvious reason: if communication is a necessary good, no source of information can be closed off. Because the positive provisions refer to media indistinctly, it must be

[5] More recently, the Supreme Court ruling of February 28, 2018 (95/2018), exonerated R. Vera, who as user@cassandra mocked the ETA attack against Carrero Blanco in the Franco era as "humiliation of the victims" and "glorification of terrorism." The family of Carrero Blanco had requested a verdict of not guilty because they considered that a guilty verdict would have been disproportionate to the act. The court ruled that no risk of violent crime existed.

[6] The legislative proceedings related to the new Directive can be followed at http://eur-lex.europa.eu/legal-content/EN/TXT/?uri=consil:ST_15651_2017_INIT (accessed January 13, 2021). The position of the French, Spanish, and Portuguese delegations can be seen in their Working Paper of October 2, 2017, that was sent to the Council (WK 10644/2017 INIT) Final text Directive (EU) 2018/1808 of the European Parliament and of the Council of November 14, 2018 amending Directive 2010/13/EU on the coordination of certain provisions laid down by law, regulation, or administrative action in Member States concerning the provision of audiovisual media services (Audiovisual Media Services Directive) in view of changing market realities.

[7] See, for example, the 57 organizations that requested the elimination of a requirement that access and storage providers filter content (Malcolm 2017). See also their open letter to the European Union (Civil Liberties Union for Europe 2017) https://www.eff.org/deeplinks/2018/10/effs-letter-eus-copyright-directive-negotiators (accessed January 13, 2020).

understood that all media are included, even those of the past and the future; this is the case in UDHR Article 19."

Private individuals also hold other rights closely related to their communication rights. For example, they enjoy the universal right to Internet access, which amounts to a right to share and participate in Internet culture, to create and be recognized as authors of content, and to have access to education and employment. This was part of the motivation of the 2003 Geneva Declaration, which is entitled "Our Common Vision of the Information Society," meant as a response to the challenges posed by information and communication technologies (ICTs), and centered on the right to communicate as a means of updating the conception and reach of communication rights for our current times.

> 1. We, the representatives of the peoples of the world, assembled in Geneva from 10–12 December 2003 for the first phase of the World Summit on the Information Society, declare our common desire and commitment to build a people-centered, inclusive and development-oriented Information Society, **where everyone can create, access, utilize and share information and knowledge,** enabling individuals, communities and peoples to achieve their full potential in promoting their sustainable development and improving their quality of life, premised on the purposes and principles of the Charter of the United Nations and respecting fully and upholding the Universal Declaration of Human Rights.[8]

The universality and interdependence of rights enshrined in the UDHR and the Geneva Declaration subserve the development and democratization of our societies. The 2003 declaration was more focused on describing a philosophy than it was on proposing a specific program of implementation. In the 15 years since the declaration was made, the vision that it presents has gradually taken shape through initiatives led by organizations such as the International Telecommunications Union to define specific universal rights for the information society.

Here, I would like to emphasize an essential point. Universal rights are rights of individuals who hold subjective rights and who are able to exercise those rights. The "person-based" or "people-centered" nature of fundamental rights lies at the heart of the principles of communication that I will consider later, and it therefore imposes an ethical obligation on policies and policymakers.

The information society is not a closed society. Nor is it a place for a privileged few. Rather, it extends across the globe and should become even more universal among people, countries, and media. Indeed, universality lies, as expressed by the United Nations (2008, See, for example, the following statement by UN in December 2008 https://www.un.org/en/chronicle/article/are-human-rights-universal), at the "core" of human rights, and it connects with the principles of interdependence, indivisibility, equality, and nondiscrimination. This relates to another research topic in communication law, namely minorities and how to guarantee communication rights to groups that are minorities owing to their members' language, ethnicity, disability, age, or any other sociopolitical reality that may put such a group at a disadvantage in relation to others. The principles of universality and justice demand the creation of conditions that ensure equality for minority groups, sometimes based on their differences relative to the majority.

Communication rights, previously known in general terms as "freedom of expression" and also referred to as the "right to freedom of expression and information," were fully defined in the International Covenant on Civil and Political Rights. These rights **include the freedom to "seek, receive and impart" information, and they are characterized by six key features** (INCL 2015) that are especially relevant in the Internet-based society. This amounts to a quite vehement stance despite criticisms of the UN system of rights. Though other authors

[8] See the website related to the 2003 Geneva Declaration here: https://www.itu.int/net/wsis/geneva/index.html (accessed January 13, 2020).

in this volume will return to this topic in greater detail, I wish to highlight that the following are among the principles of communication rights:

- They apply to all without distinction. Any discrimination based on language, color, race, sex, religion, or opinion is void.
- Their geographic area is universal and knows no borders. This universality is guaranteed by the Internet, unless services or sites are blocked, as they still are in many countries.
- Their scope, while not limitless, is broad and affects "information and ideas of all kinds." The UN Human Rights Committee employs the term "expression" in a broadly defined way to include not only political, cultural, and artistic expression, but also "controversial, false and even shocking expressions."
- They include the right not only to receive information but also to impart or disseminate information. They protect radio listeners, broadcasters, witnesses of events or public protests, and protesters themselves. In other words, both active and passive exercise of the communication rights is guaranteed.
- They demand that states create guarantees to protect them and eliminate any abridgments of these rights.
- Finally, they include dissemination of ideas or messages in any form or medium.

Communication law and international texts hold that among subjects, professionals enjoy greater protection than private individuals. These professionals include journalists, full- or part-time reporters, bloggers, and those who own or publish their own media. They exercise universal communication rights (the "function of informing," as Desantes stated in 1976) on the basis of authority tacitly delegated to them from private individuals. From this authority derive professionals' special privileges or corporate rights, such as professional confidentiality and conscientious objection. The UN has reaffirmed the rights of journalists to gain access to places and events, the right to nondiscriminatory press accreditation, and the right of journalists not to identify their sources[9] – a right that is unprotected in many jurisdictions, including in several US states.

The signing of the covenant in 1966 therefore prohibited restricting access of professionals and denying freedom of movement to foreign media or human rights observers.

## Related Universal Rights

Though communication rights were already linked to such rights as the right to culture and education and to copyright in the human rights documents of 1948 and 1966, it was not until the first Geneva Summit (Padovani and Pavan 2006; Corredoira 2007) that these links and the complimentarily of these rights became clearer, especially for an Internet-based society. As I mentioned before, within European doctrine (Desantes Guanter 1974; Sanchez Férriz 1975; Derieux 2010a, 2010b), communication rights contain and complete the "right to freedom of expression" and other, older conceptions of "communication rights" from previous centuries.

The working hypothesis that I propose is to consider the content of communication rights (and their three components of seeking, receiving, and imparting information) as relevant for information relationships in the past and today, after the invention of the Internet.

There is a clear parallel between, on one hand, these three components (Corredoira 2006, 2007) and, on the other hand, the right to culture and education. This parallel can be found in Articles 19 and 27 of the UDHR (see Table 3.1).

[9] Comment, 45. States should recognize and respect that element of the right of freedom of expression that lies behind the limited journalistic privilege not to disclose information sources.

**Table 3.1** Related universal rights.

| *Communication rights* | *Relevant UDHR article(s)* | *Dimension of the Geneva Declaration* | *UDHR articles dealing specifically with the Information Society* |
|---|---|---|---|
| SEEK | Art. 19. "Everyone has the right to freedom of opinion and expression; this right includes freedom to hold opinions without interference and **to seek**, receive and impart information and ideas through any media and regardless of frontiers." | ACCESS/ INCLUSION | Art. 21.1. **"Universal, ubiquitous, equitable and affordable access to ICT infrastructure and services,** constitutes one of the challenges of the Information Society and should be an objective of all stakeholders involved in building it. ..." |
| | Art. 27.2 "Everyone has the right to the protection of the moral and material interests resulting from **any scientific, literary or artistic production of** which he is the author." | CREATE/ PRODUCE | **55.** "We reaffirm our commitment to the principles of freedom of the press and freedom of information, as well as those of the independence, pluralism and diversity of media, which are essential to the Information Society. **Freedom to seek, receive, impart and use information for the creation, accumulation and dissemination of knowledge are important to the Information Society.** We call for the responsible use and treatment of information by the media in accordance with the highest ethical and professional standards...." |
| RECEIVE | Art. 19. "this right includes freedom to hold opinions without interference and to seek, **receive** and impart information and ideas through any media and regardless of frontiers". | CONSULT | |
| IMPART | Art. 19. "this right includes freedom to hold opinions without interference and **to seek**, receive **and impart information and ideas through any media and regardless of frontiers."** | SHARE | |
| | Art. 27.1. "Everyone has the right freely **to participate in the cultural life** of the community, to enjoy the arts and to share in scientific advancement and its benefits." | USE | 53. "The creation, dissemination and preservation of content in diverse languages and formats must be accorded high priority in building an inclusive Information Society.... It is essential to promote the production of and accessibility to all content – educational, ... scientific, cultural or recreational—in diverse languages and formats." |

The UDHR also generously affirms that "everyone has the right freely to participate in the cultural life of the community, to enjoy the arts and to share in scientific advancement and its benefits" (Article 27.1).

The Geneva Declaration is not a "new" proclamation of rights. Rather, it is the application of existing principles to the realities of the Internet, based on the idea that access is a right that facilitates other rights. The WSIS is therefore not claiming a new right but is instead launching a public campaign to raise awareness about the challenges to communication rights posed by a globalized society that faces the serious risk of a digital divide. Here, it is appropriate to invoke the ideas of Padovani, Raboy, and d'Arcy mentioned at the beginning of this chapter and that refer to communication rights, concretely through the concept of the right to communicate.

The right to culture is not based on utopian considerations and does not automatically entail free access to the Internet from the home or on mobile phones. And the state has a different role to play when taking on the (philosophical) challenge of ensuring the right to culture or the (practical) challenge of ensuring Internet access. What we might call the "right to universal Internet access," which is reminiscent of the concept of a universal telephone service discussed a decade ago, has several dimensions: infrastructure, access or connection to the Internet, and access to services. Here, technical universality (access) connects with universality of subjects and of content.

## Notes on the Technical Universality of Communication Rights: The Universality of Internet-Based Modes of Expression

We wrote in the Introduction to this volume that the "right to impart and disseminate information" – to use the wording of the International Covenant on Civil and Political Rights – needs to be rethought in the face of the challenges posed by a population that is always connected or hyperconnected to mass media outlets through personal devices such as smartphones, tablets, and laptops. A telephone allows a user to follow a TV series, rent a film on YouTube or iTunes, and subscribe to a daily newspaper that will never be delivered to the home in paper form – or even be available in print. The device serves as a communication terminal through which the subscriber can send messages as well as participate and vote in events and debates. This is now the reality in many countries of the world thanks to smartphones and to networked societies, and it should prompt a rethinking of both the law and ethics of communication.

The limits of innovations centered on the mobile phone have not been reached. Innovators are working with the idea of devices or microchips inserted beneath the user's skin and wearables – even glasses connected to a support or medium that helps us to exercise our communication rights.

The universality of technology and of media refers not only to an individual's access or mode of connection to media but also to the tangible and intangible systems and media that, in the language of copyright law, "are known today or that will be invented in the future."[10] Such a conceptualization gives universal reach to platforms and media in which creativity is expressed, whether or not those media have yet been invented.

In parallel with a freedom of information that should be universal and neutral relative to the type of platform, copyright should not restrict "access to information" or be neglected as new

[10] See, for example, Spanish legislation (Real Decreto Legislativo 1/1996, *Texto Refundido de la Ley de Propiedad Intelectual*).

forms of communication freedom are invented in the future. Rights cannot be constrained to the existing media or channels for disseminating news, ideas, and opinions.

These rights have been taking shape since the time of town criers who announced news in the streets and markets and continue to do so in today's era of media services, apps, and Tweets by journalists, which enrich debate and media. A commentary[11] from the UN Human Rights Committee indicates that the technical media and forms of expression used to disseminate information extend from oral and written forms to sign language and even to nonverbal expression such as images or works of art. These "media," then, include books, newspapers, pamphlets, flyers, posters, advertising, and legal documents. They may be transmitted audio visually, electronically, or through the Internet.

News media ("the press") is of particular importance among the various information media in a democratic society. These rights are universal, including during elections. Censorship has no place; instead, a strong relationship should exist between citizens and representatives such as members of parliament or congress. The UN commentary continues: "The free communication of information and ideas about public and political issues between citizens, candidates and elected representatives is essential. This implies a free press and other media able to comment on public issues without censorship or restraint and to inform public opinion. The public also has a corresponding right to receive media output" (2011, n. 13).

Access to websites, Internet service providers, or search engines should not be restricted. If some restriction exists, it should be compatible with the exceptions enumerated in Article 19.3 of the covenant and proportional to the problem or threat. In general, specific content should not be prohibited[12] or blocked simply because it criticizes a government or state. These principles may seem self-evident, but they merit remembering.

Despite all the positive aspects of technical capabilities, and though access to the Internet is essential for the proper enjoyment of universal communication rights, there are challenges related to the current state of the Internet, in which private entities have amassed great power over online means of expression.

In Chapter 5 of this volume, Cetina Presuel warns that states and private actors risk confusing a "standardization" of what communication rights mean and where their limits should lie. Both private platforms and governments are relying on private rules and attempts to apply local laws globally in order to obtain uniform rules that allow them to police content online. In doing so, they are moving away from a view of a universal application of communication rights based on dialog and consensus and are instead attempting to arrive at common rules by imposition.

In turn, Julie Cohen (2017) warns that, in particular, powerful social media platforms may cause us to stray away from the "technologies of freedom" framework proposed by de Sola Pool (1983) and referenced by Monroe Price in the Preface of this volume, because "rather than predominantly stimulating the development and exercise of conscious and deliberate reason, today's networked information flows are optimized to produce what social psychologist Shoshana

[11] See Comment no. 34, Human Rights Committee (UN 2011).

[12] Cfr. Comment "Any restrictions on the operation of websites, blogs or any other internet-based, electronic or other such information dissemination system, including systems to support such communication, such as internet service providers or search engines, are only permissible to the extent that they are compatible with paragraph 3. Permissible restrictions generally should be content-specific; generic bans on the operation of certain sites and systems are not compatible with paragraph 3. It is also inconsistent with paragraph 3 to prohibit a site or an information dissemination system from publishing material solely on the basis that it may be critical of the government or the political social system espoused by the government".

Zuboff calls instrumentarian power: They employ a radical behaviorist approach to human psychology to mobilize and reinforce patterns of motivation, cognition, and behavior that operate on automatic, near-instinctual levels and that may be manipulated instrumentally" (p. 77).

## Return to First Principles: Inalienable Content of the Rights to Seek, Receive, and Impart Information

In light of the universal character of the subject and object of communication rights, which subsequent chapters will flesh out in greater detail, I turn now to analyzing the content of these rights. All rights, to be considered as such, must be defined by duties and capabilities, which in the case of communication rights include the ability to seek, receive, and impart all types of information and opinions.

### The Right to Seek Information

The right to seek information is understood (Desantes Guanter 1974, p. 93) as the ability of information professionals, information media more broadly, and the general public to directly access sources of information and opinions and receive this content without any limit whatsoever. From the theoretical and practical points of view, this is undoubtedly the most difficult ability to accept and to identify as being contained within communication rights. So far, with the exception of some published rules, the capability to seek information has not been regulated in both its facets – that is, the right of all individuals and the duty of those managing information sources. Though professional customs and practices strongly facilitate access to government offices, the reality of common practice suggests a more negative picture.

In direct conflict with this ability to research is the possibility of declaring information to be classified. This problem is evident in cases of official secrets and secrecy in summary judicial proceedings. It cannot be denied that the government – essentially the political and executive powers – has the right, under specific circumstances, to classify information that may affect internal or external security. However, it must be pointed out that, to avoid abuse, this right to official secrecy should be applied as restrictively as possible, and the length of time that information can remain classified should be proscribed. This question will be covered in detail in the third part of this volume.

The right to seek information **includes the right to access public information**, for which policies of transparency and information access should be implemented by the organizations and public bodies managing the information, without concern for the source, date, or storage medium of the information. This is a key point in journalism, documentation sciences, history, and archiving. The only possible limitations, which would have to be fixed, would be those established by law in a way that maximally guarantees the security and privacy of the individual. Some of these questions, such as those about sources and transparency, will be explored in greater depth by other authors in this volume. These questions are crucial in this era in which "open government" defines relations between government and governed.

Studies of corporations and nongovernmental organizations (NGOs) have revealed a proliferation of so-called press offices or communication departments that serve to disseminate information to external users. The freedom to seek information goes even further than this in order to arrive at the ultimate sources of information.

An increasing number of people have exercised their right to seek information through the Internet. However, various factors have led the universal subject – the general public – to adopt a passive attitude and to delegate searches to professionals. This makes sense in light of the legal and practical difficulties for the average individual to research information.

## The Right to Receive Information

Taking a reductionist view, one could imagine that receiving, reading, hearing, purchasing, and subscribing to content are fairly straightforward for all the types of users described earlier. In reality, exercise of the right to receive information has various facets that one should not oversimplify. The ability to receive content – sometimes referred to as the ability to choose content – carries with it the possibility of receiving all kinds of information and opinions, as well as the possibility of refusing to receive such information and opinions. In a hyperconnected society, the receipt of messages is often involuntary. Spam, social web notifications, and messages from other "push technologies" constantly bombard the user. The channels for receiving information, ideas, and opinions change and evolve over time, but they currently include the following:

free access to newspapers;
paid subscriptions for paper or electronic publications;
pay-per-view content (TV, music, news);
content bundles (for example, press and music, or television and books);
newsfeeds from social websites;
electronic alerts and newsletters;
channels containing advertising;
undesired advertising; and
video streaming (Internet, radio, and TV);

Given the possibility of receiving content over 360°, 24 hours a day, 365 days a year – music, radio on the subway, WIFI on airplanes, tablets, and TV in airports – one speaks today of the "right to disconnect" as another part of the "right to receive." A good example is the US court decision in *Hill v. Colorado* (2000), which talks about a "right not to receive information"[13] that is part of freedom of speech in US law.

At the global level, we can say that actively exercising the right to receive or not receive information requires information pluralism (Lecaros 2003, pp. 57–80) – that is, the freedom to create media. The right to receive or not receive information presupposes the freedom to create media, because without such media, there would be no information to receive. Any restriction or administrative condition imposed on the creation of media, in the form of a requirement for authorization, licenses, or concessions, disrupts the ability to create – sometimes gravely so – and reduces media pluralism. This, in turn, disrupts the ability to choose information – that is, to receive it or not. I fear that in developing countries pluralism is scarce. This discrimination can be reduced only by providing Internet access.

Unfortunately, in many countries, the notion that radio and television are state property, as was indeed the case in Europe until the liberalization of the telecommunications industry at the end of the 1990s, has led to a system of licenses and concessions that regulates the existence of audiovisual media. Another challenge to the ability to receive information is legislation that restricts freedom of information. Such legislation runs the gamut from laws that enshrine censorship – which, as we have seen, threaten social websites such as Twitter and Facebook – to content-publishing platforms such as YouTube and even cloud sites like Google Drive, as well as to regulations that restrict specific types of

[13] *Hill v. Colorado* (2000), available at https://www.law.cornell.edu/supct/html/98-1856.ZS.html (accessed January 13, 2021): "Unlawful for any person within 100 feet of a health care facility's entrance to 'knowingly approach' within 8 feet of another person, without that person's consent, in order to pass 'a leaflet or handbill to, display a sign to, or engage in oral protest, education, or counseling with [that] person.'"

information for religious, social, economic, or political reasons. Any restriction on the dissemination of information is a direct attack on the right to communicate. Of course, freedom has its risks, but they are less evident than the risks that come with the absence of freedom.

Another threat to the ability to receive information, which has been and remains present in many countries, is the excessive presence of the state in media ownership, to the point that private initiatives are squashed or such initiatives must compete with state-run operations at an unfair disadvantage, if for no other reason than that state-run media can draw on government funding and even supplement their budgets from private advertising. Under these circumstances, the right to receive information is annulled or at least weakened, and the state has its own powerful media.

At the opposite extreme lies the hyperconcentration of wealth in private hands in the United States, which has included the development of large media conglomerates. This situation also affects the ability to receive information. When none of the media in a country is public, some voices in that society may go unrepresented, and many perspectives will be neglected, especially in highly fragmented societies. This situation may be exacerbated by the current state of the online news market, characterized by the central role of social media platforms in providing access to the news. These players, whose ownership is also concentrated in a few hands, have an outsized role in controlling both revenue streams for media companies, as they control large parts of the advertising market, and the flow of information itself, as they command large audiences and dictate what news content can reach them, as well as how and when it will do so (see Cetina Presuel and Martínez Sierra 2019).

Other threats to exercising the freedom to receive information, as well as threats to the freedom of selecting information, which all individuals should have, could be mentioned. The most positive solution is to encourage the creation of news companies that have a clear commitment to independence and a strong sense of responsibility as expressed by Nieto[14] (1973). Several such examples of new media have emerged in recent years, such as journalist societies (*sociétés de rédacteurs*). These may not resolve problems completely, but they do allow business risks to be spread over diverse stakeholders.

## The Right to Impart Information

The right to impart information is the third and last component of the right to communicate established by the UDHR. The right to seek information was the most difficult to exercise in the pre-Internet era. But things are different in the Web 3.0 era. No one questions the right to impart information; in fact, it is the oldest of the first claims to "freedom of expression, printing and press." The very term "freedom of expression" or "right of expression" puts us in direct contact with dissemination of information. As a result, we can affirm, without exaggeration, that the concept of expression – intimately tied to the concept of dissemination – forms the basis of the rights that I have been analyzing in this chapter.

These rights are complex because not all subjects among individuals, professionals, and organizations can disseminate information. Here I define *information* as the sum total of ideas and opinions. What makes these rights difficult to understand is the so-called universal subject (the general public): we must understand whether and how the public, without access to news media and without being journalists, can participate in the dissemination of information, news, and opinions. Few options were available before the social Web appeared. One solution was writing letters to the editor, in which an individual could give his or her opinion on certain information

[14] Spain's first professor of media business and its first author to write on the subject.

or even offer information. Another option was the so-called right to rectification in the event that an individual wished to correct false information in the media.

In the Internet era, individuals can participate in the dissemination of information and opinions through several channels:

- user blogs, including children's blogs;
- posts on social sites;
- comments in forums on daily newspaper websites;
- opinions sent to the radio via WhatsApp;
- weather photos provided by viewers of national TV news programs;
- online competitions; and
- opinions sent to TV programs by SMS.

In democracies, a particularly important time for citizen participation in the diffusion of information is during election campaigns. During these, flows of ideas and information between candidates, representatives, and voters are essential for citizen participation in democracy, as the UN Human Rights Committee pointed out when it "elaborated on the importance of freedom of expression for the conduct of public affairs and the effective exercise of the right to vote. The free communication of information and ideas about public and political issues between citizens, candidates and elected representatives is essential. This implies a free press and other media able to comment on public issues and to inform public opinion without censorship or restraint."[15] Ensuring information flow requires greater press freedom and the absence of censorship. Thus, democratic states are obligated to promote information dissemination during elections.

The strong development of technologies for information sharing, coupled with the globalizing nature of today's world, is giving citizens an increasingly strong and effective presence in the information world. As a result, it is increasingly common for citizens to become disseminators of news and opinions. For example, in some cases, bloggers can acquire millions of followers and become opinion leaders. Unless they are journalists, such individuals cannot be considered qualified subjects or qualified informers in the legal sense of those terms, yet they become true centers of information dissemination.

Today, many legal possibilities exist for individuals to contribute to information dissemination. These run the gamut from "collaborative journalism," such as the consortium that covered the Panama Papers, to news media that mimic journalist societies, such as *Le Monde*; information providers that follow various entrepreneurial models from individual property to crowdfunding initiatives, such as the Dutch daily *De Correspondent* (MediaLab Press 2017); and finally classical limited companies and corporations. As *De Correspondent* cofounder and editor Ernst-Jan Pfauth declared (Wijnberg 2014), "If we call someone a subscriber, it suggests that person is a passive consumer who pays for content, reads it and that's all. What we really want is an active relationship with our readers. That is why we call them members."

In the United States, influential nonprofit journalism exists in the form of National Public Radio and the Public Broadcasting Service, which are known as "public media," though only in the sense that they have a vocation of service to the public. They are NGOs that operate from public donations and funding from the government and foundations. Organizations for investigative journalism, such as ProPublica, are growing in relevance and are seeking crowdfunding.

In all countries, a multiplicity of online media, supported by multiple technological possibilities, has taken root in recent years. These media can offer generalist content or, more

[15] Comment n. 25, Human Rights Committee (2011), Freedom of expression and political rights n. 20.

importantly, specialized content responding to a greater or lesser extent to the particular needs of a segmented public. This is an area without limits, and we are witnessing the beginning of its development.

This reality, which has only just begun if we take a historical perspective, is accelerating new possibilities for searching for, receiving, and imparting information. Unfortunately, the development of this reality is not without its dangers, which center fundamentally on the ethical use of information dissemination. These dangers also include lies, defamation, attacks on personal rights, and various other forms of insult. Let us hope that Desantes Guanter (1974) was correct when, in thinking about the possibilities for exercising the right to communicate, he said, "There is no doubt that reality will prevail and that the 'should be' will slowly but inexorably align with [the right]."

## Conclusions

Communication rights are universal because they protect everyone – this is the so-called subjective universality – including **all media and platforms** that exist today and that will be invented in the future (technical universality). These rights are also universal in the sense that they "exist regardless of frontiers" (Price 2020),[16] what we call the geographic universality of communication rights. More relevant to the messages and content of communication is the fact that these rights apply not only to any "expression" and "opinion," but also to "information and ideas of all kinds." This includes, of course, journalism, political and religious discourse, opinions contained in financial ratings, commercial advertising, and citizen participation in public affairs.

Various judicial cases, including the Costeja case[17] involving Google (on the emerging "right to be forgotten") and cases on the protection of financial opinions (for example, S&P ratings, see an example of a lawsuit against S&P in Sheffield 2015) make clear that, in the twenty-first century, communication rights serve as an expanded version of the first declarations of rights in the eighteenth century or in the First Amendment of the US Constitution. These earlier declarations aimed to defend freedoms from the Crown, just as communication rights today defend media freedom from the state.

We are witnessing a revolution similar to that brought about by the printing press, which helped end the monopoly of the monarchy and privileged classes over information. Then, as now, society is moving toward new spaces of freedom for the universal subject, for every citizen.

Within this paradigm, I would emphasize that the same communication rights apply to the dissemination of information on Twitter or a blog. Even if these sites are cost free, they deal in data traffic as a form of payment. We are also talking about the same right when a child or adolescent publishes photos on Snapchat or Instagram as we are when a reputed columnist writes a piece for the *New York Times* or *El País*.

Therefore, it is clear that the signatory states to the International Covenant on Civil and Political Rights cannot prohibit media, a new dissemination method, or a set of specific contents or broadcasters, no matter how bothersome they are to some. Since the 1990s, social

---

[16] See the Preface of this book by Professor Monroe Price as well as his book *Free Expression, Globalism and the New Strategic Communication* (2014) and other previous contributions related to Technologies of Freedom, specially Ithiel de Sola Pool university \9 1983).

[17] Judgment of the Court (Grand Chamber), May 13, 2014. *Google Spain SL and Google Inc. v Agencia Española de Protección de Datos (AEPD) and Mario Costeja González.* Available in English at: https://eur-lex.europa.eu/legal-content/EN/TXT/HTML/?uri=CELEX:62012CJ0131&from=EN (accessed January 13, 2021).

networks and the Internet more broadly have placed information within the reach of all (or nearly all) across borders, though a digital divide still exists. Given restrictions on freedom, we should think about how to guarantee other rights that become more vulnerable in the presence of such restrictions, such as rights to dignity and privacy. A court should rule that the dissemination of a given message is illegal only if it threatens to violate a more important or more personal right.

Rights, and therefore law, need to be crossborder. Access to Facebook facilitated the Arab Spring. The Cuban blogger Yoani Sánchez[18] communicated "blindly" because she was able to send out messages on Twitter but not receive any. Society will take advantage of technology to assert its communication rights, just as individuals and groups searched for alternative media and pirate radio channels to search for, receive, and impart information within the Soviet bloc between the end of World War II and the fall of the Berlin Wall in 1989. During the Franco era, Spaniards listened to Radio Libertad (Radio Freedom), which broadcasted from beyond the Pyrenees, in order to follow the news in a country where owning or publishing a newspaper was prohibited.

## References

Alandete, D. (2018). La Comisión Europea renuncia a la legislación contra las noticias falsas. *El Pais newspaper* (3 April). https://elpais.com/internacional/2018/04/02/actualidad/1522694360_002636.html (accessed July 24, 2020).

Abad Alcalá, L. (2015). "El derecho a la información y las libertades informativas en el ámbito europeo", "El derecho a la información en los textos universales." In: *Derecho de la información: el ejercicio del derecho a la información y su jurisprudencia* (ed I. Bel Mallén and L. Corredoira), 69–96. Madrid: Madrid: Centro de Estudios Políticos y Constitucionales.

Arellano Toledo, W. (ed.) (2012). *Políticas y derecho de las telecomunicaciones en Europa, Norteamérica y México*. Szeged: INFOTEC.

Bel Mallén, I. and Corredoira, L. (2015). *El ejercicio del derecho a la información y su jurisprudencia*. Madrid: Centro de Estudios Políticos y Constitucionales.

Bienkof, A. (2018). Theresa May calls for new laws to ban the abuse of politicians on social media. *Business insider* (6 February). https://www.businessinsider.com/theresa-may-abuse-politicians-social-media-twitter-facebook-bullying-laws-2018-2?IR=T (accessed July 24, 2020).

Birdsall, W.F. (2007). Web 2.0 as a social movement. *Webology* 4 (2): 5–11.

Cetina Presuel, R. and Martínez Sierra, J. (2019). Algorithms and the news: social media platforms as news publishers and distributors. *Revista De Comunicación* 1(2): 261–285.

Cohen, J.E. (2017). Affording fundamental rights. *Critical Analysis of Law* 4 (1): 76–90.

Corredoira, L. (2006). Lectura de la Declaración Universal de Derechos Humanos de 1948 en el paradigma de la nueva sociedad de la información. Estudio específico del artículo 19. In: *Libertad En Internet: La Red Y Las Libertades De Expresión E Información* (ed. L. Cotino), 57–74. Valencia: Tirant lo Blanch.

Corredoira, L. (2007). A new reading of Article 19 of the Universal Declaration of Human Rights (1948) in our information societies. *Journal Media & Cultural Politics* 3 (3): 336–347.

Corredoira, L. (2015). Los medios en Internet: entre la anarquía y la hiperregulación. In: *Periodismo en la red: géneros, estilos y normas* (ed. L. Núñez Ladeveze), 415–440. Madrid: Editorial Universitas, S.A.

Corredoira, L. (2017). *Cyberlaw Clinic UCM. Retuitear contenidos puede ser delito.* (Spanish Supreme Court STS 3804/2017). http://infosociedad.blogspot.com.es/2017/11/retuitear-contenidos-puede-ser-delito.html (accessed July 24, 2020).

Corredoira, L. and Cotino, L. (2013). *Libertad de expresión e información en Internet. Amenazas y protección de los derechos personales.* Madridf: Centro de Estudios Políticos y Constitucionales.

[18] Journalist and blogger: Diario 14 y medio: https://twitter.com/14ymedio (accessed January 13, 2021).

D'Arcy, J. (1969). Direct broadcast satellites and the human right to communicate. *EBU Review* 118: 14–18.

Danieli, Y., Stamatopoulou, E., and Dias, C.J. (eds.) (1999). *The Universal Declaration of Human Rights: Fifty Years and Beyond*. Amityville, NY: Baywood Publishing Company.

de Sola Pool, I. (1983). *Technologies of Freedom*. Cambridge, MA: Harvard University Press.

Derieux, E. (2010a). *Droit des médias. Droit français, européen et international*. Paris: Librairie Générale de Droit et de Jurisprudence.

Derieux, E. (2010b). 30 ans de droit de la communication: étapes d'une longue marche de 30 ans d'incertitude et d'inaptitude. *Legicom* 2010/2 (45): 139–153.

Desantes Guanter, J.M. (1974). *La información como derecho*. Madrid: Editora Nacional.

Desantes Guanter, J.M. (1976). *La función de informar*. Navarra: EUNSA. Ediciones Universidad de Navarra Pamplona.

Desantes Guanter, J.M., Bel Mallen, I., and Garcia Sanz, R.M. (1994). *Derecho de la Información (II). Los mensajes informativos*. Madrid: Colex.

European Commission (2017). *State of the Union 2017 – Cybersecurity: Commission Scales up EU's Response to Cyber-attacks*. https://ec.europa.eu/commission/presscorner/detail/es/IP_17_3193 (accessed July 24, 2020).

ICNL (2015). The right to freedom of expression: restrictions on a foundational right. *Global Trends in NGO Law* 6 (1): 2.

International Telecommunication Union (2003). *World Summit on the Information Society (WSIS), Geneva, Principles Declaration*. https://www.itu.int/net/wsis (accessed July 24, 2020).

International Telecommunication Union (2014). *World Summit on the Information Society (WSIS), +10 High-Level Event (Online)*. Outcome Documents. https://www.itu.int/net/wsis/implementation/2014/forum/inc/doc/outcome/362828V2E.pdf (accessed July 24, 2020).

Lecaros, M.A.J. (2003). Una mirada ética en torno al pluralismo, la objetividad y la información. In: *Veracidad y objetividad: desafíos éticos en la sociedad de la información*. (ed. Congreso International de Ética y Derecho de la Informatión), 57–80. Valencia: Fundación Coso Para El Desarrollo De La Comunicación Y La Sociedad.

Malcolm, J. (2017). Digital rights groups demand deletion of unlawful filtering mandate from proposed EU copyright law. *Electronic Frontier Foundation, EFF*. https://www.eff.org/deeplinks/2017/10/digital-rights-groups-demand-deletion-unlawful-filtering-mandate-proposed-eu (accessed September 16, 2020).

MediaLab Press (2017). *Digital News Report España 2017*. https://medialab.press/los-medios-tradicionales-siguen-siendo-los-mas-confiables-la-audiencia-digital-espanola (accessed October 15, 2020).

Nieto Tamargo, A. (1973). *La empresa periodística en España*. Pamplona: Universidad de Navarra, Servicio de Publicaciones.

O'Flaherty, M. (2012). Freedom of expression: Article 19 of the International Covenant on Civil and Political Rights and the Human Rights Committee's General Comment No 34. *Human Rights Law Review* 12 (4): 627–654.

Padovani, C. and Pavan, E. (2006). The emerging global movement on communication rights: a new stakeholder in global communication governance? Converging at WSIS but looking beyond. In: *Making Our Media: Mapping Global Initiatives Toward a Democratic Public Sphere* (ed. C. Rodriguez, D. Kidd, and L. Stein), 345–359. Creskill, NJ: Hampton Press.

Price, M. (2014). *Free Expression, Globalism and the New Strategic Communication*. Cambridge: Cambridge University Press.

Raboy, M. (2004). The WSIS as a political space in global media governance. *Continuum. Journal of Media and Society* 18 (3): 345–359.

Sánchez Ferriz, R. (1975). *El Derecho a la Información*. Valencia: Cosmos, Colección Cátedra Fadrique Furió Ceriol.

Sheffield, C. (2015). S&P settlement sets chilling precedent against free speech. *Forbes* (28 January). https://www.forbes.com/sites/carriesheffield/2015/01/28/je-suis-sp-governments-chilling-effect-on-credit-rating-agencies/#712ebf7b1a7d (accessed July 24, 2020).

Stephens, M. (2005). *Freedom of Expression: The Global Challenge*. Conferencia Dictada En Oxford. Disponible En El Programme in Comparative Media Law & Policy (PCMLP) En. http://pcmlp.socleg.ox.ac.uk (accessed July 24, 2020).

United Nations (1948). *The Foundation of International Human Rights Law*. https://www.un.org/en/sections/universal-declaration/foundation-international-human-rights-law/index.html (accessed July 24, 2020).
United Nations (2011). *Human Rights Committee 102nd Session Geneva*. http://www2.ohchr.org/english/bodies/hrc/docs/gc34.pdf (accessed July 24, 2020).
Wasserman, E. (2017). Safeguarding the news in the era of disruptive sources. *Journal of Media Ethics* 32 (2): 72–85.
Wijnberg, R. (2014). *De Correspondent Digital Newspaper Co-founder, Speech and Debate during Google Tent Madrid*. https://www.elconfidencial.com/tecnologia/2014-10-30/diez-ideas-que-marcan-como-sera-el-futuro-para-la-prensa-en-internet_427260 (accessed July 24, 2020).

# 4

# Communication Rights in the United Nations System

## From Declarations to "Soft Law"

Leopoldo Abad Alcalá

Within states' internal contexts, regulation of the communication rights arising from the Universal Declaration of Human Rights (UDHR) or the International Covenant on Civil and Political Rights (ICCPR) has been developing via a gradual process of progress and setbacks that is shaped by each country's historical and political vicissitudes. However, and despite the undeniable theoretical and philosophical reflection on the right of any person to communicate his or her ideas (a pioneer here was the Salamanca school led by Francisco de Vitoria, who formulated the idea of *ius communicationis* [Desantes Guanter 1989]), the shaping of the international legal order as a relational system whose subjects are states prevented any initiative to recognize communication rights in a universal, or even regional, way.

## The First Steps: Article 19 of the Universal Declaration of Human Rights

The failure of the League of Nations and the atrocities committed by states in World War II inspired the need for a new model of interactions for international society, with individuals taking center stage relative to the main violator of their rights: their own states.[1] This is the historical context in which the appearance of the United Nations (UN) should be understood. It was created through the Charter of the United Nations, promulgated in San Francisco on June 26, 1945 (Escobar de la Serna 2004, p. 112). In reality, this document limits itself to formulating the principle of international protection of such rights and of fundamental freedoms without developing that principle through specific rules.

It would only be with the UDHR, approved by UN General Assembly Resolution 217 on December 10, 1948, that a recognition of human rights (with communication rights occupying a principal place among them) would emerge with a truly universal will. It sought to

[1]As one of the drafters of the UDHR, René Cassin, stated, the Declaration represents "the most vigorous ... protest of humanity against the atrocities and the oppression which millions of human beings have suffered through the centuries" (Winter and Prost 2013, p. 250).

*The Handbook of Communication Rights, Law, and Ethics: Seeking Universality, Equality, Freedom and Dignity*, First Edition. Edited by Loreto Corredoira, Ignacio Bel Mallén, and Rodrigo Cetina Presuel.

subordinate – if not legally then morally – states' behavior to the rights contained within it. The undoubted rooting in natural law of the declaration, the starting point of which is the undeniable dignity of the person, led to the document becoming established as a control parameter vis-à-vis states' observance of human rights, even above their own regulations, and it confirmed the idea expressed by Hannah Arendt's "right to have rights" (Arendt 1976, p. 296). This disruptive concept would not be welcomed by everyone in the same way, which largely explains why this catalog of rights was adopted as a declaration and not as a treaty or agreement. The declaration's universal applicability[2] reduced the legal precision of a large proportion of the rights recognized in it, but the inclusiveness that inspired it prevailed over a more legalistic orientation.

Such was the importance of the declaration that it became the common denominator in institutional discourse on human rights (Von Bernstorff 2008, p. 916). It is seen as a means for international public opinion to pressure states and has become customary international law (Humphrey 1979, p. 21) or, in the words of one of its main promoters, Eleanor Roosevelt, "the Magna Carta of mankind."

The work of defending communication rights within the UN has taken place through progressive recognition of them. This process began with their inclusion in Article 19[3] of the UDHR, the influence of which is beyond any doubt, though a certain terminological imprecision in its drafting has detracted from its ability to be applied as a legal norm rather than as a specification of moral principles. Interpretations of Article 19 have been varied, ranging from those that emphasize its universal applicability to those that stress its all-encompassing conception of communicative activity, but its pioneering role in the international recognition of communication rights cannot be denied.

Arising from this Article is the process of divergence between freedom of expression and communication rights as realities that are related but distinguished depending on the purpose of each one, a difference that is referred to for the first time in the landmark work "Droit de l'Infomation," by Terrou and Solal (1951, p. 6), who consider communication rights as the core of "the Communication Law." Article 19 gave rise to the so-called dualist thesis, which differentiates between freedom of expression linked to the transmission of opinions and communication rights, whose object is transmission of information. It is true that this distinction is sometimes difficult to define: there are messages that mix both rights, and they are becoming increasingly common owing to the new communication media stemming from the omnipresence of digital technologies and the importance that social networks have acquired within the ways in which citizens access information. The debatable but accepted distinction between information and opinion (an example here is the European Convention of Human Rights (ECHR)[4] – that established case law on the matter) may not make sense in present times, and the protection derived from Article 19 of the UDHR possibly should focus more on the idea of protecting freedom of expression and opinion as all-encompassing concepts applicable to all forms of communication than on the idea of seeking, receiving, and disseminating information and opinions. Both of these rights – freedom of expression and seeking, receiving, and disseminating information and opinions – can either be encapsulated as a group of communication rights or referred to generally as "communication rights," though some simply refer

[2]Concerning the concept of universality, especially in Article 19 of the declaration, see Chapter 3 by Loreto Corredoira in this volume.

[3]"Everyone has the right to freedom of opinion and expression; this right includes freedom to hold opinions without interference and to seek, receive and impart information and ideas through any media and regardless of frontiers."

[4]English version available at https://www.echr.coe.int/Documents/Convention_ENG.pdf (accessed January 14, 2021).

to them as "freedom of expression." But the main idea should be that the UDHR refers to rights, not just freedoms, with the latter being more in line with nineteenth-century conceptions. A more modern understanding is that the freedom aspect is part of how communication rights are exercised. As Desantes explains, "Existential rights, human rights, or fundamental rights, such as the right to information, would cease to be so if they could not be freely exercised." In this way, freedom follows the fate of the fundamental right in all its weightlessness and unlimitedness. Freedom is the only way to exercise right (Desantes Guanter 2004, p. 115). Even contemporary scholars that prefer to use "freedom of expression" as a generic term would also agree that we are speaking about a right, not just a freedom (González Ballesteros 1989).

Another characteristic of Article 19 is its mixed formulation, in the sense that it recognizes negative freedoms and positive freedoms. Negative freedom appears, for example, where the Article establishes how this right includes "freedom to hold opinions without interference," which implies that the individual has a degree of autonomy when exercising his or her communicative powers. As Berlin (1968, p. 121) comments, we use the negative concept of freedom when trying to answer the question: "What is the area within which the subject – a person or group of persons – is or should be left to do or be what he is able to do or be, without interference by other persons?" In short, it is about maintaining a sphere reserved for the individual in which self-expression without interference – mainly from public authorities that often use restrictive tools such as censorship or confiscation of publications and recordings to limit these freedoms – is possible. This approach too may perhaps need to be reviewed in the new digital ecosystem. The existence of trolls, orchestrated smear campaigns, hate speech, systematic discrediting, post truth, or fake news could make us rethink the idea that the main source of interference today is not the public authorities but citizens themselves, who find it increasingly difficult to accept ideas contrary to their own. Perhaps the public authorities and private companies that operate in the communication sector, with academics and legal practitioners as catalysts, should reflect on the ideas of tolerance, respect, and acceptance of difference, so that the negative freedom included in Article 19 of the UDHR acquires real effect within the new conditions for exercising communication rights. The positive formulation, meanwhile, is characterized by the Article's recognition of three fundamental faculties: to seek, receive, and impart information.

Another particular characteristic that we can find in Article 19 is the recognition of the right to seek information; it is unusual to find such a recognition in the rest of the international regulations on freedom of information, but it has become an essential foundation for journalism. The entire current of asserting the right of access to information has developed under the auspices and inspiration of this right to seek information. As Desantes Guanter (2004, p. 103) indicates, with this recognition, factual and legal possibilities have been opened up for citizens to seek and disseminate on their own.

Finally, Article 19 of the UDHR is not hindered by the establishment of limits or conditions on the exercise of the rights recognized; it is a generic recognition of rights that places no qualifications or limitations on exercise of them, in accordance with the classical liberal position. It is not even limited by a restriction provision that would be consistent with liberal thinking. Instead, this is dealt with in the general-limitations provision of Article 29.2[5] of the declaration (O'Flaherty 2012, p. 630).

[5]"In the exercise of his rights and freedoms, everyone shall be subject only to such limitations as are determined by law solely for the purpose of securing due recognition and respect for the rights and freedoms of others and of meeting the just requirements of morality, public order and the general welfare in a democratic society."

## Consolidation: Article 19 of the International Covenant on Civil and Political Rights and Its Interpretation by the Human Rights Committee

The insufficiencies of the Universal Declaration were corrected to a certain extent by the ICCPR, adopted by the UN General Assembly Resolution 2200 A (XXI) on December 16, 1966, together with the International Covenant on Economic, Social and Cultural Rights.

However, the ICCPR establishes the first control and guarantee mechanisms of a universal nature, such as the power of states to recognize the competence of the Human Rights Committee (HRC) to hear interstate complaints (Art. 41 and 42) or individual communications (through ratification of the Optional Protocols). States often comply with the committee's reports and final recommendations because of its moral value, even though these documents have no legally binding value. Perhaps the significance of this procedure is that it has been shaping the closest thing to a UN "case law" on fundamental rights, with particular attention paid to the communication rights set out in Article 19 of the ICCPR (Joseph, Schultz, and Castan 2005).

Article 19.1 of the ICCPR establishes that "everyone shall have the right to hold opinions without interference." When it comes to this right, the covenant permits no exception or restriction. Freedom of opinion encompasses the right to change one's mind when one wishes and for whatever reason one freely chooses. No one's rights recognized in the covenant can be violated on the basis of the opinions that he or she has expressed or that have been attributed to or supposed of him or her. All forms of opinion – including those of a political, scientific, historical, moral, or religious nature – are protected. Considering the expression of an opinion as a crime is incompatible with Article 19.1.[6] Harassment, intimidation, or stigmatization of a person based on his or her opinions, including arrest, remand in custody, prosecution, or confinement, constitutes a violation of Article 19.1.[7] It also establishes that any coercive attempt to make a person maintain or not maintain an opinion is prohibited.[8] The freedom to express one's opinions necessarily includes the freedom not to express them.

The content of Article 19.2 of the ICCPR is very similar to that of Article 19 of the UDHR; the former states:

> Everyone shall have the right to freedom of expression; this right shall include freedom to seek, receive and impart information and ideas of all kinds, regardless of frontiers, either orally, in writing or in print, in the form of art, or through any other media of his choice.

In its General Comment No. 34, the UN HRC specifies that the right contained in para. 2 includes political thought, comments on personal and public affairs, door-to-door campaigns, discussion of human rights, journalism, cultural and artistic expression, teaching, and religious thought. It may also include commercial advertising. The scope of para. 2 even extends to expression that might be considered deeply offensive; this expression can only be limited in accordance with the provisions of Article 19, para. 3, and of Article 20. We cannot ignore the complementarity between Articles 19 and 20 of the covenant, the latter of which establishes that: "1. Any propaganda for war shall be prohibited by law. 2. Any advocacy of national, racial

[6]See communication no. 550/93, *Faurisson v. France* (November 8, 1996).
[7]See communications nos. 157/1983, *Mpaka-Nsusu v. Zaire* (March 26, 1986) and 414/1990, *Mika Miha v. Equatorial Guinea* (July 8, 1994).
[8]See communication no. 878/1999, *Kang v. the Republic of Korea* (July 15, 2003).

or religious hatred that constitutes incitement to discrimination, hostility or violence shall be prohibited by law." This Article has also been given a much-needed reinterpretation in recent times, but I think that consideration of this would require going far beyond this chapter's space and subject matter.

Para. 2 protects all forms of expression and the media by which they are disseminated. These forms include oral and written words and sign language, as well as nonverbal expressions such as images and artworks. The media through which expression takes place include books, newspapers, brochures, posters, banners, clothing, and legal submissions, as well as all forms of audiovisual, electronic, or Internet-based modes of expression.[9]

But the contribution of ICCPR Article 19 with respect to UDHR Article might be para. 3, which establishes limits by clarifying that:

> The exercise of the rights provided for in paragraph 2 of this article carries with it special duties and responsibilities. It may therefore be subject to certain restrictions, but these shall only be such as are provided by law and are necessary: (a) For respect of the rights or reputations of others; (b) For the protection of national security or of public order (order public), or of public health or morals.

Therefore, para. 3 cannot be used to silence defenders of multiparty democracy, democratic principles, and human rights,[10] and either can it be used to attack a person, including in the forms of arbitrary arrest, torture, death threats, and murder.[11] All such attacks must be the subject of an active and timely investigation; their perpetrators must be prosecuted;[12] and adequate reparation must be offered to the victims or, when they have lost their lives, to their representatives.[13]

Restrictions must be provided for by law; the HRC has extensively considered the concept of "law." The first of the legitimate reasons for introducing a restriction listed in para. 3 refers to respect for the rights (those recognized in the covenant and in rights-related international law) or the reputation of others (which may refer to other people on an individual basis or as members of a community).[14]

The second reason is the protection of national security, public order, or public health or morals. It is not compatible with para. 3, for example, to enforce laws to suppress information of legitimate public interest that does not harm national security; to prevent the public from accessing this information; to prosecute journalists, researchers, environmentalists, or defenders of human rights for having disseminated this information;[15] or to include in the scope of these laws categories of information such as those related to the commercial sector, banking, and scientific progress.[16] For reasons of maintaining public order, in certain circumstances it

[9]See communications nos. 359/1989 and 385/1989, *Ballantyne, Davidson and McIntyre v. Canada*, (October 18, 1990); 414/1990, *Mika Miha v. Equatorial Guinea*; 1189/2003, *Fernando v. Sri Lanka* (March 31, 2005); 1157/2003, *Coleman v. Australia* (July 17, 2006); 1022/2001, *Velichkin v. Belarus* (October 20, 2005); 1334/2004, *Mavlonov and Sa'di v. Uzbekistán* (March 19, 2009); 926/2000, *Shin v. Republic of Korea* (March 16, 2004); 736/97, *Ross v. Canada* (October 18, 2000); or 1341/2005, *Zundel v. Canada* (March 20, 2007).

[10]See communication no. 458/91, *Mukong v. Cameroon* (July 21, 1994).

[11]See communication no. 1353/2005, *Njaru v. Cameroon* (March 19, 2007).

[12]Ibid. and concluding observations on Georgia (CCPR/C/GEO/CO/3).

[13]Concluding observations on Guyana (CCPR/C/79/Add.121).

[14]See communication No. 736/97, cited in note 9.

[15]Concluding observations on the Russian Federation (CCPR/CO/79/RUS).

[16]Concluding observations on Uzbekistan (CCPR/CO/71/UZB).

may be permissible, for example, to regulate the right to deliver a speech in a particular public place[17] or to consider whether certain forms of expression constitute contempt of court.

As the HRC indicated in its General Comment No. 22:[18]

> The concept of morals derives from many social, philosophical and religious traditions; consequently, limitations on the freedom to manifest a religion or belief for the purpose of protecting morals must be based on principles not deriving exclusively from a single tradition.

These limitations must be understood in the context of the universality of human rights and the principle of nondiscrimination, and restrictions must not be excessively broad.

The HRC stated in its General Comment No. 27 that:

> restrictive measures must conform to the principle of proportionality ...; they must be appropriate to achieve their protective function; they must be the least intrusive instrument amongst those which might achieve the desired result; and they must be proportionate to the interest to be protected.[19]

The principle of proportionality must also take into account the form of expression in question as well as the medium through which it is disseminated; the covenant affords great importance to uninhibited expression in public debate about public and political figures in a democratic society.[20]

In this regard, the committee has restated that the scope of this freedom should not be determined by reference to a "margin of appreciation"[21] and that, if the committee accepts the applicability of this doctrine, the state party[22] must, in any particular case, specifically demonstrate the exact nature of the threat to any of the objectives listed in para. 3 that caused it to restrict freedom of expression.[23]

## The Present and the Future: Soft Law and Challenges Faced by the United Nations in the Defense of Communication Rights

The entire process of recognition and protection of communication rights explained so far has centered on the international order's classic model of declarations, conventions, and treaties, but the evolution of international law in contexts of permanent change, especially in the field of communication, requires a certain legal flexibility that rigid international law does not usually envisage (Feler 2015, p. 287). This is how the concept of "soft law" appeared. It can be considered to be legal in nature and, though lacking binding force, capable of affecting the

---

[17]See communication no. 1157/2003, cited in note 9.

[18]General Comment No. 22: The right to freedom of thought, conscience and religion (Art. 18): 30/07/93. CCPR/C/21/Rev.1/Add.4. https://www.equalrightstrust.org/ertdocumentbank/general%20comment%2022.pdf (accessed January 14, 2021).

[19]General Comment No. 27, paragraph 14. See also communications nos. 1128/2002, *Marques de Morais v. Angola*; and 1157/2003, *Coleman v. Australia*.

[20]See communication no. 1180/2003, *Bodrozic v. Serbia and Montenegro* (October 31, 2005).

[21]A defense of the use of said margin of appreciation can be found in McGoldrick (2016).

[22]See communication no. 511/1992, *Ilmari Länsman et al. v. Finland* (October 14, 1993).

[23]See the previously cited *Sohn* and *Shin* communications.

way in which classic legal obligations are interpreted or implemented, which therefore means that it has a certain legal relevance (Barberis 1994; Meyer 2009).

The UN and its various agencies have set about "soft law" work through reports, documents, and declarations whose purpose is to establish recommendations, suggestions, directions, advice, and proposals, including ones for *lege ferenda*. These initiatives seek to influence national and regional legislation based more on *auctoritas* than on *potestas*, and based on conviction rather than on imposition.

Examples here are too numerous to include in a study such as this one,[24] but the Windhoek Declaration,[25] crafted between April 29 and May 3, 1991, and marking World Press Freedom Day may serve as a reference point for the recognition and promotion of communication rights in developing countries. Likewise, the Santiago Declaration on Media Development and Democracy in Latin America and the Caribbean (United Nations 1994), based on UDHR Article 19, affirms that freedom of expression is the cornerstone of democracy and that democracy is a prerequisite for peace and development.

In 1993, the UN Commission on Human Rights created the position of UN special rapporteur for freedom of opinion and expression, whose annual reports have established the stance of this international organization in relation to these freedoms.[26]

The special rapporteur's 2015 report[27] addressed the use of encryption and anonymity in digital communications, taking the view that there is a need to promote such security systems to avoid any interference or harassment that limits or conditions our freedom of opinion. In the report published on May 11, 2016,[28] there is a very interesting reflection on the role played by the private sector in the digital era. The report acknowledges that freedom of opinion and expression, as we currently exercise these, owe a good part of their vitality to the private sector, which has enormous power in the digital space, acting as a gateway to information and as an intermediary for expression. In digital environments, certain important questions about applicable law and the scope of private authority and public regulation cannot be ignored.

This report emphasizes an aspect that I believe is fundamental in the understanding of the UDHR's and ICCPR's respective Article 19s: the transmission of messages of any kind (which I will discuss later) "by any type of medium of expression" requires reinterpretation. As I have said elsewhere, the excessive power of large Internet companies is changing[29] relationships

---

[24]A large number of further examples can be found in Abad Alcalá (2020).

[25]https://www.un.org/es/events/pressfreedomday/pdf/Declaración%20de%20Windhoek.pdf (accessed January 13, 2020).

[26]These annual reports can be found at https://ohchr.org/EN/Issues/FreedomOpinion/Pages/Annual.aspx (access by subscription.)

[27]Report of the Special Rapporteur to the Human Rights Council on the use of encryption and anonymity to exercise the rights to freedom of opinion and expression in the digital age (A/HRC/29/32) (Twenty-ninth session). https://documents-dds-ny.un.org/doc/UNDOC/GEN/G15/095/85/PDF/G1509585.pdf?OpenElement.

[28]Report of the Special Rapporteur to the Human Rights Council on freedom of expression, states and the private sector in the digital age (A/HRC/32/38) (Thirty-second session). https://documents-dds-ny.un.org/doc/UNDOC/GEN/G16/095/12/PDF/G1609512.pdf?OpenElement.

[29]According to data from the consulting firm NetMarketShare for May 2020 (https://netmarketshare.com), Google easily has an absolute majority in the online browser market for desktops; Chrome's market share is 68.26%, almost eight times higher than that of Firefox's 8.01% or Edge's 6.67%. In the mobile search engine categories, Google has also achieved global dominance with a 93.36% share, compared to 3.92% for Baidu or 0.95% for Yahoo! Meanwhile, in the world of social media, and according to data reported by Statista in May 2020 (https://www.statista.com/markets/424/internet; accessed January 14, 2021), Facebook has more than 2.6 billion monthly active users as of the first quarter of 2020. Among other details, the social media giant now has almost five billion users worldwide, WhatsApp (two billion users) and Instagram (340 million users) are also included.

with users, who in their powers to search for, receive, and disseminate messages are subject to the conditions established by the operators in their "conditions of use." As Garton Ash (2016, p. 48) has pointed out:

> Google may not be a country, but it is a superpower. So are Facebook, Twitter and a few other giant information businesses. They do not have the formal lawmaking authority of sovereign states. Their leaders are not accountable to their users as democratic governments are to voters .... Yet their capacity to enable or limit freedom of information and expression is greater than that of most states. The biggest of the private powers are something like virtual countries.

When it comes to the relationship between freedom of expression and other communication rights, such as access to information, on the one hand and these companies operating in the digital market on the other, this situation gives rise to scenarios that are at the very least tricky. Companies do not always have sufficient procedures for letting users oppose decisions to withdraw content or deactivate an account when they believe that the measure taken by the firm is a mistake or the result of abusive flagging efforts. Where this occurs, a private company is depriving a citizen of exercising his or her right to self-expression, to expression of an opinion, or to the sharing of information with fellow citizens. The idea that nobody should be subject to interference in their holding of opinions, which we find in the respective Article 19s of the UDHR and the ICCPR, is now as closely linked to decisions made in an office in California as it is to those made by a constitutional court.

Related to transparency of international organizations, the 2017 report issued by the UN rapporteur for freedom of expression[30] acknowledges that the UN does not have an information-access policy that is applicable to all departments and specialized agencies, and neither has it established ad hoc criteria for responding to information-access requests, a state of affairs that the rapporteur views as unacceptable. This report assesses the information-access situation within the work of international organizations. It urges all such institutions, and especially the UN, to adopt well-founded freedom of information policies, and it makes specific recommendations for organizations, member states, and civil society.

The special rapporteur's 2018 report[31] sought to answer important questions related to communication rights by proposing a framework for moderating online user-generated content that places human rights at the heart of the matter. The special rapporteur on freedom of expression's recently published report[32] warns about surveillance of certain people, proposing a legal and policy framework for regulation, accountability, and transparency in the private surveillance sector.

As a last example of this soft law, I would mention that in November 1999, the three leading figures with a remit especially focused on freedom of expression[33] – the UN special rapporteur for freedom of opinion and expression, the Organization for Security and Co-operation in Europe representative on freedom of the media, and the Organization of American States

[30]Report of the Special Rapporteur to the human rights council on the role of digital access providers (A/HRC/35/22) (Thirty-fifth session). https://documents-dds-ny.un.org/doc/UNDOC/GEN/G17/077/46/PDF/G1707746.pdf?OpenElement.

[31]Report of the Special Rapporteur to the Human Rights Council on online content regulation A/HRC/38/35 (Thirty-eighth session). https://documents-dds-ny.un.org/doc/UNDOC/GEN/G18/096/72/PDF/G1809672.pdf?OpenElement.

[32]Report of the Special Rapporteur to the Human Rights Council on surveillance and human rights (A/HRC/41/35) (Forty-first session). https://documents-dds-ny.un.org/doc/UNDOC/GEN/G19/148/76/PDF/G1914876.pdf?OpenElement.

[33]All these three representatives' declarations on communication rights can be found at http://www.osce.org/fom/66176;

(OAS) special rapporteur for freedom of expression – met for the first time under the initiative of Article 19, a human rights nongovernmental organization, and adopted a joint declaration recalling the importance of freedom of expression in the functioning of democracy, the need for media pluralism and independence, the role that this freedom plays in denouncing dishonest or criminal practices by public authorities or economic powers, and the need to tackle any attempt to limit this freedom.[34]

The challenges facing effective recognition of communication rights within the UN are continuing to grow. For example, the subject who holds these rights is being redefined, as the formulation included in 1948 ("everyone") is perhaps taking on a new meaning. The classic "Desantesian" separation of universal subject, professional subject, and organizational subject (that can be seen in this work commented on by Ignacio Bel Mallén in Chapter 7) must be understood in a more fluid way and based on the transformation of current communication models, wherein the same individual can perform the functions of any of the three subjects. In this sense, the all-encompassing protection derived from Article 19 makes more sense in the digital ecosystem in which we operate, whose concepts of emitter, receiver, channel, and so on, are constantly changing.

Finally, we cannot ignore the importance of these rights owing to their essential function in the proper functioning of the entire system of human rights (Shah and Boyle 2013, p. 266) and democracy (Barent 2005). Communication rights act as multipliers or metalaw due to their function in enabling the enjoyment of so many other rights (O'Flaherty 2012) that ensure individual development and personal self-realization (Schauer 1982, pp. 4–5) and, as Dworkin (1997) indicates, are derived from the right to human dignity, respect, and equality for all.

In order for all of this to become meaningful, a rereading of the aforementioned Article 19's that does away with the so-called digital divide is necessary, since the right to access the Internet is becoming the primary requirement when it comes to the exercise of freedom of expression and communication rights; it is the basic prerequisite for enjoying all the possibilities that the Internet has to offer.

## Conclusion

The process through which communication rights have been recognized within the UN has evolved according to the changes experienced in contemporary societies and in international law. Its first stage began with Article 19 of the UDHR as a paradigm; despite its many shortcomings, that Article served as a trigger for raising awareness of the importance of these freedoms. Its pioneering recognition of the two-fold nature (information and opinion) of communication activity has endured until today. The use of international law's classic instruments in the UN continued with the promulgation of the ICCPR, which through its optional protocols, incorporated the possibility of the UN Human Rights Committee's creation of a certain amount of "case law" on the rights recognized in that document, with special emphasis laid on the communication rights set forth in the covenant's Article 19. But a changing international context and societies in which technology is omnipresent requires new ways of approaching communication's regulatory challenges. In this regard, the UN has opted for the use of "soft law" initiatives arising from its moral authority in order to influence national legislation, replacing the conventional models used to date, as the various examples described in this chapter show.

---

[34]Principles that are reaffirmed in the 2013 declaration. See note 33.

## References

Abad Alcalá, L. (2020). *Libertades informativas en el ámbito internacional.* Madrid: Dykinson.

Arendt, H. (1976). *The Origins of Totalitarianism.* San Diego: Harcourt, Brace & Jovanovich.

Barberis, J.A. (1994). *Formación del Derecho Internacional.* Ábaco de Rodolfo Depalma: Buenos Aires.

Barent, E. (2005). *Freedom of Speech.* Oxford: Oxford University Press.

Berlin, I. (1968). *Two Concepts of Liberty.* London: Oxford University Press.

Corredoira, L. (2007). A new reading of Article 19 of the Universal Declaration of Human Rights (1948) in our information societies. *Journal Media & Cultural Politics* 3 (3): 336–347.

Desantes Guanter, J.M. (2004). *Derecho a la información. Materiales para un sistema de comunicación.* Valencia: Fundación COSO.

Dworkin, R. (1997). *Taking Rights Seriously.* Cambridge, MA: Harvard University Press.

Escobar de la Serna, L. (2004). *Derecho de la Información.* Madrid: Dykinson.

Feler, A.M. (2015). Soft law como herramienta de adecuación del Derecho internacional a las nuevas coyunturas. *Lecciones y Ensayos* 95: 281–303.

Garton Ash, T. (2016). *Free Speech: Ten Principles for a Connected World.* New Haven, CT: Yale University Press.

González Ballesteros, T. (1989). La genérica libertad de expresión y la específica libertad de información. *Cuenta y Razón* 41–48.

Humphrey, J. (1979). The Universal Declaration of Human Rights: its history, impact and judicial character. In: *Human Rights. Thirty Years after the Universal Declaration* (ed. B.G. Ramcharan), 273. The Hague: Martinus Nijhoff Publishers.

Joseph, S., Schultz, J., and Castan, M. (2005). *The International Covenant on Civil and Political Rights. Cases, Materials and Commentary.* New York: Oxford University Press.

McGoldrick, D. (2016). A defence of the margin of appreciation and an argument for its application by the Human Rights Committee. *International and Comparative Law Quarterly* 65 (1): 21–60.

Meyer, T.L. (2009). Soft law as delegation. *Fordham International Law Journal* 32 (3): 888–942.

O'Flaherty, M. (2012). Freedom of expression: Article 19 of the International Covenant on Civil and Political Rights and the Human Rights Committee's General Comment No 34. *Human Rights Law Review* 12 (4): 627–654.

Schauer, F. (1982). *Free Speech: A Philosophical Enquiry.* Cambridge: Cambridge University Press.

Shah, S. and Boyle, K. (2013). Thought, expression, association, and assembly. In: *International Human Rights Law* (eds. D. Moeckli, S. Shah, and S. Sivakumaran), 257–259. Oxford: Oxford University Press.

Terrou, F. and Solal, L. (1951). *Le Droit de l'information: étude comparée des principaux systèmes de réglementation de la presse, de la radio et du film.* Paris: UNESCO.

United Nations (1994). *Declaration of Santiago on Media Development and Democracy in Latin America and the Caribbean.* New York: United Nations.

Von Bernstorff, J. (2008). The changing fortunes of the Universal Declaration of Human Rights: genesis and symbolic dimensions of the turn to rights in international law. *The European Journal of International Law* 19 (5): 903–924.

Winter, J. and Prost, A. (2013). *René Cassin and Human Rights, from the Great War to the Universal Declaration.* Cambridge: Cambridge University Press.

# 5

# Universality vs. Standardization

## The Privatization of Communication Rights on Social Media

Rodrigo Cetina Presuel

Human rights have found the right conditions for their protection in constitutional states as they are legal systems built around a constitution as a supreme norm from which legally constituted powers emanate and yield a system of laws and institutions with the necessary means to protect the rights of their citizens. However, these constitutional systems encounter problems when their laws need to be applied outside the enclosed context of the nation-state.

For all human rights, the Universal Declaration of Human Rights (UDHR) represents an answer to these problems as it sought to ensure the international recognition of human rights beyond national constitutional frameworks by serving as the basis for building a system for international recognition and protection that understood these rights as universal insofar as they are considered as inherent to all people, to their dignity and value as human beings.[1] The UDHR presupposes that anybody "wherever they may live, possess[es] the capacity to make use of them, and in a manner that is socially as well as individually advantageous, even if this may not actually be recognized in the political arrangements of a given country" (Beetham 2009, p. 286).

A system of international treaties was built on the shoulders of the UDHR, including the International Covenant on Civil and Political Rights (ICCPR), the International Covenant on Economic Social and Cultural Rights, the International Convention on the Elimination of All Forms of Discrimination, the Convention on the Rights of the Child, among other Core International Human Rights Treaties (United Nations 2006). Additionally, the American Convention on Human Rights, the African Charter on Human and Peoples' Rights, the Arab Charter of Human Rights, the European Convention for the Protection of Human Rights and Fundamental Freedoms, and others at the regional level have international and regional human rights bodies to monitor, promote, and protect human rights (IJRCenter 2020).[2]

However, these systems of international law also have limitations. Beyond the minimum conditions for recognizing and guaranteeing human rights, and the duties created by adherence to these treaties, national constitutional orders still have space to define the extent of the

[1]General Assembly of the United Nations (1952, preamble).
[2]https://ijrcenter.org/regional (accessed January 14, 2021).

*The Handbook of Communication Rights, Law, and Ethics: Seeking Universality, Equality, Freedom and Dignity*, First Edition. Edited by Loreto Corredoira, Ignacio Bel Mallén, and Rodrigo Cetina Presuel.

rights and what their limitations may be within their own national contexts. One example is national laws that govern the exercise of communication rights online, particularly in relation to free expression within the context of social media platforms, which operate beyond national borders and jurisdictions.

For some authors, freedom of expression is the preferred term in "contemporary" national, regional and international human rights instruments because "it is deliberately broader and more expansive" (Youm 2015) than other, older names for the right. In its preamble, Article 19 of the UDHR – one such contemporary instrument – configures freedom of expression as a set of rights, not only as a freedom, fully accounting for its role in the communication process: "Everyone has the right to freedom of opinion and expression; this right includes freedom to hold opinions without interference and to seek, receive and impart information and ideas through any media and regardless of frontiers" (United Nations General Assembly 1952). In the context of online platforms, authors that still use the term "freedom of expression," for example Donahoe (2020), recognizes that we are referring to something more than just a right to speak as "it also involves the freedom to seek and receive information, as well as the freedom to form opinions." That is why this work, following others like Sánchez Férriz and Corredoira (2017), prefers to speak of *communication* rights to convey the complex and multifaceted nature of a group of rights.

Thus, communication rights are conceived as universal in subject – they are recognized to all persons – in the content of their messages – there is freedom to express information, opinions, and ideas; and in the media used to transmit such messages – "by any means of expression" (Corredoira 2007); and its geography. It is also said to be recognized "regardless of frontiers" (Paust 1982, p. 57) meaning that it includes a "right to exchange information across national frontiers" (Kessler 1985, p. 249; Price 2003, p. 57).

They are seen as essential rights that allow for personal sovereignty, individual development, and self-fulfillment (Schauer 1982; Howie 2018) based on respect and equality (Abad Chapter 4, this volume) but that are also "directly linked to the ability of citizens to live and participate in a modern society" (Barata Mir and Bassini 2016, p. 78). They, are thus directly connected to the functioning of democracy (Barendt 2005; Howie 2018) and the principles of an open society in which a plurality of voices can participate in a public sphere (Habermas 1991, 1996; Calhoun 1992), which helps these democratic societies develop through discussion that leads to informed participation allowing for decisions reflecting the best interest of their members.

While international treaties establish the minimum conditions on communication rights that must be met in order to be valid, they tend to remain silent about specific limitations and "the measure [is] within the area of discretion left to each state to decide the manner of implementation that best suits local conditions. European human rights law famously permits state parties a variable 'margin of appreciation' when implementing their convention obligations" (Keller 2011, p. 99).

Thus, within national orders, we will find variations, particularly around constitutionally compatible limits on the exercise of these rights. For example, Article 19 of the ICCPR expressly establishes that freedom of expression entails special duties and responsibilities that therefore make it subject to restrictions provided for by law, necessary to protect the rights and reputation of others, and for the protection of national security, public order, public health, or public morals. Beyond these conditions, there are variations among adherents and differences in how they perceive each other in their relation to communication rights.

## Communication Rights in a Borderless Internet

On the Internet, where technology enables near instant and borderless communication among the many, those differences can create problems. Given that a good deal of online expression happens on social media platforms and these platforms operate beyond national borders, content is often available in different territories at the same time.

Since the rules that govern expression and place limits on communication rights are defined by national law and national courts determine the instances in which specific pieces of content published on social media must be subject to a limitation according to those laws, ordering the removal or blocking of specific content can give rise to jurisdictional issues. These issues include figuring out what national law applies and if the effects of a judicial order are to be limited to a particular territory or need to be global in scope in order to meaningfully protect the rights of others. For example, in defamation cases, a court will seek to provide relief to an offended party within a national jurisdiction by mandating the suppression of content deemed defamatory, but that content may be available globally.

A defining characteristic of social media platforms is that the private companies that control them have great power to govern what is communicated on them. Within the context of social media, governance problems arise as states seek to regulate expression through traditional methods, for example, laws and the courts (Balkin 2018) that are still bound by their jurisdictional scope. This creates problems for the platforms themselves because, while they enforce their own private rules, created and adopted unilaterally, on their platforms across all borders, they have to do so while also dealing with the laws and courts of the places they operate in.

To solve jurisdictional problems related to communication rights, nations are increasingly interpreting their laws in ways that allow for their application beyond their borders, relying on regulation and judicial interpretation that allows them to "coerce or co-opt private owners of digital infrastructure to regulate the speech of private actors" (Balkin 2018, p. 2016). Social media platforms are businesses and, as such, seek to generate as much revenue as possible. For that purpose, they tend to seek the most efficient and cost-effective solutions, including adopting private community standards that can serve those purposes.

Social media platforms develop rules that allow them to sort through content that should not be deemed acceptable on their platforms through a commitment to free expression that is always conditioned by profit (Gillespie 2018). Their aim is to "find rules that align with what their users expect" (Suzor 2019, p. 18) to keep them using their platforms and to avoid government regulators from punishing them for content deemed undesirable. Resulting fines or potentially being barred from a market are not good for profit.

Ensuring that private community standards comply with as many national legal orders as possible, and can be deployed through a combination of technological and human moderation to control online expression, in order to avoid liability that may arise from what users post (Franks 2019) is, in itself, a way to seek the preservation of profit. In truth, it seems that profit comes first; enabling free expression comes a distant second.

This generates a systemic problem that yields standardized, not universal, rules for interventions in the exercise of communication rights on these platforms. Problems associated with such standardized rules include potentially imposing restrictions on communication rights that are acceptable in some countries but not in others but may also lead to enforcement that is not always necessary, suitable, and proportionate and may thus be unconstitutional. It can also lead to prior restraint and collateral censorship (Balkin 2018, p. 2016) as well as reduced transparency and accountability.

## Embracing Difference in Universal Communication Rights

While achieving pure universality may not be possible or desirable (Ugland Chapter 6, this volume), at least in western constitutional democracies, the core values that justify communication rights can be said to be universally recognized and they are generally accepted as positive rights aimed at creating a space for pluralistic expression while also ensuring that communication happens with as little governmental interference as possible.

There is wide consensus that communication rights are not absolute but often, from the perspective of comparable democratic countries, and even by the standards of some international treaties, the United States is often seen as permissive in terms of the limits it imposes on expression. European scholars often see the US conception of the right as underdeveloped as it only focuses on the liberty aspects of free individual expression but not always on the rights and obligations it implies (Fiss 1996; Yemini 2019). In the United States, freedom of speech is often seen as solely a negative right that "does not impose affirmative obligations on the government to provide information, ensure access or in any way facilitate expression" (Ugland Chapter 6, this volume). In turn, European countries are often accused of having more restrictive freedom of expression laws, at least from the US perspective (Versteeg 2017; Daskal 2019).

In the United States, even if the First Amendment of the Constitution states that "Congress shall make no law" that abridges freedom of expression and the press, save some opinions, (Justice Black's dissent in *Mishkin v. New York*[3] is an example) that are by no means the majority (Krislov 1964, p. 189), there are well-established categories of unprotected speech that have been developed in jurisprudence. Incitement to violence, individual threats (O'Brien 2010), or obscenity (Bosmajian 1976) are not protected. There are also limits on what may be said through advertising and rules against the use of profanity in broadcasting (Caldwell 1935; Emerson 1970; Buckley et al. 2008; Lipschultz 2008).

The United States Supreme Court has often balanced the right to speak without interference against governmental interests and the rights of others. The Court has developed guidelines for assessing that balance over time, even if it has been criticized as incomplete and inconsistent (Emerson 1970; Bogen 1976, 1979; Rosenthal 2011). Like in other countries, defamation is a limit of free speech in the United States, even if a high bar must be met for limiting expression on the basis of libel or slander against public officials and public figures (Arellano Toledo and Cetina Presuel 2015).

Unlike the US Constitution, European regional treaties and local constitutions contain more fleshed-out versions of communication rights and are explicit in terms of the conditions that an acceptable limit on them must meet. Article 19.2 of the ICCPR establishes a right to freedom of opinion and expression and to seek, receive, and impart information and ideas of all kinds in different media of communication, orally, in writing, in print, through art, or any other media of choice expanding the reach to any means of expression that exists or may exist. Article 19.3 of the ICCPR expressly establishes that the exercise of communication rights carries special duties and responsibilities and are, therefore, subject to the restrictions that are provided for by law and are necessary to protect the rights and reputation of others; for the protection of national security, public order, public health, or public morals.

Similarly, Article 10 of the European Convention of Human Rights (ECHR) establishes a right to freedom of expression that includes the freedom to hold opinions and impart information and ideas, explicitly embracing the idea of a right that should exist "regardless of frontiers" and be exercised without "interference by public authority" but establishing that public authorities can still institute a licensing system for "broadcasting, television or cinema enterprises" while also stating that expression is free through any media of one's choice. The second part of Article 10 of the ECHR recognizes the duties and responsibilities linked to freedom of expression, making communication rights subject to the "formalities, conditions, restrictions or penalties as prescribed by law and are necessary in a democratic society" linking them to the goal of advancing democratic objectives through duties and responsibilities and accepting other possible limitations "in the interests of national security, territorial integrity or public safety, for the prevention of disorder or crime, for the protection of health or morals, for the protection of the reputation or rights of others, for preventing the disclosure of

---

[3] *Mishkin v. New York*, 383 US 502 (1966).

information received in confidence, or for maintaining the authority and impartiality of the judiciary."

At the European Union level, Title II "Freedoms" of the Charter of Fundamental Rights of the European Union (CFREU) recognizes communication rights in Article 11 in similar terms to its ECHR counterpart. It also includes a freedom of the press clause establishing that "the freedom of pluralism of the media shall be respected" establishing a link with the possibility of creating licensing schemes for broadcast and other types of media to promote pluralism. Critics argue, however, that European policies have failed to achieve any meaningful pluralism (Westphal 2002) and that, in general, it is clear that diversity through competition in the marketplace is clearly not sufficient (Freedman 2008).

CFREU's Article 52 establishes limitations to fundamental rights, including those of Article 11, that states that "[a]ny limitation … must be provided for by law and respect the essence of those rights and freedoms" and that such limitations are subject to the principle of proportionality and only allowed if necessary and "genuinely meet objectives of general interest recognized by the Union or the need to protect the rights and freedoms of others."

However, beyond these treaties, communication rights legislation is not harmonized across the EU. Individual European countries may still have different standards for protecting communication rights and instances in which expression should not be protected.

For example, in France, "freedom of expression" is an essential freedom as incorporated in the Declaration of Human and Civic Rights on August 26, 1789. Rights that were then incorporated by reference into the French Constitution. Communication rights must be balanced with other rights and public order and may be limited "for the sake of protecting privacy, protecting the presumption of innocence, and preventing defamation and insults." France also limits expression to protect institutions and holders of public office from defamation in its freedom of the press law[4] (Art. 30) and disrespecting the national anthem or the flag in certain contexts (C. Penal Art. 433 5–1). Contrast this with protection of flag burning as a freedom of expression in the United States[5] or the aforementioned standards for defamation of public officials.[6]

Article 5 of Germany's Constitution, the German Basic Law,[7] expressly states that communication rights can be limited in general laws (laws that limit free speech to protect the public interest but do not ban specific expression), in provisions for the protection of young persons, and the right to personal honor and, in general, find limits in other basic rights (Paust 1982; Schauer 1982; Kessler 1985; Habermas 1991, 1996; Calhoun 1992; Price 2003; Barendt 2005; Beetham 2009; Barata Mir and Bassini 2016; Sánchez Férriz and Corredoira Y Alfonso 2017; Howie 2018; Donahoe 2020). There is one notable exemption to the general law requirement: "the Federal Constitutional Court allows a restriction of freedom of speech by section 130, para. 4 of the Criminal Code, which criminalizes 'disturb[ing] the public peace in a manner that violates the dignity of the victims [of the Nazi regime] by approving of, glorifying, or justifying the National Socialist rule of arbitrary force.'" France also has explicit prohibitions on inciting criminal acts in the aforementioned specific legislation about freedom of the press (Art. 23), on hate speech (Art. 24), and the denial of crimes against humanity, particularly the Holocaust (Arts. 24 and 24 bis). In contrast to this, what is usually considered hate speech and banned in other western liberal democracies can sometimes be considered protected political speech in the United States. The Supreme court has reversed a conviction

[4]Loi du 29 juillet 1881 sur la liberté de la presse.
[5]*Texas v. Johnson*, 491 US 397 (1989).
[6]*New York Times Co. v. Sullivan*, 376 US 254 (1964).
[7]Basic Law for the Federal Republic of Germany (1949).

against a Ku Klux Klan leader over racist comments[8] as it found no proof that "the speaker was inciting 'imminent lawless action' or that such action was likely to occur" (Lewis 2008, p. 159).

From a European perspective, shaped by tragic experiences of totalitarianism during and after World War II, such a permissible approach to hate speech may seem unthinkable (Lewis 2008, p. 160). This not only highlights that differences do exist; it also underscores why the existence of difference is desirable: different national contexts may call for differences on what are acceptable limits on expression. These examples illustrate that, given the vast differences of the world we live in, its cultural diversity, the different historical and political realities, and varied and inequal economic conditions of the nations of the world, there should be enough space to account for differences. That is achieved by letting national governments define limits on communication rights according to their national context, as long as they commit to the universal recognition of these rights and abide by certain rules when establishing such limits. European Union law contains prescriptive measures limiting expression to be considered extremely harmful by requiring the criminalization of certain categories of content,[9] namely incitement of terrorism, child pornography, and incitement to racial and xenophobic hatred (Keller 2011, p. 144). However, even in these cases, it is up to individual states to define the particulars in their national laws.

But, in a world where the Internet has contributed to "an interconnectedness of legal orders that has never been as intense in legal history" (Basedow 2015, p. 471) particularly through digital technologies that allow individual expression to be exercised, if not regardless of, at least in spite of, frontiers (Badiou 2003; Antweiler 2016), there is a risk of confusing homogeneity, or standardization,[10] with universality. Internet platforms do not seem to be aware that there is a distinction, or perhaps their own goals lead them to willfully ignore it, and states run the risk of falling into the same fallacy. There is the risk of confusing a universal acceptance of communication rights with a sort of legal colonialism that seeks to impose a particular interpretation of the limits of freedom of expression onto other states motivated by a need to respond to the challenges that online expression poses for both nation states and Internet companies.

Sometimes, states will seek to expand the reach of their laws when they realize that online, local laws need to be applied beyond their borders to have any real effect (Aswad 2016; Rosati 2019; Suzor 2019) in order to effectively protect citizens within their own jurisdictions. Other times, regulatory efforts may seek to navigate the complexities of national and regional competences by seeking to leverage private cooperation through online platform moderation efforts. Platforms may seek to combine their self-serving conception of free expression that seeks to advance their business goals that, at the same time, allows them to navigate the maze of differences in justifiable limits for communication rights and remain free of liability.

---

[8] *Brandenburg v. Ohio*, 395 US 444 (1969).

[9] See also Framework Decision 2002/475/JHA on combating terrorism, as amended by Council Framework Decision 2008/919/JHA of November 28, 2008, Council Framework Decision 2004/68/JHA of December 22, 2003 on combating the sexual exploitation of children and child pornography, and Council Framework Decision 2008/913/JHA of November 28, 2008 on combating certain forms and expressions of racism and xenophobia by means of criminal law.

[10] We prefer the term "standardization" drawing from Cohen's (2019, p. 217) definition of *standard*: "structured protocols for conforming the activities of multiple nodes in a network" and to convey that this false universality is based on private standards adopted by private companies for moderating speech.

## Global Community Standards Do Not Imply the Universalization of Communication Rights

As said, universal acceptance of communication rights and a commitment to their protection need not entail a homogeneous interpretation of where the limits for these rights lie. Decisions on what is protected expression and what is not, where their limits are, even relations between citizens have always been made by states, including decisions not to intervene. Thus, within constitutional frameworks for freedom of expression, there are relations in the private realm, citizen to citizen, in which private actors can impose conditions to expression.

The appearance of the Internet and its promise of lowering barriers to access and of transforming the hierarchies of communication into a democratic system with multiple senders and receivers is what may have led regulators to be particularly non interventionist in the online context (Franks 2020). In turn, this is what has led to legislation such as Section 230 in the United States[11] or the Safe-Harbor provisions in the e-Commerce Directive, in the European Union.[12]

It is within this context that social media platforms have emerged as tremendously powerful entities in terms of deciding the conditions for free expression inside their online environments (Balkin 2009; Rosen 2012; Klonick 2018). They do so through their privately adopted community standards (Peters 2017; Gillespie 2018) that they hope "apply to everyone, all around the world, and to all types of content" (Facebook 2020).

Platforms are not indifferent to communication rights and they do not ignore the differing standards for expression among countries. However, their private community standards are there to impose a *particular* view of what should or should not be protected expression and "a strong incentive to exercise control over the content each of us sees" (Suzor 2019, p. 13) except that incentive is to keep users engaged in order to generate revenue through what is called surveillance capitalism (Zuboff 2019).

For example, Facebook states in its own community standards that it is important for the platform to be "a place where people feel empowered to communicate … that's why … a set of Community Standards … outline what is and is not allowed" based on the advice of technology, public safety, and human rights experts and recognizing that content that is newsworthy and in the public interest may be allowed even if it goes against those standards (Facebook 2020).

Content moderation through the interpretation of these standards is not easy. It is a time-consuming, expensive activity with a high human cost (Roberts 2019). A company like Facebook would not undertake this enormous task just out of a commitment to free expression. If they are willing to eliminate or restrict certain content – abuse, hate speech, among other examples – it is because they want to make sure that most users spend as much time on the platform as possible interacting with content and that can only be achieved by moderation; most users will be turned off by disturbing content or turned away by harassment or violence.

Social media companies are not trying to advance the universal protection of the freedom of expression of their users (at least it is not their main priority), they are simply trying to protect their profit. Roberts (2018) expresses this eloquently:

> content moderation activities are fundamentally and primarily undertaken to protect and enhance platforms' advertising revenue, protect platforms themselves from liability, provide a palatable user experience (highly context-dependent) and, when necessary and in response to specific

[11]Section 230 of the Communications Decency Act (CDA) of 1996, Title V of the Telecommunications Act of 1996, 47 USC. § 230.

[12]Directive 2000/31/EC of the European Parliament and of the Council of June 8, 2000 on certain legal aspects of information society services, in particular electronic commerce, in the Internal Market ("Directive on electronic commerce").

> jurisdictional or regulatory rulings, to comply with legal mandates. In short, the role of content moderation is fundamentally a matter of brand protection for the firm. (p. 6)

The underlying incentive is, at the end of the day, to generate revenue. That is just a feature of the economic system that gives us Facebook, and other companies like Google, Amazon, Twitter, or Apple (Ghosh 2020, p. 51).

Facebook does recognize values associated with communication rights and has possible limits on expression. Dignity, privacy, and safety are all mentioned along with another one that seems extraneous: authenticity (Facebook 2020). Authenticity is understood as a value that can justify limiting expression on the platform allowing Facebook to eliminate content that misrepresents who a person is and what they are doing. This is justified because, according to Facebook, "authenticity creates a better environment for sharing" (Facebook 2020) and because Facebook's strategy for combating disinformation on the platform is based on banning accounts that engage in "inauthentic coordinated behaviour or artificial amplification, rather than on a content basis" (Donahoe 2020).

For a company that bases its business model around engagement, which allows them to observe their users and collect their data to turn it into advertising income, this could be taken as further evidence that the Community Standards put business first and free expression second, because ensuring less misrepresentation of who a person is helps gather useful data about them and because "a better environment for sharing" means creating more activity that engages more users.

Although Facebook's commitment to not allowing misrepresentation is doubtful it does seem to allow it when it is good for business (Isaac and Kang 2020). In fact, some authors argue that companies like Facebook are willing to allow anything, including harmful content, if it is good for business, even if it comes at the cost of deteriorating public discourse and democracy (Vaidhyanathan 2018; Ghosh 2020). Privately created standards for communication rights online are also problematic because these standards are in constant flux, changing to respond to platforms' interests, which do not always align with the protection of online expression (Waddell 2016).

Social media platforms do not contribute to advance the universality of communication rights. Rather, they are making standards for online expression more uniform, turning them into a tool for moderation that is only effective inasmuch as it advances their goals, not the values that underpin communication rights. Standard policies certainly allow for some differences, but do not embrace them. Diversity is seen as an obstacle to overcome in order to make moderation more effective. Universality, on the contrary, recognizes rights inherent to all but also embraces differences justified by different social, political, cultural, and economic contexts.

Critics that point out that social networks, and technological companies in general, have too much power over online expression, and even those that downplay the issue, both worry that "if a private commercial entity (or indeed any entity) did have the power to leverage its control of an interconnection standard into policy-setting power over unrelated matters, that would be undesirable" (Cohen 2019, p. 220).

Standardization of rules that govern online expression on these platforms gives too much power to private companies and, even if standardization can help in moderation efforts to eliminate hate speech, abuse and other undesirable content, we must remember that "monopoly power over public discourse can be pernicious even when exercised for ostensibly beneficial ends" (Douek 2020, p. 23).

But despite all of this, states not only let social media platforms exert their power over expression using platforms' private standards, they also seek to leverage these private standards, and the technological capabilities that allow for their implementation, to navigate their own jurisdictional challenges in relation to communication rights.

## The Embrace of Private Community Standards by Public Authorities

EU Regulation that sets the rules for Europol's cooperation with member states[13] establishes that Europol must support and strengthen the competent authorities of the member states in preventing and combating serious crimes (Art. 3).

Said support extends to preventing and combating crime facilitated, promoted, or committed using the Internet, including, in cooperation with member states, reporting potentially criminal Internet content to the online service providers so that they voluntarily consider if such content goes against their private standards and if it should be taken down (Art. 5). This is done through Europol's Internet Referral Unit, or IRU, part of its European Counter Terrorism Center. The IRU does not make an assessment on the illegality of online content and cannot mandate companies to take down content. Instead, the IRU "has the power to create pressure to have apparently legal content deleted by companies but bear no responsibility or accountability for doing so" (EDRi 2016).

The justification for this scheme is that Europol lacks the mandate under the European Treaties to determine the illegality of supposed terrorist content because, while all countries have a commitment to criminalize the incitement of terrorism, antiterrorist legislation is a matter of national law. To overcome this competency and jurisdictional barrier, Europol contrasts content with private platforms' community standards in order to determine, not its legality, something it cannot do, but a breach in said standards and then report it so that platforms take it down. According to a report, 90% of content referred by Europol was taken down voluntarily by private platforms (European Commission 2016), with no determination of its legality.

It is difficult to see how this complies with the EU Charter's obligation that mandates that restrictions on fundamental rights must be "provided for by law" (EDRi 2016) and how communication rights can be effectively protected against overreach by Europol and the private companies since these procedures lack transparency, due process, and adequate judicial review (Riis and Schwemer 2019, pp. 11–12), which are known problems of transferring the policing of expression from public authorities to private entities (Stalla-Bourdillon 2010; Belli and Sappa 2017; Coche 2018).

A 2018 proposed regulation (European Commission 2018) for the prevention of dissemination of terrorist content online included an article that was ultimately discarded by the European Parliament. Article 5, as proposed, attempted to give new powers to "the competent (national) authority" to refer alleged terrorist content to service providers who were then required to have operational and technical measures that allow for an expeditious assessment of the referred content against its own terms and conditions in order to then decide whether the content should be removed or the access to it disabled. The same regulation introduced, in Article 3, an obligation for Internet service providers to take "appropriate, reasonable and proportionate" actions against the dissemination of terrorist content and to protect users from such content. Article 6 established an obligation to, when appropriate, take proactive measures to protect services against the presence and dissemination of terrorist content, including the use of automated detection tools. These automated tools pose similar problems to relying on community standards to take down content, as they will surely lack transparency and may not be capable of guaranteeing due process as "automated removal tools are radical measures, which can malfunction and be misused" (Riis and Schwemer 2019).

The attempt at including this article in the proposed legislation to prevent terrorist content online is indicative of an attempt by the European Commission to extend Europol's system of

---

[13]Regulation (EU) 2016/794 of the European Parliament and of the Council of May 11, 2016 on the European Union Agency for Law Enforcement Cooperation) and replacing and repealing Council Decisions 2009/371/JHA, 2009/934/JHA, 2009/935/JHA, 2009/936/JHA, and 2009/968/JHA.

referrals on the basis of private community standards to other national competent authorities. However, unlike Europol, national authorities should already be competent in determining if content posted online should be taken down per their own national laws, and through their own national courts. This is problematic because "conditioning removals on terms and conditions and not the applicable law … increases the risk of disproportionate interference with the right to freedom of expression and access to information. In this regard, it is important to consider that there may be a variety of content that the hosting providers prohibit on their platforms, but which is not illegal" (Kuczerawy 2018).

Adopting such a regulation would give another national authority, presumably an administrative authority, the power to refer supposed illegal content to a platform to determine if it should be taken down according to the platform's own private community standards, norms that are defined according to commercial interests and without any input from users or even governments (Gillespie 2018).

This seems a pragmatic move to circumvent established national competences at the EU level that make it difficult to fight illegal content online. Since no harmonization of anti terrorism legislation is possible, public authorities seek to rely on private terms and conditions that platforms apply to their platforms across European territories. That a private company's own community standards should take precedence over already established national law and a judicial procedure with the proper guarantees is nonsensical but also potentially detrimental to communication rights. Apart from issues related to transparency and lack of due process, we must remember that those community standards are there to promote private interests first, and a public interest in communication rights second.

## Embracing Injunctions with Global Effects as a Solution to Jurisdictional Challenges

European Union Law, and European Human Rights Law, through the Luxembourg and Strasbourg courts, has developed communication rights jurisprudence, often very protective of communication rights but without necessarily contributing to harmonizing it.

The European Court of Human Rights (ECtHR) has traditionally imposed and requested "a higher level of protection of the right to freedom of expression and information than the level guaranteed at the domestic level of the defending states" in cases related to access to public information, defamation of public personalities or the conviction of journalists (Voorhoof 2015, p. 43) though, in recent years, it has seemingly failed to grasp the importance of communication rights in a democratic society (Voorhoof 2015, p. 44).[14] For Flauss (2009) the Court has focused on "the structural promotion of … freedom of expression … and … the category-specific adjustment of said freedom" but exhibiting discrepancies that undermine the authority of European Jurisprudence (p. 848). Despite this, nearly 40 years of ECtHR jurisprudence have certainly influenced the Court of Justice of the European Union (CJEU) but without "automatically adhering to the methodology of control upheld by the Strasbourg Court" (Flauss 2009, p. 849).

The EU has not focused its harmonization efforts on European constitutional principles (Keller 2011, p. 245) even if it has adopted a Charter of Fundamental Rights of the European

[14]Among the cases the author cites ECtHR January 16, 2014, *Tierbefreier E.V.v. Germany*, Appl. No.45192/09 and ECtHR January 30, 2014, *De Lesquen du Plessis-Casso v. France* (no. 2), Appl. No. 34400/10 that deal with defamation and ECtHR March 11, 2014, *Yaman Akdeniz v. Turkey*, Appl. no. 20877/10 (Dec.) dealing with the blocking of websites by public authorities.

Union with the Treaty of Lisbon (2009). Believing that each member state is entitled to determine its own limits on communication rights based on public policy objectives, the CJEU has focused instead on setting and interpreting human rights standards across EU within the context of the goal of European market integration, making sure that domestic restrictions on expression, based on public policy objectives, do not infringe European human rights obligations (Keller 2011).

Inside the single market, the CJEU has focused on jurisdictional issues related to media law and other areas such as intellectual property where it has dealt with injunctions with global effects, for example, when deciding that intellectual property rights have protection all across the EU, including EU-wide intellectual property-related injunctions issued by national courts as there is no risk of conflicting decisions.[15]

In the Costeja case,[16] the CJEU created the so-called right to be forgotten, recognized across the EU and that acts as a limit to communication rights as it can restrict the availability of personal information about individuals online. The right to be forgotten, as the right of erasure, is contained in the General Data Protection Regulation (GDPR)[17] that applies uniformly across the EU.

The CJEU has further evaluated the territorial scope of the right to be forgotten[18] concluding that "search engine operators are required to remove all the links on all the versions in the EU regardless of where the request to de-reference originates in the EU" (Samonte 2019) as a goal of the EU is to ensure a high level of data protection, which includes a right to be forgotten, all across the EU, even if the door was left open for the option of the national Data Protection Authorities "to determine the conditions which will justify a delisting on all versions of a search engine based on national standards of the protection of fundamental rights" (Samonte 2019).

As part of a regional system of human rights protection, the work of both the ECtHR and the CJEU focuses on upholding member states' commitment to human and fundamental rights, not on seeking uniformity in national rules. It is possible that slowly but surely, some uniformity and commonality of interpretation can emerge for communication rights that are, after all, universally recognized by member states and present in the Treaties that form the EU.

The problem is that private companies, and apparently organizations like Europol, are not willing to wait the time it would take to traverse the long road of jurisprudential development. Lumbering courts probably seem bad for business from the perspective of a social media company and public authorities feel the need to respond to the challenges of online expression about as fast as those challenges emerge. This is why they are opting for shortcuts, bypassing national law and national authorities to obtain faster results but that, as we just exposed, has negative tradeoffs and consequences. Courts too, also seem to be embracing the possibility of cooperation with social networks to overcome jurisdictional issues.

When an anonymous Facebook user shared an article that included defamatory comments against Austrian politician Eva Glawischnig-Piesczek, she obtained an injunction from the Commercial Court of Vienna to remove the infringing content and any text with equivalent

---

[15] *Solvay SA v. Honeywell Fluorine Products Europe BV, Honeywell Belgium NV, Honeywell Europe NV*, case C-616/10, EU:C:2012 : 445.

[16] *Google Spain SL, Google Inc. v Agencia Española de Protección de Datos*, Mario Costeja González (2014).

[17] Regulation (EU) 2016/679 of the European Parliament and of the Council of April 27, 2016 on the protection of natural persons with regard to the processing of personal data and on the free movement of such data and repealing Directive 95/46/EC (General Data Protection Regulation).

[18] *Google v CNIL* Case C-507/17.

meaning from Facebook. Facebook disabled access to the content in Austria and the Vienna Higher Regional Court upheld the injunction but limited the blocking of equivalent content, which led both parties to appeal the decision. The Austrian Supreme Court referred the question of the scope of content that should be removed and the territorial scope of the content removal injunction to the Court of Justice of the EU.[19]

Article 15 of the e-Commerce Directive prohibits the imposition of a general obligation to monitor all the information service providers transmit or store or that requires them to actively seek facts or circumstances indicating illegal activity happening on their platforms. When asked, the Third Chamber of the Court ruled that member states were not precluded by the Directive from ordering a provider to remove or block unlawful content, including content that is identical or equivalent to such unlawful information conditioned on the ability of the provider to identify identical or equivalent content without an independent assessment and could use automated tools to identify it. (For a more in-depth analysis of general monitoring obligations see Ullrich 2018; Cavaliere 2019; White 2019.)

Regarding the territorial scope of the injunction that mandated content removal, the CJEU found that the e-Commerce Directive does not preclude member states from ordering the worldwide removal of the content declared unlawful, and as a consequence, left the determination of the geographic scope of a restriction in the hands of the member states and within the framework of the relevant national and international laws.

Since freedom of expression is a matter of national law, it is not uniformly applied EU law and thus, "the national rules of civil law and civil procedure of a particular member state apply in case of personal rights and protective measures" (Morawska-Zakroczymska and Gęsicka 2019). Article 18 of the e-Commerce Directive establishes that the national laws of member states have to ensure that actions before national courts concerning platforms' online activities allow for "the rapid adoption of measures ... designed to terminate any alleged infringement and to prevent any further impairment of the interests involved." In the decision, the CJEU's interpretation of Article 18 may be too broad, interpreting that the Article does not contain "any limitation, including a territorial limitation, on the scope of the measures" (para. 49). Member states may adopt them in accordance with the Directive including the possibility of adopting injunction measures that produce worldwide effects (para. 50) as long as any "EU rules in that area are consistent with the rules applicable at (the) international level" (para. 51).

Under generally applicable principles of international law "jurisdiction is a nation's assertion of power over the people, properties, and activities within its borders" (Nunziato 2018, p. 52) and "the first and foremost restriction imposed by international law upon a State is that – failing the existence of a permissive rule to the contrary – it may not exercise its power in any form in the territory of another State."[20]

The CJEU justifies the need to allow member states to have "particularly broad discretion in relation to the actions and procedures for taking the necessary measures" contained in recital 52 of Article 18 of the e-Commerce directive that refers to the particular character of damage connected to online platforms and Internet society services, pointing out that all online content, including content that may potentially damage the interests of a third party, "is characterized by its rapidity and by its geographical extent" (para. 28).

For Cavaliere (2019) "the decision reveals a struggle to grapple with technology and the opportunities it opens" as well as the challenges related to "the limited capacity of courts to enforce their decisions beyond national boundaries." Apparently, the CJEU came to the conclusion that it is a good idea to allow injunctions with worldwide effects in order to protect the interests of a person affected by potentially unlawful online content in order to face the

[19] *Eva Glawischnig-Piesczek v Facebook Ireland Limited* (2019).

[20] S.S. Lotus (*Fr. v. Turk*) (1927) of the Permanent Court of International Justice.

challenges posed by platforms that can quickly disseminate the content across borders and jurisdictions, but taking into account other problems this may generate.

The Advocate General (AG) of the Court of Justice's opinion[21] sheds more light on the reasoning behind the CJEU decision. The AG points out that online content posted by users is constantly reproduced and altered and "constantly being exchanged between users" (para. 25). The opinion also points out that there is nothing in international law that precludes injunctions from having "extraterritorial" effects and as a consequence "the finding that the information concerned was illegal would be extended to the territories of other Member States, irrespective of whether or not that information was legal under the law designated as applicable according to the conflict-of-law rules of those Member States" (para. 95). And while the CJEU does make it clear that requirements for hosting online platforms to take down and even filter content cannot be general in scope, it does open the door for takedowns and filtering to happen worldwide in specific cases, and "potentially in a very wide range of circumstances given the obligation to remove identical content and the uncertainty surrounding the definition of equivalent (content)" (Smith 2019).

A similar case reviewed by the Delhi High Court in India[22] that references *Glawischning-Piesczek v. Facebook* reached similar conclusions. The Indian court said that the taking-down of content should happen globally as platforms have a positive obligation "to remove the offending content from that computer resource in a manner so as to ensure that access is fully disabled" (para. 83). The Court reasoned that since content uploaded to a platform is available globally, then the removal of content must be from all domains, global and local, citing that it is technologically possible to do so as platforms routinely take down content globally when it goes against its community standards (para. 87).

This indicates that the Indian court intends to leverage the technical capabilities of platforms that allow them to easily block or takedown content in multiple territories and across borders. The problem is that in very much the same way as in Glawischnig, the Ramdev case opens the door for blocking content in a very wide range of circumstances and without properly grappling with adverse effects that may result.

Since the jurisdictional question seems to have no easy answer, and because technology offers pragmatic solutions that allow for the removal of content in more than one jurisdiction with relative ease, all of the described cases could be indicative of how other states around the world may choose to navigate the jurisdictional challenge of asserting their interest in regulating the Internet at the local level while, at the same time, ensuring that they can provide effective remedy and protect their citizens across jurisdictions (Woods 2018). But, in doing this, courts may not be properly assessing the risks of such a course of action.

It is no surprise that some have called the *Glawischnig-Piesczek v. Facebook* decision a serious assault on speech that paves the way for global censorship because it seems to enable EU member states to set global standards for expression through their courts, potentially allowing "one single country (to) determine what is and is not permitted speech for everyone everywhere" and in which "the most censorship-prone country wins" (Daskal and Klonick 2019).

Similarly, *Ramdev v. Facebook* has been called deeply concerning because of potential negative effects for both platforms and users in other countries and because it could result in Internet intermediaries needing to design country specific platforms "which will splinter the Internet and effectively erode the promise of the open Internet as we know it" (SFLC.in 2019). Countries, critics argue, "do not and should not enjoy the power to implement their

[21]Opinion of Advocate General Szpunar delivered on June 4, 2019 (1) Case C-18/18 *Eva Glawischnig-Piesczek v Ireland Limited.*

[22]*Swami Ramdev v. Facebook* 2019.

laws" in ways that end up restricting speech within other nations that have their own rules for speech protection (Cavaliere 2019).

Both cases have something in common: public figures are at the center, and these people, with prominent positions of power, have managed to obtain injunctions or take-down orders that are meant to apply globally, which is, in itself, problematic. An unintended consequence of both rulings could be enabling "libel tourism" in which "plaintiffs may attempt to bring defamation cases in 'claimant-friendly' jurisdictions knowing that they could result in global takedowns" taking advantage of the fact that defamation laws are not the same around the world (Staveley-O'Carroll 2009; Little 2012; Hopkins 2019).

A critique of social media platforms is that through tiered-governance or "offering different users different sets of rules, different material resources and opportunities, and different procedural protections" they often afford the most protection to the most powerful (Caplan and Gillespie 2020, p. 2). With decisions like Glawischnig and Ramdev, courts risk doing the same.

## Conclusions: The Consequences of Standardization and Privatization of Communication Rights on Social Media

In our interconnected world, particularly through digital technologies, that allow for individual expression to be received if not regardless of, at least in spite of, frontiers, there is a risk of confusing homogeneity with universality. Social media platforms are either not aware there is a difference, or their business goals lead them to willfully ignore that such difference exists. States, however, are at risk of falling into the same fallacy if they seek to impose what is perceived as the best interpretation of communication rights online – their own, onto other states.

The cases described here contribute to enable a trend by which the enforcement of freedom of expression rules is deputized to private companies either by the use of their own private rules as the standard to decide what is legal or illegal expression, or by expanding national laws and their interpretation and giving them worldwide application when they are implemented by these social media platforms. These cases also represent a move towards a standardization of rules that govern communication rights around the world. This standardization is not agreed to by countries following traditional avenues for the adoption of similar rules such as concurrent judicial interpretations, laws that seek harmonization such as Directives or Regulations, as in the case of the EU, international treaties or even academic and societal dialog, including dialog between courts.

This standardization gives too much power to private companies that police online expression out of self-interest – the pursuit of profit – and not in the interest of protecting communication rights and other human rights. Their objective is to serve their own business goals. There is also risk that this standardization becomes a question of powerful states imposing their laws on others that are less so, including those states that have less sway on how social media platforms operate on their own territories.

Undermining local jurisdictions can generate pushback from nation-states that try to impose what they consider is the correct way of interpreting freedom of expression as they seek the global application of their laws either by following impulses that are in the right place – protecting and guaranteeing the fundamental rights of their own citizens – or by giving in to temptations to impose what is best for the rest of the world in an attempt to impose, not universalize, a common understanding of essential communication rights.

By giving in to this globalizing and privatizing impulse of local freedom of expression laws, the most powerful nation-states may be reproducing dynamics of colonialism by imposing their own interpretations of communication rights into other less powerful nations. This is just the opposite of universality. Universality requires consensus, not forced acceptance.

Finally, private standards set by private companies should have no business supplanting democratically and sovereignly adopted communication rights legislation and the fact that those private standards could, one day, be dictated by private platforms, or governments, that do not share the same commitment to universally agreed freedom of expression values should make us pause. Standardization should not be confused with a universalization of communication rights. It may, in fact, represent their subversion.

## References


Antweiler, C. (2016). *Our Common Denominator: Human Universals Revisited.* New York: Berghahn Books.

Arellano Toledo, W. and Cetina Presuel, R. (2015). El Derecho a la Información en México y EEUU: Desarrollo normativo y jurisprudencial. In: *Derecho de la Información: El ejercicio del derecho a la información y su jurisprudencia* (ed. J. Bel Mallen and L. Corredoira Y Alfonso), 143–165. Madrid: Centro de Estudios Políticos y Constitucionales.

Aswad, E. (2016). The Role of U.S. technology companies as enforcers of Europe's new internet hate speech ban. *Columbia Human Rights Law Review Online.* http://works.bepress.com/evelyn_aswad/6 (accessed September 19, 2020).

Badiou, A. (2003). *Saint Paul: The Foundation of Universalism* (trans. R. Brassier). Stanford: Stanford University Press.

Balkin, J.M. (2009). The future of free expression in a digital age. *Pepperdine Law Review* 36 (2): 444.

Balkin, J.M. (2018). Free speech is a triangle. *Columbia Law Review, Yale Law School Public Law Research Paper* 118 (7): 2011–2056.

Barata Mir, J. and Bassini, M. (2016). Freedom of expression in the internet: main trends of the case law of the European Court of Human Rights. In: *The Internet and Constitutional Law: The Protection of Fundamental Rights and Constitutional Adjudication in Europe* (ed. O. Pollicino and G. Romeo), 79–101. New York: Routledge.

Barendt, E.M. (2005). *Freedom of Speech*, 2 ed. New York: Oxford University Press.

Basedow, J. (2015). *The Law of Open Societies: Private Ordering and Public Regulation in the Conflict of Laws.* Amersfoort: Brill Nijhoff.

Beetham, D. (2009). Democracy: universality and diversity. *Ethics & Global Politics* 2 (4): 284–296.

Belli, L. and Sappa, C. (2017). The intermediary conundrum: cyber-regulators, cyber-police or both? *JIPITEC : Journal of Intellectual Property, Information Technology and E-Commerce Law* (8): 183.

Bogen, D. (1976). The Supreme Court's interpretation of the guarantee of freedom of speech. *Maryland Law Review* 35 (4): 555–616.

Bogen, D. (1979). Balancing freedom of speech. How US Supreme Court decisions can be reconciled with the First Amendment in cases to which balancing applies. *Maryland Law Review* 38 (3): 387–479.

Bosmajian, H.A. (1976). *Obscenity and Freedom of Expression.* New York: Franklin.

Buckley, S., Duer, K., Mendel, T., and Siochru, S.O. (2008). *Broadcasting, Voice, and Accountability: A Public Interest Approach to Policy, Law and Regulation.* Washington: World Bank.

Caldwell, L.G. (1935). Freedom of speech and radio broadcasting. *The Annals of the American Academy of Political and Social Science* 177 (1): 179–207.

Calhoun, C.J. (1992). *Habermas and the Public Sphere.* Cambridge, MA: MIT Press.

Caplan, R. and Gillespie, T. (2020). Tiered governance and demonetization: the shifting terms of labor and compensation in the platform economy. *Social Media + Society* 6 (2): 205630512093663.

Cavaliere, P. (2019). *Glawischnig-Piesczek* v *Facebook* on private enforcement of speech regulation and international jurisdiction. *European Data Protection Law Review* 5 (4): 573–578.

Coche, E. (2018). Privatized enforcement and the right to freedom of expression in a world confronted with terrorism propaganda online. *Internet Policy Review* 7 (4): 1–17.

Cohen, J.E. (2019). *Truth and Power: The Legal Constructions of Informational Capitalism.* New York: Oxford University Press.

Corredoira, L. (2007). Lectura de la Declaración Universal de Derechos Humanos de 1948 en el paradigma de la nueva sociedad de la información. Estudio específico del artículo 19. In: *Libertad en internet: la red y las libertades de expresión e información* (ed. L. Contino Hueso), 57–74. Valencia: Tirant lo Blanch.

Daskal, J. (2019). Internet censorship could happen more than one way. *The Atlantic* (25 September).

Daskal, J. and Klonick, K. (2019). When a politician is called a 'lousy traitor,' should Facebook censor it? *The New York Times* (June 27).

Donahoe, E. (2020). The Rights and Responsibilities of Internet Platforms. https://www.the-american-interest.com/2020/07/10/the-rights-and-responsibilities-of-internet-platforms (accessed July 13, 2020).

Douek, E. (2020). The rise of content cartels. *Knight First Amendment Institute at Columbia* (February 11).

EDRi (2016). Europol: non-transparent cooperation with IT companies. https://edri.org/europol-non-transparent-cooperation-with-it-companies (accessed July 12, 2020).

Emerson, T.I. (1970). *The System of Freedom of Expression*. New York: Random House.

European Commission (2016). Communication from the Commission to the European Parliament. The European Council and the Council delivering on the European agenda on security to fight against terrorism and pave the way towards an effective and genuine security union. https://ec.europa.eu/home-affairs/sites/homeaffairs/files/what-we-do/policies/european-agenda-security/legislative-documents/docs/20160420/communication_eas_progress_since_april_2015_en.pdf (accessed July 1, 2020).

Facebook (2020). *Community Standards*. https://www.facebook.com/communitystandards (accessed July 1, 2020).

Fiss, O.M. (1996). *The Irony of Free Speech*. Cambridge: Harvard University Press.

Flauss, J.-F. (2009). The European Court of Human Rights and the freedom of expression. *Indiana Law Journal* 84 (3): 809–849.

Franks, M.A. (2019). *The Cult of the Constitution*. Stanford: Stanford University Press.

Franks, M.A. (2020). How the Internet unmakes the law. *Ohio State Technology Law Journal* 16 (1): 10–24.

Freedman, D. (2008). *The Politics of Media Policy*. Cambridge: Polity.

General Assembly of the United Nations (1952). *Universal Declaration of Human Rights*. New York: United Nations Department of Public Information.

Ghosh, D. (2020). *Terms of Disservice: How Silicon Valley Is Destructive by Design*. Washington: Brookings Institution Press.

Gillespie, T. (2018). *Custodians of the Internet: Platforms, Content Moderation, and the Hidden Decisions that Shape Social Media*. New Haven: Yale University Press.

Habermas, J. (1991). *The Structural Transformation of the Public Sphere. An Inquiry into a Category of Bourgeois Society*. Cambridge: MIT Press.

Habermas, J. (1996). *Between Facts and Norms: Contributions to a Discourse Theory of Law and Democracy. Studies in Contemporary German Social Thought*. Cambridge: MIT Press.

Hopkins, C. (2019). Territorial scope in recent CJEU cases: *Google v CNIL/Glawischnig-Piesczek v Facebook*. https://inforrm.org/2019/11/09/territorial-scope-in-recent-cjeu-cases-google-v-cnil-glawischnig-piesczek-v-facebook-cathryn-hopkins (accessed July 8, 2020).

Howie, E. (2018). Protecting the human right to freedom of expression in international law. *Journal of Speech-Language Pathology* 20 (1): 12–15.

International Justice Resource Center (2020). Regional Systems. https://ijrcenter.org/regional, (accessed July 13, 2020).

Isaac, M. and Kang, C. (2020). Facebook keeps policy protecting political ads. *The New York Times* (January 10).

Keller, P. (2011). *European and International Media Law: Liberal Democracy, Trade, and the New Media*. Oxford: Oxford University Press.

Kessler, B.S. (1985). Politics among the airwaves: an analysis of Soviet and Western perspectives on international broadcasting and the right to exchange ideas and information regardless of frontiers. *Houston Journal of International Law* 7 (2): 237–274.

Klonick, K. (2018). The new governors: the people, rules, and processes governing online speech. *Harvard Law Review* 131 (6): 598–670.

Krislov, S. (1964). Mr. Justice Black reopens the free speech debate. *UCLA Law Review* 11 (2): 189.

Kuczerawy, A. (2018). The proposed regulation on preventing the dissemination of terrorist content online: safeguards and risks for freedom of expression. For Center for Democracy and Technology. https://ssrn.com/abstract=3296864 (accessed September 19, 2020).

Lewis, A. (2008). *Freedom for the Thought That We Hate.* New York: Basic Books.

Lipschultz, J.H. (2008). *Broadcast and Internet Indecency: Defining Free Speech.* New York: Routledge.

Lisbon (2009). The Treaty of Lisbon.

Little, L.E. (2012). Internet defamation, freedom of expression, and the lessons of private international law for the United States. *European Yearbook of Private International Law* 14: 181–204.

Morawska-Zakroczymska, Z. and Gęsicka, D. (2019). Case note to the Judgment of the Court of Justice of 3 October 2019 in case Eva Glawischnig-piesczek v. Facebook Ireland, C-18/18. *Comparative Law Review* 25 (345): 345–546.

Nunziato, D. (2018). The fourth year of forgetting: the troubling expansion of the right to be forgotten. *Journal of International Law* 39 (1): 101–151.

O'Brien, D.M. (2010). *Congress Shall Make No Law: The First Amendment, Unprotected Expression and the Supreme Court.* Lanham: Rowman & Littlefield.

Office of the United Nations High Commissioner for Human Rights (2006). *The Core International Human Rights Treaties.* New York and Geneva: United Nations.

Paust, J.J. (1982). Transnational freedom of speech: legal aspects of the Helsinki Final Act. *Law & Contemporary Problems* 45 (53): 53–54.

Peters, J. (2017). The "sovereigns of cyberspace" and state action: the First Amendment's application (or lack thereof) of third-party platforms. *Berkeley Technology Law Journal* 32: 989.

Price, M. (2003). Public diplomacy and the transformation of international broadcasting. *Cardozo Arts & Entertainment Law Journal* 21 (1): 51–86.

Riis, T. and Schwemer, S.F. (2019). Leaving the European safe harbor, sailing towards algorithmic content regulation. *Journal of Internet Law* 22 (7): 1–21. University of Copenhagen Faculty of Law Research Paper No. 2019-64. https://ssrn.com/abstract=3300159 or http://dx.doi.org/10.2139/ssrn.3300159 pp. 11–12. (accessed October 9, 2020).

Roberts, S.T. (2018). Digital detritus: 'error' and the logic of opacity in social media content moderation. *First Monday* 23 (3).

Roberts, S.T. (2019). *Behind the Screen: Content Moderation in the Shadows of Social Media.* New Haven: Yale University Press.

Rosati, E. (2019). Material, personal and geographic scope of online intermediaries' removal obligations beyond Glawischnig-Piesczek (C-18/18) and defamation. *European Intellectual Property Review* 41 (11): 672–682.

Rosen, J. (2012). The deciders: the future of privacy and free speech in the age of Facebook and Google. *Fordham Law Review* 80 (4): 1525–1538.

Rosenthal, L. (2011). First Amendment investigations and the inescapable pragmatism of the common law of free speech. *Indiana Law Journal* 86 (1): 1–76.

Samonte, M. (2019). Google V. CNIL Case C-507/17: The territorial scope of the right to be forgotten under EU law. https://europeanlawblog.eu/2019/10/29/google-v-cnil-case-c-507-17-the-territorial-scope-of-the-right-to-be-forgotten-under-eu-law (accessed July 1, 2020).

Sánchez Férriz, R. and Corredoira Y Alfonso, L. (2017). La compleja configuración de un derecho-libertad poliédrico, el Derecho a la informaicón. *Revista de derecho político* 1 (99): 11–48.

Schauer, F. (1982). *Free Speech: A Philosophical Enquiry.* Cambridge: Cambridge University Press.

Smith, R. (2019). Monitoring Online Content: The Impact of Eva Glawischnig-Piesczek V Facebook Ireland Limited. https://www.reedsmith.com/en/perspectives/2019/11/monitoring-online-content-the-impact-of-eva-glawischnig-piesczek-v-facebook. (accessed July 1, 2020).

Stalla-Bourdillon, S. (2010). Chilling ISPs... when private regulators act without adequate public framework. *Computer Law and Security Review* 26: 290–297.

Staveley-O'Carroll, S. (2009). Libel tourism laws: spoiling the holiday and saving the First Amendment? *NYU Journal of Law & Liberty* 4 (3): 252–292.

Suzor, N.P. (2019). *Lawless: The Secret Rules That Govern Our Digital Lives.* New York: Cambridge University Press.

Ullrich, C. (2018). A risk-based approach towards infringement prevention on the Internet: adopting the anti-money laundering framework to online platforms. *International Journal of Law and Information Technology* 26 (3): 226–251.

Vaidhyanathan, S. (2018). *Antisocial Media: How Facebook Disconnects Us and Undermines Democracy.* New York: Oxford University Press.

Versteeg, M. (2017). What Europe can teach america about free speech. *The Atlantic* (August 19).

Voorhoof, D. (2015). *Freedom of Expression and Information and the Case Law of the European Court of Human Rights and the Court of Justice of the EU. Overview and Highlights 2014*. New York: Columbia University.
Waddell, K. (2016). Why Google quit China – And why it's heading back. *The Atlantic* (January 19).
Westphal, D. (2002). Media pluralism and European regulation. *European Business Law Review* 13 (5): 459–487.
White, C. (2019). Defamation drama: Facebook expresses concern over 'freedom of expression' following AG opinion in defamation case. *Intellectual Property Magazine*.
Woods, A. (2018). Litigating data sovereignty. *The Yale Law Journal* 128 (2): 328–406.
Yemini, M. (2019). The new irony of free speech. *Columbia Science and Technology Law Review* 20 (119): 119–194.
Youm, K.H. (2015). Freedom of expression. *The International Encyclopedia of Digital Communication and Society*. https://doi.org/10.1002/9781118767771.wbiedcs135 (accessed October 1, 2020)
Zuboff, S. (2019). *The Age of Surveillance Capitalism*. New York: Public Affairs.

## Legislation Cited

Basic Law for the Federal Republic of Germany (1949).
Directive 2000/31/EC of the European Parliament and of the Council of 8 June 2000 on certain legal aspects of information society services, in particular electronic commerce, in the Internal Market ("Directive on electronic commerce").
European Commission (2018). *Proposal for a Regulation of the European Parliament and of the Council on Preventing the Dissemination of Terrorist Content Online*. Brussels: European Commission.
Loi du 29 juillet 1881 sur la liberté de la presse, France (1881).
Regulation (EU) 2016/679 of the European Parliament and of the Council of 27 April 2016 on the protection of natural persons with regard to the processing of personal data and on the free movement of such data and repealing Directive 95/46/EC (General Data Protection Regulation).
Regulation (EU) 2016/794 of the European Parliament and of the Council of 11 May 2016 on the European Union Agency for Law Enforcement Cooperation (Europol) and replacing and repealing Council Decisions 2009/371/JHA, 2009/934/JHA, 2009/935/JHA, 2009/936/JHA and 2009/968/JHA.
Section 230 of the Communications Decency Act (CDA) of 1996, Title V of the Telecommunications Act of 1996, 47 U.S.C. § 230.

# 6

# United States and International Communication Rights Frameworks and the Pursuit of Global Consensus

Erik Ugland

## Introduction

The United States has always been a fickle contributor to international human rights initiatives, at times providing crucial political leadership but, at other times, steering things toward its own ends or withdrawing altogether (Ignatieff 2005). Throughout these cycles, however, the US approach to communication rights has served as a stable point of reference for treaty bodies and for lawmakers and judges in other countries. That is less true today, as the US model, which is increasingly absolutist and neoliberal, looks in some ways like an outlier rather than an archetype. Nevertheless, as this chapter seeks to illustrate, there is still broad agreement across legal domains about the essential attributes of the human right to free expression, and a compelling need to forge stronger international consensus on these issues to meet the challenges of this moment.

This is clearly a period of unusual ideological tumult. Dozens of once democratic or quasi-democratic countries are now bending toward autocracy and a new cohort of populist leaders has emerged who generally eschew international cooperation and reject the primacy of human rights. At the center of these shifts, as both cause and consequence, is the diminution of communication rights,[1] which are the targets of a "global assault," according to David Kaye, the former UN Special Rapporteur on Freedom of Expression (Silva 2016). Governments in every region are now regularly and brazenly subverting free expression through both traditional methods like censorship and criminal defamation laws, and through more contemporary forms of coercion like online surveillance and filtering. And many are producing equally potent effects by their *in*action – refusing to prosecute violence against journalists and ignoring laws on government transparency, among other things.

[1]The phrase "communication rights" should be understood as encompassing freedom of speech and press (or collectively freedom of expression) and will sometimes be used synonymously with those terms. But, it actually connotes something broader – not merely freedom from government interference with expression but also access to government information and places, privileges to protect journalistic sources, available channels of communication, and a generally pluralistic media system.

*The Handbook of Communication Rights, Law, and Ethics: Seeking Universality, Equality, Freedom and Dignity*, First Edition. Edited by Loreto Corredoira, Ignacio Bel Mallén, and Rodrigo Cetina Presuel.

Many of the countries whose officials are most hostile to the free flow of information are signatories to the Universal Declaration of Human Rights (UDHR) and are parties to the International Covenant on Civil and Political Rights (ICCPR), which is enforced by the United Nations Human Rights Committee (HRC). Many are also parties to enforced regional treaties like the European Convention on Human Rights (ECHR) and the American Convention on Human Rights (ACHR). These, and other charters, assert the presumptive inviolability of freedom of expression, and while occasional transgressions are to be expected, the recent shifts are more seismic: global freedom of expression is at a 10-year low, according to the measures used by the NGO Article 19 (2019), and the Economist's Democracy Index is at its lowest cumulative level since it was developed in 2006 (Economist Intelligence Unit 2019).

More consequential is the growing resistance to the philosophical or theoretical assumptions of international human rights law, its enforcement architectures, and to the free expression principles that animate the jurisprudence of the ICCPR and regional rights regimes. All of these trends highlight abiding questions about the universality of communication rights and the viability of multilateral agreements. This chapter broadly addresses those issues but focuses on two narrower questions:

1. Can US law serve as a viable referent for identifying international media law standards, or is it too far out of step with the approaches in other countries and regions?
2. What can US law draw from ICCPR and ECHR jurisprudence, and vice versa, to find more common ground and meet the unique challenges of this moment?

This chapter is not about the political credibility of the United States on these issues but rather the relevance and appeal of its law. US law, particularly some of the landmark decisions of the US Supreme Court has, at times, served as a model for courts in other jurisdictions. This chapter explores the extent to which that remains desirable, and whether there are enough points of confluence between US law, European law (ECHR, Article 10), and international human rights law (ICCPR, Article 19) to discern the outer contours of an *international* body of media law.[2]

## Universal Rights in a Fracturing World

It would have been difficult to imagine in the waning days of the Cold War, when liberal-democratic ideas were flourishing and western political models were on a seemingly inexorable ascent, that just three decades later, the world would be in such a fractured state. But it is impossible now to deny the rise of authoritarianism and the withering of free expression around the world. Democratic norms are being cast aside, and even where those structures remain intact, they are often overwhelmed by nativist and isolationist fervor, with Great Britain/Brexit providing only the most prominent example. The "third wave" of democratization (Huntington 2011) that began in the early 1970s has stalled and we are now in a "democratic recession" (Diamond 2015), raising the ominous possibility that the broader democratic order that has evolved, however imperfectly, since World War II could fully unravel.

Part of what supported the expansion of democratic systems was the ideological coalescence around the core principles articulated in the Universal Declaration – human dignity, equality,

[2]The choice to focus on ECHR and ICCPR principles was partly a practical one, given the breadth of the subject. The ICCPR was also chosen because it is the most prominent treaty addressing free expression, and the ECHR was chosen because the European Court of Human Rights (ECtHR) has developed a rich body of precedent (via more than 1000 rulings).

and self-determination – and the assumption that the signatories (and parties to the ICCPR) would pursue democratic forms of government. Both the UDHR and ICCPR emphasize "democratic society" and "the will of the people," and Article 25 of both documents specifically guarantees universal suffrage and the right to participate in public affairs. Similar rights are guaranteed by the ECHR, which adds that limitations on freedom of expression cannot be justified unless they are, among other things, "necessary in a democratic society" (ECHR, Art. 10).

Democracy and communication rights are inextricably linked, both conceptually and in the texts and doctrine of international human rights law. Democracy also serves as an anchoring principle that ties together the diverse parties to the ICCPR. Democracy is not the only end served by robust protection of communication rights, of course. Freedom of expression is vital to individual dignity and identity, to the constituting of the self, to innovation and art, and to other aspects of human flourishing (Barendt 1985). But democracy provides a less subjective and culturally conditioned foundation upon which to start to build a system of international standards, and it is one that all parties to these agreements have vowed to embrace.

Pure universality is not possible and need not be the goal. The broad *concepts* articulated in Article 19 (UDHR, ICCPR), Article 10 (ECHR), and the First Amendment to the US Constitution, Dworkin might say, will inevitably inspire different *conceptions* in the minds of particular individuals, courts, or nations (Dworkin 1977, pp. 134–136). Some allowance for that variation is useful, provided there is a general allegiance to the core aims of those provisions – the "major premises," as Bork called them, which are revealed through the text, structure, and purposes of constitutional documents (Bork 1990, pp. 162–163).

The difficulty at the moment is that violations of communication rights are so rampant (Simon 2015) it is hard to discern what the major premises are, or if knowing them makes a difference. To a great extent, these violations reflect a simple lack of political integrity and mostly present problems of enforcement. But there is a growing tendency among some leaders to argue that their denials of communication rights are justified by their own, more culturally situated, conceptions of free expression. The US approach is akin to this but assumes that US law is unimpeachable on free expression[3] and so enforcement of external standards is an inherent compromise.

No country's law on these subjects is pristine, so there is much to be gained by consolidating ideas, and indeed much has been gained through the work of the HRC, the ECtHR, and other bodies. The most immediate risk is that that work will be undone as parties begin to withdraw, in fact or in practice. There are also other reasons to redouble efforts. Communication is now transnational, the major media companies and platforms are global, and even some journalistic work (e.g., the Panama Papers project) is done collaboratively across jurisdictions. There are also a growing number of cases in which countries seek to extend the reach of their laws, like the European Union's mandate that Google enforce EU privacy laws outside the EU.

## United States Media Law and Policy

The law and policy of the United States, particularly the judicial opinions interpreting and applying the speech and press clauses of the First Amendment, have been influential in shaping conceptions of free expression around the world, and yet US law is still idiosyncratic in the

[3]The United States ratified the ICCPR in 1992 but made a reservation on Article 20, which prohibits propaganda and certain types of hate speech, because it conflicts with the First Amendment, and disavowed enforcement of any provision that conflicts with established First Amendment principles.

extent to which enables extreme speech, indulges corporate communicators, and confines the First Amendment to situations involving government interference. Over the past 100 years, US courts have constructed a body of precedent that empowers individual speakers and forces citizens – particularly government officials and public figures – to endure a speech environment that is "uninhibited, robust and wide-open"[4] where the expected response to harsh attacks or dangerous ideas is "more speech, not enforced silence."[5] It is a libertarian system that exalts the speech of individuals while severely restricting the power of government to even incidentally impair expressive acts. At the same time, First Amendment law is largely agnostic about the quality of speech that occurs or about the health of the media ecosystem. Instead, for 100 years, starting with Justice Oliver Wendell Holmes's dissent in Abrams,[6] courts have put their faith in the invisible hand of the marketplace to help citizens separate good speech from bad.

The past century of First Amendment law has largely been one of incremental expansion. US courts are generally hostile to any government limitations on expression and the prevailing sentiment has been that every expansion of the First Amendment is self-evidently a mark of progress. That sanguine view is starting to change. Some argue that courts have fetishized the First Amendment, particularly in their more recent rulings, applying it with a kind of fanatical absolutism, stretching some First Amendment principles beyond their logical end points (Stein 2006; Shanor and Post 2015; Balkin 2016).

## The Negative-Rights Construction

Judges interpreting the First Amendment are constrained by the text, which includes only 14 words on free expression: "Congress shall make no law ... abridging the freedom of speech, or of the press." The first word, "Congress," was, according to the US Supreme Court, chosen very deliberately by the Framers to confine the amendment to situations involving federal government overreach.[7] US Courts have consistently held that the First Amendment is inapplicable to speech restrictions by private parties, and that it only establishes a shield against government encroachments (the State Action Doctrine); it does not impose affirmative obligations on the government to provide information, ensure access, or facilitate expression. Emerson pointed out 40 years ago that there is an important role for government to play in filling the gaps left by the First Amendment (Emerson 1981). But the United States remains a laissez-faire capitalist society in which private-sector solutions are favored over government ones and where public policy is heavily influenced by industry. These things, combined with the negative-rights phrasing of the First Amendment, has helped create a general ethos of non intervention in which even constitutionally permissible solutions for enhancing free-speech opportunities and improving the quality of public discourse are treated with skepticism.

Government support for public media in the United States has largely evaporated. Media ownership limits have been scaled back. Broadband access is lagging. The net neutrality rules – briefly in place at the end of the Obama Administration (Protecting and Promoting the Open Internet 2017) – have been withdrawn, and so on. Even in the context of broadcast radio and television, where most regulations pose no First Amendment problem because of

[4] *NY Times v. Sullivan* (1964), p. 270.
[5] *Whitney v. California* (1927), p. 377.
[6] *Abrams v. US* (1919).
[7] The Court has held that the principles of the First Amendment apply equally against state governments as a result of the Fourteenth Amendment requirement that states may not "deprive any person of life, *liberty* or property" (emphasis added).

the unique structural features of that medium,[8] Congress and the Federal Communications Commission have done little to ensure that broadcasters serve the public interest and have repealed or relaxed a host of regulations.

## The Marketplace Metaphor

Another important aspect of US media law is its reliance on the marketplace rationale, which suggests that truth is more likely to emerge in a system in which all citizens are free to share their ideas than in a system in which the government acts as arbiter. This metaphor is also used to justify the freeing of media companies from regulation because consumer choices, it is supposed, will drive media to adapt without the need for government action. The marketplace rationale has been critiqued for decades by scores of scholars (e.g., Barron 1973; Ingber 1984; Baker 1989; Stein 2006), who point out that it presupposes an egalitarian public sphere, which is nothing like the US media environment, which is dominated by a handful of media goliaths and internet platforms. These theorists also question the marketplace assumption, originating from Milton's *Areopagitica* (Milton 1644), that truth will ultimately prevail over falsehood: "Who ever knew truth put to the worse [against falsehood] in a free and open encounter?" The presumed answer to this question seems naive in this era of fake news, video manipulation, and online conspiracies. But "however specious the marketplace approach might be to some," Judge Learned Hand once wrote, "we have staked upon it our all."[9]

## Speakers and Speech

A third key feature of US law and policy is the way in which speakers and speech are conceptualized. With regard to "speech," the Supreme Court's earliest cases were straightforward. They involved public protesters, pamphleteers, or small publishers, and then eventually more mainstream media organizations. Since the arrival of the Digital Age, courts embraced new theories – that computer code is speech,[10] that Google's search algorithms are speech,[11] and that political contributions and independent expenditures in support of political candidates are speech.[12] These newer cases have raised some concern that the courts have boxed themselves in and, without articulating some limiting principles, will be forced to accept the idea that virtually every utterance and every movement of data is presumptively protected speech.

The courts take a similar approach to defining who is a speaker, often extending First Amendment protections to corporations. This is one of the most consequential developments in US law. The public sphere in the United States is dominated by Big Media and Big Tech and there is widespread sympathy in government, especially among Republicans, for deregulation and neoliberal economic policy. Even when regulations are passed, companies can now occasionally deflect them by invoking the First Amendment. The notion that platforms are speakers was recently reaffirmed by the influential Ninth Circuit Court of Appeals, which ruled against a conservative media company that claimed Google violated its First Amendment rights by making its videos harder to find on YouTube. In situations like these, the court held, platform owners are protected by the First Amendment, users are not.[13]

[8] *FCC v. Pacifica* (1978); *Red Lion Broadcasting v. FCC* (1969).
[9] *Associated Press v. US* (1945), p. 28.
[10] *Bernstein v. US Dept. of Justice* (1999).
[11] *Martin v. Google* (2014).
[12] *Citizens United v. FEC* (2010).
[13] *Prager v. Google* (2020).

## Speech and Press Doctrine

While US policymakers are often criticized for doing too little to nurture and enliven the public sphere, US judges are often accused of providing too much protection for free expression. Though the Supreme Court has held that certain categories of speech are either so dangerous or worthless that they receive *no* First Amendment protection – fighting words, obscenity, incitement, threats – the courts' First Amendment jurisprudence is especially solicitous of individual speakers.

The First Amendment protects profane speech (except in broadcasting). It protects insults. It protects public demonstrations of all kinds, including those led by radical groups. It protects public school students and public employees from being compelled to convey particular messages. It protects hate speech, except when it is meant to intimidate specific individuals. It protects the desecration of flags and religious symbols during political protests. And it protects virtually all nondefamatory criticism of public officials. Extremist speech, even that which advocates overthrow of the government, is protected unless coupled with action.

Defamatory speech is not protected in the United States but it is difficult for plaintiffs to win libel or slander suits. Truth is an absolute defense and criminal libel laws have largely been abolished. In addition, public officials and public figures can only win libel suits where they can show that a published statement about them is false and defamatory and was published with actual malice, that is, with knowledge that it was false or with reckless disregard for the truth.[14] This poses a very difficult burden for public plaintiffs, which some people feel has helped to poison public discourse.

Similar criticisms abound with regard to privacy. Though the word "privacy" does not appear in the US Constitution, the Supreme Court has recognized a constitutional right of privacy that protects citizens against some types of government interference, but this right is narrowly construed and rarely applied. Citizens' privacy is mostly protected through data and consumer protection laws and through some widely recognized civil tort claims, allowing plaintiffs to seek damages for, among other things, *intrusion* into their private spaces, and public disclosure of *private facts* about them.

These suits rarely succeed, in part because they often involve activities that occur in public spaces, which means the plaintiffs do not have the "reasonable expectation of privacy" required to sustain an intrusion claim, and they cannot succeed on a private facts claim because what occurs in public is considered, with rare exceptions, not private. As a result, citizens and journalists have substantial freedom to observe what occurs in public, and to photograph it, record it, and disseminate it. Law in this area is not uniform, however, and there is a lot of misunderstanding, as well as deliberate abuse, by law enforcement officials, and there are renewed legislative efforts to limit recording and access to places.

This raises a final area of US media law worth emphasizing, which is the right of citizens to gather news and information and their ability to claim special protections as journalists. US courts have generally read the speech and press clauses of the First Amendment as essentially conjoined and have rejected the notion that the press, as an institution, is entitled to unique First Amendment-based protections that are denied to the public generally. While it tolerates state and federal statutes that create special privileges, it has not held that these allowances are required by the First Amendment. Indeed, the Supreme Court in *Branzburg v. Hayes* (1972)[15] refused to recognize a First Amendment reporter's privilege in part because doing so, would force it to make arbitrary judgments about who qualifies for protection. Though lower federal courts have since recognized a First Amendment-based privilege in some contexts, they have

[14] *NY Times v. Sullivan* (1964), p. 280.

[15] *Branzburg v. Hayes* (1972).

begun to embrace a more functional concept of "journalist" that extends protections to anyone acting in a journalistic role, without regard to their experience, credentials, or institutional affiliations.

## Alignment of US and International Law (ECHR and ICCPR)

What is most striking about the law and policy of the United States, the decisions of the ECtHR, and the work of the HRC, is the extent to which they correspond. They all reflect Enlightenment ideas regarding the sovereignty and dignity of individuals and people's inherent desire to exercise reason, free of coercion, to discern the truth and make their own choices. They all embrace the same core rationales supporting free expression – democratic self-governance, the search for truth, and individual self-fulfillment (Barendt 1985, pp. 8–23) – and there is considerable doctrinal overlap and even a sharing of some common language ("malice," "chilling effect"). All three also emphasize free speech and press as societal first principles, because of the extent to which they activate and help preserve other rights. But none takes an absolutist view of free expression; all recognize, through judicial opinions (US) or the covenant/convention text (ECHR, Art 10 section [2]; ICCPR, Art 19 sections [a] and [b]) that other individual rights or state interests will sometimes supersede. To read through the HRC's General Comment No. 34 (2011), which is its comprehensive summary of Article 19 principles, referencing its previous decisions and concluding observations on country reports, is like reading a consensus statement because it so closely mirrors the prevailing approaches in the United States, Europe, and many other parts of the world.

There are some key differences to highlight, however, and areas in which the law in each of these domains could be strengthened, either by reference to the others or by addressing more emerging concerns.

### Hate Speech, Sedition, and Defamation

US courts, the HRC, and the ECtHR all recognize the difficult problem of inflammatory speech targeting race, ethnicity, religion, or other aspects of people's identity. And while all of them establish an expectation that people endure public expression even when it might "offend, shock or disturb,"[16] exceptions in the United States are exceedingly rare. Generally, only when speech directly threatens specific individuals, involves the face-to-face hurling of epithets,[17] or involves speech that is likely to incite "imminent lawless action,"[18] is it unprotected by the First Amendment. The exceptions are far more abundant under the ECtHR and ICCPR. Because this type of speech often involves peculiarly local sensitivities, a wider margin of appreciation is warranted,[19] but when the ECtHR vaguely asserts that there is "no doubt" states can suppress speech "directed against the Convention's underlying values,"[20] it gives states excessive latitude. And, while the HRC tries to limit suppression of hate speech to

[16] *Handyside v. UK* (1976) section 49.

[17] *Chaplinsky v. NH* (1942).

[18] *Brandenburg v. OH* (1969), p. 447.

[19] The ECtHR recognizes a margin of appreciation that gives member states latitude when aligning their laws with ECHR principles and ECtHR rulings (Benvenisti 1998–1999). The HRC rejects this doctrine (General Comment No. 34 section 36, 2011) but allows parties to justify departures if they can offer evidence of exigent circumstances.

[20] *Seurot v. France* (2004), p. 8.

contexts that amount to incitement (ICCPR, Art. 20 section [2]), that condition is not tied, as in the United States, to immediate lawlessness, so anything government officials perceive to be capable of stirring identity-based animosities is vulnerable to restriction.

The problem is not the suppression of noxious speech that tries to humiliate or disempower. It is that this kind of speech can sometimes be misconstrued or deliberately mischaracterized, and it can even be part of an individual's push back against some perceived domination. In Northern Ireland, a Catholic speaker's anti-Protestant tirade might have more to do with political schisms than religious ones. In Turkey, an Alevist's rant about Sunnis might, in fact, be about social class or political authority, and so on. But this kind of speech is now regularly punished by governments around the world who use social cohesion or ethnic harmony as smokescreens for the suppression of what is, in fact, political speech. Given the state of democracy around the world and the rise of these more insidious methods of suppression, the HRC and ECtHR should look for ways to create more breathing space for this kind of speech, even if they conclude the US model goes too far in the other direction.

The same is true with any restrictions targeting the denunciation of political leaders or members of royal families. The freedom of citizens to criticize and hold accountable those who wield power over them is the essence of democracy and what Kalven, Jr., (1964) called the "central meaning of the First Amendment." This principle is emphasized in all three of the legal domains addressed here. However, the HRC statement on this in General Comment No. 34 (2011, section 38) is tepid in that it merely expresses "concern" over the enforcement of laws that prohibit the disrespecting of authority figures, flags and symbols, heads of state, or the military. Such laws also present problems under Article 10, yet some member states still have *lèse majesté* laws (e.g., The Netherlands) and blasphemy laws (dozens of Council of Europe countries). These types of laws are regularly used to suppress political speech around the world, particularly in Asia, and even though they are rarely enforced in Europe, their existence is anathema to any truly democratic system of free expression.

Libel laws around the world are so varied that any kind of synthesis is impossible here but all countries, as well as the ECtHR and HRC, perhaps with continued leadership from the Special Rapporteur, could look for ways to further limit the abuse of those laws by continuing to push for the elimination of criminal libel, strengthening procedural safeguards that impose higher burdens of proof on, and quicker dismissals of, lawsuits that could potentially silence or punish speech about public issues, and also reconsidering the social merit of allowing *any* libel claims to be pressed by powerful public people who already have the money and access to rebut attacks on their reputations. These are the kinds of reforms – those focused on reclaiming more of the public sphere for robust critiques of public people and institutions – that should be priorities during this time of democratic recession.

## Newsgathering and Access

The US Supreme Court has repeatedly acknowledged the important role that journalists play and has aggressively defended journalistic *expression*, which includes things like a qualified right to publish information illegally obtained by others,[21] but it has not carved out unique newsgathering protections for the press. The Court has rejected a First Amendment-based reporter's privilege,[22] a right against searches of newsrooms by police, a right of journalists to access prisons, a right against judicial inquiries into journalists' editorial processes, and a right of journalists to break promises of confidentiality with their sources. It has repeatedly insisted

[21] *Bartnicki v. Vopper* (2001).

[22] Note that some lower federal courts have recognized such a right. The Supreme Court has not revisited the issue since its 1972 ruling in *Branzburg v. Hayes*, see note 15.

that journalists comply with all generally applicable laws, and, crucially, it has rejected the idea of a general First Amendment right of access to government information or proceedings. One exception to this is access to the courts. But, if the other branches of government chose to operate in complete secrecy, there would be no First Amendment recourse.

Whatever special protections journalists have in the United States are almost exclusively provided at the discretion of Congress and state legislatures. Congress and the states have taken some steps to protect journalists and ensure transparency, but they are imperfect and incomplete. Forty state legislatures have passed shield laws allowing journalists to protect their sources; 10 have not. Congress passed a law in 1980 restricting newsroom searches, yet it has not passed a federal shield law. And though Congress and all state legislatures have passed open records and open meetings laws, there are significant coverage gaps, inconsistencies across jurisdictions, a varied set of exemptions, endemic problems with excessive fees and delays, and enforcement mechanisms that – especially at the federal level – give each administration unusual autonomy to decide how rigorously to manage the laws. Overall, then, journalists' rights and privileges vary from one period and one jurisdiction to the next, which opens the door to both unwitting violations and deliberate abuses.

The HRC and the Special Rapporteur have both emphasized the positive obligation that parties have to make government records available and that people's right to this information is implicit in the "seek, receive, and impart information" text of Article 19 section 2. There is no similar textual hook in Article 10 of the ECHR, but the ECtHR came close to recognizing a right to government information in 2016 when it held that access must be provided where it is instrumental to someone's exercise of their free expression rights and denying access would abridge that right,[23] and it has asserted that members have a positive obligation to develop frameworks for public access to information. The United States and ECHR member states all have open government systems in place; the problem is enforcement. The HRC and Special Rapporteur have done excellent work in articulating best practices on access, but they could make these issues more of a focus in their concluding observations. It might also be time to consider a separate treaty on open government to help clarify expectations and develop a more focused system of mutual accountability.

One area of newsgathering where the United States is out of alignment with the ICCPR is reporter's privilege. The HRC writes in General Comment No. 34 section 45 that states should guarantee at least a qualified reporter's privilege. In addition, the HRC has endorsed the Johannesburg Principles on National Security, Freedom of Expression, and Access to Information, which say that even national security should not be used as a reason for blanket denials of information or as a reason to compel journalists to reveal their sources (Johannesburg Principles 1996). The ECtHR has been clear about the right of journalists to protect their sources, starting with its landmark decision in *Goodwin v. UK*, which held that source protection is "one of the basic conditions for press freedom."[24] The Council of Europe has added that member states have a positive obligation to pass laws protecting journalists and whistleblowers. In the United States, however, the liberty of reporters to protect source information or other work products depends on the constellation of state statutes, common law rules, agency guidelines, and First Amendment rulings that happens to apply in their jurisdiction.

One newsgathering issue that remains unsettled across jurisdictions and legal domains is the extent to which journalists and citizens have a right to gather news and information in public spaces and to photograph and record their observations. While citizens and journalists in the United States are generally allowed to do this, provided they do not violate people's reasonable expectations of privacy, or record people's private conversations, this is an underdeveloped

---

[23] *Magyar Helsinki Bizottság v. Hungary* (2016).

[24] *Goodwin v. UK* (1996) section 39.

area of First Amendment law that is being tested by a host of news statutes prohibiting the recording of police officers, banning photography of "critical facilities" like power plants and military bases, and restricting the monitoring of farms and hunting sites by journalists and animal-rights activists. Though Article 19 protects the right to "seek" information, the HRC has not addressed the extent to which this encompasses public recording. It is not surprising that governments around the world are responding to public concerns about privacy by imposing limits on the use of digital technology, but the same tools that are occasionally exploited by voyeurs and sensationalists are also used by people to protect themselves or to monitor police, government or other powerful figures, so legislatures and courts need to ensure that those interests are prioritized.

## Platforms, Corporate Speakers, and the Public Sphere

One of the clearest points of separation between the United States and Europe is the role of government in creating and preserving a robust public sphere. Here is where the distinction between "communication rights" and "free expression rights" is most apparent. The former term is more reflective of the European approach, which recognizes that the public sphere will always be undernourished if left to the clashing of commercial interests. It is not enough for the government to stay out of the way; it must take an active role in maintaining a vital communications ecosystem by keeping market forces in check and ensuring the availability of diverse content. According to the ECtHR, "there can be no democracy without pluralism"[25] and *government* is pluralism's "ultimate guarantor."[26] The HRC, too, asserts the need for governments to "promote plurality of the media" (General Comment No. 34 2011, section 40).

In the United States, the Supreme Court likewise emphasizes the need for the public to have access to "diverse and antagonistic sources of information,"[27] but it assumes this will occur organically through supply and demand. It has aggressively defended the autonomy of newspapers and other media companies and has rejected most government efforts to encroach on the private sector. Historically, there have been two major exceptions: public broadcasting and commercial broadcasting. But the federal government now provides only a small amount of funding for public media. Commercial broadcasters, meanwhile, used to be more closely regulated to ensure that they served the public interest. Over the past few decades, however, most broadcast regulations have been relaxed (media ownership rules, licensing requirements), eliminated (the Fairness Doctrine, right of reply), or are currently under scrutiny (children's TV requirements). Meanwhile, the US government continues to take an almost completely hands-off approach to private media, unlike in many European countries where it is more common to find content-based regulations like right-of-reply laws, stricter ownership limits, and state subsidies for private media enterprises (Schweizer et al. 2014).

Harmonizing national laws on broadcast media is not essential, but there are an increasing number of conflicts with Internet-based communication, which is inherently transnational and often facilitated by companies operating in multiple countries. France, Germany, and the European Union have all sought, in effect, to extend the reach of their domestic or regional law by requiring companies like Google and Facebook to comply with European laws outside Europe on copyright, children's privacy, data protection, and the right to be forgotten. Reconciling laws on these issues, and on emerging problems like fake news, will be nearly impossible unless there is a major shift in US First Amendment jurisprudence. If the courts continue to lean on traditional theories, which are largely indifferent to market dysfunctions

[25] *Centro Europa 7 sRL and Di Stefano v. Italy* (2012) section 128.
[26] *Informationsverein Lentia v. Austria* (1993) section 38.
[27] *Associated Press v. US* (1945), p. 20.

and to the toxicity of public discourse, legislators and policymakers will need to step in to fill the void. The First Amendment might prevent some direct media regulation but does not preclude government action altogether. The US Congress and state legislatures should embrace the ECtHR notion that they are the ultimate guarantors of pluralism and take more steps to do things like expand minority media ownership, subsidize local news, expand public media, authorize more media literacy programs, facilitate access to technology and broadband, aggressively enforce anti trust laws, and put teeth back into broadcasters' obligation to serve the public interest, among other possibilities. Without more aggressive policy action, the public sphere will continue to be poisoned and distorted, which must be acknowledged as an existential threat to democracy itself.

## Conclusion

Whether a universal system of communication rights is partly achievable depends on how narrowly one defines the ends. Because there will always be some variances between different countries' approaches, it is tempting to conclude that rights can only meaningfully be conceptualized and implemented within discrete political regimes and cultures. But, when one focuses the analysis on democratic countries, or those that aspire to be democratic – an expectation of the signatories and parties to the UDHR, ICCPR, ECHR, and other human rights declarations and treaties – one can quickly see the opportunity for synthesis, at least with regard to the major premises. And by developing an international body of *media and communication law*, at least in broad strokes, it is possible to anchor the work of domestic courts and legislatures and help resolve emerging conflicts, particularly those that cross borders. Articulating core principles also puts rogue political leaders and parties on notice that their denials of communication rights offend the norms embraced by the community of democratic nations, and enforcing those norms via treaty-based regimes has the further benefit of building solidarity and a sense of shared purpose among the member countries while simultaneously strengthening their political legitimacy.

It is clear that there is already a great deal of conceptual and doctrinal overlap on communication rights within the domains addressed in this chapter. When one reads the decisions of the ECtHR, the comments and concluding observations of the HRC, and the opinions of the US Supreme Court, it is clear that there is broad consensus about most of the core principles and foundational assumptions. What the world needs now, more than a perfect global alignment, is a recommitment to those core principles, which would, perhaps more effectively than anything else, help to halt the slide toward authoritarianism and hasten the end of the democratic recession.

## References

Article 19 (2019). *Global Expression Report 2018–19: Global Freedom of Expression at a 10-year Low* https://www.article19.org/resources/global-expression-report-2018-19-global-freedom-of-expression-at-a-ten-year-low (accessed June 13, 2020).

Baker, C.E. (1989). *Human Liberty and Freedom of Speech.* New York: Oxford University Press.

Balkin, J.M. (2016). Cultural democracy and the First Amendment. *Northwestern University Law Review* 110: 1053–1095.

Barendt, E. (1985). *Freedom of Speech.* New York: Oxford University Press.

Barron, J.A. (1973). *Freedom of the Press for Whom? the Right of Access to Mass Media.* Bloomington: Indiana University Press.

Benvenisti, E. (1998–1999). Margin of appreciation, consensus, and universal standards. *New York University Journal of International Law and Policy* 31: 843–854.

Bork, R.H. (1990). *The Tempting of America: The Political Seduction of the Law*. New York: Simon & Schuster. (1972
Diamond, L. (2015). Facing up to the democratic recession. *Journal of Democracy* 26 (1): 141–155.
Dworkin, R. (1977). *Taking Rights Seriously*. Cambridge, MA: Harvard University Press.
Economist Intelligence Unit (2019). *Democracy Index 2019*. http://www.eiu.com/topic/democracy-index (accessed June 13, 2020).
Emerson, T.I. (1981). The affirmative side of the First Amendment. *Georgia Law Review* 15 (4): 795–849.
Huntington, S.P. (2011). *The Clash of Civilizations and the Remaking of World Order*. New York: Simon & Schuster.
Ignatieff, M. (ed.) (2005). *American Exceptionalism and Human Rights*. Princeton, NJ: Princeton University. Press.
*Informationsverein Lentia and Others v. Austria* 13914/88, 15041/89, 15717/89, 15779/89, 17207/90 (1993).
Ingber, S. (1984). The marketplace of ideas: a legitimizing myth. *Duke Law Journal* : 1–91.
*Johannesburg Principles on National Security Freedom of Expression and Access to Information*. (1996). United Nations Document E/CN.4/1996/39.
Kalven, J.H. (1964). *The New York Times* case: a note on "The central meaning of the First Amendment." *Supreme Court. Review* 1964: 191–221.
Milton, J. (1644). *Areopagitica: A Speech for the Liberty of Unlicensed Printing* (ed. H.B. Cotterill 1961). New York: Macmillan & Co.
Protecting and Promoting the Open Internet. (2017). 47 C.F.R. section 8.
Schweizer, C., Puppis, M., Künzler, M. et al. (2014). *Media Policy Brief 11: Public Funding of Private Media*. London: London School of Economics.
Shanor, A. and Post, R. (2015). Adam Smith's First Amendment. *Harvard Law Review Forum* 128: 165–182.
Silva, A.C. (2016). Protecting free speech in the digital age: Q&A with UN Special Rapporteur for Freedom of Expression. *FordFoundation*. Online. https://www.fordfoundation.org/ideas/equals-change-blog/posts/protecting-free-speech-in-the-digital-age-qa-with-un-special-rapporteur-for-freedom-of-expression (accessed June 13, 2020).
Simon, J. (2015). *The New Censorship: Inside the Global Battle for Media Freedom*. New York: Columbia University Press.
Stein, L. (2006). *Speech Rights in America: The First Amendment, Democracy and the Media*. Champaign: University of Illinois Press.
United Nations Human Rights Committee. (2011). *General Comment 34* CCPR/C/CG/34.

# PART II

# Communication Rights: A Study of Subjects and Messages

# 7

# Communication Rights and Their Messages

## News, Opinions, Ideas, and Advertising

Ignacio Bel Mallén

Communication law, as an academic discipline, comprises four aspects of the "information ecosystem": subjects (journalists, the public, and owners of media businesses), objects (news, opinion, propaganda, and advertising), media (press, radio, television, and online media), and, finally, media organizations (businesses and agencies).

This chapter begins with a study of subjects and messages; other authors will also consider these areas in their respective chapters, especially in Part II of this book.

Yet, if the transmission of ideas, thoughts, opinions, information, and facts is an activity that has been present in society, even before social sciences and the law, as we know it today, emerged (Sánchez Ferriz 2003), the year 1948 saw the birth of communication rights via the Universal Declaration of Human Rights (UDHR). These rights were then strengthened through the International Covenant on Civil and Political Rights. Communication rights began as human rights, and in the 1970s, they formed the basis of communication law, as Sánchez Ferriz (1974) pointed out in the first book published in Spain on this topic, and as Desantes Guanter (1974) in Spain, Derieux and Soria (1983, pp. 57–76) in France, and Aguirre Nieto (2015, pp. 9–30) in Peru have also noted.

To study these communication rights and messages, we should analyze – as one should in the case of any legal norm – three aspects that make up their essence: the **subject(s)** at which the norm is directed, the **object** that justifies the existence of the norm, and, finally, the **contents** that lay out the effective development and exercise of the right. In this chapter, I will examine the first two of these. I will analyze the theory of the universal subject of communication rights and how it affects the active exercise of these rights. In addition, I will examine the object of the rights, which refers to the content of the information and messages.

### The Subject of the Communication Rights: Universal, Professional, and Organized

Within his analysis of the contents of the UDHR, and in direct relation to the subject as holder of communication rights, Desantes Guanter (1974, pp. 31–46) established a classification of these rights as part of the communication process. According to this classification, the communication law system can differentiate between:

*The Handbook of Communication Rights, Law, and Ethics: Seeking Universality, Equality, Freedom and Dignity*, First Edition. Edited by Loreto Corredoira, Ignacio Bel Mallén, and Rodrigo Cetina Presuel.

- the qualified or professional subject,
- the organized subject, and
- the universal subject.

The first type of subjects is those who seek, prepare, or disseminate/impart information and opinions as a professional activity. Article 19 of the UDHR includes these journalistic activities within communication rights. To carry out their work, a journalist, whether employed or a freelancer, acquires a professional qualification – hence the term "qualified." That qualification allows the journalist to perform the entire communication process.

**Journalists**, **editors**, and **news anchors** on radio and television all share this profile of "qualified subjects." The training required for such work remains hotly debated, as does the level of higher education (undergraduate or postgraduate) at which that training should be provided. Notwithstanding this controversy, no one in the twenty-first century questions that professionals require training and that such training should be provided at the university level.

I cannot deny the fact that there is a clear contrast between media professionals and academics who study the trade. Some of the first group (mostly professionals and practicing journalists) consider theirs to be simply a job, for which the necessary training is defined by the daily duties of their work. Others, some in the first group and nearly all in the second group, hold the position that those who provide information require a high level of academic training that is commensurate with the power and importance of information and communication technologies (ICTs).

There is no single answer to this dilemma. What is certain is that because messages have taken on such human, social, and legal importance, it is logical to think that those working with messages should have prior training in the ethical, legal, and social aspects of information gathering and dissemination. If this is evident for those working in general areas of the news, it is even more so for those working in specialized domains such as news that covers economics, politics, religion, and health. They need to have at least minimum training so that they are able to face the challenges of their duties.

The second category of subjects who "have a right to communicate" primarily comprises organizations that have a legal personality. These are normally **corporations**, but they can also include **other organizations** that create and develop technical media that permit news, ideas, and opinions prepared by the qualified subject to be disseminated to the general public on a mass scale. These entities are called "organized subjects" because they use financial resources to establish a structured communication process that allows dissemination of information. In other words, information media must be created and developed, whether they take the form of radio, television, press agencies, or print or digital media.

In this regard, we should take note of the profound changes that ICTs are causing in the development of media corporations. Until a few years ago, such corporations were required to have substantial economic resources, costly business models, large infrastructures, and high numbers of employees.

Today, it is easy to find content online that, in terms of quality and quantity, is highly informative. This content is produced by appropriately taking advantage of ICTs' current potential, which allows publications to adopt simplified structures and operate with a low number of workers whose daily duties are performed online. This configuration has facilitated a robust development of purely online media publications worldwide. Alongside these, there are also those websites created by the traditional media that are currently helping to boost traditional media corporations' financial results. It is true that, as an endeavor in its infancy, this development of online media publications still needs a strong dose of professionalization and, above all, adaptation to communication's ethical standards (Bel Mallén 2016).

Viable and sustainable "native" digital media exist and have been promoted – and will be promoted even more in the future – by the integration of ICTs into media, which has helped simplify the information process as much as possible in terms of people and costs.

Finally, it is necessary to mention **the general public**, the *universal subject of* communication rights. This is a term for society, which receives the information/messages prepared by the qualified subject and is disseminated/imparted by the organized subject. The universal subject is key for active participation in the media, as we shall see.

## The Three Subjects Linked in a Communication Relationship

To understand the place of the subject in the field of communication, one must understand the activities contained within the exercise of communication rights and the attitudes of the subject toward those activities. Comparison of the attitudes held by the different kinds of subject will clarify the true position occupied by the universal subject in the communication process. Let us, then, examine the relationship between subject and information.

The relationship of the universal subject, or general public, with the media can be passive, in which case, the subject simply receives information. The relationship can also be active and operational, in which case, the subject engages in searching and dissemination through collaboration with professionals and organized media.

What we have described as the public's passive attitude has changed substantially since the latter half of the twentieth century. This has been caused by the appearance and consequent development of ICTs, which have brought about a substantial change in the public's relationship with information, in such a way that nowadays people can adopt highly active positions in the information field through the use of social networks. Part of this is so-called – and hotly debated – citizen journalism, as well as, in general, the use of technologies for informational purposes. "This new approach to journalism has as many followers as it has detractors. At the epicenter of debate have been reflections on whether it is another form of journalism or, on the contrary, a mere consequence of technological innovations in the communication world and an activity that does not qualify for the status of communication profession. Fundamentally, this movement is based on the possibility that any citizen can become a reporter due to the fact that, by using a mobile device as an instrument and social networks as a conduit, he or she can send informative content to the media or to other citizens or place it on the Net to bring it to the attention of society as a whole" (Bel Mallén 2020, pp. 152–154).

Until recent times, subjects' relationship with information can be summarized as shown in Table 7.1, which indicates the attitudes toward information that are exhibited by each type of subject.

Table 7.1 A summary of subjects' relationship to information

| *Subject* | *Universal* | *Professional* | *Organized* |
|---|---|---|---|
| Attitudes of the subjects in relation to the faculties | Only receiving (Passive) | Receiving | |
| | Active reception (Critical, selective audience) | | |
| | Receiving, imparting, and seeking (Participatory) | Seeking, imparting | Imparting, disseminating |

As mentioned, the universal subject has come to share the attitudes of professional subjects (journalists) and organized subjects (businesses).

In spite of this duality among the public, the tendency, until the late-twentieth century, was for ordinary citizens to be passive and concerned only with receiving information. This left the qualified subject in the active position of information manager, and the organized subject in the active position of guarantor of the final stages of the communication process. The rise of the World Wide Web and the growth of Internet access around the world enabled the public to participate in and use digital communication to a greater extent (Corredoira 2007).

This crystallizes the duality of active and passive subjects, which stands in clear contradiction to the essence of the UDHR. This document clearly established that all subjects are both active and passive; or in the language of Article 19, that all subjects are holders of each of the three abilities (receive, impart, and seek) and that they personally enjoy the right to exercise those abilities as they see fit, without being obligated to use only one.

This right does not establish two legal realities, because any subject is active and passive at the same time. The subject does not alter his or her title by exercising (or not) certain functions. All subjects are active and passive holders of the communication rights and, from the perspective of the UDHR, are enabled to exercise the various functions or abilities conceded by that right (seeking, imparting, and receiving).

The UDHR, like Article 20 of the Spanish Constitution, is a positive example because it does not distinguish professional or other subjects in the exercise of their right. Communication rights are for all, with the only difference arising in terms of how intensely they are exercised. The communicator, or person who disseminates information, is the most active and yet most passive subject (as a receiver and as a citizen), and the general public is theoretically more passive yet can easily become active through the capabilities of modern technology.

The emergence and subsequent rapid development of information technologies has led to a wider acceptance of this conception of a subject that is both active and passive. Technologies that are widely available today provide evidence of the various possibilities available to the general public for active involvement. This involvement can take the form of participation in the communication process, through what Orihuela Covlliva (2015) and others have called "citizen journalism" – the term has its critics; I do not consider it journalism in the strict sense – and the creation of online media to disseminate all types of news, ideas, and opinions. The concept of "citizen journalism" is not without controversy because journalism differs from the simple transmission or dissemination of news by citizens. This does not invalidate the classification that I have presented. Instead, it strengthens the idea that all subjects occupy a double position that is both active and passive when they exercise their communication rights. Other researchers such as Jane Johnston and Anne Wallace explore the concept of journalist in the new digital context in Chapter 21. Lorenzo Cotino (2015) also addresses the scope of the protection of professional secrecy vis-à-vis journalists or other watchdogs.

This impersonal and general conception of the active or passive subject is expressed in Article 19 of the UDHR via the word "everyone," on whom subsequent lines of the text confer the three activities of seeking, imparting, and receiving. This situates us in the universality of the subject, which can be taken to mean that all people have a right to the set of activities contained within that right. Unfortunately, this is not the way things are in reality.

In the first moments after the declaration came into existence, and even 70 years later, in some parts of the world the concept of person, as the bearer of full human rights, has continued to be subject to limiting considerations in the sense that there are legal systems that still distinguish between the person as a being, who has a full range of rights recognized by law, and strata of society that do not have this full status because of differences in social rank (caste), religion (persecution for exercising a certain belief), or politics (for not belonging to the official party), or because they are subject to, for example, restrictions on how many children they may have on the basis of a political decision. This state of affairs means that there are still notable differences when it comes to the recognition of human rights for certain citizens.

In the field of communication rights, these differences are even more noticeable; people are treated differently according to their social or political position because communication is a basic aspect of a person's development and, therefore, controlling communication is a key element of controlling society.[1]

## Equality of Subjects and a Geographical Divide

This subjective rupture becomes even more evident if we complement the rights of subjects with the three possibilities that Article 19 concedes to everyone "regardless of frontiers" and "through any media," with the added condition that everyone can "hold opinions without interference." In effect, social and economic reality has made it impossible for physical and legal persons alike to satisfy the objectives contained in Article 19 – despite the development of ICTs.

Here are some examples of circumstances in which the universality of communication rights may be violated:

- The requirement of having large sums of money to undertake communication processes, which reduces the full exercise of the right to a very few who can own media.
- Lack of equality between genders, ethnic groups, minorities, and religions in certain countries.
- The existence of rules and regulations limiting media ownership, such as the requirement in western Europe for a license or concession from the state to provide audiovisual services, or regulations limiting the publication of certain media. Many countries have been adopting various regulations that affect cinema, radio, and television. This is even more obvious on the Internet, where not only do regulations vary, but too often media operations are hindered or suspended for purely political reasons.
- The requirement to have a state-issued license or permit to work as a journalist, which neglects the universal, global character of the three activities established by communication rights.
- The perception that communication rights continue to be an internal right of states, since many countries have not incorporated the principles and details of the UDHR, subsequent regional declarations, or the international covenants into their national rights or constitutional law. In these cases, though the international documents could act as homogenizing norms across all countries, the rights contained in those documents have not been implemented.
- The different legal treatment afforded to different media, with regulations tending to be more permissive for media with smaller audiences and more restrictive for mass media.

There are other factors that negatively affect the concept of the subject in communication rights, but the examples cited earlier suffice to illustrate the long road ahead.

## The Object of Communication Rights: Messages

To frame the issues here, it is important to point out that Article 19 of the UDHR circumscribes the object of communication rights to two types of message: information and opinion. However, as pointed out in Chapter 6, communication rights are expanded in Article 19 of

[1]This is the case in certain Communist countries, where only people belonging to the party enjoy full rights. The problem of castes and the inequalities stemming from them exists in India, and inequalities that fall upon women can be found in Muslim countries.

the International Covenant on Civil and Political Rights to include ideas: "Everyone shall have the right to freedom of expression; this right shall include freedom to seek, receive and impart information and ideas of all kinds."

In my view, where the UDHR mentions "information," it is referring to *news*, *opinions*, *advertising*, and *public relations*. These messages, together with ideas, make up the object of communication rights. Analysis of messages or contents is one of the most important matters in any journalistic discipline. Indeed, the object of communication rights manifests itself in the distinct messages that the qualified subject, sometimes directly but usually through the organized subject, disseminates to the universal subject.

Though this process is sometimes difficult and arduous, it constitutes a simple but extremely important act of justice: disseminating to all citizens the messages that they deserve. This reinforces the idea that information "belongs" to the public, to the universal subject. And it also reinforces the idea that the other two types of subject are required to respect that ownership. Messages, then, belong to the public, which tacitly gives to the other two types of subject, the duty to prepare information and convey it to society. When this reality is forgotten, and the communicator or the business owner thinks that he or she owns information, the communication process can be gravely distorted, and messages become commodified based on the interests of the communicator or business owner.

Desantes Guanter (1994) carried out a complete study of the message, starting from the basic idea of an act of justice.[2] He stated that "when referring to the message as an object of the right to communicate, we are entering the territory of objective justice." On the back of his analysis of the object, based on the UDHR and the International Covenant, he established a complete system of principles of the various messages into which the object of information can be analyzed. The principle of generality, the cardinal principle for a legal study of the message, can be broken down into principles of individuality (copyright), specialization (each type of message has its own characteristics that give it validity), and exceptionality (the possibility of blocking messages in the name of respect for other personal or social rights).

Messages can be divided based on their nature into:

- Simple messages: facts (or news) and ideas.
- Compound messages: opinions, advertising, and public relations.
- In-depth analysis of the trilogy of opinion, news, and ideas requires one to keep in mind two extremely important questions related to the communication process: objectivity, which is already desirable; and truth, which is an absolute, essential condition of information (Desantes Guanter 1976). From this perspective, the previously mentioned classification can lead to some pertinent considerations.
- Ideas, as the expression of the personal ideology of each subject, contain a high degree of subjectivity because they form part of each person's cultural heritage. In addition, they are, from this standpoint, completely suitable for dissemination, even if their contents can be difficult for other people. This is true as long as the ideas are imparted with respect. From this perspective, ideas are open to the highest degree of debate, and they enjoy the greatest freedom.
- News, as communication of a real fact, should have the greatest degree of objectivity possible and so is less open to debate – as long as that essential attribute of truth is preserved. I will address these two questions in greater detail later, in my exploration of the concept of news.
- Finally, opinion occupies an intermediate position as a basic element for appreciating ideology and for putting it into perspective with news as a function of the personal opinions of each citizen.

[2] According to the classic definition by the Roman jurist Ulpian (2nd–3rd century BCE) of the "constant and perpetual will to allot to every man his due."

In the realm of informational communication, these considerations make it possible to speak of ideas, news, and opinions as the trilogy that emerges from Article 19 and that corresponds to the two terms of "news" and "opinions" mentioned earlier. Some aspects of each of these two terms should be explored in order to situate them properly with respect to the UDHR's Article 19.

### *News as the Basis of Informational Communication*

On many occasions, communication rights have been reduced to the right to news, to the point of exaggeration. The importance of this right is fundamental, and communication rights began in close association with the "right to facts," as Sánchez Ferriz (1974) put it, because it is the basis of the deductive process described earlier, and so the requirement of truth in news is absolute. Opinions, derived from one's own ideas and weighed against news, would be incorrect if news were not true. They would be rumors and disinformation. Thus, truth is the most essential attribute of news. The phrase "right to facts" was first used in France in the 1940s and was brought into Spanish by Sánchez Ferriz (1974) and later by Corredoira and Sánchez-Ferriz (2017, pp. 11–48). It is important in the historical evolution of the right to truthful information, that is, the right to news.

Truth is one of the most difficult concepts to define ideologically and philosophically. However, that difficulty should not prevent the search for an adequate definition that can be applied to media. Doing so would solve one of the greatest problems that informational communication can encounter. To this end, it is necessary to identify what type of truth we mean within the field of communication.

The definition of news from the legal perspective, as the object of communication rights, is "a communication of facts of public importance – in other words, publishable facts. To be accurate, communication must conform to a reality that is complete and rapidly accessible to all" (Desantes Guanter 1974, pp. 51).

The attribute of truth, as a defining element, is essential (Rosentiel 2020). But the challenge in the storm, that is, the informational communication process, is to determine as rigorously as possible, to what type of truth we are referring – in other words, to understand the degree of truth that is needed to conceptualize news as such.

News is, or should be, the most accurate adaptation of facts to the reality of information. From this perspective, the truthfulness of information is directly related to its faithfulness to the events that occurred. This realism constitutes a guarantee of security when evaluating the truthfulness of information. How faithful this adaptation of facts may be depends on the circumstances. An absolute adaptation is an ontological truth – in other words, the truth of being, or a perfect resemblance between reality and information. This type of truth contrasts with logical truth or truth of knowledge.

In the field of facts or news, it is practically impossible to achieve an understanding of reality given the complexity of attaining, preparing, and disseminating the entire truth or logical truth. The communication professional or journalist rarely has the possibility to access all elements that news comprises, perhaps because of a bias in sources, a lack of time, or one or more of the many other constraints imposed by the daily process of informing. Therefore, attributing this type of truth to the journalistic process is nearly impossible, because no person can directly know all of reality and all realities, or all the components of those realities. One reason for this is that "truth is the manifestation and demonstration of real things. As a result, truth is something secondary, subordinate. Truth does not exist by itself. It is always preceded by things that are, by reality. Knowing truth does not mean finding out 'the truth'; it means, in a strict sense, bringing reality out into the open." This bringing out into the open is termed "logical truth" when the reality is known together with its surrounding imperfections. The information provider or communicator should lean toward logical truth.

### *Informational Truth, Independence, and Objectivity*[3]

Next to ontological and logical truth stands informational truth, which refers to communication undertaken by a news provider or media outlet with the highest possible degree of alignment with reality or adaptation to reality. This informational truth should adapt and subordinate itself in the greatest measure possible to logical truth which, in turn, should adapt and subordinate itself to ontological truth. The intention of the information provider should be to approach logical truth as closely as possible.

To carry out the task of adaptation, a journalist must be independent as a guarantee to the public that he or she has been able to get to the bottom of the truth without fear. A journalist will be able to acquire valuable attributes such as professionalism, knowledge, and analytical capabilities. However, independence, despite the personal dimension of "wanting to be free," is conferred on the journalist by other people and circumstances. These will inevitably tend to limit exploration of the truth. In such a scenario, the journalist's independence will be on display as the guarantee of the communication process.

Finally, there are other aspects of news that, though less essential than truth, are worth mentioning. News should be complete (it should include the entire news and all news); it should be rapidly accessible to all; and it should allow the citizen to be informed as completely and quickly as possible.

I cannot complete this analysis of news without referring to a term that, on occasion, has been rejected, not because it is intrinsically bad, but because of the difficulty and antagonism that it creates. The term is "objectivity," which is a second desirable attribute of news. This is a difficult matter, but it should not be avoided for that reason.

When we speak of objectivity, we should not think of the necessity of adapting reality to news content, as we do when we think of truth. Instead, we should think about the attitude of the news communicator toward the communication object – in other words, toward the news. Objectivity means that the news should be given form by the object and that the message containing the news should be created, according to the qualities of the object of information rather than to the qualities of the subject of it. Objectivity requires arduous effort because the journalist must, as a matter of routine, isolate the object of the information and strip away preconceived criteria, ideas, and opinions (Greene 2012).

Accordingly, objectivity does not exist to allow adaptation to reality – this is, in fact, the role of truth. Rather, it exists as an ethical duty of the information provider (Lecaros 2003, pp. 57–80). Objectivity is an attitude and not a result, and therefore it can be demanded from the communicator. Objectivity may not be fully achievable given the difficulty of stripping away all preconceptions, but this is no reason not to try. Enemies of objectivity emphasize that "neutral reporting" does not exist, given the inevitable subjectivity of all subjects. While all subjects are indeed subjective, media should nevertheless avoid translating their subjectivity into the information or news that they disseminate. If they do not do so, communicators impart "their" news instead of "the" news.

### *Opinions and Ideas*

The second facet of the object of the communication rights presented in Article 19 is opinion, which forms part of a syllogism that I laid out earlier: the first premise is ideas, the second is

[3]See Chapter 9 of this volume ("News: Objectivity and Truth") by Justino Sinova, in which various works related to this topic are considered. Among these, the following are worth highlighting: Desantes Guanter (1976), Popper (1979), Postman (1985), Lipmann (1997), Frankfurt (2006), Kovach and Rosenstiel (2007), and Universidad San Pablo CEU (2013).

news, and the conclusion is opinion. The term "opinion" includes the concept of ideas and opinions per se. I focus on this term here rather than on "propaganda" because the latter, historically associated with the concept of ideas, nowadays has a negative connotation of being based on political reality.

From the legal point of view, opinion is the preserve of the individual, since it is linked to personal ideology. Opinion is the conclusion that emerges when an individual applies his or her ideas to the living reality presented in information.

The sum total of private and group opinions constitutes so-called public opinion. While truth is the essential attribute of news, freedom is the dominant, decisive attribute of opinion. Opinions are likely to be pluralistic, so it is a violation of communication rights when private or public opinions are induced, falsified, or manipulated by groups, especially information-providing groups, that bring the citizen to the conclusion of the syllogism described earlier. Thus, absolute freedom is required in order to freely disseminate ideas.

Every citizen should be able to cultivate his or her own opinions freely, even if doing so leads that citizen to make a mistake, because opinion is not a judgment of certainty but a manifestation of probability, based on individual values, which provide the principles on which an opinion is formed. Let us recall here the words of the Universal Declaration: "freedom to hold opinions without interference." Freedom of opinion is a way of making communication rights effective. Thus, the greatest respect should be accorded to individual and group opinions, and the state should be particularly respectful of these. Pluralism should be encouraged and protected so that the media industry does not end up controlled by just a few organizations or people. In fact, in today's socioeconomic climate, dangers to the freedom of opinion can come not only from the state but also from other agencies and bodies – national and, fundamentally, supranational ones – that are sometimes unknown to the general public. These organizations can violate freedom of opinion in many ways, all illegal, including by restricting pluralism, violating journalistic independence, or forcing an individual to act against his or her own conscience.

### *Other Messages: Advertising, Public Relations, and Corporate Communication*

Let us return to the idea that I proposed at the start of this chapter. Though the classical messages within communication rights are news, ideas, and opinions, these rights should also include commercial communications, such as messages about a drink, travel, or stock market values. These communications include advertising and corporate communication intended to help a company or other institution fulfill its purpose. Advertisers have rights and obligations when "selling" or disseminating information about their products and services. In fact, advertising in Europe is highly regulated. Unfair competition, deceptive advertising, and trademarks are clearly interwoven, and there are also specific regulations for advertising that involve certain classes of products such as pharmaceuticals, toys, and financial products.

Another type of message to analyze is that related to corporate communication, one of the most important journalistic specializations. This area of specialization has not yet been clearly linked to a particular type of message. Some scholars contend that it is best situated in the field of advertising, since it deals with messages of interest to the company that generates them. Others, myself included, contend that this specialty belongs in the category of information or news messages in the sense defined earlier and therefore falls within the concept of communication rights. This debate, which is of great importance today, merits more detailed analysis both in this volume and in subsequent works.

## Final Considerations and Complementary Observations About the Communication Rights in Article 19 of the UDHR

Having concluded my analysis of the subject, I finally want to mention three points that further reinforce the strength and importance of Article 19 of the UDHR. First of all, I refer to the phrase "freedom to hold opinions without interference," which refers particularly to the subject. Here, the declaration stipulates that the abilities contained within the right should never be a cause of outside interference for the subject who is actively or passively exercising those abilities. This means that seeking information, defined broadly earlier in this chapter, should never have negative repercussions, regardless of who is seeking it.

The same can be said of the activities of receiving and imparting "information," particularly the latter, which is where problems arise more often. The declaration speaks of "interference," a term that encompasses any negative repercussion – legal, social, political, or other – that the subject may suffer for exercising the right to communicate. Herein lies, for example, the modern concept of "hate speech."

This affirmation does not invalidate negative repercussions that can arise when a subject violates a legal norm that regulates communication, even if the discretional interpretation of the norm may contravene the true sense of the expression "without interference."

The second point relates to the wording "impart information and ideas through any media" contained in the UDHR. This clearly refers to the abilities that are expressed in the article and that comprise communication rights. These abilities should be accessible to the three subjects through any present or future communication medium. As Corredoira discussed in Chapter 3 of this volume, this amounts to a declaration of technical universality, which connects subjective universality (everyone), objective universality (news, ideas, advertising, public relations, and opinion), universality of ability (ability to seek, receive, and impart), and geographic universality (an absence of borders).

Evidently, the universality cannot be total here, since there can be technical issues and limitations that prevent its complete realization. However, there should be no media limitations for people exercising communication rights. It is time to overcome the widespread, but outdated, idea that media should be more or less regulated in proportion to how widely they are distributed. The three activities of seeking, receiving, and imparting information should be completely accessible to all through all media, in accordance with the principle of technological neutrality.

Finally, the third point, mentioned previously, is that communication rights apply "regardless of frontiers." The rights are universal; they apply to everyone and to every country. That is the objective of the declaration. Clearly, achieving it will take time, but the important thing is that the article is not restricted to a particular geographical context but instead aims for communication rights to be effective in all parts of the world. They are fundamental human rights belonging to all people, wherever they may live.

## References

Aguirre Nieto, M. (2015). El Derecho de la información como Ciencia. In: *Derecho de la Información. El ejercicio del derecho a la información y su jurisprudencia.* (ed. I. Bel and L. Corredoira), 9–30. Madrid: Centro de Estudios Políticos y Constitucionales.

Bel Mallén, I. (2016). Los retos de futuro en la prensa online. In: *La prensa Digital en España 2016* (ed. J. De Toro, P. Soldado M. San Pedro et al.), 179–181. Madrid: IME/IESE Business School.

Bel Mallén, I. (2020). *La ética informativa, un reto en la era de la posverdad.* Valencia: Tirant lo Blanch.

Corredoira, L. (2007). Información del artículo Lectura de la Declaración Universal de Derechos Humanos de 1948 en el paradigma de la nueva sociedad de la información. Estudio específico del artículo 19. In: *Libertad en internet: la red y las libertades de expresión e información* (ed. L. Cotino), 57–74. Madrid: Centro de Estudios Políticos y Constitucionales.

Derieux, E. and Soria, C. (1983). *Cuestiones ético-jurídicas de la información.* Pamplona: Editorial Universidad de Navarra.

Desantes Guanter, J.M. (1974). *La información como derecho.* Madrid: Editora Nacional.

Desantes Guanter, J.M. (1976). *La verdad en la información.* Valladolid: Diputación Provincial.

Desantes Guanter, J.M. (1994). Concepto jurídico de mensaje. In: *Derecho de la Información II. Los mensajes informativos* (ed. J.M. Desantes Guanter, I. Bel, and L. Corredoira), 13 – 25. Madrid: Colex.

Frankfurt, H.G. (2006). *On Truth.* New York: Knopf.

Kovach, B. and Rosenstiel, T. (2007). *The Elements of Journalism: What News People Should Know and the Public Should Expect.* New York: Three Rivers Press.

Lippmann, W. (1997). *Public Opinion.* New York: Free Press Paperbacks.

Orihuela Covilla, J.L. (2015). *Los medios después de internet.* Madrid: UOC.

Popper, K.R. (1979). *Objective Knowledge, An Evolutionary Approach.* New York: Oxford University Press.

Postman, N. (1985). *Amusing Ourselves to Death: Public Discourse in the Age of Show Business.* New York: Viking.

Rosentiel, T. (2020). Keynote: Objectivity is not neutrality with Tom Rosenstiel, ISOJ 2020. https://youtu.be/pyPa3ccBo1Y (accessed July 25, 2020)

Sánchez Ferriz, R. (1974). *El Derecho de la información.* Mexico City: Editorial Cosmos.

Sánchez Ferriz, R. (2003). El Derecho de la Información como ordenación. In: *Derecho de la Información.* (ed. I. Bel and L. Corredoira), 31–46. Barcelona: Editorial Ariel.

Universidad San Pablo CEU (2013). "Comunicación y verdad," commencement address for the 2013–2014 academic year. Madrid. Madrid: CEU Ediciones.

# 8

# Subjects of Communication Rights

## A Special Study of Minors

Isabel Serrano Maíllo

Quality information is becoming a luxury item. In the post truth and fake news era, it is not always easy to know if the messages that we receive are news or merely hoaxes. There are more and more tools through which we can access information. We are presented with more data, more media, more devices, more immediacy. However, the divide between those whom information actually reaches and those whom it does not – between those who can transmit their messages and those who have no way of doing so – is growing. In a work with a universal scope such as this one, this is the time to return to the essence, the beginning, to rethink what communication means, what it means to be a journalist, how media must adapt to these new times, how citizen journalism fits in, and what options different individuals have to access media and information.

Among the different groups that "the public" comprises are children, migrants, the disabled, and the elderly. What of the communication rights of these groups, and of those of other groups and minorities? In this chapter, I will address some of these issues and point out others, aware of the importance of responding to the information-related challenges posed by these new times.

## Introduction to Some Preliminary Observations on Having Rights

Many authors have dealt with who holds rights (among many others, Díaz-Picazo 2005, p. 129; Goig Martínez 2006, pp. 485–510; Sánchez González 2006, p. 31; Palombella 2007, pp. 396–426; Dippel 2008, pp. 341–367; Gerards and Senden 2009, pp. 619–653). As the Universal Declaration of Human Rights (1948) recognizes in its Preamble,[1] everyone holds natural rights (such as the right to life) solely by virtue of being a person. The same is not true of "legal" rights, such as the right to vote or the right to freedom of movement; enjoyment of these is subject to the person's meeting requirements set by law (for example, nationality of the state or leave to remain in it). Most of these legal requirements concern foreigners, since

[1] It states, "Whereas recognition of the inherent dignity and of the equal and inalienable rights of all members of the human family is the foundation of freedom, justice and peace in the world."

*The Handbook of Communication Rights, Law, and Ethics: Seeking Universality, Equality, Freedom and Dignity*, First Edition. Edited by Loreto Corredoira, Ignacio Bel Mallén, and Rodrigo Cetina Presuel.

they are linked to citizenship or nationality and imply the exclusion of these persons from the enjoyment of certain rights or, at least, from the possibility of holding them under the same conditions as nationals, "Foreigners hold constitutional rights and freedoms, though they do so with a different scope" (Goig Martínez 2006, p. 493). Only citizens are holders of all constitutional rights on an equal basis. This is the objective dimension of these rights. "As individuals who exercise such rights, we are all different. That is the subjective dimension" (Pérez Royo 2007, p. 417). This statement requires us to differentiate between having rights and exercising them. The former involves possessing a status that grants ownership of something (whether a good or a right), while exercise only refers to the power to use something in accordance with that "ownership." So, a person can hold a right that he or she ultimately never exercises, but it is not possible to exercise a right that one does not hold. Even the fact of having the same rights does not guarantee that those rights will be exercised in the same way.

Moreover, there are rights that are peculiar to certain types of subjects due to those persons' professional specializations. For example, educators have academic freedom, while source protection or in the case of the media, source protection or conscience clauses are rights that, in principle, are enjoyed by journalists (Moretón Torquero 2004, p. 108), but not by members of the general public.

## Holders of Communication Rights

Universality, Article 19 of the Universal Declaration of Human Rights states, attributes rights to "everyone," as Abad, Bel, and Corredoira have discussed in previous chapters of this volume.

Communication rights are held not only by any person who spreads a message in the community and to each individual within it but also by media outlets, media companies, and journalists who directly produce news items.

According to the Constitutional Court of Colombia, "Both freedom of opinion and freedom of information can be exercised by any person and through any means of expression, but when they are exercised through the mass media, they are incorporated into the substance of the freedom of the press, which includes, in addition to the freedoms to disseminate information and opinions through the media, the right to found such media and keep them operating."[2]

With regard to journalists, continental European legal thought and, by extension, some Latin American legal minds such as Gareis, Aguirre Nieto,[3] and Gutiérrez Atala[4] take the view that "the common man exercises a right when sharing information, whereas the journalist is also fulfilling a duty when he does so" (Gareis 2003, p. 197). For this reason, in certain situations, these professionals are privileged by the position that they occupy as intermediaries between the news and the community (for example, priority in entering public places, or access to exclusive areas at sports competitions or cultural events).

[2]Judgment T-904/13, December 3, 2013, of the Constitutional Court of Colombia. https://www.corteconstitucional.gov.co/relatoria/2013/T-904-13.htm (accessed January 16, 2020).

[3]According to Aguirre Nieto (2003), "The relationship between duty and the common good implies consideration of the task of reporting as a core duty and as an act of properly rendered justice."

[4]According to Gutiérrez Atala (2009, p. 273), "The informant's obligation to comply with satisfying the public's universal right to receive, investigate, and disseminate information, and specifically these last two powers, which are tacitly delegated to the information professional, must be considered the core duty."

This means that, though any reporting of information will be legally protected, the protection will be greater when it is carried out by professional journalists through recognized media outlets. Journalists act as an intermediary; they fulfill a duty, a social mandate (Desantes Guanter 1994, p. 68), "because the active form of this right cannot be exercised by the public... What the universal subject of information, the citizen, does is tacitly delegate to the informant" (González Ballesteros 2009, p. 1915).

The European Court of Human Rights also considers this right to be universal. It could not do otherwise in view of Article 10 of the European Convention on Human Rights, which reads, "Everyone has the right to freedom of expression. This right shall include freedom to hold opinions and to receive and impart information and ideas without interference by public authority and regardless of frontiers." Since the right is universal, many rulings – for example, those in which professional secrecy[5] or the right of access to information are raised – refer to the specificity of the status of journalists.[6]

Journalists are subjects with a vocation and often have very specific characteristics such as: "an instinct born from curiosity, a special eagerness to communicate facts, a minimum level of skills in narrating those facts, and the ability to exercise judgment" (Bel Mallén, Corredoira y Alfonso, and Cousido González 1992, pp. 152–153). This does not mean that a journalist is any curious individual who knows how to write. An informant must also have training, a connection to a media outlet, and an adherence to the principles of journalism.[7]

The Inter-American Court[8] defined the professional journalist as a person for whom journalism is a job – that is, a continuous, stable, and remunerated activity. However, the court took the view that compulsory membership of a professional association or the requirement to obtain a university degree in a particular field is not compatible with the American Convention on Human Rights.

A professional journalist, therefore, must have a vocation, must have training (including that of an ethical kind), and must undertake an information-sharing activity continuously and permanently. He or she must play the role of *chien de garde* or watchdog.[9] The journalist is an organizer, advocate, and educator (Jarvis 2014, pp. 52–57), as the chapters in Part II of this book discuss in detail.

Media firms are an essential component in ensuring that the information ecosystem fulfills its social function. The public places its trust not only in the informant but also in the different media outlets (with different editorial lines) that control and are responsible for, to a certain extent, the messages that they produce. Therefore, though nobody disputes the universality of communication rights when it comes to the truthful and responsible reporting of information,

[5] See *Roemen and Schmit v. Luxembourg* (2003). http://hudoc.echr.coe.int/eng-press?i=003-707011-716180 (accessed January 15, 2021) *Ernst and others v. Belgium* (2003) http://hudoc.echr.coe.int/eng-press?i=003-795697-812799 (accessed January 15, 2021), *Tillack v. Belgium* (2007), http://hudoc.echr.coe.int/eng-press?i=003-2189531-2328879 (accessed January 15, 2021), *Nagla v. Latvia* (2013), http://hudoc.echr.coe.int/fre?i=001-122374 (accessed January 15, 2021), among others.

[6] See *Guseva v. Bulgaria* (2015), for example, http://hudoc.echr.coe.int/eng?i=001-152416 (accessed January 15, 2021).

[7] Ruling from the United States District Court for the District of Oregon in the case *Obsidian Finance Group v. Crystal L. Cox* (2011). https://www.leagle.com/decision/infdco20140807903 (accessed January 15, 2021).

[8] Advisory opinion OC-5/85 of November 13, 1985, on Compulsory Membership in an Association Prescribed by Law for the Practice of Journalism. Articles 13 and 29 of the American Convention on Human Rights.

[9] Judgment of the European Court of Human Rights, *Sunday Times v. United Kingdom (No. 2)* (1991). http://hudoc.echr.coe.int/rus?i=001-57708 (accessed January 15, 2021).

the existence of the qualified subject (the journalist) and the organizational subject (the media outlet) has become indispensable. "Professional and business are the extremes of a base that makes possible the persistence of independent information from the moment when that information is produced not for their own benefit but for that of the subject emanating from the law" (Desantes Guanter 1991, p. 16).

This means that when we talk about journalism, we refer, albeit not exclusively, to its institutionalized form. That said, in these "post truth" times when fake news proliferates, "we can trust social networks not as information channels but only, perhaps, as an initial warning that something may be happening" (Ortega Gutiérrez 2017, p. 66). The exception is when pages on such networks or blogs are created and managed by communication professionals or traditional media.[10] But it is true that the emergence of new forms of media that are alternatives to traditional ones is forcing the concept of the information medium to be redefined. This does not mean that these are going to replace traditional media, or that "new content producers are replacing journalists, though they are forcing them to change" (Orihuela 2018, p. 484). Recentering, immediacy, and, above all, interaction are taking place: "We are witnessing the transformation of unidirectional communication into a complex network that connects us in a multidirectional way" (Pantoja Chavez 2011, p. 225).

As Desantes Guanter warned, "Citizens will always find that they are technically inferior relative to professionals when it comes to exercising the right to seek information. Obviously, the press or the media in general are much better equipped to enter the news arena, since they have specialized personnel at their service" (Desantes Guanter 1974, p. 75).

## Holders of the Right to Receive Truthful Information

Receiving information is the most universal facet of communication rights. It does not imply that a person can specify means, types, price, or accessibility when it comes to the news published by the media. Therefore, there is no right to require the media to broadcast particular news items (especially when one of the inherent qualities of information professionals is exercise of judgment in selecting): "According to the law, the right to receive information only has an objective dimension. For this reason, it is not technically organizable or capable of being protected by the courts" (Pérez Royo 2007, pp. 417–418). We could claim there has been a violation of the right if the information were untrue or manifestly false, but there would be very limited or even no legal consequences, unless the information infringed any other right or protected legal good (honor, privacy, dignity, and so forth) or unless damage could be demonstrated. However, some authors believe that it is possible to demand accountability and have recourse to the courts: "We refer to the right to the truth or, at least, the right to know about what is of interest to us, beyond and above what others want us to know. This imposes, at least on the public authorities, a duty of objectivity" (Corredoira y Alfonso and Sánchez Férriz 2017, p. 43).

It is clear that the right to receive information includes the requirement that the information is true (Ausín and Peña 2003) or at least genuine. However, "we must be realistic in acknowledging that our democratic system today guarantees communication rights better than it does the right of all to be truthfully informed which, in theory, the various media

---

[10] In this regard, see *Reno v. American Civil Liberties Union* (1997) https://www.law.cornell.edu/supremecourt/text/521/844 (accessed January 15, 2021) or France's Law 2010-1 of January 4, 2010, on journalists' professional secrecy.

outlets satisfy, including, ultimately, the publicly owned media in their activities, though their actual role in this regard is not always exemplary" (Alzaga Villaamil 1998, p. 112).

## Holders of the Right to Seek Information

Investigation – as a duty and as a right – constitutes one of the basic pillars on which good journalism and reputable media outlets are built. The right to seek information "exists even when it is not recognized and regulation of it has not crystallized in countries' legislation" (Desantes Guanter 1974, p. 74). Authors such as Sánchez de Diego Fernández de la Riva (2013), Cotino Hueso (2017),[11] Guichot Reina (2014),[12] Villaverde Méndez (1995),[13] Palomares Herrera (2017),[14] and Morales González (2015)[15] share this position. Furthermore, they assert the fundamental nature of this right, though not all states have passed legislation in this area. In Spain,[16] for example, this right to seek information has been linked to the right of access to public information (which is not a fundamental right) instead of to freedom of information (which is), as is the case in Germany,[17] Ireland,[18] Italy,[19] and France[20] "the Conseil d'Etat has affirmed in two cases that the right of access to administrative documents is a 'fundamental guarantee, accorded to citizens for the exercise of their public liberties in the sense of Art. 34 of the Constitution of France.'"[21]

---

[11] "These references mean that the total or partial consideration of access to information as a fundamental right in Spain is inescapable" (Cotino Hueso 2017, p. 315).

[12] "After some vacillating case law, in 2009, it seems to have been accepted that the right of access to public information is part of ECHR Art. 10's freedom of expression; this included an express admission that the court's case law on this point has evolved" (Guichot Reina 2014, pp. 22–23).

[13] "The object of the right to receive information is not only the state's duty not to interfere with the receipt of information by the passive recipient, but also a right to information owed by the state, which has the obligation to make said information available to any interested party, since it is presumed that everything the state possesses is a public matter.... It seems clear at this point that the information contained in administrative files and records [Art. 105b] is not different in nature to information that is the object of the right to receive it from Art. 20.1d" (Villaverde Méndez 1995, p. 119).

[14] "Recent Spanish regulations are still reluctant to consider the right of access as a fundamental right, despite the powerful legal and institutional role that it has had in other regulations" (Palomares Herrera 2017, p. 151).

[15] "[There has been an] evolution in the interpretation of international human rights law, which has long considered access as a fundamental right and an integral part of the right to receive information" (Morales González 2015, p. 121).

[16] Article 105b of the Spanish Constitution of 1978; Law 19/2013, of December 9, on Transparency, Access to Public Information, and Good Governance.

[17] Federal Act Governing Access to Information held by the Federal Government (Freedom of Information Act) (First adopted: 2005. Last modified: 2013).

[18] Freedom of Information Act (First adopted: 2003. Last modified: 2014).

[19] Law 241 of August 7, 1990, Reorganization of the law relating to the right to civic access and disclosure requirements, transparency, and dissemination of information by public authorities (last modified: 2016).

[20] Loi no. 78–753 du 17 juillet 1978 portant diverses mesures d'amélioration des relations entre l'administration et le public et diverses dispositions d'ordre administratif, social et fiscal; **Loi** no. 2000–321 du 12 avril 2000 relative aux droits des citoyens dans leurs relations avec les administrations; Loi no. 79–18 du 3 janvier 1979 sur les archives.

[21] https://www.rti-rating.org/country-data/France (accessed January 15, 2021).

The opposite position has been taken in Sweden,[22] Portugal,[23] the United States,[24] Norway,[25] Finland,[26] Brazil,[27] Peru,[28] and Ecuador,[29] among others. The latter line seems to have been followed by the European Court of Human Rights since 2009, following the *Társaság a Szabadságjogokért v. Hungary* (April 14, 2009) and *Kenedi v. Hungary* (May 26, 2009) judgments. From these starting points, the court seems to have progressed toward recognizing right of access as a fundamental right.

As I have said, the right to seek information refers to access to public information, transparency, and good governance, but it is important to understand that a true right to know also includes certain information aimed at promoting pluralism.

The Portuguese Constitution, for example, deals with the right of access to the public media outlets for political parties, unions, business organizations, and social organizations (Art. 40).[30] The Ecuadorian Constitution recognizes this right in relation to political groups (Art. 115)[31] and indigenous communities (Art. 57.21),[32] and that of Paraguay in relation to political and social groups (Art. 31).[33] Cyprus has established a constitutional obligation for there to be programs for its Greek and Turkish communities, with reserved hours for each of them. The country also requires both languages to be used in official communications.[34] The Romanian Constitution,[35]

[22] The Freedom of the Press Act (1766).

[23] Article 48 1976 Constitution; Law no. 46/2007 of August 24, 2007, that Regulates Access to and the re-use of administrative document (First adopted: 1993. Last modified: 2007).

[24] Freedom of Information Act (1966) and OPEN Government Act of 2007.

[25] Act of May 19, 2006 No. 16 relating to the right of access to documents held by public authorities and public undertakings (Freedom of Information Act) (First adopted: 1970. Last modified: 2006).

[26] Article 12 1999 Constitution. Act on the Openness of Government Activities (First adopted: 1951. Last modified: 2016).

[27] Law No. 12,527, of November 18, 2011, which provides for access to information pursuant to the caption of Article 5, item XXXIII; Article 37, Paragraph 3, item II; and Article 216, Paragraph 2 of the Federal Constitution.

[28] Law on Transparency and Access to Information (First adopted: 2003).

[29] Article 81 Constitution 2008; Organic Law of Transparency and Access to Public Information (First adopted: 2004).

[30] Article 40 of the Portuguese Constitution: "1. Political parties and union and professional organizations, as well as organizations representing economic activities and other social organizations with a national scope, have the right, according to their relevance and representativeness, and according to the objective criteria specified in the law."

[31] Article 115 of the Constitution of Ecuador: "The state, through the media, will guarantee in an equitable and equal manner electoral promotion that encourages debate and the dissemination of all candidates' proposed programs."

[32] Article 57.21 Constitution of Ecuador: "The reflection of the dignity and diversity of [Ecuador's] cultures, traditions, histories, and aspirations in public education and in the media; the creation of their own social media in their languages and access to others without any discrimination."

[33] Article 31 of the Constitution of Paraguay: "Media outlets emanating from the state will be regulated by law in their organization and in their operation, and democratic and pluralistic access to them from all social and political sectors must be guaranteed, with equal opportunities."

[34] Article 171.1 of the Constitution of Cyprus: "There shall be programs both for the Greek and the Turkish communities in radio broadcasts and on television."

[35] Article 31 of the Constitution of Romania: "The public radio and television services are independent. They must ensure the exercise of the right to air time for significant social and political groups."

like that of Spain (Art. 20.3),[36] refers to significant political and social groups. This same line is followed by the Inter-American Court of Human Rights, for which "freedom of expression requires the media to be virtually open to all without discrimination, or, more precisely, that there are no individuals or groups that, a priori, are excluded from access to such media."[37] The Supreme Court of Justice of Argentina[38] has stated that "it is necessary to guarantee equal access for all groups and individuals to the mass media so that there are no individuals or groups that, a priori, are excluded from access to such media."

The right of access to the media therefore seems to be the recognized power of groups that are significant in a given community "to contribute to the programming" (Menezes Barros 2015, p. 72) of publicly owned media outlets for transmission and dissemination of their ideas.

Along with these groups, it is necessary to consider populations affected by the digital divide – for example, people in poverty (Akanbi 2012), disabled people (Scholz, Yalcin, and Priestley 2017), the elderly (Abad Alcalá 2016), in short, the most vulnerable groups of people. It can be concluded, therefore, that the right of access to state-operated media is not yet guaranteed for all (Magdaleno Alegría 2006, p. 246).

## Children as Holders of the Right to Receive and Impart Information

The Universal Declaration of Human Rights of 1948 refers to children as being "entitled to special care and assistance" (Art. 25). Children were included to ensure (under the cover of human rights) their well-being and protection. In 1948, minors were not yet considered to hold rights, on the basis that they had no legal capacity to act. The child's legal guardians were the people who had to look after every aspect of his or her well-being and decide on any matter that might affect any of his or her fundamental rights. The 1989 Convention on the Rights of the Child offered the first general recognition of minors fully holding certain rights that (depending on their degree of maturity) they could freely exercise (Art. 2).[39] Political leaders

[36] Article 20.3 of the Spanish Constitution: "The law shall regulate the organization and parliamentary control of the social communications media under the control of the state or any public agency and shall guarantee access to such media to the main social and political groups, respecting the pluralism of society and of the various languages of Spain."

[37] Inter-American Court H.R., Advisory Opinion OC-5/85 of November 13, 1985, on compulsory membership in an association for journalists (Article 13 and 29 of the American Convention on Human Rights). Para. 34. http://www.corteidh.or.cr/docs/opiniones/seriea_05_ing.pdf (accessed January 15, 2021).

[38] Judgment of the Argentine Supreme Court, October 29, 2013. http://www.saij.gob.ar/corte-suprema-justicia-nacion-federal-ciudad-autonoma-buenos-aires-grupo-clarin-sa-otros-poder-ejecutivo-nacional-otro-accion-meramente-declarativa-fa13000170-2013-10-29/123456789-071-0003-1ots-eupmocsollaf (accessed January 15, 2021).

[39] Article 2 of the Convention on the Rights of the Child: "1. States Parties shall respect and ensure the rights set forth in the present Convention to each child within their jurisdiction without discrimination of any kind, irrespective of the child's or his or her parent's or legal guardian's race, colour, sex, language, religion, political or other opinion, national, ethnic or social origin, property, disability, birth or other status. 2. States Parties shall take all appropriate measures to ensure that the child is protected against all forms of discrimination or punishment on the basis of the status, activities, expressed opinions, or beliefs of the child's parents, legal guardians, or family members." These rights would be: freedom of expression and the right to information (Art. 13); freedoms of thought, conscience, and religion (Art. 14); the rights of association and assembly (Art. 15); and, finally, the rights to privacy, honor, and reputation (Art. 16).

such as Hillary Clinton (1973) or authors such as Janus Korczak (1929) had previously demanded this legal recognition, on which there is now an almost absolute consensus. But though children are recognized as having rights (Cowden 2016), their exercise of them is conditioned by their maturity and best interests (Fortin 2005).

Children and young people hold communication rights, including "freedom to seek, receive and impart information and ideas of all kinds, regardless of frontiers, either orally, in writing or in print, in the form of art, or through any other media of the child's choice" (Art. 13, Convention on the Rights of the Child) This includes states' obligation to ensure "that the child has access to information and material from a diversity of national and international sources, especially those aimed at the promotion of his or her social, spiritual and moral well-being and physical and mental health" (Art. 17, Convention on the Rights of the Child).

Before the Internet existed, concerns focused on the messages that children might receive from the media (Garitaonandía, Fernández, and Oleaga 2004). The attempt to address this involved rules that regulated the rating of programs by age or the broadcast of television or advertising content during times when children would be watching (the Television without Frontiers Directive of 1989[40] and the Audiovisual Media Services Directive of 2018).[41] These rules included bans on certain types of content (violence, pornography, and so on) and established protected times of day when airing certain advertisements (ones with xenophobic or sexist content or ones that promote gambling, alcohol consumption, tobacco, and so on) was forbidden. This concern persists but extends to the fact that minors have become content producers and, therefore, responsible for,[42] and sometimes victims of,[43] the messages that they create (bullying, sexting, hate crimes, harassment, pornography, and so on.)

## The Age of the "Children" and Young People Who are the Object of Protection

The Convention on the Rights of the Child defines a child as "every human being below the age of eighteen years." It should be understood that this definition refers only to the scope of application of the rights of the convention and not to the age of majority, a status that depends on each country's own laws. In most countries in Europe and Latin America, and most states of the United States, the age of majority is 18; it is 15 in Indonesia, 17 in North Korea, 20 in

[40] Council Directive 89/552/EEC of October 3, 1989 on the coordination of certain provisions laid down by law, regulation or administrative action in member states concerning the pursuit of television broadcasting activities.

[41] Directive (EU) 2018/1808 of the European Parliament and of the Council of November 14, 2018 amending Directive 2010/13/EU on the coordination of certain provisions laid down by law, regulation or administrative action in member states concerning the provision of audiovisual media services (Audiovisual Media Services Directive) in view of changing market realities. https://eur-lex.europa.eu/eli/dir/2018/1808/oj (accessed January 15, 2021).

[42] *El Economista*, September 14, 2014: "The Superior Prosecutor's Office is warning of an increase in use of social networks among minors in commission of acts of violence in school." http://ecodiario.eleconomista.es/interstitial/volver/reform/espana/noticias/6076858/09/14/Fiscalia-Superior-alerta-de-un-aumento-del-uso-de-las-redes-sociales-entre-menores-para-cometer-violencia-escolar.html#Kku8i5oDZXOE59Io (accessed January 15, 2021).

[43] *Europa Press Social*, September 14, 2014: "The State General Prosecutor's Office is warning of an increase in sexual images that minors are creating of either themselves or one another and sharing on social networks, indicating their 'total lack of awareness' of the consequences of such behavior." http://www.europapress.es/epsocial/menores-00645/noticia-fiscalia-alerta-aumento-imagenes-contenido-sexual-menores-redes-sociales-20140913125835.html (accessed January 15, 2021).

South Korea, and so on. It is worth adding that the age of majority does not prevent certain legal limitations from persisting until a person reaches a higher age. For example, in Japan, one comes of age at 18 but cannot smoke, drink, or gamble until the age of 20. In the United States, one comes of age at 18 too but cannot drink until the age of 21.

However, the definition given by the convention is simplistic and has created certain interpretative problems from a legal perspective. It cannot be disputed that all children enjoy certain rights from birth (the right to life, the right to physical and moral integrity, the right to a name, and so on), but the exercise of others requires a certain degree of maturity (freedom of religion or association, privacy, and so on). Seeing matters in another way may suppose a lack of protection for children, in the physical world but also the digital one, where "creating an identity and social relationships … is not only time consuming and sometimes risky but also possibly difficult to manage" (Livingstone 2014, p. 285). It would have been desirable for there to be some form of categorization by age (according to maturity criteria) in the convention to encourage a unified interpretation when it comes to the exercise of rights (Martínez Pastor et al. 2017, p. 24), though having one would also have been complicated, since categorization may depend on each country's cultural and socioeconomic factors.

In Europe, for example, the European Data Protection Regulation[44] sets the minimum age to consent to the processing of personal data at 16 (states may lower this age, but never below 13), on the understanding that minors below that age are not mature enough to understand the consequences of handing over their personal data.

## Conclusions

Communication is changing. New ways of reporting and new actors on the news scene are emerging alongside traditional media. Children, among others, have become storytellers (for example, YouTubers and Instagrammers). They exercise a right, but they are not always aware of the responsibility that doing so entails. They are responsible for what they do or say in the digital world, just as they are in the physical world, be it harassing someone, bullying, posting someone's intimate photos, being insulting, committing hate crimes, or supporting terrorism. In these cases, if the conduct is criminal, they may be tried if they have reached the criminal age established by their country (which ranges from 7 years in Switzerland to 18 in Belgium; it is set at 8 in Scotland (under review); 12 in Costa Rica, Brazil, Holland and El Salvador; 13 in France or Greece; 14 in Spain, Germany, China, and Chile; and 16 in Japan).

As for enforceability of civil liability, though the general rule is that the person responsible for a damage is its cause or author (Schwartz 2003, p. 280), juvenile law may attribute to children's legal guardians liability for the minor's act. This is based on a presumption of guilt of people who, having the duty of guardianship over others (minors), act carelessly, allowing or giving occasion for the latter to harm third parties.

[44]Regulation (EU) 2016/679 of the European Parliament and of the Council, of April 27, 2016, on the protection of natural persons with regard to the processing of personal data and on the free movement of such data. Article 8.1: "Where point (a) of Art. 6(1) applies, in relation to the offer of information society services directly to a child, the processing of the personal data of a child shall be lawful where the child is at least 16-years old. Where the child is below the age of 16 years, such processing shall be lawful only if and to the extent that consent is given or authorised by the holder of parental responsibility over the child. Member states may provide by law for a lower age for those purposes provided that such lower age is not below 13 years." https://eur-lex.europa.eu/legal-content/EN/TXT/HTML/?uri=CELEX:32016R0679&from=ES (accessed January 14, 2020).

This means that, even if minors are recognized as holding communication rights, parents will be civilly responsible for the damages caused by their children. The basis of this responsibility is *culpa in vigilando*, which in theoretical terms assumes that parents and guardians are exempt from liability only when they prove that they have been diligent persons as regards the conduct of minors under their authority.

Every right implies a duty.

## References

Abad Alcalá, L. (2016). *Alfabetización mediática para la E-inclusión de personas mayores.* Madrid: Dykinson.

Aguirre Nieto, M. (2003). El Derecho de la información como ciencia. In: *Derecho de la información* (ed. I.B. Mallén and L. Corredoira y Alfonso), 47–64. Barcelona: Ariel.

Akanbi, B. (2012). Bridging digital divide and the impact on poverty in Nigeria. *Computing, Information Systems a Developed Informatics* 3 (4): 81–87.

Alzaga Villaamil, O. (1998). *Derecho Político Español según la Constitución de 1978*, vol. 2. Madrid: Editorial Ramón Areces.

Ausín, T. and Peña, L. (2003). El deber de veracidad. In: *Palavras e pensamentos. Uma perspectiva analítica* (ed. J.L. Falguera, J.M. Saguillo, A. Zilhão et al.), 443–453. Santiago de Compostela: Universidade de Santiago de Compostela.

Bel Mallén, I., Corredoira y Alfonso, L., and Cousido González, P. (1992). *Derecho de la Información. Sujetos y medios.* Madrid: Colex.

Clinton, H. (1973). Children under the Law. *Harvard Educational Review* 43: 487–514.

Corredoira y Alfonso, L. and Sánchez Férriz, R. (2017). La compleja configuración de un derecho-libertad poliédrico, el derecho a la información. Referencias históricas. *Revista de Derecho Político* 99: 11–48.

Cotino Hueso, L. (2017). El reconocimiento y contenido internacional del acceso a la información pública como derecho fundamental. *Teoría y Realidad Constitucional* 40: 279–316.

Cowden, M. (2016). *Children Rights.* New York: Palgrave MacMillan.

Desantes Guanter, J.M. (1974). *La información como derecho.* Madrid: Editora Nacional.

Desantes Guanter, J.M. (1994). *La Información como deber.* Madrid: Editorial Ábaco de Rodolfo Depalma.

Díaz-Picazo, J.M. (2005). *Sistema de derechos fundamentales.* Madrid: Thomson Civitas.

Dippel, H. (2008). Human rights: from societal rights to individual rights. *Boletim da Faculdade de Direito: Universidade de Coimbra* 2: 341–367.

Fortin, J. (2005). *Children's Rights and the Developing Law.* New York: Cambridge University Press.

Gareis, T. (2003). Derechos y deberes de los profesionales. In: *Derecho de la Información* (ed. B. Mallén and C.Y. Alfonso), 193–221. Barcelona: Ariel.

Garitaonandía, C., Fernández, E., and Oleaga, J.A. (2004). Las tecnologías de la información y de la comunicación y su uso por los niños y los adolescentes. *Doxa* 3: 45–64.

Gerards, J. and Senden, H. (2009). The structure of fundamental rights and the European Court of Human Rights. *International Journal of Constitutional Law* 7 (4): 619–653.

Goig Martínez, J.M. (2006). Derechos de los extranjeros. Estatus constitucional y tratamiento legislativo. In: *Dogmática y práctica de los derechos fundamentales* (ed. S.S. González), 485–510. Valencia: Tirant lo blanch.

González Ballesteros, T. (2009). Voz: Libertad de Información. In: *Diccionario Crítico de Ciencias Sociales* (ed. R. Reyes), 1915–1918. España/México: Plaza y Valdés.

Guichot Reina, E. (2014). Transparencia y acceso a la información pública en España: análisis y propuestas legislativas. Fundación Alternativas working paper no. 170/2011.

Gutiérrez Atala, F. (2009). Derecho de la información, base de la profesión periodística. *Estudios de Comunicación y Sociedad* 12: 7–23.

Jarvis, J. (2014). *Geeks Bearing Gifts.* New York: CUNY Journalism Press.

Livingstone, S. (2014). Developing social media literacy: how children learn to interpret risky opportunities on social network sites. *Communications* 39 (3): 283–303.

Magdaleno Alegría, A. (2006). El derecho de acceso a los medios de comunicación públicos de los grupos sociales y políticos significativos en el estado social y democrático de derecho. *Teoría y Realidad Constitucional* 18: 226–227.

Martínez Pastor, E., Serrano Maíllo, I., Vizcaíno Laorga, R. et al. (2017). *Los niños ante la publicidad.* Madrid: Universidad Complutense de Madrid.

Menezes Barros, C. (2015). *El derecho de acceso de los grupos sociales a los medios de comunicación. Especial consideración del ordenamiento jurídico brasileño.* Madrid: Universidad Complutense de Madrid.

Morales González, G. (2015). El derecho de acceso a la información pública en la Ley de Transparencia: Una aproximación constitucional. *Eunomía. Revista en Cultura de la Legalidad* 8: 93–125.

Moretón Torquero, A. (2004). El secreto profesional de los periodistas y la empresa de comunicación: ¿Un conflicto de lealtades? *Revista Jurídica de Castilla y León* 4: 99–145.

Orihuela, J.L. (2018). Los medios de la Gente. *Razón y Palabra* 22: 481–487.

Ortega Gutiérrez, D. (2017). *Retos de la libertad de información.* Madrid: Dykinson.

Palomares Herrera, M. (2017). Estudio comparado sobre transparencia y derecho de acceso en el ámbito internacional y su influencia en España. *Revista de Derecho* 6: 123–153.

Palombella, G. (2007). From human rights to fundamental rights. *Archiv für Rechts-und Sozialphilosophie* 93 (3): 396–426.

Pantoja Chavez, A. (2011). Los nuevos medios de comunicación; las redes sociales. *Tejuelo* 12: 218–226.

Pérez Royo, J. (2007). *Curso de Derecho Constitucional.* Barcelona: Marcial Pons.

Sánchez de Diego Fernández de la Riva, M. (2013). Transparencia y acceso a la información pública ¿son lo mismo?: Por un derecho fundamental a acceder a la información pública. In: *Libertad de expresión e información en Internet: amenazas y protección de los derechos personales* (ed. L.C.Y. Alfonso and H. Lorenzo Cotino), 304–313. Madrid: Centro de Estudios Políticos y Constitucionales.

Sánchez González, S. (ed.) (2006). *Dogmática y práctica de los derechos fundamentales.* Valencia: Tirant lo Blanch.

Scholz, F., Yalcin, B., and Priestley, M. (2017). Internet access for disabled people: understanding socio-relational factors in Europe. *Cyberpsychology: Journal of Psychosocial Research on Cyberspace* 11.

Schwartz, G.T. (2003). Liability for damage caused by others under USA law. In: *Unification of Tort Law: Liability for Damage Caused by Others* (ed. D. Busnelli), 279–284. London: Kluwer Law International.

Villaverde Méndez, I. (1995). *Los derechos del Público.* Madrid: Tecnos.

# 9

# News
## Objectivity and Truth

Justino Sinova

## Objectivity Matters; Denial of It Kills

The term *objectivity* is constantly reproved in the professional world of journalism, where one frequently hears people say something that has become a cliché: "Objectivity is impossible." That statement is often asserted with such forcefulness that an apparently irrefutable axiom now prevails: "Objectivity does not exist." The conceptual crusade against objectivity is not limited to newsrooms; it has also invaded academic milieus. I have often described[1] this theory that objectivity is impossible as illogical because it is akin to affirming that sincerity, truthfulness, and honesty are impossible for humankind. Ultimately, denying that human beings have the ability to act with objectivity is equivalent to denying that they do not have the capacity to behave according to reason and reducing them to intellectually diminished beings who can only be guided by instinct.

We ought to ask ourselves, then, why there is this insistence on defiling a concept that is clearly demanded outside these professional fields by those who want to know about current events. An explanation that is generous to the denialists is that the concept of objectivity that they are talking about is of a different kind. This is the only way to understand the controversy. A statement that one hears from many of them, for example, comes from Eco: "A journalist cannot be objective because he cannot describe absolute truth" (Eco 1998, pp. 66–67). This betokens the mistaken view that objectivity and truth can be equated.

## Professional Offerings of Objective Work

Contrasting with the denialist attitude found in the professional fields of journalism and academia are the frequent promises about objective output that media companies make to their audiences so that the latter trust their messages, even as internally they try to cover up the

[1]This work builds upon updates and advances on notes, speeches, essays, and papers written by the author and also updates and builds upon some work published, partially, and as part of the author's academic output. Published work is referenced in the final bibliography as Sinova (2000, 2012, 2013).

*The Handbook of Communication Rights, Law, and Ethics: Seeking Universality, Equality, Freedom and Dignity*, First Edition. Edited by Loreto Corredoira, Ignacio Bel Mallén, and Rodrigo Cetina Presuel.

outbursts about objectivity that affect their newsrooms. Here is a small sample of the commitments to objectivity that media outlets publicly make in their editorial guidelines:

- "Editorial independence, objectivity, and rigor and not manipulating content are *El Mundo*'s basic editorial objectives as well as fundamental rights for its readers" (*El Mundo* Editorial Guidelines)[2].
- "Absolute impartiality does not exist, but an article is objective when the journalist does not introduce his or her opinions or feelings into it and provides only verifiable information" (*El Mundo* style guide 2007)[3]
- "Spanish Law 17/2006, of June 5, establishes the public service of state-owned radio and television as an essential service for democratic life. State radio and television are governed by rigor, independence, neutrality, and objectivity, and they facilitate citizen participation, guaranteeing access for significant political and social groups."[4]

One could go on forever listing examples of promises of objectivity made in the journalism world. On the one hand, intellectuals such as Karl Popper (1987) have defended scientific objectivity and attacked, in Popper's words, the "form of relativism that maintains that objectivity and the ideal of truthfulness are totally inapplicable to the social sciences."[5] On the other hand, there are those who have rejected any hint of objectivity. Starting with objection to a journalism technique that was in vogue in the 1960s in the United States, they have transferred the concept of the person to narrative. An example here is Umberto Eco (1998), who considers the issue "obsolete" because "there cannot be truly objective news."

## The Professional Effort that Journalism Requires

My starting point is the need for a strategy to produce information-bearing messages. It would be absurd for it not to be this. It would be tantamount to asserting that a person does not have to make any effort to accomplish a task. The journalist's work begins with the selection of content, which consists in declining to tackle many events and instead opting to concentrate on a few. The media offers a very small part of daily reality: A television newscast contains 20 or 30 items, while 150 to 200 stories make it into a printed newspaper.[6] What we call "current affairs" is reduced to just this. The journalist's next task is to craft news items, give them headlines, assess their importance, decide whether or not to supplement them with visuals, and choose their place in the media outlet. The journalist makes a constant assessment of the information that he or she handles, even when it comes to the task of writing a text, because writing also implies the need to choose the format, the words, the rhythm, the length, and the style.

Opposing those who assail the concept and practice of objectivity are many professionals who consider it essential and, in their information-sharing activity, put into practice the values that underpin objectivity, even if they do not speak the accursed word that divides minds. We can see this if we look at the testimony of some outstanding journalists. John Lee Anderson

---

[2] *El Mundo* Editorial Guidelines, December 1990, Article 2. https://www.elmundo.es/em/codigo-etico.html (accessed January 15, 2021).
[3] *El Mundo*, style guide, 2007. https://www.elmundo.es/em/codigo-etico.html. (accessed January 15, 2021)
[4] https://www.aggylon.com/clients/9/rtve. (accessed January 15, 2021).
[5] See also Popper (1992).
[6] The online versions of media outlets provide a much greater number of information-bearing messages because they constantly incorporate the news that is taking place. Even so, such a volume of information touches on only a minimal part of reality's boundlessness.

(2006, p. 13) says: "**I try** not to take a side. Sometimes I have my own sympathies with one side or another, but **I try** not to let them color my reporting. I spent years researching Che's life, but I have also written a profile of Pinochet and tried to delve into *pinochetistas'* lives. I don't mean that I sympathized with them, but I took an interest, and there was no difference in the professional rigor that I applied from one person to the next."[7] Benjamin Bradlee, the legendary executive editor of the *Washington Post*, wrote in his memoirs (1996, pp. 481, 576): "Since Watergate, I have always **looked for** the truth after hearing the official version of the truth, after listening to all the versions that the matter at hand's different masters of manipulation give me." And he adds that "the best newspapers remain **committed** to a **conscientious search** for the truth."

Fernández Areal (1997, p. 121), a journalist and professor of journalism, writes, "Our **duty**, as public communicators, is to **seek** the truth, transmit the truth, communicate the truth, not deceive, not misrepresent, not mislead." Kovach and Rosenstiel (2007), veteran journalists and expert writers, emphasize that "journalism's first **obligation** is to the truth" and that "its essence is a **discipline** of verification." One of the two reporters who worked on Watergate, Carl Bernstein (quoted in Kovach and Rosenstiel 2007, p. 61), said that "journalists **strive** to obtain the best possible version of the truth." And, as a culmination of this brief bunch of testimonies, it is worth mentioning that of a journalist, businessman, business advisor, and professor of law and ethics, Carlos Soria (1997, pp. 139, 144) who asks journalists to "**play fair**," which "requires the exercise of transparency and honesty with oneself and with the public" and "**rectitude of intention**." The information-sharing process is rounded off by the recipient's effective knowledge of that informed reality, which is also essential in the journalist's own employment relationship (Soria 1988).

## Overcoming Subjectivism

What takes individuals outside their bubbles of subjectivism that isolate them from the world is the effort through which they are able to moderate their natural, though not infinite, self. The German philosopher Josef Pieper[8] has described the process of knowledge in a simple way that is useful for our purpose of understanding the function of information sharing: "Willingness has to take unprecedented action by allowing itself to be determined, in knowing, only by the thing, … by forcing itself to be silent, to pass unnoticed and, through doing so, to be able to perceive." Thus, the act of knowing requires effort, courage, personal decisiveness. Professor Desantes (1976, pp. 38–41), finding support in Pieper, adds that "the subject will do everything possible to adapt his or her knowledge to reality and nothing to mask, with some subjective ingredient, the impression of reality on his or her intellect." And, consequently, information provision consists in "the prevalence of reality through all the subjective receiving and emitting filters that punctuate the passage of information." Nobody would deny the interposition of subjective filters, but one cannot give a filter the fatalistic capacity to permanently block things from passing through.

It follows that overcoming subjectivism depends largely on a "human factor" and on a personal disposition – on a willingness, in short. In journalism practice, that personal willingness has been translated into, for example, personal detachment, equanimity, fairness, honorableness, honesty, impartiality, independence, integrity, neutrality, consideration, and rectitude of

---

[7]I have used bold to highlight words that allude to the need for the intellectual effort that journalism requires in terms of the journalist's submitting his or her own opinions and feelings – subjectivity, in a word – to understanding and communicating reality.

[8]Quoted in Soria (1997, pp. 139–144).

intention. (These are synonyms that many claim are substitutes for the term *objectivity* but that do not encompass all its meaning.) According to journalism ethics, for journalists to fulfill their task of providing an information-dissemination service to the public, they must practice all the professional virtues that lead them to select, to understand that reality, to elaborate information-bearing messages, and to spread knowledge of that reality – that is, the possible truth. Therefore, the "human factor" defines an essential condition for there to be an attainment, when transmitting information, of efficacy in communicating the truth about what merits dissemination. Simply put, the first thing journalists must do to provide information well is to want to do just that, and starting on that basis, they will achieve their purpose by putting into practice the personal skills that their profession requires of them. Conveying the truth is not easy, but nor is properly carrying out any profession or trade.

In short, we can state that without a firm personal willingness aimed at ascertaining the truth, it will be difficult to obtain appropriate information. "Life without truth is not livable," wrote Ortega y Gasset (1983, pp. 39–40), who defined man as "the being that absolutely needs the truth" and that "zoologically" should be classified "more as a truth eater than as a meat eater." In reality, we all understand that information of any kind must be truthful. This quality of information was masterfully described by Professor José María Desantes (1994, p. 75) when he stated that truth is "the essential constituent of communication materialized in the message," to the point that truth is "information itself."[9] When truth is lacking, information disappears and, consequently, society loses a fundamental value that belongs to it. "Civilizations," says Harry G. Frankfurt (2007, p. 43) in a short but resounding study of truth written based on common sense, "have never managed to prosper, and nor will they be able to do so, without enormous quantities of reliable information about events."

We speak of logical truth – that is, of knowledge's fit of reality, or, in other words, of correspondence with facts.[10] As is well known, history abounds with skeptical theories of truth. To "describe" is to show the truth, "to represent something to provide a comprehensive idea of it." Information consists in offering a reality transcribed in a verbal or iconic formula that is suited to being understood. It is about offering data and not opinions, superficial impressions, or incomplete versions.

## Crimes of Journalism when Truth has been Pushed Aside (or the Classic Mistakes that Journalists Make when Truth does not Matter)

It would be useful to recall notable cases from recent years – for example, the closing of *News of the World*[11] and the case of the journalist Jayson Blair, who was cast out from *New York Times* in 2003[12] – though the list may be long. I will describe seven crimes of journalism that are committed when the truth does not matter.

[9]"An essential and unavoidable component of Information," Desantes adds, "is truth, which is the common denominator of all messages."

[10]See in this regard Popper (1992, pp. 51, 285, 286).

[11]Its disappearance was announced on July 7, 2011, and came after leaks, phone hacking, and other types of malpractice. https://www.theguardian.com/media/blog/2011/jul/07/news-of-the-world-closes-live-coverage (accessed January 15, 2021).

[12]And the newspaper itself published a text asking for forgiveness. https://www.nytimes.com/2003/05/11/us/correcting-the-record-times-reporter-who-resigned-leaves-long-trail-of-deception.html (accessed January 15, 2021).

1. **The invention of reality**. The main transgression within journalism is the invention of reality and the spread of fake news, sometimes in error, sometimes out of a desire to fabricate. The latter is the common form of lying: recounting something that never was.

   The height of such fiction came when a concocted report won a Pulitzer, the most prestigious journalism award, in 1981. A piece titled "Jimmy's World" was published on the front page of *Washington Post*; the newspaper had to confess the piece was a fraud produced by one of its reporters, and it apologized to its readers.[13] Almost one century earlier, one of the great manipulators in the history of journalism, William Randolph Hearst, had sent an illustrator named Frederic Remington to Havana to produce illustrations of abuses committed by the Spanish, but when Remington told him that nothing was going on, Hearst sent him a telegram that read as follows: "You furnish the pictures and I'll furnish the war." The incident culminated in the Spanish being blamed for the destruction of the battleship Maine, an event that was a prelude to the war.
2. **Journalistic production of an event**. Very close to a total lie is the fabrication of an event to create a story, with journalists as the main actors in the invention. Readers who reach the final pages of Gabriel García Márquez's memoirs come across an astonishing confession: in his days as a journalist, the writer organized a demonstration so that he had a story to file. He had been sent by his newspaper, *El Espectador*, to the city of Quibdó, the capital of the Chocó department in Colombia, to report on popular protests against the government, but he found that nothing was happening there. He decided to fabricate the news. In his own words (2002, pp. 535–536), "Our professional problem was simple: we had not undertaken that expedition … to report that there was no news. … Primo Guerrero [the newspaper's correspondent] then suggested we pull another [sic] demonstration out of the bag, and nobody came up with a better idea." García Márquez reveals that the governor collaborated with him and that "this was how news invented by necessity [sic] ended up being the only true news [sic], magnified by the press and radio across the whole country." According to him, that "demonstration" from "out of the bag" caused the government to correct its course, but he cannot hide the fact that it was a carefully organized lie. That said, none of this prevents the novelist from calling in his memoirs for truth in information.
3. **Fictions created to occupy a space in the media**. At other times, journalists are necessary collaborators in the fiction. This happens when groups of people organize events with the sole purpose of capturing a space in the media. In many of these cases, the news is not in the event but in the event's artificiality, and those behind it achieve their goal when, as almost always happens, journalists do not investigate or reveal the true causes that lie behind the event.

   Other times journalists are necessary contributors to a fiction. It occurs when groups of people organize events with the sole purpose of conquering a space in the media.

   There is an abundant body of novels, films, and other fictional works that depict reporters who make up stories and create objective or deliberate falsifications. Tom Wolfe described the scenario in his novel about the news world, *The Bonfire of Vanities*. The novel's reporter, who has been informed about a demonstration that is due to take place, goes to the scene, finds no crowd, and asks someone who is there about what is going on. The demonstration will begin, he is told, "soon's Channel 1 gets here." The reporter sees that the place is half empty. "But where are the people?" "They'll be here," he is told, "soon's Channel 1 gets here." And indeed, when television cameras come and are finally

[13] In his memoirs, Bradlee (1999, pp. 514–535) laments the 1981 episode, which tarnished the acclaim that the newspaper had won through Watergate.

set up, a group of people performs a protest that lasts for exactly as long as the cameras are rolling. It was an exclusive promised to the television station, which will now have a subject for its broadcast – a fictional one that will be presented as news.

4. **Yellow journalism**. Many truth-masking practices are typical of what is known as yellow journalism, which appeals to recipients' emotions and feelings and takes advantage of their sensitivity (it is synonymous with sensationalism), not hesitating to use gross falsehoods and the variety of lie that involves distorting facts. Yellow journalism alters the rules on assessment, magnifying small things and shrinking big ones.

   It is an adulterated license that Vargas Llosa did not fail to notice in his analysis of what he called "showbusiness civilization." He wrote that, "In our era, negative aspects of political life have often been magnified in an exaggerated and irresponsible way by yellow journalism, the result being that public opinion has come to believe that politics is a task for people who are amoral, inefficient, and prone to corruption" (Vargas Llosa 2012, p. 133). Bradlee (1999, p. 576) uses the term "kerosene journalism" for a form of yellow journalism that comes about when "reporters pour kerosene on whatever smoke they can find, before they determine what's smoking and why. The flames that result can come from arson, not journalism." Nobel laureate Heinrich Böll (2009) described the perverse methods and consequences of yellow journalism in a shocking and dramatic novel.

5. **A fondness for showbusiness and entertainment**. The passion for showbusiness and entertainment, a peculiarity of our time, causes damage when it is applied to news production. The medium most focused on entertainment, television, has also shrouded its information-sharing spaces in the atmosphere of "emotional gratification" and has become a limited vehicle for information. Neil Postman (1991, pp. 91, 111) defines the phenomenon as "disinformation" and says it takes the form of information that is "deceitful, mistaken, irrelevant, fragmented, or superficial; information that creates the illusion that we know something when in fact it distances us from knowing."[14]

   This anomaly has also been noticed by Vargas Llosa (2012, pp. 219, 220), who considers it harmful to communicating the truth: "The audiovisual media … are condemned to skim the surface of things and are much more impeded than are books in terms of freedom of expression and creation. … A regrettable but incontrovertible reality: images on screens are more fun, more entertaining; but they are always sparse, often insufficient, and in many cases incapable of saying, in the complex field of individual and historical experience, what courts demand from witnesses: 'the truth and the whole truth.' And their critical capacity is therefore very low."

6. **The truth, hidden or altered by opinion**. Journalists sometimes help to hide the truth under their own opinion. Differentiating between recounting facts and setting out opinions is a duty to the truth, but since the end of the last century, journalists have been superimposing their opinions on the transmission of information, to the point where it is now difficult to find a story free of its author's explicit judgments in some media.

7. **The compensating routine**. A custom that has the apparent purpose of appropriately informing people but that achieves the opposite objective, namely confusing them, has become widespread. This is a compensating routine, through which a variety of opinions on the same subject are constantly expressed, as though all opinions have the same value or equal importance. It is what has sometimes been called "journalism of statements," in which the various opinions end up hiding the significance of the fact.

---

[14]The expression "emotional gratification" that I have used is also a concept that Postman applies to television.

In this case too, it must be recognized that journalists in the public media are bound by the rules imposed by politicians, but this custom has been transferred to the rest of the media, and so the compensating routine has become a strongly rooted professional habit. The journalist, impelled by that appearance of neutrality, refrains from assessing the weight of opinions and ends up attributing all of them the same importance. An inevitable victim of this approach is journalism: "To construct newspapers by accumulating large amounts of other people's opinions," writes journalist and professor Furio Colombo (1997, p. 56), "leads to the loss of credibility and the end of journalism."[15]

Journalists must push themselves when it comes to the task of evaluating opinions, since not all are equal, and nor do they all deserve the same treatment. "Unfortunately, all too often journalistic balance is misconstrued to have this kind of almost mathematical meaning, as if a good story is one that has an equal number of quotes from two sides": This opinion from Kovach and Rosenstiel (2007, p. 108) shows the method's falseness; it is unfair and therefore goes against the truth.

## Conclusions

The term "objectivity" refers to an attitude, a disposition, a willingness. As it is something that depends on personal effort, it cannot be impossible; it will be difficult at least, but difficult does not necessarily mean impossible. And, in addition to being possible, it is required, not only from the journalist but also from every person who performs a task for others. As Soria (2012) has written, "Objectivity is difficult and resides in struggle."

It is undeniable that journalists cannot face the great challenge of discovering and spreading the truth alone. It is necessary for their efforts to be supported by their environment, nearest and farthest; I would indicate the following conditions to this end:

1. The practice of truthful information will not be possible without a **climate of political and social freedom** that respects the circulation of messages. Freedom of information and opinion creates the setting in which journalism must take place, as the journalist and academic Ignacio Bel Mallén comments in this volume.[16] In this, the public authorities – parliament, the government, the justice system – have a special responsibility to create suitable legislation that protects the dissemination of information and opinions, prevents politicians of any stripe from imposing abusive restrictions, and makes it easier for the justice system to ensure compliance with the law and impose accountability. Parties, unions, economic groups, and pressure groups can pose risks to information-sharing activities when they use their social power to impose their preferences or their silences on the media.

   Among the external conditions that can ruin freedom of information is what is now generally called "political correctness." Applying restrictions to language, limiting the subjects open to debate, or coordinating the giving of praise and the reproving of certain criticisms are consequences of this custom that occupies important areas of social life and ends up acting as a coercion of freedom.
2. The practice of disseminating truthful information will not be fully possible without a **climate of internal freedom in the media**, one that respects journalists' professional independence. In information-media companies, the selection, elaboration, and

[15]This is the remedy he suggests: "All that remains is the path, honest and stubborn, of facts verified independently, using sources, however authoritative they may be, as but one of the news's possible construction materials".

[16]See. Chapter 7.

evaluation of content is the job of newsroom professionals, whose independence must not only be allowed but also protected by the company's management. Is this a contradiction or an inconsistency concerning a company's legitimate decision-making capacity? Absolutely not. In the task of information dissemination, the company that owns a media outlet is involved in the same duties as the journalism professional. Journalists have a duty to the public through their company because communication rights impose a superior and preferential duty. The legal status of journalists' conscientious objection, which has constitutional recognition in Spain (Art. 20.1.d of the 1978 Constitution), is related to this conflict.

Through its being devoted to disseminating information, a news-media company is affected by obligations that serving the fundamental right to information imposes. Desantes described news-media companies as having "shared responsibility for the information" that they disseminate. "They are not," he wrote, "manufacturers of media, but servers of messages through the media that they own for the purposes of responsibility and even profits; but they do not own these media in the prevailing civil sense in which, for example, they own the company's buildings or machinery." A glance at the media-business landscape allows us to verify that running through its outlets is the responsibility that is derived from the concept of a duty to serve, and they have understood the need to respect journalists' independence with the ultimate aim of serving the public's right to information.

When Eugene Meyer, at the age of 57, bought a small, bankrupt newspaper that would eventually become known worldwide – the *Washington Post* – he understood the newspaper as "a public good that must serve people in a democracy." In a speech on March 5, 1935, when he was nearing two years at the head of the newspaper's management, he explained the principles of the *Post*, among which was the following: "The newspaper's duty is to its readers and to the public at large, and not to the private interests of its owner." And he added, "In the pursuit of truth, the newspaper shall be prepared to make sacrifice of its material fortunes, if such course be necessary for the public good."[17]

3. To provide truthful information to the public, one must exercise **personal independence**. Journalists' work has a duty to provide information to the public, and the public needs and wants to be served by independent journalists. What are they independent of? Everything that could decisively condition their reporting duty: independent of information sources, which they should cultivate as a professional treasure trove, but to which they should not be subordinate; of the institutions, groups, and individuals about which they must provide information; of commercial firms and interest groups, whose activities they must sometimes denounce; of interests that, for other professionals are legitimate, but for journalists are lethal.

   The most threatening dependency is political activism. With the party-political press having disappeared in western countries, organization-based activism is less frequent today. There is, however, an activism that we could call "psychic" or "psychological"; it also nullifies the journalist's scope for disseminating information. Azorín (cited in Valverde 1971, p. 376) described the journalist in the same way he depicted a politician – as someone who "quickly becomes aware of a change in the atmosphere in a nation and adapts to the new atmosphere." The then-journalist added, "Those who do not see this are blind."

[17]This was emotionally retold by his daughter (Graham 2002, p. 69), who, over time, served very effectively as the newspaper's publisher.

The famed American journalist Maggie Gallagher (cited in Kovach and Rosenstiel 2007, pp. 96–97) attempted to define the journalist's scope of independence in the following terms: "I think it's possible to be an honest journalist and be loyal to a cause. It's not really possible to be an honest journalist and be loyal to a person, a political party or a faction. Why do I say that? I think it relates to my basic belief that there is some relationship between journalism and one's perception of the truth. One can believe that certain things, ideas, proposals, would be good for America and can openly state that. But to be loyal to a political party, a person or faction means that you do not see your primary goal as commitment to speaking the truth to people who are your audience." And she adds, "The more a journalist views himself as a participant in the events, and has loyalty to sources, the less able he or she is to really consider himself or herself a journalist." The journalist's personal independence depends on effort; nobody is independent without wanting to be so and without fighting to achieve it.[18]

The history of journalism is full of appeals to make the truth emerge from between the lines and the images of the information. The veteran journalist Walter Lippmann (1997, pp. 109–110) advised his young colleagues: "Always take a vigilant attitude toward yourself, and ask yourself over and over again this question: Am I definitely seeking the truth and not simply trying to win a contest? Because the key question is whether, like scientists or specialists, journalists put truth first or second. If they put it second, they become devoted to the perfidious god of success. Or they become conceited individuals who are trying to win a contest. But to the extent that they put the truth first, they raise themselves into the company of those who know how to savor and enjoy the best things in life."

## References

Anderson, J.L. (2006). *La mirada del periodista*. Zaragoza: Asociación de la Prensa de Aragón.

Böll, H. (2009). *The Lost Honor of Katharina Blum*. New York: Penguin.

Bradlee, B. (1996). *La vida de un periodista*. Madrid: Aguilar.

Bradlee, B. (1999). *A Good Life: Newspapering and Other Adventures*. New York: Touchstone.

Colombo, F. (1997). *Últimas noticias sobre el periodismo*. Barcelona: Anagrama.

Desantes, J.M. (1976). *La verdad en la información*. Valladolid: Diputación Provincial de Valladolid.

Desantes, J.M. (1994). El derecho a la noticia, in Derecho de la Información (II). In: *Comunicación social* (ed. J.M. Desantes, I. Bel, and L. Corredoira). Madrid: Colex.

Eco, U. (1998). *Cinco escritos morales*. Barcelona: Lumen.

Fernández Areal, M. (1997). *Información y mentira*. Pontevedra: Diputación de Pontevedra.

Frankfurt, H.G. (2007). *Sobre la verdad*. Barcelona: Paidós.

García Márquez, G. (2002). *Vivir para contarla*. Barcelona: Mondadori.

Graham, K. (2002). *Personal History*. New York: Knopf.

Kovach, B. and Rosenstiel, T. (2007). *The Elements of Journalism: What Newspeople Should Know and the Public Should Expect*. New York: Three Rivers Press.

Lippmann, W. (1997). *Public Opinion*. New York: Free Press Paperbacks.

Ortega y Gasset, J. (1983). Investigaciones psicológicas. In: *Obras Completas*, Vol. 12 (ed. M. Cervantes Saavedra), 333–453. Madrid: Alianza Editorial.

Popper, K.R. (1987). *La miseria del historicismo*. Madrid: Alianza.

Popper, K.R. (1992). *Conocimiento objetivo*. Madrid: Tecnos.

---

[18] I discussed the journalist's independence in "Periodismo y militancia," closing lecture of the international congress of the SEP (Sociedad Española de Periodística; Spanish Journalism Society), held at the University of Valladolid in 2012 (Sinova 2012). I also discussed it in "Periodismo" (Sinova 2000).

Postman, N. (1991). *Divertirse hasta morir: El discurso público en la era del "show business."* Barcelona: Ediciones de la Tempestad.
Sinova, J. (2000). Periodismo. In: *Diez palabras clave en ética de las profesiones* (ed. A. Cortina and J. Conill), 59–72. Estella: Verbo Divino.
Sinova, J. (2012). Periodismo y militancia. In: *La investigación en periodismo político en el entorno de los nuevos medios* (ed. S. Berrocal and E. Campos), 257–286. Madrid: Sociedad Española de Periodística (SEP).
Sinova, J. (2013). Comunicación y verdad, Lecture, Opening Ceremony, Academic Year 2013–2014 at Universidad San Pablo CEU in Madrid, Spain.
Soria, C. (1988). La buena fe en la relación laboral informativa. *Comunicación y Sociedad* 1 (1): 149–165.
Soria, C. (1997). *El laberinto informativo: una salida ética*. Pamplona: Eunsa.
Soria, C. (2012). Prólogo. In: *La objetividad como rutina periodística* (ed. M. Francisca Greene). Pamplona: Eunsa.
Valverde, J.M. (1971). *Azorín*. Barcelona: Planeta.
Vargas Llosa, M. (2012). *La civilización del espectáculo*. Madrid: Alfaguara.
Wolfe, T. (2002). *The Bonfire of Vanities*. New York: Collins.

# 10

# Journalists, Confidentiality, and Sources

Lorenzo Cotino Hueso

Two aspects of the protection of information sources (Lazkano Brotóns 2004, p. 3) are relevant to a book about communication rights and ethics such as this one. On the one hand, journalists and democracy-guarding watchdogs have the right to secrecy, to not identify their sources of information if they are asked to do so, and to not suffer any burden or harm for refusing to share this information. At the same time, this right has another increasingly important dimension: it entails special guarantees against investigations, searches, and interception of their data and communications related to their information sources. Unlike other forms of professional secrecy, in this case, what is protected is not the content (which is normally published by the journalist) but its source or origin (Navas-Sánchez 2019, p. 5).

International treaties do not expressly regulate the right to professional secrecy, though it is considered to be part of communication rights. It should be remembered that the UDHR expressly protects a person's right to "seek, receive and impart information of all kinds" (Art. 19), while the ICCPR protects the "freedom to seek, receive, and impart information and ideas of all kinds" (Art. 19.2). An authoritative interpretation of this right from the United Nations affirms "the limited journalistic privilege not to disclose information sources."[1]

[1] UN Human Rights Committee, General Comment No. 34, Article 19, *Freedoms of opinion and expression*, September 12, 2011 https://www.refworld.org/docid/4ed34b562.html (accessed January 15, 2021) Also, in Concluding observations on Kuwait, CCPR/CO/69/KWT.

*The Handbook of Communication Rights, Law, and Ethics: Seeking Universality, Equality, Freedom and Dignity*, First Edition. Edited by Loreto Corredoira, Ignacio Bel Mallén, and Rodrigo Cetina Presuel.

## Recognition and Regulation of Protection of Journalists' Sources

### International Recognition and Regulation

The right not to reveal sources and the right to secrecy are recognized in the most important international declarations, though these are not legally binding.[2] The Special Rapporteurs' Joint Declaration on Freedom of Expression[3] begins by affirming the confidentiality of sources. Recently, the expression of this right was highlighted in Point 7 of the Global Charter of Ethics for Journalists of 2019 by the International Federation of Journalists.[4] Some declarations and UNESCO call for its legal regulation. It has also been stated that "a minimal international construction of the content of this right would be desirable" based on Article 19 of the ICCPR (Lazkano Brotóns 2004, p. 12). Most notable here are the Perugia Principles of 2018.[5]

### International Recognition in Europe and Latin America

This right has been most strongly recognized within the Council of Europe, especially since the ECtHR case *Goodwin v. UK*, March 27, 1996. Until then, it was considered more as an ethical rule rather than as a legal one, and it was not uniformly regulated by states (Lazkano Brotóns 2004). It was a disputed court decision, approved by 11 to 7. Since Goodwin, there have been about 20 rulings that have created consolidated, specific, and advanced case law (ECtHR 2011–2015; Bychawska-Siniarska 2017, pp. 102–111). Likewise, between 2000 and 2016, the Council of Europe issued various nonbinding yet very important declarations, resolutions, and reports on this right, as well as en masse surveillance of journalists and their sources.[6]

---

[2] Point 6 of the *Bordeaux Declaration*, IFJ, International Federation of Journalists (1954) https://research.uta.fi/ethicnet/country/ifj-declaration-of-principles-on-theconduct-of-journalists; Point 14, Resolution 1003 *Ethics of journalism* COE, Council of Europe-Parliamentary Assembly July 1, 1993 (42nd Sitting). https://assembly.coe.int/nw/xml/XRef/Xref-XML2HTML-en.asp?fileid=16414&lang=en (accessed January 15, 2021); and Principle 4 of the *International Principles of Professional Ethics in Journalism*, UNESCO General Assembly, Paris, November 21, 1983 https://research.uta.fi/ethicnet/country/international-principles-of-professional-ethics-in-journalism (accessed January 15, 2021).

[3] International Mechanisms for Promoting Freedom of Expression, December 19, 2006. http://www.oas.org/en/iachr/expression/showarticle.asp?artID=746&lID=1 (accessed January 15, 2021).

[4] 30th IFJ World Congress in Tunis on June 12, 2019. https://www.ifj.org/who/rules-and-policy/global-charter-of-ethics-forjournalists.html (accessed January 15, 2021).

[5] Jointly drafted under Posetti's leadership with Blueprint for Free Speech, Reuters Institute for the Study of Journalism, RISJ, World Association of Newspaper and News Publishers, WAN-IFRA, and Signals Network (Posetti, Dreyfus, and Colvin 2019).

[6] By Committee of Ministers, in 2000, *Recommendation No. R (2000) 7 of the Committee of Ministers to member states on the right of journalists not to disclose their sources of information*, March 8. https://bit.ly/3csEZHE. Also in 2016, Recommendation CM/Rec(2016)4 on the protection of journalism and safety of journalists and other media actors, April 13, 2016 (1253rd meeting). https://search.coe.int/cm/Pages/result_details.aspx?ObjectId=0900001680 6415d9#_ftn1 (access by registration). By Parliamentary Assembly, in 2010. *Report on the protection of journalist' sources from the Council of Europe*. https://www.coe.int/en/web/freedom-expression/safety-of-journalists. In 2011 *Recommendation 1950 on the protection of journalists' sources.* http://assembly.coe.int/nw/xml/XRef/Xref-XML2HTMLEN.asp?fileid=17943&lang=en. *Resolution 2045 2015, Mass surveillance*, April 21, 2015 (12thSitting)https://assembly.coe.int/nw/xml/XRef/Xref-XML2HTMLEN.asp?fileid=21692&lang=en.

Within the EU, the resolutions of 1994 and 2014 stand out.[7] The most remarkable aspect, in any case, which I discuss in my analysis at the end of this study, is regulation of the protection of whistleblowers, even when in the exercise of communication rights they directly make public disclosures. In Latin America, the protection of sources is generally protected by Article 13 of the American Convention on Human Rights (the Pact of San José), November 7–22, 1969. Various regional declarations do include this right.[8] To date, and as far as is known, there is no specific court decision or ruling on this right (Chocarro 2017a, 2017b). Various countries regulate this right constitutionally and legally.

## Recognition in National Regulations and in Different European Countries

Posetti analyzed the regulations of 121 states for UNESCO; she calls for greater and "explicit and clear protection" in constitutions or legislation (Posetti 2017, pp. 9–10). It should be noted that since 2007 most countries in the world have improved their regulation (85% of Arab, Ibero-American, and Caribbean states; 75% of states in Asia and the Pacific; 66% in Europe; and 56% in Africa) (Posetti 2017, p. 8). There is a particular need for regulation on protecting sources in view of advances in and control over digital technologies. The report calls for: regulation that is clearly imposed in a very limited and strict way when it comes to exceptions to the right; a guarantee that the restrictions are enacted by a judicial decision (or by an independent authority), and with the possibility of appeal; the classification of violation of the right as a crime; and the supplementing of regulation with protection for whistleblowers (Posetti 2017, p. 136).

A comparative analysis of European countries (Banisar 2007; Mörä and Korpisaari 2012; Posetti 2017) reveals most have some type of legal protection. Section 383 of Germany's Civil Procedure Code grants journalists the right not to disclose sources unless they consent to it. In addition, Section 53 of the same code authorizes radio and print journalists to refuse to testify about the content or source of the information. Chapter 3 of Sweden's Freedom of the Press Act protects sources that provide information to a journalist under the condition of anonymity. This protection does not apply in cases of high treason, espionage, or unlawful release of an official document (Chapter 5, Art. 3, The Fundamental Law on Freedom of Expression, Sweden, Chapter 2, Art. 5). In the UK, (Public Interest Disclosure Act 1998, Contempt of Court Act 1981) no court can require a person to disclose a source, and neither is he or she guilty of contempt of court for refusing to disclose it. Spain regulates professional secrecy in Article 20 of its Constitution of 1978; it is judicially protected, though the provision has not been the subject of legal development of the constitutional general regulation.

Since 2007, regulations have been incorporated in various European countries, as well as in the Netherlands, Greece, and smaller jurisdictions such as the Holy See and Andorra. In Slovakia, the right is regulated by Law No. 167/2008 and the amendment thereto, Amendment

[7]The European Parliament's Resolution on the Confidentiality of Journalists' Sources, January 18, 1994, and Conclusion 31 of the EU Council's *EU Human Rights Guidelines on Freedom of Expression*, Foreign Affairs meeting Brussels, May 12, 2014. http://www.consilium.europa.eu/uedocs/cms_data/docs/pressdata/EN/foraff/142549.pdf (accessed January 15, 2021).

[8]Chapultepec (1994). *Chapultepec Declaration*, Hemispheric Conference on Freedom of Expression, Mexico, March 11, 1994 No. 3. http://www.concortv.gob.pe/file/2015/04-declaracion-chapultepec.pdf (accessed January 15, 2021). Also in Point 8 of the *Declaration of Principles on Freedom of Expression*, October 2–20, 2000, IACHR Inter-American Commission on Human Rights (2000a). http://www.cidh.oas.org/Basicos/Spanish/Declaracionle.htm (accessed January 15, 2021). And this organization's Lima Principles (principles 6 and 9), of November 16, 2000. http://www.oas.org/es/cidh/expresion/showarticle.asp?artID=158& (accessed January 15, 2021).

Law No. 221/2011. Iceland ratified a new law in 2011; in 2010, Estonia amended its Criminal Code. France strengthened the protection of sources with a law that entered into force in 2010 (LOI no. 2010–2011 du 4 Janvier 2010, see Art. 109 (2) of France Code of Criminal Procedure). Ireland has incorporated this right in its case law.

## The Concept of "Source," the Content and Foundation of the Right, and the Duty to Maintain Secrecy and Silence

### The Broad Concept of "Source" and the Scope of Protection

"Sources" are the locus from or through which news flows and where journalists can turn when they are looking for material. The ECtHR Case *Nagla v. Latvia*[9] (at para. 81, follows the Observation of 2000 (COE 2000, p. 7)). It defines "journalistic 'source'" as "any person who provides information to a journalist," and it also defines "information identifying a source." The ECtHR has extended the concept of information that has to be protected even to "the unpublished part of the information provided by a journalist" as well as his or her notes (ECtHR case *Telegraaf Meda v. The Netherlands;*[10] ECtHR case Saint-Paul Luxembourg[11]).

The ECtHR has been very generous in its interpretation and has extended the protection of sources in several of its judgments since 2003 (ECtHR Case *Roemen*[12] February 25, 2003, and following). In *Nagla v. Latviathe*, ECtHR makes it clear that the law also protects new information and storage media – for example, laptops, external memories, memory cards, or hard drives. The ECtHR additionally holds that protection also applies to sources' workplaces, residences, vehicles, and mobile devices such as smartphones and tablets. Likewise, the metadata generated in communications are protected (ECtHR case *Big Brother Watch and others*[13] *v. UK*). As I will discuss later, there are special guarantees regarding searches and investigations in all these areas.

Protection also extends to all data related to contacts entered into with the source (mode, duration, frequency), even when the police or the court already knows the source's identity (ECtHR case *Becker v. Norway*[14]).

### The Content of the Right to Maintain Secrecy and Silence: Right or Duty?

As has been argued, the law implies that when the public authorities, the police, or, especially, courts, as well as parliamentary committees, ask about sources, there is a right to secrecy and silence – to not reveal them – and refusal cannot give rise to negative consequences (COE, Recommendation No. R (2000) 7, principle 7; Navas-Sánchez 2019, p. 5). It should be clarified that this right does not protect against a breach of the obligations to appear in court as a witness or as a defendant or before the corresponding institutions. Nor does this right protect against lies. A different matter is whether, when a journalist is the defendant, they have a general right not to testify.

The journalist's right is independent of the unlawful acts or crimes that the source has committed (disclosure of secrets, breach of confidentiality, data protection breaches, and so forth)

---

[9] *Nagla v. Latvia*, July 16, 2013.
[10] *Telegraaf Meda v. The Netherlands*, November 22, 2012.
[11] Saint-Paul Luxembourg, April, 18, 2013.
[12] *Roemen and Schmit v. Luxembourg*, February 25, 2003.
[13] *Big Brother Watch and others v. UK*, September 13, 2018.
[14] *Becker v. Norway*, October 5, 2017.

(ECtHR Cases *Tillack v. Belgium*[15] and *Nagla v. Latvia*). The journalist is protected even in cases where the source discloses information in bad faith and for the purpose of causing harm (ECtHR, *Financial Times Ltd and others v. UK*[16]).

If we move from law to ethics, we find that the confidentiality of sources is positioned as a "classic duty" of journalism – as an "obligation," "commitment," and ethical, deontological, and behavioral principle (Posetti 2017, pp. 18, 137 et seq); Sixth Principle of Perugia and Bordeaux declaration (IFJ 1954). This duty is usually included in codes of conduct.

However, legally it is a journalist's right, not an obligation. As a right, it depends on the will of the journalist to avail – or not avail – themselves of it. Legally, it is clearly not the case that this ethical duty can become an obligation. An obligation not to disclose the source will be enforceable in some cases. For example, if such a duty was set in a confidentiality contract, the disclosure will bear the consequences and damages provided in the contract (Puerto 1992; Navas-Sánchez 2019, p. 5). In collective labor agreements, breach of the duty by the journalist may be treated as an infraction, one that can be considered as "very serious" misconduct (Moretón Toquero 2004, pp. 131, 137).

In some countries, there is some form of regulation when it comes to the duty of maintaining secrecy. In Sweden, willful or negligent breach of the duty can lead to a prison sentence or a fine. It is also an obligation in Slovakia.[17]

### The Right's Basis

This right is not a privilege for journalists or sources. Rather, it is an instrument to ensure and increase the flow of information (Lazkano Brotóns 2004). It is a guarantee of communication rights and not of freedom of expression (Navas-Sánchez 2019). The statement by the ECtHR[18] in *Goodwin v. UK* (para. 39) is important in this regard:

> 39. Protection of journalistic sources is one of the basic conditions for press freedom.... Without such protection, sources may be deterred from assisting the press iinforming the public on matters of public interest. As a result, the vital public-watchdog role of the press may be undermined and the ability of the press to provide accurate and reliable information may be adversely affected.

The right transcends the private rights and interests of the journalist, and their source "cannot be considered a mere privilege" (ECtHR, Nagla case, para. 97). In any case, its purpose is not for a source to use the press to escape personal legal or criminal liability (ECtHR case *Stichting Ostade Blade v. The Netherlands*[19]).

## Special Guarantees Against Searches and Investigation and the Technological Activism of Journalists and Their Sources

Protection of sources is guaranteed not only by the journalist's secrecy or silence, but increasingly by specific guarantees against investigations, interception of communications, indiscriminate searches of files, confiscation of materials, and so forth. (COE, Recommendation No. R (2000) 7, Principle 6). And it should be remembered that secrecy also includes the protection

[15] *Tillack v. Belgium*, November 27, 2007.
[16] *Financial Times Ltd and others v UK*, December 15, 2009.
[17] In Sweden, Chapter 5, Article 3, The Fundamental Law on Freedom of Expression, Chapter 2, Article 5. In Slovakia, Article 4 Source Protection Law No. 167/2008 and No. 221/2011 (Posetti 2017, p. 115; Posetti, Dreyfus, and Colvin 2019, p. 11).
[18] *Goodwin v. UK*, March 27, 1996.
[19] *Stichting Ostade Blade v. The Netherlands*, May 27, 2014.

of workplaces, residences, vehicles, and mobile devices, and this therefore implies special guarantees regarding searches of these places.

If this right did not protect against such searches, it would be merely formal and not material (Lazkano Brotóns 2004). As the ECtHR has stated, such investigations are more serious restrictions than mere requests or orders issued by the police or a court to journalists so that they directly reveal the identity of their sources. As the ECtHR states in *Ressiot and others v. France*[20] these investigations give police and courts access to all the data and information protected by secrecy that journalists hold. Therefore, a very strict analytical test must be applied.[21]

As far back as the case of *Ozgür Gündem v. Turkey*,[22] the ECtHR deemed the measure of seizing the files, documents, and library of a newspaper disproportionate. And Principle 7 COE, Recommendation No. R (2000) 7 indicates that secrecy is a guarantee against indiscriminate access to such data by searches, controls, seizures, confiscations, phone tapping, and so on.

These guarantees are increasingly important when it comes to the use of new technologies by both journalists and their sources. In the twenty-first century, national security legislation and blanket and selective surveillance have become increasingly important. Journalists' confidential communications are frequently caught in mass surveillance "networks." Surveillance is "eroding," "compromising," and "undercutting" traditional guarantees (Posetti 2017 and Posetti, Dreyfus, and Colvin 2019).

In addition to protecting access to journalists' data, information, and sources with these strong guarantees, the aim is to mitigate or eliminate a chilling effect Puerto Olga, C. (1992) that is, to avoid a situation where sources, knowing that they may be subject to searches and investigations, refrain from leaking information into the public domain. Similarly, the intention is to prevent journalists from feeling inhibited or afraid as they go about their work. That is why it is necessary to be very restrictive even with the possibility that investigations are carried out, even though in the end, the journalist has not been registered or tracked down: "While it is true that no search or seizure took place in the present case, the Court emphasizes that a chilling effect will arise wherever journalists are seen to assist in the identification of anonymous sources" (*Sanoma II, Sanoma Uitgevers B.V. v. The Netherlands*,[23] para. 71 and *Financial Times Ltd and others v. the UK*, para. 70).

For these guarantees to apply, it is not necessary to fully prove that the purpose of the search and seizure was to find out the identity of the source. It is sufficient that such measures, due to the broad, vague, or indiscriminate way in which they were authorized or executed, did not exclude such a possibility (ECtHR, Saint-Paul Luxembourg)[24] of ascertaining the identity of the source in question or, even, those of the journalist's other sources (ECtHR Case *Nagla v. Latvia*).

In addition to preventions against indiscriminate surveillance, guarantees are stronger if electronic surveillance is selective and specific with respect to journalists and their sources. These investigations are only justified by an "overriding requirement in the public interest."

In the case of *Big Brother Watch and others v. UK*,[25] the surveillance system that was analyzed did have special guarantees and requirements regarding investigations and selective searches pertaining to a journalistic source. However, it was understood that there was a violation of Article 10 ECHR because the system did not extend these special guarantees to other

---

[20] *Ressiot and others v. France*, June 28, 2012.

[21] Along these lines, ECtHR cases Röemen, February 25, 2003; *Ernst and others v. Belgium*, July 15 2003; and *Nagla v. Latvia*, July 16, 2013.

[22] *Ozgür Gündem v. Turkey*, March 16, 2000.

[23] *Sanoma Uitgevers B.V. v. The Netherlands*, September 14, 2010.

[24] Saint-Paul Luxembourg, April, 18, 2013.

[25] *Big Brother Watch and others v. UK*, September 13, 2018.

collateral intrusions of access to the journalist's communications data. The Grand Chamber's decision is pending.

In the United States, the issue of investigations and searches targeting journalists and their sources is worrying. Since 2015, there have been special requirements when it comes to investigations undertaken by the Department of Justice.[26] It is necessary to "consult with the Criminal Division" before the investigation, and there are stipulations that the information was sought through alternative means and that negotiations with the journalist have been initiated, in addition to the fact that the information sought is "essential." However, the scope of these guarantees is very limited: agencies other than the Department of Justice are not subject to the obligation, and the requirements do not apply to data collection and investigations based on other laws. And it has been pointed out that the wide range of legal mechanisms available for surveillance is "overwhelming" (Posetti 2017, p. 21). Thus, the applicable regulations linked to national security can be very varied: the FISA Amendments Act of 2008, the amended program of Section 215.3, or Executive Order 12333 may apply. This is having a chilling effect that has been denounced in reports issued by PEN America (2015), Human Rights Watch, and the ACLU (2014).

## Technological Training and Measures and the Growth of Collaborative Activism

In the face of indiscriminate and selective surveillance of journalists and their sources, of increasing importance is "digital defense" and the use of encryption (Perugia Principle 5), awareness of the risks run by journalists and their sources, greater knowledge, and technological training.

Likewise, risks must be explained to the source (Perugia Principle 7). It is necessary to ensure that communications are secure and that encryption systems are used. This entails not only training but also costs (Posetti 2017, pp. 2, 8; see also pp. 103 et seq.) and secure deletion of data (Perugia Principle 9). The Perugia principles even recommend the possibility of "going back to analogue methods" to ensure sources are protected (Perugia Principle 4).

It is very important to point out that encryption systems, security tools, secure mailboxes, and guarantees of technological anonymity are becoming increasingly important (Perugia Principle 10). UNESCO has provided important information to journalists (Henrichsen, Lizosky, and Betz 2015). And, in particular, it is necessary to underline the important joint initiatives undertaken by the media and NGOs concerning tools to ensure source anonymity and vetting. The Government Accountability Project (2017) stands out in this regard, as do, especially, the activities undertaken and technologies developed collaboratively by the Whistleblowing International Network (https://whistleblowingnetwork.org/Home); Global Investigative Journalism Network (https://gijn.org); Associated Whistleblowing Press (www.awp.is); Hermes Center for Transparency and Digital Human Rights (https://www.globaleaks.org and https://www.hermescenter.org); and Free Press Unlimited (https://www.freepressunlimited.org). These associations and consortia work collaboratively with hundreds of nongovernmental organizations (NGO) and media outlets. They provide technological tools to allow communication with whistleblowers and the disclosure of public information.

---

[26] Department of Justice (2015). Annual report. Department of Justice Use of Certain Law Enforcement Tools to Obtain Information from, or Records of, Members of the News Media; and Questioning, Arresting, or Charging Members of the News Media, https://www.justice.gov/criminal/file/888316/download (accessed January 15, 2021). Office of the Attorney General (2015). *Memorandum to all Department employees*, January 14. http://www.justice.gov/file/317831/download (accessed January 15, 2021).

So that journalists and their sources are aware of possible surveillance, it is also important for there to be transparency about mass surveillance carried out by states or private actors. Unfortunately, and on different scales, cases such as Snowden or Cambridge Analytica do happen. In this regard, in the ECtHR case *Youth Initiative for Human Rights v. Serbia*[27] it was held that it was a matter of public interest and mandatory to provide information on people subjected to technological surveillance by the Serbian intelligence services. Failure to provide this information prevented the NGO from exercising a watchdog role.

## Journalists' Requirements Regarding Diligence and Limits to the Right

### Diligence and Public Interest Requirements and the Need to Disclose the Source to Demonstrate Diligence

The journalist's right is conditioned by diligence and vetting of the truthfulness of the information provided by sources, as well as by analysis of the information's relevance or public interest (Moretón Toquero 2014; cf. Fernández Miranda Campoamor 1990). As Perugia Principle 4 states, the material and its public interest should be verified, and documents and datasets should be published in their entirety if possible.

The journalist must be diligent and act in good faith, publishing reliable and accurate information and respecting journalistic ethics.[28] The need for "accurate and reliable information" is recalled in *Sanoma II Uitgevers B.V.*, para. 50; *Weber and Saravia*, para. 143; *Goodwin*, cited previously, para. 39; *Roemen and Schmit v. Luxembourg*, para. 46, and *Big Brother Watch and others v. the UK*, September 13, 2018 (para. 487).

The right not to reveal sources does not protect journalists if they are ones who commit illegal acts and crimes to obtain information, such as when they illegally intercept communications (ECtHR case, *Brambilla and other v. Italy*[29]). Such acts are not protected by freedom of expression. The right to protection of sources is also different from the limits of investigative journalism and the exclusion of the protection of ECHR Article 10 with respect to hidden or deceitful recordings made of people who have an expectation of confidentiality, as the ECtHR has pointed out in various rulings.[30]

Notwithstanding the above, journalists do not have to disclose their sources, even if the sources – not the journalist – have committed crimes by obtaining secrets or confidential materials. The journalist is protected even if their sources acted in bad faith and have been pursued by the police and the courts as a result. This possible illegality or bad faith does not affect the journalist's right.

A controversial issue arises when the journalist must reveal a source to prove diligence and truthfulness. If possible, the journalist must use other sources, evidence, and objective data to verify the veracity of the information, without compromising a source. However, that may be insufficient (Moretón Toquero 2012; Navas-Sánchez 2019, p. 10). In these cases, the journalist must choose between identifying a source to avoid being convicted and accepting the punishment imposed for not being able to demonstrate the truthfulness of the facts reported (Pradera 1994).

---

[27] *Youth Initiative for Human Rights v. Serbia*, June 25, 2013.

[28] *Fressoz and Roire v. France*, January 21, 1999; Navas-Sánchez (2019, p. 9).

[29] *Brambilla and other v. Italy*, September 23, 2016.

[30] Among others, *Haldimann v. Switzerland*, February 24, 2015; *Bremner v. Turkey*, October 13, 2015, and *Alfha Doryforiki v. Greece*, February 22, 2018.

The ECtHR has not offered a clear answer regarding these situations. In *Stângu and Scutelnicu v. Romania*,[31] para. 52, the ECtHR requires journalists to provide a solid factual basis for the prosecuted allegations, though this does not imply an obligation to disclose the names of the people who had provided the information used as a basis for writing their article.

### This Right is only very Exceptionally Limited and has Judicial Guarantees

The right to secrecy is a right that can be limited. However, for a journalist to be obliged to reveal sources or for searches and selective investigations to be a possibility, a very strict level of analysis and scrutiny must be passed. Since *Goodwin v. UK*,[32] March 27, 1996 (para. 39), the ECtHR has affirmed that "such a measure cannot be compatible with Article 10 of the Convention unless it is justified by an overriding requirement in the public interest."

This highly restrictive scrutiny or test must be carried out by a judicial or independent authority. Judicial oversight cannot be merely formal, and a severe analysis of all the interests involved must take place (*Görmüs et al. v. Turkey*[33]). The ECtHR strongly emphasizes that to limit this right there must be no alternative; it must be the only possible means available. And it is up to the authorities, and not the journalist, to demonstrate the absence of these other alternatives or their ineffectiveness. Exceptions to this right are limited to crimes of special gravity and involve situations in which the testimony or information required from the journalist is absolutely essential for the establishment of the truth during proceedings.

In addition, analysis by a court or by an independent authority must be prior to the investigations and seizure or search of documents, materials, instruments, and communications.[34]

Only for justified reasons of urgency could an investigation without prior judicial review be warranted. But there must be a procedure to identify and isolate the material subject to a search so that, until a judicial decision has been made, the data and evidence cannot be effectively accessed by the authorities (ECtHR Case *Sanoma II*;[35] Navas-Sánchez 2019, p. 8).

## Journalists and Other Subjects Who Have the Right and Those Under an Obligation

The right to secrecy and not to reveal sources was initially recognized vis-à-vis journalists and, in some regulations, journalism "professionals." However, it is becoming increasingly difficult to determine who such people are. It is at least clear that it is not possible to require registration or a license to practice journalism and, therefore, to have this right.

In any case, as I have already indicated, this right is an instrument and guarantee of communication rights and not a privilege. That is why there has clearly been some momentum when it has come to recognizing this right not only in the case of journalists but in that of different types of democracy-guarding watchdog – for example, leaders of social networks, NGOs, and individuals who investigate matters of public interest. As UNESCO states (Posetti 2017, p. 136), "Broadening the legal definition of 'journalist' … is desirable."

[31] *Stângu and Scutelnicu v. Romania*, January 31, 2006.
[32] *Goodwin v. UK*, March 27, 1996.
[33] *Görmüs et al. v. Turkey*, January 19, 2016.
[34] *Sanoma II*, September 14, 2010, para. 90–92; *Nagla v. Latvia*, July 16, 2013.
[35] *Sanoma II*, September 14, 2010.

It should be remembered that this expansion of the subjects' right of access to information has occurred little by little. That said, the UN has taken different positions on whether it recognizes the right vis-à-vis "every member of the public" or only a few qualified individuals who are recognized as journalists.[36] More clearly, in the Ibero-American sphere, the right of access to information is recognized for all, especially since the case of *Claude Reyes et al. v. Chile*, September 19, 2006.[37]

Since 1985, in more than 150 rulings,[38] the ECtHR has affirmed the importance of the role played by democracy-guarding watchdogs against abuses of power. Initially, reference was made to the media. However, the range of persons has been expanding in recent years. In the ECtHR case *Magyar Helsinki Bizottság v. Hungary*,[39] it was stated that the special protection of Article 10 ECHR "is not limited to the press but may also be exercised by, among others, non-governmental organisations" (para. 166). The status "also extends to academic researchers and authors of literature on matters of public concern. The Court would also note that, given the important role played by the Internet in enhancing the public's access to news and facilitating the dissemination of information, the function of bloggers and popular users of the social media may also be assimilated to that of 'public watchdogs'" (para. 168).

More than looking at the status of the person concerned, the key is the information of public interest that is disseminated in the context of secrecy and the right not to reveal the sources. Today, the focus is more on the "identification of 'acts of journalism,' rather than occupational or professional descriptors" (Posetti 2017, p. 136). In the same vein, Ugland (2008) has affirmed that the US Supreme Court should adopt a definition of the press that focuses on the functions that it performs and not on the identity or characteristics of those who perform those functions. As Chief Justice Burger wrote: "The First Amendment does not 'belong' to any definable category of persons or entities: it belongs to all who exercise its freedoms" (*First Nat'l Bank v. Bellotti*,[40] 435 US 765, 802 [1978] [Burger, C.J., concurring]).

Regarding subjects who are bound, the right to secrecy and not to disclose sources, obliges the public authorities, the police, courts, parliamentary commissions, and other public bodies that ask a journalist to identify their sources. They cannot impose burdens or restrictions if the journalist refuses to do so.

In principle, it is a right against everyone, including individuals. However, whether the right is able to protect the journalist against the editor of the media outlet, other hierarchical superiors, coworkers, and so on is a debatable and controversial issue. The workplace context can make this guarantee especially difficult (Fernández Miranda Campoamor 1990, p. 44; Escobar Roca 2002, p. 214).

---

[36]Thus, the English version (no. 44) of the "UN norms" recognizes the right of "all members of the public" (Report of the Special Rapporteur on the promotion and protection of the right to freedom of opinion and expression, UN Doc. E/CN.4/2000/63, January 18, 2000). The same thing can be found in Ibero-American or African declarations. However, the HRC General Comment No. 34 of 2011 states that access to public information is given to the media so that it can provide the results of the committee's activity to the public (UN General Comment No. 34, 2011, no. 18). However, the right extends to other persons who have special ties to oversight and surveillance of the public authorities, such as authors who publish on the Internet (No. 44) or associations defending human rights (UN HRC Communication No. 1470/2006, 28 of March 2011, *Nurbek Toktakunov vs. Kyrgyzstan* (particularly para. 6.3 and 7)).

[37]Inter-American Court. Case *Claude Reyes et al. v. Chile*, September 19, 2006. Available at https://www.corteidh.or.cr/docs/casos/articulos/seriec_151_ing.pdf (accessed January 15, 2021).

[38]Since *Barthold vs. Germany*, March 25, 1985, and *Lingens v. Austria*, July 8, 1986.

[39]*Magyar Helsinki Bizottság v. Hungary*, November 8, 2016.

[40]*First Nat'l Bank v. Bellotti*, 435 US 765, 802 (1978) (Burger, C.J., concurring).

The right also places an obligation on those who want to undertake searches, interceptions of communications, and investigations of journalists. They must comply with legal requirements. In this sense, communications operators, intermediaries, and platforms from which data are requested, must be aware of the special guarantees emanating from this right.

## The Protection of Sources and Whistleblowers when they Directly Disclose Information into the Public Domain

As Perugia Principle 7 states, whistleblowers and informants are a subset of confidential journalistic sources, though not all of them seek to involve the media in their attempts to reveal information of public interest, and nor do they all require confidentiality.

In recent years, regulation regarding and protection of whistleblowers and the like who leak or reveal information as a way of warning of illegal activity have become more and more important. The ECtHR has gradually recognized the protection of these sources (Bychawska-Siniarska 2017, pp. 102–107) since *Guja v. Moldova*,[41] para. 72. It repeated this recognition in *Heinisch v. Germany,* July 21, 2011. In *Matúz v. Hungary*,[42] the ECtHR recognized the need to protect a public disclosure that was made directly – without internal complaints or ones to the relevant institutions – because it was considered that this was an appropriate measure "for want of any effective alternative channel."

Recommendation CM Rec (2014) 7 of April 30, 2014, by the Committee of Ministers, on the protection of whistleblowers, has been very important in stimulating regulation in many countries in Europe.[43] In any case, mention must be made of Directive (EU) 2019/1937 of the European Parliament and of the Council of October 23, 2019, on the protection of persons who report breaches of Union law.[44] This directive must be transposed into the internal legislation of all states before December 17, 2021.

Its Recital 31 states that "persons who report information about threats or harm to the public interest obtained in the context of their work-related activities make use of their right to freedom of expression." It also asserts that "Whistleblowers are, in particular, important sources for investigative journalists. Providing effective protection to whistleblowers from retaliation increases legal certainty for potential whistleblowers and thereby encourages whistleblowing also through the media. In this respect, protection of whistleblowers as journalistic sources is crucial for safeguarding the 'watchdog' role of investigative journalism in democratic societies" (Recital 46).

Despite the above, the protection that this Directive gives to whistleblowers (Art. 15) "shall not apply" if there are "specific national provisions" to protect communication rights for those who disclose information directly to the press. This is certainly strange, and it can be explained by the fact that the Directive, in theory, does not regulate freedom of expression, a properly constitutional matter of states.

What is relevant here is that the Directive offers a structure of three subsidiary steps: the internal complaint in the organization, the external complaint to the competent institutions, and, ultimately, the "public disclosure," that is, "to persons who make such information

[41] *Guja v. Moldova*, February 12, 2008.

[42] *Matúz v. Hungary*, October 21, 2014.

[43] EU Council (2014). *EU Human Rights Guidelines on Freedom of Expression*, Foreign Affairs meeting Brussels, on May 12, 2014, http://www.consilium.europa.eu/uedocs/cms_data/docs/pressdata/EN/foraff/142549.pdf (accessed January 15, 2021).

[44] https://eur-lex.europa.eu/legal-content/en/TXT/?uri = CELEX%3A32019L1937.

available in the public domain, for instance, directly to the public through online platforms or social media, or to the media, elected officials, civil society organisations, trade unions, or professional and business organisations" (Recital 45). "Public disclosure" or "to publicly disclose" are defined as "the making of information on breaches available in the public domain" (Art. 5.6). Regulation of this is contained in Article 15. Direct public disclosure is the last option: "The reporting person should be able to choose the most appropriate reporting channel depending on the individual circumstances of the case" (Recital 33).

The reporting person or whistleblower will be protected if they "has reasonable grounds to believe that: (i) the breach may constitute an imminent or manifest danger to the public interest, such as where there is an emergency situation or a risk of irreversible damage; or (ii) in the case of external reporting, there is a risk of retaliation or there is a low prospect of the breach being effectively addressed, due to the particular circumstances of the case, such as those where evidence may be concealed or destroyed or where an authority may be in collusion with the perpetrator of the breach or involved in the breach."

As Recital 82 states, it is necessary to guarantee "the confidentiality of the identity of the reporting person during the reporting process and investigations triggered by the report." The identity should only be disclosed "to safeguard the rights of defence of persons concerned." However, confidentiality will not be guaranteed if the reporting person has revealed their identity intentionally.

The Directive regulates the "immunity" (Recital 92) of the person who discloses information, if "the reporting person had reasonable grounds to believe that reporting or public disclosure was necessary." The exemption does not extend to the disclosure of "superfluous" information (Recital 91). It is affirmed that there will be liability under national law for those who have made disclosures "not necessary for revealing a breach" (Art. 21.4).

The Directive affirms that there must be exemption and legal immunity when access to information and its disclosure is illegal under civil, administrative, or employment law. However, if obtaining or disclosing information is a criminal offense, protection of the source will depend on the legislation of each state (Art. 21.3). There must also be protection if the disclosure affects trade secrets.[45]

In addition, there is a requirement for the reporting person to have analyzed the information to ascertain that it is true. The reporting person must have "reasonable grounds to believe that the information on breaches reported was true" (requirement for protection, Art. 6.1). Similarly, the reporting person may be penalized and could have to pay compensation if he or she deliberately leaked inaccurate or misleading information. The "public disclosure of inaccurate or misleading information" generates a right to compensation under national law. And there may be sanctions "where such inaccurate or misleading information was reported or publicly disclosed deliberately and knowingly" (Recital 101, see Art. 23.2,)

## Conclusions

In this chapter, I have described the highly significant process of regulating the right to secrecy and the right not to disclose information sources at the international, regional, and national levels. Since the 1996 Goodwin case before the ECtHR, Europe has perhaps been the place where there has been the most developed recognition of this guarantee. Since then, around 20 rulings have distilled and specified a clear legal regime, with strong and concrete guarantees. These rulings have been assimilated by the different European states, as well as by other international declarations that, though not binding, are very influential. Beyond the law, the

[45] See especially Recitals 97 and 98.

Perugia Principles are entirely relevant and mark the path forward. In various regions of the world and in many states, the protection of this right must continue to be implemented as an integral part of communication rights. And this necessary regulation must also be adapted and updated to meet new challenges.

Secrecy of sources enjoys a special and strong protection, which implies the application of a very strict test to possible limitations on it. Likewise, it implies a guarantee of the competent body, which can only be a court or, where appropriate, an independent authority that authorizes an intervening over or restriction of this right when there are very good reasons to do so. The substance of this right entails the refusal to reveal sources when requested by the public authorities to do so. As has been said today, in legal terms, we now speak essentially of a right and not of a duty, despite the fact that ethically and professionally an obligatory nature is stressed. On the other hand, the scope and types of information that should not be disclosed have to be interpreted very broadly.

Today, the true guarantee is no longer the right not to reveal sources if the journalist is asked to do so. Now, the key is that sources cannot be discovered or hacked via blanket or selective intercepts of communication undertaken using the Internet. Certainly, technological developments and the protection of public and national security have put this right at risk. In any case, the right has been updated against these new threats.

Another legal challenge is whether this right is going to be extended to all democracy-guarding watchdogs, or even to all those who divulge information of public interest. The trend clearly must be in that direction. However, this generalization or extension of the right must involve some precautions to avoid abuses of it or fraud. It should be recalled in this regard that this right does not protect a lack of professionalism or diligence, and it does not protect people who commit unlawful acts to obtain information if they are journalists or other kinds of communication professionals. It is also striking that we are in the process of giving protection not only to journalists and social communicators, but also directly to sources. In this sense, the European Union's recent Whistleblower Protection Directive is especially pertinent. In the coming years, we will witness, on the one hand, a clear momentum that facilitates the flow of information of public relevance, by protecting both journalists and their sources. But on the other hand, the risk of mass or selective surveillance on the Internet may work in the opposite direction and be a brake on the flow of information. We must get behind the first, most positive momentum in favor of democracy.

## References


Banisar, D. (2007). Silencing sources: an international survey of protections and threats to journalists' sources. Privacy International Global Survey Series. https://ssrn.com/abstract=1706688 (accessed September 16, 2020).

Bychawska-Siniarska, D. (2017). *Protecting the Right to Freedom of Expression under the European Convention on Human Rights - A Handbook for Legal Practitioners.* Council of Europe. https://edoc.coe.int/en/fundamental-freedoms/7425-protecting-the-right-tofreedom-of-expression-under-the-european-convention-on-human-rightsa-handbook-for-legal-practitioners.html (accessed September 16, 2020).

Chocarro, S. (2017a). *Guía básica para operadores de justicia en América Latina.* Center for International Media Assistance National Endowment for Democracy. https://www.cima.ned.org/publication/estandaresinternacionales-de-libertad-de-expresion-guia-basica-para-operadores-dejusticia-en-america-latina (accessed September 16, 2020).

Chocarro, S. (2017b). *Caja de herramientas para escuelas judiciales iberoamericanas: formación de formadores en libertad de expresión, acceso a la información y seguridad de periodistas.* UNESCO y Red Iberoamericana de Escuelas Judiciales (RIAEJ). https://unesdoc.unesco.org/ark:/48223/pf0000251593 (accessed September 16, 2020).

COE (2000). Recommendation No. R (2000) 7 of the Committee of Ministers to member states on the right of journalists not to disclose their sources of information, 8 March. https://www.coe.int/en/web/freedom-expression/committee-of-ministers-adopted-texts/-/asset_publisher/aDXmrol0vvsU/content/recommendation-no-r-2000-7-of-the-committee-of-ministers-to-member-states-on-the-right-of-journalists-not-to-disclose-their-sources-of-information?_101_INSTANCE_aDXmrol0vvsU_viewMode=view (accessed October 7, 2020).

ECtHR, Research Division (2011). *Internet: Case-Law of the European Court of Human Rights. Council of Europe/European Court of Human Rights.* June 2015. https://www.echr.coe.int/Documents/Research_report_internet_ENG.pdf (accessed Septemberv 16, 2020).

Escobar Roca, G. (2002). *Estatuto de los periodistas.* Madrid: Tecnos.

Fernández-Miranda Campoamor, A. (1990). *El secreto profesional de los informadores.* Madrid: Tecnos.

Government Accountability Project (2017). *Working with Whistleblowers: A Handbook for Journalists.* https://www.whistleblower.org/wp-content/uploads/2017/11/whistleblowerguidejournalism.pdf (accessed September 16, 2020).

Henrichsen, J., Lizosky, J., and Betz, M. (2015). *Building Digital Safety for Journalists.* Paris: UNESCO.

Human Rights Watch and ACLU (2014). *With Liberty to Monitor All: How Large-Scale US Surveillance is Harming Journalism, Law and American Democracy.* https://www.hrw.org/report/2014/07/28/liberty-monitor-all/how-large-scale-us-surveillance-harming-journalism-law-and

International Federation of Journalists (1954). *Bordeaux Declaration.* https://research.uta.fi/ethicnet/country/ifj-declaration-of-principles-on-theconduct-of-journalists (accessed October 7, 2020).

Lazkano Brotóns, I. (2004). *La protección de las fuentes periodísticas en el sistema europeo de derechos humanos. Zer: Revista de estudios de comunicación.* https://www.ehu.eus/ojs/index.php/Zer/article/download/5317/5173 (accessed September 16, 2020).

Mörä, T. and Korpisaari, P. (2012). Reporter's privilege in the era of the Internet. https://ssrn.com/abstract=2031491 (accessed September 16, 2020)

Moretón Toquero, A. (2004). El secreto profesional de los periodistas y la empresa de comunicación: ¿un conflicto de lealtades? *Revista Jurídica de Castilla y León* 4: 99–146.

Moretón Toquero, A. (2012). *El secreto profesional de los periodistas: de deber ético a derecho fundamental. Centro de Estudios Políticos y Constitucionales (España).* https://recyt.fecyt.es/index.php/doxacom/article/view/36066 (accessed September 16, 2020).

Moretón Toquero, A. (2014). La protección de las fuentes de información: la integración del modelo español con la jurisprudencia del TEDH. *Estudios de Deusto: revista de la Universidad de Deusto* 62 (2): 121–144.

Navas-Sánchez, M.M. (2019). Libertad de prensa y derecho de los periodistas a mantener la confidencialidad de sus fuentes de información. *El profesional de la información* 28 (4). http://www.elprofesionaldelainformacion.com/contenidos/2019/jul/navas.pdf (accessed September 16, 2020).

PEN América (2015). Global chilling: the impact of mass surveillance on international writers. https://pen.org/research-resources/global-chilling (accessed 16 September 2020).

Posetti, J. (2017). *Protecting Journalism Sources in the Digital Age.* Paris: UNESCO.

Posetti, J., Dreyfus, S., and Colvin, N. (2019). *The Perugia Principles for Journalists. Working with Whistleblowers in the Digital Age.* https://www.blueprintforfreespeech.net/en/news/blueprint-launches-perugia-principles-for-journalists-working-with-whistleblowers-in-the-digital-age

Pradera, J. (1994). La cláusula de conciencia y el secreto profesional de los periodistas. en AA.VV. Debate, Centro de Estudios Constitucionales in Madrid, Spain (24 de enero de 1994).

Puerto Olga, C. (1992). When reporters break their promises to sources: towards a workable standard in confidential source/breach of contract cases. *University of Miami Law Review* 47 (2): 501–536.

Ugland, E. (2008). Demarcating the right to gather news: a sequential interpretation of the First Amendment. *Duke Journal of Constitutional Law & Public Policy* 3: 113–189.

# 11

# Addressing the Risks of Harms Caused by Disinformation

## European vs. US Approaches to Testing the Limits of Dignity and Freedom of Expression Online

Divina Frau-Meigs[1]

The advent of social media platforms and their subsequent emergence as a de facto public sphere for the expression of ideas and opinions can be perceived as a double-edged sword for democratic societies. On the one hand, they extend the scope of communication and democratize expression. On the other hand, they extend the scope of disinformation and curtail the integrity of information and of election processes (Morgan 2018). Issues of truth and trust have been the most researched in all sorts of academic fields, from political science to cognitive sciences (Bradshaw and Howard 2018). Much less researched, the issue of harm to the public sphere can be related to the communication category of "harmful content and harmful behaviour" (O'Connell 2005; McGonagle 2007). The most obvious harm has been to freedom of expression and opinion, as disinformation alters the integrity of information, and the quality of the decision-making citizens can derive from their media. But a less obvious risk of harm relates to dignity as disinformation often comes with hate speech, character assassination, racist and ethnic slandering which, in turn, may affect an individual or a group with added segregation, loss of self respect, and reputation torts.

The role of social media platforms like YouTube, Twitter, and Facebook is critical to the considerations about dignity, either in the US marketplace of ideas where the framework is commercial liability or in the European public service paradigm where the right to be informed remains key to social exchanges and cultural identity. In the United States, where most of the global social media platforms were invented and are located, the First Amendment shields the media from the liability for the spread of disinformation, as reconfirmed by Section 230 of the Communications Decency Act of 1996 that gives platforms the status of publishers, not responsible for content. In the EU, Article 10 of the European convention on Human Rights adds "duties and responsibilities … as are prescribed by law and are necessary in a democratic society, in the interests of national security, territorial integrity or public safety, for the prevention of disorder or crime, for the protection of health or morals, for the protection of the reputation or rights of others, for preventing the disclosure of information received in

[1]The author was part of the European Commission High Level Expert Group on online disinformation and of the French High Authority on Communications (CSA) taskforce that audited the platforms on COVID-19 disinformation.

*The Handbook of Communication Rights, Law, and Ethics: Seeking Universality, Equality, Freedom and Dignity,* First Edition. Edited by Loreto Corredoira, Ignacio Bel Mallén, and Rodrigo Cetina Presuel.

confidence, or for maintaining the authority and impartiality of the judiciary" (European Court of Human Rights 1950). In other words, freedom of expression is compounded with social considerations that go under the general umbrella of human dignity.

Neither the United States nor the EU have an Article 1, like the Universal Declaration of Human Rights whose first lines of Preamble state "the recognition of the inherent dignity and of the equal and inalienable rights of all members of the human family is the foundation of freedom, justice and peace in the world." Article 1 also threads together freedom and dignity: "All human beings are born free and equal in dignity and rights. They are endowed with reason and conscience and should act towards one another in a spirit of brotherhood."

Additionally, Article 3 connects it to "life, liberty and security of the person" confirming that it is a right, not a moral notion attached to a specific belief system. So, dignity is not an adjunct to human rights, it is asserted both as a preamble and as the first article, which means that it is supposed to be implemented pragmatically, not just principled (Schachter 1983; Shultziner 2003). Dignity then is not just a normative, moral position that insists on social justice, it is also an operational ethical action that emphasizes autonomy, engagement, and cooperation so as to ascertain the consequences of one's actions in everyday life. Thus, loosely defined, dignity carries with it the values of empowerment and self-development and it can benefit from media freedoms.

As a right, dignity affects all citizens, whatever their political system and it should not be different for online social media and services. Defining such intangible attributes as dignity of self and the integrity of one's persona in mass and social media is not easy (Caulfield and Chapman 2005). It is easier for the law to evaluate loss of property than to evaluate loss of self-esteem. Yet, when dealing with the social media, the intangible assets related to "digital identity," i.e., sharing of data and building one's influence and reputation online, point to ways people build their public and private personas. Dignity then has to do with self-development and freedom, beyond legal parlance (Lash and Featherstone 2002; Frau-Meigs 2011). As Rotenberg puts it, "rights are not services" that can be resolved with mere torts and damages regulation (Rotenberg 2000). The threat lies in the risk that rights that are being protected in the real-world public sphere are being outsourced to private interests in the virtual sphere, that are both judge and party, like Facebook or Google. This will compel individuals to pay for them as services, with disparities between those citizens wealthy enough to obtain extra protection to their privacy and dignity and those who aren't or won't. Hence, the importance in seeing the contributions of the European Union to the debate, especially through the prism of its active mobilization against disinformation, conducive to the drafting of an extensive Action Plan to combat disinformation (EC 2018) that lead to a Code of Practice on disinformation (COP 2018).

What are the new vulnerabilities of dignity in relation to online disinformation? What are the challenges to dignity in the online environment that could affect dignity offline? Who are the people most likely to be perpetrators against dignity and who are the most likely to be hurt by dignity infringements? How do the practices of users affect dignity and how can the social media platforms factor it in the design of their services? How can such practices inform Internet regulation so as to find solutions for harmonized levels of respect for dignity that also preserve freedom of expression, across states or via global governance across nations?

## Characteristics of Disinformation that Affect Dignity: Establishing Potential Risks of Harm to Information

In the case of disinformation, the information-communication perspective focuses both on the producers and their motivations and on how this affects the receivers of such news and the reasons they amplify them, effectively becoming the accomplices of the perpetrators. This mediated dimension is recognized in the definition of disinformation proposed by the High Level Expert Group (HLEG) of the EU that was set up in 2018:

> We define it as false, inaccurate, or misleading information designed, presented and promoted to intentionally cause public harm or for profit. The risk of harm includes threats to democratic political processes and values, which can specifically target a variety of sectors, such as health, science, education, finance and more. It is driven by the production and promotion of disinformation for economic gains or for political or ideological goals, but can be exacerbated by how different audiences and communities receive, engage, and amplify disinformation. (HLEG 2018, p. 11)

The challenge to dignity in media comes from the blend of verified facts with fraudulent, fabricated constructs and with user practices that can be viralized by astroturfing, networks of fake followers, targeted advertising, organized trolling and meme campaigns. "It can also involve a whole array of digital behaviour that is more about circulation of disinformation than about production of disinformation, spanning from posting, commenting, sharing, tweeting and re-tweeting, etc" (HLEG 2018, p. 11).

The definition does not deal with already recognized forms of illegal or harmful content such as defamation, hate speech or incitement to violence or terror, that are covered by EU regulation. It attempts to define a new risk of public harm, to democratic processes and values. And it points to a new sort of "digital behaviour" that relates not only to the actors and producers of such harmful content but to the amplifiers and their practices.

The Data and Society Research Institute proposes a typology of such actors and their intended harms: Internet trolls, gamergaters, hate groups and ideologues, conspiracy theorists, influencers, hyper partisan news outlets, and politicians. Such a typology is useful to determine the type of abuse and the resulting type of harm. It shows that the characteristics of perpetrators are to test the range of what is acceptable or not in society, in terms of dignity and democracy. Their types of abuse are not just psychological or even physical but also political, and most of them are based on "deliberately offensive speech and the desire to create emotional impact in targets" (Marwick and Lewis 2017, p. 5). They act as "bullies" and harass their targets, that tend to be feminists (gamergaters), non whites (hate groups, Internet trolls), migrants (ideologues, conspiracy theorists).

In their attacks on the dignity of the person, these perpetrators and amplifiers tend to claim "free speech," and they rail against political correctness as curtailing their rights. They push for a polarized form of discourse: us vs. them, subterranean affiliations, collusion of interest, and insider machinations. They present themselves as victimized by minorities, feminists, etc. They accuse others of trying to stifle their free speech. They express anxieties related to loss of status, marginalization, and displacement. They are in favor of populism and nationalism and against mainstream media painted as biased against them. They are "united by a hatred of liberalism, feminism and multiculturalism" (Marwick and Lewis 2017, p. 11). Their discursive and psychological actions have real-life consequences as evinced by the "Blue Lives Matter" counter protest to the "Black Lives Matter" rally in Dallas 2016, organized by the "Heart of Texas" Facebook group, allegedly also manipulated by the Internet Research Agency (IRA), a troll farm used by Russia for interference in the US elections of 2016 (Geraghty 2017).

The actors most likely to attack dignity are considered to be part of the alt-right in the United States, and they are also to be found in Europe, with the addition of extreme left elements. In Europe, additional actors are signaled in the research who generate formats of disinformation that include hybrid threats and third-party intervention in democratic processes (Rožukalne 2015; Stratcom 2017). The resulting risks of harm to dignity are likely to have offline consequences like terrorist attacks, anti-Semitic attacks, revenge porn, scapegoating of some minority groups. They too compromise "free speech" and instrumentalize it to serve their attacks on dignity.

Such ambiguity allows them to go under the radar of detection for abuse and harm to dignity. Ambiguity is cultivated to wage infowars and bypass censorship on social media as exemplified by the cases of Alex Jones (founder of YouTube channel InfoWars.com) or Milo Yiannopoulos (contributor to Breitbart News website) whose accounts were eventually banned from Facebook and Twitter. It is also cultivated to enable this loose coalition of perpetrators to dissociate themselves from over-scandalizing issues or figures while maintaining their overall offensive stance (Marwick and Lewis 2017, p. 17). Accordingly, a typology that reflects the cultivation of ambiguity as a strategy can alert us to the issue by focusing on hybrid profiles, typical of harm offenders, that try to cover their tracks and are pure player influencers, born digital: the fan/torch-bearer, the humorist/polemicist, the columnist/launderer, the partisan/extremist, and the troll/informer (Frau-Meigs 2021). They tend to fall under the four categories of online risks or "4Cs": Content (abusive speech), Conduct (bullying and ostracism), Contact (offline solicitations threats), and Consent (commercial or political pressure and laundering of vilifying fakes via social and mass media) (Millwood Hargrave and Livingstone 2006; Frau-Meigs 2011).

Connecting the types of abuse (and their perpetrators) with the attendant types of harm (and their victims) makes it possible to map the risks of harm caused by disinformation to dignity and freedom of speech at the same time (see Table 11.1).

The various 4Cs of disinformation present challenges for certain categories of people at risk in terms of harmful content as they are victimized: women, minorities, the poor, migrants, and immigrants. Their right to dignity as empowerment and self-development can be curtailed and reduced. This can increase the sense of a two-tiered citizenship, where some categories of people are intimidated, as evinced in tactics to prevent minorities to go out and vote in some disinformation strategies during the 2016 presidential campaign in the United States. This goes against dignity and freedom as rights that are egalitarian and people-centered, aiming at social justice and solidarity.

**Table 11.1** Relationship between abuse and resulting harm in the case of disinformation.

| | *Psychological (content)* | *Physical (conduct + contact)* | *Political and commercial (conduct + consent)* |
|---|---|---|---|
| Types of abuse (perpetrator, amplifier) | insult | threat | leaks and gates |
| | stereotype | hack | interference |
| | scapegoating | intimidation | activism |
| | ostracism | bullying | conspiracy |
| | assault on reputation/identity | harrassment | click-bait |
| | ⇩ | ⇩ | ⇩ |
| | Refers to mind | Refers to body | Refers to body politic |
| Types of harm (victim) | fear | violence | destabilization |
| | loss of self-esteem | injuries | polarization |
| | anxiety | self-harm | speculation, hoaxcrash |
| | hate speech | immobility (not voting) | election and market fraud |
| | self-censorship | isolation | blackmail |

## The Role of Mass Media and Social Media: Propaganda, Publicity, and Polarization

Taking advantage of the opportunity the Internet proffers for collaboration, communication, and peer production, these perpetrator groups target vulnerabilities in the news media ecosystem to increase their visibility among and across their closed communities to broadcast their polarized messages. Harmful online content may take many forms with the platforms providing a mix of these types of contents, with users facing different harms in relation to each. This is amplified by the "transverse effect" of disinformation (transborder, transmedia, and translanguages) that is cumulative and changes the scope of harm (Frau-Meigs 2018). The characteristics of the fake news crisis, as generated and amplified by mass and social media, in relation to dignity lie in the increasingly intrusive inroads into privacy and identity, and in the lack of accountability of the various actors involved, including the online platforms.

Mass and social media have greatly benefited from the appeal of "fake news" and particularly the conspiracy theories kind, despite their potential for harm. Among the perpetrators, Danah Boyd counts hyperpartisan networks and politicians themselves, who have propagated opinion or faith-based "news" in a manner that is very difficult to disprove or refute. And such media outlets meet increasingly with elected politicians, such as Donald Trump, Jair Bolsanero, or Vladimir Putin, who promote their warped views as ideologues and white male supremacists without running the risk of being indicted. Trump's Tweets are agenda setting for such mainstream media as Fox News and CNN alike for instance (Vargo, Guo, and Amazeen 2017). Fringe theories have become a full-fledged industry in the United States and Russia, with ramifications in Asia for cheap click-labor that creates "astroturfing," that is the illusion that a whole virtual audience follows and believes in such extremist fake news. Social media hyperpartisans and influencers use this strategy for fake news laundering, as the mainstream media will cover them, because of the buzz and click-bait they generate (Berthier 2017; Wardle and Derakhshan 2017).

Social media also have a vested interest in disinformation as it has become part of their business model. Disinformation has exploded since 2012, date when Facebook and Twitter were incorporated in NASDAQ, the US stock exchange ICTs. They had to prove themselves to their shareholders and bring benefits. The result has been the introduction of advertisement in the newsfeed of Facebook and the upsurge of Audience Network, Facebook's ad agency. Two online ad agencies are left online, in a typical US duopoly, Adsense by Google and Audience Network by Facebook (Frau-Meigs 2019). The capacity to engage audiences and communities, and to have access to metrics of engagement and participation, is what goads the platforms for which increased traffic means profit. This publicity shift, in turn, creates a stronghold on mass media that becomes dependent on social media for their existence and that impairs their capacity to invest in quality verified information. When publicity becomes political advertising, especially during electoral campaigns, the borders become porous with propaganda and may induce extremist groups and third-party threat actors or states to use their influence to derail democratic processes, as witnessed by the tainted US elections of 2016, the Brexit referendum revealed by the Cambridge Analytica scandal or the insurrectionist rioting of the Capitol in January 2021.

As a result, the matrix of disinformation harm organizes itself in two axes: the political communication axis of polarization/radicalization and the commercial communication axis of advertising/propaganda (see Figure 11.1) These two axes show the role of influence by perpetrators (mostly third-party threat actors) on the one hand, and the role of engagement by audiences (including victims) on the other hand (Frau-Meigs 2018).

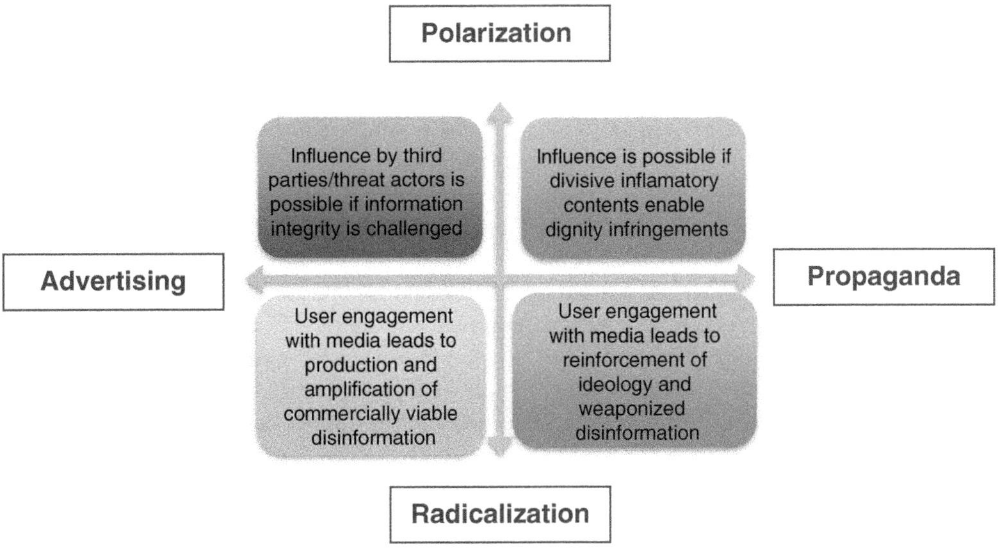


**Figure 11.1** Matrix of disinformation (Frau-Meigs 2021).

Such challenges of influence operations and manipulations in the mass and social media can be related to Article 10, as risks of harm caused by disinformation lodge themselves in all the social dimensions of human dignity considered as "compounding" freedom of expression.

1. The interests of national security, territorial integrity or public safety can be challenged by troll factories in Saint-Petersbug for instance (Kim et al. 2018).
2. The prevention of disorder or crime can be visible in examples such as the Pizzagate that connects Hillary Clintons to child trafficking in Washington, DC.
3. The protection of health or morals is exemplified by the plethora of fake-vax provoking outbreaks of measles in Italy and France (Chiou and Tucker 2018).
4. The protection of the reputation or rights of others takes the shape of deepfakes that portray stars and politicians in compromising situations and enable blackmail and intimidation.
5. The prevention of the disclosure of information received in confidence can be evidenced in cases of revenge porn such as in gamergate case.
6. The maintenance of the authority and impartiality of the judiciary has led to high-level court cases such as *IRA v. USA*, to ascertain that troll factory's role in polarization and destabilization of US public opinion.

The examples considered suggest the need to balance dignity against technological inroads and commercial interests of platforms and fake news business; the need for the protection of human dignity with appropriate regulatory standards; the need to consider ethics of media, old and new, taking a "media as eco system" approach (Frau-Meigs 2011, 2019). This sets into question practices that are contrary to human dignity, like deepfakes that modify the values in the speech of a well-known politician such as Barack Obama (though this deepfake was originally fabricated by University of Washington researchers to raise awareness on the issue). It requires a balancing act between commercial interests in the Internet as a "new free marketplace of ideas" (Pollicino 2019) and the protection of online freedoms as rights are not services (Flew, Martin, and Suzor 2019).

## The Challenges of Finding Proportionate Solutions

An examination of the relationship between abuse and harm (see Table 11.1), combined with the matrix of disinformation (see Figure 11.1), points to several types of measures to protect and promote dignity while not compromising online freedoms, and not recurring to "hard" legislation as it could lead to a *priori and a posteriori* forms of censorship. In democratic perspectives, it is crucial not to collapse all categories and contradictions and to display, as explicitly as possible, the array of solutions that protect and promote dignity. The "soft" approach suggests the promotion of guidelines and codes of conduct and a general plea for transparency as a way of preserving both dignity and freedom of expression and of information. Such a multipronged approach also works with three legal and political checks and balances: accountability, proportionality, and legitimacy, to which revision mechanisms have to be added for real effectiveness.

Accountability, in the case of infringements to dignity by disinformation perpetrators, is associated with the social responsibility of platforms for instance and their legitimacy to function as a de facto public space though they are driven by a commercial business model (Helberger, Pierson, and Poell 2018). It implies identifying accountability gaps that lead to less social justice and more infringements on dignity such as hate speech. Implementing a comprehensive plan of action to build accountability requires a series of steps, such as creating a set of harm and abuse indicators and track their enforcement and infringement (see Table 11.1).

Proportionality applied to disinformation and infringements to dignity focuses on filtering and warning mechanisms and their appropriateness according to the victims' status (youngster, adult, minority ...). Proportionality recognizes that Internet enhances freedoms but also increases the number of risks of harm to dignity. But it is also about the proportionality of limitations and cautions about the intended purpose of filtering, so as to avoid distortion or abuse. So, it is about creating guidelines that take into account the context of diffusion of material and the cultural sensitivity and the diversity while also being age-sensitive and appropriate.

Legitimacy applied to disinformation and infringements to dignity tries to forestall the criticism from freedom of expression fighters (be it alt-right, influencers ...), that filtering or monitoring is just an alibi for legitimizing censorship of all kinds. Legitimacy is predicated on a clear and explicit explanation of how the restrictions taken are in compliance with Article 10 of the European Convention on Human Rights. It protects the risk of censorship with a two-tiered barrier of protection, usually behind a competent national authority, and a review mechanism that is independent. It is often associated with transparency and monitoring mechanisms with civil society oversight.

As a result of such balancing act requirements, the multipronged solutions are distributed across a diversity of actors.

- Self-regulation: fact-checking is the new response of the mass media and social media platforms.
- Regulation: transparency is the main request of the public sector.
- Education: Media and information literacy is fostered to ensure informational resilience in the users and preparedness among the population at large as well as decision-makers in political candidates and parties (Frau-Meigs, 2018).

Such gatekeeping of dignity implies a kind of coregulation, where all actors are involved in governance, with its obligations and reciprocities (UN IGF Dynamic Coalition on Platform Responsibility 2017). "Civil society actors seem to be attributed a triple role: monitor, review, and call upon other sectors when infringement is detected. Public service actors are required to encourage, to promote awareness and to enforce major human rights. The private sector is expected to develop and update services that are consumer-friendly" (Frau-Meigs 2011). It does evince a move away from sanctioning to monitoring and public reviewing, which in itself, is pedagogical!

## Co regulated Self-regulation: The EU Approach with the Code of Practice on Online Disinformation

The elaboration of the EU Code of Practice is an unheard-of attempt to apply just such principles to disinformation, with a multistakeholder strategy. The European Commission has been dealing with its own balancing act with four overarching principles: transparency, diversity of information, credibility of information, and cooperation. It brought together a taskforce (HLEG) to assess the scope of online disinformation composed of all stakeholders: researchers, media sector, platforms, consumers, and civil society associations. The taskforce came up with a report that advocated for support for media literacy and for fact-checking, supporting dignity with the diversity principle to strengthen quality of information and call attention to the disproportionate power relations between media institutions and social media platforms. It also promoted credibility by requesting the platforms to design solutions to reduce disinformation and implement them in favor of information trustworthiness (HLEG report 2018).

The most striking outcome was the proposal of a Code of Practice (COP) for the platforms that looked for ways to make them aware of the issues related to advertizing, polarization, and integrity of information and integrity of elections, without censoring them. The signatories (Google, Facebook, Twitter, and Mozilla), agreed to be transparent about disinformation, political advertising, and issue-based advertising. The main thrust was thus on the political advertizing part of the disinformation matrix (see Figure 11.1), in the hopes that it would curb polarization and propaganda by third-party states, by draining the political advertising manna. Issue-based advertising in particular was targeted, as an attempt not to curtail freedom of expression but to disclose it publicly so that the users would be aware of the spread of fake news (Nenadić 2019). The platforms consented to it because they feared regulation and they feared their field of activity would be constricted in the European single market (including taxation). They also realized they were not able to moderate on their own issues of hate speech and calls to radical extremism and polarization (Frau-Meigs 2018).

The code of conduct was an exercise in governance, with the plan for setting it up discussed by all stakeholders as well as the monitoring during the implementation. The EU stipulated that "After one year, if self-regulation fails, the creation of a stricter regulation is foreseeable, if a legal basis is found in European Treaties." The EU also set up a revision mechanism, the Sounding Board, composed of a subset of the taskforce to oversee its setting up (Sounding Board 2018).

The overall assessment of the Code's effectiveness took place in 2019–2020. And the mechanism of independent scrutiny was entrusted to the European Regulators Group for Audiovisual Media Services (ERGA). ERGA issued its report in 2019 and it was adopted by the EU in 2020, after considerable evidence was obtained, with 15 progress reports and three EC evaluation reports. Basically, the conclusion expresses mixed results. The report shows progress in the area of dignity and risk of harm, with a new oversight instrument. The creation of a database of political advertizing is a real progress (Leerssen et al. 2019). However, additional layers of transparency and public oversight need to be included. According to ERGA, "the lack of transparency of the platform's internal operations and decision-making processes remains and represents a risk." (ERGA 2019). The weak point for dignity infringements remains "issue-based ads" where the reporting is lacking from most platforms. This impairs the adequate assessment of the implementation, especially as access by researchers and independent parties remains mostly unavailable.

So, the initial conclusions on the "European approach" are that it has successfully created a risk of harm caused by disinformation, identifying key principles and scoping the challenges and their complexities. It has also made significant steps to create a common answer to disinformation, especially by targeting political manipulation by third-threat parties. The EU has also moved to press on the COP, adding other platforms to the signatories (including Chinese TikTok) and asking for analytics for impact evaluation and an iterative process for gathering extra evidence. The secondary and yet important effect of the process has been the collaboration of platforms with government for sharing intelligence if not information. They are able to point to threat actors and disclose their tactics and procedures and take down their websites or accounts (Frau-Meigs 2019). So, influence operations and countermeasures are covered and could help the civil dimension instead of the military one, especially in the area of counternarratives to disinformation.

But this soft European approach faces two constraints: "On the one hand, it faces the power of global platforms shaped in the US tradition which, to a significant extent, differs from the European approach in balancing freedom of expression and data protection. On the other hand, the EU approach confronts the resilience of national political traditions in member states, in particular if the measures are based on recommendations and other soft instruments" (Nenadić 2019).

Effectively, the "US approach" based on free speech is remaining strong and promotes the vision of the Internet as the new marketplace of ideas (Pollicino 2019). It also shields the global platforms behind the Telecommunications Law of 1996 and especially Article 230 of Communications Decency Act of 1996 where the tech companies' status enshrines their total immunity as long as they act "in good faith." If they acted in bad faith, they could become liable to social responsibilities and considered as carriers and lose their current immunity.

The other constraint, the EU national level, has indeed shown resistance. The COP has not prevented some countries like France or Germany from moving to hard regulation. Germany first produced "NetzDG" in 2018, ostensibly to fight hate speech online. France has produced two laws, one on "the manipulation of information during elections" in 2019 and one on "online hate speech" in 2020 (since declared partly unconstitutional). Both country laws have not embedded proportionality, and their legitimacy and implementation has come under very heavy criticism.

But the European approach could be facilitated by a different strategy from the COP and its self- and coregulatory stance. This strategy is inspired by the US approach, with regulatory compliance. Compliance is a regulatory process that ensures that organizations such as the social media platforms conform to some over-arching rules that relate to public interest and are in line with standards or policies to that effect (Frison-Roche 2017). Such an approach could both address the issue of risk of harm caused by disinformation and the issues of the status of the platforms in the process, as they are part of an environment with a prevalence of monopolies that can limit freedom of expression as much as dignity.

## COVID-19 Infodemic: The Litmus Test Toward Compliance Law for Dignity?

While the situation seemed to be at a standstill between European and US approaches, with each power involved in strong-arm tactics, the COVID-19 pandemic crisis of 2020 has provided a litmus test to soft regulation as the platforms have had to deal with an infodemic of fake-vax. They have responded in a manner that makes them liable to compliance regulation, of their own accord. Basically, their response has been, on the one hand, to modify their early design and to use moderation and human intervention in the post design. In both cases, they respond to human dignity as a vital priority as mentioned in Article 10: health and the global common good.

The platforms have adopted various sets of compliance controls to face the infodemic, as revealed during auditions conducted in France during April and May 2020, by the French Conseil Supérieur de l'Audiovisuel (CSA). Among the compliance controls used by social media, a whole series of measures were adopted, as encouraged by the COP: deplatformization, modification of search algorithms, flagging, demonetizing, fact checking, and human moderation. For instance, of its own accord, Facebook decided to support the global health community and to give people access to accurate information and stop misinformation and harmful content.[2]

By doing so, Facebook effectively recognize recognized the existence of "harmful content" and "risk of harm" and the need to curtail it in the name of a higher good: health. But this points to the reality of Facebook becoming an editor and publisher of content not only a distributor. This works if Facebook invokes its social responsibility, "in good faith," because, like media, it obeys to its social obligations and it also works if Facebook is de facto a crucial digital operator in which case, compliance regulation applies.

In the first hypothesis, warnings send the message of solidarity and social responsibility and they create a precedent: what is valid for the COVID infodemic becomes valid for any kind of influence operation and disinformation. The message sent is not neutral because Facebook invites its users to share public resources and to go to news and advice on UN World Health Organization and national public websites. It implies an expected behavior of the user (be careful about fakes) as it did in the past to "get out the vote" and it implies editorial responsibility of the platform.

The second hypothesis, the action of Facebook as a crucial operator, responds to the obligation to combat disinformation as laws against hate speech and against disinformation are in place in many European countries. Facebook obeys a "monumental goal" set by public authorities with public interest at large (Frison-Roche 2017). The social media platform is then free to choose the modalities of its compliance, internally and it has to act ex ante to fight disinformation, not on its own will and good faith, and incidentally, to promote quality information (pushing users toward public providers of health information).

The impact on risk of harm, due to disinformation, is interesting because the social media platforms find themselves proposing affirmative, positive solutions, pointing to verified information, and demonetizing and debunking fake information. The issue of their social responsibility is visible in their choice of solutions, some of them being human and machine-learning moderation. These two hypotheses lead to qualified legal implications, though of a different nature as, in the first case, Facebook becomes a publisher whereas in the second case its status stays within compliance regulation. The mindsets may be different but the results are the same for risk of harm: the implicit-made-explicit recognition of its existence whether the US or European approach.

## Conclusion

In conclusion, it seems that the path is set for detecting and preventing disinformation, which is advocated by compliance regulation and also by several actors in the governance process. Constant vigilance is needed to protect the integrity of information in democratic societies. This supports a culture of accountability and transparency in the public eye, as online expression can lead to detrimental infringements to dignity offline. Global Internet governance will need to accommodate such realities of online/offline reciprocal impact.

---

[2] See https://economictimes.indiatimes.com/news/international/business/covid-19-facebook-scrambles-as-use-soars-in-time-of-isolation/articleshow/74703490.cms (accessed January 15, 2021).

## References


Berthier, T. (2017). *Les 3 F du HoaxCrash: Fausses données, Flash Crash et Forts profits.* Paris: Chaire de Cyberdéfense & Cybersécurité Saint-Cyr.

Bradshaw, S. and Howard, P.N. (2018). Challenging truth and trust: a global inventory of organised social media manipulation. Computational Propaganda Research Project, Oxford Internet Institute. https://comprop.oii.ox.ac.uk/wp-content/uploads/sites/93/2018/07/ct2018.pdf (accessed September 17, 2020).

Caulfield, T. and Chapman, A. (2005). Human dignity as a criterion for science policy. *PLoS Med* 2 (8): e244.

Chiou, L. and Tucker, C.E. (2018). Fake news and advertising on social media: a study of the anti-vaccination movement. Working Paper No. 25223. Cambridge, MA: The National Bureau of Economic Research. https://papers.ssrn.com/sol3/papers.cfm?abstract_id=3209929 (accessed Septemebr 17, 2020).

Code of Practice on Disinformation (2018). https://ec.europa.eu/digital-single-market/en/news/code-practice-disinformation (accessed September 17, 2020).

European Commission (EC). (2018). Action plan against disinformation. European Commission contribution to the European Council. https://ec.europa.eu/commission/sites/beta-political/files/eu-communication-disinformation-euco-05122018_en.pdf (accessed September 17, 2020).

European Court of Human Rights (1950). *European Convention on Human Rights.* https://www.echr.coe.int/Documents/Convention_ENG.pdf (accessed September 17, 2020).

European Regulators Group for Audiovisual Media Services (ERGA) (2019). Report of the activities carried out to assist the European Commission in the intermediate monitoring of the Code of Practice on Disinformation. Slovakia: European Regulators Group for Audiovisual Media Services. http://erga-online.eu/wp-content/uploads/2019/06/ERGA-2019-06_Report-intermediate-monitoring-Code-of-Practice-on-disinformation.pdf?fbclid=IwAR1BZV2xYlJv9nOzYAghxA8AA5q70vYx0VUNnh080WvDD2BfFfWFM3js4wg (accessed September 17, 2020).

Flew, T., Martin, F. and Suzor, N.P. (2019). Internet regulation as media policy: rethinking the question of digital communication platform governance. *Journal of Digital Media and Policy* 10 (1): 33–50.

Frau-Meigs, D. (2011). *Media Matters in the Cultural Contradictions of the Information Society.* Strasbourg: Council of Europe Publishing.

Frau-Meigs, D. (2018). Societal costs of fake news. IPOL, Directorate General for Internal Policies, European Parliament, 1–40. https://www.europarl.europa.eu/RegData/etudes/STUD/2018/626087/IPOL_STU(2018)626087_EN.pdf (accessed January 15, 2021).

Frau-Meigs, D. (2019). *Faut-il avoir peur des "Fake news"?* Paris: Documentation Française.

Frau-Meigs, D. (2021). Les enjeux de la réception: comment mesurer l'influence de la désinformation. In: *Les Guerres de l'information : enjeux politiques et outils techniques* (ed. C. Marangé and M. Quessard). Paris: Presses Universitaires de France.

Frison-Roche, M.-A. (2017). *Tracer les cercles du Droit de la Compliance.* Working Paper. http://mafr.fr/fr/article/le-bon-usage-de-la-compliance (accessed September 17, 2020).

Geraghty, J. (2017). What Russia really wants: a divided, paralyzed America. *National Review.* https://www.nationalreview.com/corner/what-russia-really-wants-divided-paralyzed-america (accessed September 17, 2020).

Helberger, N., Pierson, J., and Poell, T. (2018). Governing online platforms: from contested to cooperative responsibility. *The Information Society* 34 (1):1–14.

High Level Expert Group on Fake News and Online Disinformation (HLEG) (2018). Final report. https://ec.europa.eu/digital-single-market/en/news/final-report-high-level-expert-group-fake-news-and-online-disinformation (accessed September 17, 2020).

Kim, Y.M., Hsu, J., Neiman, D. et al. (2018). The stealth media? groups and targets behind divisive issue campaigns on Facebook. *Political Communication* 35 (4): 515–541.

Lash, S. and Featherstone, M. (eds.) (2002). *Recognition and Difference Politics, Identity, Multiculture.* London: Sage.

Leerssen, P., Ausloos, J., Zarouali, B. et al. (2019). Platform ad archives: promises and pitfalls. *Internet Policy Review* 8 (4). doi: 10.14763/2019.4.1421.

Marwick, A. and Lewis, R. (2017). Media manipulation and disinformation online. Data and Society Research Institute. https://datasociety.net/library/media-manipulation-and-disinfo-online (accessed September 17, 2020).
McGonagle, T. (2007). La protection de la dignité humaine dans le secteur européen de l'audiovisuel. *Iris Plus* 1–8. https://rm.coe.int/16807833e7 (accessed September 17, 2020).
Millwood Hargrave, A. and Livingstone, S. (2006). *Harm and Offence in Media Content: A Review of the Evidence.* Bristol: Intellect.
Morgan, S. (2018). Fake news, disinformation, manipulation and online tactics to undermine democracy. *Journal of Cyber Policy* 3 (1): 39–43.
Nenadić, I. (2019). Unpacking the "European Approach" to tackling challenges of disinformation and political manipulation. *Internet Policy Review* 8 (4): 1–22.
O'Connell, R. (2005). Harmful content. Report prepared for the Council of Europe, Strasbourg. https://rm.coe.int/0900001680926470 (accessed January 15, 2021).
Pollicino, O. (2019). The Internet is a new free marketplace of ideas. *Media Laws EU*, 23–25. http://www.medialaws.eu/wp-content/uploads/2019/05/2.-Pollicino-1.pdf (accessed September 17, 2020).
Rotenberg, M. (2000). *Protecting Human Dignity in the Digital Age.* Paris: Unesco.
Rožukalne, A. (2015). Internet news about Ukraine and the "audience agenda": topics, sources and the audience aggressiveness. *Journalism Research* 8 (1): 17–37.
Schachter, O. (1983).Comment: human dignity as a normative concept. *American Journal of International Law* 77: 848–854.
Shultziner, D. (2003). Human dignity – functions and meanings. *Global Jurist* 3 (3): 16–39.
Sounding Board (2018). The Sounding Board's unanimous Final Opinion on the so-called Code of Practice on 24 September 2018. https://ec.europa.eu/digital-single-market/en/news/code-practice-disinformation (accessed September 17, 2020).
Stratcom (2017). Internet trolling as a tool of hybrid warfare: the case of Latvia. https://www.stratcomcoe.org/download/file/fid/3353 (accessed September 17, 2020).
UN IGF Dynamic Coalition on Platform Responsibility (2017). Platform regulations: how platforms are regulated and how they regulate us. http://bibliotecadigital.fgv.br/dspace/handle/10438/19402 (accessed September 17 2020).
Vargo, C.J., Guo, L., and Amazeen, M.A. (2017). The agenda-setting power of fake news: a big data analysis of the online media landscape from 2014 to 2016. *New Media & Society* 20 (5): 1–22.
Wardle, C. and Derakhshan, H. (2017). Information disorder: toward an interdisciplinary framework for research and policymaking. [Report No. DGI(2017)09]. Strasbourg: Council of Europe. September 17, https://firstdraftnews.org/wp-content/uploads/2017/11/PREMS-162317-GBR-2018-Report-de%CC%81sinformation-1.pdf?x56713 (accessed September 17, 2020).

# 12

# The Law and Ethics of Journalism in a Changing World

## New Professional Realities and Challenges for Communication Professionals

Fernando Gutiérrez Atala

### Introduction: A Profession Under Threat and Turning away from Quality

Analyzed from different perspectives (employment, profession, and representativeness, among others), journalism has been experiencing a deep crisis for several years. It is undergoing clear changes that are altering spaces for creation and exchange between media producers and audiences through different channels and codes (Mogollón and Gutiérrez 2006). This critical moment could be understood as one of the consequences of globalization, which has provoked a crisis of meaning in modern society (Bauman 2000). The media is gradually losing its power as an information provider as a result of social networks and democratizing technology (Chadwick 2013). Its role is being eroded, since information and knowledge cannot be separated from power (Campás 2011).

Journalism, as an activity, has always been sensitive to the social and technological changes with which it is interrelated, and the influence between them is becoming reciprocal. There is sufficient empirical evidence to take the view that we are witnessing a paradoxical situation that, at the very least, is calling journalism's traditional essence into question. In addition to this loss of influence, the current advances in, and deployment, of technology represent a considerable modification in journalism's practices and routines (Almirón and Jarque 2008). Information is becoming abundantly available, and it is circulating in exorbitant quantities, but unfortunately these characteristics do not translate into news of better quality. That is, journalists are failing to appropriate new spaces to generate added value. And, perhaps unknowingly, they are handing over their spaces to the audience (Picard 2009). This can be largely attributed to the new conditions for managing and disseminating information, which stem from technological advances and cultural changes, in which entertainment plays a decisive role (Pellegrini et al. 2011).

In this sense, the turning of news into showbusiness, infotainment, and the media's adaptation to various digital applications have made the quality of journalism one of the key topics in debates about the media in recent decades (Gómez-Mompart and Palau-Sampio 2013). The media is losing credibility (García, Bezunartea, and Rodríguez 2013), and journalism is becoming devalued (Picard 2009).

*The Handbook of Communication Rights, Law, and Ethics: Seeking Universality, Equality, Freedom and Dignity*, First Edition. Edited by Loreto Corredoira, Ignacio Bel Mallén, and Rodrigo Cetina Presuel.

The first studies on this concept were theories based on gatekeeping and newsmaking; in these, guidelines were set out to establish the newsworthiness criteria that make an event attractive to the media and the way in which the news-construction process is conducted (Gutiérrez Coba 2006, p. 31). That said, in the view of Gómez-Mompart and Palau-Sampio (2013), one should speak of "'journalistic quality' rather than 'informative quality,' given that what is of interest is not only the product but the entire information and communication production process."

Another area that is causing a deterioration in journalism's provision of information is social factors. Parreño (2015) considers there to be two causal factors behind the decline in journalistic quality: the ongoing economic crisis of the media sector and adaptation to information and communication technologies. In her opinion, these have directly affected working conditions by causing the generation gap to widen owing to the media's hiring of new, unskilled personnel. She demonstrates how this situation has changed journalistic practice, based on the adaptation of processes and the accelerating sense of immediacy, created by technological evolution. Trying to define or characterize journalistic quality is a complex task, since studying it entails an epistemological difficulty. Yet, at the same time, making this attempt may represent the key to journalism's survival as a service to the citizen and as a democratic space.

What is clear is that the quality of the journalism output offered to the public today is determined by the configuration of broad influences within journalistic production processes, as I will explain later. My starting point here will be the assumption that journalism work should guarantee that changes produced by information technologies in society do not alter citizens' democratic right to receive information that has been prepared based on excellent quality criteria (Parreño 2013).

For Shoemaker and Reese (2014, pp. 8–9), the determining factors that affect the development of journalism practice occur at five levels of influence: (a) individual, in relation to the journalist herself as creator of journalism stories; (b) journalism routines that are established in the profession and, therefore, have tacitly been validated; (c) organizations, based on the decision makers in the media themselves; (d) social institutions that encompass advertisers, audiences, and interest groups; and (e) the system, understood as the social system or societies' ideologies.

Hanitzsch et al. (2010, pp. 11–12), meanwhile, classify these influences according to six dimensions: (a) political, in the form of both political representatives and lobbyists who operate in the political field; (b) economic, relating to the need for advertising as a way of financing media companies; (c) organizational, relating to decision-making processes in the media; (d) procedural, in relation to the time and space limitations with which journalists work; (e) professional, in terms of work practices established according to the profession's cultural conventions; and (f) reference groups, which determine the journalist's work and which comprise both the audience and other diverse actors such as colleagues, friends, or family.

Regardless of the categorization that is used when organizing these conditioning factors, it is essential to bear in mind that the development of influences from a hierarchical level "supposes important distinctions between the levels of analysis and places the individual journalist in a network of organizational and ideological limitations" (Reese 1999, p. 48). Journalists' ideological factors are therefore also limited by institutional constraints, which additionally depend on the social context in which journalists and the media operate.

In the Latin-American context, studying influences on journalistic practice has become a central pillar of academic interests. Through multiple perspectives and different methodological developments, journalists have become fundamental subjects of study when it comes to delving into journalism-production processes.

Accordingly, using the categorization proposed by Oller-Alonso and Meier (2012), studies on systemic influences – for example, the risks involved in journalism practice in Mexico following an increase in violence and the consequences of that violence on news practice (Hughes and Márquez 2017) – have been carried out. There have also been studies of the pressures exerted on journalists by political and various social actors in Argentina, Chile, Colombia, Ecuador, and Mexico (Gutiérrez-Atala et al. 2016) and on the conditioning of journalism's autonomy in Colombia and Mexico by physical threats, overlapping forms of inequality, and clientelism (Hughes et al. 2016).

Lastly, if we turn to studies that concern the journalist's ideology and productive routines, we find research focused on: the role of journalists with reference to the use of digital information tools and their performance, particularly on Twitter (Tandoc, Cabañes, and Cayabyab 2018); the role of women in journalism culture and as a producer of news content in Argentina (Amado 2017); the relationship between journalists and political power, and the restrictions that this sector creates for access to and dissemination of information (Gutiérrez-Atala et al. 2016); and the importance of university-level training for journalists' professional practice in Ecuador, Chile, and Mexico (Gutiérrez-Atala, Domínguez-Panamá, and Odriozola-Chéné 2017).

## Technology, Audiences, and Attacks on Identity: What are Journalists?

Problematizing the journalists' identity, their frames of reference, and their ideas about the impact of their work on the social processes of the community to which they belong is relevant in terms of the meaning of information and what moves subjects to produce and distribute it. In a context of major transformations for the sector, as a result of the incorporation of information technologies, there also seem to be observable changes in the ways in which news services are devised, in the construction of journalists' relationship with citizens, and in ways to intervene in the community – that is, everything sustained in the relationship and direct interaction of people with each other and with organizations, renouncing the mediating role traditionally exercised by the media.

Is journalism a profession with a future? The question is being repeated in view of the media business model, which is currently exhibiting signs of crisis. The ways in which the news is delivered are not subject to innovation and do not seem to fit what the information-consuming public needs, despite the fact that this public is constantly changing and transforming as well as developing new information needs. In view of this situation, and according to Picard (2009), journalists cannot continue delivering news in the way in which they have traditionally been doing or simply rehashing news that has already appeared on other channels. They must contribute something new that adds value.

In this area, new technologies are foreshadowing a fatal end for journalists (Ramonet 2011), since easily accessing or disseminating information is now widespread. Technological changes, the streamlining of the news's production flow, and the use of devices that streamline communication and the flow of news require reflection, as they are necessarily leading to a reordering of routines. In addition, journalists' lack of credibility is applying permanent pressure, since the power exerted by the editorial line over them does not always allow them to publish with absolute freedom. It is important, in this sense, to understand that journalism is a public-interest service and that the democratic system is sustained by it because, generally, the information transmitted by the media is people's only reference when it comes to knowing about what is going on in the world and to making decisions. For De Pablos-Ceollo and Mateos-Martín (2003), "Democracy requires an information system for its citizens that allows: the possibility of comparing different points of view, access to quality information, publicizing of events as opposed to any forms of secrecy, and the most thorough participation possible in collective decision-making procedures."

On the other hand, as Ure and Schwarz (2014, p. 21) point out, "Identity appears to be a source of meaning and motivation for the actions undertaken by social actors. It makes them feel recognized and equal to their peers. Identity, in fact, supposes a certain degree of identification with values and practices, and it serves as a differentiating element in exchanges with other social actors. In terms of the professional field, such identification is reinforced and consolidated by obtaining some measure of satisfaction with what one is doing, from which confidence and a healthy pride in oneself are derived."

In the case of journalism, professional identity is a source in which to find meaning in one's professional and social work. It can be turned to in demotivating times (such as the present moment), since undertaking journalism has historically been associated with little professional training, poor working conditions, media concentration, and pressures on press freedom.

Why pay attention to journalists' self-perception and identity today? Because according to various theoretical positions, journalism appears to be a profession whose social function is under serious threat, and journalists seem to be becoming a practically extinct species. This idea will be contested in the final paragraphs of this text.

Article 19 of the Universal Declaration of Human Rights states, "Everyone has the right to freedom of opinion and expression; this right includes freedom to hold opinions without interference and to seek, receive and impart information and ideas through any media and regardless of frontiers" (Oficina del Alto Comisionado para los Derechos Humanos 2020). As is therefore evident, the subject who holds communication rights is the person herself, the citizen, the public. Until now, the journalist has turned the exercise of this universal right into an activity and a professional duty as a result of society's tacit delegation. But what if that tacit delegation vanished as a result of social pressure and the global impact of phenomena that are damaging journalism's image, such as post-truth and fake news? To what extent can journalism's professional identity be changed? And what, then, is the challenge for the academic world?

As Suárez-Villegas states, a profession is "an institutionalized social practice that assumes a special function in the defense and promotion of fundamental forms of good for the person" (2009, p. 120). This is why reporting alone does not mean one is acting as a journalist; this work also requires one to be aware that one is carrying out a task that entails taking on a responsibility vis-à-vis those at whom the information is directed (Ure and Schwarz 2014, p. 23).

According to Manuel Castells, (2003 quoted in Ure and Schwarz 2014, p. 24), "It is advisable to distinguish the concepts of identity and role. Whereas identities organize meaning, understood as the symbolic identification of the objective of the act, roles organize functions." However, in this case, roles do not refer to the tasks carried out by the journalist to build an informative news item – that is, to journalistic routines – but to the objective that the journalist hopes to achieve vis-à-vis the recipient of the information and, furthermore, society.

## Journalism, Law, and Ethics: An Inextricable Triad

A complex informational scenario such as that currently faced by communicators requires not only high doses of reflection regarding informational function and the constant transformations that it is undergoing, but also a workforce that supports it – that is, sufficient human capital for new times. The situation makes it increasingly necessary to think about a shift toward a journalist with a new profile – one that is multifaceted, diverse, and complex, and, within which, the coupling of ethics and law plays a fundamental role.

Thus, the transformations that the new knowledge society is imposing are translating into modifications not only for journalism as a profession but for each communication professional in particular. In this sense, the key to understanding how the different professional roles are changing is understanding the evolutions mainly brought about by technological advances, evaluating their social consequences, and determining the population's communication needs.

However, defining specific profiles can be a difficult task in periods when the profession faces scenarios that clearly entail multifunctionality. Though journalism, as a discipline, is the subject of debate within the academic world, this discussion has not managed to move into the social sphere, so it cannot be taken for granted with a deep critical sense, which is why the different conceptual approaches fail to offer something that balances theory and practice (Deuze 2005). In this sense, there is an urgency to explore a new concept that is a meeting point between these two spheres, analyzing and planning them based on new social, cultural, and economic realities, which will give rise to a transformation in ways of thinking about this profession and of doing journalism.

In the case of journalists, it will only be possible to fulfill the profession's fundamental role if those who claim to be professionals have special training, skills, and judgment, as well as a high level of ethical responsibility, which also means that ethical training is necessary. All this would be a foundation that allows them to be understood and acknowledged by the community that they are part of, with the cognitive, normative, and sociological-construction capacities of the work that they perform (Singer 2003). Obviously, there is still work to be done.

In this context, the reflective proposals offered in this text aim to afford a leading role to professional-training institutions, owing to the direct relationship that they have with journalists' current circumstances. However, this role does not necessarily indicate a limitation in news offerings (since the market itself should regulate the levels of saturation within the profession) but rather an intervention from the social perspective – that is, to establish the bases for greater coherence between the professionalization of journalism as an activity and the true possibilities of undertaking it in today's society. In other words, there ought to be a redefinition of the professional profile so that ethical and legal perspectives occupy an elemental role.

Having properly trained journalists goes far beyond their being technically proficient. It is an ethical necessity that requires urgent attention and reflection. What Desantes proposed (1994) is tangible proof of this, since he predicted the present by postulating that, as a derivation of universal communication rights, the tree of professional duties would continue to grow and develop new branches according to the new connections that the work of information provision produced. Therefore, there is an urgent need to recover journalism's humanistic perspective, giving a deserved place to the so-called evaluative disciplines deserve within curricula – disciplines that make the future professional capable of appreciating human acts and weighing them up with reference to the information that is produced for the public (Aguirre 1998).

Almost three decades ago, Soria (1991) pointed out that there are historical reasons for ethical needs in relation to journalists. One of these reasons is identity and professional competence, in the sense that reporters' responsibility lies in their identification with the purposes of news. The communication professional possesses a cultural professionalism – that is, one that goes beyond the merely technical or political. Accordingly, the profession, by assuming some of the discipline required itself, shelters itself from external intervention, which may run the risk of being inappropriate or excessive for the freedom that is required in the news environment. For this reason, journalists need to view their profession with a certain perspective, to go deeper into the social responsibility that they have voluntarily assumed, and to approach this issue more positively, with a little more conviction.

Subjects such as ethics and law are therefore the sound foundation on which other knowledge rests, and they must be as central as technology, languages, or journalism genres, which overstate technical knowledge. The capacity for appropriately assessing shapes a suitable environment for recognizing in the appropriate and pertinent training not only a desirable situation, but a duty that cannot be ignored by the professional reporter, according to the social role that journalism work has. After all, as Desantes (1994) said, social communication is too serious to leave to dilettantism, improvisation, or frivolity. In order to provide the social service that the journalism profession demands, it is necessary to undertake training; being able to provide a service means being in a position to perform it. No one can offer what they do not have.

Media organizations that aim to respond to the public's demands for news must be able to call on professionals who have the relevant training in this area. A lack of training would represent not only a serious technical failing but a great attack on the ethical exercise of the profession, because for the reporter to be able to provide the social service that journalism as a profession demands, training is required, since providing a service means being able to perform it. No one who is incapable can attempt to fulfill his duty, let alone to satisfy a universal right as important for each individual as communication.

## The Need for Professional Empowerment

The question is a pertinent one: Are we witnessing a lag, a delay in the process of transforming information that is globally available, democratized, and within everyone's reach into a superior input that provides utility to the society in which each individual lives their life? Everything seems to indicate that the answer is yes. As Carbonell (2011) states, technology and socialization of it bring about tensions and divisions in our ethological and cultural structures. Therefore, not only must we be concerned with fostering and arriving at that knowledge, but we are now also facing the most difficult of challenges: achieving an effective dissemination of knowledge, so that the right conditions exist to advance toward a society of thinkers.

We might ask ourselves: Is the knowledge society a utopia? Are we really living in it? According to Subirats (2011), it is such a vague concept that any position could be defended; it depends on what one wants to express and what is hoped for, on what the concept's expectations are and what it represents. She points out that the very opposite is true: we are moving away from it as awareness of our ignorance grows, and as the information and knowledge available expands.

Are today's societies, victims of an avalanche of information and knowledge, increasingly ignorant? And more importantly, what is the role and task of, and what are the challenges facing, the media and journalists under these circumstances? All professions, but in particular journalists, must accept that they work in a different society, one that has a broader media landscape and new professional conventions. An environment dominated by technology and interactivity defines not only a new terrain for the actions of journalism professionals, but it may also be the beginning of new forms and processes involving the public and the audience that could even pull us toward a reconceptualization of communication professions.

Though this new scenario will effectively mean changes in the media, what should remain unchanged in the new era is journalism as a profession. But there will also be transformations in the tasks of the communication professional – that is, there will be new journalism and new journalists. The confluence of the role of sender and receiver, feedback dynamics, and the greater ease with which things can be published on networks may mean substantial change in the traditional concept of professional reporting. Beyond the matter of technology, it is clear that society requires a more skilled journalist. Because of the enormous availability of information, professional journalists will be able to access it in abundance as they undertake the news-production process.

All of the above can only be achieved by enhancing two of the reporter's important characteristics. First, solid training. The journalist must have greater training, in both information science and general culture. The immediacy and speed with which news will need to be conveyed will require an ability to make as few errors as possible. Transmitting information immediately will not be an excuse for disinformation or errors. Professionalism among reporters is increasingly necessary, making it more vital than ever to add depth to their identity and training. For new tasks, the journalist needs to master the current tools, be well trained in a way that allows versatility to be combined with subject specialization and media specialization, and have the talent to offer well-crafted content.

Journalists experience versatility in different ways, Scolari et al. (2008) state. Though professionals have always been versatile in small media organizations (where they have to do everything), reporters at an online newspaper naturally accept versatility as part of the process of technological integration and convergence. However, in large traditional companies, this transition, which can often generate conflict and instability, remains an ongoing process. This process of continuous renewal, Scolari et al. say, lies in the fact that the skills that communication professionals have will hardly serve them throughout their entire working life: they must be constantly updated, in terms of both the use of technologies and work procedures.

However, media companies have not always understood and assimilated this situation, approaching it more from a resource-based perspective rather than in terms of results and news quality. Companies squeeze too much from their resources and do not invest in training. This can dilute and homogenize the news product and risks damaging the quality of their work (Salaberría 2008). The question is: How can this challenge be tackled? What must be done to ensure the mission of empowering journalists to achieve the goal of effective mediation between news and the public?

## Conclusions and Proposals for the Immediate Future

Based on the analysis presented in the previous paragraphs, several ideas and proposals for reflection emerge. These can be summarized as follows:

1. Providing reporters with the relevant tools to promote informational negotiation. It can be said that information nowadays is increasingly taking on a negotiable nature – that is, information is a product that can be negotiated with the source that is in possession of the raw material. In this sense, the relationship between journalists and sources has often been characterized as a dance or a transactional negotiation (Túñez 1999). A "transaction" is defined as a deal or agreement, and as the action and effect of compromising – that is, according to *Merriam-Webster*, "com[ing] to a settlement or agreement by mutual concession."

   Understanding informative negotiation, therefore, as the process in which the reporter interacts with the source, transacting to obtain information, we can say that mastering the topic, subject to transaction, is the key tool in ensuring the success of that transaction for the reporter. The quantity and quality of the information that is obtained and published depends largely on the result obtained in the negotiations between sources and journalists. This will even influence how the media outlet will ultimately present that information to its audience.

   The empowered journalist is better able to enter into dialog with sources, and therefore, to question and verify her interpretation of reality and confront other alternatives – that is, to negotiate over the way of looking at the events that are occurring and dominating the daily schedule. Besides, this approach makes possible differentiation from the Internet's powerful (but dangerous) flows of pseudoinformation. It is a magnificent possibility to make a quality journalism product, with the necessary added value that identifies it and positions it before the community, in accordance with what I have set out in the preceding paragraphs.

Ultimately, what is at stake in the negotiation between journalists and sources is the definition of what will be understood to be newsworthy information. Not surprisingly, sources and journalists are involved in a fight for control of events. In such a situation, empowerment allows the reporter to negotiate with sources under optimum conditions, to select content much more appropriately, and to avoid the tainting of the news, since they are using the direct knowledge provided by the sources (García 2003).

The important thing is to promote a balanced dialog between the reporter and the source and, therefore, also to benefit the negotiation, since sources are recognized as valid interlocutors through which their view of the facts can be made public. This relationship is only possible and effective when journalists present themselves to news sources as critical and well-prepared professionals.

2. Reflecting on whether journalists, as professionals, are sufficiently educated and trained to avoid manipulation, which is often disguised as help or collaboration from sources with an agenda. Though this matter is complex in its own right, if we add to the picture the precariousness of some media organizations, the lack of resources, and excessive work demands, an environment is generated that is detrimental to the free and safe undertaking of communication work.

   Therefore, everything seems to indicate that professional qualifications would be the most effective tool to exercise control over sources, from the point of view of knowing who they are, what their interests are, and what their persuasion strategies are. In addition, the urgent need for professionals to adapt to this already changed and constantly evolving reality must be addressed. The reporter is understood to be a mediator or information manager, which leads to the argument that the journalist, in this context, is far from disappearing, as might be thought, despite the great avalanche of news from the new digital media and audiences' increasingly important and risky participation in defining the media agenda. Accordingly, we can then refute the pessimistic ideas expressed at the beginning of this text, projecting a positive vision with a future, to the extent that the dynamics that have been familiar until today are modified.

3. Final consideration should be given to the demand for appropriate autonomy. The tasks described earlier aim to grant journalists a sufficient level of professional autonomy to allow them to carry out their informational duties correctly and to adequately tackle the social, cultural, and professional changes brought about by innovations and the permanent and continuous reinvention of journalism, with the incorporation of new rules and new values within the debate on quality (Deuze 2004, 2005). This requirement is directly related to values linked to professional ethics, such as responsibility, credibility, and independence.

   Studies abound that show a predominance of journalists with passive, neutral characteristics, an excessive emphasis on dissemination, little analytical aptitude, a sense of servility as they perform their activities, and a permanent feeling of their autonomy being under threat. For this reason, the suggestions made here aim to promote reflection and the conception of specific proposals emanating from universities to improve the operating conditions faced by thousands of journalists, who are dealing with a mosaic culture (Moles 1975), in which no idea is necessarily general, but in which many ideas are important and hierarchization is practically impossible, because there is no common thread between ideas. Such a context turns the news reality into a chaotic and difficult scenario for the journalist, so the aim is for the ideas expressed here to be useful for fostering a relevant professional environment that allows reporters to fulfill their indisputable role and social service.

## References


Aguirre, M. (1998). *El Deber de Formación en el Informador*. Pamplona: Ediciones Universidad de Navarra.

Almirón, N. and Jarque, J.M. (2008). *El mito digital. Discursos hegemónicos sobre Internet y periodismo.* Barcelona: Anthropos.

Amado, A. (2017). Las periodistas desde los estudios del periodismo: perfiles profesionales de las mujeres en los medios informativos. *Cuestiones de Género: de la igualdad y la diferencia* 12: 325–346.

Bauman, Z. (2000). *Modernidad líquida*. México DF: Fondo de Cultura Económica.

Campás, J. (2011). La sociedad de la crisis de sentido. In: *La Sociedad de la Ignorancia* (ed. A. Brey, D. Innerarity and G. Mayos), 105–126. Barcelona: Pelícano.

Carbonell, E. (2011). La sociedad de la ignorancia. In: *La Sociedad de la Ignorancia* (ed. G. Mayos and A. Brey), 11. Barcelona: Península.

Chadwick, A. (2013). *The Hybrid Media System*. New York: Oxford University Press.

De Pablos-Coello, J.M. and Mateos-Martín, C. (2004). Estrategias informativas para acceder a un periodismo de calidad, en prensa y TV. Patologías y tabla de "medicación" para recuperar la calidad en la prensa. Ámbitos. *Revista internacional de comunicación* 11–12: 341–365.

Desantes, J.M. (1994). *La información como deber*. Ábaco: Buenos Aires.

Deuze, M. (2004). What is multimedia journalism? *Journalism Studies* 5 (2): 139–152.

Deuze, M. (2005). What is journalism? Professional identity and ideology of journalists reconsidered. *Journalism* 6 (4): 442–469.

García, E. (2003). La negociación informativa en el Periodismo Especializado. In: *El Periodismo de Fuente* (ed. F. Esteve and Á. Lozada), 85–98. Salamanca: Publicaciones Universidad Pontificia de Salamanca.

García, M., Bezunartea, O., and Rodríguez, A. (2013). El Valor Agregado Periodístico como herramienta para establecer los criterios definitorios de un periodismo de calidad. In: *La calidad periodística. Teorías, investigaciones y sugerencias profesionales* (ed. J.L. Gómez-Mompart, J.F. Gutiérrez-Lozano and D. Palau-Sampio), 44–55. Castellón de la Plana: Publicacions de la UJI, colección Aldea Global.

Gómez-Mompart, J.L. and Palau-Sampio, D. (2013). El reto de la excelencia. Indicadores para medir la calidad periodística. In: *La calidad periodística. Teorías, investigaciones y sugerencias profesionales* (ed. J.L. Gómez-Mompart, J.F. Gutiérrez-Lozano, and D. Palau-Sampio), 18–34. Castellón de la Plana: Publicacions de la UJI, colección Aldea Global.

Gutiérrez-Atala, F., Odriozola-Chéné, J., and Domínguez-Panamá, J.J. (2017). La satisfacción de los periodistas de Ecuador, Chile y México frente a la formación universitaria y sus implicancias en el ejercicio profesional. *Revista de Comunicación* 16 (1): 76–96.

Gutiérrez-Atala, F., Odriozola Chéné, J., Ferreira Jiménez, J. et al. (2016). El peso de la presión Social y política: estudio de las limitaciones que condicionan el desempeño de los periodistas en cinco países latinoamericanos. *Anuario electrónico de estudios en Comunicación Social «disertaciones»* 9 (1): 84–102.

Gutiérrez Coba, L. (2006). Análisis de la calidad informativa, primer paso hacia el cambio. http://palabraclave.unisabana.edu.co/index.php/palabraclave/article/view/1227 (accessed October 6, 2020).

Hanitzsch, T., Anikina, M., Berganza, R. et al. (2010). Modeling perceived influences on journalism: evidence from a cross-national survey of journalists. *Journalism & Mass Communication Quarterly* 87 (1): 5–22.

Hughes, S., Garcés-Pretelt, M., Márquez Ramírez, M. et al. (2016). Rethinking professional autonomy: autonomy to develop and to publish news in Mexico and Colombia. *Journalism* 18 (8): 956–976.

Hughes, S. and Márquez, M. (2017). Examining the practices that Mexican journalists employ to reduce risk in a context of violence. *International Journal of Communication* 11: 499–521.

Mogollón, H. and Gutiérrez, S. (2006). Internet como fuente de información en un contexto de glocalidad y necesidades informativas en Venezuela. *Razón y Palabra* 49: 1020.

Moles, A. (1975). *La comunicación y los Mass Media*. Mensajero: Bilbao.

Oficina del Alto Comisionado para los Derechos Humanos. https://www.ohchr.org/EN/UDHR/Documents/UDHR_Translations/spn.pdf (accessed September 17, 2020).

Oller-Alonso, M. and Meier, K. (2012). *La cultura periodística de España y Suiza*. Madrid: Fragua.

Parreño, M. (2013). Periodistas; entre la democracia y el mercado. In: *La calidad periodística. Teorías, investigaciones y sugerencias profesionales* (ed J.L. Gómez-Mompart, J.F. Gutiérrez-Lozano, and D. Palau-Sampio), 105–118. Castellón de la Plana: Publicacions de la Universitat Jaume I, colección Aldea Global.

Parreño, M. (2015). La calidad periodística mediante el análisis del discurso de los profesionales de la información. *Estudios sobre el mensaje periodístico* 21 (2): 1137–1147.

Pellegrini, S., Puente, S., Porath, W. et al. (2011). *Valor Agregado Periodístico: la apuesta por la calidad de las noticias.* Santiago: Ediciones UC.

Picard, R. (2009). Por qué los periodistas merecen ganar poco. http://www.soitu.es/soitu/2009/06/18/actualidad/1245340380_187306.html (accessed September 17, 2020).

Ramonet, I. (2011). *La explosión del periodismo. Internet pone en jaque a los medios tradicionales.* Argentina: Capital Intelectual S.A.

Reese, S. (1999). Hacia una comprensión del periodista global. el modelo de investigación de "jerarquía de influencias". *Comunicación y Sociedad* 12 (2): 47–68.

Salaberría, R.Y. (2008). La convergencia tecnológica en los medios de comunicación: retos para el periodismo. *Trípodos* 23: 44–45.

Scolari, C., Micó Sanz, J.L., Navarro Guere, H. et al. (2008). El periodista polivalente: Transformaciones en el perfil del periodista a partir de la digitalización de los medios audiovisuales catalanes. *Zer* 13 (25): 37–60.

Shoemaker, P.J. and Reese, S.D. (2014). *Mediating the Message in the 21st Century: A Media Sociology Perspective.* New York: Routledge.

Singer, J.B. (2003). Who are these guys? the online challenge to the notion of journalistic professionalism. *Journalism* 4 (2): 139–163.

Soria, C. (1991). *La hora de la ética informativa.* Barcelona: Mitre

Suárez Villegas, J. (2009). La crisis de identidad del periodista y la ética profesional. *Estudios sobre el Mensaje Periodístico* 15: 119–134.

Subirats, M. (2011). La sociedad del conocimiento y las dificultades de su producción. In: *La sociedad de la ignorancia* (ed. G. Mayos and A. Brey), 87–103. Barcelona: Península.

Tandoc, A., Cabañes, J.V., and Cayabyab, Y. (2018). Bridging the gap. *Journalism Studies* 6: 857–871.

Transaction. 2020. In Merriam-Webster.com. Retrieved 10 july, 2020, from https://www.merriamwebster.com/dictionary/transaction

Túñez, M. (1999). *Producir noticias: cómo se fabrica la realidad periodística.* Santiago de Compostela: Tórculo.

Ure, M. and *Schwarz*, C. (2014). Las identidades del periodismo argentino: estudio cualitativo de la percepción de los propios periodistas. Konrad Adenauer Stiftung- Universidad Católica Argentina. https://bit.ly/2MKpG5k (accessed October 6, 2020).

# PART III

# Studies in Comparative Communication Law

# 13

# Data Protection as a Limit to Communication Rights

## A General Vision of Data Protection in Europe

José Martínez Soria

### Data Protection and Communication Rights: The Practice of a Tense Relationship

This chapter deals with the question as to how, from a European perspective, the balance between freedom of expression and the protection of personal data can be achieved. Freedom of expression and freedom of information are essential for any democratic society.[1] The provision of a wide range of opinions and media is directly affected by the automated processing of personal data. Take the following example: If a citizen thoroughly investigates an issue on the Internet and, finally writes a blog, a multitude of personal data is automatically processed. In this way, the citizen is constantly caught between the right to freedom of expression and the right to protection of personal data (Erdos 2015, p. 2).

In democratic societies, it is normal that we can access diverse media and opinions without restriction. However, a glance at other countries quickly shows that this is unfortunately anything but self-evident (UN-CCPR, Communication No 1180/2003, section 7.2). Precisely for this reason, it would be fatal if the important right to data protection did not help and protect, but rather restricted individuals in the wrong way (Scheuer and Schweda 2011, p. 7).

In the following, I will examine the scope of communication rights and data protection in the EU. This scope is defined by the Charter of Fundamental Rights and the European Convention on Human Rights. However, both human rights systems do not contain any explicit statement about the appropriate balance between the fundamental rights concerned. A central statement can be found in Article 85 para. 1 General Data Protection Regulation (GDPR), which is examined in detail. According to this provision, the EU leaves the balance between the fundamental rights concerned to the member states. The benchmark is the principle of proportionality as developed in the case law of the Court of Justice of the European Union (CJEU) and the European Court of Human Rights (ECtHR). The most important judgments are examined in the chapter.

---

[1] ECHR, No. 5493/72, A 24, section 49 – Handyside (Pl.) December 7, 1976.

*The Handbook of Communication Rights, Law, and Ethics: Seeking Universality, Equality, Freedom and Dignity*, First Edition. Edited by Loreto Corredoira, Ignacio Bel Mallén, and Rodrigo Cetina Presuel.

## The Scope of the Freedom of Expression or Information

Freedom of expression and information is guaranteed in Article 11 of the EU-Charter of Fundamental Rights (CFR). It is "one of the essential foundations of a democratic society."[2] Without this freedom, a democratic community cannot exist. However, the fundamental right does not only have a social function, but also ensures the autonomy, dignity and personal development of the individual[3] (Erdos 2015, p. 2).

The freedom of the media, which is anchored in Article 11 para. 2 CFR, takes into account the importance of the mass media and their function in the formation of public opinion, which goes beyond the formation of a single individual opinion. It is about the special role of the mass media to spread news and, at the same time, to initiate public debates. The ECHR has also emphasized this double task of the mass media as being in the general interest. The high status of media pluralism is also stressed by the courts.[4] The plurality of the media serves the diversity of opinion. Article 11 para. 2 CFR contains a basic decision in favor of diversity of opinion which may curtail the freedom of media (business), if necessary.

The ECHR does not contain a separate fundamental right for the media; in this respect, the freedom of expression of Article 10 ECHR is applicable (cf. Article10 para.1 sentence 3 ECHR). However, the provision of Article 11 para. 1 CFR corresponds in content to the provision of Article 10 ECHR. Therefore, according to Article 52 para. 3 sentence 1 CFR, the guarantee must not fall short of this regulation.

The provision of Article 11 para. 1 CFR contains a uniform guarantee, the freedom of expression in the broader sense – "liberté d'expression."[5] According to para.1 sentence 2, it includes the "freedom to hold opinions"/ "liberté d'opinion", i.e., the freedom to have an opinion and to disseminate it. It may appear surprising to consider the freedom of opinion as a subset of the freedom of expression, but such an approach corresponds to the provision of Article 10 para. 1 ECHR. Furthermore, freedom of expression includes "freedom of information", i.e., the freedom to receive and process information and ideas. To classify freedom of expression and freedom of information as two different fundamental rights, as is the case in individual states, contradicts the wording of Article 11 para. 1 CFR as well as the fact that freedom of information includes the reception and transmission of information.

The guarantees of Article 11 para. 1 CFR as well as those of Article 11 para. 2 CFR primarily contain a negative obligation[6] but it also provides for states' positive obligations.[7] The two fundamental rights convey enforceable rights, not mere principles within the meaning of Article 52(5) CFR. Article 11 CFR obliges the Union under Article 51 para. 1 CFR. The member states are (only) obliged under this provision to the extent that they implement Union law. The obligation does not extend to private individuals. Nevertheless, the law among private individuals is of great importance. Norms of private law that violate fundamental rights

---

[2]CJEU Cases C-340/00 K/Cwik, (2001) May 24, 2014, ECR I 10269 para.18; C-112/00 Schmidberger, June 12, 2003, ECR I 5659 para.79; C-274/99 Connolly/K, March 6, 2001, ECR I 1611 para.39. See also Jarass (2016, Art. 11, para. 4).

[3]ECHR, Case No.13585/88, October 24, 1991 para. 59b; ECHR, Case No.13585/88, April 23, 1992, para. 59b.

[4]CJEU, Case C-368/95 Familiapress (1997) ECR I 3689 para.18; ECHR, No.10890/84, para. 69.

[5]Advocate General Trstenjak in CJEU Case C-316/09, 24.11.2010 No. 81.

[6]CJEU Case C-219/91 Ter Voort (1992) ECR I 5485 para. 36.

[7]ECHR Case No.28274/08 para. 44.

are inapplicable. In addition, private law provisions must be interpreted in conformity with fundamental rights. Finally, regulations implementing positive obligations can lead to an obligation on the part of private individuals.[8]

The form and presentation of the communication are also covered by Article 11 para. 1 CFR. The expression is protected by word, writing, pictures, or symbols.[9] Furthermore, the manner and the way in which communication is transmitted are also protected even in cross-border contexts. In this respect, it is irrelevant which medium is used. Article 11 para. 1 CFR applies to statements on the Internet and to business advertising.

Moreover, the freedom of information in Article 11 para. 1 CFR protects the receipt of information as well as opinions. This concerns both the receipt and the active procurement of information. In particular, it covers the reception of information via the Internet and in advertising.[10] The acquisition and use of the necessary equipment is also protected. In general, it should be assumed that the information is generally accessible. Likewise, the (passive) reception of opinions and information as well as all activities to obtain the opinions and information are protected. In addition, the processing of information is covered, including its storage. Finally, negative freedom of information is protected, for example, against imposed information (Jarass 2016, Article 11 para. 14).

According to Article 52 para. 1 CFR, the freedom of expression and information can be restricted. In addition, Article 52 para. 3 sentence 1 requires that Article 10 para. 2 ECHR (and the case law on it) is observed; the latter also applies to freedom of information. The interpretation is supported by the practice of the European Court of Justice which has also applied Article 10 para. 2 ECHR to restrictions of broadcasting companies.[11]

The authorization of Article 16 ECHR to restrict the freedom of opinion and information of foreigners in case of political activities is not applicable to EU foreigners. However, the exception of Article 16 ECHR is likely to apply to third-country nationals.

Restrictions of the rights from Article 11 must be provided for by law according to Article 52 para. 1 sentence 1 or Article 10 para. 2 ECHR; a legal basis is necessary (Schladebach and Simantiras 2011, p. 792). Furthermore, the legal provision must be sufficiently defined, i.e., "formulated in such a precise manner" that "the persons concerned can arrange their conduct, if necessary, after obtaining expert advice."[12] Contradictory regulations lack sufficient predictability. On the other hand, a margin of interpretation is permissible. Finally, the accessibility of the regulation must be guaranteed.[13]

## The Scope of the Right to Data Protection

### Charter of Fundamental Rights of the European Union

The protection of personal data is guaranteed in Article 8 CFR. This fundamental right is becoming increasingly important as one of the important parts of the protection of private life in the modern information society due to the rapid development of the communications

---

[8] CJEU Case C-250/06 United Pan-Europe (2007) ECR I 11135 para. 41.

[9] ECHR Case No.33629/06 para. 47.

[10] CJEU Case C-101/01 Lindquist (2003) ECR I 12971 para. 86.

[11] CJEU Case C-245/01 RTL Television (2003) ECR I 12489 para. 69.

[12] CJEU Case C-274/99 Connolly/K (2001) ECR I 1611 para. 42.

[13] ECHR, Case No.35083/97 para. 5.

media (Stern/Sachs/Johlen GRCh Article 8 para. 1). Accordingly, a specific fundamental right was created. The protection previously concretized in secondary law was raised to the level of primary law. This fundamental right conveys a negative obligation protecting against encroachments by those obliged to respect fundamental rights; in addition, it also contains certain positive obligations. Article 8 CFR is an enforceable right not to be interpreted as a mere (charter) principle within the meaning of Article 52 (5) CFR. Secondary law must be interpreted "in the light" of the fundamental right, i.e., in conformity with the fundamental right.

Article 8 CFR obliges the Union and its bodies (BeckOK InfoMedienR/Gersdorf EU-GRCharta Article 8 para. 10). According to Article 51 para. 1, first sentence, the member states are only obliged to implement Union law. Private individuals are not covered by this obligation (Raschauer and Riesz 2015, Art. 8 para. 2). Nevertheless, the effects of this fundamental right among private individuals are of great importance, for example, in Internet search engines.[14] Norms of private law that violate Article 8 CFR are inapplicable. Furthermore, the provisions of private law must be interpreted and applied in the light of the fundamental right, i.e., in conformity with fundamental rights (Jarass 2016 Art. 8 para. 3).

An encroachment on fundamental rights exists if personal data within the meaning of Article 8 para. 2 sentence 1 CFR is "processed" by persons obliged to respect fundamental rights. Processing is understood to mean any collection, storage, use, blocking, or deletion of data. This also includes the mere disclosure of personal data and the presentation of data on the Internet.[15] It is irrelevant whether the processing leads to a disadvantage.[16] The obligation to observe fundamental rights also applies to the conclusion of international agreements, for example, on data transfer.

As Article 8 para. 2, first sentence CFR confirms, processing personal data is generally allowed, if the data subject has consented to the processing (Kingreen 2016, Article 8 para.13). Consent should not be seen as a justification (for lack of a proportionality test), but as an exclusion of interference (Mehde 2006, § 21 para. 38; Bernsdorff 2019 Article 8 para. 2).

Para. 2, sentence 1 presupposes a voluntary nature of the consent, which must be assessed in the light of all the relevant circumstances (Augsberg 2015 Article 8 para.12). Furthermore, the data subject must be adequately informed before consent is given. The mere notification of a future publication of the data is not sufficient.[17] Consent cannot generally be given beforehand, but only for a specific purpose, which is why this purpose must be defined as precisely as possible before consent is given (Raschauer and Riesz 2015, Article 8 para. 23). Finally, the exclusion of an interference according to para. 2 p. 1 only applies if this corresponds to "good faith." Good faith is generally lacking in case of illegal purposes.

Restrictions of the right to data protection are possible on the basis of Article 52 para. 1 CFR, while observing the requirements of Article 8 para. 2 CFR. In addition, according to Article 52 para. 3 sentence 1 CFR, the requirements of Article 8 para. 2 ECHR must be observed. Every restriction of the fundamental right requires a legal basis according to Article 8 para. 2 p.1 and Article 52 para. 1 p.1 CFR. The legal basis must provide "clear and precise rules as to the scope and application of the measures in question" so that the addressees can base their conduct on it. In particular, the purpose of the processing must be specified, as can be seen from Article 8 para. 2 p.1 CFR.

---

[14] CJEU Case C-131/12 Google Spain (2014) para. Rn.69, 71, 81, 97, 99.

[15] CJEU Case C-92/09 Schecke (2010) ECR I 11063 para. 60.

[16] CJEU Case C-465/00 Österreich. Rundfunk (2003) ECR I 4989 para. 7.

[17] CJEU Case C-92/09 Schecke (2010) ECR I 11063 para. 63.

### Under EU Secondary Law

The European Data Protection Directive 95/46/EC (EDPD) has been in force in the European Union since 1995. However, because the member states of the European Union have not uniformly implemented and interpreted the Directive, there was a need for improvement.

With the aim of harmonizing and simultaneously modernizing EU data protection law, the European Parliament and the Council of the European Union adopted the General Data Protection Regulation (Regulation (EU) 2016/679, GDPR) on April 27, 2016. It has been applicable in all member states since May 25, 2018.

The basic data protection regulation strengthens the rights of data subjects and the enforcement powers of data protection supervisory authorities. High fines may be imposed in the event of data protection infringements. At the same time, GDPR is intended to promote the free movement of personal data within the European Union. Article 85 GDPR instructs the national legislators of the EU member states to harmonize freedom of opinion and information with the right to data protection (Taeger/Gabel/Westphal, 3. Aufl. 2019, DS-GVO Art. 85 para. 11; BeckOK DatenschutzR/Stender-Vorwachs DS-GVO Art. 85 para. 2). How this is to be done is unclear.

Until now, this process has been carried out in accordance with the case law of the CJEU, in that the fundamental rights concerned must be taken into account when interpreting the former DSRL and the national law implementing it, especially when balancing the interests in accordance with Article 7 lit. f DSRL (now Article 6 para. 1 subpara. 1 lit. f GDPR). The greater the public's interest in information, the more it must take precedence over the protection interest of the person concerned (Nettesheim 2019, p. 474).[18]

If, however, one takes the provision of Article 85 para. 1 GDPR literally, it has an explosive power for the full harmonization of data protection in Europe that should not be underestimated: as soon as freedom of opinion or information is affected, it is not the GDPR that would apply, but national law. However, the scope of application of the directly applicable provisions of the GDPR would be severely restricted. Virtually every publication affects freedom of information and freedom of opinion. And ultimately, data protection law is a communication regulation. It has therefore been proposed that Article 85 para. 1 GDPR should merely be seen as a mandate for the national legislator to adapt existing national law. Such a conclusion would indirectly result from an interpretation of Article 85 para. 2 GDPR, since only this Article provides for exceptions to the GDPR. This interpretation is in line with the primary objective of the GDPR, namely to standardize data protection law. However, such an interpretation reduces Article 85 para. 1 GDPR to a purely declaratory provision because, in these cases, the provisions of the GDPR would take precedence over national law anyway (Schantz and Wolff 2017, p. 15.)

## Balancing the Rights in the Jurisprudence of the CJEU and the ECtHR

Balancing the fundamental rights of data protection and of communication in the framework of Article 85 GDPR must necessarily take into account the previous case law of the CJEU and ECtHR. The following judgments are relevant in this respect.

[18]See ECHR Case von Hannover No 59320/00, No 40660/08 and 60641/08, (paras. 2, 3, 4, and 5), Case Mosley No. 48009/09; Case No. 39954/08.

## Promusicae

For the first time, the CJEU balanced the fundamental right to data protection and the right to information in the Promusicae judgment.[19]

The CJEU rejected an obligation to provide information on personal data of users of access providers but left it up to the member states to introduce such rights. By means of the information claims, right holders tried to overcome the problem that they are not easily able to identify infringers, but are dependent on the assistance of the providers who have the relevant data in connection with the IP addresses of the users. The massive infringements of rights within the framework of file-sharing systems in particular, but also other forms of rights violations, had brought the rights holders to the scene. In view of the negative attitude of state courts, some of the rights holders were forced to resort to criminal investigations; the primary objective of such proceedings was not criminal prosecution, but the acquisition of the relevant data.

The central point of dispute in the ruling was the relationship between data protection law and the (copyright-based) right to information. The facts of the case concerned a constellation that was almost classic for claims for information due to rights violations: the association Promusicae, as representative of rights holders, requested Telefónica España to release personal traffic data of Telefónica users in order to more effectively enforce its claims against the infringers, namely the personal and identity information on certain IP addresses on certain days to which Promusicae could attribute a participation in the file-sharing network Kazaa. Spanish law did not, however, provide for any corresponding claims for information or restrictions in data protection in favor of private individuals. At first sight, the CJEU's decision leaves it to the discretion of the member states to decide whether they introduce corresponding rights to information and how they balance the requirements of data protection law to this end. However, such an opening also has considerable indirect legal policy consequences both for the harmonization of copyright and liability law in the EU, which is currently under scrutiny, either at EU level or at national level.

The risks that arose for the harmonization of liability and copyright law as a result of such an opening up were obvious: there are still considerable differences in the treatment of claims for information in the member states. Decisions from Germany, which categorically reject the information claims and identification obligations for providers, are countered by decisions from other member states, which oblige providers to give access to the corresponding data to private individuals (Spindler 2008, p. 574). As already described, however, claims for information are closely related to the liability of the providers and possible principles of only subsidiary recourse, since rights holders cannot be left completely defenseless by being caught between Scylla – data protection with regard to the infringer – and Charybdis – the impossibility of recourse to providers (Spindler 2008, p. 577). Harmonization, therefore, seemed urgently necessary from a European law perspective in order to create a balanced system of accountability. Unfortunately, the CJEU's comments, particularly on the fundamental rights test and barriers, were not very clear-cut and only referred to a general proportionality test (Coudert and Werkers 2010, p. 65), which left the member states, as well as the Commission, a relatively large margin of maneuver with regard to secondary legislation. This solution, a decentralized balancing process, based on the general principle of proportionality, still marks the European path today.

---

[19] CJEU Case C-275/06 Promusicae.

## Österreichischer Rundfunk

The judgment in the case "Österreichischer Rundfunk"[20] further developed European data protection law. The main proceedings in the Österreichischer Rundfunk case were based on legal disputes between two Austrian employees (Neukomm/Lauermann) and their employer, the Österreichischer Rundfunk (ORF). ORF and some of its employees objected to the fact that, on the basis of Austrian law, the annual remuneration is communicated to the Court of Auditors, together with their names, for inclusion in its public annual report.

In particular, the question of whether Directive 95/46/EC (EDPD) was applicable was controversial since it was a case with purely domestic implications. EDPD was a particular directive, being the only Community legal act that explicitly addressed the protection of fundamental rights; at the same time, it ensured the free movement of data between member states. The CJEU concluded that the Directive was applicable to this case, due to specific character of the data protection as a human right.

In the opinion of the CJEU, the provisions of Directive 95/46 must be interpreted in the light of fundamental rights, in so far as they concern the processing of personal data that may lead to restrictions on fundamental freedoms and, in particular, the right to respect for private life, which, according to settled case law, are among the general principles of law whose observance the Court must ensure[21] and which have also been expressly included in Article 6 para. 2 EU-Treaty. Whereas Article 8 para. 1 ECHR establishes the principle that public authorities may not interfere with the exercise of the right to respect for private life, para. 2 declares such interference permissible where it is provided for by law and constitutes a measure necessary in a democratic society in the interests of national security, public policy, the economic well being of the country, the maintenance of law and order and the prevention of criminal offenses, the protection of health and morals, or the protection of the rights and freedoms of others.

The collection of personal data concerning the professional income of individuals for disclosure to third parties falls within the scope of Article 8 ECHR. The ECHR has ruled in this respect that the term "private life" may not be interpreted narrowly and that, in principle, it is not possible to exclude professional activities from the concept of "private life."[22]

Though the mere storage by an employer of personal data relating to the salaries paid to staff does not, in itself, constitute an infringement of the right of the persons concerned to respect their private life and therefore an interference within the meaning of Article 8 ECHR, the disclosure of such data to a third party does, irrespective of the subsequent use of the information disclosed. Whether the information transmitted is to be regarded as sensitive and whether the persons concerned have suffered any disadvantages as a result of the operation,[23] is not decisive.

The CJEU then examines whether the interference was permissible. It discusses the specific requirements of Article 8 ECHR, but leaves the assessment to the referring courts as to whether such publication is necessary and proportionate in relation to the objective of the Austrian law to keep the income of the employees within reasonable limits. In particular, they would have to examine whether this purpose could be achieved just as effectively if the personal data were made available only to the supervisory bodies. Furthermore, the question

---

[20] CJEU Case *Rechnungshof v. Österreichischer Rundfunk and others*, May 20, 2003, C-465/00.

[21] Cf. see, inter alia, CJEU Case C-274/99 *P Connolly v Commission* [2001] ECR I-1611, para. 37.

[22] See in particular ECHR, *Amann v. Switzerland* of February 16, 2000, Recueil des arrêts et décisions 2000-II, section 65, and *Rotaruc v. Romania* of May 4, 2000, Recueil des arrêts et décisions 2000-V, section 43.

[23] In this sense, the judgment in *Amann v. Switzerland* ECHR case *Amann v. Switzerland*: February 16, 2000, section 70.

arises whether it would not be sufficient to inform the public only of the remuneration, and other benefits in kind, to which employees of public bodies are entitled on a contractual or statutory basis, without indicating the amounts received by the employees in question in a given year, which may depend to varying degrees on their family and personal situation.

The ORF case thus provided the Court of Justice with its first opportunity to comment on the right to data protection, especially in connection with the Data Protection Directive (Siemen 2004, p. 316). The ruling of the Court of Justice fleshes out that the Data Protection Directive has a very broad scope of application, which may also extend to purely domestic situations. The Directive thus extends the protection guaranteed by the direct application of the fundamental freedoms, which are restricted in their application to cross-border cases.

## Bodil Lindqvist

Questions as to which acts are covered by data protection law at all and which are relevant for the freedom of information and opinion, had initially remained open. In particular, it was unclear whether someone who refers to different persons on an Internet page and makes them identifiable either by their names or in some other way, is thus performing an act which constitutes, under Community law, automated processing of personal data. The Bodil Lindqvist case[24] allowed the CJEU to clarify these issues.

Mrs. Lindqvist set up an Internet site in her parish in Sweden to facilitate access to information for confirmands. Information was provided on Mrs. Lindqvist, who was a catechist in the parish, and 18 of her colleagues who were not aware of the existence of the site. When Mrs. Lindqvist learned that the website had been disapproved of by some colleagues, she immediately took the site down. However, the Swedish Public Prosecutor's Office initiated criminal proceedings for a violation of the Swedish Personal Data Act (PUL), which transposed EDPD into Swedish law.

In contrast to the Austrian Broadcasting Corporation case, no economic connection was discernible in Mrs. Lindqvist's activities; rather, they were of an honorary and religious community nature. In order to assess whether such activities also fall within the scope of EDPD, the Court had to examine, in greater detail, the system of exceptions provided for in the first and second indents of Article 3 para. 2.

The CJEU stresses the conflict of objectives of the Directive between ensuring the free movement of data and respect for fundamental rights. However, it sees no reason to doubt the compatibility of the Directive with general principles of Community law, in particular fundamental rights. A balance between the conflicting rights and interests must therefore be struck in the specific case, i.e., at national level, when applying the implementing legislation. In the present case, Mrs. Lindqvist's freedom of expression must therefore be weighed against the protection of the privacy of the persons concerned. Not only must the national authorities interpret their national law in accordance with the directive, but they must also ensure that this interpretation does not conflict with the Community fundamental rights or other general principles of Community law, such as the principle of proportionality.

In conclusion, it is therefore the responsibility of the national courts to take account of the right of expression, but the provisions of the Data Protection Directive, as such, do not conflict with the general principle of freedom of expression.

[24] CJEU Case C-101/01 Criminal proceedings against Bodil Lindqvist, November 6, 2003.

The Lindqvist judgment highlighted the importance of data protection in the Community legal order, and that the Court of Justice strives to take this into account by ensuring a high standard of protection (Siemen 2004, p. 320).

In summary, the judgments confirm that data protection is a protection of fundamental rights, which is not guaranteed at Community level by general principles of law alone. It is not the EU that provides for a balance between these fundamental rights but continues to leave this task to the member states.

## Satamedia (CJEU and ECtHR)

The balance between freedom of expression and freedom of information is at the heart of the Satamedia judgment of the ECtHR[25] and the CJEU.[26] The ECtHR ruled that the ban on the publication of tax data of Finnish citizens by the Finnish authorities does not violate freedom of expression and information.[27] Rather, the authorities had found an appropriate balance between freedom of opinion and information (Article 10 ECHR) and the right to respect for private life (Article 8 ECHR). In particular, the publishing house could not invoke exceptions to Finnish data protection rules that allow data processing for journalistic purposes.

The applicants were two cooperating media companies, Satakunnan Markkinapörssi Oy and Satamedia Oy, which have published an annual list of income and assets of the Finnish population in their magazine *Veropörssi* since 1994. The underlying data had previously been published by the Finnish tax authorities in accordance with national law. Later on, Satamedia also offered an SMS service that made it possible to retrieve relevant information about a specific person. The processing of the data to the extent in question, which in 2002, the year in question, covered approximately one-third of the Finnish population, was objected to by the Finnish Data Protection Commissioner as it constituted unlawful processing of personal data. The exceptions provided for in the Finnish Data Protection Act for journalistic activities do not apply to the present case.

After the Data Protection Committee did not share the opinion of the Data Protection Commissioner, administrative court proceedings were subsequently instituted. In the course of this procedure, the CJEU had to determine the scope of application of the exception for journalistic activities provided for in Article 9 of Directive 95/46/EC, on which the national regulations are based, upon submission of the Finnish Supreme Administrative Court. In the opinion of the CJEU, this exception was to be interpreted narrowly in order to protect the fundamental right to privacy. The Supreme Administrative Court thereupon ruled in the final instance in favor of the data protection commissioner and prohibited the two companies from carrying out the activities in question because the public interest did not require publication of the data to the extent in question.

In its judgment, the ECtHR came to the conclusion that the Supreme Administrative Court had convincingly struck the necessary balance between freedom of opinion and information and the right to privacy as required by the ECtHR judgment. In the view of the ECtHR, therefore, weighty reasons would have been required to replace this assessment with its own. Finally, the Court emphasized that the judgment did not prohibit the publication of tax data in general, but only to the extent in dispute. The Finnish policy of making tax data publicly

---

[25] *Satamedia Oy v. Finland* ECtHR, (June 2018). *International Legal Materials*, 57 (3): 437–489.

[26] CJEU Case *Tietosuojavaltuutettu v Satakunnan Markkinapörssi Oy and Satamedia Oy*, December 16, 2008.Case C-73/07.

[27] Judgment 21.7.2015 – Complaint No 931/13.

available was based on the need to ensure that the public could control the activities of government authorities. Giving the public access to official documents undoubtedly serves to ensure the availability of information to enable a debate on matters of public interest. Such access, though subject to clear legal rules and restrictions, has a constitutional basis in Finnish law and has been widely guaranteed for many decades (McCully 2018, p. 438).

The magazine *Veropörssi* stopped publishing the data in question in the years after 2009 and the SMS service was discontinued. However, this was not a direct consequence of the judgment, but rather an economic decision of the applicant. The ECHR also held that the prohibition of discrimination (Article 14 ECHR) was not violated: The two companies had not been treated unequally in comparison with other newspapers, which also published tax data, as the scope of the data published in the other media was significantly smaller. Therefore, the companies were not in a comparable situation.

## Google Spain

The consequences resulting from a violation of data protection and personal rights in relation to the information rights of the population were the subject of the Google Spain judgment.[28] Mr. González found that entering his name in the search engine Google, a link appeared to an edition of a Spanish daily newspaper in 1988, which referred to an auction of his property in connection with a garnishment order for social security debts. Mr. González requested that the newspaper and Google either delete the pages in question or modify them so that the personal data concerning him no longer appeared there. The newspaper replied that this was not possible; Google replied that, as provider, it had nothing to do with the content of the pages. The Spanish court dealing with the case referred the matter to the CJEU. The CJEU found that a provider does indeed carry out processing of personal data within the meaning of Directive 95/46 and must therefore be regarded as the controller of that processing. A person affected by the publication of private data has a "right to forget," regardless of whether the posting of the data was originally unobjectionable. Google therefore had to remove the link.

The CJEU created a right for citizens to demand that the company deletes search results that violate personal rights and stressed that personal rights "in general" take precedence over the public's interest in information (judgment May 13, 2014, ref. C-131/12). The CJEU first had to establish that European data protection law applies to Google at all. The search engine provider wanted to evade responsibility by arguing that its servers, which process the data, are located in the United States and not in Spain or anywhere else in the EU. This did not convince the CJEU: Google is active in Europe and carries out advertising activities there that are closely linked to the search results. According to Article 4(1a) EDPD, this leads to the applicability of European data protection law.

In terms of content, the CJEU's ruling places Google under an obligation to delete search results if they violate the personal rights of European citizens. There may even be an obligation to delete information that is lawfully disseminated on the Internet and is protected by the freedom of communication. Google cannot invoke the media privilege under data protection law.

The judges highlighted that the fundamental rights to respect for private life and to the protection of personal data can be significantly affected by a search engine. The significant impact on the rights exists on top of the dissemination of information on individual websites. Entering a name could lead to a list of results that "potentially concerns numerous aspects of private life" and could result in a "more or less detailed profile of the person sought."

---

[28] CJEU Case C-131/12 *Google Spain SL, Google Inc. v. Agencia Española de Protección de Datos (AEPD)*, Mario Costeja González.

The CJEU only allows a different assessment "in particularly well-founded cases," but remains more than vague in this respect and mentions only in general terms the "public interest in access to information, which may vary depending, among other things, on the role that the person plays in public life" as a reason for legitimation (Streinz 2014, p. 1143).

The judgment puts Google in a situation where deleting data is always the most convenient solution. If unpleasant search results are criticized, Google will always take a high risk to refuse deletion in the future – there is the threat of fines, which will be even more severe after the data protection reform. The public interested in access to information, on the other hand, has no lawyers and no right of action before the CJEU (Dörre 2014, p. 281).

However, anyone who hoped that the CJEU will create a fundamental "right to be forgotten" in the ruling has been disappointed (Knebel 2018, p. 98). In the last part of the judgement, the CJEU only briefly deals with this question and comes to the conclusion, in very general terms, that an originally legitimate search result could became illegal after a certain period. Whether this can be affirmed in the specific case is a matter for the national court to examine. However, there is much to be said for the fact that, after the expiry of 16 years, "no particular reasons" exist which could justify an overriding interest of the public in obtaining certain information (Streinz 2014, p. 1143).

## Buivids

In its decision of February 14, 2019,[29] the CJEU delivered an opinion on the relationship between data protection and freedom of expression. The decision concerns the fundamental question of the significance of data protection law when personal data are published on the Internet as part of an expression of opinion or reporting. The decision concerned a private individual who had recorded and published a conversation with police officers on his mobile phone. The question was whether this event was protected by the rules for journalistic data processing on which the Court was not competent to decide. However, it stressed that the concept of journalism should be interpreted broadly, as freedom of expression is of great importance in any democratic society (para. 51 of the decision). Private individuals could therefore also be "journalists" in this sense (para. 55). For the question as to whether personal data may be published on the Internet, the CJEU wants to base itself primarily on the case law of another court, namely that of the ECtHR on the relationship between the right to respect for private life and the right to freedom of expression (para. 66). In this context, the ECtHR has developed a number of criteria which belong more to the right of the press or the right of expression. The CJEU expressly mentions these criteria (para. 66):

- contribution to a debate of general interest;
- the data subject's level of awareness;
- subject of the report;
- the previous behavior of the data subject;
- content, form, and effects of the publication;
- the manner and circumstances in which the information was obtained; and
- their accuracy.

The result suggests that the CJEU wants to apply the same standards to the publication of personal data on the Internet as under general press law or the right to make statements (Stähler 2019, p. 462). The decision was still issued on the basis of the old Data Protection Directive, but it is also relevant for the interpretation of the GDPR. Here, the legality of publications is judged according to Article 6 and 9 GDPR and the "media privilege" according to Article 85 GDPR.

[29] CJEU Case Buivids, February 12, 2019, C-345/17.

## Conclusion

The relationship between data protection and communication rights is regulated in Article 85 para. 1 GDRP. Paragraph 1 mandates the member states to strike a fair balance between the right to data protection under Article 8 para.1 ECHR and the rights to freedom of expression and information under Article 11 para. 1 ECHR (Kühling and Martini 2016, p. 286). Behind this provision, lies the general objective of the Regulation to further reduce differences between member states in data protection (Recital 9 et seq.) and to reduce obstacles to the free movement of data within the internal market (Schantz 2016, p. 1841). However, in some respects, the Regulation gives leeway for the national legislator and thus combines elements of a regulation with those of a directive (Pötters 2015, p. 12). While the objective of a proportionate balance between data protection and freedom of opinion, media and information binds member states according to the ECHR, the choice of means and the specific regulation is left to the individual states (Albrecht and Janson 2016, p. 503 et seq.; Benecke and Wagner 2016, p. 602). In doing so, however, member states are bound by Union law and above all by the guarantees of the CFR and thus also by the case law of the CJEU. In its recent judgements, Google Spain and Buivids, the Court set some markers for weighing up data protection and freedom of information on the Internet. According to its jurisprudence, on the one hand, the sensitivity of the information and, on the other hand, the public interest in it, which may be based on its topicality, must be taken into account. It must be stressed that the judgments of the ECHR are elementary for interpreting data protection and communication rights under EU law in light of Article 52 para. 3 CFR (Buchner and Tinnefeld 2018, para. 9).

## References

Albrecht, J.P. and Janson, N.J. (2016). Datenschutz und Meinungsfreiheit nach der Datenschutzgrundverordnung. *Computers und Recht* 32 (8): 500–509.

Augsberg, S. (2015). Article 8 GRC. In: *Europäisches Unionsrecht* Vol. 1, 7e (ed. H. von der Groeben, J. Schwarze and A. Hatje). Baden-Baden: Nomos.

Benecke, A. and Wagner, J. (2016). Öffnungsklausel in der Datenschutz-Grundverordnung. Gestaltungsspielräume für ein nationales Datenschutzrecht. *DVBl* 131 (10): 600–608.

Bernsdorff, N. (2019). Article 8 GRC. In: *Charta Der Grundrechte Der Europäischen Union*, 2e (ed. J. Meyer and S. Hölscheidt). Nomos-Verlag.

Buchner, B. and Tinnefeld, M.-T. (2018). *Datenschutz-Grundverordnung*, 2e. Bundesdatenschutzgesetz: DS-GVO/BDSG.

Coudert, F. and Werkers, E. (2010). In the aftermath of the Promusicae case: how to strike the balance? *International Journal of Law and Information Technology* 18 (1): 50–71.

Dörre, T. (2014). Haftung des Suchmaschinenbetreibers für Suchergebnisse. *GRUR-Prax* 10: 281.

Erdos, D. (2015). From the Scylla of restriction to the Charybdis of license? Exploring the present and future scope of the 'special purposes' Freedom of Expression Shield in European data protection. University of Cambridge Faculty of Law Legal Studies Research Paper Series, Paper No. 20/2015. http://www.law.cam.ac.uk/ssrn (accessed September 17, 2020).

Jarass, H.D. (ed.) (2016). *Charta der Grundrechte der Europäischen Union: GRCh*. Munich: C.H. Beck.

Kingreen, T. (2016). Article 8 EMRK. Calliess/Ruffert, EU-/AEUV-Kommentar, 5e.

Knebel, S. (2018). Die Drittwirkung der Grundrechte und -freiheiten gegenüber Privaten 2018.

Kühling, J. and Martini, M. (2016). Die DSGVO und das nationale Recht Munster: Vertagshaus Monsenstein und Vannerdat OHG.

McCully, J. (2018). Introductory note to Satakunnan Markkinapörssi Oy.*International Legal Matters* 57 (3): 437.

Mehde, V. (2006). Datenschutz. In: *Handbuch der Europäischen Grundrechte* (ed. S. Heselhaus and C. Nowak), 25. Munich: Beck C.H.

Nettesheim, M. (2019). Datenschutz und Meinungsäußerungsfreiheit - Zur Reichweite der Freistellung allgemeiner Meinungsäußerungen nach Article 85 Abs. 1 DSGVO. *Zeitschrift für das gesamte Medienrecht* 50 (6): 473–481.

Pötters, S. (2015). Primärrechtliche Vorgaben für eine Reform des Datenschutzrechts. *Recht der Datenverarbeitung RDV* 2015: 10–16.

Raschauer and Riesz (2015). Article 8 GRC. In: *GRC-Kommentar: Charta der Grundrechte der Europäischen Union* (ed. M. Holoubek and G. Leinbacher). Wein: MANZ-Verlag.

Schantz, P. (2016). Die Datenschutz-Grundverordnung – Beginn einer neuen Zeitrechnung im Datenschutzrecht. *Neue Juristische Wochenschrift 2016* 69 (26): 1841–1847.

Schantz, P. and Wolff, H. A. (2017). *Das neue Datenschutzrecht.* Munich: Beck CH.

Scheuer, A. and Schweda, S. (2011). Der Schutz personenbezogener Daten und die Medien. *Iris Plus, Die Grenzen der Nutzung persönlicher Daten 2011–6*, 7–29.

Schladebach, M. and Simantiras, N. (2011). Grundstrukturen des unionalen Rundfunkrechts. *EuR* 2011: 784–807.

Siemen, B. (2004). Grundrechtsschutz Durch Richtlinien/Die Fälle Österreichischer Rundfunk u.a. und Lindqvist – Anmerkungen zu den Urteilen Des Europäischen Gerichtshofes in den verbundenen Rechtssachen C-465/00. C-138/01 und C-139/01 und C-101/01 - EuR 2004. 306–321.

Spindler, G. (2008). Die Tür ist auf" – Europarechtliche Zulässigkeit von Auskunftsansprüchen gegenüber Providern Urteilsanmerkung zu EuGH. *Promusicae/Telefónica, GRUR 2008* 7: 574–577.

Stähler, T.P. (2019). Verarbeitung personenbezogener Daten – Journalistische Tätigkeit – Heimliche Filmaufnahmen. *Europäischer Gerichtshof, Urteil vom 14.2.2019 – Rs. C-345/17 (Buivids)* 459–464.

Streinz, R. (2014). Europarecht: Löschungsanspruch gegen verantwortlichen Suchmaschinenbetreiber. *JuS* 12: 1140–1143.

# 14

# Regulation of Internet Intermediaries and Communication Rights

Joan Barata

## Introduction. Who Are the Intermediaries?

In 2018 the Committee of Ministers of the Council of Europe (CoE) adopted a Recommendation "on the role and responsibilities of Internet intermediaries,"[1] which described these actors as "[a] wide, diverse and rapidly evolving range of players," which:

> facilitate interactions on the internet between natural and legal persons by offering and performing a variety of functions and services. Some connect users to the internet, enable the processing of information and data, or host web-based services, including for user-generated content. Others aggregate information and enable searches; they give access to, host and index content and services designed and/or operated by third parties. Some facilitate the sale of goods and services, including audio-visual services, and enable other commercial transactions, including payments.

The CoE also emphasizes the importance of intermediaries as framers of users' freedom of expression through moderation and ranking of content. This takes the CoE to the conclusion that intermediaries "exert forms of control which influence users' access to information online in ways comparable to media, or they may perform other functions that resemble those of publishers." In addition to this, "intermediary services may also be offered by traditional media, for instance, when space for user-generated content is offered on their platforms."

The intermediaries have thus become main actors in the process of dissemination and distribution of all types of content. They also play a very prominent role in ensuring the "visibility" of the content produced by traditional media, such as the written press or even radio and television. As a matter of fact, it has become increasingly frequent that this kind of content is consumed as the result of a recommendation or its appearance on social networks and all types of platforms, and not because of direct access by users (Pew Research Center 2018).

---

[1]Available online at: https://rm.coe.int/1680790e14 (accessed January 16, 2021).

*The Handbook of Communication Rights, Law, and Ethics: Seeking Universality, Equality, Freedom and Dignity*, First Edition. Edited by Loreto Corredoira, Ignacio Bel Mallén, and Rodrigo Cetina Presuel.

However, it is also clear that the interests that modulate the decisions taken by intermediaries (particularly those related to content) are not solely and necessarily the protection of the right to freedom of expression. Intermediaries are undoubtedly commercially driven entities and follow ad-based business models (which might translate into the promotion of socially undesirable or harmful speech). Other pressures (not always of economic nature) are also relevant: need to show responsibility when dealing with "problematic content" within different societies, managing pressure coming from parliamentary committees or media and public opinion, handling "threats" of regulation from governments and legislators, and being able to properly respond to the behavior of business rivals (Keller 2019a). Intermediaries are also subjected to different national legal regimes that may empower national (legal, regulatory) authorities to issue direct orders imposing several possible obligations on them (content removal, user identification, account deactivations, etc.). It is also important to note that national legislation usually defines the degree of legal liability of intermediaries for the dissemination of third-party content on the basis of the way content is moderated under the factors mentioned earlier.

All these factors frame intermediaries' adoption of diverse sets of rules and specific reporting, internal mechanisms for enforcement and appeals that govern the way content is privately moderated.

This means that, from a legal point of view, the discussion on how to protect freedom of expression and properly apply its limits has evolved into the more specific issue of how to regulate content moderation by online intermediaries and which kind of liability regime must be derived from the corresponding system. It is obvious that different regimes will also have a diverging impact on the exercise of the right to freedom of expression.

The debate on content moderation regulation contains a main tension challenging to manage. On the one hand, states and certain civil society groups tend to ask intermediaries to make greater efforts to eradicate harmful and undesirable content, especially manifestations of hatred, disinformation, certain forms of propaganda, references to criminal acts, and other similar behaviors. On the other hand, organizations dedicated to the protection and promotion of freedom of expression, international human rights organizations, and even some governments have expressed their concern that global private companies such as Google or Facebook often restrict or simply eliminate ideas, opinions, and other content published by users on the basis of internal rules that are considered unjustified, abusive, and ambiguous (and more important, contrary to applicable international and regional freedom of expression legal standards).

This tension also reveals different ways of understanding freedom of expression in a globalized world, even between states fitting all under the category of liberal democracies.

## Who Is the Speaker? Who Is Liable?

*Freedom of expression and liability from the perspective of the legal systems of the United States and the European Union*

As it has been noted, the CoE puts a special emphasis on the fact that intermediaries play a very important role creating the conditions or providing a platform for the exercise of the right to freedom of expression. Moreover, in the context of the European Union, the IT companies Facebook, Microsoft, Twitter, and YouTube signed a Code of Conduct with the European Commission in May 2016 with the objective of "countering illegal speech online."[2] Other relevant initiatives are the Communication of the European Commission on tackling

[2]Available online at: https://ec.europa.eu/newsroom/just/item-detail.cfm?item_id=54300 (accessed January 16, 2021).

illegal content online of 2017[3] and the companion Recommendation of 2018.[4] The Code starts with the acknowledgment of the "collective responsibility and pride in promoting and facilitating freedom of expression throughout the online world." The parties also:

> stress the need to defend the right to freedom of expression, which, as the European Court of Human Rights has stated, is applicable not only to "information" or "ideas" that are favourably received or regarded as inoffensive or as a matter of indifference, but also to those that offend, shock or disturb the State or any sector of the population.

This perspective, based on the idea that intermediaries facilitate and enable the exercise of the right to freedom of expression by their users cannot be found, at least with the same meaning and implications, in the US legal system, where intermediaries, and not users, are recognized and protected as holders of the right to freedom of expression contained in the First Amendment of the Constitution. Therefore, these companies can oppose their constitutional right to freedom of expression against any user who has seen how their posts have been withdrawn or even their account cancelled. Goldman (2019) has summarized the arguments used by several US Courts that dismiss claims to consider certain intermediaries' decisions as a violation of the First Amendment rights of the respective users. In this context, it is particularly interesting to mention the recent decision in *Prager University v. Google LLC.*[5] As Goldman (2020) has pointed out, the Court made very relevant statements is this area, including:

> Despite YouTube's ubiquity and its role as a public-facing platform, it remains a private forum, not a public forum subject to judicial scrutiny under the First Amendment PragerU runs headfirst into two insurmountable barriers – the First Amendment and Supreme Court precedent. The Internet does not alter this state action requirement of the First Amendment.

It must be noted that the main and most relevant argument here is the confirmation by the Court that intermediaries have a First Amendment right to moderate content.

This decision is also of particular importance, as it dismisses a possible use of the term "public forum" as analog to the idea of a public space of protected speakers, usually taken from the decision of the US Supreme Court confirming the ruling of the California Supreme Court (in application and interpretation of the State's Constitution) in the *Pruneyard Shopping Center v. Robins* case[6] (Keller 2018, p. 15). In other words, and according to this jurisprudence, the fact that intermediaries provide an openly accessible space to speak, neither deprives this space from its intrinsically private nature, nor creates an obligation for the former to protect users' right to freedom of expression.

The US legal system, applicable to intermediaries, cannot be explained solely on the exclusive basis of the First Amendment. A fundamental and more important element is the provision contained since 1996 in section 230 of the Communications Decency Act (CDA).[7] This

[3] Communication of the European Commission to the European Parliament, the Council, the European Economic and Social Committee and the Committee of Regions on Tackling Illegal Content Online. Towards an enhanced responsibility of online platforms. COMM (2017) 555 final. September 28, 2017.

[4] Commission Recommendation of March 1, 2018 on measures to effectively tackle illegal content online. C (2018) 1177 final.

[5] *Prager University v. Google* 2020, Case No. 18-15712 (9th Cir. Feb. 26, 2020). Available online at: http://cdn.ca9.uscourts.gov/datastore/opinions/2020/02/26/18-15712.pdf (accessed January 16, 2021).

[6] 447 U.S. 74 (1980). Available online at: https://supreme.justia.com/cases/federal/us/447/74 (accessed January 16, 2021).

[7] 47 U.S.C. section 230 (2012).

legal provision has a long history and development (Klonick 2018, p. 1604), and is applicable to a wide variety of online content with a few exceptions (mainly intellectual property rights and federal crimes which are covered by specific legislation). The importance of section 230 vis-à-vis intermediaries is the fact that (a) it provides intermediaries with complete immunity for third-party content they host, and (b) it includes a so-called good Samaritan clause that also gives immunity to intermediaries for the content they decide to take down on the basis of a good faith understanding that it is illegal or merely objectionable. It is therefore obvious that, despite the importance of the First Amendment in this area, section 230 introduces more substantive and procedural benefits to intermediaries, as well as a higher level of legal certainty (Goldman 2019).

The debate is more open in Europe. In Germany, the Higher Regional Court of Munich ruled that a comment posted by a right-wing politician was, according to Facebook, in violation of its internal content rules, nevertheless it constituted an exercise of freedom of expression protected under the German constitution. Facebook was thus ordered to reupload the comment and reinstate the user's account, which had been deleted for 30 days. It is not clear whether this decision will be confirmed by higher courts, but it is relevant in the sense that the Court establishes that the right to freedom of expression of Facebook users is to be protected in practically equal terms as vis-à-vis state institutions and that, when applying their own internal content moderation rules, intermediaries need to consider these constitutional standards.[8]

There have been similar cases in some European countries and other places across the globe, though this still cannot be considered as a consolidated jurisprudential approach confirmed by higher courts in general. The most recent case when drafting this text is the decision of a Civil Court in Rome to reactivate the Facebook account of the far-right party CasaPound and pay € 800 for each day the account had been closed. Similar to the German case, the account had allegedly violated Facebook's internal anti hatred policies. However, the Court considered that the decision of the platform created an unacceptable exclusion or limitation of the voice of CasaPound in the Italian political debate.[9]

Thus, courts have considered, in some cases, the adoption of positive measures to protect certain forms of online speech when the role and presence of a specific platform within the public sphere has direct implications on the exercise of fundamental rights (notably freedom of expression or right to non discrimination) and or affects basic national and European constitutional principles (such as pluralism) (Ketteman and Tiedeke 2019). This is, of course, still a very open question, that would deserve future proper and consistent elaboration from the side of national constitutional courts and the European Court of Human Rights.

In any case, it is important to underscore that the debate in Europe about the existence of possible "positive" obligations for states to protect individuals' freedom of expression vis-à-vis intermediaries' content moderation decisions is still at a very early stage, though some scholars have already established interesting connections between the traditional media law principle of pluralism and diversity (and the correlative powers that legislators and regulators may have in this area) and the introduction of possible restrictions and obligations to the way platforms manage content. Such restrictions and obligations are not necessarily based on the need to avoid illegal content but rather on the promotion of the

---

[8] *Themel v. Facebook Ireland*, OLG München, Beschluss August 24, 2018 – 18 W 1294/18, See a description and analysis of the case at Columbia University Global Freedom of Expression Database: https://globalfreedomofexpression.columbia.edu/cases/heike-themel-v-facebook-ireland-inc (accessed January 16, 2021).

[9] *CasaPound v. Facebook Tribunale di Roma*, December 12, 2019 - R.G. 59264/2019. See a description and analysis of the case at Columbia University Global Freedom of Expression Database: https://globalfreedomofexpression.columbia.edu/cases/casapound-v-facebook (accessed January 16, 2021).

dissemination and access to certain types of content. Authors like Leerssen (2015) admit that for users "the identification of direct state action currently remains essential for an appeal for their free speech rights against online services." However, he also invites bodies like the European Court of Human Rights to further "explore the horizontal dimension of free-speech rights online, and depart from a strict distinction between public and private responsibilities for the observance of these claims" (Leerssen 2015, p. 113). There is no doubt that this is a matter that may change some of the foundations and traditional constitutional approaches to the role and methods to protect freedom of expression in our societies, thus introducing us to what has been called "digital constitutionalism" (De Gregorio 2019). In addition to this, some interesting analyses on the interplay between artificial intelligence (AI), content moderation, and freedom of expression can already be found (Llansó et al. 2020).

At the level of the European Union, it is important to outline that, so far, there are several legal provisions imposing content moderation and supervision obligations to platforms that, at the same time, require the need to take into consideration users' right to freedom of expression. Important examples include:

- General Data Protection Regulation:[10] Article 17 on the right to erasure or right to be forgotten establishes that data subjects, when deciding on requests grounded on the mentioned right, need to give prevalence to the exercise of the right of freedom of expression and information.
- Copyright Directive:[11] Recital 70 states that "steps taken by online content-sharing service providers in cooperation with right-holders should be without prejudice to the application of exceptions or limitations to copyright, including, in particular, those which guarantee the freedom of expression of users."
- Audiovisual Media Services Directive:[12] Recital 49 determines, with regards to video-sharing platforms, that besides the obligations contained in the Directive, they are entitled "to take stricter measures on a voluntary basis in accordance with Union law, respecting the freedom of expression and information and media pluralism."

Regarding liability, the general legally applicable regime has remained fundamentally intact since its adoption in 2000: the e-commerce Directive[13] establishes liability exemptions for intermediaries under certain conditions of lack of knowledge of illegal activity or information and expeditious removal and disabling upon knowledge (Art.14). The Directive also includes an important provision regarding the absence of any legal obligation for providers to monitor content (Art. 15).

In brief, intermediaries enjoy liability immunities inasmuch as they perform a role of a mere technical, automatic, and passive nature. This requirement of "passivity" is compatible with

[10] Regulation (EU) 2016/679 of the European Parliament and of the Council of April 27, 2016 on the protection of natural persons with regard to the processing of personal data and on the free movement of such data, and repealing Directive 95/46/EC.

[11] Directive (EU) 2019/790 of the European Parliament and of the Council of April 17, 2019 on copyright and related rights in the Digital Single Market and amending Directives 96/9/EC and 2001/29/EC.

[12] Directive (EU) 2018/1808 of the European Parliament and of the Council of November 14, 2018 amending Directive 2010/13/EU on the coordination of certain provisions laid down by law, regulation or administrative action in member states concerning the provision of audiovisual media services (Audiovisual Media Services Directive) in view of changing market realities.

[13] Directive 2000/31/EC of the European Parliament and of the Council of June 8, 2000 on certain legal aspects of information society services, in particular electronic commerce, in the Internal Market.

certain activities identified by the case law of the CJEU.[14] In addition to this, voluntary proactive measures to monitor, detect, and remove illegal content online do not necessarily lead the online platform in question to lose the benefit of the liability exemption. Intermediaries become liable in cases where they fail to act expeditiously to remove or to disable access to the illegal content upon obtaining knowledge or awareness, or they are simply proven to have overlooked a particular illegality when implementing voluntary and proactive monitoring measures in such a way as to create actual or constructive knowledge that strips them of immunity.

This being said, it is also true that there are some trends in EU law that point toward the reinforcement of monitoring responsibilities of intermediaries and also the introduction of modulations in the general liability exemption system precisely on the basis of the induction of new active monitoring obligations for platforms.

Just to mention a couple of examples, Article 17 of the Copyright Directive establishes that, in some cases "online content-sharing service providers shall be liable for unauthorized acts of communication to the public, including making available to the public, of copyright-protected works and other subject matter, unless the service providers demonstrate that they have: made, in accordance with high industry standards of professional diligence, best efforts to ensure the unavailability of specific works and other subject matter for which the right-holders have provided the service providers with the relevant and necessary information; and in any event", Article 28b of the Audiovisual Media Services Directive encompasses a series of duties of video-sharing platforms concerning the prevention and moderation of content that constitutes hate speech and child pornography, affects children's physical and mental development, violates obligations in the area of commercial communications, or can be considered as terrorist. National authorities (mainly independent media regulatory bodies) are given the responsibility of verifying that VSPs have adopted "appropriate measures" to properly deal with the types of content mentioned earlier (alongside other undesirable content). This includes the guarantee that platforms properly revise and enforce their Terms of Service; have appropriate flagging, reporting, and declaring functionalities; implement age verification or rating and control systems; establish and operate transparent, easy-to-use, and effective procedures to resolve users' complaints; and provide media literacy tools (Barata 2020).

In the case of Eva Glawischnig-Piesczek,[15] the CJEU and the Advocate General (AG) Szpunar seem to endorse an interpretation of Articles 14 and 15 that finds that specific monitoring obligations are valid and possible only when they do not put intermediaries in the position of becoming liable under the parameters of Article 14. This may lead to the conclusion that these obligations are acceptable inasmuch as they can be fulfilled with recourse to "passive" automated search tools and technologies. Conversely, and according to the AG, applying human error-correction protocols to fulfill the obligation of finding content "identical" to the previously identified as illegal may make the platform (Facebook, in this case) lose its immunity in terms of Article 14 (Keller 2019b).

## Intermediaries and the Enforcement of the Law

The debate around these new legal provisions and its implementation refers to the possibility of legally compelling platforms to incorporate in their Terms of Service and enforce rules and limits already contemplated by the law. This is already a problematic issue, as the recent experience in Germany has shown.

[14] See, among others, the *L'Oreal* case (Judgement of July 12, 2011, case C-324/09), and the *Google France* case (Judgment of March 23, 2010, joined cases C-236/08 to C-238/08).
[15] Judgment of October 3, 2019, case C-18/18.

On January 1, 2018, the Netzwerkdurchsetzungsgesetz (Network Enforcement Act, or NetzDG), came into force.[16] This rule was the subject of a great number of debates and criticisms by that time, as it was considered by organizations that defend fundamental rights online as disproportionate, inadequate, and promoting private censorship on the Internet.[17] In a nutshell, the NetzDG obliges large platforms (those with more than two million users in Germany) to provide them with mechanisms to report a wide range (22 specifically) of criminal categories already included in the German penal legislation. Once the corresponding complaint is received, it is up to the platform to determine whether the content is actually illegal. According to NetzDG, in cases of "manifestly illegal" content, the platforms must remove it within 24 hours. In cases where such determination is more complex, the removal must be carried out within seven days. Non compliance with such obligations is sanctioned with fines of up to € 50 million. Likewise, platforms are obliged to publish "transparency reports" that reflect the decisions adopted regarding content moderation.

The NetzDG can be considered as a truly unique law both in relation to the type of obligations that it imposes on this type of providers, as well as to its extension and intensity, and the seriousness of the penalties it contemplates in cases of contravention of its provisions. Though the effectiveness of the NetzDG as a tool to combat and eliminate certain forms of illegal online content is still pending today with reliable data, the truth is that NetzDG's fame reached worldwide scale and its approval by a liberal European democracy has been explicitly appreciated and used as inspiration by authoritarian or semi-authoritarian regimes in other parts of the world as justification for approving considerably restrictive rules. These regimes include Russia, Venezuela, Belarus, Honduras, Malaysia, Singapore, and the Philippines.

A norm of the characteristics of the NetzDG entails an obvious risk of over-removal of contents. If a Damocles sword hangs over the platforms in the form of large fines for those cases in which they have failed to consider a certain content as illegal, it is clear that these companies will feel pushed to eliminate any content that raises the slightest suspicion of being illegal. The impact on the exercise of freedom of expression is evident, especially if we take into account the fact that, purely, we are not faced with a strictly private decision, but rather with a limitation materially implemented by a private company, though on the basis of an obligation derived from a legal norm whose compliance is verified by the authorities.

As a matter of fact, these cases imply no less than the delegated exercise of the power (typically statutory to date) to determine the legitimate scope of freedom of expression and, more importantly, act accordingly (especially as regards the withdrawal of the corresponding content). Being true that all these decisions can ultimately be subject to jurisdictional control, the impact of the immediate removal of a certain piece of content can hardly be compensated by a judicial decision favorable to the author's claims.

However, there is another emerging trend that would go beyond this, and basically will represent the adoption of legal and regulatory frameworks aimed at obliging platforms not only to enforce general legal restrictions in areas such as hate speech, terrorist content, protection of children, and so on, but also to adopt additional rules and principles that would go beyond such general restrictions. In other words, platforms may acquire the legal obligation to establish speech limits that are neither contemplated in the laws, nor would be acceptable, due to international standards and constitutional protections, if they were adopted or enforced by public entities. In addition to this, platforms would face legal responsibilities and even liability in case they fail to properly incorporate and enforce such rules.

[16]September 1, 2017. Federal Law Gazette I, p. 3352 ff.

[17]https://www.article19.org/wp-content/uploads/2017/09/170901-Legal-Analysis-German-NetzDG-Act.pdf (accessed January 16, 2021).

The Online Harms regulatory initiative in the United Kingdom represents a good example of this trend. At the time of writing this chapter, the Government published, in April 2019, an extensive White Paper,[18] which was the object of an extensive public consultation. In February 2020, an initial response was published, pointing at some more specific details in a few areas.[19] The main development in the Initial Consultation Response was the shift to a differentiated duty of care. This, we are told, means that for lawful but harmful content seen by adults, intermediaries will be free to set content standards in their terms and conditions (T&Cs). The interest of the regulator will be in ensuring that the T&Cs are enforced transparently and consistently – and perhaps effectively, depending on which section of the Initial Response you read.

Similarly, we are told that the regulator will be concerned with systems and processes to deal with online harms, not requiring the removal of specific pieces of legal content.

It is interesting to note that the initial Paper constantly acknowledges the need to deal not only with actual illegal content but also with content that is categorized as "harmful," "threatening the way of life in the UK," or "unacceptable," to mention just a few examples. It is, in any case, clear that such categories do not necessarily coincide with illegal content but, on the contrary, they refer to legal and protected expressions that the authors of the Paper do not want to be disseminated in the United Kingdom, at least through online platforms.

In fact, the Paper clearly admits on page five that certain types of content "even if they may not be illegal in all circumstances, can also cause serious harm." The Paper does not include any assessment to support, on the basis of specific data, what constitutes its main assumption or starting point: "the prevalence of illegal and harmful content online," or the online widespread use of "illegal and unacceptable content and activity." An additional example would be the threatening reference to the fact that "hostile actors use online disinformation to undermine our democratic values of principles." Despite the fact that the Paper provides some references or data to justify its interventionist approach, it also needs to be underscored that, in most cases, information provided is general, focusing not only on the problems in the United Kingdom, and not necessarily conclusive.

It could then be legitimately asked how this – in many cases – legal but harmful content can be defined in a precise way. A minimum degree of detail would be needed inasmuch as this kind of content will be the object of a series of legal obligations imposed on platforms and encapsulated in a new category called "duty of care," which basically means them being forced to adopt a series of measures aimed at mitigating the impact of unacceptable content, including of course, deletion.

In any case, it needs to be pointed out that in light of the most recent response by the Government, and as analyzed by Graham Smith (2020a), a more detailed approach to differentiated duty of care can be found: for lawful but harmful content seen by adults, intermediaries will be free to set content standards in their terms and conditions. The interest of the regulator will be in ensuring that the Terms of Service are enforced transparently and consistently. More importantly, it appears that the regulator will be concerned with systems and processes to deal with online harms, not requiring the removal of specific pieces of legal content.

There is no doubt that, in any case, such regulatory mechanism has a clear and state-originated impact on the exercise of the right to freedom of expression and therefore UK authorities might be creating the conditions for an unacceptable online version of the well-known chilling effect, where online speakers cannot be certain under which circumstances

[18] Available online at: https://www.gov.uk/government/consultations/online-harms-white-paper/online-harms-white-paper (accessed January 16, 2021).

[19] Available online at: https://www.gov.uk/government/consultations/online-harms-white-paper/public-feedback/online-harms-white-paper-initial-consultation-response (accessed January 16, 2021).

their speech would be protected or restricted. As previously mentioned, this is a relevant departure from the already problematic approach to the regulation of Terms of Service contained in the AVMSD, inasmuch as, in the UK model, this delegated regulation does not relate to the general and legally established speech boundaries but to the discretionary and evolutive will of a regulatory body, as authors like Graham Smith (2020b) have clearly and critically pointed out.

In contrast with the UK example, the French Government has also published a report[20] aimed at elaborating proposals to "make social media platforms more accountable." The approach of this document is significantly different from the UK's approach, as it focuses on the definition of a public intervention that is subject to "particular preventions," on the explicit basis of the principles of proportionality and necessity. In this sense, new legal obligations to be imposed on platforms would not focus on content issues but rather on transparency and accountability, also including the special need to protect the integrity of all users. The details of the proposal cannot be described here but, as mentioned, the French version of a new "duty of care" for platforms represents the adoption of a targeted regulation that would establish new rules to improve the transparency of platforms with regard to their internal rules and processes, as well as the accountability of the decisions they take. This would also imply a better communication with civil society organizations and a more comprehensive reporting vis-à-vis government bodies. In this scheme, discussions about the legality or legitimacy of content would apparently remain in the hands of judges and regulators.

## Intermediaries' Regulation and Human Rights

As it has been shown so far, social media platforms apply their own rules to various actions that we do online. Among them, probably the most important activity affected by these private rules, is speech. This is a challenging territory, as freedom of expression is protected by international law as a human right.

Likewise, every state in the world has in place a set of national rules governing the dissemination of ideas, information, and opinions. Sometimes these rules are aligned with international standards. Yet, not always.

Platforms' own Terms of Service navigate in these murky waters, which include, apart from universal rules, a complex set of regional and national norms, distributed across a patchwork of jurisdictions. Despite the private nature of platforms' Terms of Service, comparisons to legal standards are inevitable. Platforms may and sometimes actually do find the "inspiration" for their standards in already existing national and international concepts and principles. In this context Balkin (2018) has created the well-known reference of the "free speech triangle," where, in one corner, there are states and other public bodies and supranational organizations, in the second corner, one can find Internet companies (social media, search engines, ISPs, etc.) while, in the third corner, we have speakers and legacy media.

Global platforms may be forced to apply local laws through local authorities when speech can be associated to a specific physical territory. Platforms are also being asked by relevant bodies of the international system and civil society to align their practices with international human rights law. All these normative inputs do not only affect the way social media entities design their internal rules but also their implementation by the same private bodies. In this regard, Klonick (2018) accurately describes them as the New Governors in the digital era.

[20] "Creating a French framework to make social media platforms more accountable: Acting in France with a European vision," May 2019. Available online at: https://minefi.hosting.augure.com/Augure_Minefi/r/ContenuEnLigne/Download?id=AE5B7ED5-2385-4749-9CE8-E4E1B36873E4&filename=Mission%20Régulation%20des%20réseaux%20sociaux%20-ENG.pdf (accessed January 16, 2021).

One could, first of all, ask about the relationship between the "rule of law," i.e., speech legislation and regulations enshrined in legal norms emanating from public bodies and platforms' content rules. There is a possible discussion on whether and how platforms must incorporate legal notions to their own community guidelines. In fact, as shown very much in detail by Klonick (2018), there is no doubt that content-moderation policies of Silicon Valley big social media companies were initially rooted in US First Amendment values, norms, and objectives.

Beyond these general principles, the relationship between content moderation and legal systems becomes particularly complex in cases when different national regimes create different, and sometimes incompatible, rules applicable to one single and global digital territory. Along the same lines, there are situations when international law is not completely defined, thus requiring a proper understanding of the context, the nature of the speaker, and many other relevant circumstances in order to properly frame the application of certain notions (for example, the prohibition of hate speech). Last, but not least, platforms receive and need to consider the execution of orders from public bodies (courts, regulators, etc.) on the basis of national norms that may, at the same time, contravene international standards.

It could be argued that international and regional standards may not necessarily be relevant to this debate, as platforms are entitled to have their own internal rules, which would not automatically replicate or incorporate otherwise applicable legal standards. This argument would be particularly successful in the US context, where, as it has been shown, so far users are not considered to hold First Amendment rights vis-à-vis online platforms.

This being said, it must also be stressed that in his 2018 thematic report to the Human Rights Council,[21] the United Nations Special Rapporteur on the promotion and protection of the right to freedom of opinion and expression David Kaye, directly addressed platforms, requesting them to recognize that "the authoritative global standard for ensuring freedom of expression on their platforms is human rights law, not the varying laws of States or their own private interests, and they should re-evaluate their content standards accordingly." A proper discussion on how and to what extent platforms may incorporate international standards to their content policies (in case this recommendation is fully accepted) still needs to take place. Yet the essential issue here is that, independently from the detailed rules and standards that platforms may have (and which would not necessarily equate to the myriad of national legal norms governing speech), according to the mentioned international documents, platforms would at least need to adhere to and use universal human rights law as a general guiding and interpretative framework for the establishment and enforcement of such norms.

In any case, it is important to note that adherence to human rights law has become at least a soft reference commonly made by platforms' representatives when publicly presenting and defending their content moderation practices, though no clear, explicit, or strong commitment can be found at this point.

To mention just a few examples, in July 2019, Twitter announced that the company would allow public officials and other relevant political representatives to publish certain types of content that might violate specific content rules of the company whenever, at the same time, "it may be in the public interest to have access" to it.[22] Twitter's view is based on the fact that "these leaders have outsized influence and sometimes say things that could be considered controversial or invite debate and discussion. A critical function of our service is providing a place where people can openly and publicly respond to their leaders and hold them accountable." Related to this, Twitter's CEO Jack Dorsey tweeted in 2018 that the company's values

---

[21] Available online at: https://www.ohchr.org/EN/Issues/FreedomOpinion/Pages/ContentRegulation.aspx (accessed January 16, 2021).

[22] https://blog.twitter.com/en_us/topics/company/2019/publicinterest.html (accessed January 16, 2021).

need to be rooted in human rights law. It is thus obvious that the involved platforms are deliberately using, at least, what can be called a "human rights language."[23]

After this, in May 2020 the same company decided to hide (yet not delete) a Tweet by US President Donald Trump in the midst of the coronavirus crisis behind a warning that it "glorifies violence." The Tweet warned people in Minneapolis protesting against the killing of a black man, by a white police officer, that he would send the military to intervene and stated that "When the looting starts, the shooting starts." Also in May 2020, Twitter decided to add a warning label to other two Tweets by Trump, as they were considered to contain potentially misleading information about voting processes, and with the aim of providing additional context around mail-in ballots in particular. During June 2020 the company also hid this other Tweet from the President: "There will never be an 'Autonomous Zone' in Washington, D.C., as long as I'm your President. If they try they will be met with serious force!," after a clash between protesters and law enforcement in the capital. Twitter added the following notice: "We've placed a public interest notice on this Tweet for violating our policy against abusive behavior, specifically, the presence of a threat of harm against an identifiable group." This means that the company kept the Tweet up but restricted the ability of users to interact with it. All these measures triggered a series of statements and threats by the President himself (including a contested and dubiously enforceable Executive Order[24]) particularly vis-à-vis the possible introduction of changes in the current and applicable legal regime. Such a matter cannot be analyzed in this chapter.

In parallel, several media outlets have disclosed a Facebook's document on fact-checking practices and rules applied by the company, which underscores that content "with the primary purpose of expressing the opinion or agenda of a political figure" is not eligible for such a tool. Considering that fact-checking is one of the instruments used by Facebook to reduce the dissemination of the so-called fake news (or, more technically, disinformation), this would mean that statements (at this point I am only focusing on organic content) posted by "political figures" may not be, as a general principle, subjected to the mentioned type of scrutiny, and therefore remain exempted from measures applied to false or misleading content, including deletion.[25] In addition to this, in a blog post, Facebook's VP of Global Affairs and Communications Nick Clegg has somewhat elaborated on the basis and consequences of such policy, invoking the already existing "newsworthy policy." This policy means that if someone makes a statement or shares a post that breaks Facebook's community standards, it will still be allowed on the platform provided that the public interest in seeing it outweighs the risk of harm. Speech from politicians will thus be treated, as a general principle, as newsworthy speech. A very interesting expansion of a policy already in place, taken to a controversial height.[26] The post states that decisions on content published by politicians "will account for international standards."

However, during the coronavirus crisis, amidst the racial protests across the United States and, in view of then upcoming presidential election in November 2020, the platform changed this approach regarding these matters. In a post published on June 26, 2020, Mark Zuckerberg reiterated that "seeing speech from politicians is in the public interest, and in the same way that news outlets will report what a politician says, we think people should generally be able to see it for themselves on our platforms." However, he also announced that Facebook will start labeling some of the content they leave up so that

[23]Available online at: https://twitter.com/jack/status/1027962500438843397?lang=en (accessed January 16, 2021).

[24]https://www.whitehouse.gov/presidential-actions/executive-order-preventing-online-censorship (accessed January 16, 2021).

[25]https://www.facebook.com/help/publisher/182222309230722?ref=MisinfomrationPolicyPage (accessed January 16, 2021).

[26]Available online at: https://about.fb.com/news/2019/09/elections-and-political-speech (accessed January 16, 2021).

people who share this content can also condemn it. However, and regarding specifically the so-called newsworthiness policy, "if we determine that content may lead to violence or deprive people of their right to vote, we will take that content down" even in cases where "a politician or government official says it."[27]

It is clear that the content moderation–international standards–national legal systems relationship is becoming more complex and intricate. In addition, current proposals put in place, and particularly Facebook's proposed Oversight Board, seem to be insufficient for this purpose: according to its Charter, the Board will "pay particular attention to the impact of removing content in light of human rights norms protecting free expression." This notion of "paying particular attention" is a bit puzzling for any legal reader, as it seems to refer to something lighter than merely "applying."[28] In addition to this, the more recent white paper published by Facebook's Vice President Monika Bickert does not provide further light on these very sensitive matters.[29] Only the actual "case law" of the Board will show us how this extremely vague provision is to be understood. On May 6, 2020 the appointment of the first group of members of the Board was publicly announced.[30] At the moment of making the final revision of this text, the regular work of this body has not yet commenced.

## Conclusions

New technologies have brought unprecedented change to human communications and have undoubtedly expanded the possibilities and scope of the exercise of the right to freedom of expression. This has also triggered new societal risks that pushed the introduction of undesirable rules and mechanisms restricting to the right to freedom of expression (either by public or private entities, or a combination of both).

How to solve these complex tensions is a debate that remains open between governments, platforms, media, activists, and a great diversity of subjects involved. Any effective solution will require an effort of imagination, especially for jurists, to find mechanisms and categories different from those used so far to correctly address the exercise of freedom of expression and properly define and enforce its limits.

## References

Balkin, J. (2018). Free speech is a triangle. *Columbia Law Review* 118: 2011–2056.

Barata, J. (2020). Regulating content moderation in Europe beyond the AVMSD. LSE Media Blog. https://blogs.lse.ac.uk/medialse/2020/02/25/regulating-content-moderation-in-europe-beyond-the-avmsd (accessed September 17, 2020).

De Gregorio, G. (2019). The rise of digital constitutionalism in the European Union. *International Journal of Constitutional Law*. https://ssrn.com/abstract=3506692 (accessed September 17, 2020).

Goldman, E. (2019). Why Section 230 is better than the First Amendment. *Notre Dame Law Review Reflection* 95 (1): 33–46.

[27] https://about.fb.com/news/2020/06/meeting-unique-elections-challenges (accessed January 16, 2021).

[28] Available online at: https://fbnewsroomus.files.wordpress.com/2019/09/oversight_board_charter.pdf.

[29] Available online at: https://about.fb.com/wp-content/uploads/2020/02/Charting-A-Way-Forward_Online-Content-Regulation-White-Paper-1.pdf (accessed January 16, 2021).

[30] https://www.oversightboard.com/news/announcing-the-first-members-of-the-oversight-board (accessed January 16, 2021).

Goldman, E. (2020). YouTube isn't a state actor (DUH) – PragerU v. Google. *Technology & Marketing Law Blog* (2 March). https://blog.ericgoldman.org/archives/2020/03/youtube-isnt-a-state-actor-duh-prageru-v-google.htm (accessed 17 September 2020).

Keller, D. (2018). Who do you sue? *Hoover Institution. Aegis Series Papers* 1902.

Keller, D. (2019a). Facebook restricts speech by popular demand. *The Atlantic* (22 September). https://www.theatlantic.com/ideas/archive/2019/09/facebook-restricts-free-speech-popular-demand/598462 (accessed September 17, 2020).

Keller, D. (2019b). Dolphins in the net: Internet content filters and the Advocate General's Glawischnig-Piesczek v. Facebook Ireland opinion. Stanford CIS White Paper. http://cyberlaw.stanford.edu/blog/2019/09/filtering-facebook-introducing-dolphins-net-new-stanford-cis-white-paper-or-why (accessed September 17, 2020).

Kettemann, M.C. and Tiedeke, A.S. (2019). Back up: can users sue platforms to reinstate deleted content? A comparative study of US and German jurisprudence on "must carry." *GigaNet*. https://www.giga-net.org/2019symposiumPapers/05_Ketteman_Back-Up-Can-Users-Sue-Platforms.pdf (accessed September 17, 2020).

Klonick, K. (2018). The new governors: the people, rules, and processes governing online speech. *Harvard Law Review* 131: 1598–1670.

Leerssen, P. (2015). Cut out by the middle man. the free speech implications of social network blocking and banning in the EU. *JIPITEC* 1: 99–119.

Llansó, E., Van Hoboken, J., Leerssen, P. et al. (2020). Artificial intelligence, content moderation, and freedom of expression. Transatlantic Working Group on Content Moderation Online and Freedom of Expression. https://www.ivir.nl/publicaties/download/AI-Llanso-Van-Hoboken-Feb-2020.pdf (accessed September 17, 2020).

Pew Research Center (2018). News use across social media platforms. https://www.journalism.org/2018/09/10/news-use-across-social-media-platforms-2018 (accessed October 1, 2020).

Smith, G. (2020a). Online harms revisited. *Cyberleagle*. https://www.cyberleagle.com/2020/06/online-harms-revisited.html (accessed September 17, 2020).

Smith, G. (2020b). Online harms deconstructed – the initial consultation response. *Cyberleagle*. https://www.cyberleagle.com/2020/02/online-harms-deconstructed-initial.html (accessed September 17, 2020).

# 15

# Imperiling Community Memory
## The European Right to be Forgotten's Tampering of Search Engine Results

Kristie Byrum

Citizens of the world seeking important or, at times, mundane information about a variety of topics, simply type the request into a search engine and instantly the answers appear on the smart device, coloring the screen with multiple answers for the recipient. The inquisitive fingers then wander over the responses, allowing the viewer to assume a self-directed exploration of the chosen topic. Yet, there may be something flawed about the purity of this experience. In the United States, respondents can rest assured that the information is thorough. Yet, this is not the case in countries in the European Union as the European General Data Protection regulation allows for search engine data removal under the Right to be Forgotten provision. When addressing communication rights across international borders, the legal aspects of the European Right to be Forgotten (RTBF; a provision of the European General Data Protection Regulation) emerge as we contemplate how online information is governed and exchanged across geographic borders. For residents of all continents, the availability of information on global search engines and "who" controls the availability of content are paramount issues. For journalists and historians, the removal of information is particularly troubling as information becomes harder to find, or worse yet, history is ostensibly rewritten as the community memory is distorted by holes in the search engine results.

While the European General Data Protection Regulation offers the right to be forgotten for online search engines, the United States' First Amendment stops similar actions from being taken in the United States. Google recently won a legal victory stating that Google does not have to apply the RTBF provision across the globe. While French privacy regulator CNIL tried to apply the law globally, the Court of Justice of the European Union ruled that global delisting requests do not apply globally and that data protection authorities in Europe maintain rights (KU Leuven 2020). This action beckons a call for further exploration of the public sphere for social, political, and economic discourse. Furthermore, the ability to readily retrieve accurate information remains in question within the framework of global boundaries. The European Right to be Forgotten requires global citizens to scrutinize the existence of a virtual public sphere for debate regarding social, economic, and political issues. Renowned German philosopher and sociologist Jürgen Habermas pointed to the public sphere as a place for discussion of public events. In his seminal book, *The Structural Transformation of the Public Sphere—An Inquiry into a Category of Bourgois Society* (Habermas 1991), he asserts that the public sphere manifests an identity as a place where individuals can unite, discuss collective social problems,

*The Handbook of Communication Rights, Law, and Ethics: Seeking Universality, Equality, Freedom and Dignity*, First Edition. Edited by Loreto Corredoira, Ignacio Bel Mallén, and Rodrigo Cetina Presuel.

and, through that discussion, ultimately influence political action. Reminiscent of the Greek city-state (polis), the public sphere affords the opportunity for public debate and formation of opinions. Habermas's work, recognized as a foundation for subsequent theories on the public sphere, characterized the decline of the political sphere and the rise of the changing forces of media. These crucial forces included the introduction of commercialism and private gain into the public sphere, transforming the bourgeois public sphere and adapting the way that citizens address political concepts. Lessons regarding the public sphere may also be gained by looking at the evolution and practice of public relations. Edward Bernays, often characterized as the father of public relations and who was the nephew of Sigmund Freud, provided the world with the book, *Crystallizing Public Opinion* in 1923, proffering insights about how consensus is gained through appropriate public dialogs and displays. Bernays coined the term public relations counsel for those who perform this type of work, providing a viable alternative to negative connotations including "propagandist" or "publicist," and through his writing, the notion of two-way communication emerges (Bernays 1923). Bernays deftly informed subsequent thinkers about the role of communication in the public sphere. The two-way communication paradigm provided a solid foundation for subsequent communication models, including those prevalent in public relations theory and practice (Grunig and Grunig 1992).

As we examine the transformation of the public sphere, it is also relevant to consider the role of thought leaders in the flow of information. Today, thought leaders emerge in the social media space, providing "followers" with particular views, opinions, and endorsements. This public sphere is further influenced by the availability of rich media, technology-enabled production techniques for videos, infographics, and imagery. While literature often points to notable public opinion luminaries like Bernays and Walter Lippman, the author of *Public Opinion* (1922), the role of the information recipient and the information "receiver" take on more gravitas in the formulation of public opinion. Lippman often critiqued the ease of public opinion and pointed to the role of citizens in forming beliefs in a representative democracy. While Bernays, at times referred to as the "father of public relations," underscored the significant influence of thought leaders in society, who help shape and determine salient discussion points for society. In their early writings, neither Lippman nor Bernays may have anticipated the technology-enabled atmosphere that pervades modernity, yet both contribute theoretical insights that resonate today, as we contemplate the role of communication in society. Lippman writes, "The world that we have to deal with politically is out of reach, out of sight, out of mind. It has to be explored, reported, and imagined. Gradually, he makes for himself a trustworthy picture inside of his head of the world beyond his reach" (Lippman 1922, p. 20).

The casual smartphone user who receives Tweets or brief alerts from news organizations, and occasionally accesses a search engine to find more in-depth information about a specific topic is using these technology tools to create what Lippman called the "picture inside our heads." In his critique of mass media, Lippman suggested media remain susceptible to manipulation and that the media signal the occurrence of an event through the journalistic process of the selection of news and the discernment of societal happenings. Bernays' seminal writings suggest a role for an opinion leader to manage the movements of the "herd," as they gather public opinion. Bernays suggests that the passivity of viewers results in the formulation of public opinion by simple exposure to mass media outlets, which at the time of his writing, encompassed newspapers, posters, and advertising: "People accept facts which come to them through existing channels. They like to hear new things in accustomed ways. They have neither the time nor the inclination to search for facts that are not readily available to them" (Bernays 1923, p. 146). Consistent with this tenet, contemporary media consumers must acknowledge the "mainstreaming" of social media and recognize that it has become a medium for information, whether it is deemed accurate or offers a channel for the spread of false information. Citizens today gain information as it actively pours over the transom of the smartphone, buzzing, beeping, and bearing characters with tiny bytes of information. Furthermore,

Bernays suggests that the reader operates passively, letting their opinions gain shape by what enters their lives. Today, this situation seems relevant considering the inclination of Digital Age citizens to gain no more information than what arrives in front of their eyeballs from a media channel such as a television station, newspaper, or online media, or morsels of information from another individual in the form of a Tweet, a text, or a shared hyperlink to a news story, often accompanied with a pithy statement of opinion. In the contemplation of the right to be forgotten, perhaps the "average" citizen does not care to use the search engine in a meaningful way, so why is it imperative to retain information on the search engine at all? Yet, it may also be argued that citizens of the world use search engines many times a day to gather information and curate their own "world" of information. While Digital Age citizens may conduct an ambitious search for information by tapping search terms into Google and the like, information continually streams into their consciousness through email, social media, mobile applications, and other message carriers in the digital milieu. This cacophony creates a modern day manifestation of a condition that Habermas diagnosed, indicating the decline in the public sphere and the naiveté of citizens to simply embrace the "publicity" and stunts of communicators in multiple realms, most notably the political sphere. A stylistic show has emerged in Digital Age democracies reflecting the richness of the media production channels.

While Habermas has written extensively on the decline of the bourgeois social sphere as a venue for a spirited public debate that allows for the formation of public opinion and open dialogs among citizens, he points a chastising finger at public relations practitioners and the "advertisers" as culprits in the demise. Specifically, Habermas attacks staged publicity as a "transmutation" that pervades the entire public sphere in the political realm. Before the expanded public sphere, the transactions themselves are stylized into a show. Publicity loses its critical function in favor of a staged display; even arguments are transmuted into symbols to which, again, one cannot respond by arguing but only by identifying with them (Habermas 1991, p. 206). Habermas further points to the employment of advertising in the mass media-dominated public sphere as a way to influence votes and, in the face of this political marketing, the electorate disintegrates as a public (1991, p. 217). Does the online sphere remain analogous to a "world" where individuals seek information, exercise access, formulate public opinion, and engage in the physical world through social, economic, and political conditions? Or rather, does the passive viewer simply absorb ideas as they come over the transom, failing to exert rational questioning or question the fluid assumptions of arguments. Distrust in legitimate news sources and traditional institutions rises in the atmosphere of populism characterized by a media "echo chamber" that allows for the reinforcement of existing attitudes and beliefs. So now, we must face the digital milieu and attempt to understand how search engines, social media, and the right to be forgotten can lead to misunderstandings and misperception in the public sphere.

The European Right to be Forgotten further complicates the matter. Europe's adoption of the European Data Protection Regulation translates into the implementation of the right to be forgotten in 28 countries across Europe, the ability to request data removal about one's past is considered a human right, thus creating a legal mandate for Google, Bing, and other data controllers to remove data that is deemed inadequate, irrelevant, or no longer relevant. The United States presents itself as a country that ardently opposes the right to be forgotten by virtue of the existence and adherence to the First Amendment to the Bill of Rights of the US Constitution. While Constitutional theorists articulate a multitude of theories about the framers of the Constitution. One of the most relevant for this discussion is the marketplace of ideas theory. US jurisprudence has adopted the concept of the Marketplace of Ideas, transmitting notions first articulated by John Milton in 1644 in *Areopagitica* into the contemporary landscape. Milton wrote this tract to protest against censorship and today it has become a well-regarded essay for the defense of freedom of expression. The World Wide Web's marketplace of ideas operates 24 hours a day, seven days a week. While Europeans embrace tenets of privacy over the free flow of information in society, US audiences, imbued with the light of the First Amendment, seem to understand its freedoms were molded into the legal code as the very first amendment of the Bill of Rights adopted by the country's founding fathers. In distillation, the First Amendment prohibits the passage of any laws that would encumber freedom of speech and freedom of the press. Therefore, under the most rigid interpretation of the law, the First Amendment would preclude the implementation of the Right to be Forgotten in the United States. By examining theories of the US First Amendment, in tandem with the rationale for the European right to be forgotten legislation, we rapidly encounter a conflict of principles and practice. The fork in the road between the US treatment of web delinking and that of the right to be forgotten may gain enlightenment from the theoretical framework of the Marketplace of Ideas that has been central to Supreme Court arguments for preservation of freedom of speech and press since the nation's inception. The Marketplace of Ideas theory presumes that ideas should have the opportunity to compete in the marketplace in an effort to gain acceptance.

As we apply the Marketplace of Ideas concept to the web's search engine, we encounter a critique of the marketplace that questions whether it is authentically transparent, offers accurate information, and provides access of the market's information to humans operating with rational thought. Therefore, it may be argued that the right to be forgotten disrupts the information marketplace by compromising the inventory of information available online. In the United States, corresponding movements to delink information from common search engines like Google taint the First Amendment and arbitrarily centralize power of the information in an omnipotent information source, in many cases, a private individual making à la carte information decisions, based on variable rules. The implementation of such a system warps truth, and the available information for citizens to glean truth is, in fact, dictated by a private power source. In the case of the right to be forgotten, the European Union has enacted a law that transfers regulation of the activities to a private company, in this case the search engines, that exercise discretion over the information available on a given subject. This government intervention led by the European Union leads to an incomplete search, delivered with multiple holes. The cascading results of government intervention and information regulation, for example, propel the systematic handicapping of journalists who may attempt to investigate a story or present information into the marketplace for consideration by citizens. Ordinary information-seekers suffer too, because the Marketplace of Ideas is compromised and once-valued transparency now gives way to a murky sea of information that has some tidbits of retrievable data but is absent of possible salient information that is simply gone forever, digitally erased after search engine delinking.

## The Public Stage, Online Personas, and Digital Governance

In light of the RTBF provisions, the World Wide Web reveals an evolution of the public stage, the maintenance and availability of online personas and the legal regulation of digital governance of news and information. The cornucopia of historical content available with just a few keystrokes ushers in a new virtual "public stage," where citizens increasingly struggle to define their reputation and protect the integrity of private information. So, the question then becomes: How do Digital Age citizens safeguard their online personas? The ability to sculpt one's own persona becomes particularly challenging when others actively contribute content and display images 24 hours a day, seven days a week, 365 days a year. The World Wide Web hums with stories created by one's self and by others – composing a persona not only derived by the individual, but also by the online community. In contemplation of this contemporary situation, it has been proposed that the right to be forgotten does not distinctly represent an infringement on the right of expression nor does it function as a privacy guarantee, but the right to be forgotten establishes an environment whereby an individual may aptly construct a personal, though revisionist, narrative. By enfranchising the individual this way, the right to be forgotten matures into a societal-level concern about society's memory and memory rights (Tirosh 2017). Human memory is a complicated facet of the human condition.

In the book, *Seven Sins of Memory* (2001), Harvard University professor Daniel Schacter points to the human memory's malfunctions calling them "sins," including transience, absent-mindedness, blocking, mis-attribution, suggestibility, bias, and persistence. However, these sins of memory resemble human qualities, not those found in algorithmically generated memory found in online search engines. Through memory, humans have an ability to self-regulate the historical onslaught of information that would be too painful to bear, but the digital memory offers no latitude of forgiveness – rather it returns the pleasant, the untoward, and the deplorable to the surface with just a few keystrokes. Therefore, in the Digital Age we, as beings, are reduced to the conclusions that can be drawn from our online search engine results.

Who we "are" online defines us, yet, without any way to remove unpalatable information, these depictions become a reputational concern. For Europeans, the obstruction to preserving one's reputation was exceedingly repugnant, paving the way for the acceptance of the right to be forgotten. Yet, the US perspective on the reputational dimension is somewhat different, as the United States espouses a culture of transparency that does not generate barriers between the private and public spheres. To counteract movements for information removal, the strategic act of writing more and speaking more about one's self on a particular topic provides an alternative that allows the individual to harvest a certain gradient of control over information about themselves (Janes 2016). Pop psychology underscores transparency in personal affairs by advocating open avenues for discussion; citizens call for transparency in accounting; and politics suggest that the ability to shed light into a situation creates a higher level of accountability. As individuals though, many Webizens want to simultaneously see and be seen in the online environment, until something gains the light of day that does not cast them in most favorable shadow. Today, we operate in a transitory time in our global digital history, a time when decisions about information handling, storage, and recall will influence our world for generations to come. The confluence of legal principles with digital operations, cultural mores, and individual beliefs creates an international quandary for those responsible for implementing global information policies, most notably the right to be forgotten.

The connection between media governance and cultural memory remains undeniable. Some scholars assert the Spanish court's decision and the institutionalization of the concept into European law denote the beginning of a new era that links media governance and regulation to society's information processes (Tirosh 2017). Furthermore, some scholars indicate that the right to be forgotten contributes to contemporary scholarship on memory, because it legitimizes the governance of personal and collective memories (Periera, Ghezzi, and Vesnic-Alujevnic 2014). In an examination of archival practices, researchers say that the right to be forgotten will not completely harm preservation (Dulong de Rosnay and Guadamuz 2016). The pair assert that the right to be forgotten is actually a misleading term, because the de-linking that occurs after the individual's request does not permanently remove the item from the original source, thus not promoting a total "disappearance" of the data. The concept of the archive is addressed later, but digital citizens have come to rely on Google as a personal archive, making the mission to find information more onerous by tracking down individual sources. This can be found in contemporary news organizations in which the institutions preserve their own archives, but when Google delinks them, the news item, though remaining covertly in the news archive, becomes less accessible on the search engine. This places an additional burden on information gatherers, including journalists or common citizens seeking information to help them make decisions.

As global citizens march into the digital era where items cannot so easily be forgotten, it has been suggested that we are entering a "postscarcity" culture whereby the ability to shape one's online reputation and persona become more viable, yet simultaneously unwieldly, because of the continued return of information (Hoskins 2014). The scarcity culture of days gone by, constantly creating content that was "fixed" in time, stand in stark contrast to the media of today that is malleable, based on the user's whim, and morphs through the transmission of online media, giving social media greater power to depict the human being. In what has been called, the "circulation of the self," the individual, culture, and society are reconstituted in real time, creating a digital "present" (Hoskins 2014). Yet the right to be forgotten stands as a "resentiment" of the postscarcity age, countering a memorial force that is uncertain about the prospects for erasing or forgetting (Hoskins 2014). Forgetting and remembering represent the dual functions of memory, and the notions of individual and collective memory cross multiple disciplines, including psychology, sociology, anthropology, history, and communication. The classification of European search engines as data controllers has thrust open the door for the arbitrary censorship of information and concepts on a global level. As citizens living in a democracy, we must explore the underbelly of the distortion that could occur analyzing the impact of memory holes and other destructive forces in information curating.

## Internet Archives and the Link to Big Data

With the preservation of images and information online, individuals become frozen in time with the presentation of data, whether outdated or unavailable for viewing. As individuals, we conduct searches about other individuals, whether screening an employee or gaining background information about a potential romantic partner. The constant gaze of the Internet archive does not allow for individuals to change, evolve, or be "different" than they once were a decade ago, a year ago, or a month ago. Cheng (2016) suggests delinking and removal of the information is the wrong path, and that an alternative solution may be to allow individuals to update information, and thus not counter freedom of expression. By creating a "right of reply" and facilitating contextualism, Cheng suggests a "right to be different," thus altering the concept of the person frozen in time. It has also been suggested that instead of contemplating the binary thinking of "forgetting" vs. "remembering," alternative methods could be employed, including "reordering" instead of delisting (deMars and Callaghan 2016). These lines of query may be the most fertile for individuals attempting to find a way to incorporate a similar right to be forgotten in the United States.

In sum, however, the movements toward World Wide Web governance must appropriately consider the future of big data. Challenges for regulating the World Wide Web archive and retrievability of information remain intertwined with the complicating notions of big data practices. By analyzing the right to be forgotten through the big data prism, Koops (2011) suggests three speculative frameworks for a semblance of digital forgetting. The first approach encompasses the idea that personal data should be deleted in "due time;" the second approach adheres to a social "clean slate" that diminishes the data used against a person; and the third perspective relinquishes social stigmas and allows people to express themselves in online media. The absence of consensus and the ability for private corporation and government regulators to come to grips with ethical management of the information leaves Digital Age citizens adrift, fearful of how their personal information will be used and concerned about the misappropriation of their personal information that will in some way harm them. The clamor for access to the digital archive and the robust memory of the World Wide Web resides in a general need to understand the other. As a society, we are seeking to know who is that person we work with, how can I learn more about that person's habits, personal life, hobbies, and what may we have in common that could bind us together. We have a longing to engage with the other in the present sense. While we are all citizens, some have achieved a new social and legal status – that of a public figure with profound name recognition to a public official elected by the people to serve the public. In an effort to outmaneuver the search engines, individuals who want to manage their online reputation now resort to third-party, private services to perform search engine optimization services for private individuals.

The notion of collective memory is one addressed by scholars in multiple fields, including those in sociology, history, psychology, and medicine. One of the most intriguing interpretations, when contemplating the role of the search engine and the right to be forgotten, is the discussion that collective memory is both a cognitive and social process (Casey and Oliviera 2011) and collective memory emerges from material artifacts and collective consciousness (Fine and Beim 2007). This idea is advanced when considering that sociomaterial traces of memory are stored in archives, allowing for future retrieval and analysis (Ocasio, Mauskapf, and Steele 2016), and that a metanarrative emerges from the logics that emerge from the archives. For the sake of argument, the search engines of today then become a vital instrument in the shaping of the metanarrative by determining the ranking, availability, scope, and societal nuances attached to information retrieved after a search engine query. But, the power of the search engine transcends beyond the ability to color the world by painting search engine results in a very specific way. The search engines also possess the power to discern social, economic, and political concerns of citizens, based on their search engine history, and can use that information for material gains, including financial, political, or social advancements.

The search engines themselves aggregate vast data warehouses full of data. The search data itself, when interpreted collectively, can decipher topics of interest to people living in a certain part of the country, including political leanings, public opinion on social issues, and a myriad of other conclusions based on information, not simple hunches. By examining this data, researchers can now discern what is on the societal "collective mind," allowing the World Wide Web to serve as an associative memory for users (Poritz 2007). Yet this "collective mind" created through what has been called a search engine oligarchy (Poritz 2007) derives value and creates nervousness among the individual data specimens. For example, Poritz states that netizens may not understand that simply entering a single word into a search engine could help another person or corporation derive a strategy for investments, politics, or marketing. But, in that reality, the knowledge is what creates the squeamishness in collective privacy. The formation of subsequent laws such as existing prohibitions against insider trading may develop in the future to address these privacy concerns (Poritz 2007).

## Across Geographic Borders

While elected officials may still suffer the eye of scrutiny found in a RTBF-free environment, the larger, global informed citizenry may face a new predicament. The delinking of information chisels away at the totality of available information, leaving voters in a position that could be manipulated by a power source, in this case, a private data controller. We live in a world of porous boundaries between political and social culture, converging on devices like a smartphone. The formation of public opinion occurs through the transmission and reception of information. Today, public opinion encounters a complicated, confusing journey as information from multiple authors travels through the Internet to search engines and ultimately arrives in the eyes and ears of the recipient. The ability of public opinion to gain a critical mass differs from heritage of coffee shops devoted to various trade groups and political parties. In fact, some would argue that the World Wide Web is analogous to a gigantic coffee shop, shopping mall, or robust marketplace that allows for the exchange of ideas and formulation of public opinion. The notion of public opinion appeared in the seventeenth century with John Locke's writing, *An Essay Concerning Human Understanding* (Locke 2001). US Constitutional Father James Madison recognized the imperative for an educated citizenry who possessed the capacity to form collective opinions, and envisioned an enlightened majority would have the capacity to mobilize against an illegitimate regime (Gabrielson 2009). Yet, by deconstructing public opinion, we can observe the impact of political opinion on society. For example, beliefs comprise the basic building block of public opinion, and, if these beliefs influence our behavior patterns, they become an attitude. As a result of this sequence, a reader who retrieves information on a search engine begins to develop beliefs and attitudes from the immediate rendering of the search engine results. If the rendered information is riddled with holes, the reader suffers a crippling defeat before they even start to digest the information.

## Impact on National Sovereignty: Geographic Censorship

The ability for the European Union to influence online data policies that influence the availability of information on the World Wide Web, indicates a potential infringement on national sovereignty not only among European countries, but also indicates that the United States may experience aspects of censorship that fly in the face of the First Amendment. Moreover, the ability for a single individual working at a search engine to make these critical decisions seems arbitrary at best. "While privacy in the new age of information is undoubtedly important, the right to be forgotten harms more than it helps. It allows a single individual to determine what the rest of the world sees, threatening to censor the World Wide Web in its adolescence. It undermines national sovereignty and democratic values by promoting one culture's adherence to privacy over another culture's freedom of expression" (Cunningham 2016).

## Conclusion: Further Global Implications

The right to be forgotten represents a movement of global significance. The procedures for information-sharing and data governance across international borders requires significant study, legal collaboration, and an appreciation for various cultural traditions. The incorporation of the right to be forgotten by all members of the European Union requires monitoring and observation. The departure of the United Kingdom from the European Union leaves the right to be forgotten hanging in a political balance, and scholars call for more thoughtful consideration of information context, the data protection landscape, and freedom of information concerns (Townend 2017). A study of media coverage of the right to be forgotten yielded insights that a chasm exists between the language used to describe the right to be forgotten in media outlets in the United States and the United Kingdom, further suggesting that national identity, political orientation, and capitalism play a role in the news coverage treatment (Shahin 2016). While Google deals with pressures to honor take-down requests across multiple domains, scholars thoughtfully suggest approaches, including Svantesson's (2015) "Model code for determining the geographical scope of delisting under the right to delisting" that considers the context for information and a consequence focused approach.

The European Right to be Forgotten provides a legal model for other countries attempting to define measures for data removal. Russia enacted a law in 2016 that requires search engine operators to remove information if the information distribution violates the law, is not accurate or factual, or has lost its importance (Andryuschchenko 2016). In the Netherlands, one of the countries of the European Union, the right to be forgotten matured through several judicial decisions before it was mandated through the European Data Protection Regulation

(Verheij 2016). A Belgian court has ruled that the right to be forgotten is part of the constitutionally guaranteed "right to be left in peace" in one's private life (Ginsberg 2016). The absence of a consensus of administration across Europe portends a tumultuous time for Google and other search engines legally responsible for the administration. The application of national sovereignty to control over the information in one's own country become a challenge amid the cacophony of the Digital Age. The presence of subversive and other information outside government auspices continues to grow amid hacking, virtual private networks, and innovative technology tools that utilize satellites and new mobile technologies. The global information society is coming of age with a movement to reduce information in the name of personal privacy under the European Data Protection Regulation's right to be forgotten.

The contemplation of the Right to Be Forgotten occurs amid the digital revolution and changing dynamics of information flow across borders. Facebook acknowledged the acceptance of advertisements from foreign entities that have meddled with the US Presidential election in 2016 (Shapiro 2017). This phenomenon suggests the marketplace may be undergoing false market forces, and further suggests that the era of online digital governance will guide how citizens perceive the world.

## References


Andryuschchenko, E. (2016). Right to be Forgotten on the Internet in Europe and Russia. *Conhecimento & Diversidade, Niteroi* 8 (15): 14–25.

Bernays, E. (1923). *Crystallizing Public Opinion*. New York: Ig Publishing.

Casey, A.J. and Oliviera, F. (2011). Reflections on organizational memory and forgetting. *Journal of Management Inquiry* 20: 305–310.

Cheng, A. (2016). Forget about the Right to be Forgotten: how about a right to be different? *Auckland University Law Review* 22: 106–141.

Cunningham, M. (2016). Free expression, privacy, and diminishing sovereignty in the information age: the internationalization of censorship. *Arkansas Law Review* 69: 71–115.

deMars, S. and Callaghan, P. (2016). Privacy and search engines: forgetting or contextualizing? *Journal of Law and Society* 43 (2): 257–284.

Dulong de Rosnay, M. and Guadamuz, A. (2016). Memory hole or right to delist? *RESET*. Online. doi: 10.4000/reset.807.

Fine, G.A. and Beim, A. (2007). Introduction: interactionist approaches to collective memory. *Symbolic Interaction* 30: 1–5.

Gabrielson, T. (2009). James Madison's psychology of public opinion. *Political Research Quarterly* 62 (3): 431–444.

Ginsberg, J. (2016). Global view: Europe's Right to be Forgotten pushed to new extremes after belgian court rules that individuals can force newspapers to edit archive articles. *Index on Censorship* 45 (3): 60–61.

Grunig, J. and Grunig, L. (1992). Models of public relations and communications. In: *Excellence in Public Relations Management and Communications and Communications Management* (ed. J. Grunig), 285–324. Hillsdale, NJ: Lawrence Erlbaum Associates, Inc.

Habermas, J. (1991). *The Structural Transformation of the Public Sphere*. Cambridge, MA: MIT Press.

Hoskins, A. (2014). The Right to be Forgotten in post-scarcity culture in Ghezzi. In: *The Ethics of Memory in the Digital Age* (ed. A. Pereira and L. Cesnick-Alujevic), 50–64. Basingstoke: Palgrave Macmillan.

Janes, J. (2016). Forget me not: is the appeal of the Right to be Forgotten more about anonymity or control? *American Libraries* 47 (6): 30–31.

Koops, B. (2011). Forgetting footprints, shunning shadows. A critical analysis of the Right to be Forgotten in big data practice. *Scripted* 8 (3): 229–256.

KU Leuven (2020). *Google v. CNIL*: The CJEU determines the territorial scope of the right to de-referencing. https://www.law.kuleuven.be/citip/blog/google-vs-cnil-the-cjeu-determines-the-territorial-scope-of-the-right-to-de-referencing (accessed January 16, 2021).

Lippman, W. (1922). *Public Opinion.* Provo, UT: Renaissance Classics.
Locke, J. (2001). *An Essay Concerning Human Understanding* [Electronic Resource]. Blacksburg, VA: Virginia Tech.
Ocasio, W., Mauskapf, M., and Steele, C. (2016). History, society and institutions: The role of collective memory in the emergency and evolution of societal logistics. *Academy of Management Review* 41 (4): 676–699.
Periera, A., Ghezzi, A., and Vesnic-Alujevnic, L. (eds.) (2014). *The Ethics of Memory in the Digital Age.* Basingstoke: Palgrave Macmillan.
Poritz, J. (2007). Who searches the searchers? Community privacy in the age of monolithic search engines. *Information Society* 23: 383–389.
Schacter, D. (2001). *The Seven Sins of Memory: How the Mind Forgets and Remembers.* Boston, MA: Mariner Books, Houghton Mifflin Harcourt.
Shahin, S. (2016). Right to be Forgotten: how national identity, political orientation and capitalist ideology structured a transatlantic debate on information access and control. *Journalism and Mass Communication Quarterly* 93 (2): 360–382.
Shapiro, L. (2017). Anatomy of a Russian Facebook ad. *Washington Post* (November 1). https://www.washingtonpost.com/graphics/2017/business/russian-ads-facebook-anatomy/?utm_term=.137f0ee4cc7c (accessed September 17, 2020).
Svantesson, D. (2015). Limitless, borderless, forgetfulness? Limiting the geographical reach of the "Right to be Forgotten." *Oslo Law Review* 2: 116–138.
Tirosh, N. (2017). Reconsidering the "Right to be Forgotten" memory rights and the right to memory in the new media era. *Media, Culture & Society* 39 (5): 644–660.
Townend, J. (2017). Data protection and the "right to be forgotten" in practice: a UK perspective. *International Journal of Legal Information* 45 (1): 71–115.
Verheij, A. (2016). The Right to be Forgotten – a Dutch perspective. *International Review of Law, Computers & Technology* 30 (1–2): 32–41.

# 16

# The Crime of Historical Denialism as a Limit to the Freedom of Expression

## A European Glance

Germán M. Teruel Lozano

### Introduction: The Crime of Historical Denialism and a "Humble" Balance Regarding Its Harmonization in Europe

The Treaty on European Union, signed on February 7, 1992 in Maastricht, created the Union "recalling the historic importance of the ending of the division of the European continent and the need to create firm bases for the construction of the future Europe." In this context, the protection of our collective memory, especially the memory of the Holocaust and the repudiation of the serious crimes of genocide and against humanity that led to the destruction of our continent in a past still recent, is fundamental. As well as the fight against those anti-Semitic or xenophobic speeches that precisely could serve as a breeding ground for them. Both issues have justified that the majority of European countries, and the Union itself, had promoted legislative measures to punish not only hate speech, but more specifically, the denialist discourses of the Holocaust and other serious crimes. In the face of these "assassins of memory" (Vidal-Naquet 1993), Europe has opted to turn to its most powerful weapon: criminal sanctions.[1] As Emanuela Fronza (2018, p. 23) unequivocally warned, "Due to the highly symbolic potential of judicial proceedings and punishments, law and criminal trial are seen as key instruments for establishing memory." The problem with these regulations, as will be studied in this chapter, is that the criminalization of these speeches implies an interference to the freedom of expression that presents serious doubts of constitutionality. To this end, the chapter begins by looking at the legislative panorama in Europe to then analyze the conflict that arises when such crimes clash with other fundamental freedoms, according to the decisions of the main European courts.

The first country to specifically criminalize historical denialism in Europe was France, which in 1990 passed legislation known as the Gayssot Law, a reform of the law relating to freedom

---

[1] For a broad study on criminalization of denialist speech in Europe, see Fronza (2018) and Teruel Lozano (2015). A synthesized analysis, at Cajani (2017). Moreover, information on the domestic implementation of Framework Decision 2008/913/JAI of the Recommendation, November 28, 2008, on tackling specific forms of racism and xenophobia through the use of criminal sanction can be found in Eur-Lex: https://eur-lex.europa.eu/legal-content/ES/NIM/?uri=CELEX:32008F0913 (accessed January 18, 2021).

*The Handbook of Communication Rights, Law, and Ethics: Seeking Universality, Equality, Freedom and Dignity*, First Edition. Edited by Loreto Corredoira, Ignacio Bel Mallén, and Rodrigo Cetina Presuel.

of the press. This legislation provided for a specific model of indicting those who questioned [*contesté*] the existence of crimes against humanity according to the definition given by the Charter of the International Military Tribunal and which had been sentenced in either a French or international jurisdiction (Art. 24. bis *Loi du 29 juillet 1881 sur la liberté de la presse*). The legislation was amended in 1992, and more recently in 2014 and 2017. Of great interest in France has been the debate around the possibility of extending denialist offenses to crimes which, albeit not brought before an international tribunal, can nevertheless be considered to fit such definitions, as is the case with the Armenian genocide, to which French public opinion is particularly sensitive. So much so that since 1995 various proposals have been made to criminalize denial of any crime of genocide, war, or against humanity. In 2012 in particular, attempts were made to criminalize the denial of crimes of genocide that were recognized as such by a French law (as in the case of the Armenian genocide, Act n. 70, January 29, 2001). However, the *Conseil Constitutionnel* in its Decision no. 2012-647 DC, February 28, 2012 considered that these kinds of laws, as political acts, were not capable of justifying a restriction on freedom of expression.

Following this, Austria, in 1992, and Germany, in 1994, reformed their Criminal Codes to place sanctions on the "Auschwitz lie" (*Auschwitzlüge*); penalizing those who deny, trivialize, or justify Nazi crimes. Not long afterwards, in 1995 many countries laid out specific forms of this offense: Belgium followed Germany's example in criminalizing the "Auschwitz lie," and Portugal and Spain added criminal offenses with specific details. Portugal, in its criminal offense of racial, religious, or sexual discrimination, included a specific reference to actions involving denialism of any war crime or crime against peace, as a specific form of defamatory speech that is motivated by discrimination. Spain also foresaw the crime of denialism by extending it to the denial or justification of genocide; but it was declared partially unconstitutional under the Spanish Constitutional Court Judgment no. 235/2007, November 7, which referred to the act of mere denial (as will be examined in more detail further on). In 2015, it was heavily modified. In its latest reform, the Spanish legislature criminalized denialist speech as a form of hate speech, albeit with particular nuances.

Taking these provisions as a reference point, it could be said that a bottom-up initiative ended up being a top-down process (Fronza 2018, p. 13): one year later, in 1996, the European Union adopted the first regulatory provision targeting denialist speeches in Joint Action 96/443/JAI concerning action to combat racism and xenophobia. This called upon states to criminalize public apologias, with racist and xenophobia intent, of crimes against humanity and human rights violations, as well as the "public denial of the crimes defined in Article 6 of the Charter of the International Military Tribunal appended to the London Agreement of 8 April 1945 insofar as it includes behavior which is contemptuous of, or degrading to, a group of persons defined by reference to color, race, religion or national or ethnic origin" (I, JA). However, the effectiveness of the Joint Action was limited.

Later, the Joint Action had been superseded by Framework Decision 2008/913/JAI, November 23, on combating certain forms and expressions of racism and xenophobia by means of criminal law, which succeeded in gaining approval following a "tiring" legislative *iter* that began in 2001 with the Commission's proposal (Teruel Lozano 2015, p. 96). This European legislation, which continues to be the reference guide in this area to this day, urged the criminalization of denialist speech by setting out the proposal for an offense within the framework of hate speech (Art. 1). Specifically, these apply if the criminal conduct is directed at a target group or its members (defined by certain "protected" characteristics: race, color, religion, heritage, etc.), and if the conduct is "likely to incite" violence or hate. This effectively imposes a requirement of potential or hypothetical endangerment. But, to my understanding, this does not prevent member states from opting to require specific endangerment when implementing the Decision in order to safeguard freedom of expression (Art. 7 of the same Decision). Furthermore, the Framework Decision has set aside the initial trend of calling for the criminalization only of Nazi crimes (which still fall under Art. 1(1)(d)) by proposing to criminalize denialism of any war crime or crime against humanity (Art. 1(1)(c)). The various acts punished by the Framework Decision include "publicly condoning, denying or grossly trivializing" these crimes. And the basic formulation of the offense may be restricted by incorporating any of the additional qualifications provided for the Decision. These clauses attempt to restrict the effect of the legislation on denialism of any war crime or crime against humanity, yet it also creates some contradictions as will be discussed later. The Framework Decision provides for such conduct to be punishable by "a maximum of at least between 1 and 3 years of imprisonment" (Art. 3[2]).[2]

Hence, in the light of this European act, a significant number of member states proceeded to implement or reform the relevant offenses in their national law, though there is no single model in Europe for criminalizing denialist statements. Furthermore, there are countries that have opted to not create specific offenses, criminalizing these statements under basic offenses relating to provocation of hatred and discrimination or under those relating to threats and insults. This results in a "humble" balance of the harmonization, which has been recognized by the European Commission itself in its report on the implementation of the Framework Decision, in which it cautions that member states "have not implemented in total and/or in the correct manner all of the provisions in the Framework Decision, specifically those related to the offences of denial, apologia and gross trivialisation of certain crimes."[3]

Nonetheless, despite all these differences, 21 member states have a specific offense relating to denialist statements. However, among these states, some have only criminalized denialism of those crimes to which their socio-political landscapes are more sensitive: for example, Germany, Austria, Belgium regarding Nazi crimes; or Poland and Hungary both criminalize the denial of Nazi and Communist crimes.[4] Additionally, there are many states that have not included any further qualification to the offense beyond requiring simple denial, justification, or trivialization of such crimes in a public manner, setting themselves apart from the tendency proposed by the European Framework Decision to treat denialist offenses as a form of incitement to hatred or violence.[5] It must also be pointed out that only four countries have included the requirement

---

[2] Cfr Teruel Lozano (2015, p. 108 ss) and Lobba (2011, p. 134).

[3] Cf. Report from the Commission to the European Parliament and the Council on the implementation of Framework Decision 2008/913/JAI, of the Recommendation on combating certain forms of racism and xenophobia via criminal law, SWD(2014) 27 final, January 27, 2014.

[4] The case of Poland is very interesting. In 1998 the Act on the Institute of National Remembrance criminalized historical negationism of crimes committed against Polish by Nazi or Communist (Art. 55). In 2007 and 2018 it was amended. But this last amendment has led to significant controversy. On the one hand, a new Article 55a criminalized "Whoever claims, publicly and contrary to the facts, that the Polish Nation or the Republic of Poland is responsible or co-responsible for Nazi crimes committed by the Third Reich." After a great national and international outcry, it was amended to become a civil offense. And, on the other hand, the 2018 Amendment also introduced a specific reference to crimes against Polish citizens by "Ukrainian nationalist" (Art. 2.a), which was found to be unconstitutional by the Polish Constitutional Court.

[5] Only Cyprus, Bulgaria, Greece, and Spain have incorporated the requirement that such behavior must incite violence or discrimination. In the case of Italy, the interpretation of the offense is unclear on this point but, due to its systematic location, it seems that it would be necessary to connect the denialist statement with incitement or provocation. Portugal provides an alternative by punishing conduct involving incitement as well as that which is insulting or threatening. Malta also punishes different acts based on their offensive character, i.e., when there is an incitement to violence or discrimination, when they are threatening or insulting, or when they are capable of disrupting public order. The latter is also the option chosen by Germany and Lithuania, and Spain views it as an aggravating feature. Lithuania and Slovenia also provide for the punishment of denialist conduct where it is threatening or insulting. In the Spanish case, it was considered a lesser offense where the denialist conduct harmed the dignity of the person without an incitement to hatred or violence.

that the crimes being denied or questioned must be recognized by a Court and, in the case of Greece, by the law,[6] something which was considered unconstitutional by the French *Conseil Constitutionnel*,[7] as it was said. Finally, the different penalties laid out by the various countries must also be taken into account, despite the efforts toward harmonization in this area also.

Therefore, we find ourselves faced with a "crime which varies according to geography," as E. Fronza (2012, p. 12) concludes.

## The Boundaries of the Freedom of Expression: When is an Interference to Freedom Justified by Historical Denialism According to European Courts?

Denialist speech, and in particular Holocaust denialism, is clearly harmful: "both individuals and societies suffer harm as a result of Holocaust denial," which constitutes an "affront to human dignity" and which shows "its capacity to pollute and corrupt public discourse," as acknowledged by L.B. Lidsky (2008, p. 1093). However, does the recognition of this harm lend legitimacy to the restriction of the freedom of expression via criminal sanction? In other words, as we have seen, is it constitutionally admissible for the European tendency to punish these speeches under different criminal laws?

I do not believe so. First, because democratic criminal law requires that offenses are justified by particular harm to constitutional interests. However, as discussed earlier, denialist offenses in many European countries penalize mere discourse of a denialist nature, without requiring further qualification. They presume harmful effect without proper evaluation of the impact, whether an insult, or a provocation to violence. As D. Fraser has recognized, "There must be serious doubt within the traditional confines and limitations of criminal law discourse that Holocaust denial causes or is likely to cause specific and identifiable harm" (Fraser 2010, p. 519). It is unclear, then, which constitutional interest is protected by these offenses: human dignity, public order, public peace, the right to non discrimination, or still others? And, for many academics, it is not possible to consider collective memory as a constitutional interest worth criminal safeguarding (Manes 2007, pp. 2–3; Fronza 2012, p. 133).

Furthermore, though we may consider these statements harmful, this does not immediately deprive them of constitutional protection. The freedom of expression exists precisely to protect speech which is harmful and offensive (Scanlon 1972). In Dworkin's words, referring to Holocaust denialism: "freedom is important enough even for sacrifices that really hurt" (Dworkin 1996, p. 226). We must recognize that, however much we may dislike it, denialist statements are a communicative act that purports to display a message and, as such, a priori would fall under the freedom of expression. Moreover, depending on the content of the discourse, it may fall under the protection of either ideological freedom or academic freedom.

However, not all courts have recognized the above in Europe. In particular, the European Court of Human Rights (ECtHR) has developed a doctrine in which Holocaust denial is *ratione materiae* excluded from Convention protection under Article 17 ECHR,[8] an application which has been branded "absolutist," as a "pure content-based restriction" (Pech 2009).[9] This approach contrasts with the one previously taken by the ECtHR, which with Holocaust

---

[6] The countries which include these provisions are France, Luxembourg, Slovakia, and Greece.

[7] Decision no. 2012-647 DC, February 28, 2012.

[8] *Roger Garaudy v. France*, June 24, 2003, ECtHR and, after, *M'Bala M'Bala v. France*, October 20, 2015, ECtHR.

[9] Cfr. Mishra (2018), Teruel Lozano (2015, p. 133 ss, 2017), and Caruso (2011, p. 352).

denialism may be covered under Article 10 ECHR, but, using Article 17 ECHR, the test for necessity in a democratic society would be lowered to a mere verification of whether the conduct at stake had content and motive of a denialist nature.[10] Furthermore, the severe position held by the European Court with the Holocaust denialism diverges from the one established in cases of revisionism relating to the events of World War II,[11] in which the Court has favored ensuring a broad debate and recognized that it is not the duty of judges to interfere in discussions between historians;[12] nor in the case of other war crimes,[13] or genocidal crimes other than the Holocaust, as confirmed in the leading case at present, heard by the Grand Chamber of the ECtHR: *Perinçek v Switzerland*, October 15, 2015. Thus, in the jurisprudence of the ECtHR, we see varying levels of scrutiny depending on the type of denialism in question and the Holocaust is seen as a "unique" event that merits specific protection.[14] The problem is that the justification offered for this by the Court in establishing this unequal footing is, in my view, unconvincing and contrary to the heart of freedom of expression. Let us examine why.

According to the European Court's case law, the difference between Holocaust denialism and denialism of other crimes is that the former is a "clearly established event," which is negated for spurious motives that are necessarily anti-Semitic: "There could be no doubt that disputing the existence of clearly established historical events, such as the Holocaust, did not constitute historical research akin to a quest for the truth. The real purpose of such a work was to *rehabilitate the National-Socialist regime* and, as a consequence, to accuse the victims of the Holocaust of falsifying history. *Disputing the existence of crimes against humanity was, therefore, one of the most severe forms of racial defamation and of incitement to hatred of Jews.* The denial or rewriting of this type of historical fact undermined the values on which the fight against racism and

[10] *Hans-Jürgen Witzsch v. Germany*, April 20, 1999, ECtHR and *Hans Jorg Schimanek v. Austria*, February 1, 2000, ECtHR. More recently, though the Court does not mention Article 17, it seems that it maintains this position by stating: "the applicant sought to use his right to freedom of expression with the aim of promoting ideas contrary to the text and spirit of the Convention. This weighs heavily in the assessment of the necessity of the interference" (*Williamson v. Germany*, January 31, 2019, ECtHR).

[11] Cf. *Lehideux & Isorni v. France*, September 23, 1998, ECtHR; *Chauvy & others v. France*, June 29, 2004, ECtHR; and *Monnat v. Switzerland*, September 21, 2006, ECtHR.

[12] For example, in the case *Lehideux & Isorni v. France*, September 23, 1998, the ECtHR concluded that "the events referred to in the publication in issue had occurred more than forty years before" and affirmed "the efforts that every country must make to debate its own history openly and dispassionately." In the same judgment, the Court affirmed that "it is not its task to settle this point, which is part of an ongoing debate among historians about the events in question and their interpretation." In a similar pronouncement, in the case *Chauvy & others v. France*, June 29, 2004, the ECtHR set that "it is an integral part of freedom of expression to seek historical truth and it is not the Court's role to arbitrate the underlying historical issues, which are part of a continuing debate between historians that shapes opinions as to the events which took place and their interpretation." On this point, see also *Monnat v. Switzerland*, September 21, 2006, ECtHR, where it referred to historical debate as "a sphere in which it is unlikely that any certainty exists".

[13] *Orban & others v. France*, January 15, 2009, ECtHR.

[14] On this point, see the critique in Fronza (2018, p. 112) about the ECtHR doctrine that recognizes the "unique" nature of the Holocaust. Lobba (2017, p. 128) also questions this position of the ECtHR and he concludes: "As we sought to demonstrate, the unique legal treatment reserved to Holocaust denial – upheld in Perınçek – is hard to justify and falls to be increasingly challenged by other groups of victims who feel that their dignity deserves equal protection. Future cases will tell if the Court continues to stand by this dichotomy or opts for progressive harmonization of its principles on denialism." Furthermore, albeit prior to this judgment, a discussion of the varying levels of scrutiny by the ECtHR and the Commission can be read in Pech (2009).

anti-Semitism was based and constituted a serious threat to public order. *It was incompatible with democracy and human rights and its proponents indisputably had designs that fell into the category of prohibited aims under Article 17 of the Convention.*"[15] However, other crimes such as the Armenian genocide would indeed be debatable and their calling into question would not necessarily amount to an incitement nor imply motives contrary to the Convention, as concluded by the Court in the aforementioned *Perinçek v. Switzerland* case, in which it found that criminal punishment of an individual who had questioned the legal qualification as a genocide of the Armenian massacre amounted to a Convention violation. In this case, the European Court concluded that the criminal penalty was not necessary in a democratic society, taking into account: "that the applicant's statements bore on a matter of public interest and did not amount to a call for hatred or intolerance, that the context in which they were made was not marked by heightened tensions or special historical overtones in Switzerland, that the statements cannot be regarded as affecting the dignity of the members of the Armenian community to the point of requiring a criminal law response in Switzerland, that there is no international law obligation for Switzerland to criminalize such statements, that the Swiss courts appear to have censured the applicant for voicing an opinion that diverged from the established ones in Switzerland, and that the interference took the serious form of a criminal conviction."[16]

Ultimately, we end up with the same contradiction: is it possible to simultaneously assert that Nazi crimes are "clearly established historical events"[17] and state that "historical investigation is by definition open to disagreement and debate, and does not lead to any definitive conclusions or objective and absolute truths?"[18] This seems to reiterate my previous conclusion: "with the category of 'clearly established historical events', the ECtHR seems to have created a 'bespoke fit' for Holocaust denialism, which leads to the paradox that the broad scientific 'consensus' must be weighed against the legal imperative for its recognition" (Teruel Lozano 2015, p. 149). The Holocaust has thus become a "taboo" (Alcácer Guirao 2013, p. 338) for the ECtHR, but taboos or dogmas do not fit with freedom of expression, even more when we are facing public discourses, where "the core right of participatory democracy [...] requires that people remain free to challenge the new dominant narratives as well as remnants of old ones" (Weinstein 2010, p. 35).

In a similar fashion, the German Federal Constitutional Court denied constitutional protection to Holocaust denialism in its judgments of 1994 (*BVerfGE* 90, 241) and 2009 (*BVerfG*, 1BvR 2150/08), albeit without the establishment of a doctrine as radical as the one pursued by the ECtHR (Grimm 2010, pp. 650–561). For the German Constitutional Court, the foundation of its proscription would be, in the case of simple factual statements, that the statements were untrue, and where mixed with opinion, the grounds for denying these constitutional protections would lie, in that the same may be considered offensive by Jewish victims living in Germany, who deserve special protection, and may be presumed to disturb the public peace where such opinions are

[15] *Roger Garaudy v. France*, June 24, 2003, ECtHR (emphasis added).

[16] *Perinçek v. Switzerland*, October 15, 2015, ECtHR. In *Williamson v. Germany*, January 31, 2019, the ECtHR has followed this argument but with a different result as the case was in Germany. In particular, the Court has declared inadmissible the complaint about the conviction by German courts for denying the Holocaust on Swedish TV. It has recognized a broad margin of appreciation and the Court has reiterated "that it has always been sensitive to the historical context of the High Contracting Party concerned when reviewing whether there exists a pressing social need for interference with rights under the Convention and that, in the light of their historical role and experience, States which have experienced the Nazi horrors may be regarded as having a special moral responsibility to distance themselves from the mass atrocities perpetrated by the Nazis."

[17] *Roger Garaudy v. France*, June 24, 2003, ECtHR.

[18] *Perinçek v. Switzerland*, October 15, 2015, ECtHR, section 117.

publicly expressed. As Grimm (2010, pp. 560–561) has explained: "Denial of the Holocaust therefore denies [present generation of Jews in Germany] identity. If the German state allows such denial of Jewish identity, it contributes to creating an atmosphere of insecurity for German Jews or at least nourishes the impression that Germany no longer distances itself from what it had done to the Jews, whereas an official recognition that these events happened and that their denial will be prosecuted provides a safeguard against their repetition." This doctrine, however, also presents problems. First, if we consider the Holocaust as a statement of fact then it becomes a "notorious" event and therefore judiciarily indisputable, or judges will have to apply a test of veracity to complex historical events improper of its jurisdictional role. In this sense, when we encounter pseudo-scientific denialist texts, there is no alternative but to put on trial the academic methods used within them. This, as acknowledged by E. Fronza (2012, p. 150, 2018, p. 137), may risk trading the paradox of content for the paradox of method, where judges must evaluate, in each case, whether an academic consensus exists – as referred to by the ECtHR – or, harder still, whether scientific methodology has been correctly observed. Secondly, if we prohibit Holocaust denial statements as a ***malum in se*** presuming its harm, we will create a restriction on pure content as the European Court has done, in a way that we have considered incompatible with the heart of the right to the freedom of expression. The German Court itself has recognized the unacceptability of banning opinions which reside in a "purely intellectual" domain (*BVerfG*, 1BvR 2150/08) and, as D. Grimm (2010, p. 561) wrote commenting on this sentence, "[t]he criminalization of the Holocaust denial symbolizes this deep conviction and, thus, is an uniquely German justification. As such, this justification would not be applicable to a prohibition of Holocaust denial in countries that do not have to bear the same historical responsibility." For that reason, the restrictions on freedom of expression should be justified in the actual offensiveness of the discourse in question, taking into account its content along with various other contextual factors.

Indeed, the Belgian Court of Arbitration, in its Judgment no. 45/96, July 12, 1996, has also legitimized the criminalization of Holocaust denial with no further qualification and has justified a criminal offense based on an abstract endangered, in considering these statements harmful to the Jewish community. However, the Court recognized that the judge had the ability to rebut the presumption of offensiveness balancing, on the one hand, the tendency to condone or rehabilitate National Socialism, and, on the other, considering whether such discourse could fall under the protection accorded to scientific freedom. The French *Conseil Constitutionnel* also seemingly rejects that denialist discourse *prima facie* constitutes an abuse of the freedom of expression for its disruption of public order and the rights of third parties (Decision no. 2016-745 DC, January 26, 2017, section 194).

Moreover, despite its shortcomings, I believe the most nuanced position today is the one put forward by the Spanish Constitutional Court and summarized in STC 135/2007 of November 7.[19] In its judgment, the Court diverged from the ECtHR doctrine by rejecting a

[19] In this case, the Constitutional Court considered the constitutionality of the offense criminalizing the denial of genocide (Art. 607.2 PC.) and declared it partially unconstitutional, annulling the criminalization of the mere denial of these crimes. For the Court, simply "denying" cannot "even slightly" be considered to create such climates of hostility. However, with regards to "justifying," the Court ruled that it was possible to consider this element in such a manner and, consequently, admitted the constitutionality of its criminalization. Prior to this ruling, two cases should be mentioned in which the Constitutional Court first dealt with the issue of denialism. First, STC 214/1991 November 11: Violeta Friedman, a Jewish woman and prisoner in a concentration camp, who initiated a civil process in protection of her right to honor in relation to statements made in media by Leon Degrelle where he denied the Nazi genocide of the Jewish people and attributed their invention to them. Secondly, STC 176/1995, December 11, also ruled on protection regarding the crime of insulting for which the editor of a publishing house that had published a comic about Hitler with neo-Nazi and Holocaust denialist content had been convicted. For an in-depth analysis, see Teruel Lozano (2015, p. 348 ss) and to the bibliography cited therein.

"militant" conception of Spanish democracy on the grounds that Spanish Constitution lacks a provision analogous to Article 17 ECHR. On the basis of this, the Spanish Constitutional Court has enshrined the principle of harm as justification for any limit to the freedom of expression: the scope of Constitutional protection "cannot be restricted by the fact that such rights may be used for the dissemination of ideas or opinions that are contrary to the essence itself of the Constitution unless this actively undermines constitutional rights or goods." Denialist discourse would therefore be potentially protected under the freedom of expression, unless its offensive character is evidenced. Thus, "the statements, doubts and opinions regarding Nazi actions with respect to Jews and concentration camps, however reprehensible or distortionary they may be—and which are indeed reprehensible and distortionary when denying historical evidence—are protected under the right to freedom of expression (Art. 20.1 CE), in relation to the right to ideological freedom (Art. 16 CE)." Given the above, when would punishment of these behaviors be legitimate? According to the Spanish Constitutional Court, in the following cases: (a) indirect incitement to serious crimes such as genocide, even when they are not "clearly capable" of directly inciting the commission of such crimes; (b) provocation of hatred toward certain groups which gives rise to the "actual danger" of creating a climate of violence and hostility that can result in specific acts of discrimination; and (c) insulting or degrading speech regarding a group of people: expressions which are "denigrating, racist or humiliating" toward a nationality or ethnic group. Here, the concept of honor would fall within the protection accorded to human dignity. This is a doctrine which, in my opinion, has the benefit of expressly adopting the principle of harm as a justification of any limit to freedom of expression, but which disadvantages the consistency of the evaluation of offensiveness, especially when applied to criminal offenses, given that it permits the formulation of crimes based on a hypothetical or potential risk. The judicial evaluation of this potentiality of risk requires judges to ultimately apply a "bad tendency" test, which has been rightly struck down by US jurisprudence, as it is based on pure intention or inclination (Sottiaux 2011). From my point of view, only where there is temporal imminence and a high likelihood of materialization of the harmful acts in question, or rather, where there is a "clear" and "present" danger, as formulated by the US Supreme Court,[20] will the test of potential dangerousness have enough substance to justify a restriction on the freedom of expression.[21]

---

[20] This test sprang from the pen of Judge O.W. Holmes in the *Schenck v. United States* sentencing (*Schenck v. United States*, 249 US 47 (1919)), and was gradually imposed on the "bad tendency" test that originated from the English *common law* (*Debs v. United States*, 249 US 211 (1919); *Frohwerk v. United States*, 249 US 204 (1919); or, moreover, *Abrams v. United States*, 250 US 616 (1919)). The test was evolving (*Dennis v. United States*, 341 US 494, 584 (1951); *Yates v. United States*, 354 US 298 and others (1957)) until in *Brandenburg v. Ohio*, 395 US 444 (1969), the Supreme Court, in a decision *per curiam*, expressed the current formulation of the test of "clear and present danger," defining it as: "the principle that the constitutional guarantees of free speech and free press do not permit a State to forbid or proscribe advocacy of the use of force or of law violation except where such advocacy is directed to inciting or producing imminent lawless action and is likely to incite or produce such action." There are thus two factors to take into account when determining whether an intervention is legitimate: 1. The subjective intention to incite; 2. Whether the discourse is capable of imminently producing any illegal action.

[21] In this regard, at the international level, the Johannesburg Principles on National Security, Freedom of Expression and Access to Information, adopted in November 1996, establish that, in order to limit the freedom of expression for threats to national security, as well as for incitement and the capacity to provoke imminent violence, it is necessary to require "a direct and immediate connection between the act and the probability or the event of such violence." See also the dissenting opinions of Justice A. Asúa, followed by Justice Fernando Valdés, and of Justice Juan Antonio Xiol in the Judgement of the Spanish Constitutional Court n. 177/2015, July 22.

Thus, in answer to the initial question, we can conclude that there is not a common response in Europe to historical denialism as a limit to freedom of expression: there is a long distance from the "*ratione materiae*" restriction for Holocaust denialism at the European Court's jurisprudence to the Spanish Constitutional Court decision, going by the intermediate positions of others' Constitutional Courts, as we have studied. For that reason, maybe the lowest common denominator is the European Framework Decision, which excludes content-based restrictions to freedom of expression and proposes to punish denialist discourses as a form of hate speech, demanding that the prohibited statements may incite violence or hatred and are directed against a target group or its members. And, a question remains open: is it a good policy to criminalize denialism?

## Conclusions

It is possible, therefore, to criminalize denialist discourse in a way that respects the freedom of expression along with other fundamental freedoms but, at the same time, answering this last question, in my opinion, we must be cautious and move away from a criminal justice system with a purely symbolic purpose (Fronza 2018, p. 157 ss). The purpose of criminal law is to protect constitutional interests, not to safeguard collective remembrance, however important it may be as an integral element of our society. A. Merli (2008, p. 29) has argued with great clarity: "In a mature democratic society, it is not the responsibility of the State to coercively educate adult citizens in accordance with the dominant social values (which are open to pluralistic debate), converting criminal law 'into a tool for the cleansing of the soul.'"

Criminal due process must not become a "theatre" (Osiel 2005, p. 106; Fronza 2018, p. 23).

Accordingly, my conclusion is that it is not a good policy to enact a specific offense punishing historical denialism. The criminalization of genuinely harmful statement (i.e., insults, threats, or a real risk of violent or discriminatory acts) is already covered by common offenses, making it unnecessary to foresee a specific one directed at denialist discourse. Moreover, these specific offenses, such as crimes that punish hate speech or historical denialism, have a weak offensive content that is insufficient to justify a criminal limit to freedom of expression. They protect "supra-individual" goods such as public order or public peace, a peaceful climate that must be assessed by the judges on the basis of socio-political criteria.

In addition, these offenses run the risk of seeming to impose an "official truth," with the consequent risk that denialists who are convicted will portray themselves as martyrs (Lidsky 2008, p. 1099). Furthermore, as Teachout states, "you can respond to poisonous ideas by censoring them and throwing those who disseminate them in prison, but that will only serve to drive the ideas underground where the poison will fester and spread" (Teachout 2006, p. 675).

In summary, I believe that there is no better option than to traverse the most arduous of paths: civic education, so that it is society itself which confronts these hateful statements. The state may intervene to support this civil reaction, and it may develop public policies promoting speeches that counteract denialist poison in accordance with our democratic values. But it must not resort to censorship and criminalization. This is because, as C. Esposito (1958, p. 52) acknowledged years ago, what we cannot do is "transform the State into a dogmatic Church to protect ourselves against the infidels."

## References

Alcácer Guirao, R. (2013). Libertad de expresión, negación del Holocausto y defensa de la democracia. Incongruencias valorativas en la jurisprudencia del TEDH. *Revista Española de Derecho Constitucional* 33 (97): 309–341.

Cajani, L. (2017). Legislating history: the European Union and the denial of international crimes. In: *Law and Memory* (ed. U. Belsavusau and A. Gliszcynska-Graias), 129–148. Cambridge: Cambridge University Press.

Caruso, C. (2011). Ai con ni dell'abuso del diritto: l'hate speech nella giurisprudenza della Corte Europea dei Diritto dell'Uomo. In: *Lo strumento costituzionale dell'ordine pubblico europeo* (ed. L. Mezzetti and A. Morrone), 339–352. Turin: G. Giappichelli

Dworkin, R. (1996). *Freedom's Law*. Cambridge: Harvard University Press.

Esposito, C. (1958). *La libertà di manifestazione del pensiero nell'ordinamento italiano*. Milan: Giuffrè.

Fraser, D. (2010). 'On the Internet, nobody knows you're a Nazi': some comparative legal aspects of Holocaust denial on the WWW. In: *Extreme Speech and Democracy* (ed. I. Hare and J. Weinstein), 551–537. Oxford: Oxford University Press.

Fronza, E. (2012). *Il negazionismo come reato*. Milan: Giuffrè.

Fronza, E. (2018). *Memory and Punishment*. Berlin: Springer.

Grimm, D. (2010). The Holocaust denial decision of the Federal Constitutional Court of Germany. In: *Extreme Speech and Democracy* (ed. I. Hare and J. Weinstein), 557–561. Oxford: Oxford University Press.

Lidsky, L.B. (2008). Where's the harm?: free speech and the regulation of lies. *Wash & Lee Law Review* (65): 1091–1101.

Lobba, P. (2011). La lotta al razzismo nel diritto penale europeo dopo Lisbona. *Osservazioni sulla Decisione Quadro 2008/913/GAI e sul reato di negazionismo. Ius* 17 (3): 109–158.

Lobba, P. (2017). Testing the 'uniqueness': denial of the Holocaust vs denial of other crimes before the European Court of Human Rights. In: *Law and Memory* (ed. U. Belsavusau and A. Gliszcynska-Graias), 109–128. Cambridge: Cambridge University Press.

Manes, V. (2007). Attualità e prospettive del giudizio di ragionevolezza in materia penale. *Rivista Italiana di Diritto e Procedura Penale* 2–3: 739–765.

Merli, A. (2008). *Democrazia e diritto penale: note a margine del dibattino sul cosiddetto negazionismo*. Naples: Edizioni Scientiche Italiane.

Mishra, P. (2018). Truth on trial: law, memory and freedom of expression in Europe. *Soas Law Journal* V (I): 71–129.

Osiel, M.J. (2005). Politiche della punizione, memoria collettiva e diritto internazionale. In: *Giudicare e punire. I procesi per crimini di guerra tra diritto e politica* (ed. L. Baldissarra and P. Pezzino), 105–117. Naples: L'ancora del Mediterreaneo.

Pech, L. (2009). EU-wide criminal prohibition. Jean Monnet Working Paper, 10.

Scanlon, T. (1972). A theory of freedom of expression. *Philosophy & Public Affairs* 1 (2): 204–226.

Sottiaux, S. (2011). 'Bad tendencies' in the EctHR's 'hate speech' jurisprudence. *European Constitutional Law Review* 7 (1): 40–63.

Teachout, Peter R. (2006). Making Holocaust denial a crime: reflections on European anti-negationist laws from the perspective of U.S. constitutional experience. *Vermont Law Review* 30: 655–692.

Teruel Lozano, G.M. (2015). *La lucha del Derecho contra el negacionismo: una peligrosa frontera*. Madrid: CEPC.

Teruel Lozano, G.M. (2017). El discurso del odio como límite a la libertad de expresión en el marco del Convenio Europeo. *Revista de Derecho Constitucional Europeo* (27). https://www.ugr.es/~redce/REDCE27/ReDCEsumario27.htm (accessed January 18, 2021).

Vidal-Naquet, P. (1993). *Assassins of Memory*. New York: Columbia University Press.

Weinstein, J. (2010). Extreme speech, public order, and democracy: lessons from the *Masses*. In: *Extreme Speech and Democracy* (ed. I. Hare and J. Weinstein), 23–61. Oxford: Oxford University Press.

17

# Hate Speech in the United States and Abroad

## Finding Common Ground

Chris Demaske

Prior to the global explosion of social media platforms, the United States was able to stay relatively removed from most speech issues in other countries. With its historical commitment to near total freedom of expression under the First Amendment, the United States has long prided itself on its unique relationship to this particular freedom, a relationship that has separated it from the rest of the world. This separatist perspective has led to the United States being at odds with most international laws regarding speech restriction. With the growing usage of social media, those minor disagreements are now manifesting as major legal clashes. The flood gates of information are wide open and we need to find a way to have agreement at some level on how to treat speech issues in the digital world.

One of the most pressing of those issues today is the regulation of hate speech. As with previous free-speech debates, this one finds the United States defending the "right of the racist to express her views," (Baker 2009, p. 146) placing it at odds with much of the international community. Much has been written about the tension between the United States and the international community regarding the topic of hate speech restriction, particularly in the past decade as the Internet has made it increasingly impossible to separate communication boundaries. With very few exceptions, most of that scholarship concludes that the divide between the United States and the rest of the world cannot be bridged and, subsequently, calls either for the United States to completely change its position or vice versa. I don't believe that to be the only solution. This chapter proposes that, despite the differences in our legal and philosophical approaches to speech protection, there is a common ground to be found between the international commitment to human dignity and the US emphasis on self-realization and autonomy. By focusing on the commonalities between the United States and Europe, as opposed to the differences, we can begin to conceive hate speech regulations that will benefit members of both communities and will address one of the most contentious free-speech issues on the Internet today.

*The Handbook of Communication Rights, Law, and Ethics: Seeking Universality, Equality, Freedom and Dignity*, First Edition. Edited by Loreto Corredoira, Ignacio Bel Mallén, and Rodrigo Cetina Presuel.

## The US Experience

The US commitment to freedom of expression is grounded in the First Amendment to the US Constitution which reads: "Congress shall make no law ... abridging freedom of speech, or of the press." While this may sound like a clear mandate to require absolute protection for all speech, that is not the reality of its application. Almost from the very beginning, the legal system has been grappling with establishing the parameters of which speech must be protected, which speech should likely be protected, and which speech is not worthy of protection. How these decisions are made is at the crux of the debate over whether or not some level of hate speech should be restricted.

Traditional perspectives on the importance of the role of free speech in an open society can be traced back to Enlightenment philosophy, particularly to John Stuart Mill (1859). Mill, a nineteenth-century British philosopher whose work was heavily influenced by enlightenment philosophy, called for an almost absolutist protection of speech. Much of his reasoning was attached to his conception of truth and the role of speech in promoting the protection of and search for it. He proposed that we must hear opinions that are true as well as those that are false because it is through the collision of the two that truth emerges. Without this collision, society could miss out on replacing an erroneous position with a true one or true positions could lose their validity and become dead dogma. In short, Mill believed that restricting the expression of any opinions would have serious negative consequences not only for members of current society but also for future generations. Mill's influence can be seen in one of the earliest and extremely influential Supreme Court cases, *Abrams v. United States.*[1] In *Abrams*, Justice Oliver Wendell Holmes wrote:

> But when men have realized that time has upset many fighting faiths, they may come to believe even more than they believe the very foundations of their own conduct that the ultimate good desired is better reached by free trade in ideas—that the best test of truth is the power of the thought to get itself accepted in the competition of the market, and that truth is the only ground upon which their wishes safely can be carried out. (p. 630)

That language from Holmes is arguably the most influential dissent in speech case law because it ushered in our commitment to truth and wrapped the commitment within the cloak of the "Marketplace of Ideas," a discursive tool still employed today in arguments for speech protection. Mill's influence can also be seen in the development of contemporary First Amendment theory. Theorists such as Thomas Emerson (1963), Martin Redish (1982), C. Edwin Baker (1989), and Robert C. Post (2000) have incorporated Mill's assessment of truth into their own understanding of free speech in society and found it to include assuring self-fulfillment/ self-realization and participation in the political process. Of particular importance to this chapter is the concept of self-realization. Martin Redish (1982) explained the usage of the term in relation to First Amendment theory in this way:

> This term has been chosen largely because of its ambiguity: it can be interpreted to refer either to development of the individual's powers and abilities—an individual "realizes" his or her full potential—or to the individual's control of his or her own destiny through making life-affecting decisions—an individual "realizes" the goals in life that he or she has set. (p. 621)

In other words, one of the key reasons that we ultimately protect speech is to protect the ability for each individual to have a meaningful life. This concept underlies much of First Amendment case law.

[1] *Abrams v. United States*, 250 US 616 (1919).

Through Supreme Court rulings, a complicated system of free speech has developed. Far from the absolutist language "congress shall make no ..." the system includes the application of various tests and doctrines to determine the parameters of speech protection. For the purposes of this chapter, the most significant are the content-neutrality principle, fighting-words doctrine, and true-threats doctrine. One way to explain these principles and doctrines is to consider their application in key First Amendment cases that touched on the possibility of hate speech restriction. To be clear, in the United States we have no legal category of "hate speech." Having said that, the government has, at times, tried to restrict certain types of harmful speech targeted toward members of certain groups. Most notable of those cases is the 1992 ruling in *R.A.V. v. St. Paul.*[2] This case focused on the constitutionality of the St. Paul Minnesota Bias Motivated Crime Ordinance. The ordinance prohibited the display of a symbol "which one knows or has reason to know arouses anger, alarm, or resentment in others on the basis of race, color, creed, religion or gender" (p. 380). The ordinance was challenged after a teenager, charged under the ordinance after he and some of his friends fashioned a cross out of a broken chair and burned it on an African-American neighbor's lawn, was charged under it.

In a unanimous decision, the Supreme Court found the statute to be unconstitutional. Justice Scalia, writing for the majority, explained: "The dispositive question in this case, therefore, is whether content discrimination is reasonably necessary to achieve St. Paul's compelling interest; it is not" (p. 396). In other words, the Court relied heavily on application of the content-neutrality principle. The content-neutrality principle in First Amendment analysis refers to limiting, except in rare specified situations, the government from restricting speech based on the content of the message. The state of Minnesota argued, and the Minnesota Supreme Court agreed, that:

1. The ordinance was necessary to curtail increasing incidents of intolerance based on race, religion, and gender.
2. The speech restricted within the ordinance fit into the category of fighting words, a category of speech that has no First Amendment protection.

The US Supreme Court disagreed. Justice Scalia wrote that, while "burning a cross in someone's front yard is reprehensible," St. Paul had options available to prevent such acts "without adding the First Amendment to the fire" (p. 396). The majority pointed out that the ordinance was both content and viewpoint based in that it required the government to restrict speech based on its "hostility – or favoritism – to the underlying message expressed" (p. 386). and, as a result, the possible speech being restricted would not fit into the fighting-words category – which is a content-neutral category.

Given that by its very nature, hate speech is defined by its viewpoint, under the ruling in *R.A.V. v. St. Paul*, it appears that no hate speech restrictions could be held constitutional. However, the Supreme Court would rule on another hate speech related case in 2003. *Virginia v. Black*[3] focused on a Virginia State law that made it a felony "for any person ... with the intent of intimidating any person or group ..., to burn ... a cross on the property of another, a highway or other public place" (p. 343). According to the statute language, any cross burning "shall be considered prima facie evidence of an intent to intimidate a person or group" (p. 343). The statute in *Black* differed in significant ways from the ordinance in *R.A.V.* First, the Virginia statute called out only one type of speech – cross burnings with the purpose to intimidate. In *R.A.V.*, the ordinance was broader, sweeping into it any speech that "arouses anger, alarm or resentment." Second, the Virginia restriction did not single out any specific

2 *R.A.V. v. St. Paul*, 505 US 377 (1992).

3 *Virginia v. Black*, 538 US 343 (2003).

targets. In other words, under the Virginia statute, anyone no matter race, gender, religion, etc., could be considered a target of intimidation. In *R.A.V.*, the ordinance clearly specified race, color, creed, religion, or gender as the only possible targets. Third, while the Court in *R.A.V.* focused on the application of fighting words doctrine, the Court in *Black* relied on true-threats doctrine. The Court defined true threats as "those statements where the speaker means to communicate a serious expression of an intent to commit an act of unlawful violence to a particular individual or group of individuals" (p. 359). True threats is also a content-neutral category. In *Black*, the Court found that while the statute singled out a specific expression of speech – the burning cross – the statute was still content neutral because it only restricted the use of the symbol with an intent to intimidate or threaten. Finally, Justice O'Connor, writing for the plurality, spent significant time outlining the particularly virulent history of the burning cross in US society. That discussion was used to support the constitutional acceptability of restricting that one particular expression. This approach is distinctly different from the reasoning in *R.A.V.* that did not appear to address the State's asserted concern over protecting particularly vulnerable groups from certain types of messages. In *R.A.V.*, history of abuse and intolerance toward the groups singled out in the ordinance were not taken into consideration.

The above review, while not comprehensive, sheds light on some of the key justifications for protecting hate speech. Under this reasoning, the possible harms of hate speech cannot be considered as a valid justification for speech restriction. Restricting hate speech, under this reasoning, runs three risks. The first being the slippery slope concern, a concern that passing one law restricting speech will ultimately take us down a path toward more restrictions. Second, the repercussions could mean that the social, economic, or political majority would use those very restrictions to silence dissident or minority groups. Finally, many traditional scholars contend that restricting hate speech will only mask the hatred between groups, not dissipate it. The above discussion also points to a particular conception of the individual, one in which the individual can only remain autonomous, self-realized, and self-fulfilled if left to speak freely. The response to hateful speech, under this schema, is more speech not regulation of speech (Strossen 2018). As Steven Heyman (2009) has noted, it shifts the conversation away from a rights-based approach and instead forces First Amendment issues to be seen as a contestation between "the right to free expression and various social issues" (p. 160). This rights-based approach is actually more aligned with the international community and, as such, indicates perhaps the key difference between the United States and the rest of the world.

## Hate Speech Regulation Outside the United States

While the United States adamantly protects hate speech, other countries are embracing the need to limit certain types of speech in order to combat the harms that it causes. To this end, countries outside the United States deal with complex layers of laws intended to promote human rights and, in the process, attempt to balance the exercise of freedom of expression against competing interests, similar to the rights-based approach alluded to by Heyman. While this chapter is unable to discuss each of these in-depth, the following review illustrates the differences between the United States and international approaches and, through that review, will also open up a space for considering similarities.

At the international level, two of the most impactful covenants addressing the prohibition of hate speech are the 1965 International Convention on the Elimination of All Forms of Racial Discrimination (CERD) and the 1966 International Covenant on Civil and Political Rights (ICCPR). Article 4 in CERD requires that:

> States Parties condemn all propaganda and all organizations which are based on ideas or theories of superiority of one race or group of persons of one colour or ethnic origin, or which attempt to justify or promote racial hatred and discrimination in any form, and undertake to adopt immediate and positive measures designed to eradicate all incitement to, or acts of, such discrimination. (p. 3)

Article 4 takes a particularly firm stance against racist hate speech, laying out specific regulations including restricting the dissemination of ideas based on racial superiority, dissemination of ideas based on racial hatred, incitement to racial discrimination, and incitement to acts of racially motivated violence. As of January 2020, there were 182 parties to CERD and 88 signatories. Many countries have attached reservations to their ratification of CERD, including the United States, which filed a reservation citing conflicts with the First Amendment.

The forceful position taken in Article 4 concerning the restriction of racist hate speech has led to many countries refusing to sign it. To attempt to give more shape to the understanding of punishable racist speech, address long-term concerns, and align the article more closely with other international human rights laws, CERD adopted its General Recommendation (GR) 35 (2013) "Combating Racist Hate Speech." For example, GR 35's elaboration on what constitutes racist hate speech stated:

1. All dissemination of ideas based on racial or ethnic superiority or hatred, by whatever means;
2. Incitement to hatred, contempt or discrimination against members of a group on grounds of their race, color, descent, or national or ethnic origin;
3. Threats or incitement to violence against persons or groups on the grounds in 2. above;
4. Expression of insults, ridicule or slander of persons or groups or justification of hatred, contempt or discrimination on the grounds in 2. above, when it clearly amounts to incitement to hatred or discrimination;
5. Participation in organizations and activities which promote and incite racial discrimination (p. 4).

Clearly, this language in GR 35 will help to guide the interpretation and application of Article 4. This elaboration in GR 35 will not, however, change the US position, as the only constitutionally regulable speech listed in the five points would be those related to incitement.

Articles 19 and 20 of the ICCPR also address the tensions between protection of freedom of speech and protection from racist speech, but it does so in a way that is less expansive and thus slightly less contentious than Article 4 in CERD. Article 19(2) establishes a firm commitment to freedom of expression for individuals and for the media but it tempers that commitment with language in Section 3 that reads in part, that the speech rights subject to certain restrictions: "(a) For respect of the rights or reputations of others; (b) For the protection of national security or of public order, or of public health or morals" (p. 176). Speech protection must be balanced against other rights, particularly those rights associated with human dignity. Article 20(2) includes additional stipulations that could also impact free-speech protections. Specifically, it reads:

1. Any propaganda for war shall be prohibited by law.
2. Any advocacy of national, racial or religious hatred that constitutes incitement to discrimination, hostility or violence shall be prohibited by law (p. 178).

While the language in Article 20(2) does not have to implicate speech, many rulings by the Human Rights Committee have done just that. The United States has registered reservations concerning Article 20(2), citing again conflicts with the First Amendment.

At the regional level, and here I am emphasizing predominantly Europe, there are two key documents regarding the possibility of hate-speech restriction. The Charter of Fundamental

Rights of the European Union came into effect in December 2009 and is legally binding on every EU member state. It holds:

> Conscious of its spiritual and moral heritage, the Union is founded on the indivisible, universal values of human dignity, freedom, equality and solidarity; it is based on the principles of democracy and the rule of law. It places the individual at the heart of its activities, by establishing the citizenship of the Union and by creating an area of freedom, security and justice.

Article 11 sets out the right to freedom of expression and information but that is tempered by among other articles, Article 21, which focuses on non discrimination. The Charter was drafted by the European Union and is interpreted by the Court of Justice of the EU.

The Charter is sometimes confused with other human rights provision. For example, the European Commission Against Racism and Intolerance (ECRI) is the human rights body of the Council of Europe (CoE) (2015), an intergovernmental organization with 47 member states of which 28 are EU members. The CoE was created in 1949 in an effort to promote greater unity among its members and to defend human rights and promote democracy. The ECRI's role is to monitor matters concerning racism, xenophobia, antisemitism, intolerance, and racial discrimination. The ECRI works closely with authorities in member states, as well as international organizations such as the EU and the United Nations. Its primary goal is to provide guidance to policy makers. In 2015, the ECRI released its General Policy Recommendation (GPR) No. 15 that focused specifically on hate speech. GPR 15 first defined hate speech as speech that "is based on the unjustified assumption that a person or a group of persons are superior to others; it incites acts of violence or discrimination, thus undermining respect for minority groups and damaging social cohesion" (p. 1). The recommendation called on governments to act swiftly, promote self-regulation of the media, raise public awareness to the consequences of hate speech, withdraw support (financial or otherwise) from political groups who use hate speech, and to criminalize the most extreme forms of hate speech. In this recommendation, however, the ECRI tempered its call for hate-speech restriction against maintaining a commitment to freedom of expression, holding that the measure should not be used to curb freedom of expression.

In addition to international and regional limitations on hate speech, most countries have their own laws restricting certain types of hate speech under varying circumstances and applying to specific groups. Those laws differ widely. Some of them focus on physical harms associated with threats, intimidation, and incitement. Many of those countries specifically call out public incitement to hatred and/or incitement to genocide. Other laws and regulations are more broadly focused on human dignity concerns and might restrict language or expression that ridicules, insults, invokes rancor, or is offensive. The regulations may apply only to race or religion but often extend to include other categories including color, nationality, ethnicity, gender, sexual orientation, gender identity or expression, mental or physical disability, and/or age. Some countries are even broader in their set of protections. Canada, for example, covers "any identifiable group" (Canadian Criminal Code 2019, p. 347) and Croatia prohibits discrimination based on differences "of race, religion, language, political or other belief, property, birth, education, social position or other characteristics, gender, color, national or ethnic origin, violates fundamental human rights and freedoms recognized by the international community" (Croatian Penal Code 2004, p. 69). The mechanisms for regulation also vary country-by-country with prohibitions established through regional laws, national statutes, or constitutions. The penalties for violating those regulations can range from monetary fines to 10-years imprisonment.

How these regulations are written, what groups are protected, what penalties are assessed and in what ways they are enforced are mainly driven by the history of that particular country.

For example, Germany, in response to the atrocities committed against the Jewish population during the Holocaust, created laws designed to restrict hate speech in regard to group defamation, use of propaganda by Nazi organizations, and incitement of hatred against minorities (National Legislative Bodies 1949). In 2017, the language from the German Penal Code laid the groundwork for the passage of the Act to Improve Enhancement of the Law in Social Networks, otherwise known as the Network Enforcement Act (NetzDG). The much criticized law is intended to reduce hate speech on social media sites by holding social media intermediary companies (such as Facebook and Twitter) responsible questionable content. Fines for failure to do so within a timely fashion can run up to 50 million euros. In early 2020, in response to increased far-right, fascist violence, Chancellor Angela Merkel proposed to intensify NetzDG by requiring companies not just to remove content but also to report it to authorities (Brady 2019). Hate speech online would carry stiffer penalties than offline hate speech in an effort to highlight the increased reach of comments made online. While Germany is the most extreme example of hate-speech legislation, the range of penalties and speech restricted varies from other strict countries such as France (EURACTIV Network 2019) to more balanced countries such as Canada (Walker 2018). No matter how stringent or lenient these laws are, they all have a similar basis for restricting speech – protecting human dignity.

## Finding Common Ground

In terms of the United States, free-speech considerations have driven the legal debate over hate-speech restriction. As we saw in terms of *R.A.V. v. St. Paul*, any legislation focused on restricting hate speech will have a nearly impossible bar to pass. That bar, of course, is the US Supreme Court's reliance on the content-neutrality principle and content-neutral doctrines such as fighting words and incitement. Even the ruling upholding Virginia's constitutional right to restrict cross burnings with the intent to intimidate was housed within the content-neutral framework of true threats. That reliance on the principle of content neutrality in hate-speech cases sheds light on more fundamental and universal concerns related to free-speech protection. For example, it illustrates the fear of government suppression, concerns of government overreach (the slippery slope argument), and the assumption that society will be best served by protecting virtually all speech. By allowing open debate, any falsehoods will inevitably lose out in the Marketplace of Ideas. Ultimately, underpinning all of this is an assumption that individuals are autonomous and that as such 1) only their speech needs to be protected in order to support self-fulfillment and self-realization, and 2) the only fear of silencing that they should be concerned about is from government censorship. The best response, then, to speech we don't like – such as hate speech – is more speech, not suppression of speech.

Outside the United States, discussions surrounding restricting some level of hate speech have been more grounded in a human rights framework. As such, though most countries with anti hate speech legislation also have some stated protection of freedom of expression, the focus is less on the rights of the individual to speak and more so on the human rights of the person being targeted by the hate speech. They do attempt to balance speech protections against the harms associated with hate speech; however, the balancing is weighed more heavily in favor of protecting human rights. Much of the hate-speech legislation in the international community is based on historic concerns of oppression, discrimination, and genocide. However, those laws also pay heed to the threat of government overreach. Despite those concerns, most countries outside the United States see more value in restricting hate speech than in protecting it.

Clearly, there are significant differences in our legal and philosophical approaches to speech protection, but there is a common ground to be found between the international conception of human dignity and the First Amendment conception of self-realization. Despite our differences in how best to protect and promote self-realization or human dignity, the United States and the rest of the world have articulated a commitment to ensuring this for every citizen. Of course, the US conception of self-realization and non-US notions of human dignity aren't the same.

In 2012, Jeremy Waldron released a book in which he argued that hate-speech restrictions were necessary in order to protect human dignity. He explained: "A person's dignity is not just some Kantian aura. It is their social standing, the fundamentals of basic reputation that entitles them to be treated as equals in the ordinary operation of society. Their dignity is something they can rely on – in the best case implicitly and without fuss, as they live their lives, go about their business and raise their families" (p. 5). Human dignity in Waldron's interpretation is a basic right, a necessary foundation for a well-ordered society. In addition, Waldron attempted to further define the concept by differentiating between the philosophical understanding of the concept and the social and legal status. He says: "It [dignity] is a matter of status – one's status as a member of society in good standing – and it generates demands for recognition and for treatment that accords with that status. Philosophically, we may say that dignity is inherent in the human person – and so it is. But as a social and legal status, it has to be established, upheld, maintained and vindicated by society and the law and this … is something in which we are all required to play a part" (p. 60). Building on this understanding of dignity, in relation to the social and legal spheres, Waldron finds hate speech to undermine human dignity and so asserts that some level of restriction is necessary to counter its negative effects.

Waldron's book touched a nerve among Constitutional law scholars, generating much attention aimed at dismantling Waldron's position. For example, James Allan (2013) proclaimed Waldron's book to be "ultimately unpersuasive and unsatisfying" (p. 63). He specifically critiqued Waldron for not offering clear explanation of "how exactly he thinks hate speech undermines this assurance of good standing and how laws against such speech themselves undermine that undermining" (p. 66). Robert C. Post took issue with the ability of hate-speech legislation to promote the well-ordered society because, according to Post, such restrictions instead of fostering human dignity actual remove "guarantee of political equality in the formation of public opinion" embedded within the protection of free speech (Post 2017, p. 656). Other well-respected US constitutional law scholars, including Nadine Strossen, James Weinstein, and Ronald Dworkin, have also debated Waldron over his position (Gannoway 2013). Finally, C. Edwin Baker, one of the major proponents of self-realization, also weighed on Waldron's work. Baker (2012) specifically raised questions about how Waldron – and the rest of Europe, according to Baker – defines dignity. He asserted that Waldron's position on dignity is that "it involves the legal right to control other people's thoughts and attitudes or at least some of their expressions of their thoughts, attitudes, and beliefs" (p. 62). Baker maintained instead that dignity "encompasses a person's status as an agent who has a right and, to some extent, the ability to have and express attitudes and beliefs" (p. 62). Baker's premise, which serves as representative of many First Amendment scholars, is that "1. that legitimacy of the legal orders depends on it respecting people's equality and 'autonomy' and 2. … that as a purely formal matter, the legal order only respects people's autonomy if it allows people in their speech to express their own values" (p. 63).

The aim here is not to enter into the debate about Waldron's position per se but instead to use this debate to highlight the salient differences and similarities between human dignity and self-realization. What is clear from the above debate is that similarities abound. Specifically, both conceptions are aimed at the individual. Even though the human dignity approach is more community centric, that does not mean that the US reliance on self-realization does not take community into account. In fact, self-realization is often tied to the ability to participate fully in a well-functioning democracy. A key difference, of course, that becomes glaringly apparent from the debate is the role of speech in promoting dignity or self-realization. At first glance, it appears that this is the major sticking point. In other words, is it more beneficial to individuals and society at-large to restrict some hate speech or is it better to protect the greatest amount of speech possible? I don't mean to oversimplify the debate, nor the appropriate response, but I do want to posit that this, to me, seems to be treated typically as an either/or scenario when really it is a matter of degree. How much speech restriction is enough to better promote human dignity and self-realization for all, or how much is too much, discouraging people from being able to hold their own thoughts and opinions and thus impeding that same end? The response from many traditional free-speech advocates seems out of touch with the way in which speech silences, harms, and disenfranchises members of socially and politically disempowered groups. In addition, it fails to take into account the global nature of communication systems today and the acceleration of the spread of hatred over social media. However, by acknowledging the primary space where most of the world seems in agreement – a commitment to promoting individual self-fulfillment – we can begin to conceive hate-speech regulations that will benefit members of both communities and will address one of the most contentious free-speech issues on the internet today.

## The Social Media Problem

Restrictions or the recommendation of restriction of hate speech are not new. Europe and much of the rest of the world began to incorporate at least some level of restriction into the development of their human rights laws following World War II. In the decades since then, those restrictions have been given shape and expanded. In the United States, legal attempts at restricting hate speech can be traced back to the 1950s when in *Beauharnis v. Illinois* (1952) the Supreme Court in a 5–4 decision found that a state law prohibiting libel against a class of citizens of a certain race, color, creed, or religion was constitutional under the First Amendment. The movement to restrict hate speech would take on speed starting in the mid-1980s when scholars began arguing for hate-speech restriction on college campuses. That movement ebbed a bit through the 2000s but has picked up momentum again. That renewed interest in hate-speech restriction can be tied to two elements: the exponential spread of hate speech through social media and the increase in motivated violent attacks. It is my position that those two elements taken together don't just suggest that the United States consider some level of hate-speech restriction, they require it. Here is but a small sampling of examples where violent acts can be traced to social media origins:

- In the United States, murders and attacks with an online hate-speech connection can be traced back nearly a decade. In 2012, white supremacist Wade Michael Page posted in online hate forums before he went on to murder six people at a Sikh temple in Wisconsin. In 2015, Dylan Roof self-radicalized online before he murdered nine people at a black church in South Carolina. In 2018, Robert Brown had been active on Gab, a Twitter-like site used by white supremacists before he killed 11 elderly worshippers at a synagogue in Pennsylvania. In August 2019, Patrick Crusius posted a white nationalist, anti-immigrant manifesto on 8chan and then went to a Walmart in El Paso and killed 22 people. 8chan, which rebranded itself as 8kun following the El Paso shooting, is a site that has been linked with white supremacism, neo-Nazism, racism, anti-Semitism, and hate crimes. In December 2019, just days before the end of the year, Grafton Thomas attacked a Rabbi in his home with a machete during Shabbat and Hanukah observances. Those are just the most publicized incidents of attacks. According to the Federal Bureau of Investigation, attacks motivated by bias or prejudice reached an all-time high in 2018.

- Over the course of the past decade, Japan has seen increasing hate-speech rallies and online attacks on ethnic minorities. One of these events was the 2009 attack on the Kyoto Korean School in which ultranationalist groups shouted racist and xenophobic messages at the elementary school, damaged school property, and posted video footage. This incident resulted in a district ruling that the hateful rallies were not protected speech and that the rallies constituted racial discrimination under CERD. That ruling was upheld by the Osaka High Court.
- In what is one the worst recent hate-based killing sprees, Brenton Tarrant killed 51 people and injured 49 others in two Mosques in Christchurch, New Zealand. Tarrant, who has been described as a white supremacist and member of the alt-right, live-streamed the first attack on Facebook. According to Facebook, the video had only been viewed 4000 times before it was removed (Kharpal 2019). The New Zealand Office of Film and Literature Classification has classified the video as "objectionable," making it a criminal offense in the country to distribute, copy, or exhibit the video. Approximately one dozen arrests have been made for possessing or sharing the video or Tarrant's manifesto.
- In October 19, Stephen Balliet also recorded himself as he went on a killing spree near a synagogue in Halle, Germany. He uploaded his video to Twitch, a live-streaming platform owned by Amazon. Twitch removed the material but not before it was archived on right-wing sites. Balliet also linked his crime to the June 2019 murder of Walter Lubcke, a German politician who had been a vocal supporter of immigration. Lubcke was killed execution style.
- These anti-Semitic attacks in Germany and the United States have led to the newly proposed Merkel law discussed previously and most recently in January 2020 to testimony before the House Committee on Homeland Security from the Anti-Defamation League (Cortellessa 2020). Jonathan Greenblatt, head of the ADL, pushed for passage of the Online Safety Modernization Act, which would increase enforcement and create tougher penalties for online harassment and cybercrimes. He proclaimed: "It's long overdue for the social media companies to step up and shut down the neo-Nazis on their platforms" (p. 1).

Research into the area of online hate speech lends credence to Greenblatt's concerns. For example, UK scholar Raphael Cohen-Almagor (2018) published results in 2018 based on a study of hate sites over a 10-year period, as well as interviews with more than 40 experts in Internet security, and human rights from Canada, the United States, Israel, France, England, Ireland, and Portugal. His study focused exclusively on racist, white supremacist websites. Ultimately, he concluded that "there is sufficient evidence to suggest that speech can and does inspire crime" (p. 39). In 2017 Karsten Müller and Carlo Schwarz published a working paper, which has drawn considerable attention. The authors reviewed anti refugee rhetoric on "Alternative for Germany," the Facebook page associated with the far-right party. Specifically, Müller and Schwarz reviewed the composition of the users on the page and their location and then compared that with more than 3300 anti refugee incidents in Germany. They concluded: "Our findings suggest that social media has not only become a fertile soil for the spread of hateful ideas but also motivates real-life action" (p. 42). More recently, several scholars at Cardiff University used computational criminology to study the relationship between online hate speech that targets people based on their race or religion and offline racially and religious motivated crimes (Williams et al. 2020). The study focused on crimes in London over an 18-month period. According to the researchers, "the findings renew our understanding of hate crime as a process, rather than as a discrete event, for the digital age" (p. 93).

## Conclusion

The purpose of this chapter was to address two questions: can the United States and the global community find common ground in the debate over hate-speech restriction and why is it important that they do so at this time in history? Given the escalating incidents of violence and the documented role of hate speech on social media sites as a contributing factor, it is clear that 1) leaving the decision up to service providers is not sufficient and 2) it is time for the global community, including the United States, to figure out a new path forward. Undoubtedly, the United States has a distinct social and legislative history that will keep it from creating the types of intensive anti-hate speech laws in place in some parts of the world. However, through our mutual respect for individual dignity and self-realization, a conversation can start that might help move us closer to more compatible ideas about hate-speech restriction, particularly in regard to social media.

## References

Allan, J. (2013). Hate speech law and disagreement [Review of *the Harm in Hate Speech*, by J. Waldron]. *Constitutional Commentary* 29: 59–79.

Baker, C. (1989). *Human Liberty and Freedom of Speech*. New York: Oxford University Press.

Baker, C. (2009). Autonomy and hate speech. In: *Extreme Speech and Democracy* (ed. I. Hare and J. Weinstein), 139–157. Oxford: Oxford University Press.

Baker, C. (2012). Hate speech. In: *The Content and Context of Hate Speech: Rethinking Regulation Responses* (ed. M. Herz and P. Molnar), 57–80. Cambridge: Cambridge University Press.

*Beauharnais v. Illinois*, 343 US 250, (1952)

Brady, K. (2019). Germany announces plans to combat far-right extremism and online hate speech. DW Akademia. https://www.dw.com/en/germany-announces-plans-to-combat-far-right-extremism-and-online-hate-speech/a-51049129 (accessed September 17, 2020).

Canadian Criminal Code (2019). Hate propaganda. Section 318(1). https://laws-lois.justice.gc.ca/eng/acts/c-46/section-319.html (accessed September 17, 2020).

Cohen-Almagor, R. (2018). Taking North American white supremacist groups seriously: the scope and challenge of hate speech on the Internet. *International Journal for Crime, Justice and Social Democracy* 7 (2): 38–57.

Cortellessa, E. (2020). ADL tell Congress to curb online hate speech if social media giants won't. *The Times of Israel*. https://www.timesofisrael.com/adl-tells-congress-to-curb-online-hate-speech-if-social-media-giants-wont (accessed September 17, 2020).

Croatian Penal Code (2004). Racial and other discrimination. Article 174. https://www.unodc.org/res/cld/document/croatia-criminal-code_html/Croatia_Criminal_Code_1997.pdf (accessed September 17, 2020).

Emerson, T. (1963). *Toward a General Theory of Free Speech*. New York: Random House.

EURACTIV Network (2019). France adopts touch line against online hate speech. https://www.euractiv.com/section/politics/news/france-adopts-tough-law-against-online-hate-speech (accessed September 17, 2020).

Gannoway, A. (2013). Waldron takes questions. *NYU Law Magazine*. https://blogs.law.nyu.edu/magazine/2013/waldron-takes-questions (accessed September 17, 2020).

Heyman, S. (2009). Hate speech, public discourse, and the First Amendment. In: *Extreme Speech and Democracy* (ed. I. Hare and J. Weinstein), 158–181. Oxford: Oxford University Press.

Kharpal, A. (2019). Facebook says video of New Zealand mosque shootings was viewed 4,000 times before being removed. *CNBC*. https://www.cnbc.com/2019/03/19/facebook-new-zealand-mosque-shootings-video-viewed-4000-times-before-removal.html (accessed January 18, 2021).

Mill, J.S. (1859). *On Liberty*. London: Longmans, Green, Reader and Dyer.

Müller, K. and Schwarz, C. (2017). Fanning the flames of hate: social media and hate crime. *SSRN Electronic Journal*: 1–37.

National Legislative Bodies (1949). Germany: Basic Law for the Federal Republic of Germany. https://www.refworld.org/docid/4e64d9a02.html (accessed 2 February 2020).
Post, R. (2000). Reconciling theory and doctrine in First Amendment jurisprudence. *California Law Review* 88: 2353–2374.
Post, R. (2017). Legitimacy and hate speech. *Constitutional Commentary* 944: 651–659. https://scholarship.law.umn.edu/concomm/944.
*R.A.V. v. St. Paul*, 505 US 377, (1992)
Redish, M.H. (1982). The value of free speech. *University of Pennsylvania Law Review* 130 (3): 591–645.
Strossen, N. (2018). *Hate Speech: Why We Should Resist is with Free Speech, Not Censorship.* New York: Oxford University Press.
UN Committee on the Elimination of Racial Discrimination (CERD) (2013). General recommendation No. 35: Combating racist hate speech. https://www.refworld.org/docid/53f457db4.html (accessed February 2, 2020).
Waldron, J. (2012). *The Harm in Hate Speech.* Cambridge: Harvard University Press.
Walker, J. (2018). Hate speech and freedom of expression: legal boundaries in Canada. https://lop.parl.ca/sites/PublicWebsite/default/en_CA/ResearchPublications/201825E (accessed January 18, 2021).
Williams, L.W., Burnap, P., Javed, A. et al. (2020). Hate in the machine: anti-black and anti-Muslim social media posts as predictors of offline racially and religiously aggravated crime. *British Journal of Criminology* 60: 93–117.

# 18

# Political Communication and Electoral Campaigns in Europe

## The Search for International Standards

Rafael Rubio

Many years ago, when the Internet was just a distant dream, Ted Nelson (Nelson and Brand 1974) wrote, "If you are interested in democracy and its future, you'd better understand computers." Today, it is impossible to address the debate on democracy without taking the impact of technology into account (Hindman 2009).

## Communication, Technology, Democracy, and Voting

The use of technology has always affected democracy, but it has had a powerful impact on our political ecosystem in recent years. As time goes by, it is becoming increasingly evident that we are witnessing the major impact that the Internet is having on social and economic models. And though it is true that technology has also had an impact on the political sphere, those changes have not been accompanied by real changes to political spaces; the state continues to be "the point of reference and the obligatory framework where assumptions regulating social life are established and where the ordering and evaluative principles of coexistence are democratically expressed and defined (De Vega 1998)." Initially, there was a certain bedazzlement to technology's capacity to be an ally of democracy. It was thought that democratization would enable a strengthening of the citizen's role in politics, increasing pluralism in society, and improving mechanisms of control and participation through new organizational forms of a horizontal nature, giving rise to a new, more open, and more engaged public sphere.

This initial blind faith has been replaced by alarm at the dangers posed by the use of technology. The appearance of new inequalities around the digital divide; greater control over citizens; The demise of traditional media and ascend of social platforms and search engines, silencing sectors of the population in the public debate; the replacement of public spaces with closed ones; the lack of Credible news sources and the creation of a climate of general suspicion, increasing cynicism and apathy among citizens; and volatility and low engagement: these trends have given rise to the so-called The Dictatorship of Data, "algocracy," "computopia," or "weapons of math destruction," the terms used to indicate the overall threat that has arisen.

*The Handbook of Communication Rights, Law, and Ethics: Seeking Universality, Equality, Freedom and Dignity*, First Edition. Edited by Loreto Corredoira, Ignacio Bel Mallén, and Rodrigo Cetina Presuel.

Added to these "structural" dangers are those that attempt to impede or alter how technological systems function, causing distrust in the ability of democracy to face these new threats and distorting the functioning of the democratic system – for example, cyber attacks or disinformation operations (Rodríguez Andrés 2018), in which technology plays a key role (Rubio 2018), against the electoral process.

## Digital Transformation and Political Communication

In the context that I have just described, political communication and electoral campaigns have been radically transformed and a new paradigm is emerging. The existence of new channels, the Internet and social networks through which citizens can access political information is affecting who plays the leading role in transmitting messages that, in the past, was held almost exclusively by political parties. The increase in the selection of being available has led to communication that has come to be known as "audience democracy" (Manin 1997; Sartori 1998). Traditional mass advertising has been replaced by new forms of communication, which allow messages to be tailored to specific segments of the public, bringing about a very high degree of personalization. Communication is being concentrated within small, homogeneous groups, and campaigning techniques have returned to a one-to-one approach (of the kind used in the nineteenth century), or to many-to-many "mass customization" facilitated by technology (Pine 1993).

Electoral campaigns are where the highs and lows of audience democracy are revealed. Additionally, "[a]lthough on a theoretical level, electoral campaigns continue to be conceived as an enormous and symbolic dialogue between voters and those who are eligible, changes in the communicative ecosystem fully affect this theoretical collective dialogue, to the extent that 'it ends up making the inspiring principles succumb of the behavior of homo sapiens before the requirements and urgencies of homo videns'" (De Vega 1998). The Internet is transforming the ways in which people make electoral decisions and exercise their vote; it is transforming the very concept of political communication, and especially the concept of campaigning, since the ultimate success of a campaign may depend on effective use of the Internet.

A campaign collects data in order to be able to reach each voter at the right time and to disseminate the most appropriate messages and calls to action for that voter, whether those calls are for donations or the sale of advertising materials. And messages that have the ability to change voting intentions are saved, only being sent out in the campaign's final days.

These transformations occur both at the level of social changes and in the development of disinformation strategies, which take advantage of these new ways of winning power. They are located in indeterminate territories and, though suspicions may be raised, they are difficult to identify. They take advantage of a new concept of time, in which the immediacy of news affects decision making, and where the effectiveness of the response depends on its speed and involves a plurality of actors: parties, the media, citizens, and private companies.

They affect new channels, which occupy an important place in the organization, financing, and distribution of campaign information and the traditional conception of certain fundamental rights at risk. We might speak of platforms as a battlefield, websites and platforms as weapons and news as ammunition. This is why Mark Zuckerberg compares this new environment to the arms race that took place during the Cold War.

## Political Communications and Electoral Campaigns: Ethics and Law

The health of democracy has always been closely related to communication and public opinion. In a representative democracy, rulers must act in the name and in the interest of the people. This dynamic is accentuated in the knowledge society, where the status of information as the "raw material" of democracy has been confirmed. It is true that lying has always been a structural element of politics, but its power over public opinion was balanced by communication rights and media plurality. The impact of technology breaks these balances, calling into question various democratic pillars.

The idea of political communication as something that goes far beyond elections is gaining ground (Blumenthal 1982). Having become widespread, information technology has caused an "overexposure" of reality, which is being "attacked" by an increasing number of channels that make this information public and by the expansion of the possibilities for information to enter the public space. Accordingly, the likelihood of keeping information hidden has decreased. As a consequence, citizens are demanding greater volumes of information. Public opinion also deteriorates significantly, and starts distancing itself from reality. Democracy becomes a temporary convergence of opposing interests in which there is only one possible winner. Though these dangers threaten the entire democratic process, they are to be monitored with particular caution when it comes to elections, where communication exchanges affect how citizens form opinions and make decisions.

There are a number of vulnerabilities and manipulations that are becoming a new form of attack with a clear impact on public opinion than the traditional or more obvious attacks. Some even argue that such attacks have a more perverse aim, for example, provoking a more restrictive reaction when it comes to the use of information, which could cast doubts on the differences between how liberal democracies and illiberal democracies should react.

The frequency and virulence of these attacks has highlighted the need to search for answers. Any regulation will be insufficient if it is not accompanied by ethical behavior. There is no doubt that questions of communication within politics, its role in society, and the development of human beings and their dignity are essentially ethical in nature.

Each political regime has had its own political ethics as far as the role of communication is concerned. An idea that is becoming more and more widespread is that regulations are not enough to guarantee the right connection between public opinion and public powers and that citizens, communication professionals, and politicians need to exercise civic virtue in order to avoid a corruption of institutions and a trivialization of political debate.

## Hybrid Threats, Hybrid Answers

Here, we are dealing with the dissemination of false content using technology, the purchase of segmented advertising, the use of platforms to organize domestic or international influencing operations, and the amplification of hate speech. The hybrid – technology-based and communication-based – nature of threats requires the responses offered to be hybrid and to be undertaken in different fields beyond the legal sphere, within a comprehensive strategic plan. Security, which seeks to protect people's rights and the democratic processes they engage in, might be the first priority. This includes protecting communication infrastructures that are a priority for national security and creating specific organizations to tackle disinformation, such as those found in the United Kingdom, the Czech Republic, Sweden, or Spain (at election time).

Attacks on basic infrastructure related (though not exclusively) to democracy also pose a threat, because they can paralyze certain institutions, weakening confidence and reinforcing perceptions of democracy's fragility. This has led certain countries to declare elections to be critical infrastructure. This is the case in the United States, Sweden, and the European Union, which put in place specific initiatives to protect elections held in 2019.

Carrying out research is also necessary to enhance our knowledge of the techniques used for disinformation and their true impact on democracy and elections, as intergovernmental organizations such as IDEA or OSCE and public institutions such as the European Commission, the European Parliament, the Council of Europe, the Venice Commission, and NATO have long been doing. Along the same lines, there is a need for education that allows technology and its effects to be confronted and that makes it possible to detect threats, protect privacy, and evaluate information by discerning the truth. Such education would cultivate citizens who are capable of entering into dialog and making the decisions that are essential in a democracy.

Another approach that has developed throughout the world is the use of fact-checking mechanisms[1] and other tools that allow users to verify whether information is true. But this is not enough; institutions need to prioritize the construction of narratives that are their own and that are ongoing. The media is indispensable in this endeavor, and so strengthening its diversity and sustainability is advisable.

In order to be able to offer solutions of this type in a global and hyperconnected world, cooperation when it comes to prevention, prosecution, awareness raising, and media literacy is essential. Collaboration in the following areas is therefore necessary:

- public-private cooperation involving electoral authorities, academics, political actors, platforms, the media, and platforms to detect threats, distribute official information, and even debunk hoaxes;
- between industry and governments to strengthen digital security;
- between technology companies, governments, and education systems to strengthen education;
- between technology companies and fact-checking organizations; and
- between different national governments (because threats to democracy are both national and international).

International cooperation covers aspects such as the international protection of communication systems, prevention of their misuse, the identification of attacks' origins, the collection of evidence, and pursuit of the attackers. In this sense, by sharing information and positive experiences with one another, all the actors involved will also contribute to identifying appropriate solutions for these common problems.

During elections, it is necessary to increase the security of electoral mechanisms, to work on education, and to strengthen cooperation systems between the different actors involved in campaigns – not only political and institutional actors, but also companies and civil society. There is a need to provide the electoral authorities with sufficient resources and training to tackle these new challenges on a sure footing. Self-regulatory measures for social platforms and technology service providers must also be explored.

## Self-regulation

Another approach is the self-regulation that is undertaken by social platforms and focused on transparency about the advertising appearing on them, the algorithms that automatically select the information provided to users, the reporting of fake news and profiles, and the promotion of more reliable information. A version of this that incorporates ethical standards is the preferred choice of the European Parliament and the European Commission (HLEG 2018). The Commission recommends distinguishing sponsored content from organic content; adapting advertising policies so that they reinforce transparency and avoiding incentivizing disinformation; ensuring responsibility is exercised during data processing, strengthening protection of the relevant fundamental rights; enhancing control over fake accounts and bots; and facilitating access to information in the hands of Internet platforms for verification purposes (Magallón 2019).

[1] All of which have come together since 2015 in the International Fact-Checking Network (IFCN).

Facebook, Instagram, Twitter, and Google have adopted a series of measures that includes, for example, limiting the purchase of political advertising to authorized users; restricting information that comes from certain sources; making it obligatory to label the origin of messages from such sources; deleting fake accounts; and creating an "election committee" to collaborate with academic researchers to study this phenomenon and possible solutions to it.

Codes of conduct can also emerge from collaboration between platforms and institutions. For example, a code of conduct against online hate speech has been developed by the European Commission in conjunction with Facebook, Microsoft, Twitter, and YouTube. Such codes can satisfy different international standards, and ideally, they should lead to the creation of an independent, international self-regulatory organization.

The media should also heighten its transparency and independence through ethical, sectoral, or medium-specific codes (Bel 2015), and, along with platforms, it should even adopt common standards of behavior.

## The Search for European Standards

We cannot resign ourselves to understanding political communication as an independent reality that has its own rules and is detached from moral and legal considerations. Therefore, within a comprehensive perspective, it is especially important to seek balanced legal formulas so that the measures proposed protect individual and political rights while respecting, as far as possible, the commercial viability of the platforms on which debate takes place.

Though the use of technology has always had an impact on democracy, when that use so clearly affects the democratic process, special legislative attention is required. Despite this, there are very few European countries that have seriously addressed this issue by contemplating reforms to their legislation (Magallón 2019; Corredoira 2020).

A series of constitutional values is at stake, as are the principles contained in the UN texts that Gomá, Corredoira, and Bel comment on in this volume. On the one hand, we have fundamental rights such as freedom of expression, the right to communicate, the right to honor, the right to privacy, and the right to participate in political life and, on the other hand, we have democratic stability and security.

Difficulties include the technical knowledge required to understand the nature of the activities and their direct and indirect consequences within the democratic ecosystem; the difficulty of ascertaining the effects of disinformation activities on society's and private individuals' behavior; and the fact that attacks take place on private global platforms, regulation of which gives rise to new complexities. Debate here has become more relevant, and even to a certain extent more urgent following events such as the Coronavirus health crisis (where disinformation, in addition to causing social uncertainty, could have serious effects on health).

Communication rights are one of the pillars on which the contemporary democratic political system is based. Traditional communication entailed a plural model linked to truthfulness as a guarantee of an independent and objective public sphere, with the establishment of minimum constitutional limits to defend personality rights (honor, privacy, and personal reputation) as well as to protect children and young people, and with subsequent protection mechanisms.

Though these forms of protection traditionally sought to combat a state's monopoly on information and to guarantee plurality, the adequacy of that model is being questioned today. As Cotino (2008) states, "Traditional mass media has ceased to be a basic pillar of the democratic system, or, at least, it has ceased to be the only one. The democratic edifice is sustained by many other pillars online." Technology has brought about an explosion in communication actors, transforming the information ecosystem. This proliferation of communicators has harmed pluralism by privatizing the concept of the public sphere, decoupling information from responsibility and causing it to become fragmented and radicalized (Rubio 2018).

Hence, social threats now exist alongside the traditional limits of freedom of expression such as libel or slander. Two threats to democracy can therefore be observed. The first is the creation of a social climate that may provoke democracy-endangering instability – that is, "social alarm." The other is direct influence on electoral results that distorts decision-making, vote-casting, and ballot-counting processes.

Regulation must rise to a broad set of challenges: authorship of and responsibility for things published; the ability to remove or flag content; segmentation of content with subsequent collection, storage, processing, and use of personal data (García Mahamut 2015, 2017); "hate speech" (Cabellos Espierrez 2018); the deletion of certain accounts and the conditions under which that deletion can be carried out; the establishment of replication mechanisms adapted to the Internet era (Abad 2015); particular public bodies' fulfillment of the obligation to provide information; and the prohibition of preventing specific citizens' access to such information (for example, via blocking of certain users on social platforms).

In the context of electoral campaigns, there is also a need to respond to the possibility that other subjects, inside and outside a country's borders, might take part in the electoral campaign and even buy advertising; to ban the publication of certain types of content at specific times in the electoral process – for example, the prohibition of surveys for a certain period of time or the prohibition of political messaging (both online and offline) and political advertising for a certain period of time before an election; and to have speedy complaint procedures and swift legal solutions in place for when these are needed.

## Existing Regulations in Europe[2]

Within the European Union (Magallón 2019; Corredoira 2020), there are different examples of state-level legal responses to the problems that I have indicated.

Germany (Network Enforcement Act 2017) has transferred oversight obligations to the companies that own social platforms with more than two million users, even in the case of offenses not committed in Germany. They are the ones that have to block or remove illegal content within a maximum period of 24 hours; if they do not do so, they face fines of up to 50 million euros.

In France, the law on combating fake news during election periods seeks to identify and stop deliberate publication of false or misleading facts on an online platform in the period prior to an election. The law obliges platforms to immediately remove any unlawful content that is published on them and to implement a mechanism for people to notify the platform of any fake news; they are also bound by certain "enhanced-transparency obligations" regarding advertising sales and the costs thereof. In addition, it establishes a specific emergency appeal procedure that is based on the designation of a specific court, which must issue a ruling within a maximum period of 48 hours and has the right to block the content and demand that the platform stop campaigns containing it.

In Italy ("DDL Gambaro," Senato della Republica 2017), an attempt was made to pass a law setting fines of up to 5000 euros for anyone who publishes or distributes disinformation, as well as fines of up to 10 000 euros for anyone who undertakes hate speech or campaigns against the democratic process. However, the bill was rejected. Bills have also failed to pass in Croatia and Ireland.

---

[2] https://www.poynter.org/ifcn/anti-misinformation-actions/(accessed January 18, 2021); London School of Economics. Beyond Regulation: Approaching the challenges of the new media environment. (2018). Link: https://bit.ly/2WA1Avs (accessed January 18, 2021).

## Conclusions: Measures to be Implemented

It would be advisable to establish a series of basic general guidelines that could be adapted to this complex, ever-changing phenomenon and that, in relation to the European model, would make it possible to effectively tackle the transformation that communication is experiencing within democratic ecosystems across the world.

**Disinformation:** The threats that we are witnessing cannot become an excuse to curtail freedom of expression. There is thus a need to clearly define behaviors not permitted in law and to justify the proportionality and necessity of measures in relation to the objective defended.[3] Disinformation is the communication and distribution on the Internet – mainly on social networks – of fake news, half-truths, or highly subjective information that is presented as objective and true. Said disinformation is published in an organized or profit-driven manner; and its purpose is to destabilize and polarize public opinion on matters of general interest or social sensitivity, and it damages trust in the authorities and public representatives.

**Segmentation:** Personal data allow the information provided to citizens to be segmented almost to the point of personalization, especially because segmented advertising can be purchased on social platforms that have a very wide variety of data about those citizens. Data protection measures ensure that personal data, which for the most part are held by private companies, are processed fairly and transparently, as well as according to the specific, legitimate, and known purposes for which they were collected. It is necessary to find standards that guarantee data subjects' ownership of, access to, and control over their data as well as the security of that data. It may be necessary for measures to be confined to ensuring the especially sensitive nature of political opinions and making sure that processing of them is only possible on the basis of clear guarantees determined by law, especially in the context of elections.

**The responsibilities of tech platforms:** It is essential to define the status of technology platforms and to clarify their responsibility over the content published on them.[4] Other important issues in this regard are the ability to restrict access when credible allegations of illegality are made; the requirements and responsibilities of clarity, transparency, and accountability (De la Chapelle and Fehlinger 2016) that are applicable to platforms' operations; the income linked to political advertising that platforms receive; and the requirements for implementing oversight measures, at all times maintaining the principles of necessity and proportionality.

Along with the responsibility that they bear regarding content, platforms have a responsibility to their users. In this regard, it will be necessary to recognize the role of citizens as controllers of power and as an active part of public opinion,[5] as well as to establish the differences between different publishers of information if, as is the case in an electoral campaign, it is deemed necessary to establish different obligations. The debate here centers on whether or not it is advisable to allow people to participate anonymously in online political debate, and whether it is possible to delete profiles without state oversight when there are suspicions that they are bots that create inauthentic public opinion or are implicated in inappropriate or illegal behavior. It is also necessary to address the possibility of establishing legal requirements to demand data from platforms when such data may help to identify those who have undertaken certain acts, such as the purchase of advertising.

---

[3] *Mathieu-Mohin and Clerfayt v. Belgium*; *Ždanoka v. Latvia.*

[4] *Delfi as v. Estonia.*

[5] *Magyar Helsinki Bizottság v. Hungary. Animal Defenders International v. the United Kingdom. Delfi as v. Estonia.* Court of Justice of the European Communities (Grand Chamber) of December 16, 2008, preliminary ruling in case C 73/07.

**Equality and communication rights for all:** Favorable conditions need to be promoted[6] so that people can express their opinions and ideas without feeling afraid to do so. If we accept that platforms play a key role in shaping public opinion, to counteract the digital divide it is necessary to establish a series of obligations related to people's ability to access technology. Platforms would need to be required to offer the news in a fair and pluralistic way and avoid excluding specific groups from political debates. These obligations become stronger in election periods, when the state has a duty to guarantee the right to vote and to ensure that the necessary information on the different political options can reach citizens.

**The electoral campaign:** In election periods, the importance of the right to vote in free elections makes it necessary to add new extraordinary restrictions to the exercise of freedom of expression. It must be assumed that attacks undertaken during campaigns are a threat to the right of individual political participation and have impacts on the political system. Electoral regulation must not only protect voters' communication rights and the freedom of their decision making, but it must do so by guaranteeing the principles of objectivity, political neutrality, transparency, and equal opportunities among the different candidates. This raises the need to establish special procedures: Who can prohibit the dissemination of information in the campaign when it is suspected that this information may not be true, and under what conditions may they do so?[7] When is a message considered to be "advertising," as opposed to a case of individual expression that has been widely shared? Are advertising and political communication subject to different control mechanisms?

**Specific regulations:** Technology is bringing about changes in the handling of information, and legislation must regulate these new circumstances in the context of election campaigns. And such regulation, as it relates to elections, has traditionally been devised as a special legal regime. Its application is time limited; and it deals with a very particular set of actors (the government, candidates, and the media); and it establishes particular rules in relation to certain types of conduct.

**Jurisdiction:** The applicable jurisdiction can be established based on the location of the actions, the devices, the people, the place where the action has its effects, and the nationality of the victim (Brenner and Koops 2005). Also desirable in this regard would be clear rules on legal procedure, standard criteria for decision making, and a transnational system for appeals (De la Chapelle and Fehlinger 2016).

**Competent authorities:** Another challenge is to design an order capable of balancing, not only judicial and nonjudicial systems, but also the jurisdictions of different national authorities. This raises questions about the viability of a competent international authority for resolving international conflicts that arise. From the point of view of judicial responses, the major challenge is collaboration and information sharing, which should be covered by legal provisions.

**Public–private partnerships:** The link between administrative and judicial authorities and social platforms, at both national and international levels, is essential to ensure the detection and prosecution of threats and the timely implementation of the necessary responses; the mandatory nature of such measures must be established by law.

**Global approach:** Information can be found in different places, far from national jurisdictions, and it may take fragmented forms, which complicates the task of determining its origin and authorship. The need for a transnational perspective must translate into scope for accessing and preserving evidence to ensure the availability of data on external servers or in the cloud. Mutual legal assistance aimed at improving international cooperation is also required.

---

6 *Ahmet Yıldırım v. Turkey. Cengiz and Others v. Turkey.*

7 *Dink v. Turkey.*

It is only from such a comprehensive and flexible perspective that it will be possible to: guarantee transparency when it comes to sponsored political content; restrict targeting options for political advertising; reduce revenue for disinformation providers; provide greater clarity on how algorithms work; allow third-party verification; make it easier for users to discover and access different news sources that represent alternative points of view; introduce measures to identify and close fake accounts and address the problem of automatic bots; and facilitate the work of fact checkers, researchers, and public authorities for the purpose of continuously monitoring online disinformation. In short, this is the approach required to defend freedom of expression, communication rights, and the right to privacy, with the aim of achieving pluralistic communication in the new multimedia ecosystem.[8]

## References

Abad, L. (2015). El derecho de rectificación. In: *Derecho de la información. El ejercicio del derecho a la información y su jurisprudencia* (ed. I. Bel and L. Corredoira), 319–348. Madrid: Centro de Estudios Politicos y Constitucionales.

Bel, I. (2015). El autocontrol individual y corporativo de la actividad informativa. In: *Derecho de la información. El ejercicio del derecho a la información y su jurisprudencia* (ed. I. Bel and L. Corredoira), 509–530. Madrid: Centro de Estudios Politicos y Constitucionales.

Blumenthal, S. (1982). *The Permanent Campaign*. New York, NY: Simon and Schuster.

Brenner, S. and Koops, B.-J. (2005). Approaches to cybercrime jurisdiction. *Journal of High Technology Law* 4: 1–46.

Cabellos Espierrez, M.Á. (2018). Opinar, enaltecer, humillar: respuesta penal e interpretación constitucionalmente adecuada en el tiempo de las redes sociales. *Revista Española de Derecho Constitucional* 112: 45–86.

Corredoira, L. (2020). European regulatory responses to disinformation. Special attention to election campaigns. *Derecom* 29. Brussels.

Cotino, L. (2008). Nuevas tecnologías, desafíos y posibilidades para la libertad de expresión. Paper 3rd Jornadas de Derecho Constitucional Constitución y libertad de expresión, November 2008, UNED Barbastro (Huesca).

De la Chapelle, B. and Fehlinger, P. (2016). Jurisdiction on the Internet: from legal arms race to transnational cooperation. Centre for International Governance Innovation and Chatham House. https://www.cigionline.org/sites/default/files/gcig_no28_web.pdf (accessed September 17, 2020).

De Vega, P. (1998). Mundialización y Derecho Constitucional. La crisis del principio democrático en el constitucionalismo actual. *Revista de Estudios Políticos* 100: 14–15. https://doi.org/10.18042/45191

García Mahamut, R. (2015). Partidos Políticos y derecho a la protección de datos en campaña electoral: tensiones y conflictos en el ordenamiento español. *Teoría y Realidad Constitucional* 35: 309–338.

Garcia Mahamut, R. (2017). Elecciones y protección de datos: los grandes desafíos para la Unión Europea. In: *Hacia un nuevo Derecho Europeo de Protección de Datos* (ed. A. Rallo and G. Mahamut), 481–512. Valencia: Tirant lo Blanch.

Hindman, M. (2009). *The Myth of Digital Democracy*. Princeton, NJ: Princeton University Press.

HLEG (2018). A multi-dimensional approach to disinformation. Report of the Independent High level Expert Group on fake news and online disinformation. http://ec.europa.eu/newsroom/dae/document.cfm?doc_id=50271 (accessed September 17, 2020).

Magallón, R. (2019). La (no) regulación de la desinformación en la Unión Europea. Una perspectiva comparada. *Revista de Derecho Político* 106: 319–347.

Manin, B. (1997). *The Principles of Representative Government*. Cambridge, UK: Cambridge University Press.

[8] *Salov v. Ukraine.*

Nelson, T. and Brand, S. (eds.) (1974). *Computer Lib: You Can and Must Understand Computers Now*. Nashville, TN: Nelson.

Network Enforcement Act 2017, BR-Drs. (536/17).

Pine, B.J., II. (1993). *Mass Customization: The New Frontier in Business Competition*. Boston: Harvard Business School Press.

Rodríguez Andrés, R. (2018). Fundamentos del concepto de desinformación como práctica manipuladora en la comunicación política y las relaciones internacionales. *Historia y comunicación social* 23 (1): 231–244.

Rubio, R. (2018). Los efectos de la posverdad en la democracia. *Revista de Derecho Político* (103): 190–226.

Sartori, G. (1998). *Homo Videns*. London: I.B. Taurus.

Senato della Repubblica 2017, XVII Legislatura. N. (2688).

## Council of Europe

Council of Europe, Recommendation CM/Rec(2007)15 of the Committee of Ministers to member states on measures concerning media coverage of electoral campaigns.

Council of Europe, Recommendation CM/Rec(2016)1 on protecting and promoting the right to freedom of expression and the right to private life with regard to network.

Council of Europe, "Internet and electoral campaigns—Study on the use of internet in electoral campaigns" has been prepared by the committee of experts on media pluralism and transparency of media ownership (MSI-MED) of the Council of Europe.

(DGI2017)11

Council of Europe, Recommendation CM/Rec(2018)1 on media pluralism and transparency of media ownership.

Council of Europe Recommendation CM/Rec(2018)2 on the roles and responsibilities of internet intermediaries.

Council of Europe, Convention 108+, Modernized Convention for the protection of individuals with regard to the processing of personal data (June 2018).

Council of Europe, Consultative Committee of the Convention for the Protection of Individuals with regard to the processing of personal data, Report on Artificial Intelligence. Artificial intelligence and data protection: challenges and possible remedies, of 25 January 2019.

Council of Europe, Declaration by the Committee of Ministers on the manipulative capabilities of algorithmic processes, of 13 February 2019.

Council of Europe, Committee of Experts (MSI-AUT), Draft Recommendation of the Committee of Ministers to member States on the human rights impacts of algorithmic systems, of 26 June 2019.

Council of Europe, Cybercrime Convention Committee (T-CY), Guidance note no. 9,

Aspects of election interference by means of computer systems covered by the Budapest Convention, 08.07.2019.

Council of Europe, Parlamentary Assembly, Resolution 2254 (2019) on Media freedom as a condition for democratic elections.

Council of Europe Report on "the use of the Internet & related services, private life & data protection: trends & technologies, threats & implications."

Recommendation CM/Rec(2010)13 on the protection of individuals with regard to automatic processing of personal data in the context of profiling.

Ministers of Justice Resolution (2010)No. 3 on data protection and privacy in the 3rd millennium, MJU-30 (2010) RESOL.

Parliamentary Assembly Resolution 1843 (2011) on the protection of privacy and personal data on the internet and online media.

Committee of Ministers Recommendation CM/Rec(2012)3 on the protection of human rights with regard to search engines.

Committee of Ministers Recommendation CM/Rec(2012)4 on the protection of human rights with regard to social networking services.
Committee of Ministers Declaration (2013) on Risks to Fundamental Rights stemming from Digital Tracking and other Surveillance Technologies.
Committee of Ministers Recommendation CM/Rec(2014)6.
Committee of Ministers Recommendation CM/Rec(2018)2 on the roles and responsibilities of internet intermediaries.
Committee of Ministers Declaration Decl(2019)1 on the manipulative capabilities of algorithmic processes.
European Commission for Democracy through Law (Venice Commission) et al., Joint Report on Digital Technologies and Elections. (June 2019).

## European Union

European Commission, Communication from the Commission to the European Parliament, the Council, the European Economic and Social Committee and the Committee of the Regions on "Tackling online disinformation: a European Approach", COM(2018) 236 final.
European Commission, Communication from the Commission to the European Parliament, the Council, the European Economic and Social Committee and the Committee of the Regions on "Securing free and fair European elections", COM(2018) 637 final.
European Commission, Commission Recommendation on measures to effectively tackle illegal online content (March 2018).
Directive 2000/31/EC of the European Parliament and of the Council on certain legal aspects of information society services, in particular electronic commerce, in the Internal Market ("Directive on electronic commerce").
Regulation (EU) 2015/2120 of the European Parliament and of the Council of 25 November 2015 laying down measures concerning open internet access and amending Directive 2002/22/EC on universal service and users' rights relating to electronic communications networks and services and Regulation (EU) No 531/2012 on roaming on public mobile communications networks within the Union.
BoR (2016) 127. BEREC Guidelines on the Implementation by National Regulators of European Net Neutrality Rules.
The General Data Protection Regulation (GDPR) (EU) 2016/679.
European Commission, High-level group of experts ("HLEG") to advise on policy initiatives to counter "fake news" and disinformation which is spread online. Final Report, March, 2018.
European Commission, High-level expert group on artificial intelligence, A definition of AI: main capabilities and disciplines, 8 April 2019.
European Commission, Free and Fair Elections. Guidance Document. Commission guidance on the application of Union data protection law in the electoral context. A contribution from the European Commission to the Leaders' meeting in Salzburg on 19–20 September 2018.
Opinion by the European Data Protection Supervisor on online manipulation and personal data (2018).
European Parliamentary Research Service (2019) "How artificial intelligence works," "Why artificial intelligence matters."

19

# One Servant Cannot Serve Two Masters

## A Struggle for Divided Loyalties of Media Regulation in Hong Kong

Grace Leung and Richard Wu

### Introduction

Governance through regulation has undergone different waves of changes in the past few decades because of rapid changes in technologies and political environments. Between 1980 and 1990, the theme was "de regulation" in the western nation-states, which followed the inevitable trend of technological convergence that leading to a transformation of the media landscape (Wilson 2000). However, the United States and Europe de regulated their markets for different reasons. The former intended to stimulate competition and end the monopoly of AT&T (Wilson 2000, p. 107) while the latter developed a more relaxed attitude after the "decline in ideology" and "rise of pragmatism and populism" in European politics (Van Cuilenburg and McQuail 2003, pp. 191–197). The classical deregulation pattern from monopoly to liberalization and then competition (Feintuck 1999; Hutchison 1999) was widely treated as the ideal pattern in the west. Some scholars (Wilson 2000; Mosco 2004, p. 125) regarded economic incentives, like enhancing competitiveness in the information economy, as the major driving force. However, other scholars (Venturelli 1998; Hutchison 1999) argued that pluralism and public interests were the ultimate policy goals. For example, Venturelli (1998, p. 22) contended that the information policy laid down by the European Commission documents, like the 1994 Bangemann Report, represented a "revised social contract" of the European government to secure a space of publicity for its citizens' enjoyment in the new information society. It was hoped that liberalization of the market would eventually protect the state and society through the core value of democracy (Feintuck 1999, p. 6; Hutchison 1999).

In such a reform process, many governments revamped their regulators by strengthening their policy-making power or expanding their jurisdictions. The regulators were given more power to make policy decisions through their professional expertise and judgements (Wilson 2000, p. 61; Lung and Livingstone 2012). Against this background, the United Kingdom established a unified regulator for different media sectors, i.e., the Office of Communications (OFCOM), which became a regulatory model for other countries. Lung and Livingstone (2012) considered that OFCOM demonstrated a third-way approach of New Labour (1997–2010) in balancing state ownership and neoliberalism. The UK government preferred a light

*The Handbook of Communication Rights, Law, and Ethics: Seeking Universality, Equality, Freedom and Dignity*, First Edition. Edited by Loreto Corredoira, Ignacio Bel Mallén, and Rodrigo Cetina Presuel.

touch in media regulation and the "quasi-governmental" OFCOM had a special duty to advance the interests of citizens and consumers in media issues.

In 1997, the regulatory regime in Hong Kong largely mirrored the British colonial system that existed before the handover. To remain competitive, the city followed "international best practices"[1] by revamping the regulatory structures including the establishment of a unified regulator akin to OFCOM called the Communications Authority (CA). As stated in its mission statements (Communication and Technology Branch 2006), the CA was set up to ensure regulatory efficiency, enhance market competition, and protect public interest. Since its inception, radical political changes have taken place in the local regulatory environment and the function of this unified regulator is shifting from protecting economic and public interests to serving political ends. This chapter evaluates the performance of the CA as a regulatory agency in this process, focusing on its performance in the public sphere under the constraints of Chinese state capitalism.

This chapter is based on a historical analysis of secondary source documents and case studies in local media industries. It first explains the media regulatory philosophy for nation-states with a neoliberal tradition to provide the context for understanding the practices and justification of regulation in market economies and democratic countries. We then use the CA as a case study to see how she has regressed from a "semi-independent" regulator promoting public accountability through market competition to a bureaucrat serving political accountability to the Beijing government. This shift does not merely reflect a change of regulatory policy but also a change of governance strategies that threaten the local government's credibility, public accountability and legitimacy (Wong 2015). On the basis of three incidents, we demonstrate how CA has gradually shifted from an impartial market facilitator to a partial arbitrator adopting political loyalty as the determining criterion to control market players. Lastly, we project the future development of communications regulation in Hong Kong.

## Media Regulatory Philosophy for Nation-States with a Neoliberal Tradition

In nation-states with a neoliberal tradition, laws and semi-independent statutory bodies are adopted as tools for licensing regulation, establishing common technical standards, and formulating practice codes for commercial media. The latter include newspapers, radio, television, Internet, and telecommunications. The goals of media regulation in such places include protecting public interest, promoting market competition, enhancing diversity and arbitrating between different stakeholders' interests (Feintuck 1999; Freedman 2008; Flew, Iosifidis, and Steemers 2016). Media regulation is considered necessary in these places because communication media fall between private (market) and public (democracy) domains. The use of laws and semi-independent statutory bodies as regulatory tools ensures a delicate balance between restraining the government power as well as overt market force (Sjøvaag 2014). Ideally, laws provide an objective standard to measure the practices of the market players (Feintuck 1999, p. 29). Finally, media regulation enables the media to play the role of the "fourth estate" through protecting public opinion, securing citizens' access to information and their freedom of expression (Hutchison 1999).

[1]European Commission (EC) (1997). Green paper on the convergence of the telecommunications, media and information technology sectors, and the implications for regulation. *Towards an Information Society Approach.* https://ec.europa.eu/digital-single-market/en/news/green-paper-convergence-telecommunications-media-and-information-technology-sectors-and (accessed January 18, 2021).

Moreover, an impartial statutory body administering media regulation can inspire public confidence as it keeps an arm's length from the government and maintains its relative independence and autonomy through legal protection (Schulz, Valcke, and Irion 2014). It is also an approach adopted by governments with a neoliberal tradition to differentiate media policy from politics to enhance regulatory efficiency and effectiveness. As Lasswell, Lerner, and Fisher (1951, p. 88) explained, an implicitly neutral ideological assumption of the policy making process frees itself from undesirable connotations like "partisanship" and "corruption" associated with politics. As Chakravartty and Sarikakis (2006, p. 2) argued, the governments of the United States and United Kingdom were able to remove political undertone from their media policies. Both governments succeeded in creating a public perception in their countries that market expansions through deregulation and intensified privatization of broadcasting policy were "apolitical" measures.

However, scholars differed on whether governments should adopt neoliberalism and deregulation measures, i.e., opening up the market and introducing competition with minimal government intervention (Freedman 2008, p. 47), as the ideal model of media regulatory policy exemplified by various directives promulgated by the European Commission in the late 1980s. Some (Negrine and Papathanassopoulos 1991; Sepstrup 1991) argued for adoption of neorealism to construct a European Information Society on the basis of the philosophy of Kant, Weber, Habermas, and Marx. Likewise, Hitchens (2006, p. 49) asserted that promoting pluralism and diversity in the media market as a means to reclaim the public sphere was a core value of media regulation and supported neoliberalism as a guiding regulatory philosophy. Venturelli (1998) asserted that neoliberalism was compatible with the political rights and freedom of participation in the public sphere in a democratic society, while admitting that a "post liberalist" regulatory framework focuses more on information rights of participants and a participatory public sphere. In recent decades, neo liberal media policy has also been criticized for turning an audience into consumers. It also led to commodification of knowledge, expansion of commercial space, and concentration of ownership (Hamelink 2002, pp. 252–253). De regulation became a state-driven initiative to restructure the market to achieve political or ideological ends (Freedman 2008, p. 49). Therefore, de regulation as a governance strategy was gradually replaced by re regulation in Europe (Grande 2011). Moreover, scholars like Freedman (2008, p. 1), Chakravartty and Sarikakis (2006), and Flew, Iosifidis, and Steemers (2016), were not convinced about possible separation between media policy and politics. They argued that the role of nation-state has simply changed, and not diminished, in the face of market liberalization. To a great extent, individual nation-states still retain the power to regulate their media sectors.

The preceding discussion provides the theoretical context for understanding the origin of, and rationale for, communication regulation under the Anglo-American model. Such a regime is premised on a rule-of-law system which regulates business corporations through consistent incentives and disincentives, with a guiding principle of protecting consumer rights through regulation of private economic activity by public authority (Freedman 2008, p. 64).

## Hong Kong Communications Regulation with a Neoliberal Tradition from British Colonial Days

Lauded as the freest economy by Friedman and Friedman (1980, p. 34) since its colonial days, Hong Kong's economic miracle was largely based on a "positive non-interventionist" (Hanson 2012) or laissez-faire approach in enhancing the city's economic competitiveness. In spite of a lack of direct elections in its legislature, Hong Kong has enjoyed press freedom and freedom of expression guaranteed by the Basic Law, its "mini constitution," as well as its Bill of Rights Ordinance. Hong Kong is the home[2] to many international media conglomerates like the *Asian Wall Street Journal* and CNN International, as well as publications with anti-Communist backgrounds like *The Epoch Times*, which is funded by Falun Gong, a religious organization banned in Mainland China. As a global financial center, Hong Kong enjoyed a high degree of information freedom both before and after 1997 (Tables 19.1 and 19.2). According to the Press Freedom Index, reported by the Reporters Without Borders, Hong Kong was ranked 18th in the world and 2nd in Asia in 2004, which was only after Japan.[3]

However, in certain sectors like banking and communication, the government justified its intervention through regulation to enhance efficient and effective distribution of public resources, such as allocation of electromagnetic bandwidth (Chen and Lin 2002, p. 4). The global discourse on the promise of the information technology coincided with UK right-wing politics in the early 1990s. It enabled Hong Kong, which was still a British colony at that time, to undergo rapid liberalization of its communications sectors for nearly a decade. The highly regulated communication sectors, i.e., the telecommunication and television markets, were opened up to promote competition and provide more consumer choices.

Such a de regulatary move to the communications sectors was also a direct response to similar reforms undertaken by neighboring countries like Singapore and Malaysia. The latter exerted pressure on Hong Kong to revamp its regulatory policy and the local policymakers had to respond to external pressure, particularly over de regulation and liberalization of the communications markets.[4] There was an urgent need for regulatory reform as Hong Kong was keen to preserve economic momentum and integrate into the global information economy. The rationale behind such regulatory reforms was to enhance market efficiency. Such policy direction was also in line with the regulatory philosophy of financial secretaries after the reunification with China, as reflected in their approaches of "leading by market, facilitation by government" and "big market, small government" (Wong 2015). Tables 19.1 and 19.2 demonstrate the efforts of Hong Kong in its development of communication laws over the past century.

Apart from adopting new communications laws, Hong Kong has also implemented policy reforms for its communications sectors over the past three decades. Table 19.3 sets out various policy initiatives to open up the local communications markets before and after 1997. Both the telecommunication and broadcasting sectors were regulated under a sectoral approach to promote market vitality and attract foreign investment (Mueller 1997, pp. 30–31). When telephone and television ordinances were revamped in 2000, new provisions regulating anti-competitive behavior and abuse of dominant position were incorporated into these ordinances. Though both sectors underwent regulatory changes, the pace of reform varied differently. The telecommunication market was largely opened up within a decade. In contrast, the local free terrestrial television market remained largely unchanged for more than six decades. Such difference in the pace of reform reflects the concerns of local government over a complete liberalization of the television sector. Against this backdrop, the government proposed to set

---

[2]Carrie Yau, Secretary for Information Technology and Broadcasting (Designate) (June 5, 2000) "Informatisation of Hong Kong Special Administrative Region" at the *High-level Forum on "City Informatisation in the Asia-Pacific Region"* in Shanghai.

[3]Ng, K.C. (2015) "Hong Kong press freedom sinks to new low in global index," *The South China Morning Post*, 13 February.

[4]Carrie Yau (November 6, 2001) the speech by the Secretary of Information and Technology Bureau at the Plenary Session on "*Facilitating Infrastructure*" *of the XIIth World Productivity Congress.*

**Table 19.1** Hong Kong laws relating to communications sectors, 1925–1988.

| *Title of ordinance* | *Chapter* | *Year* |
|---|---|---|
| Telephone | 269 | 1925 |
| Telecommunications | 106 | 1936 |
| Television | 52 | 1964 |
| Control of Obscene and Indecent Articles | 390 | 1987 |
| Broadcasting Authority | 391 | 1987 |
| Film censorship | 392 | 1988 |

Source: Mueller 1997, p. 44.

up a unified regulator, the CA, to harmonize the two regulatory regimes for the telecommunications and broadcasting sectors in 2006.

The CA was established on the basis of similar neo liberal philosophy to administer sector-specific rules to fulfill the pro-competition policy goal (Chen and Lin 2002, p. 5). The broadcasting sector was treated in the same manner as other economic sectors. The regulator at that time, i.e., the Broadcasting Authority, played an impartial role in balancing the interests of different stakeholders, i.e., the policymakers, the operators, the investors, and the general public. The public choice theory advocated by Buchanan and Tullock (1962), which adopted an economic approach to make political decisions, explained well the broadcasting regulation at that time. In a free society like Hong Kong, political decisions on its broadcasting policy were made through standard consultation procedures that took the interests of different stakeholders into account. It was also evident that the local government made rational decisions to cater for public interest at that time.

In the Consultation Paper on the Establishment of the CA released in 2006, the government explained the need for a unified regulator. To begin with, a unified regulator was necessary because of technological and market developments in the communications sectors (paras. 16–19). Second, the need for fair competition in a converging market also called for a unified regulator. Competition in the local communications sector is still regulated by "sector-specific" laws. Such a regulatory framework would become ineffective as the broadcasting and telecommunications markets intertwined with each other. For example, anti competitive practices might arise but the impact of which could only be assessed if the entire communications sector is treated as a single market. Moreover, new opportunities for business synergies would arise in the era of convergence, and the regulator had to understand the converging markets to avoid inhibition of progress. A unified regulator could also better cope with "cross-sectoral" competition in a converging environment (paras. 20–23). Third, a unified regulator

**Table 19.2** Hong Kong laws relating to communications sectors after 1997.

| *Title of ordinance* | *Chapter* | *Year* |
|---|---|---|
| The Broadcast Ordinance (repelled former Television Ordinance, Cap 52) | 562 | 2000 |
| The Telecommunication Ordinance (Repelled Telephone Ordinance, Cap 269) | 106 | 2000 |
| Unsolicited Electronic Messages Ordinance | 593 | 2007 |
| Communication Authority Ordinance | 616 | 2012 |

**Table 19.3** Market liberalization policy for telecommunications and television industries before and after 1997.

| *The telecommunication industries* | | *Commercial TV industries* | |
|---|---|---|---|
| *Year* | *Policy* | *Year* | *Policy* |
| 1925 | Hong Kong Telephone (HKT) was established (parent company was UK's Cable and Wireless) | 1957–2016 | ATV (formerly known as RTV, from pay to free TV) provided service |
| 1984 | The PNETS license was created to authorize new mobile telephone services | 1967–now | TVB (free-to-air, dominant player) began service |
| 1993 | Setting up of the Office of Telecommunication Authority | 1975–1978 | Commercial TV (free-to-air) provided service |
| 1995 | Early termination of HKT's exclusivity over local telephone service<br>Three new FTNS licenses were issued in July | 1987 | Setting up the Broadcasting Authority |
| 1998 | Early termination of HKT's exclusivity over external communication service with a compensation of HK$ 6.7 billions | 1990 | Satellite TV (by subscription) was introduced |
| 1999 | Opening up of the IDD market | 1993 | Cable TV (pay-TV) provided service |
| 2003 | Complete open-up of the fixed telephone network services | 2003 | Launch of Now TV and Hong Kong Broadband (pay TV) |
| 2004 | Introduction of 3G telephony | 2007–2020 | Rolling out of digital TV to replace the old analog system |
| 2009 | Introduction of 4G telephony | 2012 | Issue of two new free-to-air TV licenses<br>Establishment of the Communication Authority |

Source: Hong Kong Yearbook (HKSAR 1990–2012); Mueller 1997.

would benefit both the regulator and operators. It provided "one-stop-shopping" and consistency in regulatory approach to the industry players, thereby reducing administrative burden and enhancing efficiency. The regulator could also pool together expertise to deal with issues arising from a converging environment (para. 24). Fourth, regulation of the broadcasting and telecommunications sectors called for similar expertise. Thus, operational synergy and efficiency could be accomplished by merging the broadcasting and telecommunications regulators into one unified regulator (paras. 25–26). Finally, a unified regulator could promote efficient utilization of public resources, bring about innovations, and increase competition in the communications sectors. All these benefit consumers in Hong Kong (para. 27). The market-driven and technological-driven narratives of the consultation paper therefore reflected the "economic-oriented" regulatory philosophy of the local government toward the communications sectors at that time.

## Emergence of a Neoliberal Communications Regulator with State Capitalism Ideology

Hong Kong increased its economic reliance on its motherland after the signing of the Close Economic Partnership Arrangement in 2004 when Hong Kong became volatile after the Asian financial crisis. In the same period, China grew into the second-largest economy by 2010, 10 years after its accession to WTO. In 2012, Xi Jinping, took over presidency of China and became the most powerful leader since Chairman Mao (Gueorguiev 2018). In the same year, C.Y. Leung, a patriotic professional turned politician, succeeded Donald Tsang and became the third Chief Executive. After becoming the local leader, Leung actively implemented pro-Beijing policy in Hong Kong (Cheng 2020, p. 698).

With a decline in its economic contribution to China, Xi tightened the ideological grip of Hong Kong through implementing national education reform and massive acquisition of local media with Chinese capital. Paradoxically, the unified regulator, i.e., the Hong Kong Communication Authority, was also established in this year. In the past decade or so, however, both the government and regulator got into one political controversy after another. The following incidents demonstrate how communication regulation in Hong Kong has rapidly changed from a regime based on economic considerations to one dependent on political concerns.

The first incident concerned the opening-up of the terrestrial television market. Against the backdrop of a pro-competition policy goals as discussed earlier, the Hong Kong government announced the issuance of free-to-air TV licenses and invited interested players to bid in 2009. It also suggested that no limit would be set on the number of successful bidders (Nip 2013). This exercise attracted three existing pay television operators, i.e., Hong Kong i-Cable, Now TV, and Hong Kong Television Network (HKTV), to apply due to the benefit of economy of scale.

The predecessor of CA, Broadcasting Authority, went through all the regular consultation process and made a recommendation that all three applicants should be granted licenses to the Executive Council, i.e., the top decision-making body headed by the Chief Executive. To the surprise of many, the Executive Council only accepted the bidding of two players but rejected HKTV in 2013. HKTV was headed by Ricky Wong, an entrepreneur who made his fortune from operating an international call-back service in the 1990s. Wong was shocked by the decision because he claimed that he was invited by a senior government official to make the bid in 2009 (Chow 2013). This decision led to a strong outcry from the general public (SCMP 2013). Instead of adhering to the liberalization policy to promote competition in the television market, the Executive Council was perceived to screen out an applicant who failed to obtain the blessing from Beijing before making the bid (Kawase 2014).

The HKTV licensing saga was unacceptable to the local business community and public at large for several reasons. First, it was against the public expectation that a competent and popular operator was rejected by the local government (Chow 2014). Second, the whole licensing procedure violated the public-choice principles perceived to be important by the local community for several decades (SCMP 2013). Those principles include transparency and consistency in policy decision-making processes, protecting community interests as a policy goal, and government accountability in policy decision-making. The unexpected change of licensing criteria in the middle of the consultation process, without prior notification, would affect future investors' confidence in the government's policies (Chan 2013). Third, the government suddenly redefined its administrative style from non interventionist to interventionist with the regulator's decision by declining to accept the recommendation from the latter, instead of respecting its professional advice like it had in the past. Obviously, the government gave up the old "light-handed" philosophy and adopted a new interventionist approach in its regulation of communication sectors. A regulatory approach, based on meritocracy, has given way to one dependent on political affiliation and loyalty.

The second incident was a follow-up of the licensing saga for HKTV. After failing to secure a free-to-air television license, HKTV acquired a mobile television license and spectrum from China Mobile Hong Kong (CMHK). The latter held broadcast spectrum and a unified carrier license that allowed the licensee to offer mobile television services. HKTV planned to relaunch UTV, i.e., the mobile TV channel operated previously by CMHK, as HKTV in 2014.[5] HKTV also planned to broadcast television programs through over-the-top television format. However, CA disputed HKTV's use of the most advanced technical parameter under the Digital Terrestrial Multimedia Broadcasting (DTMB) standard on the ground that use of such a technical parameter would affect the existing free-to-air signals.[6] HKTV challenged the regulator's ruling and applied for judicial review of the decision. Unfortunately, HKTV lost the judicial review case and could not roll out a mobile TV service as planned.[7]

This saga demonstrated that both the government and regulator have deviated from the regulatory policy to promote technological convergence and "cross-sectoral" competition. In 2000, the local government claimed to adopt a "technological neutral" approach in passing the new Broadcasting Ordinance. Ironically, when HKTV opted for a more advanced technical parameter, i.e., DTMB, to provide over-the-top television service, the regulator rejected such a choice of a technically compatible transmission mode for fear that a mobile TV service would create new competition with the existing terrestrial television market. If technological convergence was already envisaged by the government in 2000, it was a legitimate expectation of the public that the regulator should adopt a flexible regulatory approach to promote "cross-platform" competition. It was therefore inconceivable for the regulator to discourage a new type of television service that could have brought more market competition. This incident was inexplicable if there was no political consideration on the part of the regulator.

The HKTV saga also sees a *de facto* redefinition of the relationship between the government and regulator. The local government, as represented by the Executive Council, took a more proactive role from CA in the final stage of licensing. Before 2012, the government preferred to take a consensus approach in making decisions for important public policy, in which it respected the expert opinions of the regulator as its members represented different sectors or adopted the reports prepared by top international consultant companies (Chong, Zhao, and Chan 2013). But this time, the Executive Council did not consider the expert opinions of the regulator when making final decisions. A dominant role of the Executive Council over the CA in the decision-making process was obvious. Moreover, the CA later revealed that the Broadcasting Authority had recommended that three free television licenses be granted in the past.[8] Such a disclosure reflected an open disapproval of the regulator over the government decision. The mutual respect and trust between the government and this statutory body, which was crucial to the success of the local communications regulation, has been fast disappearing over the past decade.

[5]Staff Reporter (2014) "China experts say Hong Kong TV deal likely to require dual approval" *BBC Monitoring Asia Pacific*, January 7.

[6]Government Information Services (2014) "OFCA's statement on issues raised by HKTV on provision of broadcast-type mobile television services", *Hong Kong Government News*, March 17.

[7]Refer to HCA 39/2014.

[8]Refer to the minutes of Panel on Information Technology and Broadcasting, Special meeting on 2 December 2013. http://www.legco.gov.hk/yr13-14/english/panels/itb/papers/itb1202cb4-188-1-e.pdf (accessed January 18, 2021).

The final incident witnessed how CA lost its credibility to the general public when it could not fulfill a watchdog role to the media industry. The market was surprised to learn two years later that TVB, the dominant player, was actually controlled by a Shanghai media tycoon Li Ruigang who was supposed to be an unqualified person according to the Broadcasting Ordinance without informing the CA. This information was disclosed by the Security and Futures Commission (SFC) in May 2017 when TVB was involved in a buy-back activity on the stock market. The Panel of SFC even doubted whether CA received true information on the real shareholding structure of TVB (Cheng 2017). TVB, however, did not receive any form of "punishment" for this "negligence." In March 2020, CA suddenly allowed TVB to drop its license requirement to broadcast RTHK, the local public broadcaster, shows 3.5 hours a week on its Chinese-language channel. TVB always complained that RTHK programs affected its revenues. This arrangement had lasted for three decades and people doubted whether this decision was really serving public's interest (Lum 2020).

In December 2019, CA received over 20 000 complaints from ordinary citizens over TVB's bias news reports in mid-June on the protests but CA found the complaints unsubstantiated.[9] In contrast, CA repeatedly gave RTHK "serious warnings" over different programs. One was related to a guest's comments regarding the way the police confronted protesters at two universities at November 2019.[10] The other was related to a satirical program, "The Headliner," from which CA received 3300 complaints saying it had "denigrated" and "insulted" the police force. The CA ruled that the complaints "in respect of accuracy of factual contents ..., denigration and insult on the police, and expression of a sufficiently broad range of views" were justified.[11]

However, a former panel member of the Broadcasting Authority, Stephen Chan, recalled similar complaints were received against a Legislative Councilor from the same satirical program in 2011 but the regulator viewed that it was a common practice to use satire to parody public figures or government officials and ruled the complaints unsubstantiated.[12] The inconsistency in ruling outcomes and apparently different standards applied towards different players made viewers lose trust in this official complaint channel that was available for them to express their concern on media players' behaviors.

## Political Interests Preceding Public Interests

The experience of the CA showed that no matter what the original rationale was based on, there are strong political constraints on the pursuit of a media policy oriented towards public interest in a fast changing society. As Freedman (2008) argued, media policy is never separate from politics. Policymakers have to strive to advance their policy agenda even in the United States and United Kingdom where pluralist values like competition, transparency,

---

[9]Refer to TVB corporate information, see Television Broadcasts Limited (December 1, 2019) "Complaints about TVB news reports unsubstantiated", https://corporate.tvb.com/article/9cc7ae79a7ea67a1859a0103bc3ae567.html (accessed January 18, 2021).

[10]RTHK (2020) "RTHK given 'serious warning' over police comments," RTHK, April 20. https://news.rthk.hk/rthk/en/component/k2/1521689-20200420.htm (accessed January 18, 2021).

[11]RTHK (2020) "RTHK warned over 'gratuitous attack' on police," RTHK, May 19. https://news.rthk.hk/rthk/en/component/k2/1527074-20200519.htm (accessed January 18, 2021).

[12]MingPao (2020) "舞台劇演《求其新聞》主持 涉社會話題 陳志雲：有得睇要快啲睇", *MingPao*, May 26. https://ol.mingpao.com/ldy/showbiz/news/20200526/1590432712047 (accessed January 18, 2021).

accountability, and scientific values all shape and constrain media policy development in these democratic countries.

Modeled on OFCOM in the United Kingdom, the CA in Hong Kong originally adhered to the ideal of adopting economic principles to communication regulation. Indeed, the public choice theory (Brown 1996, p. 179) aptly explains the media regulation of the local government in its early days after the handover in 1997 when government administration still closely adhered to the practice of "rule by consensus." At that time, different stakeholders in the media sectors, or even the public, could form political groups to express their concerns and opinions to influence the policy decisions of the local government. One good example was the selection of technical parameter for the digital terrestrial television platform before 2007. At the beginning, the local government preferred the European standard, i.e., Digital Video Broadcasting (DVB), a technical standard widely used in Europe, Australia, and New Zealand. After consultations, the industry recommended a new standard developed by China, i.e., DTMB as television programs produced in Hong Kong could be indirectly transmitted to Mainland cities. Eventually, the government accepted the industry's recommendation.[13] This incident reflected that a more effective and rational policy decision could be reached through consultations and negotiations between stakeholders.

However, such a decision-making pattern cannot work when the government refuses to engage in dialog or make policy decisions based on economic principles or public interest. After the rejection of HKTV's application for free-to-air license as discussed earlier, many Hongkongers still hoped that the government was willing to negotiate on the basis of providing more consumer choices. Therefore, they organized rallies to support HKTV as well as put pressure on the government to rectify her decision on HKTV license (SCMP 2013). In the end, they were disappointed to find out that the government did not listen to public opinion or bother to engage in dialog with the community. The government was therefore criticized as making policy decisions to appease Beijing than to be accountable to Hong Kong people (Cheng 2020, p. 698).

As illustrated by the incidents discussed previously, both the government and regulator have redefined their regulatory paradigm and philosophy, their role, and their relationship with other stakeholders. First, political correctness is more important than meritocracy as a guiding criterion in the decision-making process. Second, the government no longer respects the regulator in decision-making and openly intervenes in communications regulation. Third, the local government no longer focuses on business vitality as a policy goal of broadcasting regulation like it did before. It increasingly treats the broadcasting regulation as an integral part of the political and cultural processes of nation-building (Kitley 2003, p. 3) like the Beijing government. In the past, Hong Kong was an international hub of free media and mainly governed by business logic. However, the local government has gradually "repositioned" the broadcasting sector to become a domestic medium regulated by "national" concerns in the past decade.

## Conclusion: Communications Regulation Under State Capitalism

Communications regulation reflects the political characteristics of a society. In the case of Hong Kong, a shift of regulatory paradigm is taking place in a rapidly changing political-economic environment. A free-market philosophy rooted in the Anglo-American tradition is giving way to a state capitalism ideology originating in a socialist country. The licensing

---

[13]Refer to the official website for DTV service in Hong Kong, https://www.digitaltv.gov.hk/eng/index.htm (accessed January 18, 2021).

incidents discussed in this chapter showed that both the government and regulator in Hong Kong had gradually changed their regulatory goals from public good to national good by ignoring public interest and market competition. The neo liberal policy ideal in the past is increasingly irrelevant to the current regulatory regime as Hong Kong rapidly integrates with China both politically and economically. In retrospect, the unified communications regulator established in Hong Kong has been an organization in paradox from its inception because such a semi-independent regulator cannot serve two masters, i.e., the state interest at one end and the public interest at the other, particularly when they diverge in opposite directions. It is in the state's interest to turn the local media sector into a propaganda machine for the government, but it is in the public interest to safeguard pluralistic voices through market power so that people's voices can be represented in the public sphere.

According to Wong (2015), the government's non intervention regulatory approach in the past did not merely reflect an economic policy to favor the business sector. It was also a governance strategy to maintain a delicate balance between socialist and capitalist rent seekers. If the SAR government gave up this position, it might lose its ideological credibility and become vulnerable to lobbyists. Without the mandate from a democratic system, the government would rapidly lose authority or even legitimacy for effective governance. With this paradigm shift in communications regulatory philosophy, Hong Kong is also declining rapidly as a regional media capital. Reporters Without Borders, a leading international organization that safeguards press freedom, relocated from Hong Kong to Taiwan in 2017 (Wang 2017).

The global ranking of the city in the World Press Freedom Index dropped to 73rd in 2019.[14] With a fast-shrinking media sector, the CA plays a diminishing role in market regulation. In the future, it is likely that the unified regulator will increasingly have less "regulatory space" to develop more diversified communications sectors for Hong Kong. In recent years, CA has continued to lose its credibility when some of its decisions have apparently become arbitrary towards RTHK, the public broadcaster, due to its perceived lack of political loyalty to the government.[15]

As demonstrated by the incidents discussed, both local government and regulator increasingly failed to make policies or decisions in accordance with public opinions. As a result, many aggrieved Hongkongers took initiatives to boycott the dominant operator (Ives and Li 2019), which was widely perceived to enjoy "hegemony" over the local free-to-air television market for several decades. As result, viewership dropped significantly, and the share price has also fallen sharply in the past few years.[16] Eventually, the failure to introduce market competition through communication regulation led to a no-win situation in the media sectors of Hong Kong.

## References

Brown, D. (1996). The invisibility factor: the limits of public choice theory and public institutions. *Washington University Law Quarterly* 74: 179–221.

[14]Refer to the website of Reporter without Border, see RSF. Hong Kong RSF https://rsf.org/en/hong-kong (accessed January 18, 2021).

[15]RTHK (2020) "有港台節目顧問團成員發起運動冀市民投訴通訊局不公". https://news.rthk.hk/rthk/ch/component/k2/1527329-20200520.htm?archive_date=2020-05-20 (accessed January 18, 2021).

[16]TVB's stock price per share was over HK$50 at 2015 but dropped to less than HK$12 by January 2020. Refer to a finance trading site like Yahoo Finance, "Television Broadcast Limited HKSE." https://finance.yahoo.com/quote/0511.HK (accessed January 18, 2021).

Buchanan, J. and Tullock, G. (1962). *The Calculus of Consent: Logical Foundations of Constitutional Democracy.* Ann Arbor: University of Michigan Press.
Chakravartty, P. and Sarikakis, K. (2006). *Media Policy and Globalization.* Edinburgh: Edinburgh University Press.
Chan, K. (2013). Politics played no part in HKTV license decision: CE. *China Daily* (October 22).
Chen, E.K. and Lin, P. (2002). Competition policy under laissez-faireism: market power and its treatment in Hong Kong. *Review of Industrial Organization* 21 (2): 145–166.
Cheng, J.Y.S. (2020). *Political Development in Hong Kong.* Singapore: World Scientific Publishing Co. Ltd.
Cheng, K. (2017). Chinese media mogul revealed as owner of Hong Kong broadcaster TVB, in potential regulatory breach. *The Hong Kong Free Press* (May 11).
Chong, T., Zhao, S., and Chan, T. (2013). Hong Kong government rating slumps to new record low amid HKTV row. *The South China Morning Post* (November 15).
Chow, V. (2013). Public outcry over rejection of Ricky Wong's free-to-air TV license bid. *The South China Morning Post* (October 16).
Chow, V. (2014). Revolution put on hold as HKTV wins online support but still no license. *The South China Morning Post* (June 26).
Communication and Technology Branch (2006). Consultation on the establishment of the communication authority. https://www.info.gov.hk/archive/consult/2006/ca_e.pdf (accessed October 7, 2020).
Feintuck, M. (1999). *Media Regulation, Public Interest and the Law.* Edinburgh: Edinburgh University Press.
Flew, T., Iosifidis, P., and Steemers, J. (2016). Global media and national policies: the return of the state. In: *Global Media and National Policies* (ed. T. Flew, P. Iosifidis, and J. Steemers), 1–15. London: Palgrave Macmillan.
Freedman, D. (2008). *The Politics of Media Policy.* Cambridge Malden: Polity Press.
Friedman, M. and Friedman, R. (1980). *Free to Choose: A Personal Statement.* Orlando: A Harvest Book.
Grande, E. (2011). De-regulation and re-regulation of public utilities: the new regulatory state in the European system of multi-level governance. In: *The New Regulatory State* (ed. L. Leisering), 57–79. London: Palgrave Macmillan.
Gueorguiev, D.D. (2018). Dictator's shadow: Chinese elite politics under Xi Jinping. Centre d'étude français sur la Chine contemporaine. *China Perspectives* 2018 (1–2): 17–26.
Hamelink, C. (2002). The civil society challenge to global media policy. In: *Global Media Policy in the New Millennium* (ed. C. Fanthome), 251–260. Luton, UK: University of Luton Press.
Hanson, D. (2012). Positive non-interventionism: the policy that unleashed Hong Kong. *AEIdeas* (March 22). https://www.aei.org/economics/positive-non-interventionism-the-policy-that-unleashed-hong-kong (accessed September 18, 2020).
Hitchens, L. (2006). *Broadcasting Pluralism and Diversity: A Comparative Study of Policy and Regulation.* Portland: Hart Publishing.
HKSAR. (1990–2012). *Hong Kong Yearbook.* Hong Kong: Information Service Department.
Hutchison, D. (1999). *Media Policy: An Introduction.* Oxford: Blackwell Publishers.
Ives, M. and Li, K. (2019). Hong Kong protesters' new target: a news station seen as China's friend. *The New York Times* (July 14).
Kawase, K. (2014). HKTV at odds against Beijing over China mobile deal. *Nikkei Asian Review* (January 8).
Kitley, P. (2003). First principles – television, regulation and transversal civil society in Asia. In: *TV Regulation and Civil Society in Asia* (ed. P. Kitley), 3–34. London: Routledge.
Lasswell, H.D., Lerner, D., and Fisher, H.H. (1951). *The Policy Sciences: Recent Developments in Scope and Method.* Stanford, CA: Stanford University Press.
Lum, A. (2020). Hong Kong's TVB axes RTHK programmes after watchdog's rule change but smaller rivals likely to continue airing shows. *The South China Morning Post* (6 March).
Lung, P. and Livingstone, S. (2012). *Media Regulation: Governance and the Interests of Citizens and Consumer.* London: Sage.
Mosco, V. (2004). *The Digital Sublime: Myth, Power and Cyberspace.* Cambridge, MA: MIT Press.
Mueller, M. (1997). *Telecom Policy and Digital Convergence.* Hong Kong: City University of Hong Kong Press.

Negrine, R. and Papathanassopoulos, S. (1991). The internationalization of television. *European Journal of Communication* 6 (1): 9–32.
Nip, A. (2013). TV licensing row shows up fickle policy, critics say. *The South China Morning Post* (October 16).
Schulz, W., Valcke, P., and Irion, K. (2014). *The Independence of the Media and Its Regulatory Agencies: Shedding New Light on Formal and Actual Independence against the National Context.* Bristol, UK; Chicago, IL: Intellect Books.
SCMP Staff Reporters (2013). Thousands protest to 'defend Hong Kong's core values' after failed HKTV license bid: HKTV chairman Ricky Wong says rule of law at stake as thousands protest at license decision. *The South China Morning Post* (October 21).
Sepstrup, P. (1991). *Transnationalization of Television in Western Europe.* London: John Libbey.
Sjøvaag, H. (2014). The principles of regulation and the assumption of media effects. *Journal of Media Business Studies* 11 (1): 5–20.
Van Cuilenburg, J. and McQuail, D. (2003). Media policy paradigm shifts: towards a new communications policy paradigm. *European Journal of Communication* 18 (2): 181–207.
Venturelli, S. (1998). *Liberalizing the European Media: Politics, Regulation and the Public Sphere.* Oxford: Oxford University Press.
Wang, A. (2017). Taiwan moved up six spots on this year's World Press Freedom Index. *The Washington Post* (May 4).
Wilson, K.G. (2000). *Deregulating Telecommunications: U.S. And Canadian Telecommunications, 1840–1997.* Lanham: Rowman & Littlefield.
Wong, R.Y.C. (2015). Positive non-interventionism as governance Strategy. https://wangyujian.hku.hk/?p=6365&lang=en (accessed October 7, 2020).

# 20

# Latin American Thinking in Communication and Advances in Communication Rights

Rolando Guevara-Martínez

## Introduction

The historical tradition of communication sciences in Latin America is separate from the northernmost part of the continent, i.e., English-speaking America. In the twentieth century, important Spanish and Portuguese-speaking thinkers emerged and contributed to a very specific vision of the region with important contributions to the discipline and the understanding of communication rights. In this chapter, we highlight some of the most important Latin-American authors who have left their mark in the field of communication, among them authors such as José Marqués de Melo, Luis Ramiro Beltrán, José Luis Aguirre, and Antonio Pasquali[1] who passed away at the end of 2019, leaving behind great contributions to the study of communication rights. The emphasis will be on the latter, as he managed to make a synthesizing model of the Latin-American proposal on communication with its own meaning. Following the model articulated by this Venezuelan thinker, it has been possible to generate a contrast with the classic definitions of communication and to generate an alternative paradigm to proposals from the Northern, English-speaking parts of the continent. Later, we will analyze some experiences in the region, which represent the problems of the Latin American context, selecting some of the most emblematic legal cases of Mexico and the Inter-American Court of Human Rights in order to present a balanced view that includes theory and the empirical evidence that helped observe the advances in communication rights and how each case can be seen from the perspective of the proposals made by the intellectuals represented in this chapter.

[1] Italian by birth, migrated to Venezuela at the age of 19 where he adopted the country and developed as a Latin-American intellectual. He wrote a large number of works that influenced the academy, in particular the Communication field. One of his most important works was *"Comprender la Comunicación"* (2007), which was originally written in 1978 and republished almost 30 years later to adapt it to technological challenges.

*The Handbook of Communication Rights, Law, and Ethics: Seeking Universality, Equality, Freedom and Dignity*, First Edition. Edited by Loreto Corredoira, Ignacio Bel Mallén, and Rodrigo Cetina Presuel.

## Interconnections in the Communicational Thinking of Latin-American Authors

One of the most important thinkers in Latin America was José Marqués de Melo. In 2018, his work was inspired by Luiz Beltrão, a Brazilian thinker who is credited with creating the concept of *folkcommunication*, which seeks to counterbalance the dominant Anglo-Saxon lines of thought of communication theory.[2] For both authors, focusing communication on the medium leaves out the human part of the action.

José Marqués de Melo considered that "Popular communication is characterized by the use of artisanal mechanisms of symbolic diffusion to translate into unintelligible messages previously transmitted by the cultural industry" (2007).

For this author, communication is also generated in communities and is a retroactive process that is fed by various sources, one of them being the local culture or the so-called popular culture. For the author "popular communication is a process of intermediation between the culture of the elites (erudite or massive) and the culture of the working classes (rural or urban)" (2007). José Marqués de Melo spoke about "communicational exclusion" derived from the colonial heritage and in which certain sectors of society are excluded and lagging behind due to linguistic or ethnic discrimination. Multiculturalism derived from miscegenation has also brought a different perspective to the Anglo-Saxon and European thinking that instrumentalize the concept and focus specifically on the individual and their rights.

The deep Latin-American inequality further accentuates these symbiotic relationships between those who produce content and those who must absorb it with little to no ability to replicate it. José Marqués de Melo considered that popular beliefs and traditions are wiped out in the media by more postmodernist and semi-erudite positions. Under these arguments, the past and the future are interconnected in a complex body of words, sounds, and images, which shows that tradition and modernity are two faces of a society that progresses without losing its identity. Popular traditions are incorporated into the contemporary media agenda to preserve cultural identities destined to stagnation (2007).

The proposal of popular communication is contrasted with the Anglo-American paradigm whose proposal is to see the mass media as a form of knowledge (2010). This paradigm has promoted a strong parallel development between the educational and media systems. The universalization of the educational system, according to the author, has generated a population informed and educated enough to demand better content. This media literacy has become another form of education that has transformed media into knowledge. Meanwhile, in the Latin-American paradigm we observe another perspective: the media as a reflection of society. As José Marqués de Melo refers:

> Anglo-American societies affirmed themselves precociously as nations (18th century), inspired by the ideals of representative democracy. That is why they attributed to the mass media the function of the "fourth power", establishing not only a regime of coexistence with the government machinery, but constitutionally preventing the possibility of creating obstacles to its free expression. In contrast, Latin American societies came to emerge late (19th century) as independent nations. Opting for authoritarian systems of political organization, reproducing the Iberian aristocratic models. For this reason, the mass media, journalism and later the electronic mass media are given a diffuse role of social control. Hence the legislative fury that plagues power holders, trying to create media filters, handcuffing their owners or corrupting their professionals. (2010)

---

[2] In our opinion, these Latin-American authors propose a discussion of communication focused more on society and the human being. Please see the book "*Historias de las teorías de la comunicación*" (1997) by Armand Matterlart, in order to go deeper into the "theories of communication."

This author's approach to the role of the media and society reflects on the similarities shared in the region. In this way, while José Marqués de Melo confronted the paradigms formulated to John Dewey (2011) and Charles Cooley (2005), Antonio Pasquali confronted the paradigm proposed by Marshall McLuhan (2003), understanding communication as a basic element of human life and communication freedom as the base element of a democratic, plural, representative, and equitable society. Antonio Pasquali used elements of Kant's philosophy (inherent, causality, and community) to refound communication and eliminate the utilitarian, technical, and instrumentalist perspective that we currently have on communication.

## Influential and Critical Thinking of Communication in Latin America

Another of the most important thinkers in Latin America in the communication sciences was Luis Ramiro Beltrán, who died in 2015. In the last century, he was one of the contributors to communicative theory and a staunch critic of the classical notions of communication. Luis Ramiro Beltrán contributed to comparative theory to break away from Anglo-Saxon traditions. His bet was always for the democratization of communication and, like Antonio Pasquali, communication rights were *lemotivs* of all his work. In the book *"Un adiós a Aristóteles: la comunicación horizontal"* he stated:

> the traditional definition of communication is one that describes it as the act or process of transmitting messages from sources to receivers through the exchange of symbols (belonging to codes shared by them) through signal transport channels. In this classical paradigm, the main purpose of communication is the attempt of the communications to affect in a given direction the behavior of the receiver; that is to say, to produce certain effects on the way of feeling, thinking and acting of the one who receives the communication or, in a word, persuasion. Feedback is considered instrumental in ensuring the communicator's goals are achieved. (Beltrán 2007, p. 75)

Luis Ramiro Beltrán considered that there are sufficient reasons to reform the concept of communication and go beyond the proposals prepared by Marshall McLuhan. He agreed with the vision of Antonio Pasquali in the criticism of this Canadian theorist and his idea about "the medium is the message," since he considered that communication is much deeper than the medium. Both Latin-American authors began to shape the concept of horizontal communication. The fundamental idea sustains that the traditional conception is not compatible with democracy and does not protect the freedom of communication. An alternative idea to the concept, and more specific to the region, reconfigures the focus on the functions of communication. Instead of thinking about what the media (*effects orientation*) does to people, one could reorient towards *function orientation*, that is, discover what these media do for people (Beltrán 2007).

The work of these authors was not only theoretical but also critical and participatory in the public life in the region. In the 1990s, Luis Ramiro Beltrán published a book called *"Comunicación para el desarrollo en Latinoamérica: una evaluación sucinta al cabo de cuarenta años"* (1993) in which he took stock of communication in Latin America in the last four decades. He specifically emphasized the role of the mass media and the cultural imposition of the northern superpowers throughout the region, governments and power groups who have colloquially understood communication as a unilinear model that mechanically transmits active information to passive receivers (Beltrán 2007, p. 77). Luis Ramiro Beltrán, on the contrary, assumed that there is no transmission; there is only provocation of meanings already existing in people who, by decoding the symbols, actively participate (p. 77). For Latin-American actors, communication is a dynamic process loaded with many elements that interact with each other since they come from social relations and not only from unilateral exercises.

In a similar sense, José Luis Aguirre is another Latin-American thinker of communication theory that follows a similar line to the previously mentioned authors. This author considers that the human interrelation that occurs in dialog is the most authentic form of communication and that no medium such as radio and television can predominate in the definition of the concept of communication:

> Every medium (radio, newspaper, television, and even other technological forms or resources that we can use to exchange content) is a simple device, they are simply resources for the extension of the pre-existing human capacity to communicate. Furthermore, because the medium is an artificial channel or an artifact that carries encrypted messages, but there is no human communication that can do without the use of natural channels at the beginning and at the end of the process. (Aguirre 2013)

The ethnic diversity of the region is one of the greatest strengths for experimenting theoretically with comparative communication. José Luis Aguirre agrees with the efforts of Antonio Pasquali to differentiate the concepts of information and communication. Communication as a process that happens in concrete scenarios of the community in which the inhabitants must recognize each other, re signify their qualities and diversity to achieve dialog (Aguirre 2009).

In light of the aforementioned, we consider that the contribution of all these Latin-American thinkers can be integrated into a model of communication freedom proposed by Antonio Pasquali. The pentagonal prism, as explained later, can define the five angles of communication freedom, which we can later demonstrate by means of a brief overview of the situation of these freedoms, particularly from their dimension of freedom of expression (but not only this type of freedom) in some Latin-American countries and some of the emblematic cases of the Supreme Court of Mexico and the Inter-American Court of Human Rights. Each case is useful for us in order to understand the proposals of Latin-American theorists and their contribution to communication rights.

## An Approach on Human Rights and Communication in Latin America

In 2009, at the Conference of the International Association for Media and Communication Research (IAMCR) held in Mexico City, in which the central theme was "Communication and Human Rights," Antonio Pasquali gave a conference called "Rights of Man and Communication in Latin America" (2012). In the conference, he established that there is a very common mistake in thinking that communication rights (or freedom of communication, as he also called it) are limited to freedom of expression. After making a distinction between the two concepts, he considered the need for a broader and updated definition of the totemized freedom of expression.

Antonio Pasquali questioned how a new edition of Article 19 of the Universal Declaration of Human Rights for the digital age would be drafted. This author invited its re reading and statements made in the past:

> Everyone has the right to freedom of opinion and expression; this right includes freedom to hold opinions without interference and to seek, receive and impart information and ideas through any media and regardless of frontiers.[3]

[3] Universal Declaration of Human Rights (1948), Article 19.

He recognized that despite it being a sexagenarian Article from the pre digital era, it was still in good health in our time. It was based on its core aspect since the freedom to communicate or to express oneself is the *sine qua non* condition of human relationship.

Pasquali decoded how to better assume the modern complexities of that form of freedom, interpreting Article 19 through a pentagonal prism. Full freedom to communicate would then have five faces of a pentagon with the freedom of code, freedom of channel, freedom of access to sources, freedom of message or contents, and freedom of recipient audiences "regardless of borders" (2012, pp. 120–122).

This proposal by Antonio Pasquali is relevant to analyze the situation of freedom of communication in Latin America in the face of progress and possible setbacks in the region.

Though digital communication in most Latin-American countries is not as restricted as in other countries of the world, there is still a significant lag in two aspects. First, in how the right to communication is perceived, and second, in how, based on a fragmented idea, it is fairly legislated.

In another text by Pasquali, which follows the line of the lecture given at the IAMCR Conference in Mexico City with important contributions to the communication rights, called "*La Comunicación Mundo. Releer un mundo transfigurado por las comunicaciones*" (2011), He established that "there is an implicit tendency to identify genus and species, as if the communication rights were exhausted by freedom of expression" (p. 55). This way of perceiving communication and relating it to freedom of expression is an outdated idea that has remained among academics and politicians for more than two centuries. Antonio Pasquali's proposal is to raise the concept to broader levels of understanding, to an anthropological aspect. This new concept defines five fundamental faces of communication, as mentioned, which form a pentagonal prism that exemplify[4] here:

1. *Freedom of code* (e.g., language rights or new computer codes).
2. *Freedom of channel* (e.g., right to impart information, which is materialized with newsprint, radio broadcasting frequencies, or equipment used in the dissemination of information, or by any other means tending to the communication and circulation of ideas and opinions).
3. *Freedom of access to sources* (e.g., right to investigate, seek, and receive information; the right to free access to timely and truthful information from multiple sources; the right of access to information, as well as the related issues of transparency and accountability).
4. *Freedom of message or contents* (e.g., right to freedom of opinion and expression, including not being disturbed by opinions with reasonable limitations such as propaganda for war and any advocacy of national, racial, or religious hatred that constitute incitements to violence or to any other similar illegal action against any person or group of persons on any grounds including those of race, color, religion, language, or national origin either orally, in writing, in print, in the form of art, or through any other medium of one's choice).
5. *Freedom of recipient audiences*, "regardless of borders" (e.g., this possibility cannot be understood without the right of access to information and communication technologies, as well as to broadcasting and telecommunications services, including broadband and Internet access; for which we consider that it necessarily involves the ideal devices for receiving signals and the corresponding media and digital literacy).

[4] In accordance with the American Convention on Human Rights (1969), Article 13 (Freedom of Thought and Expression); and the Political Constitution of the United Mexican States (2013), Article 6.

Antonio Pasquali was resounding with his statement in the IAMCR Conference, expressing the following:

> To say today that a society enjoys full freedom of communication implies, then, checking for the simultaneous presence of those five structural components.... To barely tolerate the fourth freedom to pretend to the world that *freedom of expression* does exist, while tightly controlling its other four aspects—which many authoritarian governments currently do—is to reduce this freedom to fiction and caricature, or to safeguard a freedom with 18th century arguments that pleads for backing with 21st century arguments. (Pasquali 2012, p. 122)

Protecting, expanding, and improving the sense of communication is a pending task in the twenty-first century. The moral and logical bases were the task of the communicative theory of Antonio Pasquali while the Law should be the executing arm of the new conception of communicative thought. "Every new freedom needs a sheriff" was a phrase that the Venezuelan thinker said in one of his last interviews. Though it sounds paradoxical, any new freedom acquired in modernity needs legislation in this regard. And to achieve this freedom, Pasquali adds, it is necessary to use an international body that applies supranational laws in a globalized world, even more punctually,

> the idea in the medium and long term of creating International Courts empowered to judge certain macroeconomic crimes or particularly disastrous attacks (of a political, technological or economic nature) against the communication right of individuals and societies, remains as a non-chimerical hope that should start to be considered. (2007, p. 285)

This last idea is directly related to the justiciability not only for communication rights but also for human rights, as we will see later.

## Elements of Context of the Regional Struggle

The ideas outlined by the authors from decades ago have been reflected in some parts of Latin America. In Chile, for example, freedom of expression has expanded after the dictatorship. Freedom of communication for journalists and the media has made significant progress thanks to the enactment of the Press Law[5] (Castellón and Jaramillo 2010). Various Chilean laws indirectly assumed censorship through legal arguments. Journalism was regulated by the Advertising Abuse Act, which aimed to protect citizens from press abuse. In the execution, the agency allowed the prior censorship of the publication of certain newspapers with contents that "dishonored" people.

In Mexico, there have also been moments of censorship in journalism and in the mass media. During the 2012 elections, citizens formed an important front against one of the country's largest media corporations: *Grupo Televisa* (Gómez-Robledo 2015). A movement arose at the *Universidad Iberoamericana* after a visit of one of the candidates (and later, the winner of the presidency) Enrique Peña Nieto. When the media tried to misrepresent the protests by arguing that they were created by outside agitators, the students created a video showing their credentials to prove otherwise. This situation unleashed a movement called #Yosoy132 (hinting at the number of students who showed their credentials) from which numerous demonstrations and debates emerged to demand the democratization of the media. This frontal confrontation with big media opened new spaces for bilateral communication regarding the increasing penetration of social networks, reducing the company's power of

[5] Law 19.733 on Freedom of Opinion and Information and the Exercise of Journalism (2001).

influence for the first time. In the following years, Grupo Televisa suffered a dramatic drop in its stocks due to the public's transition to new media for entertainment and information.

The fight for freedom of expression in Mexico still suffers from many obstacles in its path. Though the government does not directly repress citizens as in previous times, criminal organizations now intimidate journalists and activists in the country. In the last decade, there have been around 300 murders of journalists who denounced human-trafficking networks, criminal organizations, and other illegal activities (Aristegui Noticias Network 2019). These actions have prevented freedom of expression from being freely exercised in the country.

This lack of sensitivity to the universal communication rights responds to an economic dynamic that technifies the concept and turns it into a simple instrument of commercial exploitation.

According to the reviewed authors, communication needs to be viewed from human need and from those angles that do not imply an economic activity or form of political control. It must also be a liberating element for minorities and a space for historically repressed groups to express their culture and language.

Regarding this issue, Jesús María Aguirre (2010) asks what strategies must be organized for the great continental task of generating indigenous means and forms of expression that give voice to marginalized or silenced peoples in a globalized world. One response that seems to give glimpses of hope in various Latin-American countries is community radio and the allocation, though scarce, of the radio spectrum to telecommunications projects as they have managed to give voice to some indigenous peoples and communities.

Latin-American authors propose to review communication, relating it more to the social processes that create them. This humanistic turn breaks with the classic instrumentalism proposed in other disciplines. Nowadays, it is necessary to review media legislation to adapt it to the human rights and communication scenario, since there are several emblematic cases and local contexts in Latin-American countries that warrant a thorough review.

## Emblematic Cases in Mexico

There are several cases where communication rights have had challenges in Mexico. One of the most cited cases on freedom of expression[6] is the one of the newspaper *La Jornada* vs. the magazine *Letras Libres*. In this case, the newspaper considered suffering moral damage to its detriment by the publication of the column "*Cómplices del terror*" (Accomplice of terror) in the magazine, in which it was stated that the newspaper had links with a terrorist organization in Spain. The case was resolved in favor of *La Jornada*, considering that such publication affected the reputation of the company. The final resolution referred to the following:

> The First Chamber determined that the right to freedom of expression protects not only the substance of information and ideas, but also the way or tone in which they are expressed, in the same way it pointed out that legal entities may also see their right to honor through the disclosure of facts concerning its entity, when another person defames or demeans it in the consideration of others. The fact that a journalistic note refers to conduct that could be considered illegal does not necessarily translate into the imputation of a crime. Although some expressions could be considered offensive in isolation, in relation to what they intend to communicate and the factual situation, their offensive significance decreases. Therefore, the second instance sentence was finally confirmed.

The conclusion regarding this case is that the media, as legal entities, also have the right to honor and this case is an example of how the abusive exercise of the freedom of expression of another information company was limited.

[6] Supreme Court of Justice of the Nation-Mexico. Direct Appeal ("Amparo") 28/2010.

Another interesting case[7] In the last years arose from one of the most important social networks in the world: Twitter. This is a case that involved, on the one hand, the right of access to information and, on the other, the alleged privacy of public officials. The Prosecutor of Veracruz State, Jorge Winckler Ortiz, blocked the account of journalist Miguel Ángel León Carmona, who collaborates with various local media, on Twitter. On Twitter, blocking a user prevents the blocked user from accessing the posts of the blocking user and any other interaction with them. The journalist was using the Prosecutor's account to find out about the events and official announcements and to denounce clandestine graves. When he was blocked by the Prosecutor, the journalist's defense filed an *amparo* (constitutional relief) against him for violations of freedom of expression and access to information. The case was ruled in favor of the journalist, who argued that this action limited his "journalistic work, thereby restricting the possibility of seeking, receiving and imparting information of public interest, and constitutes a discriminatory act by excluding him from knowing such information" (Article 19, Civil Organization 2019). This case was ruled upon and resolved by the Mexican Supreme Court of Justice of the Nation and its decision resulted in the Prosecutor, Jorge Winckler Ortiz, having to allow the journalist access to his social network Twitter, under penalty that a Federal Judge could request the legal representation of the company Twitter in Mexico to directly perform the unlocking.

Another relevant case[8] was the one of the poet Mardonio Carballo Manuel, a Náhuatl language speaker, that in 2015 was reviewed by the Mexican Supreme Court for considering that his linguistic rights were being violated, particularly due to the entry into force of the Federal Telecommunications and Broadcasting Law on August 13, 2014. The Supreme Court stated the following:

> Mardonio Carballo Manuel requested the protection of the federal justice against the first paragraph of Article 230 of the Federal Telecommunications and Broadcasting Law. In his claim, Mardonio Carballo Manuel alleged that Article 230 violates his rights to freedom of expression, to participate in cultural life and to non-discrimination, as well as the rights of indigenous communities.

The claim alleged that the new Federal Telecommunications and Broadcasting Law restricted his freedom of expression and did not allow the use of his language.[9] The Veracruz poet also alleged in the document that not only his individual rights were violated but also the collective rights of other people of indigenous origin.

The ruling was in favor of the poet, who set a precedent in the communication rights by laying the foundations of language rights.

## Emblematic Cases of the Inter-American Court of Human Rights

In recent decades, various cases related to communication rights have been reviewed by the Inter-American Court of Human Rights. We compile the most significant ones in Latin America.

---

[7] Supreme Court of Justice of the Nation-Mexico. Appeal in Review ("Amparo") 1005/2018.

[8] Supreme Court of Justice of the Nation-Mexico. Appeal in Review ("Amparo") 622/2015.

[9] Federal Telecommunications and Broadcasting Law (2014) originally set forth in Article 230, first paragraph, the following: "In their transmission, licensed broadcasting stations shall use the national language. The foregoing is without prejudice to the use of the corresponding language of the indigenous people by the concessions for indigenous social use."

The first of these is the Chilean case known as "The Last Temptation of Christ,"[10] argued in 2001 and whose sentence was delivered on February 5 of that year. The lawsuit originated from judicial censorship of the movie "The Last Temptation of Christ," which was prohibited from being shown by the Chilean State and whose action directly affected the freedom of expression of the Chilean people. The lawsuit was filed by the Association of Lawyers for Public Freedoms Attorney General in representation not only of several individuals directly affected, but also "of the rest of the inhabitants of the Republic of Chile." The resolution concluded that with

> respect to the persons in whose name the case is being promoted, the Chilean State has ceased to fulfill its obligation to recognize and guarantee the rights contained in articles 12 (Freedom of Conscience and Religion) and 13 (Freedom of Thought and Expression) in connection with Articles 1.1 (Obligation to Respect Rights) and 2 (Domestic Legal Effects) of the American Convention on Human Rights, of which Chile is a State party.

The ruling determined that the projection of the film was an obligation of the State.

Another case reviewed by the Court in 2001 was the so-called *Ivcher Bronstein v. Peru*, Case.[11] The Inter-American Commission on Human Rights submitted this application so that the Court could decide whether the State violated, to the detriment of Mr. Baruch Ivcher Bronstein, Articles 8 (Judicial Guarantees), 13 (Freedom of Thought and Expression), 20 (Right to Nationality), 21 (Right to Property), and 25 (Right to Judicial Protection), all of them in relation to Article 1.1 (Obligation to Respect Rights) of the Convention. The document assured that the State arbitrarily deprived Mr. Ivcher Bronstein, a Peruvian citizen by naturalization, majority shareholder, director and president of the Board of Directors of Channel 2 *"Frecuencia Latina"* of Peruvian television of his nationality in order to displace him from the editorial control of said Channel and to restrict his freedom of expression.

The Court ruled in favor of Mr. Ivcher Bronstein, who alleged, with certainty, that he was being hindered from free access to communication channels. The case was a positive precedent in the search for freedom of expression and other related rights in Latin America.

A third case carried out in 2004 featured *Herrera Ulloa v. Costa Rica*.[12] In this case, the affected person was declared liable for defamation by the State for the partial publication of various reports from a Belgian newspaper that attributed to the diplomat Félix Przedborski, *ad honorem* representative of Costa Rica at the International Atomic Energy Organization in Austria, the commission of serious illicit acts. The Court determined that the State should give compensation to Mr. Herrera for having blocked his right to freedom of expression and recommended that modifications be made to local laws to match the Court's findings. The latter case is further proof of the advances in freedom of expression. The State of Costa Rica sought to hinder the communication channels of the newspaper "La Nación" that Mr. Herrera owned. Regarding the resolution, it was concluded that:

> On September 7, 2001, the Court required the State to adopt, without delay, as many measures as necessary, in order to leave without effect the registration of Mr. Mauricio Herrera Ulloa in the Criminal Registry of Offenders, until the case was definitively resolved by the organs of the Inter-American system for the protection of human rights. Likewise, the Court requested the State to suspend the order to publish in the newspaper "La Nación" the "extract" of the condemnatory sentence issued by the Criminal Court of Trials of the First Judicial Circuit of San José on November 12, 1999, and the suspension of the order to establish a "link", in La Nación Digital, between the defendant articles and the operative part of that judgment.

---

[10] Inter-American Court of Human Rights. "The Last Temptation of Christ," Case-Chile-(2001).

[11] Inter-American Court of Human Rights. *Ivcher Bronstein v. Peru*, Case (2001).

[12] Inter-American Court of Human Rights. *Herrera Ulloa v. Costa Rica*, Case (2004).

## Latin-American Authors of Communication and the Future

The proposal of the reviewed Latin-American communication authors is still now valid in order to analyze the present and future cases of the region, though it is clear that new challenges are arising in the digital age.

For this reason, these theoretical proposals are relevant in order to address the technological changes and innovations that impact Latin America, as societies become more dependent on digital environments and nations begin to legislate on social aspects related to communication.

For example, one of the current communication rights issues in the region is the one related to net neutrality that cannot be overseen. There can be no open Internet without communication rights such as freedom of expression and the right to information, and even others such as language rights, since censoring and blocking on the Internet also violates these rights.

Some/Certain cases in the Latin-American region invite us to imminently rethink the concepts behind freedom of expression, and even communication rights, and analyze them from a point of view where the human being must be at the center.

Antonio Pasquali's proposal revolves precisely around the humanism that must be implicit in communication rights. For the author, the Internet has strengthened communication, but it poses a series of challenges that must be conquered. Andrés Cañizález (2010) considers that the main purpose of this author was to rehumanize communication and his action is purely human where a clear distinction must be made of the concept of information. Antonio Pasquali understood that information is a unilateral relationship between institutionalized knowledge (also called the mass media) and mass receiver. This situation occurred mainly in the second half of the twentieth century until the arrival of the Internet. Unlike information, says Cañizález, communication is understood as: "the permanent relationship as creation and recreation of language and any symbolic form between social subjects, beyond any specialized technique" (2010, p. 10). Communication occurs by any means and has meanings that go beyond the way they are manifested.

## Conclusions

The cases introduced represent an example of the challenges and advances for communication rights in Latin America. As we observed in the works of the Latin-American theorists we have reviewed in this chapter, there is a communication paradigm in the region that seeks to separate itself from the Anglo-Saxon tradition. The sociocultural conditions of Latin-American countries, with a rich, multicultural history, but that have suffered of exploitation by the powerful and of a marked inequality, have also fostered the generation of intellectuals who offer different views that can be contrasted against the dominant theories, which have been formed in a reality different from that of Latin America. José Marqués de Melo, Luis Ramiro Beltrán, and José Luis Aguirre have laid the basis for a re foundation of the concept communication rights.

In particular, the legacy of Antonio Pasquali has resided in the moral perspective that communication assumes, and therefore, concludes that better communication will result in a better community. Better media quality will result in better communication. In some cases, the lack of legislation has led to judicial precedents through which the communication rights have been updated as a result of experiences that civil society has gone through and the cases it has pursued. In this way, one of the indicators to find and understand communication rights in Latin America can be identified through the relevant decisions of the courts that have traditionally analyzed issues related to the dimensions of freedom of expression. And, above all, in an international jurisdiction, in this case regional Latin-American jurisdiction, through certain key decisions of the Inter-American Court of Human Rights.

The cases presented in this document are legal precedents that help open the discussion on communication rights in Latin America, each of the cases representing various issues in both *offline* and *online* communication. Our Latin-American theoretical foundation, based on the work of these authors, has laid the foundations for profound changes in communication legislation that is yet to be fully realized.

Our perspective on communication rights in the region is that it will continue to expand in some countries, while others will stagnate for political and/or economic reasons. Governments will have to guarantee respect for human rights and the intervention of international courts will be increasingly recurring.

In this sense, Antonio Pasquali´s work is timely, as he opportunely established the idea that an international organization should apply supranational laws and that there should be international tribunals that have powers to judge attacks against communication rights of individuals and societies.

Communication will continue to evolve, in its multiple dimensions, our ability to communicate, and fundamental rights that allow for communication without restrictions is still a pending task of our times and the times to come.

## References


Aguirre, J.L. (2009). Comunicación sin identidad: las cara de una latinoamerica con sellos culturales propios. *Punto cero* 14 (19): 7–18.

Aguirre, J.L. (2013). *El derecho a la comunicación base para la construcción de la comunidad.* Cochabamba, Bolivia.

Aguirre, J.M. (2010). Diálogo con la obra de Pasquali. *Revista Latinoamerica de Comunicación: Chasqui* 109: 5–8.

Aristegui Noticias Network (2019). *Redacción/AG.* https://aristeguinoticias.com/2910/mexico/mas-de-300-periodistas-asesinados-en-la-ultima-decada (accessed September 18, 2020).

Article 19 Civil Organization (2019). La Suprema Corte emite precedente relevante sobre bloqueos en redes sociales de servidores públicos. https://articulo19.org/la-suprema-corte-emite-precedente-relevante-sobre-bloqueos-en-redes-sociales-de-servidores-publicos (accessed September 18, 2020).

Beltrán, L.R. (1993). *Comunicación para el desarrollo en Latinoamérica: una evaluación sucinta al cabo de cuarenta años.* Lima, Peru: Johns Hopkins University.

Beltrán, L.R. (2007). Un adiós a Arístóteles: La comunicación "horizontal". *Revista de la Carrera de Ciencias de la Comunicación de la Universidad Católica Boliviana San Pablo* 12 (15): 69–91.

Cañizález, A. (2010). Pasquali y la comunicación humana. *Revista Latinoaméricana de Comunicación: Chasqui* 109: 9–12.

Castellón, L. and Jaramillo, O. (2010). Libertad de expresión en Chile: avances significativos de la década. *Revista Latinoamericana de Comunicación: Chasqui* 109: 48–52.

Cooley, C.H. (2005). El yo espejo. *Cuadernos de Información y Comunicación* 10: 13–26.

Dewey, J. (2011). *John Dewey: seleccion de textos.* Medellín, Colombia: Universidad de Antioquia.

Gómez-Robledo, M. (2015). Qué fue de #YoSoy132, Los 'líderes' del que fuera uno de los movimientos más grandes de México siguen activos. https://elpais.com/internacional/2015/04/02/actualidad/1427927341_113541.html (accessed September 18, 2020).

Marqués de Melo, J. (2007). Mutações em folkcomunicação: revisitando o legado Beltraniano. Razón y palabra: Primera revista electrónica en Latinoamérica especializada en comunicación (60). www.razonypalabra.org.mx/anteriores/n60/mmelo.html (accessed September 18, 2020).

Marqués de Melo, J. (2010). *Comunicación Multicultural en Iberoamérica. Historia contextual y comparada.* Sao Paulo, Brasil: INTERCOM – Sociedade Brasileira De Estudos Interdiciplinares Da Comunicação.

Mattelart, A. (1997). *Historias de las teorías de la comunicación.* Barcelona, España: Paidós Comunicación.

McLuhan, M. (2003). *Understanding Media: The Extensions of Man*. Corte Madera, CA: Gingko Press.
Pasquali, A. (2007). *Comprender la comunicación*. Caracas, Venezuela: Gedisa.
Pasquali, A. (2011). *La Comunicación Mundo: releer un mundo transfigurado por las comunidaciones*. Zamora, Spain: Comunicación Social Ediciones y Publicaciones.
Pasquali, A. (2012). Comunicación y Derechos Humanos. In: *Colección Alternativas* (ed. A. Vega Montiel), 184. México: UNAM.

# 21

# Media Disorder and the Future of Journalism

## International Developments and the Challenge of WikiLeaks

Jane Johnston and Anne Wallace

The question of who is a journalist and what is journalism was thrown into the international spotlight in 2019 when WikiLeaks founder Julian Assange was arrested in London and his status as a journalist (or not) became a matter of heated global debate. At issue was whether Assange's manner of publishing, described as a "publish and be damned" approach (Greste 2019) with "No filter. No conscience" (Parker 2019), was as a journalist; and, whether WikiLeaks, described as "not so much a publisher as it was a combatant in information warfare" (Lake 2019), was journalism. The debate divided opinion globally. Questions of "real" and "conventional" journalism were posed, name calling occurred, emotions ran high. One of Assange's most outspoken supporters, documentary film-maker and journalist John Pilger described the denunciation of Assange and WikiLeaks as "a disgrace." Pilger argued "Julian Assange is every bit as much a journalist as I am. What has changed is the digital revolution [which] has allowed information to be much more widely available and WikiLeaks is the first organisation that has adapted to that" (Pilger 2019).

Whether Assange should be afforded the title "journalist" and the activities of WikiLeaks "journalism" is not just a question of semantics. It is illustrative of a wider issue confronting law and policy makers around the world about who should be considered a journalist before the law, in cases where source anonymity is at stake, in matters of national security and terrorism, and in relation to privacy and data protection (West 2014; Johnston and Wallace 2017, 2018). But this is not just an issue for courts, legislators, and policy makers. Scholars have questioned whether "bloggers, dilettantes, and do-it-yourselfers" (Ugland and Henderson 2007, p. 241) should be included in definitions; whether "real" journalists should somehow make up an "A-list" (Singer 2007, p. 80); or, whether the bar should be set at some sort of "press exceptionalism" level that demands an agreed degree of accountability (West 2014). At the same time, Jay Rosen has challenged "disaffected newsroom 'traditionalists,' who look upon changes in journalism since the rise of the web with fear and loathing" (Rosen 2013). A journalist, he argues, is simply a "heightened case of an informed citizen, not a special class." Rosen has called for an end to the question of "Who's a journalist?" arguing "it leads nowhere so drop it" (2013). Yet, despite his call, the question has not gone away. The arrest of Julian Assange and the case of WikiLeaks has breathed new life into the question, reinvigorating it on a grand scale with major long-term implications (Chomsky 2016; Goodale 2019; Pilger 2019).

*The Handbook of Communication Rights, Law, and Ethics: Seeking Universality, Equality, Freedom and Dignity*, First Edition. Edited by Loreto Corredoira, Ignacio Bel Mallén, and Rodrigo Cetina Presuel.

This chapter uses this case as a springboard to re-examine this long-standing debate in an era in which "bright line distinctions" between "old" and "new" journalism in the twenty-first century (New Zealand Law Commission 2013, p. 4) have been virtually obliterated. In the chapter, we draw on the substantial academic literature about the changing status of journalism plus the legal definitions, precedents, and political frameworks that continue to be reviewed and reframed by law and policy makers, regulators, and others, who wrangle with the complexity of journalism's transition to the digital era. It presents an analysis of how the legacy media and other commentators responded to Assange's arrest on April 11, 2019, and, importantly, the public response to the question of "who is a journalist" and "what is legitimate journalism" more broadly. Together, this analysis raises a Pandora's box of themes and issues about free speech, democracy, accountability, and whether the nineteenth-century concept of journalism has had its day. The chapter concludes by considering the future of journalism and public communication as it continues down the path of digital disorder and uncertainty in the 2020s.

## A Decades-Old Debate

In its report into the *When the New Media Meets the News Media* in 2013, the New Zealand Law Commission noted how:

> before the advent of the internet there was little practical necessity to consider the question: who are the "news media"? The "news media" simply comprised the public service broadcasters and corporates which between them produced the nation's daily newspapers, television and radio news and current affairs programmes. (2013, p. 63)

Yet, while the advent of the Internet and the shift to digital in the past two decades put a bright marker on the era of uncertainty, it was not the beginning of this field of inquiry. In 1943 Bryant Kearle searched for clarity in encyclopedic and dictionary definitions of journalism noting that constrained definitions did not leave room for "inevitable change" (Kearle 1943, p. 42). Like contemporary scholars and policy makers until quite recently, he used the term "new media" to press the need to keep boundaries fluid, rejecting a single orthodox view of journalism. Kearle's argument, now almost 80 years old, could have been proposed in the digital era:

> Starting from scratch, then, the proper definition must be broader than those now current; it must not be based solely on what is included in "journalism" teaching now; but it must not be so broad as to be non-defining. The definition must have intelligent limitations, yet it must have "maneuverability," adaptability to changing conditions. (Kearle 1943, p. 42)

This key argument is reflected in the current literature (Alonzo 2006; Singer 2007; Ugland and Henderson 2007; Peters and Tandoc 2013; Shapiro 2014; West 2014; Fulton 2015; Johnston and Wallace 2017). However, where Searle departs from some of the more recent literature, is in the fundamental shift from describing journalism as a stand-alone field to one converged with communication more broadly (Peters and Tandoc 2013; West 2014). He cites his contemporary, Professor of Journalism Edward N. Doan, as remarking: "instead of studying the field of journalism we ought to be thinking in terms of the whole field of timely communication" (Kearle 1943). Kearle concluded that "it seems inevitable that what we now call journalism must take over the whole study of mass communication" (1943, p. 43). He even went as far as to extend the definition to public relations and advertising – certainly a bridge too far for many contemporary thinkers. Yet, when we consider how the allied fields of "advocacy," "brand," and "influencer" journalism have become part of the journalistic remit (Bull 2013; Bachman 2019), it becomes apparent how broadly the business of news has expanded.

Kearle's definition of journalism centered on "the conveyance of timely information, ideas, counsel guidance, emotional attitudes and advertising to a varying audience by means of organized media and written, oral or pictorial symbols" (Kearle 1943, p. 44). The expectation that those activities must be carried out by a certain type of "worker" is superfluous to his definition – an issue that is a recurrent theme in this chapter.

Importantly, Kearle also noted that "no single, precise, correct definition exists for any word" journalism included. On this point, he has remained in good company over the years. Shapiro argues that "Definitions … do not gain life or durability by authorial fiat; rather, they evolve through a steady trend in usage and metamorphosis" (2014, p. 562) and Johnston and Wallace (2017) suggest that while legal definitions "may present pragmatic solutions, they also need to be flexible and reflexive enough to respond to and reflect constantly changing contexts" (2017, p. 25). Such change is reflected in how courts in many parts of the world have been approaching the question of how to define journalists over more than a decade. In 2006 a California state appeals court became the first US court to explicitly recognize that "Internet journalists" should be afforded the same journalists' privilege granted to traditional print and broadcast journalists, in effect, determining that:

> Bloggers and other private Internet publishers who disseminate news fulfill the same function as the mainstream press: informing the public. In addition, bloggers benefit society by providing increased access to the marketplace of ideas and thereby combat the effects of media consolidation. (Alonzo 2006, p. 752)

In a 2008 case relating to data protection, the European Court of Justice determined the term "journalistic purposes" could apply to individuals as well as organizations and did not depend on the medium of publication; the key was whether "the sole object of processing the personal data is to disclose to the public information, opinion or ideas" (*Satakunnan Markkinapörssi Oy and Satamedia*, cited in Roth 2010, p. 553). In an earlier case, the court took a similar view, finding that the wording of the relevant law was deliberately designed not to restrict its application to institutional media (*Tietosuojavaltuutettu v. Satakunnan Markkinapörssi Oy and Satamedia*, Oy C -73/07 2008).

This is reflected in the interpretation of Article 10 of the European Convention for the Protection of Human Rights and Fundamental Freedoms (freedom of expression) by the European Court of Human Rights, which found that: "The function of the press includes the creation of forums for public debate. However, the realisation of this function is not limited to the media or professional journalists" (*Társaság a Szabadságjogokért v. Hungary* para 27). Hovlid notes that in Társaság the Court referred to the press as "one of society's watchdogs" and not "the watchdog" (2009) leaving the interpretation of Article 10 open for interest and activist groups and individuals to contribute to public debate.

In 2014 the US 9th Circuit Court of Appeals overturned a 2011 judgment that had ruled against allowing journalistic privilege to a blogger in a defamation case. The court held unanimously that there was no difference between a journalist who works for a media outlet and a blogger, citing First Amendment protections. In the words of Justice Andrew Hurwitz:

> The protections of the First Amendment do not turn on whether the defendant was a trained journalist, formally affiliated with traditional news entities, engaged in conflict of-interest disclosure, went beyond just assembling others' writings, or tried to get both sides of a story. As the Supreme Court has accurately warned, a First Amendment distinction between the institutional press and other speakers is unworkable. (*Obsidian Finance Group, LLC v. Cox* 2014, pp. 11–12)

In the same year, the New Zealand High Court found that a "blogger can be legally defined as a journalist, and likewise that a blog can be journalism, even if the work is carried out for a non-mainstream media outlet" (*Slater v Blomfield* 2014, para 83). The judge found that reports in the blog in question contained "genuine new information of interest over a wide range of topics" and the blog, Whale Oil, was "not of such low quality that it is not reporting news" (*Slater v Blomfield* 2014, para 62).

These cases highlight the flexibility that is now called for in legal interpretations to respond to the current and dynamic media environment. One way of navigating through the morass is, as Shapiro suggests, to focus more on the practice than the practitioner. He notes how: "Egalitarian discomfort with the idea of professional distinction should diminish if one seeks strictly to recognize what constitutes journalistic activity, rather than who is a journalist" (Shapiro 2014, p. 556). Shapiro proffers the following definition which, albeit quite vague, is durable and flexible for the current time. He defines journalism as comprising "the activities involved in an independent pursuit of accurate information about current or recent events and its original presentation for public edification" (Shapiro 2014, p. 561). Shapiro is not alone in this distinction. Broadly speaking, definitions are separated around the function of journalism (i.e., the nature and purpose of journalism) and the professional or institutional approach (i.e., its links to media organizations and professional association), with the general leaning toward the functional definition as being more useful (Johnston and Wallace 2017; Hovlid 2019).

In the now burgeoning literature on this topic, certain characteristics are repeatedly debated and balanced against each other in discussion of definitions. Popular among these are questions relating to originality, objectivity, public interest, breaking news (versus commentary), receiving payment for work, membership of a professional body, and adhering to a code of ethics. What is broadly missing from much of the discussion, however, is that definitions on their own are neither inherently useful nor transportable. As statute would suggest, they are mostly worthwhile when invoked within a specific context and it may be expected that judges will have to determine the application on a case-by-case basis. In recently deliberating about a new definition in the Journalist Sources Protection Act 2017 in Canada, one member of parliament commented along these lines:

> We have so many platforms nowadays that it is hard to pin down who exactly is a journalist ... and what counts as traditional media versus new media. It is important to work with fairly broad definitions of "journalist" and "media" even if that means judges have to make their own calls about that as necessary. (Laverdière 2019)

That Act settled on the following definition:

**Journalist:** a person whose main occupation is to contribute directly, either regularly or occasionally, for consideration, to the collection, writing or production of information for dissemination by the media, or anyone who assists such a person (Journalist Sources Protection Act 2017).

However, it is interesting to note that the Act did not define "the media."

## Journalism Goes Full Circle

A "Special Report into the News Media" by *The Economist* in 2011 examined what it called: "A great historical irony at the heart of the current transformation of news" (*The Economist* 2011, p. 14). Consistent with Kearle's earlier insights, as well as contemporary scholars such as Rosen, who have questioned whether journalism must be related to a dedicated profession or specialist group of actors, the report found that the twentieth-century modern construct of journalism is now outdated. It notes how, prior to the nineteenth century, there were no dedicated journalists. Newspapers had small, local circulations, containing news, gossip, opinion, and ideas intended for particular social circles or communities, with little distinction between producers and consumers. "They were social media," it points out (*The Economist* 2011, p. 14). As businesses grew, so did the specialists who were employed to write the news in the new monetized spaces built around advertising. Thus, journalists and journalism, as we have come to know them, evolved. The report notes:

> The mass-media era now looks like a relatively brief and anomalous period that is coming to an end. But it was long enough for several generations of journalists to grow up within it ... And when you've built your whole career on that, it isn't easy to say, 'well, actually, that was just a phase'... The biggest shift is that journalism is no longer the exclusive preserve of journalists. (*The Economist* 2011, p. 14)

This "phase" also included a second element – the role of the news source – which had consolidated the traditional journalist in her or his position. In his book *The Power of News*, Michael Schudson talks of the "new movement in the 1990s ... that seeks to institutionalize ways in which the general public, rather than journalists or government officials, could help set the news agenda" (1995, p. 30). Schudson's argument was reflective of John Dewey's earlier ideas of the role of citizens in a democracy, supporting the new concept of "public journalism" (Rosen 1995). Proposing this view, Rosen said the press "should nourish or create the sort of public talk that might get us somewhere, what some of us would call a deliberative dialogue," (Rosen 1995, p. 35). This line of thinking signaled a shift from the well-established dominant elite sources within the bureaucracy that, together with the professional journalist, had dominated not just the news agenda but had established it as "the most pervasive and authoritative vehicle in society for ... promoting social control" (Ericson, Baranek, and Chan 1989, p. 5).

Within two decades, the digital era was to change this. *The Economist* reported that by 2011 there was not only a "new wave" of journalists but the separation between sources and journalists was now also blurred. The tools of production were enabling "the people formerly known as the audience" to become publishers (Rosen 2006), usurping the role of the expert source, alongside the role of the expert journalist. Likewise, the line between journalism and activism was now also blurred. *The Economist* reported that among this "new wave" was Julian Assange and WikiLeaks.

## Assange, WikiLeaks, and Media Disorder

Fast forward from *The Economist*'s 2011 report to the arrest of Julian Assange in 2019. That eight-year period saw a robust literature and commentary develop about the "boundaries of journalism collapsing" (Rosen cited in *The Economist* 2011, p. 11). This escalated in the April/May period of 2019, following Assange's arrest, resulting in both a tirade of criticism and condemnation and an outpouring of support and admiration. Our following brief analysis of how this was reported by legacy media, and the public responses to that coverage, centers on that period. We also pick up some of the most recent reports up until the end of 2019 during the period Assange was being held in Britain's Belmarsh prison.

Essentially, what was at the center of the disputed title was, first, how the US government defined a journalist for the purposes of the charges and, second, how this lined up with notions of free speech, democracy, and the United States' Constitutional First Amendment. Reuters reported in April 2019 that the United States had bypassed the "thorny issue of press freedom" by focusing on Assange as a hacker (Wolfe and Layne 2019). However, one month later, 17 charges under the Espionage Act were laid (Zhao 2019). In the week following the arrest, Eli Lake from Bloomberg noted: "As Julian Assange awaits his extradition hearing in the UK, the debate over what to call him and his organization, WikiLeaks, is once again important" (Lake 2019).

The US government was clear on this when the Justice Department's Assistant Attorney General for National Security John Demers denied Assange journalist status, telling the mainstream media: "The department takes seriously the role of journalists in our democracy and we thank you for it. It is not and never has been the department's policy to target them for reporting ... But Julian Assange is no journalist" (Zhao 2019).

Ironically, in the week following his April arrest, Assange was also awarded a European Parliament (GUE/NGL) Award for Journalists, Whistleblowers & Defenders of the Right to Information. Nobel Peace laureate Mairead Maguire, accepting the award on his behalf, condemned the international media for its lack of support "while the UN working group on arbitrary detention defines him as innocent" (Maguire 2019). WikiLeaks lists a further 17 awards for journalism on its website (WikiLeaks 2015).

The public response to the negative stance against Assange and WikiLeaks was palpable. A YouTube video clip posted by Canadian *National Post* journalist Christie Blatchford titled "Julian Assange is no journalist," in which she calls Assange a "madman" and denounces him as a journalist, resulted in an influx of criticism and vitriol, including challenges to who had the right to define a journalist, reproaches of legacy media, and responses to attacks on Assange (Blatchford 2019). Of 574 comments that responded to the video clip, very few supported the criticism of Assange.[1] One comment fiercely challenged the right of any one journalist to decide who is, and is not, a journalist: "You as a 'journalist' don't get to decide who's a journalist; that's up to the public at large." Another reinforced this line of commentary, posing the question: "Somehow you are implying journalism is some sacred profession for those special ones that are initiated is it?" And another continued to raise questions about what was journalism:

> Please define journalist. Do you need a degree to be called one? Do you need to fill out some form or pay for a sticker on your car? No. Anyone can create news and commentary. Everyone is a journalist. You have no right to say otherwise.

Further commentary challenged legacy media's abilities to deal with big issues such as global security and terrorism, often centering on questions of truth and trust and the fact that the news media had used material from WikiLeaks while simultaneously rejecting the organization's legitimacy. For example, one person commented: "You're right, he isn't a journalist. Journalists spin and twist the truth ... to fit the flawed, biased ideological narratives they are selling. He was a harbinger of the full damn truth." Several people called the legacy media the purveyors of "fake news," pointing to the irony of how "media corporate clones use his sources and [call] him a non-journalist."

As momentum continued to grow in the reporting and commentary about Assange and WikiLeaks in the months following his arrest, the question of Assange's status as a journalist and WikiLeaks as a media publisher was never far from the news agenda. WikiLeaks editor-in-chief, Kristinn Hrafnsson, himself a three-times investigative journalist of the year in Iceland, travelled to Assange's home country of Australia to urge support for the WikiLeaks founder from the Australian government, media, and public. He pointed to "a polarisation within the media fraternity," indicated by poor attendance at an Australian Press Club event, but also found "a growing recognition among principled journalists and media workers that enormous issues are at stake" (Grenfell 2019). Hrafnsson told the Australian media:

> The case of Julian Assange is, in all senses, the turning point. It is the biggest and the most serious attack on journalism and the free press in decades, if not 100 years. If this extradition goes ahead,

[1] The comments remain in the "comments section" following the video clip.

journalists around the world will have lost so much that it will be very hard, if not impossible, to get back the rights that we had before. (Grenfell 2019)

Others, like James Goodale from *Harpers* also questioned why legacy journalists had so often ignored the story. Goodall proposed the real reason they had not supported Assange was that they "simply don't get it" and he cautioned the media to take heed. He said the focus should not be on whether Assange meets the usual definition of a journalist or whether other journalists approve of what he does. "That's not the point. The point is that he carries out the functions of a journalist, has First Amendment protections (as they do), and should not be prosecuted for what he does. If he is, we are all worse off for it," (Goodale 2019).

Their words reflected an urgency focused on the ramifications for free speech and democracy emanating from the Assange/WikiLeaks story. Renowned free speech and democracy advocates rallied behind Assange and railed against his indictment, calling to account the challenges to journalism inherent in the case. Media scholar Noam Chomsky argued: "Julian Assange has performed an enormous service to all the people in the world who treasure the values of freedom and democracy and who therefore demand the right to know what their elective representatives are doing," (Chomsky 2019). John Pilger called the situation: "a campaign against journalists and particularly the public's right to know" (Pilger 2019). Many argued that a likely outcome of Assange's indictment will be a chilling effect on media reporting. Harvard law professor Yochai Benkler pointed out in *The Guardian* how sections of the indictment against Assange were "vastly overbroad and could have a significant chilling effect," a response supported by Columbia University's Carrie DeCell (Pilkington 2019).

## Interpreting Journalism in Law

It remains to be seen whether the US decision to indict Assange under that country's espionage laws will be successfully challenged on First Amendment grounds. A decision to exclude Assange and WikiLeaks from the benefit of that protection would throw wide open the question as to how the right to freedom of opinion and expression is to be understood in countries that have similar constitutional or legislative protections (such as Canada and New Zealand). For example, the New Zealand High Court decision in *Slater v. Bromfield* concerned the privilege granted to journalists under that country's law of evidence. Whether the New Zealand Supreme Court would take a similar view of the status of a blogger, or an individual or organization similar to Assange and WikiLeaks, when interpreting the right to freedom of expression in section 14 of the *Bill of Rights Act 1990* (NZ) is unknown.

In countries that do not have such constitutionally enshrined protections, including Assange's country of citizenship, Australia, the position is even less clear. Australia is a signatory to the International Covenant on Civil and Political Rights, which encompasses a commitment to the Universal Declaration of Human Rights. However, it has not taken the further step of enshrining the protections embodied in the covenant (including the right to freedom of opinion and expression expressed in Art. 19 of the UDHR) in its federal constitution, and though the Australian High Court has found an implied freedom of political communication, this has been fairly limited in its application to date (Hardy and Williams 2014, p. 802). Several Australian states have enacted their own Human Rights Charters, but these are ineffectual in relation to matters of national security which is a federal responsibility.

In 2018 the Australian federal government introduced the National Security Legislation Amendment (Espionage and Foreign Interference) Bill 2018, which amended the federal Criminal Code to create sweeping new offenses in relation to national security, including long jail terms for the unauthorized holding of, or dealing with, sensitive government information.

This legislation would clearly enable an Australian government to prosecute individuals and organizations who undertook similar activities to those alleged against Assange and WikiLeaks in the current US court proceedings. This was pointed out in Parliamentary debate on the legislation, by Senator Andrew Bartlett who observed:

> These laws are attempts to criminalise and attack people like Julian Assange. Let's not forget that Julian Assange is acknowledged as and registered as a journalist, and actually won a Walkley Award for his work exposing governments acting against their own citizens. (Bartlett 2018)

In fact, under this legislation a new section (S122.5(6)) proposed as the Criminal Code contained a defense for an individual who could prove that they dealt with the information in the "public interest", in their "capacity as a journalist engaged in fair and accurate reporting" (National Security Bill 2017). Following strong protests by Opposition parliamentarians, media, and civil liberties groups, and referral to a Parliamentary Joint Committee on Intelligence and Security, these requirements were watered down by:

- removing any requirement for journalists to demonstrate that their reporting was "fair and accurate";
- ensuring the defense is available where a journalist reasonably believes that their conduct was in the public interest;
- clarifying that the defense is available for editorial and support staff (including editors, lawyers and administrative staff) as well as journalists themselves;
- ensuring the defense is available where administrative support staff are working at the direction of a journalist, editor or lawyer who reasonably believes that conduct was in the public interest (Supplementary Explanatory Memorandum 2018, pp. 2–3).

Another interesting amendment to the proposed legislation, which was unremarked upon in parliamentary debates, was the deletion of the word "journalist," so that the defense can now be called in aid of any person acting in their "capacity as a person engaged in the business of reporting news, presenting current affairs or expressing editorial or other content in news media," (Criminal Code Act 1995 (Cth) Schedule section 122.5(6)). So though politicians who spoke during the debate on the amended legislation persisted in referring to the provision as the "journalist defense," in fact, the defense is now defined in terms of the functions performed by the individual in question, rather than their membership of a profession or calling, designated as "journalist." This amendment was clearly designed to open the defense to a wider category of individuals, other than those working in traditional media forms. Indeed, the legislation does not contain any definitions of the key terms that would have to be satisfied to meet the defense – including "news media," "reporting," "current affairs" – leaving a great deal of scope for the courts in determining to whom and to what activities this defense will apply. Whether an individual and organization carrying out the same type of activities as Assange and WikiLeaks could take advantage of that defense if they were prosecuted under the legislation, would depend on the approach a court takes to interpreting those terms.

A similar approach has been adopted in another new security provision introduced by the Australian Federal Parliament, which requires Internet service providers to collect and retain user data for two years; a regime designed to facilitate access to that data by security agencies (*Telecommunications (Interception and Access) Act 1979* (Cth) Chapter 4). In the case of information held by someone "working in a professional capacity as a journalist" access can only be obtained through the issue of a specific type of search warrant called a "journalist information warrant" (*Telecommunications (Interception and Access) Act 1979* (Cth) ss 180G; 180H). However, the Act provides no definition of "journalist"; which would, again, leave it up to the courts to decide whether an individual (such as Assange, and an organization such as WikiLeaks,) would be entitled to the arguably somewhat inadequate protection offered by the special warrant provisions (Media, Entertainment and Arts Alliance 2019).

It may be an appealing solution for parliaments to leave these types of provisions vague, so that key terms come to be defined, and refined, through judicial interpretation. There is also a clear argument that this is also a sensible approach at a time in which the media and news reporting is continuing to undergo significant changes in form and composition. However, for those operating in these news environments, it creates a significant level of uncertainty as to the level of protection they are entitled to in terms of freedom of opinion and expression. That uncertainty in itself may have a chilling effect on the exercise of those rights.

## Concluding Remarks

An irony in the debate over whether Wikileaks is journalism is that Assange has reportedly said it was not a journalistic operation. In 2010 he told the New Yorker that: “We come not to save journalism but to destroy it”, noting how journalism had to be ground down into the ashes before a new structure could be formed (Hooten 2019). Assange’s legal team and many others, nevertheless, are firmly of the opinion that he is a journalist and WikiLeaks is a publisher. This is, of course, necessary if Assange is to attract the legal protections afforded to a journalist. It also reflects the belief of many that Assange and his activities do, in Shapiro’s terms noted earlier, involve “an independent pursuit of accurate information about current or recent events and its original presentation for public edification” (2014, p. 561). Assange’s ideas of finding a new structure for journalism may have come out of a totally different motivation to that of governments and courts in responding to the need for new definitions, however, the outcome may well be the same; that is, a significant shake-up of what constitutes journalism, and most certainly the definition of “what is a journalist?”.

Several other observations can be made that speak to journalism now, historically, and in moving forward. Notably, while the public commentary on YouTube we considered in this chapter was from a limited source, there was no denying it decried the legacy media’s claim to journalistic authority and its dominance, even relevance, in the current era. This points to the need for further study to better understand public expectations of journalism and of civil society’s demands for a greater voice and of new media models. We also note how the contemporary distinction between producers and consumers is history repeating itself; so too, the idea that journalism was, historically, inherently a social function. Schudson reminds us that “Reporting is not an ancient art. It is a historically specific, historically created activity ... It does not maintain itself untouched as the world around it changes” (1995, p. 95). “News is culture,” he points out (1995, p. 31). That culture, then, must surely reflect the time and place where news is reported, published and consumed.

It may be that, as governments and courts grapple with definitions around the functions and acts of journalism rather than the person who performs those functions and acts, and, as the role of sources in co creating the news continues to trend upward, the notion of the nineteenth-century “invention” of the journalist (Schudson 1995, p. 94) will simply disappear. Arguably, this is already well under way as narrower “journalistic rights” move toward broader “communication rights” in legal, political, social and cultural contexts just as Kearle predicted they would 80 years ago.

## References

Alonzo, J. (2006). Restoring the ideal marketplace: how recognizing bloggers as journalists can save the press. *NYU Journal of Legislation and Public Policy* 9: 751–780.

Bachman, I. (2019). Advocacy journalism. *Oxford Research Encyclopedia* https://oxfordre.com/communication/view/10.1093/acrefore/9780190228613.001.0001/acrefore-9780190228613-e-776 (accessed September 19, 2020).

Bartlett, A. (2018). Commonwealth of Australia, parliamentary debates. 4265–4266. https://parlinfo.aph.gov.au/parlInfo/search/display/display.w3p;query=Id:%22chamber/hansards/9eef6b31-3509-4f19-aff2-298cba8a8db6/0006%22;src1=sm1 (accessed September 19, 2020).

Blatchford, C. (2019). Julian Assange is no journalist. *YouTube*. https://www.youtube.com/watch?v=Uw9jiA4po3k (accessed September 19, 2020).

Bull, A. (2013). *Brand Journalism*. London: Routledge.

Chomsky, N. (2016). Noam Chomsky in support of Julian Assange. *YouTube*. https://www.youtube.com/watch?v=gxLa6jtF01g (accessed September 19, 2020).

Criminal Code Act 1995, s122.5(6) (Austl.).

Ericson, R., Baranek, P., and Chan, J. (1989). *Negotiating Control: A Study of News Sources*. Toronto: University of Toronto Press.

Fulton, J. (2015). Are you a journalist? New media entrepreneurs and journalists in the digital space. *Javnost – The Public* 22 (4): 362–374.

Goodale, J.C. (2019). More than a data dump: why Julian Assange deserves First Amendment protection. *Harpers*. https://harpers.org/author/jamescgoodale (accessed September 19, 2020).

Grenfell, O. (2019). WikiLeaks editor Kristinn Hrafnsson addresses the Australian Press Club. *World Socialist Web Site*. https://www.wsws.org/en/articles/2019/12/04/hraf-d04.html (accessed September 19, 2020).

Greste, P. (2019). Julian Assange is no journalist: don't confuse his arrest with press freedom. *Sydney Morning Herald*. https://www.smh.com.au/national/assange-is-no-journalist-don-t-confuse-his-arrest-with-press-freedom-20190412-p51di1.html (accessed September 19, 2020).

Hardy, K. and Williams, G. (2014). Terrorist, traitor, or whistleblower? Offences and protections in Australia for disclosing national security information. *UNSW Law Journal* 37 (2): 784–819.

Hooten, A. (2019). Love him or hate him or simply don't care, Julian Assange's fight for freedom concerns us all. *Sydney Morning Herald* (December 17). https://www.smh.com.au/national/love-him-or-hate-him-or-simply-don-t-care-julian-assange-s-fight-for-freedom-concerns-us-all-20191202-p53g1q.html (accessed September 19, 2020).

Hovlid, E. (2019). Finding a judicial definition of journalism: a challenging exercise in the digital age. In: *Human Rights, Digital Society and the Law: A Research Companion* (ed. M. Susi), 209–224. London: Routledge.

Johnston, J. and Wallace, A. (2017). Who is a journalist? Changing legal definitions in a de-territorialised media space. *Digital Journalism* 5 (7): 850–867.

Johnston, J. and Wallace, A. (2018). Law defining journalists: who's who in the age of digital media? In: *The Routledge Handbook of Developments in Digital Journalism Studies* (ed. S. Eldridge and B. Franklin), 15–27. London: Routledge.

Journalist Sources Protection Act (2017). https://www.parl.ca/DocumentViewer/en/42-1/bill/S-231/royal-assent (accessed September 19, 2020).

Kearle, B. (1943). Journalism–what is it? A re-definition. *Journalism Quarterly* 20 (1): 40–44.

Lake, E. (2019). Is Assange a journalist? It depends on who what year you ask. *Bloomberg*. https://www.bloomberg.com/opinion/articles/2019-04-17/is-julian-assange-a-journalist-it-depends-what-year-you-ask (accessed September 19, 2020).

Laverdière, H. (2019). Open parliament debate, House of Commons Hansard #209. https://openparliament.ca/debates/2017/9/29/helene-laverdiere–2.

*LLC. v. Cox*, 740 F.3d 1284, (2014)

Maguire, M. (2019). Nobel Peace Laureate Mairead Maguire on her request to visit Julian Assange, World Summit of Nobel Peace Laureates. http://www.nobelpeacesummit.com/nobel-peace-laureate-mairead-maguire-on-her-request-to-visit-julian-assange (accessed September 19, 2020).

Media, Entertainment, & Arts Alliance (2019). Journalist information warrants. *MEAA*. https://pressfreedom.org.au/journalist-information-warrants-d47b402ae071 (accessed September 19, 2020).

National Security Bill (2017). Schedule 2, Part 1, Division 122 s122.5(6)

National Security Legislation Amendment (Espionage and Foreign Interference) Bill 2018, section 2(1)(122) (Austl).

New Zealand Law Commission (2013). The news media meets the "new media". Report no. 128. Law Commission of New Zealand, Wellington. http://r128.publications.lawcom.govt.nz (accessed September 19, 2020).

Parker, K. (2019). Julian Assange is not a journalist. *AP News.* https://apnews.com/52f4a2f42dba4f6b9afe026e57d51e96 (accessed September 19, 2020).

Peters, J. and Tandoc, E.C. (2013). 'People who aren't really reporters at all, who have no professional qualifications': defining a journalist and deciding who may claim the privileges. *New York Journal of Public Policy Quorum* 34: 34–63.

Pilger, J. (2019). John Pilger on Julian Assange, latest in Venezuela. *ABC Radio National Drive with Patricia Karvelas.* https://www.abc.net.au/radionational/programs/drive/john-pilger-on-julian-assange,-venezuela-latest/11084078 (accessed September 19, 2020).

Pilkington, E. (2019). Julian Assange's charges are a direct assault on press freedom, experts warn. *The Guardian* (April 12). https://www.theguardian.com/media/2019/apr/12/julian-assange-charges-press-freedom-journalism (accessed September 19, 2020).

Rosen, J. (1995). Public journalism: a case for public scholarship. *Change* 27(3): 34–38.

Rosen, J. (2006). The people formerly known as the audience. *Pressthink* (June 27). http://archive.pressthink.org/2006/06/27/ppl_frmr.html (accessed September 19, 2020).

Rosen, J. (2013). Look, you're right, okay? but you're also wrong. *Pressthink* (February 13). http://pressthink.org/2013/02/look-youre-right-okay-but-youre-also-wrong (accessed September 19, 2020).

Roth, P. (2010). Data protection meets Web 2.0: two ships passing in the night. *UNSW Law Journal* 32 (2): 532–561.

Schudson, M. (1995). *The Power of News.* Cambridge MA: Harvard University Press.

Shapiro, I. (2014). Why democracies need a functional definition of journalism now more than ever. *Journalism Studies* 15(5): 555–565.

Singer, J. (2007). Contested autonomy. *Journalism Studies* 8 (1): 79–95.

*Slater v Blomfield* NZHC 2221 (N.Z.), (2014).

Supplementary Explanatory Memorandum (2018). National Security Legislation Amendment (Espionage and Foreign Interference) Bill 2017. The Parliament of the Commonwealth of Australia.

*The Economist* (2011). Special report: the news industry. http://www.economist.com/sites/default/files/special-reports-pdfs/bulletins-from-the-future.pdf (accessed September 19, 2020).

Ugland, E. and Henderson, J. (2007). Who is a journalist and why does it matter: disentangling the legal and ethical arguments. *Journal of Mass Media Ethics* 22 (4): 241–261.

West, S.R. (2014). Press exceptionalism. Harvard Law Review 27: 2434–2462.

WikiLeaks (2015). What is WikiLeaks? https://wikileaks.org/What-is-WikiLeaks.html (accessed September 19, 2020).

Wolfe, J. and Layne, N. (2019). Assange hacking charge limits free speech defence: legal experts. Reuters (April 12). https://www.reuters.com/article/us-ecuador-assange-usa-legal-analysis-idUSKCN1RN2RZ (accessed October 7, 2020).

Zhao, C. (2019). "Julian Assange is no journalist": WikiLeaks founder indicted on 17 new charges under espionage act. U.S. *Newsweek* (May 23). https://www.newsweek.com/julian-assange-no-journalist-wikileaks-founder-indicted-17-counts-espionage-1434739 (accessed September 19, 2020).

# PART IV

# At the Intersection of Law and Ethics: Challenges in the Age of Algorithms, Disinformation, and Post-Truth

# 22

# Public Communication and Sustainability in a Post-Truth Era[1]

María José Canel

## Introduction

On September 24, 2015, the 193 member states of the UN signed an extensive intergovernmental agreement in New York. Titled *Transforming our World: the 2030 Agenda for Sustainable Development* (UN 2015b), the initiative pursues comprehensive sustainability. It sets 17 goals in areas as diverse as health, education, urban development, natural resources, technological development, the labor market, and institutional quality.

This agreement fits within the agenda advanced by the UN since the Universal Declaration of Human Rights was signed in 1948. The text emphasizes states' responsibility to respect, protect, and promote the human rights and fundamental freedoms of all, and it includes the approaches, planning mechanisms, indicators, and monitoring devices that the UN has been deploying to ensure compliance with the declaration's provisions.

The 2030 Agenda is, the agreement says at its beginning, "a plan of action for people, planet and prosperity. It also seeks to strengthen universal peace in larger freedom. We recognize that eradicating poverty in all its forms and dimensions, including extreme poverty, is the greatest global challenge and an indispensable requirement for sustainable development" (UN 2015b, p. 1).

Is such a global movement of states toward sustainability credible, and can we trust that it will take place?

This chapter aims to answer this question with a coincidence in timing pointed out by Lockie (2017) in mind: 2016 is the year when the implementation of this sustainability agenda began, but it is also the year when dictionaries (for example, those of Oxford Dictionaries) added the term *post-truth*. This word threatens to shake up the common benchmarks for interpreting concepts that are at the heart of the UN agreement – for example, human dignity, prosperity, progress, peace, and freedom.

The coincidence in timing is also relevant because a significant part of the debate on post-truth revolves around denialist discourse on climate change. This discourse, according to critics, downplays scientific evidence in order to advance a specific ideological position (Murphy

[1] I am very grateful to Tom Corckett for his most valuable help with English writing.

*The Handbook of Communication Rights, Law, and Ethics: Seeking Universality, Equality, Freedom and Dignity*, First Edition. Edited by Loreto Corredoira, Ignacio Bel Mallén, and Rodrigo Cetina Presuel.

2016; Lockie 2017; Ihlen et al. 2019). Post-truth ignores the science developed in relation to sustainability.

But this chapter focuses not so much on the relationship between post-truth and science but on that between post-truth and communication, since it is based on the assumption that within this relationship may lie one of the critical factors when it comes to making the advances in sustainable development that states have set for themselves. For as Lockie states, "If 2016 is to be known as the year in which the world turned a corner on sustainable development and the mitigation of climate change, it will require more than blind optimism or luck" (2017, p. 4). It requires, I would venture to say by way of an introduction to this chapter, there to be true knowledge of the situation and the problem, and also the determination of states to make progress to be authentic. In this chapter, I adopt the assumption that communication is one of the critical factors for this truthfulness and authenticity, as well as, ultimately, for the success of the 2030 Agenda. This is a highly relevant perspective to this volume's focus on communication rights and ethics.

The issue of post-truth has become especially critical in the context of the global crisis caused by COVID-19, the recovery from which, as initial assessments assert, will not involve a straightforward return to normality. Even if the spread of the virus can be contained soon, "there will be vast political, economic, social, technological, legal and environmental consequences which will last many decades" (Nesta 2020). A true and authentic motivation on states' part to jointly advance towards the comprehensive sustainability described in the 2030 Agenda will also be decisively important for dealing with the post-COVID-19 world.

This chapter is structured as follows. After considering the features of a post-truth context, I will explore the challenge of communicating the intangible value of the 2030 Agenda. In the final part of the chapter, I describe the risks facing a true sustainability agenda and propose streams of work aiming for one.

## Communicating Sustainability in a Context of Post-Truth

In this chapter, I adopt Canel and Luoma-aho's definition of *public sector communication* (2019, p. 33):

> Goal-oriented communication inside organizations and between organizations and their stakeholders that enables public sector functions within their specific cultural and/or political settings, with the purpose of building and maintaining the public good and trust between citizens and authorities.

One of the central ideas of this definition as it relates to the theme addressed in this chapter is that communication has the potential to enrich and strengthen relations between public entities and publics when common objectives are pursued. Applied to the case at hand, communication could unite different actors (governments, public authorities, companies, NGOs, and so on) under the 2030 Agenda. But it could also have the opposite effect if, as happens in a post-truth context, the communication undertaken is not real communication.

Oxford's dictionaries added the word *post-truth* in 2016, defining it as: "Circumstances in which objective facts are less influential in shaping public opinion than appeals to emotion and personal belief" (Oxford Dictionaries 2016). Many authors assert that this is not a new way of handling the truth (Harsin 2015; Lockie 2017; Macnamara 2018; Gil and Jiménez 2019; Ihlen et al. 2019). Nevertheless, the Brexit and Trump campaigns have perhaps served as catalysts for the post-truth "phenomenon," to the point where *post-truth* became 2016s "word of the year" (d'Ancona 2017; Russo 2017; Wilber 2017).

Based on a summary of the characteristics attributed by different authors to post-truth that I put forward in a previous work (Ball 2017; d'Ancona 2017; Davis 2017; Russo 2017; Canel 2018; McIntyre 2018; Waisbord 2018; Gil and Jiménez 2019; Ihlen et al. 2019), in what follows, I present some features that I consider to be essential to the relationship between this term and the 2030 Agenda.

Post-truth consists in affirming falsehoods, even when evidence to the contrary is presented or experts demonstrate that the opposite of those falsehoods is true. Post-truth has changed our way of relating to facts (Waisbord 2018), as it involves "alternative facts" that replace real ones (McIntyre 2018). It seems that we have "given way to a society without truth, or, as it would be translated in German, to a society that had left facts behind (*postfaktisch*)" (Gil and Jiménez 2019, p. 251). This poses a major threat to the 2030 Agenda: to the extent that the truth and veracity of data lose relevance, it will become difficult to establish clear benchmarks for the goals that countries set for themselves in this agreement.

But post-truth is not just a denial of the factual. In my judgment, it entails something more complex and deeper: post-truth occurs because emotions carry more weight than evidence. It is "a certain relativism where personal values, beliefs and emotions take precedence" (Ihlen et al. 2019, p. 2). What counts are not facts but "the feelings that are generated by the news and the attitudes of the recipient who follows it" (Gil and Jiménez 2019, p. 251).

The post-truth communicator thus appeals to emotion and even to hatred, aware that feelings are a powerful lever for mobilization. Therefore, post-truth trivializes content, presenting informed analysis on the same footing as bombastic claims or rumors. When we receive and buy into post-truth content, we do so because we have cognitive biases that "make us feel that our conclusions are based on good reasoning even when they are not" (McIntyre 2018). Thus, a nice story, a good metaphor, or the right special effects could hide the weakness of a poor argument about forward or backward steps on the path toward the sustainability set out in the 2030 Agenda.

The literature also agrees in attributing a moral judgment of censure to post-truth. Within post-truth reasoning, what is right and what is wrong is no longer relevant; discourse serves particular goals, regardless of what is true and what is not (Ihlen et al. 2019, p. 2). Post-truth communication may banalize the threat that sustainability faces and open the door for each actor to compose a description of the situation that best suits its interests. Moreover, this is something that could be done with impunity, because in a post-truth context, the common benchmarks used as a basis for prioritizing and assessing fall apart.

## Post-Truth and Political Correctness

"The Elevation of Sensitivity over Truth": this is the name of Granath and Ullén's (Granath and Ullén 2019) work on the political correctness that permeates media coverage. On the back of an analysis of *Time*, they conclude that politically correct phrases have been used since the 1990s to convey evaluative subjective opinions as if they were objectively informed facts. It seems that political correctness may have served as a vehicle for post-truth.

The term "political correctness" refers to the objectives pursued through political guidelines on language or behavior that are intended to avoid offending or disadvantaging certain people or groups in society (Moller 2016).

For the purposes of this chapter, what is relevant is politically correct communication's relationship with the truth. In this respect, the analysis of those who see Donald Trump's political incorrectness as one of the reasons for his electoral victory in the 2016 presidential election is becoming more pertinent. It is worth asking: What is it about political incorrectness that is attractive?

A study by Conway III, Repkea, and Houck (2017) shows that during the 2016 campaign, the restrictive communication rules that are particular to political correctness and a chronic emotional reluctance to follow those rules increased support for the Republican candidate. People are fed up with identity politics – so Conway III states in a version of this research aimed more at a nonspecialist audience – as well as with the ideologization of discourse that courses through this imposition of communication norms (Conway III 2018).

In my view, however, the explanation for the attractiveness of political incorrectness goes deeper (or at least wider) than its being a mere rebellion against imposition, since political correctness is related to post-truth. I agree with Domínguez and Reutner when they state that political correctness is associated with what a group accepts as valid, while political incorrectness is linked to what that group disapproves of on the basis that it is not in line with its values (Domínguez and Reutner 2018). Political correctness contains a moral judgment of things, and perhaps those who oppose it also do so because they do not agree with what political correctness establishes as good or what incorrectness regards as bad. In short, such political correctness has contributed to fragmenting the judgments that a community makes about what is right and what is wrong.

This fragmentation of opinions about the values that we share is well conveyed by Moller (2016), who takes the view that political correctness's attempt to advance the legitimate interests of certain groups in the public sphere comes at the cost of conflicting with other values that are also desirable to the community, because that attempt often produces "an internal schism that threatens us with collective irrationality" (Moller 2016), Moller illustrates this irrationality with the following subtle irony: while criticizing those who refer to personnel who provide assistance as "secretaries" is a manifestation of political correctness, calling for higher salaries for such personnel is not. By the same token, it is not politically incorrect to donate money to the fight against gay marriage, but it is politically incorrect to write an opinion piece against it, even if that piece made its argument in an extremely careful and dispassionate way. Therefore, political correctness can jeopardize the ability to share the dearest common values (Moller 2016, p. 4). In other words, formal compliance with rules imposed on public discourse runs the risk of overshadowing reality. Applied to the case in hand, it could be said that the 2030 Agenda is in danger of entangling itself in a politically correct form of sustainability, in which governments, companies, and NGOs would be complying with the brief stated in the UN agreement (for example, reporting investment data in fulfilment of the targets) even if no real progress were being made. Politically correct communication would thus help to conceal a negative reality – of poverty, poor health conditions, or inequality – and could serve to hide an entirely inauthentic motivation on the part of the actors involved in the sustainability challenge.

## Communication as a Source of Post-Truth

The literature associates the development of a post-truth society with public relations, spin, propaganda, and, ultimately, communication (Lockie 2017; Ihlen et al. 2019). Macnamara 2018 coined a term to convey this relationship: "postcommunication." This is a one-way, propagandistic, top-down form of communication that seeks not mutual benefit but the interests of the communicating organization.

Waisbord's (2018) argument operates along the same lines: post-truth derives from a change in the conditions in which communication unfolds today and, as a result of that change, shared evaluations of reality have become difficult, making it impossible to arrive at the truth. Waisbord maintains that the digital revolution has led to the development of new forms of propaganda and deception and that the commercialization of the media has fragmented public opinion, hindering consensus.

As a consequence of these changes, Waisbord's argument continues (2018, p. 6), social forces arise that "eagerly or distractedly take part in distorting facts and perpetuating falsehoods." What is thus generated is public opinion that is not supported by facts, that becomes resistant to rectifications, and that consumes information to reaffirm prejudices and biases. Factual data is put at the service of narratives by blurring the border between fact and fiction, between truth and lies. Ultimately, the collective effort to reach agreement on the correspondence between assertions and reality is undermined, truths become partial, and politics is reduced to a conflict between different sides.

At this point, it is worth asking: If narratives have contaminated the truth, what role remains for communication within a global sustainability challenge? Will communication have to be eliminated? Aside from the fact that such a thing is not possible, I agree with Lockie (2017) in distinguishing communication (this author speaks instead of *spin*) from what he calls "post-truth politics": whereas the latter entails manipulation of reality, the former does not necessarily do so. And "while 'governance by focus group' tended to gravitate toward the political middle ground, post-truth politics clearly gravitates to the extremes" (Lockie 2017, p. 3).

Bringing different actors toward consensus is at the heart of public-sector communication, in line with the conceptualization presented at the beginning of this chapter. But it is difficult to verify whether such a purpose is being fulfilled, since generating the cohesion or trust that are associated with consensus is something of an intangible nature.

## An Added Challenge: Communicating an Agenda of Intangible Value

The challenge of communicating sustainability in a time of post-truth becomes even greater if one takes into account that the 2030 Agenda is about something intangible. Its objective (it aims for comprehensive sustainability), approach (solidarity: "no one will be left behind"), and method (consensus: its progress is based on partnerships) are of an intangible nature. And because it is intangible, everything about the 2030 Agenda is as vague as it is relevant, just as the unity with which a country reacts to the COVID-19 pandemic is vague and relevant. These are intangible realities, and their value will determine the direction taken and progress made by societies.

Nevertheless, what we have here are intangible realities that are reflected in tangible realities. For example, sustainable development goal (hereafter SDG) 16, which entails the pursuit of peace, justice, and strong institutions, sounds abstract and vague, but when it is achieved, it will improve food security or reduce unrest and conflicts that result from inadequate access to water. The 2030 Agenda's intangible value translates into concrete realities.

In analyzing the intangibility of the 2030 Agenda, I will deploy the following definition of *intangible asset*:

> A nonmonetary asset (without physical substance) that enables and gives access to tangible assets, that is activated through communication, and that is built on past events (and linked to the behavior of the organization); therefore, it gives rise to a resource that is identifiable and from which a future (long-term) benefit/value (social, monetary, and so forth) is expected to flow, potentially, for both the organization and stakeholders/citizens. (Canel and Luoma-aho 2019, p. 77)

Two characteristics included in this definition are relevant for the purposes of my argument (Canel and Luoma-aho 2019; see also, 2017). First, creating an intangible asset requires past facts – that is, particular organizational behavior. An intangible good derives from positive experiences and, though it can be managed, it is not built from scratch. It will not suffice, then, for governments to affirm, "We are sustainable," if nothing about their governance supports that assertion. But second, facts alone are not enough. Since an intangible asset exists to the extent that someone attributes it to something, communication work that activates recognition of good organizational behavior is required.

Paradoxical as it may seem, a focus on intangibility forces public-sector managers to base their communication on the provision of something real and tangible – achievements – without which there would be no possibility of value. An intangible asset, by definition, demands a comparison be made between what is being talked about and the actual behavior of the organization, in a similar vein to what can be found in the 2030 Agenda.

## The Intangible Value of the 2030 Agenda: A Review of the Facts

Supported by previous work (Canel and Luoma-aho 2017, 2019) in which I analyzed the characteristics of intangible resources that are applicable to public sector organizations, I point out some of their features that in my understanding are applicable to the 2030 Agenda.

First, an intangible asset lacks physical substance, and if the majority of the realities with which public authorities work are nonmaterial, so is the 2030 Agenda. For example, the agreement signed in 2015 contains several intangible notions: education, quality employment, innovation, health, social welfare, gender equality, integration of diversity, and fair and inclusive growth (UN 2015b). In addition, and as I have already mentioned, the sustainability that the 2030 Agenda pursues is not only environmental but also comprehensive, since it aims to act in all areas of public management: health, education, poverty, inequality, urban planning, and so forth. Finally, to achieve the goals, countries deploy not only material resources but also – and principally – something that is intangible: agreement and consensus, the foundation on which partnerships, the working method set out in SDG number 17 to achieve the other goals, are established.

Second, it is also possible to apply to the 2030 Agenda the characteristic that an intangible asset needs activation of communication to exist. This is based on the potential of narratives to create a collective agency, summoning energies to achieve a common goal (Koschmann, Kuhn, and Pfarrer 2012). When it is possible to craft a consistent message around what we are and what we do, it is easier for everyone to collaborate (Canel 2018). This is what is at stake as attempts are made to advance the 2030 Agenda.

It is worth analyzing the frameworks or approaches of the narratives that are used in the text of the agreement signed in New York to generate semantic room with which to advance tangible realities. Table 22.1 summarizes the information from the frames deployed.

Narratives help not only to define common goals but also to collaboratively diagnose a situation: they generate consensus on the key data that define the global state of sustainability, as well as on setting priorities (Gabriel and Gauri 2019); and they provide guidance on operationalizing assessment of compliance (Elias and Holliday 2018; Simcock and Wittich 2019).

However, the task of communication that countries have to undertake is not only about narratives but also about making the message reach the public. For this reason, the UN combines its agenda with work in different areas of communication: campaigns (see, for example, "Project Everyone," www.project-everyone.org), fiction (see the comics or stories [UN 2020a] or the SDG Toolkit [UN 2020b]), technology (see the mobile applications available at https://www.sdgsinaction.com), or strategy (see, for example, Hackenesch et al. 2016; Halonen et al. 2017).

However, this communication would be useless if there were no facts supporting the message. Relevant in this regard is what the UN has established to monitor advances in the agenda: the text includes a consensus on what countries will measure to gauge the progress made to date and how and how often they will do so. And they will be held accountable.

**Table 22.1** The 2030 Agenda's framing of sustainability.

| | |
|---|---|
| What | "It is a plan of action for people, planet and prosperity;" "A comprehensive, far-reaching and people-centered set of universal and transformative goals and targets." |
| Why | "Because eradicating poverty is an indispensable requirement for sustainable development"; because "we don't have a plan B because there is not planet B" (Ki-moon 2016). |
| What for | "To strengthen universal peace in larger freedom"; "To attain a shared prosperity." |
| With what consequences | There will be "new opportunities for shared value." |
| How | through partnering, "in a revitalized Global Partnership"; deploying a common language and shared purposes. |

Source: created by the author based on the UN agreement (UN 2015b).

Accordingly, the 17 SDGs have 169 targets associated with a total of 232 indicators. For example, with regard to SDG 1, "Eradicate poverty in all its forms everywhere," countries will have to report tangible realities such as "Proportion of population living in households with access to basic services" (UN 2015a).

This is transparent and regular monitoring; the data that countries will provide for it will be accessible and processable (see point 47 of the declaration on follow-up and review of the agreement), and they will be used to produce comparative snapshots (see for example GlobeScan 2019 or the annual report on sustainable development at https://www.sdgindex.org).

In short, the 2030 Agenda will need both reality management – sustainability advances supported by objective data – and communication that manages perceptions accordingly. The 193 countries will then have to work both on "presentation" (narratives, logos, stories, speeches), and on "substantive" management (behaviors, facts, achievements, data).

## Advancing Sustainability Through Intangible Resources

With the support of previous works (from which I take the definitions that I mention later) (Canel, Piqueiras, and Ortega 2017; Canel 2018; Canel and Luoma-aho 2019), and based on the idea that intangible resources combine factual aspects with narratives, I propose implementing the 2030 Agenda through intangible resources.

Because intangible resources provide measures of tangible growth, the data produced in monitoring the 2030 Agenda will make it possible, for example, to assess the fulfillment of the promise of sustainability (it is the intangible resource *brand*), the recognition by stakeholders of sustainable behavior (*reputation*), the experience of public service (*satisfaction*), and the ability of an organization to generate and manage knowledge about what contributes to sustainability (*intellectual capital*).

The intangible resource of *organizational culture* (the capacity of an organization to align its different publics under common goals) is useful for bringing about a convergence of the efforts of public-sector employees by aligning them with the SDGs. Working on *legitimacy* (the capacity of an organization to ensure its publics give it the right to exist) of the 2030 Agenda will help in exploring and understanding the standards on which people make their judgments about sustainability. *Transparency*, a very relevant intangible asset in SDG 16, can help practices to not only be in bureaucratic compliance with the law but also to constitute a form of relationship between citizens and public authorities, with real consequences for sustainable economic and social growth.

There are two intangibles that seem to cut across the 17 SDGs. *Social responsibility* (the capacity of an organization to be and be seen to be committed to the common good) is related to the whole agenda because the sustainability that the latter pursues is comprehensive in nature. In partnering (a 2030 Agenda working method), *engagement* (the capacity to involve publics in public processes) is also a cross-cutting intangible resource. Partnerships will emerge if there are common interests – if doing things together generates more value than doing them separately does (Beisheim and Simon 2016; ESADE 2019). For this reason, other intangibles will mediate here – for example, *trust* (the capacity of an organization to be granted discretion from its publics in the use of public resources within contexts of uncertainty, and from which a certain compliance emerges) or *social capital* (an organization's capacity to bring about social cohesion).

## Conclusion: A True 2030 Agenda Versus a Post-Truth 2030 Agenda

To what extent is the global movement of states toward the intangible value of sustainability threatened by post-truth communication that enshrines political correctness? What can communication do so that the 193 states work on the real situation and are driven by an authentic motivation?

In this concluding section, I provide a list of what I consider to be risks and suggest some lines of action.

1. *Dealing with the risk of irrelevant data via agreements on certification systems*

I have argued in this chapter that a post-truth context threatens to shake the foundations of the 2030 Agenda, and I now refer more specifically to the factual and objective data on which to support the measurement of outcomes, the verification of goal achievement, and the elaboration of diagnoses. To the extent that truth and the truthfulness of data become less relevant, it will become difficult to establish clear benchmarks on the goals and targets that this agreement sets. If data are seen as irrelevant, pro-sustainability policies will also be post-truth policies.

The effort made by the states in determining the 232 indicators with which they will measure tangible progress in each of the targets has been important. But there is still a long way to go, as such indicators are only a first step followed by organizations at all levels of public administration as well as all sectors as they attempt to adapt these indicators to each specific context. For the 2030 Agenda to be successful, the data must be reliable, and they must also be given the same value by all parties.

A relevant line of work in this field is the development of certification systems with which to establish indicators or values on which there is agreement (consider, for example, Bonsucro, a multistakeholder organization established in 32 countries that promotes measurable standards of economic viability that take into account the environmental and social impact of cane-sugar production; UN and KPMG 2016, p. 10).

2. *Dealing with the risk of trivializing substance by sharing and combining scientific rigor and humanistic richness*

A post-truth 2030 Agenda would also be one in which stories, metaphors, or special effects divert attention from the strength of the data. Combating such a risk is an important challenge, because the comprehensive sustainability for which countries aim is full of technicalities. In line with what I have argued in this chapter, it is worth stating that the way forward may not be so much to avoid these stories, since it is necessary to communicate in line with publics that live within the post-truth era's particular "communication conditions." Of particular relevance here, in my view, are Lockie's (2017) proposals to disseminate science with what he calls solidarity, or Macnamara's (2018) suggestion that we go beyond science by revisiting the cultural studies of the Chicago School that support a humanistic approach to communication. Also pertinent here are the contributions of Gomá, Bel, and Corredoira in the first part of this book on dignity, freedom, and universality of communication.

3. *Dealing with post-truth politically correct sustainability with integrated reporting relevant to organizational change*

I have argued that politically correct communication can be used as cover where countries seek to hide their sustainability shortcomings. This is what happens when organizations do not take genuine steps and deceive themselves via sustainability reports in which they simply reallocate undertaken actions and resources used to date for the purposes of goal fulfillment.

What is developing around the integrated report (see, for example, Colglazier 2015; GRI and UN Global Compact 2015) is of value. The UN encourages organizations to use this practice not for image-related issues of making stakeholders know about the progress made in sustainability, but so that a real picture of the situation leads to an undertaking of strategic organizational changes. It is about self-transformation with a view to becoming truly sustainable. This requires new ways of reporting based on the principles of "Stakeholder inclusiveness, sustainability context, materiality, completeness, balance, comparability, accuracy, timeliness, clarity and reliability" (GRI and UN Global Compact 2015, p. 27).

Committing to integrated reporting that is clearer and more thorough, transparent, and authentic also includes finding measures of intangible resources that complement the assessment of progress made on the tangible level. In my opinion, the evaluation framework agreed by the countries lacks indicators of the intangible resources that would allow the intangible value of the 2030 Agenda to be captured: measures of legitimacy, trust, reputation, transparency, social responsibility, and so forth. As I argued earlier, these intangible resources are ways to implement the SDGs.

4. *Dealing with the fragmentation of values with communication aimed at finding common ground*

I will end this chapter by emphasizing the risk that the 2030 Agenda runs of being a post-truth, postpolitical pact (that is, one whose meanings are hollow) that has been agreed by postpoliticians (those who fabricate realities as they please), is supported by banal diagnoses, and lacks shared stories and narratives. As a result of politically correct post-truth communication, states could end up in a post-2030 Agenda era defined by postsustainability, and such a thing would render the global agreement for sustainability irrelevant due to a fragmented consensus. It would be an agenda that never found channels for communication about shared values and prioritizing criteria. In the aftermath of COVID-19, when the parameters for distributing resources will have to be modified, this would be especially dangerous. If such a thing were to happen, sadly it would be time to apply Russo's view (2017) that the truth has become so painful – it was impossible to jointly move towards sustainability – that it was necessary to take refuge in post-truth. Under post-truth, "the art of the lie is shaking the very foundations of democracy" (d'Ancona 2017, p. 1), and therefore, it is also shaking the foundations of a 2030 Agenda that might end up being innocuous, empty, and misleading.

I propose to answer the call made by various authors to use communication in a quest for what we have in common (Russo 2017; Macnamara 2018; Waisbord 2018; Ihlen et al. 2019)

**Table 22.2** A true 2030 Agenda versus a post-truth 2030 Agenda.

| *Risks of a post-truth 2030 Agenda* | *Streams of work to make progress in sustainability* |
|---|---|
| Weak, confusing, sparse, or alternative data | Developing certification systems |
| Gimmicky, banal, and trivializing stories about the sustainability problem | Disseminating combining scientific rigor with the humanization of communication |
| Politically correct sustainability devoid of reality | Deploying integrated reporting for organizational change |
| Fragmentation of agreements, views, opinions, and values | Gearing communication to value common ground |

in order also to make progress when it comes to sustainability (López and Monfort 2017). In this regard, what Macnamara notes about the word *communicate* itself is significant: it comes from the Latin *communis* (*community* or *commonness*) and from the Latin verb *communicare* (create or build), and thus, "communication is by definition a *two-way* interactive process aimed, not only at persuasion, but at coming together to share meaning and understanding – not necessarily agreement, but understanding, accommodation, adaptation, co-orientation" (2018, p. 12).

Table 22.2 summarizes risks and proposed streams of work.

All that remains for me to do is to return to the concept of public sector communication that I presented at the beginning of this chapter to highlight how communication geared toward the common good will be a critical factor for the truthfulness and authenticity that the success of the 2030 Agenda requires. Because "when common ground is emphasized, relativism that denies the possibility that a society enjoys something shared can be struggled, and a greater capacity for communicability and dialogue between different opinions, outlooks, and beliefs can emerge. Far from losing cultural diversity, democracy can be protected from the onslaught of subverted meanings" (Canel 2018, p. 134). Truthful and authentic communication is what will save from post-truth the human dignity for which the comprehensive sustainability of the 2030 Agenda aims.

## References


Ball, J. (2017). *Post-Truth: How Bullshit Conquered the World*. New York, NY: Connected Editions.

Beisheim, M. and Simon, N. (2016). *Multi-Stakeholder Partnerships for Implementing the 2030 Agenda: Improving Accountability and Transparency*. New York, NY: German Institute for International and Security Affairs.

Canel, M.-J. (2018). *Comunicación De La Administración Pública. Para gobernar con la sociedad*. Ciudad de México: Fondo De Cultura Económica.

Canel, M.-J. and Luoma-aho, V. (2017). Qué aportan los bienes intangibles a la Administración Pública? In: *La Comunicación de la Administración Pública. Conceptos y Casos Prácticos de los Bienes Intangibles* (ed. M.-J. Canel, P. Piqueiras, and G. Ortega), 29–50. Madrid: Instituto Nacional de la Administración Pública.

Canel, M.-J. and Luoma-aho, V. (2019). *Public Sector Communication. Closing Gaps between Citizens and Organizations*. Boston: Wiley-Blackwell.

Canel, M.J., Piqueiras, P., and Ortega, G. (eds.) (2017). *La Comunicación de la Administración Pública. Conceptos y Casos Prácticos de los Bienes Intangibles*. Madrid: Instituto Nacional de la Administración Pública.

Colglazier, W. (2015). Sustainable Development Agenda: 2030. *Science* 349 (6252): 1048–1050.

Conway III, L.G. (2018). How a cultural revolt against" "political correctness" helped launch Trump into the Presidency. http://eprints.lse.ac.uk/88850 (accessed April 30, 2020).

Conway III, L., Repkea, M., and Houck, S. (2017). Donald Trump as a cultural revolt against perceived communication restriction: priming political correctness norms causes more Trump support. *Journal of Social and Political Psychology* 5 (1): 244–259.

d'Ancona, M. (2017). *Post-Truth: The New War on Truth and How to Fight Back*. London: Ebury Press.

Davis, E. (2017). *Post-Truth: Why We Have Reached Peak Bullshit and What We Can Do about It*. London: Little, Brown Book Group.

Domínguez, P. and Reutner, U. (2018). La corrección política y el control ideológico-cognitivo de la realidad. *Odisea No 18: Revista de Estudios Ingleses* 18: 23.

Elias, J. and Holliday, J. (2018). Who gets "left behind"? promises and pitfalls in making the global development agenda work for sex workers – reflections from Southeast Asia. *Journal of Ethnic and Migration Studies* 45 (14): 2566–2582.

ESADE (2019). La contribución de las empresas españolas a los objetivos de desarrollo sostenible. Segundo informe. https://obrasociallacaixa.org/documents/10280/825331/la_contribucion_de_las_empresas_espanolas_a_los_ods_segundo_informe_es.pdf (accessed April 30, 2020).

Gabriel, I. and Gauri, V. (2019). Towards a new global narrative for the sustainable development goals. In: *Sustainable Development Goals: Harnessing Business to Achieve the SDGs through Finance, Technology, and Law Reform* (ed. J. Walker, A. Pekmezovic, and G. Walker), 53–70. Chichester, UK: John Wiley & Sons.

Gil, A. and Jiménez, R. (2019). Special issue on post-truth. *Church, Communication and Culture* 4 (3): 251–254.

GlobeScan (2019). Globescan-SustainAbility survey 2019. Evaluating progress on the SDGs. https://globescan.com/evaluating-progress-sdgs (accessed January 19, 2021).

Granath, S. and Ullén, M. (2019). The elevation of sensitivity over truth: political correctness and related phrases in the Time magazine corpus. *Applied Linguistics* 40 (2): 265–287.

GRI and UN Global Compact (2015). SDG compass. The guide for business action on the SDGs. https://sdgcompass.org/wp-content/uploads/2015/12/019104_SDG_Compass_Guide_2015.pdf (accessed April 30, 2020).

Hackenesch, C., Kloke-Lesch, A., Kock, S. et al. (2016). Towards a "Sustainable Development Union": why the EU must do more to implement the 2030 Agenda (No. 6/2016). http://hdl.handle.net/10419/199770 (accessed April 30, 2020).

Halonen, M., Persson, Å., Sepponen, S. et al. (2017). *Sustainable Development Action – the Nordic Way: Implementation of the Global 2030 Agenda for Sustainable Development in Nordic Cooperation*. Copenhagen: Nordic Council of Ministers.

Harsin, J. (2015). Regimes of posttruth, postpolitics, and attention economies. *Communication, Culture & Critique* 8 (2): 327–333.

Ihlen, Ø., Gregory, A., Luoma-aho, V. et al. (2019). Post-truth and public relations: special section introduction. *Public Relations Review* 45 (4): 101844.

Ki-moon, B. (2016). Press conference at COP22. https://www.un.org/sustainabledevelopment/blog/2016/11/secretary-generals-remarks-to-the-press-at-cop22 (accessed April 30, 2020).

Koschmann, M.A., Kuhn, T.R., and Pfarrer, M.D. (2012). A communicative framework of value in cross-sector partnerships. *Academy of Management Review* 37 (3): 332–354.

Lockie, S. (2017). Post-truth politics and the social sciences. *Environmental Sociology* 3 (1): 1–5.

López, B. and Monfort, A. (2017). Creating shared value in the context of sustainability: the communication strategy of MNCs. In: *Corporate Governance and Strategic Decision Making*, 119–135 (ed. O.L. Emeagwali). Rijeka: InTech.

Macnamara, J.R. (2018). Public relations and post-communication: addressing a paradox in public communication. *Public Relations Journal* 11 (3): 1–20.

McIntyre, L. (2018). *Post-truth*. Cambridge, MA: MIT Press.

Moller, D. (2016). Dilemmas of political correctness. *Journal of Practical Ethics* 4 (1): 1–22.

Murphy, R. (2016). Conceptual lenses to bring into focus the blurred and unpack the entangled. *Environmental Sociology* 2 (4): 333–345.

Nesta (2020). There will be no "back to normal." https://www.nesta.org.uk/blog/there-will-be-no-back-normal/,últimoacceso30deabrilde2020 (accessed April 30, 2020).
Oxford Dictionaries (2016). Post-truth. https://www.oxforddictionaries.com (accessed April 30, 2020).
Russo, G. (2017). Donald Trump and the era of post-truth. La Voce Di New York. http://www.lavocedinewyork.com/en/news/2017/05/18/donald-trump-and-the-era-of-post-truth (accessed April 30, 2020).
Simcock, P. and Wittich, W. (2019). Are older deafblind people being left behind? A narrative review of literature on deafblindness through the lens of the united nations principles for older people. *Journal of Social Welfare and Family Law* 41 (3): 339–357.
UN (2015a). Global indicator framework for the sustainable development goals and targets of the 2030 Agenda for Sustainable Development. https://unstats.un.org/sdgs/indicators/indicators-list (accessed April 30, 2020).
UN (2015b). Transforming our world. The 2030 Agenda for Sustainable Development. https://www.un.org/ga/search/view_doc.asp?symbol=A/RES/70/1&Lang=E (accessed April 30, 2020).
UN (2020a). The SDG communicator. Stories and advice to engage citizens for sustainable development. https://sdg-communicator.org (accessed April 30, 2020).
UN (2020b). The SDG Toolkit. http://sdgtoolkit.org (accessed April 30, 2020).
UN & KPMG (2016). SDG industry matrix. https://sustainabledevelopment.un.org/content/documents/9786CRT046599SDG_Food_Bev_24Feb_WEB_FINAL.pdf (accessed April 30, 2020).
Waisbord, S. (2018). The elective affinity between post-truth communication and populist politics. *Communication Research and Practice* 4(1): 17–34.
Wilber, K. (2017). *Trump and a Post-truth World*. Boulder, CO: Shambhala Publications.

# 23

# Freedom of Expression in Social Networks and Doxing

Pedro Anguita R

## Introduction

Internet development in the 1990s quickly gave way to the so-called Web 2.0, which allowed active user interaction, not only receiving content but also creating and disclosing opinions and information produced by themselves or by third parties mainly through the possibility of personal blogs provided by a growing number of new technological platforms.

Then the explosive development of social networks began, which quickly became the so-called applications, which started incorporating the new generation of mobile phones called "smartphones." The combination of the above factors has made it possible, as never before in the history of humankind, to exercise one of the human freedoms most valued by men and women, freedom of expression. Some see the Internet and social networks as a vast democratic paradise, without censorship or limits where everyone can communicate, inform themselves, and be entertained, against their critics who warn about the dangers and intolerance that are prevailing in such space, an anarchic and chaotic place where violence, bullying, irrationality, and nonsense prevail.

The invention of the printing press in the fifteenth century and the subsequent development of newspapers and journals sometime later always required the existence of directors and editors, i.e., responsible people who had to decide, based on specific criteria and principles, on what to publish. Such decisions had consequences. Those who exercised such powers were eventually accountable to their readers and society as a whole, but also legally accountable to the courts of law. So, before the development of the Internet, there was never the possibility that a person could exercise his or her freedom of expression by producing and publishing content without responsible intermediaries. Freedom of expression could also be exercised orally in public places, such as squares or streets, and also by displaying posters or painting walls. Such were the possibilities of citizen expression. Because of this necessary intermediation, the press received in 1791 an explicit mention in the First Amendment issued in the United States – one of the first declarations of fundamental rights – which provided for it:

*The Handbook of Communication Rights, Law, and Ethics: Seeking Universality, Equality, Freedom and Dignity*, First Edition. Edited by Loreto Corredoira, Ignacio Bel Mallén, and Rodrigo Cetina Presuel.

> Congress shall make no law respecting an establishment of religion, or prohibiting the free exercise thereof, or restricting the freedom of expression, or the press or the right of the people peaceably to gather, and make a request to the Government for a redress of grievances.

A couple of years ago, early constitutionalism on the European continent had enshrined in the Declaration of the Rights of Man and Citizen adopted by the French National Constituent Assembly on August 26, 1789: "the free communication of thoughts and opinions is one of the most valuable rights of man. Every citizen may freely speak, write, and publish, except when he has to answer for the abuse of this freedom in cases determined by law." The text already emphasizes that there would be limits to the exercise of this freedom, which the legislators will have to be responsible for later on.

In the twentieth century, two relevant texts in respect of freedom of expression were the American Declaration of the Rights and Duties of Man and the Universal Declaration of Human Rights, both drawn up in 1948. The first document enshrined in Article IV the right of all individuals to freedom of research, opinion, expression, and propagation of thought by any media.

The Universal Declaration of Human Rights issued four months after the American Declaration introduced a very significant novelty in the protection, which had historically been afforded to freedom of expression. By guaranteeing to everyone for the first time (Art. 19) the three dimensions of the communicative process: the research, reception, and publication of both information and opinions, elements that are considered an integral part of the right to freedom of opinion and expression. Together with the right not to be disturbed, a right that can be exercised without restrictions as to borders, and what we are interested in emphasizing, by any means of expression, as had already been recognized by the American Declaration (Article IV).

## Freedom of Expression Through Social Networks

Before referring to the regulation of freedom of expression, it is important to make a brief conceptualization of what is understood by social networks. It has been defined as a service that allows people to do at least the following three things: build a public or semi-public profile within a defined system; articulate a list of other users with whom they share a connection; and observe and browse their list of connections and those made by others within the system (Boyd and Ellison 2007).

The international human rights treaties already described developed open, broad, and general wording of the various forms of exercising freedom of expression, where they did not list exhaustively the supports covering its exercise. In this sense, they were far-sighted, assuming that technological development in human communication would continue. Therefore, from the perspective of international law, from the mid-twentieth century onwards, there was normative protection regarding the freedom of expression for future forms of technological communication that had not yet been invented. This trend continued within the Inter-American Human Rights System when the American Convention on Human Rights was adopted in 1969. Article 13 recognizes, under the heading of *Freedom of Thought and Expression*, the right to such freedoms, which we can articulate in more contemporary terms, as communication rights, to respond to their three-fold dimension: to seek, receive, and impart information and ideas of all kinds, regardless of frontiers, either orally, in writing, in print, or the form of art, *or through any other procedure of one's choice*. According to this latter section, freedom of expression through the Internet, whether through a website, a blog, social networks, or all kinds of applications, is protected by the American Convention on Human Rights, also known as the Pacto de San José. Thus, the

Inter-American Commission on Human Rights (from now on IACHR) has interpreted it, which since 2002 expressed "the right to freedom of expression in terms enshrined in Article 13 of the American Convention protects both the traditional media and the expression spread through the Internet."[1]

An important regulation in the exercise of communication rights provided by the American Convention was the prohibition by law of any propaganda in favor of war and any advocacy of national, racial, or religious hatred that constitutes incitement to violence or any other similar unlawful action against any person or group of people for any reason whatsoever, including race, color, religion, language, or national origin. (Art. 13 No. 5). This last restriction is important because, as we have warned, it is not only the Internet and social networks that promote hatred on national, racial, or religious grounds. Violent content is also circulating that threatens people's physical integrity because they support or defend political options or moral preferences, which are not covered by the protection of freedom of expression, which is strongly defended and promoted by the Inter-American Human Rights System. It has been suggested that this system unify the general standards for the exercise of freedom of expression on the Internet, which may reduce the wide margin of discretion of intermediary companies that currently allow third parties to affect the rights of other people (Cabrera 2017, p. 220).

The European Union, on its side, in the last general text on human rights, approved in 2000 its Charter of Fundamental Rights where the right to freedom of expression is enshrined in Article 11, together with freedom of information, including freedom of opinion and freedom to receive and impart information and ideas without interference by public authority and regardless of borders, respecting the freedom of the media and its pluralism. The Charter of Rights does not refer to supports, procedures, forms, or means, so it includes and extends to all communicative acts expressed through all the possibilities of expression that the Internet makes possible, such as social networks, blogs, and web pages. The jurisprudence of the European Court of Human Rights on freedom of expression has not distinguished different limits depending on whether the message is spread through social networks or otherwise (Díez Bueso 2018).

The normative regulation of social networks has been different in the United States, European, and Latin-American legal systems and therefore the role that the law has had in the problems that have been generated by said platforms (Arévalo Mutiz et al. 2011).

Finally, a group of freedom of expression rapporteurs has highlighted the importance of the Internet for the exercise of freedom of expression. Thus, the group composed of the United Nations (UN) Special Rapporteur on Freedom of Opinion and Expression; the Organization for Security and Cooperation in Europe (OSCE) Representative on Freedom of the Media; the Organization of American States (OAS) Special Rapporteur on Freedom of Expression; and the African Commission on Human and Peoples' Rights (ACHPR) Special Rapporteur on Freedom of Expression and Access to Information, have issued several joint statements on the defense of freedom of expression. In the one prepared in July 2019, the group set out the challenges of exercising this freedom for the next decade.

The text highlights some negative externalities of the digital environment, referring to disinformation; incitement to hatred; discrimination and violence; terrorist recruitment and propaganda; arbitrary and illegal surveillance; interference with the use of encryption technologies and anonymity; and the power of online intermediaries. The joint declaration calls in one of its relevant points to create an environment that allows the exercise of freedom of expression with regulatory systems that adequately protect such freedom especially, but not only, in the case of the digital environment.[2]

---

[1] IACHR. Complaint before the Inter-American Court of Human Rights against the Republic of Costa Rica No. 12.367, Case La Nación Mauricio Herrera Ulloa and Fernán Vargas R. January 28, 2002. Para. 97.

[2] All joint declarations available at: http://www.oas.org/es/cidh/expresion/showarticle.asp?artID=1146&lID=2 (accessed January 19, 2021).

The statement highlights a list of problems associated with the development of the Internet, such as discrimination and violence that exists, which are linked to the problem that we will be addressing next.

## Doxing

The development of the Internet and the creation of a digital universe have generated illicit behavior with the emergence of new information technologies similar to those that occurred in the pre-Internet era. It is so in the area of crimes against property, fraud, scams, and computer theft; criminal figures in the field of people's rights, such as reputation and private life; and crimes against public order and the protection of democratic institutions. A new catalog of illegality has also emerged from the Internet, taking advantage of the characteristics and vulnerabilities of the Internet, such as damage, sabotage, improper access, and espionage of computer systems. Doxing (or doxxing) belongs to latter behaviors that have been developed under protection of the development of the Internet, and in which there are no national or international regulations since it is a complex action to deal with from the regulatory point of view.

Doxxing is a complex, gendered communicative process by which one or several person(s) (doxxer/doxxers) seek private or personal identifying information about another individual (subject/target) and widely distributes it through undesired online mass media channels without the consent of that person, who would be made vulnerable by mass media disclosure (Eckert and Metzger-Riftkin 2020).

Doxing, according to one of the few available definitions included in the online edition of the Cambridge dictionary "is a term used in the Internet medium to refer to the practice of investigating, collecting and spreading information about a person who was specifically selected for a particular purpose or as a vendetta" (https://dictionary.cambridge.org/es/diccionario/ingles/doxing). Some authors have also defined doxing as an act that "involves releasing someone's personal details onto the Internet in an easily accessible form" (Douglas 2016, p. 199). Etymologically, doxing originates from the abbreviation of documents "docs," from which it is stylized as "dox."

Doxing is essentially using intelligence, skills, and imagination to search the Internet for information about another person, their life records and information that identifies or can identify a person, tracked information that usually falls into the category of what the law defines as personal data. The most common information that is available about a person using popular and general search engines and other more specific information, are the full real name, nicknames, age, sex, email address, websites where they have registered; the social networks to which they belong with all their opinions and moral, social, and political preferences that they have expressed; home or work address; telephone number; the educational institutions they attended their entire work history, and information related to family and friends. Another source of information may be the telephone number, which is why it is recommended not to publish it on social networks. There is a so-called reverse search service that can provide a person's address from the telephone number. Usually, this information is obtained from web portals of free access to the public, databases of public access and especially in the social networks to which the person under investigation belongs.

Another form of doxing, often called social engineering, consists of obtaining background information on a person by means of deception or simulation through people who make up their family or friendship circle. Entering a person's name in any search engine provides a lot of information about its users, especially if they belong to social networks such as Facebook, Twitter, Myspace, Instagram, or LinkedIn that provide a significant volume of private content.

In all its forms, doxing often relies on the gathering of dispersed information that may already be semi-public but this should not detract from the fact that the act of doxing is often perpetrated by a "malicious actor who wields an individual's personal information as a tool to harass, threaten, intimidate, and injure that person" (MacCallister 2017, p. 2454).

Despite the growing awareness of protecting our data, users often exhibit high levels of disclosure – privacy settings are in the minority – and very low levels of security. Sometimes, the mechanism for obtaining background information that is difficult to obtain is hacking or other surreptitious procedures in which access is gained without the authorization of the holder. In general, the collection of personal data from an individual usually stems from the person's decision to spread the information. There is a substantial difference between doxing and hacking, as the former does not pursue an economic purpose, either by appropriating direct money, or through extortion or deception unlike other forms of computer crime, in which it is usually the motivation. In doxing, there is no intention of appropriating and illegally obtaining an economic gain.

The second essential element in doxing after researching and collecting information is disclosing it, communicating it to others, and the Internet. There is no wrongdoing just for researching and collecting information from a person. The motivation for doxing, in many cases, occurs for an altruistic motive, which is why we speak of positive doxing, such as reporting a person or institution that has carried out acts outside the law, in order to develop business and risk analyses and scenarios, and also for other negative purposes, such as extorting, harassing, coercing, or victimizing or publicly exposing a subject. Sometimes, depending on a country's constitutional or legal system, doxing can be protected under the protection of freedom of expression, for example, when images of people gathering to promote racial, sexual, or xenophobic hatred or discrimination, or extremist political ideas associated with either the right- or the left-wing are released and data such as their home or workplace is disclosed.

In certain countries, such background disclosure actions could be considered a violation of the right to privacy and the protection of their data. Thus, two types of doxing could be considered: the lawful one where a legitimate purpose is pursued, such as the detention of persons who have transgressed the law, to identify them and prevent their illegal acts from going unpunished. Such actions, despite their meritorious purposes, are not outside the error margin, as sometimes doxing is based on precedents, such as audiovisual material that was not true, where an error in identity can occur, attributing the authorship of the actions to the wrong people. Such mistakes have increased in recent years.

Douglas reminds us that doxing should be further differentiated from related concepts such as blackmail, gossip, or defamation (Douglas 2016). Doxing does not include demanding something (e.g., money) from a subject to prevent personal information being released. The threat of doxing may constitute blackmail but doxing itself may not be. Unlike doxing, defamation necessarily involves something that damages the reputation or right to honor of the person described and it usually involves untrue facts. Doxing may seek to harm someone's reputation, but it does not create false statements as libel might; it is not a form of written defamation. Doxing is also different from mere gossip as it is not based on hearsay or innuendo, it is based around releasing the actual identity of a person and personal data associated to that identity.

Doxing is also substantially different from concepts such as cyber-bullying, which involves aggressive behavior, such as insulting, harassing, defaming, or threatening, by sending messages, showing videos or pictures through social networks. Such actions are what accompany doxing, when a massive attack begins against a person, but they are different, though they can go together. That is, the same person can attack another through social networks with all sorts of expressions and threats and, in parallel, accompany with data that reveals information that is possible to obtain from the Internet, such as phone number, address, email, or profiles that could have been held across different social networks.

Judged from instances of doxing we have seen around the world, we can assume what a person experiences associated with a particular fact or who expressed their opinion, real or not, and after an accusation of a reprehensible act, become viralized. The place where they live is revealed and the simultaneous attack of thousands of insults and death threats, both personal and to family, where they are warned, for example, where they live, their working place, and a high number of details about their lives.

It is not difficult to think of the fear that invades the victims of such attacks and the fear they feel for a long period of time just by going out on the street. This is the main effect that doxing has on people: the feeling of a threatening environment of which they can be victims day and night. The above can only generate a condition of anxiety and emotional stress since they cannot find a protective space where they can take refuge while the exhibition lasts. In short, it causes a notable and inevitable change in the person's usual living conditions, with effects on their studies, work, relationships, etc. The most vulnerable victims are minors, who lack experience and skills to adequately face such a complex situation.

## Types of Doxing

Therefore, there are several categories of doxing. A positive one is the investigations carried out by the institutions in charge of criminal prosecution and also by the police investigation corps in order to investigate antecedents or identify a person who has broken the law. Prosecutors' offices today often begin searching the Internet for records of an accused or suspect, which they then include in their reports. Another type of doxing that is also legitimate is Internet searches by people who require some type of service or work. They can be professionals such as doctors, lawyers, architects, psychologists, and tradesmen of all kinds. In both cases, they will investigate relevant or significant antecedents in order to decide about their hiring. Such an activity, as it only concerns the interested party, is not disclosed to third parties, as it only aims to assess the provider's capabilities, not to alert or communicate to the rest of the community. However, there are also cases of people who, after ending the contractual relationship with a provider, are considered harmed when not defrauded and instead of deducing actions before the courts or consumer protection institutions try to take justice into their own hands, they proceed to disclose the background of the service provider to discredit them through social networks sometimes including images of the effects of work poorly done, for example, a poorly built wall, a pet with sequelae, or medical malpractice. While such actions may be covered by the right to freedom of expression of the affected contractors, their counterparts who often have a conflicting version will find it an unfair attack on their reputation, which is why they often bring legal action against the users or social network platforms where they appear.

In the latter cases, depending on the context, the legal claims are accepted by the courts in some legal systems, which look at self-guardianship and private revenge with distrust, and which do not resort to formal instances constitutionally and legally responsible for resolving conflicts. There are some variations of what we have called positive doxing. In China, for example, digital media searches, blogs, and discussion forums are called *Human Flesh Search Engine*, among other things, to combat corruption in government bureaucracy. This activity is based on the interaction and collaboration between many people through social networks, hence its name, which seeks to identify people suspected of having committed a crime or socially repugnant actions.

There is, on the contrary, another type of doxing that is negative since the objective pursued by the doxer is to harm another person or certain groups through the mechanism of seeking, collecting, and disclosing their personal data.

Through the disclosure of the personal background of a person, the intention is to cause damage to their psychological or physical integrity. At the very least, negative uses of doxing seek to generate a hostile environment or even real-world retaliation against doxed individuals.

The motivation to undertake such actions is usually diverse, but those that we are interested in analyzing in this work are those that have a political character since they affect the conditions of deliberative dialog that is the one that should develop the public debate in a democratic society. Non political doxing is used as a vehicle to seek revenge, damage, and retaliation, and thus is a form of online vigilantism in which the objective is for someone to obtain justice by their own hand outside the judicial system and win, where personal interests prevail. This is different from so-called political doxing, which is a more common type of doxing (Lopez 2018, p. 84).

For this reason, the most frequent victims are communicators, journalists, radio and television program hosts, professional politicians, or public personalities dedicated to all kinds of activities that express their political or moral options on the occasion of a news event or for any other reason.

One of the most serious doxing cases in Europe happened in December 2018, where a German tweeter published data on politicians, journalists, presenters, YouTubers, musicians, and actors.[3] Though much of what was disclosed was unimportant or outdated, it did display private email addresses and phone numbers, home addresses, and even banking details, including private conversations, in chats on some social networks. But anyone who is not a public person and who expresses their ideological preferences on social networks can be a potential victim of doxing. Sometimes doxing can originate in news or videos viralized in social networks and then picked up by the media, increasing its diffusion exponentially.

One of the most telling examples is the now-famous incident on January 18, 2019, at the Lincoln Memorial in Washington, DC, when a group of high-school students from a Catholic school in Covington, Kentucky, joined an anti abortion march with another group of African-American Jews who were honoring the deaths of that community in the Vietnam War.

The main US media reproduced an incomplete version of the conflict, giving a partial and distorted perspective of what happened due to the lack of diligence and professionalism in the journalistic investigation. The first version they broadcast was based on a short video they showed on their covers with titles such as: opening research to students wearing red hats with the slogan of the Trump *Make America Great Again* election campaign who harassed an Indian war veteran. The video was uploaded to the social networking platforms Instagram, Twitter, and YouTube, which received millions of views and was widely shared. So the news and the video for a few minutes was about a group of white teenage students where Nick Sandmann appeared in the foreground, laughing loudly in front of and within walking distance of Nathan Phillips, an older Native American man, as he played the drum and sang. The images of the tense confrontation quickly became viral, creating outrage throughout the US political class. It was on a fake Twitter account that the first video was broadcast, seen at least 2.5 million times, and retransmitted at least 14 400 times until the account that uploaded it to that social network was removed.

Pictures of Sandmann and background information such as the school he attended quickly began to circulate on social networks. Soon after, a much more extensive version of the first video circulating that lasted nearly two hours was released and uploaded to Facebook by a protester who was part of Phillips' Black Hebrew Israelites group. The long version shows a group of five African-American Hebrew men protesting the

[3] https://www.handelsblatt.com/today/politics/data-leak-20-year-old-german-hacker-confesses-in-doxxing-case/23841212.html?ticket=ST-19218321-VhVGNpdgGbb3jveQX1Bd-ap5 (accessed January 19, 2021).

oppression of centuries, which mocked and hurled insults. Before the Sandmann scene, this group of men appear with the students exchanging pleasantries, in a context different from that of a group of white boys making fun of an older African-American man. Phillips had told the media that the students surrounded him, and he was harassed, but the extensive video showed that he was the one who approached them, and then for several minutes, he beat his drum a few inches from Sandmann's face, who remained smiling and silent. Sandmann received thousands of insults, hate speech, and was accused of being racist, intolerant, and discriminatory. He received many death threats and warnings that an attempt would be made on his life at his high school, in his neighborhood, and at home. Sandmann's father even claimed that his son *was* "the victim of the most sensational Twitter attack on a minor child in the history of the Internet."[4]

Sandmann's parents sued CNN, *The Washington Post*, and NBC Universal for their coverage of the incident, seeking compensation for damages caused by the emotional distress of both Sandmann and his family for more than US$200 million each, where they are still considering suing at least 10 other media entities. Previously, the media refused to make a correction to the news coverage. A federal court in Kentucky dismissed the lawsuit against *The Washington Post* in July 2019, though it was reconsidered and refiled in October of that year. On July 24, 2020, an agreement was announced between Sandmann and the newspaper. In January 2020, CNN entered into a settlement agreement with Sandmann for a sum of money and conditions that were not disclosed.

The Sandmann case could constitute a reference on news coverage and its propagation through social networks since there are many cases of doxing and lynching that occur on such platforms without consequences for the participants of such actions. If doxers begin to be exposed to legal consequences for their actions, they may begin to discourage the radical violence that exists on Internet-based social networking platforms.

The Sandmann case also originated a few weeks after it occurred, one of the first bills in the world to sanction the practice of doxing, though only in cases of minor victims. The bill filed in the Kentucky State Senate seeks to make it a crime to post a minor's personal information online with the intent to harass, abuse, or frighten. Thus, it would be a crime, for example, to disclose personal information of minors, such as the address of their home or the school they attend, with the intention of threatening them. While this is a well-inspired initiative, both the United States and other countries around the world should be aware that ambiguous wording of the sanctioned conduct could affect users' freedom of expression. After several decades of discussion, we know that the limits of the public debate must be as wide as possible, and be open, strong, and uninhibited, particularly in the field of political activity. For this reason, there are critics of such initiatives since they also argue that the laws already contain sanctions for threats of death or injury and, in general, against the physical integrity of people, cases of cyberbullying, and also for violent discourse or the promotion of hatred and discrimination. Though in most of the most popular social networks, there are community rules that prohibit the nonconsensual disclosure of private information of third parties, in a significant number of cases, technology companies still do not have timely and effective actions to end massive doxing or threats. However, in 2012, California incorporated section 653.2 into its Penal Code, which prohibits the distribution or publication of personally identifiable information with the intention of placing a victim in reasonable fear for their safety, a norm which the accused in *People v. Shivers*, for electronically distributing a harassing message via Twitter (McIntyre 2016, p. 122) was claimed to have breached.

[4] See NBC News at https://www.nbcnews.com/news/usseparar.

## Political Doxing

While the Sandmann case was clearly political in nature, the proliferation of doxing actions that have such a motivation do not arise from a demonstration like the Sandmann case, but from statements or decisions made by elected representatives of citizens or government figures. Hand in hand with a growing atmosphere of polarization in the political debate in many countries, it is understandable that violence is being transferred from the streets and public squares to the world of the Internet and social networks. Though violence and political conflicts are clearly not born in social networks, they end up reflecting and reproducing what happens in real life.

Doxing in other regions of the world, such as the southern cone of Latin America, emerged for very unique reasons. In the 1980s, human rights groups looking for the victims and disappeared of political violence began to go to the workplaces of military personnel suspected of being responsible for such crimes taking with them banners and drums denouncing impunity and the passivity of justice. They began in Argentina, where they were called *escrache* and then moved to Chile after the restoration of democracy in the early 1990s when they were called *funas*. They were symbolic acts by family members and victims of moral reproach in the face of impunity and the absence of punishment for those responsible. The Internet had not reached the current level of development.

But today, both the escraches and the funas have become increasingly political. In Chile, for example, an interesting case occurred with parliamentarians belonging to the Chamber of Deputies who voted against a constitutional charge brought against the president of the republic. A political leader urged through Twitter: "We must find out the houses of those parliamentarians who have betrayed the people ... because, just as they follow families who cannot pay a mortgage and the police go to evict them, well, we are going to go to their houses." The deputies, feeling threatened in their right to freedom and personal security, filed an action of protection against the speaker, but the courts of justice dismissed the judicial appeal because they did not notice a real threat to the victims. Also, in Chile, a criminal judge was subjected to doxing followed by multiple death threats and accused of being a traitor for having left a prisoner in custody by the police in the context of the so-called social explosion in that country that began in October 2019.

Both cases reported have in common that the victims of the doxing, parliamentarians, and a judge are public individuals, the former elected by popular vote and the latter in office according to promotion after a civil service career. From a doctrinal point of view, which has been recognized by relevant jurisprudence both in Europe and on the American continent, a person's public status implies a lower threshold of protection for their reputation and privacy in the case of a conflict with freedom of expression. However, in the case of doxing, it is difficult to frame the actions of investigation, collection, and diffusion of a person, even if they have the quality of being a public person in the exercise of freedom of expression. There is no doubt that every type of public authority in a democratic society must be subject to demanding and severe public scrutiny and the harshest and most severe criticism on the exercise of their powers and the evaluation of both their decisions and judgments. But disclosing one's home address or telephone number through social networks seems to be an activity that is difficult to protect under the right to freedom of expression. This is just a way of dissenting from decisions that do not challenge what has been decided but only seek to instill fear in those authorities. However, while they may be inhibited in the exercise of their duties, individuals in the public office often enjoy institutional protections not available to private individuals and must have greater strength and character to resist doxing. But no person, authority or not, can be required to perform heroic acts.

Finally, we must point out that though in many internal legislations of each country, there is usually the penal figure of the crime of threatening the life and physical integrity of another person, such a criminal figure does not adequately fit with the elements that make up doxing. First, the crime of threat requires that it be credible and serious, i.e., that there is some certainty that the threat will be carried out, and second, that it be credible, i.e., not vague or nonsensical that instills in the victim the fear of being the victim of a crime. Doxing basically consists of the investigation, compilation, and disclosure of the personal background of the affected person, where sometimes, there is not even the slightest threat, as others usually formulate it.

## Is It Time to Regulate Social Networks?

The criminalization of illicit expressions such as doxxing will necessarily imply a regulation of freedom of expression. In addition, one must bear in mind the difficulties that countries have to regulate technology companies such as social networks that do not have an establishment or domicile (Ferrer-Serrano 2013). We have already explained the risks that such regulation will entail. Furthermore, it will involve assigning responsibilities to people who disclose personal data of third parties and those who might have social networks. So far, social networking technology platforms such as Facebook, Instagram, and Twitter, and others such as Google have enjoyed broad immunity by claiming that they cannot take responsibility for the content that users express or upload to their technology platforms by being mere intermediaries. They also tend to put forward technical reasons, claiming that they cannot control what the millions of people are doing on their platforms every day. This position is legally recognized in several countries around the world, including the United States, where most of the technological platforms have developed around the world. In 1996, when the Internet was beginning, the Federal Communications Decency Act was passed in 1996, and section 230 added shortly afterward.[5] This section was specifically designed to exempt Internet technology companies from legal liability.

Section 230 provides:

> No provider or user of an interactive computer service shall be treated as a publisher or issuer of any information from any other information content provider.

The rule was issued when the social networks and large companies that exist today, such as Facebook, Twitter, or Instagram, did not yet exist, nor did other companies such as YouTube or the most widely used search engine in the world, Google. However, all these companies enjoy the status conferred on them by Section 230, which qualifies them as platforms and not as content publishers, as this is the activity inherent in what the media do. It is this qualification that needs some discussion and where only two alternatives fit. Defining technology companies as media would imply understanding that they operate under explicit editorial principles or lines, which inspire or guide the selection of content, being responsible for the sources and procedures for obtaining and verifying the information they disclose. On the other hand, if we consider that social networks are mere platforms for distributing neutral content, they would lack all the features attributable to the media described earlier.

When the development of social networks began, they had few rules, did not label content uploaded by users, and did not remove them. The exceptions were few: contents covered by intellectual property protection laws were not allowed, and neither was child

---

[5] Communications Decency Act, 47 USC section 230 (1996). Also called Title V of the Telecommunications Act of 1996, legislation enacted by the US Congress in 1996 primarily in response to concerns about minors' access to pornography via the Internet.

pornography, which gets sanctioned in a large community of countries. Nowadays, instead, urged by the growing problems generated through their platforms, and whose starting point was the increasing spread of fake news that circulated in 2016 during the presidential elections in the United States, social networks started to increase the rules and mechanisms to control the qualified contents incompatible with their principles and operation rules. Its compliance initially relied on the development of technological tools such as algorithms but, in recent years, social networks have increasingly incorporated many people whose function is to detect content that violates their community rules.

This new role, which all social networks now apply with nuances, became evident with the two disputes at the end of May 2020 between President Trump and Twitter. The first began with the President's Tweet on May 26, where he expressed his rejection of the postal vote, a form of voting widely used in the United States. He said:

> THERE IS NO WAY (ZERO!) that mail ballots are not fraudulent. They will steal the mailboxes, forge the ballots, print them illegally, and sign them fraudulently. The Governor of California is sending ballots to millions of people, no one...

Trump was alluding to a statement made by Gavin Newsom, Governor of that state a few days earlier about his plan to vote massively in that way in the November 3 presidential election in the context of the pandemic generated by COVID-19.

Twitter did not remove the President's Tweet but added at the end of it, the warning: "Get the Facts about Voting by Mail," a tag linking to a short note produced by Twitter, indicating that Trump's claims about the mail ballots were "unsubstantiated." All this, according to reports on the subject by media sources such as CNN, *The Washington Post* and experts who claimed that absentee voting rarely linked to election fraud, followed by a "what you need to know" section where Twitter corrected what it believed were false claims by the US president.

The second incident occurred only three days later. On May 29, 2020, President Trump called the protesters criminals in a Tweet about the looting and disorder in Minneapolis, Minnesota, after the death of George Floyd, warning that "when the looting starts, the shooting starts." Twitter decided to hide the Tweet but did not remove it, though it did place a warning: "This tweet violated Twitter's rules on the glorification of violence." However, Twitter has determined that it may be in the public interest for the Tweet to remain accessible. Next to the warning, a link saying "view" led to President Trump's hidden Tweet.

Perhaps both cases symbolically represent the changes that social networks are implementing about their new policies of warning about fake news and fighting against the language that glorifies violence, especially by linking to the figure of President Trump. However, what is relevant about the incidents is the edition that Twitter made in both cases. Editing usually means the preparation or direction of a text, book, or magazine, in its formal and content aspects, where notes or comments usually follow. As Twitter has done, it made an editorial decision so that, after the incidents with President Trump, it could hardly claim that it is a mere neutral platform that only distributes content from its users. With this critical change, Twitter and the rest of the social networks that decide to intervene or edit their users' content will have to assume their responsibilities. The current absence of effective legal action to defend victims of doxing has been a prominent reason why it has been proposed in the United States that lower federal courts adopt a new standard that could criminalize malicious doxing (MacCallister 2017).

The US judiciary has already set some rules about public debate on social networks, in a case that once again had President Trump as its protagonist who prefers to express himself through social networks than in traditional press conferences. *Knight First Amendment Institute at Columbia University v. Trump*, was a case that arose from a lawsuit filed by the Knight First

Amendment Institute at Columbia University on behalf of seven individuals who had been blocked by the president after criticizing his policies.[6] The New York Federal Court of Appeals for the Second Circuit ruled that the President of the United States could not silence users who thought differently because that would violate the First Amendment passed in 1791 to protect freedom of expression. Judge Parker said: "In resolving this appeal, we remind the litigants and the public that, if the First Amendment means anything, it means that the best response to a disadvantaged speech on matters of public concern is more dialogue, not less." The decision held that the US Constitution "does not allow a public official who uses a social networking account for any official purpose to exclude people from dialog because they express opinions with which the official disagrees." The ruling noted that the country's government and its representatives are currently the subjects of an "open and strong debate," indicating that while these discussions can often be "uncomfortable and unpleasant," they are "nevertheless a good thing."

## Conclusions

Freedom of expression has a new field of expansion following the development of the Internet and the emergence of social networks. However, within this unprecedented opening in human history for human communication, there are growing disruptive behaviors that affect the exercise of freedom of expression. One of these behaviors is the so-called doxing, which consists of investigating, compiling, and spreading private background information on the social networks of a person who inhabits it, and instills fear especially in the context of a news item linked to the political field where violence and tension are progressively increasing in many regions of the world.

In several countries of the world, there are legal initiatives or laws that approved that sanction reprehensible actions through social networks such as online harassment called cyberbullying, particularly in cases of minors in the area of school education. However, there are difficulties for the co legislator powers to regulate behaviors such as doxing because it could restrict the legitimate exercise of political criticism that in a democratic society should be very broad, uninhibited, and robust.

As social networks are not merely content distribution platforms currently, since they carry out media activities, they should have the responsibilities that the media have. Social networks are the new public spaces where those who wish to make their opinions known can express themselves in a poorly ordered manner.

There are still a few high courts of justice in the world that have ruled on the exercise of freedom of expression on social networks. The normative regulations on some behaviors such as the doxing we have analyzed, which, together with other older ones, threaten to turn social networks into a space of intolerance, violence, irrationality, and hate instead of the deliberative, peaceful, rational, and respectful place that once promised to be, do not yet exist.

## References

Arévalo Mutiz, P.L., Navarro Hoyos, J.A., García Leguizamón, F. et al. (2011). Modelos de regulación jurídica de las redes sociales virtuales. *Revista Vía Iuris* 11: 109–136.

---

[6] *Knight First Amendment Institute at Columbia University v. Trump*, No. 1:17-cv-5205 (S.D.N.Y.), No. 18-1691 (2d Cir.). (2019).

Boyd, D.M. and Ellison, N.B. (2007). Social network sites: definition, history, and scholarship. *Journal of Computer-Mediated Communication* 13 (1): 210–230.

Cabrera, A. (2017). La regulación del derecho a la libertad de expresión en Internet: estándares interamericanos y el caso de Facebook. *Voz Iuris* 33 (1): 209–222.

Ferrer-Serrano, R.L. (2013). El tránsito de las redes sociales hacia un nuevo concepto extraterritorial de los Estados («netstates»). In: *Libertad de expresión e información en Internet: amenazas y protección de los derechos personales* (ed. L. Corredoira and L. Cotino). Madrid: Centro de Estudios Políticos y Constitucionales.

Díez Bueso, L. (2018). La libertad de expresión en las redes sociales. *IDP. Revista de Internet, Derecho y Política* 27: 5–16. http://dx.doi.org/10.7238/idp.v0i27.3146

Douglas, D.M. (2016). Doxing: a conceptual analysis. *Ethics and Information Technology* 18: 199–210. https://doi.org/10.1007/s10676-016-9406-0

Eckert, S. & Riftkin-Metzger, J. (2020). Doxing. Wiley Online Library. https://doi.org/10.1002/9781119429128.iegmc009 (accessed 30 September 2020).

MacIntyre, V. (2016). "Do (x) you really want to hurt me?": Adapting IIED as a Solution to Doxing by Reshaping Intent. Tul. J. Tech. & Intell. Prop., 19, p. 111–134.

Lopez, J. (2018). Límites en las Redes Sociales: Qué podemos y qué no podemos hacer. *Economist and Jurist* (1 March), p. 78. https://www.economistjurist.es/articulos-juridicos-destacados/limites-en-las-redes-sociales-que-podemos-y-que-no-podemos-hacer (accessed July 19, 2020).

MacCallister, J. (2017). The Doxing dilemma: seeking a remedy for the malicious publication of personal information. *Fordham University Law Review*. https://ir.lawnet.fordham.edu/flr/vol85/iss5/44 (accessed September 19, 2020).

# 24

# The Emerging Threat of Synthetic Media
## A Consideration of Journalists' Responsibilities

Muira Nicollet McCammon

## Introduction

The ethical decisions made by journalists have long been a subject of significant study (Voakes 1998; Coleman and Wilkins 2004), with much of the scholarship focusing on ways to improve moral judgments made in newsrooms (Patterson and Wilkins 2010). Recent research has considered the ethical performance of journalists during specific events (Fahmy and Johnson 2005; Andén-Papadopoulos and Pantti 2013) and perceptions of traditional ethical values in a changing digital scenario (Singer and Ashman 2009; Friend and Singer 2015).

One of the most significant challenges that journalists face in telling stories is the images that they pair with their prose; pictures can play an integral role in people's understanding of news, as they can also interact with texts to create new forms of understanding (Bryant 1996; Darling-Wolf and Mendelson 2008). The ways in which images are ordered, presented, and spatially situated shape their visual meaning (Fiske 1990; Edwards 1992; Mendelson 2007). Including any type of photograph in a news story has repercussions on readers as well, for photographs "… reiterate. They simplify. They agitate. They create the illusion of consensus" (Sontag 2003, p. 6). Yet, photographs can also, by their very inclusion in stories, divide readers and editors, who disagree over what types of images are appropriate for the public to see on the page. For newsrooms, photographs wield a certain meaning-making power that is often difficult to operationalize or quantify, and they allow abstract concepts to be made more real to readers, as they offer concrete images as conceptual anchors (Huxford 2001). Similarly, the texts that a journalist pairs with an image can have grave impact, as a text can narrow the meanings perceivable in a photograph (Barthes 1977) and push readers toward a certain interpretation (Fiske 1990). As Popp and Mendelson (2010) point out, a lack of a text can also shape how readers interpret an image. Absent explanations can amplify the uncertainty of a subject.

The decisions that journalists tend to make – whether to pair an image with a text or cover a certain topic – do not exist in a vacuum; they are instead part of a series of practices that they invoke in their day-to-day responsibilities in the newsroom. In this chapter, I offer a more nuanced understanding of the practices adopted by journalists in their ongoing coverage of a specific type of technology: synthetic media. Here I draw on Schatzki's (2001) definition of *practice* as "a set of doings and sayings organized by a pool of understandings, a set of rules"

*The Handbook of Communication Rights, Law, and Ethics: Seeking Universality, Equality, Freedom and Dignity*, First Edition. Edited by Loreto Corredoira, Ignacio Bel Mallén, and Rodrigo Cetina Presuel.

(p. 61). Focusing on practice theory offers us few distinct benefits. First, it allows us to avoid "focusing too much on the spectacular and ignoring the routine, the everyday practices of late modernity" (Bigo and Tsoukala 2008, p. 3). It also helps us consider "patterned actions that are embedded in particular organized contexts" (Adler and Pouliot 2011, p. 5).

Technological advances have the capacity to harm some individuals greatly and unequally; these "advances" can provide others with benefits and positive deliverables. In the case of artificial intelligence (AI) algorithms and the media products they help create, there is a profound risk in sharing information about technologies that affect and harm certain groups of people disproportionately. Historian Mar Hicks (2019) suggests that some of these technologies are so fundamentally flawed and harmful to certain minority populations that they should be abandoned. Journalists, however, do not have the power to remove certain technologies from circulation. Instead, they must navigate an inherent tension between two contradictory values. On one hand, a technology that can harm readers is obviously newsworthy; on the other hand, the news media have long been thought to have a responsibility to protect the public from harmful images that might traumatize people. According to the "informing and displaying" approach (see Morse 2019), journalists have a responsibility to inform their readers, so that they themselves can make their own judgments of a certain technological reality. In contrast, according to the divergent "taste and decency" approach (see Morse 2019), when visuals related to a specific technology might harm or encourage harm toward a subset of readers, circulating them does not serve the public's right to know.

In the twenty-first century, journalists have struggled to determine which types and aspects of AI algorithms are worth covering, and they have not reached an agreement or, as a community, implemented a set of standardized norms in deciding what images to pair with stories about machine learning that could harm certain readers (Bateyko and McCammon 2019). Much of the discourse to date has instead focused on ensuring that journalists are equipped with the technological tools that can detect deepfakes (Halper 2019).[1] Less attention has been devoted within the field of journalism studies to imagining how synthetic media products should be described, explained, and visualized. This chapter, through a textual analysis and semi-structured interviews, offers a contemporary understanding of how newsrooms covering synthetic media are attempting to negotiate and invoke certain (photo-) journalistic practices that can inform readers while not putting them at risk of technological harm.

## A Note on Terminology: Defining Synthetic Media

Over the years, communication scholars, technologists, and journalists have struggled to come up with a common terminological framework to describe artificially generated and manipulated media products. Jon Bateman (2020) in a recent piece offered the following explanation: "AI algorithms can produce realistic 'deepfake' videos, as well as authentic-looking fake photos and writing." Bateman (2020) and others (Stanton 2018; Witness 2018; Ovadya and Whittlestone 2019) refer

[1] In this piece, I follow the frameworks set forth by Chadwick, Vaccari, and O'Loughlin (2018) and Jack (2017), who clarify that online disinformation is intentional behavior that purposely misleads, and online misinformation is intentional behavior that inadvertently misleads. Some deepfakes are vehicles of disinformation, as they are rooted in intentional acts; the creator of the synthetic media would presumably know its capacity to mislead others. However, when circulated online by others, including journalists, synthetic media can turn into misinformation, if the people contributing to its distribution believe them to be truthful representations. This distinction is not especially germane for the purposes of this chapter but is worth mentioning in contextualizing the decisions journalists make in deciding whether or not to share a deepfake with their readers.

to these digital tools collectively as "synthetic media." One type of synthetic media that has become particularly disruptive is that which relies on machine learning algorithms to superimpose the facial expressions or entire body of one person onto another (GitHub 2019a, 2019b).

By focusing on a collection of items known as "synthetic media," I posit in this piece that it is insufficient to use the term "deepfake" to refer to content made with the aim of deceiving people, because it shifts the conversation from what such content *is* and assumes too much about what each person involved in circulating it intends for it to do.[2] It is important to think of AI as a field of research, which relies on a wide set of engineering practices (Russell, Norvig, and Davis 2010). Subsequently, many types of AI, such as that which directs an autonomous car, do not have immediate or direct connections to journalism practices, and that is why it is critical to differentiate between them with precision.

## Case Study: Context and Controversy

In June 2019, journalists around the world published stories about DeepNude, an easy-to-use AI application designed to create non consensual fake nudes of women. In an article that prompted many more, VICE, a popular online publication in the United States, used images of multiple celebrities – Gal Gadot, Natalie Portman, Tyra Banks, and Kim Kardashian – in order to demonstrate how the technology worked (Cole 2019).[3] Within 24 hours after the first story went live, the anonymous programmer who made the application had taken it down, declaring that "the world is not yet ready for DeepNude" (Cole 2019, p. 1).

Many scholars, technologists, and academics (see Bateyko and McCammon 2019) took to social media to hail this episode as a success story: an anonymous programmer's misogynistic tool had seemingly been shut down after public outcry and journalistic coverage. But, in fact, the episode pointed to a broader reality: that journalists around the world struggled and continue to struggle to situate synthetic media products within their stories. This chapter uses DeepNude as a case study to argue the ways in which journalistic practices can amplify a subset of dangerous technologies; it also offers specific ethical and legal strategies for newsrooms to adopt in their coverage of synthetic media products. In considering this single case study, I demonstrate how the circulation of certain exploitative imagery fell short of journalism's proclaimed objective of fully documenting the elements of harmful technologies. I argue that in so doing, US journalism failed to raise certain questions about the complexity of synthetic media and I will highlight journalistic practices that create more responsible and ethical coverage.

One of the reasons why the VICE news coverage of DeepNude provides a platform for a bigger conversation about the emerging threats of synthetic media is that it shows the pre-existing need for journalists and editors to reflect further, and among themselves, on what ethical and conscientious coverage of new media entails. It also demonstrates that newsrooms are listening to readers and are prepared to change their journalistic practices in order to avoid alienating audiences. Though VICE editors initially decided to print artificially generated images of celebrities as a way of demonstrating how the AI algorithms could be leveraged to unclothe images of women, the media company later appended the following editor's note to the piece:

---

[2] We might think of synthetic media as a byproduct of a "narrow AI," as opposed to "general AI" (Broussard 2018).

[3] For context, DeepNude made it so that if users uploaded clothed photographs of women, it would subsequently undress them and produce a new, artificially generated image. The application is no longer operational.

> This story originally included five side-by-side images of various celebrities and DeepNude-manipulated images of those celebrities. While the images were redacted to not show explicit nudity, after hearing from our readers, academic experts, and colleagues, we realized that those images could do harm to the real people in them. We think it's important to show the real consequences that new technologies unleashed on the world without warning have on people, but we also have to make sure that our reporting minimizes harm. For that reason, we have removed the images from the story, and regret the error.

By the time that VICE had revised the story, the images originally included in the piece had circulated across the Internet, appearing on blogs and in other outlets' coverage of DeepNude. The entire episode called into question what journalistic practices underlie reporting on synthetic media and what methods beget an ethical and informed approach to demonstrating how AI algorithms work.

The creation and subsequent coverage of DeepNude might be best understood as a node within a network of events related to the collision of newsrooms and AI algorithms. For example, Buzzfeed (2018) published a video showing former US President Barack Obama speaking from what looked like the Oval Office. Eventually, the Buzzfeed editors reveal that what viewers have been watching is not Obama himself but rather the US comedian Jordan Peele (Mack 2018); a split screen shows that Obama's and Peele's facial expressions and lip movements have been made to match perfectly and that through AI algorithms, Peele has digitally altered Obama's face so that it mirrors his own.

Later, in 2019, weeks after DeepNude launched, Momo, a social media company, released an app that let users superimpose images of their faces onto actors in iconic movie scenes. In all of these episodes, journalists had to decide how and to what extent to explain the mechanics of generative adversarial networks (GANS), the AI algorithms needed to facilitate face-editing and face-swapping. What is significant about the DeepNude case study is that some newsrooms chose to *use* the technology themselves in order to create and subsequently publish synthetic imagery that would demonstrate its potential to readers. VICE, the first US newsroom to do so, would subsequently remove the synthetic images of celebrities from its webpage, but by that point the artificially generated photographs had already spread to major social media outlets, such as Twitter (Bateyko and McCammon 2019).

## Methods: Tracing Journalistic Practices Across DeepNude News Coverage

In this chapter, I rely partially on semiotic analysis of published articles, interviews, and editorials, wherein news organizations either published or abstained from publishing nude deepfakes that came from DeepNude. I pair this method with a textual analysis, an approach that is useful for assessing not only the surface meanings of texts but also the "underlying ideological and cultural assumptions" (Fursich 2009, p. 240) that they are making. In this circumstance, textual analysis permits us to look beyond the images themselves as well as the intentions of media practitioners (Fursich 2009) and instead examine the assumptions that underlie the norms directing their journalistic practices. By fusing these two approaches of semiotic analysis with qualitative textual analysis, we can edge closer toward meaning-making that regards each article about DeepNude; this approach takes inspiration from Larsen (1991), who urges that a text be treated as an "indeterminate field of meaning," as opposed to a "closed, segmented object with determinate, composite meanings" (p. 122).

In this process, I track journalistic practices in each piece and draw on follow-up interviews with journalists and illustrators about the decision-making processes that went into covering DeepNude. I analyzed articles published within a month after VICE broke the first story about DeepNude. I searched Lexis Nexis, Factiva, and Google News databases using the search term "DeepNude" and also filtered out articles that did not refer to "DeepNude" multiple times to ensure the sample did not include writing that only peripherally mentioned the app, its creator, and its users. This resulted in a sample of 35 articles from a variety of news outlets, including *CNET*, *Vox*, *Motherboard*, *The Washington Post*, and *MIT Technology Review*.

## Findings: Journalistic Practices Underlying DeepNude Coverage

### Harkening Synthetic Media to Other Technologies

Headlines from the likes of VICE ("This Horrifying App Undresses a Photo of Any Woman With a Single Click"), *The Washington Post* ("'The world is not yet ready for DeepNude': Creator kills app that uses AI to fake naked images of women"), and Poynter ("Are we ready for the 'deepnude' era") would have readers believe that AI-synthesized image and video content are new, that is, detached from previous technologies capable of facilitating the spread of disinformation. DeepNude, however, is a type of application that draws on a philosophy that visual media can be edited, manipulated, and distributed without the consent of those featured within it. This is the same principle underlying the logics of earlier technologies, such as Photoshop, which let users tweak images. DeepNude helped illustrate a significant choice that journalists face in how they frame synthetic media; they can link it to a history of technologies that have had the potential to harm, deceive, and denigrate the reputation of individuals, from celebrities to people on the street, or, they can sensationalize the technology, amplifying its allegedly "never before seen" effects. For example, one practice that journalists can adopt in their description of potentially harmful synthetic media is to liken it to other media, such as data breaches and revenge porn leakages. In both, it is possible to speak of them without directing readers to the parts of the Internet where they were originally discovered or sourced.

### Making Artificial Intelligence, including Generative Adversarial Networks, a Beat

Telling stories about DeepNude may ultimately be instrumental in changing the legal landscape, if reporters decide to explain the technical process behind synthetic media systems, so that people can start to make sense of AI news when they see it, and subsequently push policymakers to regulate the publication of media products facilitated by AI algorithms. Informing readers about AI in a holistic, comprehensive way means not only explaining how it works but also how it can be used to harm and impact others. Thus, in selecting what they cover, journalists preserve, amplify, and highlight topics prioritized by some technologists and reject others; this is yet another journalistic practice bound up in ethics. VICE's decision to retract its publication of synthetic images of naked women signaled that it did not support circulating artificially generated images that could be weaponized against women or cause them psychological distress.

Single articles can influence each other, in that journalists regularly swap sources and content with each other (Boczkowski 2010). As a result, readers have become accustomed to encountering news stories that are in conversation with each other (Su et al. 2015). Subsequently, meaning-making does not occur in isolation and instead results from the constant interplay of articles that speak to and about each other. Journalists covering AI and machine learning do not have total control over their stories, and thus it is worth pausing for a moment to consider the structural ways in which newsrooms could strengthen their coverage of synthetic media globally. While stories about synthetic media tend to be assigned to technology reporters, even many within that specific beat interviewed for this research admitted that they are not sufficiently informed about the technological and legal mechanics underlying manipulated media. Thus, newsrooms that commit resources to creating positions for AI reporters may prove more capable of providing more nuance and comparative understanding of how one type of AI-generated media differs from another.

## Privileging the Victim's Voice

In all reported stories, journalists wield great power in deciding who constitutes a source, because sourcing is all about allocating trust and power. Sources are a fundamental component of journalistic sense-making, as they provide journalists with facts and figures that they then verify and validate (Gans 1979). Sources can assist journalists in their pursuit of accuracy and also define reality by providing unique perspectives (Sigal 1999). Ultimately, in choosing their sources, journalists give authority and legitimacy to some groups over others (Carlson 2009).

Sourcing norms are another journalistic practice worth revisiting in the contemporary coverage of manipulated media and the populations they could threaten. Feminist scholars (Citron 2019) have encouraged academics and others writing about exploited women to remember that the traumas that they have experienced can sometimes reduce their desire to speak to the press. A challenge of synthetic media coverage is that assignments do not always permit journalists to take the time to engage directly, face-to-face with individuals negatively affected by the makers of harmful media products. To complicate matters further, the lack of trauma training in many newsrooms (Beam and Spratt 2009) has created an implicit distance between media practitioners and the networks of individuals impacted by their sourcing and reporting.

A number of stories published about DeepNude made an effort to include eyewitness accounts from women. One article, "Porn app used to doctor photos of S'pore women" (Sun 2019), begins with an emphasis on how synthetic media products can travel across the web. Singaporean David Sun begins his piece with a line that privileges the experiences of a woman affected and exploited by DeepNude: "She posted an innocuous selfie on social media more than a year ago. Last week, her photo appeared on a sex forum with a startling difference—she is naked" (p. 1). Part of what makes Sun's piece distinct is that it also provides readers with legal knowledge about what they can do if clothed images of themselves are turned into synthetic media; he interviews and privileges the viewpoint of lawyer Gloria James, who notes that doctoring photos to make people appear naked is a criminal offence under the Films Act. Unfortunately, in the United States, readers do not have the same legal rights.

Interviewing lawyers and populations directly impacted by DeepNude therefore provides journalists with a way to disempower programmers intent on exploiting women's bodies. It is also a sourcing norm that predates the arrival of synthetic media and has been deployed in the coverage of revenge porn. However, this sourcing norm is not without its complexities. Scholars have previously highlighted that readers are more likely to believe sources who are prepared to be named (Carlson 2010), and it is simultaneously known that many victims of sexual exploitation do not wish to go on record.

## Reimagining Dangerous Imagery Instead of Publishing it

In an interview, Javier Zarracina, the graphics editor at Vox, describes his initial reaction to seeing the DeepNude images published by VICE. His own illustration for a Vox story about the app included no direct mention of DeepNude or its creator. He explained, "These fake images were a little bit disturbing, so I thought that it would be better to make the story without using the images." For Zarracina, drawing a silhouette of a dressed woman was a good solution. He justified his drawing by adding, "We're talking about the use of women's bodies sexually by software, and the challenge was how to represent that without drawing a naked woman without reproducing the harm." For him, journalists need to collaborate with illustrators to find common ground in deciding what should be conveyed in a single story. "We need to find how to transmit the key points of the story using the visual language, and in that sense, we have to be respectful and measured," he warned.

In another interview, Sarah Hashemi, a motion graphic artist for *The Washington Post*, reflected a similar type of thinking when she intentionally chose imagery for a story by Drew Harwell that would demonstrate how DeepNude affects all women. "My job as the designer and animator was to make sure that I could visually convey what Drew reported," Hashemi clarified, "to express the emotion and tone of his story and not to add any additional harm to the subject of his story and others who share her story."

What we see in both these interviews are attempts by illustrators to cultivate an explicit, comprehensive, and coherent set of ethical practices applicable to the ways in which synthetic media is communicated to public audiences. Tensions can arise between journalists and illustrators about how to frame and visualize synthetic media. Ethical principles evolve and often remain in flux, and for this reason, solving ethical tensions within a newsroom requires a two-fold process. First, it requires a recognition that pluralistic societies are often home to many different ethical and value systems; second, it requires a reckoning with the fact that produced media and covered media can embody some of these very same conflicts.

## Sharing Knowledge Between Scholars, Journalists, and Readers

During interviews with the researcher, many journalists and illustrators responsible for writing about these technologies revealed their lack of training in how machine learning works; they could therefore benefit from engaging more regularly and rigorously with the rich network of historians, technologists, lawyers, and human rights lawyers who study machine-learning applications and can speak to the ways in which they harm certain members of the public disproportionately. More importantly, they need to talk among themselves and with animators, editors, and readers to share the types of practices that could reduce psychological and emotional harm. Journalists, in covering synthetic media, can make the choice to critically interrogate the messages that they are communicating to their readers, but to do so requires reflection.

Not all synthetic media involves the same networks of people. In the case of DeepNude, there was an anonymous creator who encouraged others on the Internet to upload images of women so that the app could subsequently produce images that stripped women of their clothes and made them appear naked. This type of synthetic media is distinct from Buzzfeed's video merging Jordan Peele's face with that of Obama, mentioned earlier in this chapter. In the former, there are victims, women whose bodies have been distorted and subsequently disrespected, who may avoid speaking out for fear of attracting more attention (Citron 2019). The latter, meanwhile, features the former US president, who, as a public figure, is already the target of substantive parody and disinformation campaigns.

Sharing knowledge between scholars, journalists, and readers can thus help facilitate informed conversations, both in published pieces and in the comments below them, about who synthetic media harms and who it benefits. Journalism history scholars can speak to the ways in which newsrooms have conceptualized the risks of harming their readers. Internet historians and machine-learning experts can specify how certain synthetic media generators, much like platforms, can bring together a wide set of users, from politicians to parents, teens to technologists, spies to free-speech activists; they effectively serve as a stage where people gather, argue, develop personal relationships, and jockey for divergent futures (Marvin 1988; Pearce 2011; Gillepsie 2018). Legal scholars can warn journalists of the potential legal fallout that may result from artificially generated images being published online or in print, and they can give readers a sense of what recourse they may have if images of themselves are circulating on the web; some privacy law experts, such as Citron (2018), have already begun this critical work.

### *Learning the Letter of the Law*

Most journalists interviewed about their DeepNude coverage were eager to discuss the ethics of their journalistic practices but did not profess great knowledge of how pending legislation might impact their future reporting. Many did not demonstrate an understanding of how synthetic media laws might dismantle or discount the strength of journalists' communication rights. Fortunately, as Matthew F. Ferraro (2019) explains, "Almost without exception, the pending or enacted deepfake-related bills require that, to be liable, a defendant must 'intend' for the deepfake he or she produces or distributes to cause a particular result or harm" (p. 2). That said, much of the pending legislation in the United States has received criticism from news media organizations and advocacy groups out of the concern that potential laws will limit the expression of journalists and what they are able to cover (Cahill 2019). Thus, journalists covering technologies such as DeepNude face twin challenges going forward: they must not only endeavor to cover synthetic media ethically, but they also need to track new legislation regarding its distribution so as not to violate it accidentally by publishing synthetic imagery of naked women.

## Conclusion

Visuals carry power and subsequently can complicate meaning when paired with texts. Their absence or presence in a story can concretize the abstract nature of new technologies or amplify harms to specific vulnerable populations. Synthetic media produced with the help of generative adversarial networks can facilitate face- and body-swapping in ways that can raise questions for newsrooms, especially those without fact-checkers on staff and those without in-house lawyers, because it requires journalists to contemplate which manipulated images they value, fear, and seek to problematize and who they might wish to put at risk. Images released online by journalists of nude women – even if they are synthetically made – can be weaponized in unknown ways, and once they are published, in the United States, women have no comprehensive way of limiting their circulation on the Internet.

The case study of DeepNude points to the need for newsrooms to reckon more substantively with the history of dangerous technologies. DeepNude cannot and should not be equated with the likes of nuclear bombs and other weapons of mass destruction; it is not, for example, designed to kill or cause bodily harm to its users. However, it can introduce different types of harm to readers. It can asymmetrically and unevenly disrupt the lives of women whose bodies are input as images into the application. For this reason, there is a need for media scholars to create a taxonomy of harms that can result from the amplification of digital media that can cause emotional, psychological, or physical distress among readers.

It is also clear that synthetic media complicates journalism's ethical codes, particularly around the question of *what is journalism meant to do?* (Zelizer 2017). While all digital technologies have origin stories, these are not necessarily the narratives that journalists themselves need to amplify. Instead, they have a responsibility to pause and consider the networks of individuals impacted and entangled in their coverage. Part of this process involves imagining potential readings and interpretations of their texts. Featuring programmers' narratives might call attention away from those negatively impacted by the creation, circulation, and promulgation of certain new media. Similarly, highlighting the "new" and "disturbing" aspects of synthetic media can erase its intimate relationship with older technologies, which have historically privileged the entertainment and information needs of men at the cost of women's wellbeing (Criado Perez 2019).

The central takeaway from the case study of DeepNude is that journalists' commitment to uncovering truths and documenting the evolving nature of new media can blind them to the role of ethics and of law in their own profession. Editors eager for clicks often ignore the question of who a piece, a headline, or an image might harm. The notion of "trusting our gut" does not suffice in this media ecosystem, where synthetic images of naked women, circulated without their consent, can constitute not only an invasion of their sexual privacy (Citron 2018) but also signal a symbolic refusal of a newsroom to recognize their dignity.

## References

Adler, E. and Pouliot, V. (2011). International practices. *International Theory* 3 (1): 1–36.

Andén-Papadopoulos, K. and Pantti, M. (2013). Re-imagining crisis reporting: professional ideology of journalists and citizen eyewitness images. *Journalism* 14 (7): 960–977.

Barthes, R. (1977). *Image – Music – Text*. New York: Hill and Wang.

Bateman, J. (2020). Deepfakes and synthetic media in the financial system: assessing threat scenarios. *Cyber Policy Initiative Working Paper Series*. https://carnegieendowment.org/files/Bateman_FinCyber_Deepfakes_final.pdf (accessed September 19, 2020).

Bateyko, D. and McCammon, M. (2019). After DeepNude, ideas for more conscientious coverage of synthetic media. *Columbia Journalism Review*. https://www.cjr.org/watchdog/deepnude-ai-synthetic-media-ethics.php (accessed January 20, 2021).

Beam, R.A. and Spratt, M. (2009). Managing vulnerability: job satisfaction, morale and journalists' reactions to violence and trauma. *Journalism Practice* 3 (4): 421–438.

Bigo, D. and Tsoukala, A. (2008). Understanding insecurity. In: *Terror, Insecurity, and Liberty: Illiberal Practices of Liberal Regimes after 9/11* (ed. D. Bigo and A. Tsoukala), 1–9. Oxford: Routledge.

Boczkowski, P. (2010). *News at Work: Imitation in an Age of Information Abundance*. Chicago: University of Chicago Press.

Broussard, M. (2018). *Artificial Unintelligence: How Computers Misunderstand the World*. Cambridge: MIT Press.

Bryant, M. (1996). *Photo-textualities: Reading Photographs and Literature*. Newark: University of Delaware Press.

Buzzfeed (2018). You won't believe what Obama says in this video! 1F609 *BuzzFeed*. https://www.youtube.com/watch?v=cQ54GDm1eL0 (accessed September 19, 2020).

Cahill, N. (2019). California senate approves anti-deepfake bill despite free speech concerns. *Courthouse News Service*. https://www.courthousenews.com/california-senate-approves-anti-deepfake-bill-despite-free-speech-opposition (accessed May 15, 2020).

Carlson, M. (2009). Dueling, dancing, or dominating? Journalists and their sources. *Sociology Compass* 3/4: 526–542.

Carlson, M. (2010). Whither anonymity? Journalism and unnamed sources in a changing media environment. In: *Journalists, Sources, and Credibility: New Perspectives* (ed. B. Franklin and M. Carlson), 37–48. Florence, KY: Routledge.

Chadwick, A., Vaccari, C., and O'Loughlin, B. (2018). Do tabloids poison the well of social media? Explaining democratically dysfunctional news sharing. *New Media and Society* 20 (11): 4255–4274.

Citron, D.K. (2018). Sexual privacy. *University of Maryland Legal Studies Research Paper No. 2018-25*. https://ssrn.com/abstract=3233805 (accessed September 19, 2020).

Citron, D.K. (2019), The national security challenge of artificial intelligence, manipulated media, and "deep fakes." *House Permanent Select Committee on Intelligence*. https://intelligence.house.gov/calendar/eventsingle.aspx?EventID=653.

Cole, S. (2019) This horrifying app undresses a photo of any woman with a single click. *VICE*. https://www.vice.com/en_us/article/kzm59x/deepnude-app-creates-fake-nudes-of-any-woman.

Coleman, R. and Wilkins, L. (2004). The moral development of journalists: a comparison with other professions and a model for predicting high quality ethical reasoning. *Journalism and Mass Communication Quarterly* 81 (3): 511–527.

Criado Perez, C. (2019). *Invisible Women: Exposing Data Bias in a World Designed for Men*. London: Chatto and Windus.

Darling-Wolf, F. and Mendelson, A.L. (2008). Seeing themselves through the lens of the other: an analysis of the cross cultural production and negotiation of National Geographic's "The Samurai Way" story. *Journalism and Communication Monographs* 10 (3): 285–322.

Edwards, E. (1992). *Anthropology and Photography, 1860–1920*. New Haven: Yale University Press.

Fahmy, S. and Johnson, T. (2005). How we performed: embedded journalists' attitudes and perceptions towards covering the Iraq War. *Journalism and Mass Communication. Quarterly* 82 (2): 301–317.

Ferraro, M.F. (2019). *Deepfake Legislation: A Nationwide Survey – State and Federal Lawmakers Consider Legislation to Regulate Manipulated Media*. https://www.wilmerhale.com/en/insights/client-alerts/20190925-deepfake-legislation-a-nationwide-survey (accessed May 15, 2020).

Fiske, J. (1990). *Introduction to Communication Studies*. London: Routledge.

Friend, C. and Singer, J.B. (2015). *Online Journalism Ethics: Traditions and Transitions*. London: Routledge.

Fursich, E. (2009). In defense of textual analysis: restoring a challenged method for journalism and media studies. *Journalism Studies* 10 (2): 238–252.

Gans, H.J. (1979). *Deciding What's News*. New York: Pantheon Books.

Gillepsie, T. (2018). *Custodians of the Internet: Platforms, Content Moderation, and the Hidden Decisions that Shape Social Media*. New Haven: Yale University Press.

GitHub (2019a). *Faceswap*. https://github.com/deepfakes/faceswap (accessed September 19, 2020).

GitHub (2019b). *DeepFaceLab*. https://github.com/iperov/DeepFaceLab#Where_can_I_get_the_FakeApp (accessed September 19, 2020).

Halper, E. (2019). "Deep Fake" videos could upend an election – but Silicon Valley may have a way to combat them. *Los Angeles Times*. https://www.latimes.com/politics/story/2019-11-05/deep-fakes-2020-election-silicon-valley-cure (accessed May 15, 2020).

Hicks, M. (2019). Hacking the cis-tem. *IEEE Annals of the History of Computing* 41 (1): 20–33.

Huxford, J. (2001). Beyond the referential: uses of visual symbolism in the press. *Journalism* 2 (1): 45–71.

Larsen, P. (1991). Media contents: textual analysis of fictional media content. In: *A Handbook of Qualitative Methodologies for Mass Communication Research* (ed. K.B. Jensen and N.W. Jankowski), 121–134. New York: Routledge.

Mack, D. (2018). This PSA about fake news from Barack Obama is not what it appears. *Buzzfeed*. https://www.buzzfeednews.com/article/davidmack/obama-fake-news-jordan-peele-psa-video-buzzfeed; https://perma.cc/3AGM-F8EM (accessed January 20, 2021).

Marvin, C. (1988). *When Old Technologies Were New*. New York: Oxford University Press.

Mendelson, A.L. (2007). The construction of photographic meaning. In: *Handbook of Literacy Research: Visual, Communicative and Performative Arts* (ed. J. Flood, S. Brice Heath, and D. Lapp), 27–36. Mahwah: Lawrence Erlbaum.

Morse, T. (2019). Gruesome images in the contemporary Israeli mediated public sphere. In: *Media and the Politics of Offence* (ed. A. Graefer), 233–251. Cham: Palgrave Macmillan.

Ovadya, A. and Whittlestone, J. (2019). Reducing malicious use of synthetic media research: considerations and potential release practices for machine learning. *arXiv preprint arXiv:1907.11274*.

Patterson, P. and Wilkins, L. (2010). *Media Ethics: Issues and Cases*, 7e. New York: McGraw-Hill Education.

Pearce, C. (2011). *Communities of Play: Emergent Cultures in Multiplayer Games and Virtual Worlds*. Cambridge: MIT Press.

Popp, R.K. and Mendelson, A.L. (2010). X'-ing out enemies: Time magazine, visual discourse, and the war in Iraq. *Journalism* 11: 203–221.

Russell, S.J., Norvig, P., and Davis, E. (2010). *Artificial Intelligence: A Modern Approach*. Upper Saddle River, NJ: Prentice Hall.

Schatzki, T.R. (2001). Introduction. In: *The Practice Turn in Contemporary Theory* (ed. K. Knorr Cetina, T.R. Schatzki, and E. Von Savigny), 10–23. London: Routledge.

Sigal, L.V. (1999). Reporters and officials (Excerpt). In: *News: A Reader* (ed. H. Tumber), 224–234. Oxford: Oxford University Press.

Singer, J. and Ashman, I. (2009). "Comment is free, but facts are sacred": user-generated content and ethical constructs at the. *Guardian Journal of Mass Media Ethics: Exploring Questions of Media Morality* 24 (1): 3–21.

Sontag, S. (2003). *Regarding the Pain of Others*. New York: Farrar, Straus & Giroux.

Stanton, C. (2018). November 2018 Convening Mapping Synthetic Media's Problem and Solution Space. Carnegie Endowment for International Peace. https://carnegieendowment.org/2018/11/16/november-2018-convening-mapping-synthetic-media-s-problem-and-solution-space-pub-79892 (accessed January 20, 2021); https://perma.cc/M6EZ-8CDX (accessed January 20, 2021).

Su, L.Y.F., Akin, H., Brossard, D. et al. (2015). Science news consumption patterns and their implications for public understanding of science. *Journalism and Mass Communication Quarterly* 92 (3): 597–616.

Sun, D. (2019). Porn app used to doctor photos of S'pore women. *The Straits Times*, July 11. https://www.straitstimes.com/singapore/porn-app-used-to-doctor-photos-of-spore-women (accessed January 20, 2021); https://perma.cc/XB4R (accessed January 20, 2021).

Voakes, P.S. (1998). What were you thinking? A survey of journalists who were sued for invasion of privacy. *Journalism and Mass Communication Quarterly* 75 (2): 378–393.

Witness (2018). *Mal-uses of AI-generated Synthetic Media and Deepfakes: Pragmatic Solutions Discovery Convening*. http://witness.mediafire.com/file/q5juw7dc3a2w8p7/Deepfakes_Final.pdf/file (accessed April 20, 2020).

Zelizer, B. (2017). *What Journalism Could Be*. Cambridge: Polity Press.

# 25

# Journalism Routines Depend on Clicks

## Best Practices for Using Metrics in Journalism

Mariza Zapata Vásquez

Nowadays, a click opens up a world of knowledge to us. A quick press of a button or a touch screen is all that it takes to satisfy our curiosity about something someone has said, a photo, a hyperlink, a visual, and so on. In many cases, this simple physical movement can lead to our discovering the most wonderful stories and pictures that are important to our lives – or perhaps the most perverse, tasteless, trivial, and wrongheaded ones.

And that click is how audiences' interests are now measured. It tells us whether or not they are reading us, and whether or not they are engaging with particular topics. All this happens in real time. The number of clicks may tell us whether or not we have a real presence, or whether or not we are surviving as a communication business. We depend on it; we are in thrall to this absolute power that we subject ourselves to; we lose ourselves in despair and then cannot find a way out.

In this chapter, I will outline how journalists' daily routines revolve around the audience on digital platforms, and I will also reflect on what our mission as journalists is and how we can find the right middle ground between this daily pressure that we feel to achieve the goals set each day and our disseminating quality content. The things that we do to add clicks to the metrics must be rigorous and deliberative, and they must be in line with the practices of the prudent and diligent journalist, who, in addition to hitting their target, gives the reader the chance to understand reality better.

It is indisputable that the digital transformation is directly related to our ways of acting and speaking. Companies and industries post their advertisements on the websites that report the most hourly and daily visitors (registered users and subscribers). And, based on those results, advertisements and the agenda for the journalism content to be published are segmented. It is the same logic as that applied in the case of print editions: reader numbers, sales volumes at newsstands, subscriber numbers for the print edition, the socioeconomic groups that subscribers belong to, and so forth. In recent years, a daily effort to win over and keep more digital subscribers has emerged. To repeat: the goal is to gain more of them and then not lose them.

Alongside this, media companies deploy analytical software that allows them to follow their audiences' preferences in real time, before our eyes on the screens installed in newsrooms, in reports that appear on our devices through institutional email accounts, and at daily planning meetings. What do metrics tell us? Everything ends up influencing the topical agenda.

*The Handbook of Communication Rights, Law, and Ethics: Seeking Universality, Equality, Freedom and Dignity*, First Edition. Edited by Loreto Corredoira, Ignacio Bel Mallén, and Rodrigo Cetina Presuel.

Reception of a news story is measured by identifying photos, visuals, headlines, story protagonists, theme development, and topics of focus.

And this is how misguided strategies emerge, through which communication companies and journalists become addicted to figures and begin to distort content, specifically when it comes to the elements that the reader sees first (titles, subtitles, captions, summaries, and so on). This desire to distort can lead to deception. The consequences are serious if we bear in mind that "trust is fundamental to the existence of good, and the need to contribute to furthering good does not impede the journalist's work. Rather, it is the only thing that makes it possible: it must be the pillar of a true journalistic ethos," as Ratzinger (1991, p. 287) highlights.

In addition, journalism is an intellectual activity: we link events with their context in terms of time and place, and we make sense of them so that they are understood and acknowledged by others. "Information must be understood as a cognitive ingredient," according to García-Noblejas (2000, p. 50), "[i]t is oriented toward what philosophy understands as 'species' or 'ideas': the environment in which the known thing becomes present and actualizes the faculty for knowledge of it to materialize. Information consists of actualization, of making the thing present so that knowledge emerges. The 'species' informs the faculty and is the means by which something is immediately known."

To inform is to create, because "there is something that is totally common to expression: creation," Algarra (2003, p. 146) notes. The message, as such, does not exist by itself; it needs to be created by a communicator and constructed through linguistic, visual, or audio resources. This interpretive process entails an intrinsic relationship between good and intellect. And in this process, the message, Galdón (2001, p. 50) argues, must have meaning within a historical evolution, not within isolated events. We need to explain the meaning that things have in themselves and as a result of their impact on us. This is what creates the subsequent need to analyze how, in the almost addictive search for that click, content becomes deformed and misinformed.

## Clicks Set Journalism's Agenda

We might begin by defining what *clickbait* is. *Oxford Dictionary* defines it as "Content whose main purpose is to attract attention and encourage visitors to click on a link to a particular web page" (https://en.oxforddictionaries.com/definition/clickbait). It is a pejorative term that describes content on the Internet that aims to generate advertising revenue via sensationalist headlines. Some authors indicate (Bel Mallén 2020) that it is a practice whose objective is to make users access content that does not correspond to the statement first presented to them. Others characterize it as a hook that takes the form of incomplete and dubious headlines that break the basic features of reporting or distort all the traditional rules of producing journalistic statements.

Marín (2019, pp. 18–19) describes this fixation on headlines as follows:

> Although the headlines of stories have always been very important, they are now crucial ... On the Internet, selecting what to read and what not to is much more dramatic. The reader of a digital page faces a jumble of dozens of headlines. As a result, the contest between headlines to attract the attention of this type of reader—who is usually much more distracted than readers of print editions are—becomes a vicious fight.

Headlines of this kind are devoid of meaning or newsworthiness, and they trample on the first level of reading, namely the who, what, why, when, where, and how – that is, the structural characteristics of journalism on which all our work is focused – because these things have no value here. There is no creativity applied to produce a grammatical and semantic structure that respects informative value or the main ideas of the news-story construction. They are produced based on keywords, are easy to locate, and win clicks when someone reads them. Headlines obtain better positioning as they are the part of the story that appears on search engines. Keywords go beyond the headlines, the first paragraph of the journalism piece, subheads, other paragraphs of the story, final paragraph, intertitles, captions, and so forth. While use of keywords as a way of writing headlines is part of the news-construction process in digital journalism – in contrast to the printed format, in which a grammatical sequence is respected – the digital journalist often neglects their duty to disseminate an accurate and consistent statement, depending on the audience size they wish to achieve.

There are also headlines that are expressed as direct or indirect questions, answers to which we did not find upon clicking. But, by then, the click has already been counted, and that is what matters. It all adds up, and it is a strategy for recruiting readers. A story's headline often does not respond to traditional journalistic criteria, and its ultimate goal is to keep readers on the page as long as possible rather than to inform them. Palau-Sampio (2016, pp. 67–68) also identifies clickbait with an approach to formulating titles that, in contrast to news-report headlines, appeals to curiosity via humor, emotion, or classic baits such as sex. She also indicates that it is an important resource for stimulating digital traffic and new media's ability to attract advertising.

That is why the clickbait phenomenon is framed within the so-called attention economy (Roca 2008), which relates to the competition that content generators engage in to attract the public's interest and monetize it within a market that is saturated by information stimuli, as well as to create suspense. Rigor and creativity are pushed aside in this endeavor. The media's digital evolution is no longer only technological but also linguistic and communicative. Storytelling has become a key factor in connecting with readers, whose interest is caught by language that excites and appeals to them and that calls for new linguistic and digital training (Albaladejo 2011).

These stories ultimately become news. It is a vicious circle that some digital media outlets now find it difficult to escape from. The anecdotal, domestic experiences, and trivial dialogs have become news. We no longer attach importance to context and analysis. Isolated stories yield to well-told ones, not only because of narrative or the good use of language, but because of the investigative structure of combining text and context well to achieve a better understanding of the facts. We find photo galleries devoid of stories or content and with so-called captions that offer no explanations and only respond to the desire for more page views or longer visit durations.

Let us look at some examples of electronic publications that show this focus on the anecdotal and entertainment. The homepage of www.ojo.pe, a publication based in Lima (Peru), has featured: "The moment a tiger tries to catch a wild dog"[1] and "Corazón Serrano: Lesly Águila put on weight in quarantine and shared a photo of her new figure."[2] On republic.pe, we find "Senior says goodbye to her little dog and he surprises her with moving reaction (recommended video)"[3] and "He never had a dog, his girlfriend gave him one, and the two share a tender moment."[4]

[1] https://ojo.pe/locomundo/youtube-viral-el-instante-en-que-un-tigre-intenta-atrapar-a-un-perro-salvaje-video-india-nnda-nnrt-noticia (accessed January 20, 2021).

[2] https://ojo.pe/ojo-show/corazon-serrano-cantante-subio-de-peso-en-cuarentena-y-muestra-foto-de-su-nueva-figura-web-ojo-noticia (accessed January 20, 2021).

[3] Video available at https://larepublica.pe/tendencias/2020/05/16/facebook-viral-anciana-se-despide-de-su-pequeno-perro-y-este-tiene-conmovedora-reaccion-animales-mexico-mx-redes-sociales-video (accessed January 20, 2021).

[4] Video available at https://larepublica.pe/tendencias/2020/05/17/youtube-viral-nunca-tuvo-un-perro-su-novia-le-regalo-un-cachorro-y-ambos-terminan-en-adorable-escena-video-animales-mascotas-redes-sociales-rddr (accessed January 20, 2021).

## The Page View Dictatorship

Among the content created for the digital version of Mag.com, a platform that belongs to the Lima-based El Comercio Group, of the 95 most-viewed pages for the week from May 11 to 17, 2020, 50 are stories that refer to showbusiness and film and TV figures, and 23 of them are classified as viral; a metric that measures the source of their initial access, in this case through Facebook, a social network in which information is shared over and over again and disseminates through networks of users. From this latter set, it is interesting to note that the piece "Woman makes homemade bread and her reaction to taking it out of the oven goes round the world"[5] spent the whole week at the top of the most-viewed list. One day it was accessed 801 742 times.

One would think that local economic affairs would elicit great interest but only 16 local economics news-items appear in the 95 most-viewed pages. At the bottom of the list, we found two items on sports and one about a music tutorial, accessed via WhatsApp. In analyzing the previous list, it is important to specify that the most viewed stories are accessed through social-media platforms, where they are virally distributed. This accounts for the high number of views these stories have received.

Salaverría (2014, p. 19) has linked "viral journalism to the intensive use of social networks, which affects the way in which news is selected and produced and makes journalism extremely competitive." They aim only to boost the success of stories. "Media publications ... share news on Twitter at strategic times to increase attention to it on Twitter; they include videos edited for release on Facebook. ... In short, the objective is to create journalism that becomes inoculated with the ease of a virus," he points out. Diaz Nosty (2015, p. 15) describes this as the trivialization of journalism: "The great bazaar of the media spectacle, which integrates information as a sort of miscellany of dramatic, intriguing events or ones that star celebrities, has abandoned its natural environment and infected spaces formerly protected by journalistic quality." There is no space for a critical spirit; what we find are short stories with no logical narrative thread, "barely argued and made necessary by the constructive requirements of the digital format" (Nosty 2015, p. 16).

We have new ways of communicating messages, and these have completely changed the way journalism works. We have new tools derived from the characteristics of digital language – multimedia, hypertextuality, and interactivity – and we make them available for inconsequential stories just to follow what an audience metric says. Journalism content and potential topics have to adapt to reading formats that are fragmented and dispersed, as well as delivered through different devices and in dissimilar formats of discursive representation. Access to this content is detrimental to both the journalist and the audience. The journalist becomes desperate and begins to prioritize clicks over genuine newsworthiness.

Once the selection and creation process is complete,[6] a process that entails contacting sources and checking facts, some journalists then ask themselves how the story will be represented (journalistic format, photos, audio, video, graphics), how they will hierarchize the different elements, and how they will structure the statements, the language, and so on – all in order to get clicks. This leads to referential photos that do not fit the story told, or the time it happened, or the people who are involved in it. The same is true of videos. And if there are photos, a description of the images or an explanation of the context in which they were captured is not deemed to be of interest to the reader. All that appears is a string of photographs

[5] https://mag.elcomercio.pe/virales/facebook-viral-mujer-realiza-pan-casero-y-su-reaccion-al-sacarlo-del-horno-da-la-vuelta-al-mundo-video-rdcnmg-noticia (accessed January 20, 2021).

[6] The approach of value-added journalism proposed by Pellegrini et al. (2011, p. 41) "distinguishes between two areas of professional development of news: examination of the news in the world (a selection process) and the ways in which the journalist processes that news to report on it (a creation process)."

without text that the reader looks at over and over, the aim being to increase the metric corresponding to page-viewing time. The time the reader spends looking at the written, graphic, visual, or oral story is the most important priority.

Sites' pages exploit hypertext to divert readers attention to unconnected or anecdotal content that neither contributes to nor adds to understanding of the stories being read. And interactivity is only put to use for sharing texts on social networks and making messages go viral. There is no feedback or system for direct engagement in which Internet users' comments add content to the story.

In this regard, the social network Facebook has created its business based on tracking of its users to ascertain their interests and store information about their lives, all with the aim of developing a news-distribution strategy that captures users' attention. According to Cetina Presuel and Martinez Sierra (2019, p. 270), these platforms "make editorial decisions about when and where content is made available to the user, even if those decisions are not directly implemented by a human, but through automated processes designed by humans." They add that "algorithms can work automatically, and some of them can also learn and evolve on their own, but because they are created by people, they are subject to the opinions, values, and even biases and errors of those who have programmed them" (p. 270). This is similar to decisions made in a newsroom for a print or digital news edition.

Cetina Presuel and Martinez Sierra (2019) point out that Facebook's algorithms decide what may be of interest to a particular user, when users will see particular content, and the order in which content appears. Ultimately, the goal of Facebook's algorithms is to choose what is most relevant, selecting stories and displaying them in news feeds to keep users engaged with the platform for as long as possible.

Many web pages, in their eagerness for advertising, have taken advantage of Facebook's algorithms for news sections and made use of engagement bait, whose objective is to attract users to take action on a certain publication and interact with it. This is why Facebook started a project in 2017 to delete publications and pages that used these methods and thus to ensure that user interaction is always spontaneous and authentic. User comments have become important, and in the repertoire of emotions the options "love," "haha," "wow," "sad," and "angry" are now being considered. These other emotional reactions are more important to the algorithm; they are "active" emotions that require more effort than simply clicking the "like" button by default. On top of this is time spent on the page and the date and time of the publication.[7]

## An Ethical Proposal: The Journalist's Prudence in Decision Making

Thus far in this chapter, I have sketched out an overview of the creation of digital journalism content, but a way out of the situation that I have described has to be found, and there is one. We cannot avert our eyes and be indifferent to the idea of "digital first," which embodies the shift that has taken place in newsrooms in recent years to create an agenda. It cannot be denied that this is what routines are like now, and it is making us, as journalists, dependent on page views and visit times.

Furthermore, journalists have to deal with other fronts: immediacy, multimedia, hypertextuality, temporality (in the sense not only of publishing the initial story as quickly as possible but also of constantly providing updates as it develops), universality, and interactivity, characteristics of the digital language that are affecting our ways of communicating and our actions.

---

[7] https://fg.ull.es/noticias/2020/01/08/cautiva-en-facebook/#:~:text=El%20cambio%20m%C3%A1s%20significativo%20en,empresas%2C%20marcas%20y%20medios%20de (accessed January 20, 2021).

These qualities will set the path for decision making and the choice of the most effective tools to communicate a message in the most appropriate way forward – one that will lead us to the truth and win the click we long for. We can no longer escape dependency on them and what they dictate. The only thing that remains, as a form of coexistence, is to find a fair way for that click to lead us to a more reflective text that complies with journalism's true mission.

Our way of communicating and our routines – that is, acting with deep ethical roots, being quick and efficient in defining points of view or approaches at the moment of identifying newsworthy events, verifying them in the investigative phase, and then giving them shape through the different types of languages – have changed.

Most studies of journalistic routines link them to day-to-day ways of acting. The consensus between editors and editors-in-chief focuses on what should be reported following criteria of newsworthiness such as topicality, proximity, interest, and respect for the common good, among others. But that consensus needs to be studied from the perspective of journalism – that is, the formation of habits and virtues as an indissoluble form of daily work.

The debate centers on: How to reach a consensus given that a news story has to be uploaded immediately to the platform so that users click the title that appears in the browser and do not do so on another website. Minutes matter, and a head start on the news is required to take on the competition. At this stage of the process, the journalist often acts as a repeater of messages (texts, photos, videos, things people have said, and so on) just as a way of increasing the number of clicks in their daily output. In other words, the journalist only quotes what someone else has said (source or official document), or shares information heard by chance, without offering the public the historical and social context in which the quoted material was issued.

In practice, immediacy means that no consensus is arrived at, and the journalist is the person who must evaluate which text to send, if a single headline is required to achieve good SEO (search engine optimization).[8] In this part of the process, it does not matter whether the reader, having clicked, finds a developed story; one piece of information is sufficient. The story is uploaded with the details later on. Acting prudently is vital at this point in journalistic work, as this is where the biggest mistakes are made. What is the best decision? Waiting until all the facts have been checked and contextualized and then sharing them. It may be just a number or an important statement, but it will be verified.

A routine is a habit, a permanent disposition, an active state of being that, according to the Aristotelian framework, is directly linked to prudence, a virtue that intersects with the journalist's acts. Aristóteles (2005) defines prudence as "excellence in deliberation," "intelligence" as an "ability to understand," "consideration," or "judgment." But sound deliberation is what leads us toward good. "Prudence concerns human things and those about which it is possible to deliberate. Because the activity of the prudent person is, above all, this: deliberating well …. And the good deliberator [the journalist], in general, is the one who achieves, following reasoning, the best of things achievable by man through action" (2005, 1141B., p. 190). The rigorous message, be it written, oral, or visual, requires an action, a deed, adapting reality to knowledge through verification, comparison, good management of linguistic resources, and so on. That makes the journalist a prudent, deliberative man.

José María Desantes (1988, pp. 34–25) indicates that news-making duties imply a duty of care that, in any situation, is required by law, negatively (negligence or fault) or positively demanding proportionate attention. Desantes saw the duty of care as involving attentive performance. On the other hand, he adds, negligence supposes abandonment, trivialization, carelessness, boredom.

---

[8] https://www.oxfordlearnersdictionaries.com/definition/english/search-engine-optimization (accessed January 20, 2021); A set of actions and techniques that is used to improve the search engine positioning (visibility) of a website on the Internet.

At the same time, deliberation has to do with the contingent, which varies according to individuals and circumstances (Aunbenque 2010, p. 31). It is related to our projection of what is going to happen in the future, even more so if, in view of the immediacy with which the dissemination of information in digital formats is undertaken, we have to constantly evaluate the consequences of the data disseminated and of the story told. And this evaluation is a *sine qua non* condition of prudence. Galdón (2006) states: "Journalism should take into account much more foresight of the personal and social consequences of information, both individually and as a whole.... When [messages] must be communicated, one must have the delicacy and finesse of a good surgeon to focus on them with the right perspective and gaze [and with truth]. The gaze, which fixes on or emphasizes one thing or another, is essential."

Therefore, "a disregard for prudence in journalists' narratives," Chillón (2007, p. 117), "would reduce the profession to a mere technical process that is learned through practice. The relevance of and effort involved in working with records would be disregarded, considered reflection on daily work would be excluded, and there would be use of literary and rhetorical devices with a different meaning from that of expression of informational truth."

And on that diligent path to ascertaining the truth is objectivity. Carlos Soria, in the prologue to Greene's book (Greene 2012, p. 14), defines objectivity as "an attitude, as a predisposition of reporters—in the midst of social environmental circumstances and pressures—to silence their own inner world, opening to the greatest degree their physical, intellectual, and moral eyes to adapt knowledge to reality—with the conviction that human knowledge is finite and never exhausts the known reality."

Greene (2012, p. 171) says that objectivity is not synonymous with truth, but rather a guarantee that the subject can offer regarding their disinterested pursuit of truth, and, as Soria adds, this is a matter of detachment from the journalist's own values that could skew a story and avoid controversy. It is to free oneself from prejudice to make decisions that, in the case of the prudent journalist, are indispensable when observing and processing news events. It is openness to reality, which implies respect for the nature of things and the effort to discover it, as Galdón emphasizes (1994, pp. 198–201) in describing the journalist's sense of realism, which combines with the critical sense required in considered reflection on sources and reality, to reach unrushed judgments and practical decisions, "hence critical sense is not only a 'desideratum,' a good goal, but a necessary condition for carrying out journalism activities in accordance with their nature."

Therefore, according to Soria, the obstacles to objectivity – to that effort to discover reality – are pragmatism, euphemism, and ambiguity, practices that are directly related to some journalistic content strategies, especially in digital formats. The lack of time to verify newsworthy facts, for that triangulation of content to which Greene refers, is also an obstacle, as is media politics. And now, with digital media, added to these obstacles is the obsession with the first fruits that are reaped in real time in response to stiff competition between media outlets.

## The Case of the Newspaper *El Comercio*: Producing Quality Content and Winning Clicks

But how to achieve that balance of focusing journalists' actions on the search for truth without turning away from the new business model? How can our prudent actions make us get clicks without applying misinformation trickery or lacking rigor? *El Comercio de Lima* (Peru) has long set out to give added value to its stories, which it shares on its digital version (www.elcomercio.pe), and it aims to supplement the characteristics and tools of digital language to properly tell good stories (analyzed and contextualized ones), so that its readers understand the messages published. All through a click. This is the right balance and the consensus that I previously mentioned. Chillón (2007, p. 173) specifies that the "practical truth established in that reading of Aristotle opens up the way for us to take the view that the daily, personal, and professional decisions faced by a journalist are manifestations of that interest in conveying comprehensible, useful information (in best sense of the term) that is contextualized and adapted for the public."

*El Comercio* seems to have grasped this, and though it continues to depend on clicks, it has set out to improve the content that it publishes in its digital edition. "We appreciate the number of people who visit our website, but what we value, above all, is their staying to read our content, as well as our content's being helpful and interesting to them, its changing their day, and its helping them to make decisions. The objective for the digital platform is no longer just to have people visit it, but, above all, for them to find our website engaging."[9] Moreover, "The newsroom seeks users' loyalty in metrics such as reader engagement time. Internet users are target benchmarks for traffic, and page visits are indicators for the business side, but these should not matter more than measurement of the time users spend on pages. We want fans, not sporadic readers who click and leave immediately,"[10] as is the case of the *New York Times* and some media outlets in the region such as *O Globo* in Brazil and *La Tercera* in Chile.

The daily data provided by *El Comercio*'s Digital Intelligence Unit show the topics best received by digital readers and therefore make it possible to prepare the content agenda for the printed edition. The latter benefits from the news produced for the web, which goes through an optimization process so that reading the printed newspaper complements the digital version's content. This supposes a change in the classic journalism routine.

With these added values, it can be concluded that a report "worked well" and that it marks out the path that the print edition's agenda should follow and the agenda to be prepared for the next few days. But what does "worked well" mean when it comes to daily routines? The answer is a high number of page views, a story that interested people, and good language use in the story. Based on these indicators, daily goals are set for each section in terms of the number of generic and registered users and subscribers. Averages are established per month, per week, and per day for numbers of page views, viewing times, and navigation in general. Metrics indicate the success or failure of a report or a column. Therefore, there has been a 360-degree shift in decision making. We think about digital first, then print.

But journalists know that stories must be sought out. And by using the formats and tools that the digital environment gives us, "stories are told through videos, databases are used, Twitter threads are opened up, and readers' habits are measured and understood. We know the time of day when they connect and how long they engage with stories, and from these measurements the best formats are chosen and adapted to suit each investigation," says Aurelio Arévalo, loyalty and projects editor at *El Comercio de Lima*.

Consequently, *El Comercio*'s editorial team has given priority to three clearly distinct branches: one responsible for the printed edition (of which I am a part); another for digital management that seeks to innovate to mix languages and narratives according to what the new tools provide; and a third that oversees the creation of suitable content for both editions (digital and print) of the newspaper.

As we are seeing, content-innovation projects have become important in this change. Salaverría (2014, p. 22) calls this "laboratory journalism": "The media needs to devise new editorial formulas, technologies, languages, and ways of connecting with the public. Labs are proving to be a useful tool in this regard. But, with or without them, innovation is a challenge that the media will have to tackle if it aspires to definitively turn the page on the crisis and finally open a new phase of hope for journalism."

---

[9] https://elcomercio.pe/lima/asi-es-la-transformacion-digital-de-el-comercio-noticia (accessed January 20, 2021).

[10] https://elcomercio.pe/lima/cuales-son-las-5-claves-de-la-transformacion-digital-de-el-comercio-noticia (accessed January 20, 2021).

In line with this, *El Comercio*, like the *New York Times*,[11] has given its historical archive a more active life by updating stories about heroic sporting performances or political activities via photo galleries that work well in print and digital editions.

## Journalists' Self-reinvention and Narrative Innovations: The Case of the #Notepases Campaign

It is necessary to identify the best story to tell. In this business, there is a need to keep going and to monetize; this is what we repeat to ourselves over and over again, every day in content-planning meetings. While this perspective is correct, it is also true that in the daily task of creating content and developing it in the most appropriate formats, the media as an organization and journalists themselves also take time to reflect on how we manage to reconcile the overwhelming desire to meet the daily target for number of page views with quality content. That is the challenge. Reinventing oneself as a journalist and innovating are the order of the day.

In April 2018, *El Comercio* launched the #Notepases ("don't do that") hashtag as the first journalism campaign created for the digital format and the comprehensive multimedia plan. This is a campaign on transportation in Lima that corresponded to journalism's supervisory function with an emphasis on changes in the system of public organization and the role of serving the community by effectively following up on stories. That is, the idea was for stories to have a social impact and for there to be leadership over the public agenda. In addition, the reports confirmed that readers identify with problems that require urgent attention. Journalism content that is close to readers' lives, more in empathetic terms than geographic ones, finds greater acceptance among audiences because the problems described echo their own daily experiences and because the pieces additionally propose solutions to those problems. This is why Galdón (2001, p. 51) specifies that "language must be adapted both to the type of reality in question and to readers' cultural and intellectual capacities, their habits and customs, and their backgrounds."

From April 1, 2018, to January 29, 2019, 235 stories were published on the *El Comercio* website within the #Notepases campaign. The stories generated 5.8 million page views in this period. "The report *This is what it's like to spend an hour traveling with the worst driver in Lima*[12] about a driver who ran an illegal bus service and had been issued with 147 tickets, achieved an average reading time of almost five minutes, a figure above the general average, and one that indicates readers' interest in undertaking an in-depth consultation on the subject. On social networks, the indicators were more than encouraging. We take as a priority the high level of engagement generated by the publication on Facebook, where more than 77 videos on the subject were posted, obtaining over 14 million views. On this social network, #Notepases generated more than 450 000 reactions and 94 000 comments, and the message was shared across 180 000 accounts" (*El Comercio*, May 2019).

The documentary film "The beast of Petit Thouars"[13] was then released as part of the campaign. According to *El Comercio*'s reports, the video had more than 430 000 minutes of play

---

[11] https://ijnet.org/es/story/c%C3%B3mo-el-new-york-times-ha-cambiado-partir-de-su-informe-de-innovaci%C3%B3n (accessed January 20, 2021).

[12] https://elcomercio.pe/lima/sucesos/viajar-hora-peor-conductor-lima-video-notepases-noticia-512485-noticia (accessed January 20, 2021).

[13] https://elcomercio.pe/lima/transporte/bestia-petit-thouars-coaster-pirata-resume-caos-transporte-lima-noticia-ecpm-616934-noticia (accessed January 20, 2021).

time, and it was mostly watched by a young audience aged between 25 and 34 who shared the documentary 2328 times. "Here 'sentiment' about the publication made it possible to know what the user thinks and to be attentive to any particular need that would serve as an input to expand the context or follow up on new topics" (*El Comercio*, May 2019).

Another documentary, "A license for a blind man,"[14] which was also part of the #Notepases campaign, obtained 174 000 views, 2700 reactions, 485 comments, and 2977 shares. It enjoyed a high level of virality. The link with the print edition was satisfactory: there was a video for the digital edition and a well-written story with a series of photos for the print version. They complemented and dialoged with each other.

The success[15] of these campaigns, as reflected in the high number of page views, which at a discursive level managed to supplement all of digital language's tools and characteristics with an understandable and empathetic narrative thread, led to the launch of the #Estamoshartas ("we're fed up") campaign[16] to address the theme of violence against women in Peru. The campaign is very similar to the #MeToo movement. In March 2019, 22 pieces (reports, first-hand accounts, and interviews) were published as part of the campaign, achieving 2.6 million views on Facebook. In addition, 23 373 million likes, 8474 shares, and 4274 comments were generated. The videos published on Facebook during this campaign elicited 474 368 views and 257 403 minutes of playing time.

These figures indicate volume, thousands of clicks, but success lies in the difference in the content. It demonstrates innovation with wisdom and prudence. Wisdom to search for new stories that connect with our audiences and to choose the appropriate types of language (visual, written, and verbal) that help us to better convey and construct those stories and their pertinence. And prudence in our actions, to make the fairest decisions and always to look at the whole and not at isolated events. This is how to get clicks.

## Conclusions

The digital transformation has forced media companies to change the routines they use in the news-construction process. Some have become desperate and focused their business strategies on racking up clicks. Their aim is to increase the volume of the metrics without adding value to the content they disseminate. Thus, the anecdotal, the inconsequential, and the anodyne become newsworthy events and are shared on social networks and websites, to the point of deception. All semantic and grammatical coherence is broken through the headlines to engage audiences. As I have said, SEO prevails. In such cases, its arbitrariness becomes perverse and, consequently, the duty to report a truthful and understandable message is not fulfilled. The journalist acts as a repeater of texts, photos, videos, and things that people have said solely to increase the number of clicks recorded.

Journalism routines have adapted to the demands of digital language. Two of these, immediacy and timeliness **(the constant updating of news events is part of the process of creating content in digital media)**, cannot be avoided by the media, and they have forced

[14] https://elcomercio.pe/lima/sucesos/peru-falta-ver-brevete-documental-notepases-noticia-581013-noticia (accessed January 20, 2021).

[15] In total, the #Notepases campaign's videos had had 50 million views by October 2019. It has also received several international recognitions and awards, such as Asociación Internacional de Medios de Noticias (INMA) prizes in the categories Best Community Service Campaign and Best Campaign in Latin America and an award from Grupo de Diarios América, which groups 11 media, in the category Best Innovative Editorial Offering.

[16] https://especiales.elcomercio.pe/?q=especiales/estamos-hartas-ecpm/index.html (accessed January 20, 2021).

publications to make a complete reversal in managing the news agenda and in their content-selection processes: "First digital and then print." Therefore, the demands of providing news coverage have changed, and it has become imperative to act more prudently and diligently in decision making, bearing in mind that journalism is an intellectual endeavor guided by practical morality that seeks suitable communication of knowledge. Immediacy and temporality lead to competition and confrontation between the media, conditioning the behavior of editors and journalists in general, and in the process mistakes and deceits can be committed that completely distort the nature of journalism.

From the ethical perspective that leads the journalist to the search for truth, harmony between volume and quality can be achieved, and it is possible to obtain thousands of clicks (page views) and engage readers with a well-crafted story that respects all the demands of rigor. In planning processes, which are part of journalism routines, discussions and consensus between journalists revolve around how stories will be represented: a video, a photo, a visual, a text with hyperlinks that serve to contextualize the story and allow its origins and consequences to be understood. This is why journalists rely on digital tools such as hypertextuality and multimedia, which allow the media to innovate in improving journalism content.

With the journalistic #Notepases and #Estamoshartas campaigns, *El Comercio de Lima* (Peru) demonstrated that obtaining healthy metrics and producing quality journalism can coexist in these new business strategies. Innovation is fundamental, but even more important is journalists' acting diligently, thoughtfully, and ethically as they seek out the truth as a good.

## References

Albaladejo, T. (2011). Accesibilidad y recepción en el discurso digital: la galaxia de discursos desde el análisis interdiscursivo. In: *Un nuevo léxico en la red. Universidad Rey Juan Carlos*, 15–28. Madrid: Dykinson Bookstore-Editorial.

Algarra, M. (2003). *Teoría de la comunicación: Una propuesta*. Madrid: Tecnos.

Aristóteles (2005). *Ética a Nicómaco. Alianza Editorial* (trans. J.L. Calvo Martínez). España: Alianza editorial.

Aunbenque, P. (2010). *La prudencia en Aristóteles*. Buenos Aires: Colección Mitma.

Bel Mallén, I. (2020). *La ética informativa, un reto en la era de la posverdad*. Valencia: Tirant lo Blanch.

Cetina Presuel, R. and Martínez Sierra, J. (2019). Algorithms and the news: social media platforms as news publishers and distributors. *Revista de Comunicación* 18 (2): 261–285.

Chillón, J.M. (2007). La verdad periodística. En busca de un nuevo paradigma Universitas Philosophica. *Año* 24 (48): 95–125.

Desantes, J.M. (1988). *El deber profesional de informar Lección magistral leída en la apertura del curso 1988–89*. Valencia: Fundación Universitaria San Pablo CEU

Galdón, G. (1994). *Desinformación, método, aspectos y soluciones*. Pamplona: Eunsa.

Galdón, G. (2001). *Introducción a la comunicación y la información*. Barcelona: Ariel Comunicaciones.

Galdón, G. (2006). De la objetividad a la prudencia. Hacia un paradigma informativo humanista. *Revista Comunicación y Hombre*. https://portalderevistas.ufv.es/index.php/comunicacionyhombre/article/view/82/527 (accessed July 28, 2020).

García-Noblejas, J. (2000). *Comunicación borrosa. Sentido práctico del periodismo y de la ficción cinematográfica*. Pamplona: Eunsa.

Greene, M. (2012). *La objetividad como rutina periodística*. Pamplona: Eunsa.

Nosty, B. D. (2015). La banalización del periodismo. *Cuaderno de Periodistas* 31. http://www.cuadernosdeperiodistas.com/la-banalizacion-del-periodismo (accessed September 19, 2020).

Marín, B. (2019). *La tiranía del clic*. España: Turner Publicaciones.

Palau-Sampio, D. (2016). Metamorfosis de la prensa de referencia en el contexto digital: clickbait y estrategias de tabloide en Elpais.com. *Communication & Society* 29 (2): 63–80.

Pellegrini, S., Puente, S., Porath, W. et al. (2011). *Valor Agregado Periodístico (la apuesta por la calidad de Noticias)*. Ediciones Universidad Católica de Chile. https://www.researchgate.net/publication/330094011_Valor_Agregado_Periodistico_La_apuesta_por_la_calidad_de_las_noticias/link/5c2d2ddf92851c22a3562e2c/download (accessed July 28, 2020).
Ratzinger, J. (1991). *Cooperadores de la verdad*. Madrid: Rialp.
Roca, M. (2008). Rethinking entertainment. Entrevista a Marty Kaplan. *Trípodos* 23: 135–143.
Salaverría, R. (2014). Periodismo en 2014: balance y tendencias. *Cuadernos de periodistas* 29: 9–22.

# 26

# Epilogue

Ignacio Bel Mallén and Marisa Aguirre Nieto

From the moment the idea for this book took shape, the intention was to thoroughly investigate the relationship between the law and ethics of communication, the ways in which communication professionals can protect the essential object of communication rights – information and messages – and the role played by citizens in both the enjoyment of freedoms and the fulfillment of responsibilities that communication entails in free societies. As can be seen, the scope of the work was always ambitious because it involved establishing bridges between theory and reality, detecting things on the margins that had been left undefined, and dealing with various issues that the global society has raised. As they addressed these subjects, the contributing authors – university professors and researchers, most of whom have many years of experience – detected inconsistencies, gaps in need of filling, and new situations created by the development of society itself and revolutionary advances in technology.

Upon reading the studies that the book comprises, we found well-documented responses to many of these issues that represent advances within the two subjects on which the work is founded: communication law and communication ethics. Taking the object communication rights as their starting point, the studies are based on an undeniable basic idea: the reality of communication as a broad phenomenon that amounts to a pillar of society. One's participation in social life is predicated on an awareness of what is happening; the scope of this proposition expands greatly when we begin to consider social life in global rather than local terms. From the perspective of law, there is one thing that protects this right: communication, through the creation of information based on truth and objectivity. This volume has demonstrated this point.

Across the gamut of communication activities, there exists a multitude of situations that depend on the decisions made by the information-imparting subject. Because these decisions are located in that subject's inner world, law has no place, but ethics does. The duty to inform thus becomes a bundle of ethical duties. The moment when protection of this reality took on the form of Article 19 of the Universal Declaration of Human Rights of 1948, which establishes the universal right to "freedom of opinion and expression" and is still considered the basis of communication law and communication rights, is recent history. The first part of this book offers an in-depth analysis of the universality stemming from this declaration and serves as a departure point for the subsequent chapters. One of the main pillars on which it rests is freedom in relation to subjects and their rights. However, in view of the challenges posed by

*The Handbook of Communication Rights, Law, and Ethics: Seeking Universality, Equality, Freedom and Dignity*, First Edition. Edited by Loreto Corredoira, Ignacio Bel Mallén, and Rodrigo Cetina Presuel.

the twenty-first century's permanently connected societies, it was necessary to review and rethink at least some aspects of those rights.

Article 19 of the Universal Declaration of Human Rights, analyzed at length in several chapters of the volume and from different perspectives and continents, specifies in light of human dignity – another topic studied here – the right to "seek, receive and impart information and ideas" as an aspect of the right to freedom of opinion and expression that gives shape to communication rights. However, the meaning of this right can be problematic if a distinction is not made between imparting information in traditional media such as newspapers and doing so on social media such as Twitter or Facebook.

Therefore, current technology's features pose new challenges related to communication rights that needed to be explored. The book, as a whole, addresses those realities and offers theorizing about communication rights as they have been developed in Spain, France, the United States, various Latin American countries (including Mexico, Chile, and Peru), and jurisdictions elsewhere such as Australia and Hong Kong. This focus made it possible to identify universal ideas and concepts that represent common ground between all conceptions of communication rights; our aim was to establish a path toward the universalization of concepts which, in turn, will serve to universalize communication rights.

The study of a framework for messages and subjects has turned out to be an ideal endeavor for understanding and addressing communication disorders and disinformation itself, which, curiously, is occurring in a world that is well equipped in technological terms. We know that technological progress also has the potential to become a powerful weapon capable of destroying the social order and corrupting consciences if it does not facilitate fair and truthful information – that is, if it does not comply with law and ethics. For this reason, a concept such as post-truth seems to be a concrete threat that requires thought. What value can an impressive treatment of some matter of universal interest have if it turns out to be false, deceptive, or meaningless because an explanation of it is lacking? Technology allows us to see things, connect, and be where the news is happening. But does it allow us to understand? And if technology is not conceived with reality in mind, can it inform? Does it offer time for reflection? We have confirmed that it cannot.

Another important topic that the contributors studied and investigated concerns disinformation. This book maintains that the challenge faced by dignity in the media comes from the combining of verified facts with fraudulent and fabricated constructions and with different user-focused viral techniques such as astroturfing, networks of fake followers, targeted advertising, and meme campaigns, as well as with other activities that violate users' rights – for example, doxing, organized trolling, and deepfakes.

Disinformation can also involve a wide variety of digital behaviors that are more about the flow of it than they are about its production. These behaviors range from publishing and commenting to other activities such as sharing, tweeting, and retweeting. Damage has most obviously been dealt to communication rights, since fake news alters the integrity of communication and the quality of the decisions that citizens make based on the messages they receive from the media. But a less obvious risk of harm concerns dignity, since disinformation is often accompanied by expressions of hatred, defamation, and racial and ethnic abuse which may, in turn, subject an individual or a group to greater segregation, a loss of self-respect, and reputational damage. The idea of what communication should be has been trampled on in very different ways in recent decades.

The situations that we have witnessed leave no room for doubt that some media proprietors have sold out their outlets and corrupted their journalists so that they would write according to the dictates not of their consciences but of money and power. But it is also reasonable to think that there have probably been many honest journalists who have been tainted by circumstances – ones who did not find a way to defend their rights or who had to live with the way things are out of a desire to keep their jobs, at the cost of silencing their consciences. Once again, the individual is important because the professional world places before them new realities, changes, and difficult situations that, as a professional, they must accept and resolve. The public also pays the price here.

An important part of this volume is the set of issues arising from the widespread development of ICTs that have brought about a radical change in the position of subjects in the communication field. We know, for example, that because of ICTs, any citizen can impart information and participate in debates in ways that only the organized media previously could. Accordingly, the boundaries between journalism and other forms of communication or activism become blurred; data are mixed with opinions, truths with lies, news with rumors and hoaxes (so-called fake news); and everything spreads almost immediately in a multiplatform and multimedia environment. As we can see, the overall picture is confusing. The rise of fake news has elicited concern about the consequences that it may have in relation to the future of journalism and the exercise of the communicational aspects of democracy, a subject that several chapters of the book deal with. And that is a valuable contribution, given the importance of this new and widespread phenomenon of post-truth in the context of political communication. Various digital, professional, and academic organizations are trying to tackle the issue and seek solutions, and they have published various documents on the subject. The mutation of political advertising and news into electoral propaganda shows the porosity of boundaries, and it is made more worrying by the foreign interference that has been observed in many electoral processes. When this occurs, the victim is undoubtedly, in addition to democracy, the truth and the objectivity that the news must have. What of these profound ethical issues?

Technologies innovate, change, and develop, but the essential content of rights does not, which means that the right to know the truth is still necessary, regardless of the channels, media, or systems used to transmit information. The purpose of this right to know the truth is to help each individual to form an opinion about what is happening and to arrange their life accordingly. Misinformation or a lack of information creates social disturbance because fake news, rumors, and intrigues that affect the social order proliferate. It is not right to accept what post-truth aims to achieve based on a dubious distinction between what is true and what a person feels is true; the latter is not supported by reality.

Several authors suggest that it is necessary to balance dignity against the incursion of technology and the commercial interests of platforms and the fake-news business, to protect human dignity with appropriate regulatory standards, and to consider the ethics of the media, old and new, by taking the approach of viewing the media as an ecosystem. This calls into question practices that are contrary to human dignity, such as profound falsifications that modify the values of discourse.

In addressing the economic and business aspects of media and platforms, the authors of this book agree that a balancing act is required between commercial interests on the Internet as a free market for ideas and the protection of online freedoms, as rights cannot be considered services.

Many topics have been covered, and numerous and very significant conclusions have been derived from each study, but all feature a common element: the need for ethics and law to be aligned and updated to fit the current world's new realities. The book is underpinned by the following argument: there are two realities that we must analyze and defend, when necessary, the essence of communication rights from a point of view that allows the establishment of lines of defense to ensure a genuine exercise of those rights in our times. Those two realities are ethics and law.

One cannot understand the exercise of these rights enshrined in the constitutions of most states – even in the most positivist ones – and their exercise on a daily basis without bringing into play ethical and legal considerations, united in the purpose of obtaining objective, true, and useful information for the citizen. Ethics also has an undoubted advantage over law and the unchanging permanence of the principles that shape it: truth, objectivity, professional secrecy, respect for the democratic game, and so forth. These will always be an immutable reality; they may or may not be defended by the law, but their substance will not change over time.

On the other hand, law has two serious drawbacks when it comes to responding, at any given time, to the requirements of communication rights, which are simply attributable to the changes that occur in society and in communication itself.

One is the difficulty that lawmakers face in responding quickly to the challenges posed by the information society's new communication models. The law needs time to ascertain, evaluate, and compare new realities; communication does not grant it that time. And the second negative factor is the slowness of the law to adapt to the – in many cases astonishing – changes that communication is bringing about in our time. This book contains several examples of situations in which lawmakers, seeking rapid adaptation, head down undesirable paths that, in the long run, could compromise communication rights and even their universality.

Until legal solutions arrive, it is necessary to apply ethical principles that, because they are general in nature, allow for greater adaptability. In short, law and ethics, or vice versa, are two complementary realities in the world of communication. They are mutually necessary and never exclusive but rather complementary. When they join forces, they have a positive impact on communication activity. This is the idea that the pages of this book have sought to convey, whether at the level of broad topics or in chapters that deal with and analyze very specific instances of communication activity, and especially its technological reality, even taking into account the diversity of points of view or debate between the authors.

Problems arise when the two realities, ethical and legal, are forgotten, or one seeks to absorb the other. Normally, this danger occurs more in relation to the excessive prominence of the law, which takes the view that only reason and therefore positive law must illuminate the communication reality, forgetting, if not neglecting, the ethical reality of communication. In these situations, communication suffers, journalists suffer, and, above all, the public, as recipients of information, suffers. Therefore, both realities – law and ethics – must be complementary, and communication professionals, whether they are business people or journalists, must keep in mind the search for a true exercise of communication rights.

# Index

Note: Page numbers followed by 'n' refer to notes.


Abad, L., 17
*Abrams v. United States*, 206
African Charter on Human and Peoples' Rights, 19
Aguirre, J.M., 247
Aguirre Nieto, M., 89, 101n3
Algarra, M., 304
Allan, J., 212
American Convention on Human Rights, 17, 76, 102, 123, 249, 280
Anderson, J.L., 112–113
Arab Charter on Human Rights, 17
Arab Spring, 44
Aristóteles, 308
Aristotle, 25
artistic expression, 35, 50
Ash, G., 54
Assange, J., 261
attitudes, 91, 96, 117, 192, 212, 269, 309
Audiovisual Media Services Directive, 107, 176, 177
Azurmendi, A., 9

Baker, C.E., 212
Balkin, J.M., 180
Bartlett, A., 260
Bateman, J., 293
*Beauharnis v. Illinois*, 213
Bel, I., 2, 20, 32, 90, 91, 102, 221, 275, 304
Beltrán, L.R., 243
Berlin, I., 49
Bernays, E., 186
*Big Brother Watch and others v. the UK*, 126, 128
Bodil Lindqvist, 166–167
Böll, H., 116
Bradlee, B., 113, 116
*Branzburg v. Hayes*, 80
Buchanan, J., 232
Buivids, 169
Buzzfeed, 295

Canel, M.-J., 268
Cañizález, A., 250
Carbonell, E., 152
Castells, M., 150
Castro Fariñas, J.A., 10
Cavaliere, P., 68
Cetina Presuel, R., 307
Chadwick, A., 293n1
Chakravartty, P., 230
Charter of Fundamental Rights of the European Union, 20, 61, 66, 159, 161, 281
  Article, 8, 161–162
Cheng, A., 190
Chillón, J.M., 309, 310
Cicero, 21, 22
citizen journalism, 91, 92, 100
citizen participation, 42, 43, 112
*Claude Reyes et al. v. Chile*, 130
Cohen, J., 38
Cohen-Almagor, R., 214
Colombo, F., 117
common dignity, 29
communication relationship, 91–93
  advertising, public relations, and corporate communication, 97
  independence, 96
  informational truth, 96
  news, informational communication basis, 95
  objectivity, 96
  object of communication rights, messages, 93–95
  opinions and ideas, 96–97
    subjects and geographical divide, equality, 93
communication. *see also individual entries*
  activity, 55, 315, 318
  ethics, 2, 315
  freedom, 38, 243, 244
  law, 1–3, 34, 85, 89, 231, 315
  media, 60, 229
  process, 58, 89–94, 96
  regulation, 163, 229, 230, 234, 237–238
  sectors, 49, 231–233, 235
Communications Authority (CA), 229
Communications Decency Act (CDA), 174
communicators, 92, 94–96, 150, 187, 221, 285, 304
community law, 166
community memory, imperiling, 185–193
  geographic borders, 191–192
  global implications, 192–193
  Internet archives and link to Big Data, 190–191
  national sovereignty, geographic censorship, 192
  public stage, online personas, and digital governance, 188–190
community standards, 63–66, 69
competent authorities, 224
compliance regulation, 143, 144
confidentiality, 82, 121–133
consolation, 21
Constitutional Court, 54, 101, 203
constitutional rights, 101, 202
content moderation, 63, 64, 173, 176, 177, 181, 183
content-neutrality principle, 207, 211
Convention for the Protection of Human Rights and Fundamental Freedoms, 16
Convention on the Elimination of All Forms of Racial Discrimination (CERD), 208, 209, 214
  Article 4 in, 208
Conway III, L., 270
Cooley, C., 243
copyright, 35, 37, 84, 94, 164, 176
Copyright Directive, 176
Corredoira, L., 9, 12, 20, 30, 32, 33, 35, 58, 92, 95, 98, 221



*The Handbook of Communication Rights, Law, and Ethics: Seeking Universality, Equality, Freedom and Dignity*, First Edition. Edited by Loreto Corredoira, Ignacio Bel Mallén, and Rodrigo Cetina Presuel.

cosmopolitan dignity, 28–29
cosmopolitanism, 29
Cotino, L., 92, 221
Council of Europe (CoE), 83, 122, 172, 210, 219
Court of Justice of the European Union (CJEU), 66–69, 163–170, 177
covenants, 15, 16, 35, 38, 50–52, 208, 259
COVID-19, 143, 268
Covlliva, O., 92
crimes, 60, 61, 123, 124, 195–199, 202, 214, 282, 286–288
criminalization, 62, 195–197, 201, 203, 288

D'Arcy, J., 31
data protection, 159–170, 253, 255
 freedom of expression or information, 160–161
 law, 163, 164, 166, 168, 169
 right to data protection, 161–162
Declaration of the Rights of Man and of the Citizen, 13, 16
*De dignitate et excellentia hominis* (Manetti), 23
deepfakes, 140, 293, 294, 316
DeepNude, 294–300
*De excellentia et praestantia hominis* (Fazio), 22
defense, 16, 23, 150, 260, 317
democracy, 42, 53, 55, 77, 82, 84, 85, 210, 217–220, 257, 259, 317
democratic society, 58, 60, 77, 131, 135, 159, 160, 165, 199, 200, 285, 287, 290
denialism, 196, 197, 199
denialist speech, 196, 198
De Pablos-Coello, J.M., 149
Derieux, E., 89
Desantes Guanter, J.M., 43, 49, 89, 94, 113, 114, 151, 152, 308
de Sola Pool, I., 38
Dewey, John, 243
dignity, 20–29, 135–138, 141–143, 212, 316
 cosmopolitan, 28–29
 egalitarian, 26–27
 history of, 21–23
 inviolable, 27–28
 in Kant, 23–24
 litmus test toward compliance law for, 143–144
 resistant to everything, 25
disinformation matrix, 141, 142
disinformation strategies, 138, 218
disinformation, risks of harms, 135–144
 co regulation, 142–144
 COVID-19 infodemic, 143–144
 dignity, 136–138
 EU Code of Practice, 142–144
 mass media and social media, 139–140
 potential risks of harm to information, 136–138
 propaganda, publicity and polarization, 139–140
 proportionate solutions, challenges, 141–142
disseminate information, 33, 35, 37–39, 41, 92, 101
divergences, 2
diversity, opinion, 160
Doan, Edward N., 254
Donahoe, E., 58
doxing, 279, 281–290
 freedom of expression, 282–288
 political, 287–288
 types of, 284–286
Dworkin, R., 55

Eco, Umberto, 112
*The Economist*, 256, 257
egalitarian dignity, 26–28
egalitarianism, 29
electoral campaigns, 139, 217–225
communication, technology, democracy and voting, 217–218
engagement, 274
Esposito, C., 203
ethical principles, 318
ethics, 1, 3–5, 9, 13, 25, 37, 114, 121, 125, 128, 140, 147–154, 218–219, 256, 268, 296, 299, 300, 316–318
EU-Charter of Fundamental Rights (CFR), 160
European Commission Against Racism and Intolerance (ECRI), 210
European Convention of Human Rights (ECHR), 18, 48, 60, 61, 76, 77, 81, 83, 102, 135, 141, 159–162, 165, 167, 168, 170, 198, 199
 Article 10, 199
 Article 17, 199, 202
European Court of Human Rights (ECtHR), 66, 81–83, 85, 102, 105, 122, 124–126, 128–131, 136, 159, 163–169, 174–176, 198–200, 255
European Human Rights Law, 58, 66
European Regulators Group for Audiovisual Media Services (ERGA), 142
Europol, 65–67

facial expressions, 294, 295
fake news, 79, 84, 139, 142, 150, 220, 222, 223, 289, 316–317
Fernández, R., 10
Fernández Areal, M., 113
Ferraro, Matthew F., 299
First Amendment Law, 2
First Amendment right, 83, 174
Fisher, H.H., 230
Flauss, J.-F., 66
Frankfurt, H.G., 114
Fraser, D., 198
Freedman, D., 236
freedom, 9–17, 49, 55, 58, 61, 160, 244–246, 249, 280, 281
 communication rights, 9–19
 existence of, 10–11
freedom of expression, 1, 11–12, 14, 31, 34, 41, 49, 58, 60, 61, 150, 159–161, 167, 170, 176, 181, 195–203, 244, 245, 259, 279–290
 boundaries, 198–203
 defense of, 187, 281
 doxing, 282–288
 exercise of, 175, 178, 183, 208, 224, 281, 287, 290
 importance of, 42, 55
 protection of, 211, 281, 283
 regulation of, 280, 288
 through social networks, 280–282, 288–290
freedom of information, 159–161, 163, 167
freedom of opinion, 1, 14, 16, 31, 50, 53, 54, 58, 60, 97, 101, 150, 160, 161, 163, 167, 170, 181, 244, 245, 259, 280
freedom of religion, 17, 108
freedom of speech, 13, 40, 60, 61, 78, 138, 188, 209
freedom of thought, 17
free expression, 58, 59, 62–64, 75–78, 80–82
free speech triangle, 180
Friedman, M., 230
Friedman, R., 230
Fronza, E., 195, 198, 201
fundamental rights, 13–15, 49, 50, 61, 67, 98, 159–163, 165–167, 210
 protection of, 67, 165, 167

Galdón, G., 304, 309, 311
Gallagher, M., 119
García Márquez, G., 115
García-Noblejas, J., 304
gender, 93, 207, 208, 210
General Data Protection Regulation (GDPR), 66–67, 159, 163, 169, 176, 185
 European Data Protection Directive 95/46/EC (EDPD), 163
 European data protection law, 165, 168
 European Data Protection Regulation, 187, 192, 193
General Policy Recommendation (GPR) No.15, 210
General Recommendation (GR)35, 209
Geneva Declaration, 31
Geographic Censorship, 192
Germany, 104, 108, 143, 175, 177, 178, 196, 197, 200, 201, 211, 214, 222
*Glawischning-Piesczek v. Facebook*, 69
global consensus pursuit, 75–85
Goldman, E., 174
Gómez-Mompart, J.L., 148
*Goodwin v. UK*, 83, 122, 125, 129
Google, 77, 136, 139, 142, 168, 169, 173, 185, 187, 189, 192, 193, 288
Google Spain, 168–169

Government Accountability Project, 127
Greene, M., 309
Grimm, D., 201
*Guja v. Moldova*, 131
Gutiérrez Atala, F., 101n4

Habeas Corpus Act, 12
Habermas, J., 185, 187
Hanitzsch, T., 148
hate speech, 61–64, 81, 196, 205, 207, 208, 210–213, 215, 222
  finding common ground, 211–213
  regulation, 205, 208
  regulation outside United States, 208–211
  restriction, 209–213, 215
  social media problem, 213–214
  in United States and abroad, 205–215
  US experience, 206–208
having rights, preliminary observations, 100–101
  holders of communication rights, 101–103
  holders of right to receive truthful information, 103–104
  holders of right to seek information, 104–106
  holders of right to impart information, 41–43, 245
*Heinisch v. Germany*, 131
*Herrera Ulloa v. Costa Rica*, 249
Heyman, S., 208
Hicks, M., 293
*Hill v. Colorado*, 40
hindrance, 25
historical denialism, 195–203
  crime, 195–203
  European Courts and, 198–203
  harmonization in Europe, 195–198
Hitchens, L., 230
Holmes, O.W., 206
holocaust, 61, 195, 198–201, 211
  denialism, 198–200, 203
Hong Kong, 229–234, 237, 238, 316
Hong Kong communication regulation, 230–233
Houck, S., 270
Hovlid, E., 255
HRC's General Comment No.34, 81, 82
human rights, 9–11, 14–19, 31, 48, 51, 55, 76, 102, 106, 136, 249, 280, 281
  primacy of, 14, 75
  protection of, 67, 249
Human Rights Committee (HRC), 35, 38, 42, 50–52, 76, 77, 81–85, 209
human rights law, 18, 181, 182, 213

indignity, 28
individual expression, 62, 70, 224
individual rights, 10, 12, 13, 34, 81, 248
information
  disseminating, 48, 97, 118, 147, 149
  dissemination, 3, 42, 43, 118
  impart information, 14, 16, 17, 30, 31, 39, 41, 44, 49, 58, 60, 83, 94, 98, 102, 106, 107, 121, 245, 280, 281, 317
  informational truth, 96, 309
  media, 38, 39, 90
  rights, 168, 230
  society, 30, 32–34, 318
  sources, 118, 121, 132
  technologies, 92, 148, 149

information and communication technologies (ICTs), 34, 90, 91, 93, 317
intangible resources, 272, 273, 275
intangible value, 268, 271, 272, 274, 275
Inter-American Commission on Human Rights, 249, 281
Inter-American Court of Human Rights, 106, 241, 244, 248, 251
Inter-American Human Rights System, 280, 281
intermediaries, 53, 101, 102, 131, 173–177, 179, 288
International Agreements on Human Rights, 14–16
International Communication Rights Frameworks, 75–85
international community, 205, 208, 210, 211
International Covenant on Civil and Political Rights (ICCPR), 14–17, 50, 53–55, 58, 60, 76, 77, 81–83, 121, 122, 208, 209
  Article 19 of, 50–52
international human rights law, 76, 77, 180, 209
international law, 52, 55, 68, 69, 81, 180, 181, 205, 280
international organizations, 14, 53, 54, 210, 238, 251
international standards, 77, 178, 180–183, 221
International Telecommunications Union, 31
Internet-based society, 30–44
  related universal rights, 35, **36**, 37
  right to impart information, 41–43
  right to receive information, 40–41
  right to seek information, 39
  technical universality, communication rights, 37–39
  threats to communication rights, 32–33
  universal subject, information society, 33–35
Internet intermediaries regulation, 172–183
  enforcement of law, 177–180
  regulation and human rights, 180–183
  speaker, liable, 173–183
*Ivcher Bronstein v. Peru*, 249

Jack, 293n1
Johnston, J., 255
journalism, 256–257
  clicks set journalism's agenda, 304–307
  *El Comercio*, quality content and winning clicks, 309–311
  ethical proposal, 307–309
  journalist's prudence, decision making, 307–309
  metrics in, 303–313
  #Notepases campaign, 311–312
  page view dictatorship, 306–307
  self-reinvention and narrative innovations, 311–312
journalism, law and ethics, 147–154
  clicks set journalism's agenda, 304–307
  ethical proposal, 307–309
  inextricable triad, 150–152
journalist's prudence, decision making, 307–309
  metrics in, 303–313
  professional empowerment, 152–153
  profession under threat, 147–149
  proposals for immediate future, 153–154
  technology, audiences, and attacks, identity, 149–150
journalistic quality, 148, 306
journalists, 121–133
journalists' sources
  collaborative activism, 127–128
  diligence and limits to right, 128–129
  Europe and Latin America, international recognition, 122–123
  international recognition and regulation, 122
  national regulations, recognition, 123–124
  protection of sources and whistleblowers, 131–132
  right is exceptionally limited and has judicial guarantees, 129
  right's basis, 125
  right to maintain secrecy and silence, 124–125
  source and scope of protection, 124
  special guarantees against searches, 125–127
  subjects who have right and those under obligation, 129–131
  technological activism, 125–127
  technological training and measures, 127–128

Kalven, J.H., 82
Kaye, David, 181
Kearle, B., 254, 255
*Kenedi v. Hungary*, 105
Klonick, K., 180, 181
*Knight First Amendment Institute at Columbia University v. Trump*, 289
Koops, B., 190
Kovach, B., 113, 117

language rights, 245, 248, 250
Larsen, P., 295
Lasswell, H.D., 230

Latin-American countries, 244, 245, 247, 250
Latin American thinking, 241–251
  authors of communication, 250
  communicational thinking, interconnections, 242–243
  emblematic cases, Mexico, 247–248
  human rights and communication, 244–246
  influential and critical thinking, communication, 243–244
  Inter-American Court of Human Rights, emblematic cases, 248–249
  regional struggle, elements of context, 246–247
legacy media, 180, 254, 257, 258
Lerner, D., 230
Lidsky, L.B., 198
Lippmann, Walter, 119
Livingstone, S., 228
Lockie, S., 267, 268, 271, 275
logical truth, 95, 96, 114
Lung, P., 228
Luoma-aho, V., 268

Machiavellianism, 25
Macnamara, J.R., 276, 277
*Magna Carta Libertatum*, 12
*Magyar Helsinki Bizottság v. Hungary*, 130
mainstream media, 137, 139, 258
Marín, B., 304
Marqués de Melo, J., 242
Martínez Sierra, J., 307
mass media, 93, 101, 106, 138, 139, 141, 160, 242, 243, 246, 250
Mateos-Martín, C., 149
*Matúz v. Hungary*, 131
McLuhan, M., 243
media, 37, 38, 40–42, 91, 93, 98, 101, 103, 106, 115, 117, 118, 147, 148, 160, 243, 246, 317
  concentration, 32, 150
  freedom, 43, 136, 160
  ownership, 41
  pluralism, 40, 55, 160, 176
  policy, 230, 236
  regulation, 228–238
media disorder, 253–261 *see also* disinformation
  Assange and WikiLeaks, 257–259
  interpreting journalism, law, 259–261
media regulatory philosophy, 229–230
Meier, K., 148
member states, 14, 15, 65, 67–69, 82, 83, 159, 160, 163, 164, 170, 197, 210
Mendelson, A.L., 292
Merli, A., 203
*Metaphysical Foundations* (Kant), 23, 24
Mill, John Stuart, 206
*Mishkin v. New York*, 60
misinformation, 3, 317
Moller, D., 270
Mora, F., 20
*Nagla v. Latviathe*, 124
narratives, 220, 271–273, 275, 299, 309, 310
negative freedom, 49, 161
neoliberal communication regulator, 234–236
neoliberal tradition
  British colonial days, 230–233
  nation-states, 229–230
news, 111–119
  crimes of journalism and truth, 114–117
  media, 38, 41, 42, 254, 256, 258, 260, 293, 294, 299, 300
  objectivity matters, 111
  professional effort, journalism, 112–113
  professional offerings, objective work, 111–112
  subjectivism, overcoming, 113–114
newsrooms, 111, 112, 292–300, 303, 307, 310
New York, 267, 272
New Zealand Law Commission, 254
NGO Article19, 76
Nosty, D., 306

objectivity, 94, 96, 103, 111, 112, 117, 224, 256, 309, 315, 317
obligations, 65, 124, 125, 129, 160–162, 168, 174–178, 224, 249
O'Flaherty, M., 31
Oller-Alonso, M., 148
O'Loughlin, B., 293n1
*On Duties* (Cicero), 21, 22, 24
online disinformation, 136, 142 *see also* disinformation
online expression, 58, 62, 64, 67, 144
online freedoms, protection of, 140, 317
Online Harms regulatory initiative, 179
online hate speech, 143, 214, 221
opinions, 14, 16, 17, 31, 41, 42, 48, 50, 53, 54, 89, 94, 95, 97, 116, 117, 160, 161, 167, 280
organizational culture, 273
Ortega y Gasset, J., 114
Österreichischer Rundfunk, 165–166
*Ozgür Gündem v. Turkey*, 126

Pact of San José de Costa Rica (Convención Americana sobre Derechos Humanos) 17, 19
Paine, T., 10
Palau-Sampio, D., 148, 305
Parreño, M., 148
Pasquali, A., 2, 241, 243–246, 250, 251
PEN America, 127
*People v. Shivers*, 286
*Perinçek v. Switzerland*, 199, 200
personal data, 108, 159, 161–169, 222, 223, 282, 283
personal information, 67, 190, 283, 286
personal rights, 43, 68, 168
Petrarch, 21
Picard, R., 149
Pieper, J., 113
Pinker, S., 21
polarization, 139, 140, 142, 287
  self-regulation, 220–221
political communication, 217–225, 259, 317
  digital transformation and, 218
  and electoral campaigns, ethics and law, 218–219
  European Standards, 221–222
  hybrid threats and answers, 219–222
  self-regulation, 220–221
political correctness, 117, 137, 237, 269, 270, 274
political doxing, 287–288
political interests, 236–237
political rights, 13–18, 20, 30, 34, 37, 43, 89, 94
Popp, R.K., 292
popular communication, 242
Postman, N., 116
post-truth, 150, 268–271, 274–277, 316, 317
  communication, 269, 274
  politics, 271
*Prager University v. Google LLC*, 174
Preamble and Article 1 of the Charter of Fundamental Rights, 20
Preamble and Article 1 of the International Convention of Civil and Political Rights, 20
Preamble and Article 1 of the Universal Declaration of Human Rights, 20
Preamble of the Charter of the United Nations, 20
press freedom, 42, 83, 125, 150, 231
private community standards, 59, 63, 66
private individuals, 34, 35, 160–162, 164, 169, 191, 221, 287
professional realities, 147–154
Promusicae, 164
protected expressions, 63, 179
*Pruneyard Shopping Center v. Robins* case, 174
public communication, 267–277
public information, 31, 39, 66, 104, 105, 127, 255
public opinion, 97, 186, 187, 191, 192, 218, 219, 223, 224, 237, 238, 268, 271
public–private partnerships, 224
public sector communication, 268
public sphere, 79, 80, 82, 84, 85, 185–187, 189, 229, 230
Puerto Olga, C., 126

*Ramdev v. Facebook*, 69
Ratzinger, J., 304
*R.A.V. v. St. Paul*, 207, 211
Recommendation CM Rec7, 131
Redish, Martin, 206
Reese, S.D., 148
regulations, Europe, 222
Repkea, M., 270
*Ressiot and others v. France*, 126
right of access, 49, 83, 102, 104–106, 130, 245, 248
right of expression, 17, 41, 166, 169, 188
right to be forgotten, 43, 169
right to communicate, 31
right to data protection, 159, 161–164, 166, 170

right to impart information, 41–43, 245
right to information, 18, 31, 49, 118, 164, 250, 258
right to privacy, 167, 221, 225, 283
right to receive information, 40–41
right to seek information, 39
Roberts, S.T., 63
*Roemen and Schmit v. Luxembourg*, 128
Rosen, J., 253
Rosenstiel, T., 113, 117
RTHK, 236, 238
Russo, G., 278

Salaverría, R., 306, 310
Sánchez, Y., 44
Sánchez Ferriz, R., 89, 95
*Sanoma II Uitgevers B.V.*, 128
Sarikakis, K., 230
Satamedia, 167–168, 255
Schacter, D., 189
Schatzki, T.R., 292
*Schenck v. United States*, 202n20
Schudson, M., 257, 261
Schwarz, C., 150
Scolari, C., 153
segmentation, 223
self-expression, 49, 54
self-realization, 205, 206, 211–213, 215
self-regulation, 141, 142, 210, 220
Shapiro, L., 255
Shoemaker, P.J., 148
*Slater v. Bromfield*, 259
Smith, G., 179, 180
social capital, 274
social media
  borderless Internet, 58–59
  companies, 63, 67, 181, 214, 295
  global community standards, 63–64
  hate speech, sedition, and defamation, 81–82
  injunctions with global effects, 66–70
  marketplace metaphor, 79
  negative-rights construction, 78–79
  networks, 3
  newsgathering and access, 82–84
  platforms, 38, 41, 58, 59, 63, 64, 70, 135, 141–144, 180
  platforms, corporate speakers and public sphere, 84–85
  private community standards, embrace, 65–66
  privatization of communication rights, 57–76
  solution to jurisdictional challenges, 66–70
  speakers and speech, 79
  United states media law and policy, 77–81
  universal communication rights, difference, 59–62
  US and International Law, alignment, 81–85
social networks, 32, 33, 91, 279–285, 287–290, 306, 311
  freedom of expression, 280–282, 288–290
  regulate, 288–290
social platforms, 217, 220, 222–224
social responsibility, 274
Solal, L., 48
Soria, C., 89, 113, 117, 151
Spanish Constitutional Court, 201–203
Spanish Law 17/2006, 112
speech protection, 70, 205–207, 209, 212
*Stângu and Scutelnicu v. Romania*, 129
state capitalism, 237–238
  ideology, 234–236
state legislatures, 83, 85
Stephens, M., 30
"The Stupidity of Dignity,"21
Suárez Villegas, J., 150
Subedi, S., 15
Subirats, M., 152
Supreme Court, 61, 79, 80, 84, 106, 174, 207, 213, 248, 255
sustainability, 220, 267–276
sustainability, post-truth era, 267–277
  communicating, 268–269
  intangible resources, 273–274
  intangible value, 2030 agenda, 272–273
  intangible value, communicating, 271–272
  post-truth and political correctness, 269–270
  source of post-truth, communication, 270–271
  true 2030 agenda v. post-truth 2030 agenda, 275–277
sustainable development, 34, 267, 268, 273
sustainable development goals (SDGs), 271, 273, 276, 277
Switzerland, 108, 199, 200
synthetic media, 292–299
  artificial intelligence, 296–297
  case study, context and controversy, 294–295
  coverage, 296, 297
  dangerous imagery, reimagining, 297–298
  defining, 293–294
  generative adversarial networks, 296–297
  harkening, 296
  journalistic practices, DeepNude news coverage, 295–296
  products, 293, 294, 297
  sharing knowledge, 298–299
  terminology, 293–294
  threat of, 292–300
  victim's voice, privileging, 297

*Társaság a Szabadságjogokért v. Hungary*, 105
tech platforms, 223
telecommunications, 11, 229, 231, 232, 260
*Telegraaf Meda v. The Netherlands*, 124
Terrou, F., 48
textual analysis, 293, 295
traditional media, 3, 90, 103, 108, 217, 256, 281, 316
*Transforming our World: the 2030 Agenda for Sustainable Development*, 267
transparency, 39, 54, 65, 66, 127, 128, 141, 142, 144, 180, 189, 220, 221, 223, 224, 273
Treaty of Lisbon, 67
trust, 274
truth, 79–81, 94–96, 111, 113, 114, 116, 117, 119, 206, 258, 269, 271, 309, 313, 317
truthful information, 95, 103, 117, 118, 245, 316
truthfulness, 111, 112, 128, 221, 268, 274, 276
  of information, 95
Tullock, G., 232

Ugland, E., 130
UN Charter, 14
UN Declaration, 13
unified regulator, 228, 229, 232–234, 238
United Nations System, 47–55
  soft law and challenges, 52–55
United States, 2, 60, 75–85, 185, 188, 192, 205, 208, 209, 211, 213–215, 289, 299
universal communication rights, 18, 35, 38, 59, 151, 247
Universal Declaration of Human Rights (UDHR), 7, 9, 12–16, 18–20, 30, 31, 34, 48, 49, 57, 77, 89, 92, 94, 98, 100, 106, 280, 315, 316
  Article 1 of, 20
  Article2, 17
  Article13, 17
  Article19, 3, 16, 30, 47–49, 98, 315, 316
  object of protection, children and young people, 107–108
  right to receive and impart inform, children as holders, 106–108
  universal, professional and organized, communication rights, 89–91
universality *vs.* standardization, 57–71
universal rights, 26, 34, 35, 76
Ure, M., 150
US Declaration of Independence, 13

Vaccari, C., 293n1
Vargas Llosa, M., 116
Venturelli, S., 228, 230
*Veropörssi*, 167, 168
Virginia Declaration, 13
*Virginia v. Black*, 207

Waisbord, S., 270, 271
Wallace, A., 255
*Weber and Saravia*, 128
whistleblowers, 123, 127, 131, 132
  protection of, 123, 131
WikiLeaks, 253, 257–261
Wong, R.Y.C., 238
World Summit, 30, 34
World Summit on the Information Society (WSIS), 31, 37
World Wide Web, 92, 187, 188, 190–192

yellow journalism, 116
*Youth Initiative for Human Rights v. Serbia*, 128